Perspectives in Social Philosophy

*readings in
philosophic sources
of social thought*

ROBERT N. BECK

Clark University

Perspectives in Social Philosophy

readings in philosophic sources of social thought

Holt, Rinehart and Winston, Inc.

NEW YORK · CHICAGO · SAN FRANCISCO · TORONTO · LONDON

About this book

Ten years ago, in his introduction to a collection of papers on social philosophy, Peter Laslett observed that "for the moment, anyway, political philosophy is dead."* Six years later, in the second volume of the same series, he cited some important books and noted a changed philosophical situation, although he did not feel able to proclaim the resurrection of the field. The present collection, it is hoped, will contribute materials for the basic and effective study of social philosophy necessary for its developing renewal.

A number of assumptions have guided the selection and organization of these materials. Six problems—man and society, values, authority, law, obligation, and justice—have been followed through nine major philosophic schools or "perspectives." For most social philosophies, these problems are at, or near, the center of their concerns. Of course, many selections touch on other topics, and teachers will be able, if they so choose, to develop them also. The concept of a philosophic "school" is admittedly somewhat vague; but carefully handled, it can be an important pedagogical device in aiding students to organize ideas and to trace implications.

In general, selections have been taken (where traditions are longer) from older rather than more recent sources. While many of the older sources are, to be sure, inadequate for various reasons, they are nevertheless valuable for students because of their greater familiarity, their richness in content, and their usual economy in stating essentials without entangling qualifications. As a consequence of this stress, the various perspectives could be arranged in a rough historical order, and the introductory editorial material takes brief account of this order. Teachers who prefer to approach social philosophy through its historical roots will find the selections organized to aid their interest, though more analytic approaches are not at all thereby ruled out.

---

* *Philosophy, Politics and Society,* New York: Macmillan, 1956, p. vii.

v

Most of the individuals whose writings are used in the text are generally recognized as philosophers. Where other representatives appear, it is because, while they are not so recognized, they do stand in a tradition and from it have made insightful contributions to social thought.

One omission from the book, namely fascism, may require brief explanation. While fascism may not be as important an alternative today as it was a few decades ago, some political theorists may believe it still important for study. I agree with most philosophers that fascist ideologies do not qualify as philosophy, though they have frequently borrowed indiscriminately from many philosophies. Mussolini, for example, tried to combine Machiavellian pragmatism, Gentilean idealism, and Sorelian myth making and violence with Italian nationalism. The result was hardly philosophy. Yet, for instructors who feel that courses in political philosophy should include fascism, the major philosophic materials for treating it are contained in this volume.

Editorial material has been prepared to aid the student in two ways. Part of it is descriptive and serves to help readers through the intricacies of argument. The introductions also attempt to sketch briefly the basic terms and meanings of the philosophy being considered. Particular social philosophies reflect, if they do not directly express, more general methods and conclusions, and firm understanding of the particular demands exploration of the general. Both the interconnections of philosophic concepts and the oppositions of philosophic school can serve reflective, searching, and creative learning, and this is the end that the following materials seek to serve.

R. N. B.

Worcester, Massachusetts
January 1967

Contents

Perspectives in Social Philosophy

readings in
philosophic sources
of social thought

INTRODUCTION

Social Philosophy

Students of society ask a great variety of questions about social process and its institutions. Among them, however, is a group of questions such as why one should prefer one kind of society to another, at what goals a political organization should aim, how political institutions may be judged in terms of criteria and methods, why one should obey a government, and when, if ever, one should not. However disparate they may seem, these questions illustrate two special though interrelated philosophic attitudes, one evaluative, the other analytic. The first seeks to judge society by reference to norms and values, the second analyzes and appraises arguments offered in support of special institutions and practices.

Social philosophy is the attempt by philosophers to provide guidance and answers in order to resolve these types of problems. So viewed, it is a *philosophic critique of social process with reference to the principles underlying social structure and functions.** As an introductory definition, this statement serves to mark out a field of inquiry, though it is admittedly somewhat vague and in need of refinement.

Philosophy is the key word requiring clarification in this definition. Unfortunately, the meaning of philosophy is difficult to convey in a brief phrase. It is derived from two Greek words, *philia* (love) and *sophia* (wisdom), an etymology that is helpful for an understanding of Greek philosophy, but that is not very useful for identifying all the work of philosophers throughout Western history. Wisdom to the Greek meant the understanding of "first truths" like real, good, just, even truth itself, and the application of these first truths to the problems of life. Many

---

* The term social philosophy was used by Thomas Hobbes for a general theory of human society; it also appears in the subtitle of J. S. Mill's *Principles of Political Economy* (1848). Some related expressions are political philosophy and philosophy of right, which are generally used as synonyms for social philosophy though some philosophers do suggest certain distinctions among them.

1

philosophers, however, have denied both of these meanings: they reject the existence of first truths, and they believe philosophy should be wholly "theoretical" rather than concerned with guiding conduct.

Perhaps more helpful than any brief formula would be a statement of the chief activities in which philosophers have been engaged over the centuries. Here some clarification is possible, for these activities can be arranged under four headings. First is the *speculative* activity. Surveying the results of the sciences and arts, sometimes including common sense and theology, philosophers have attempted to develop a comprehensive vision or picture of the universe. Since this constructive effort often transcends the more special disciplines, it is usually pursued by speculative rather than analytic methods. A second activity is *phenomenological* or descriptive. Here philosophers seek to provide a complete and unbiased description of basic experiences. Some experiences like guilt, obligation, and fear, are so covered by interpretation and prejudice that their real nature can be recovered only by highly disciplined efforts. Phenomenology aims to make this recovery. A third activity is *normative* and evaluative, for philosophers try to act as critics by providing standards against which individual and social conduct may be judged and guided. Fourth, in what may be called the critical or *analytic* activity, philosophers strive to achieve clarity about the meaning of basic concepts like true, false, good, and just, and of logical patterns relating to them that are central to all intellectual work.

These four activities, then, describe philosophers' work. Unfortunately, however, an ambiguity remains even here. Some philosophers see them as interrelated parts of an inclusive philosophical activity; others take them to be four kinds of philosophy from which the student must choose. These alternatives carry different implications for the meaning of social philosophy.

Before relating this material to the meaning of social philosophy, it may be well to list briefly the major kinds of problems faced by philosophers—however they decide to view the above activities. This can be done conveniently in terms of the major fields of philosophy that include first, *epistemology* or theory of knowledge. Here the philosopher asks such questions as: What is the source of knowledge? What is the criterion or test of knowledge? What is the nature of knowledge? The second field of philosophy is *metaphysics* or theory of reality. Metaphysics has traditionally relied on speculative methods, and analytic philosophers have often rejected it, seeing it as an invalid or improper discipline. The metaphysician's concern, however, is with problems such as the meaning of being, the nature of reality, and the principles for understanding the cosmos. Third is a group of inquiries generally called the *normative sciences,* which deals with such values as the good (ethics), the beautiful (esthetics), and the holy (philosophy of religion). "Science" is used in its etymological sense of "organized body of knowledge" and does not refer to modern experimental or natural science. "Normative" refers to questions of value. Social philosophy is often included here as it deals with certain values that cluster around the ideal of justice. Finally, there is a group of rather specialized fields that seek to relate some particular field, like science or education, to a more general philosophical position. In the absence of any commonly accepted name, they may be called the "philosophies of."

These many statements about philosophy must now be related to the definition of social philosophy, which has just been classified as one of the normative sciences. As the philosophic critique of the principles underlying social process, social philosophy seeks to develop the arguments that justify political and social institutions, either as they actually are or as they are imagined. If the emphasis of a philosopher is primarily evaluative, social philosophy becomes for him a branch of ethics, which is the inquiry into the good. That is, since ethics or moral philosophy deals with the most general considerations of values, social philosophy is a matter of their application to the moral questions raised by the social order. On the other hand, if the philosopher's interest is in methods of inquiry and analysis of concepts, his social philosophy will be neutral toward value and will be directed rather toward clarification of terms and arguments. More speculative philosophers may try to combine these two interests.

In any case, these approaches are alike in that they attempt to examine critically the justificatory arguments for social institutions. In this sense, social philosophy is concerned with principles "underlying" social process, real or ideal. Justification is, among other things, a recourse to principles that coherently support and clarify the conclusions that have been drawn. As has been indicated, philosophers sometimes seek these principles in their theories of value, sometimes in methods of analytic clarification, and sometimes in both ethics and analysis.

However pursued—and the selections in the text will reveal great diversity in views of social philosophy itself as well as in conclusions drawn—theories of justification of social institutions will be found to include a number of essential further considerations. Among them is, first, an attempt to understand the nature of associative life. The aspects of man's nature—needs, modes of dependence, and independence—stand in certain relationships to society and its institutions. A basic problem for any social philosophy is found in this correlative existence of man and society. Here also is suggested a second justificatory problem. Associative life reflects, or may reflect, a set of associative values toward which social process is directed. These values need clarification and justification. Third, there is the problem of power and authority of the state. Social process must be viewed with reference to control in terms of means (authority) as well as ends (values).

Fourth, social control may be specified further in terms of law and rights. Law, with its supporting institutions, is an agent of social control, but it grants to individuals certain powers and privileges. What is, or what should be, the nature of law and its assignments of rights is a central question for all social philosophies. Fifth is the problem of political obligation. The preceding factors in justificatory arguments—association, values, power, law, and rights—raise questions regarding the obligations of individuals to society and state and of state to individuals. What is the nature of these obligations? Are there limits to them? Are there conditions under which political obligations may or should be broken? Finally, much of social philosophy is directed toward fundamental understanding of the inclusive ideal for society and its institutions whose traditional name is justice.

This sketch of the basic concerns of the social philosopher may be of further aid to the student in demarking his field of inquiry. But introductory statements must remain just that; in the study of philosophy it is especially important to proceed quickly to the materials themselves. The question, "What is social philosophy?" is itself a philosophical question; it must be asked again at the end of one's investigations. Then it may be answered with greater comprehension. Meanwhile, the student should plunge into the stream of philosophic controversy to examine alternative positions and the arguments offered to justify them.

Classical Realism

Fundamental to the first position we shall study, in fact, almost its defining characteristic, is the attempt to understand man, society, and government against the background of the cosmos. The questions asked and the answers given, however diversely the particular details may be developed by individual thinkers, arise within the context of a broader theory of the nature of things and of the universe as a whole. In a general sense, the social philosophy of classical realism may be called cosmological or metaphysical.

What is classical realism? The word classical is used to indicate that this position (it is one of the oldest and most continuously active philosophies) had its origin in ancient Greece as well as to distinguish it from other forms of realism such as Scottish common sense realism and American new realism. The term realism identifies a philosophy which holds that the universe consists of real, independent, existing things, hierarchically structured and related, and forming a *cosmos* or totality within which meaning and order can become available to man. To many readers this definition may seem to be only "common sense," and indeed the realist does hold that his philosophy acknowledges and remains true to the beliefs of the "common man." Yet realism is not simply common sense; in its attempt to articulate the meaning of experience, it becomes a technically developed philosophy.

Three fundamental philosophical assertions are made by the realist.* First, he believes that metaphysics, defined as the science of being, is a valid and important discipline, and that in fact the concern for being and its principles is the central philosophical interest. Second, the realist holds in his epistemology that beings can be known by the human mind as they are in themselves. Reason is the agent

* See the platform by a contemporary professional organization, the Association for Realistic Philosophy, in *The Return To Reason,* ed. John Wild, Chicago: Henry Regnery Co., 1953, pp. 357–363.

of such knowledge—hence the realist's insistence on rationality—and truth can be grasped by man as universal, absolute, and eternal. Third, the realist asserts that knowledge of being, especially of human being, provides man with reliable norms of good and evil, both for the individual and for society.

In developing these theses, realists rely heavily on the Greek philosophical tradition as expressed by Plato (427–347) and above all by Aristotle (384–322). Even today, although perhaps in a somewhat modified form, this tradition, which articulates a number of assumptions of Greek life, is a major alternative in philosophy. One of these assumptions was suggested above by the use of the word "cosmos." This nearly untranslatable Greek word carried a number of meanings for the educated Greek. As he applied the word to the universe, he meant that reality is an ordered whole, that law and reason are written into the very nature of things, and that the world is ultimately harmonious and structured. This cosmos, in turn, is to a large extent knowable, and the instrument of knowledge is reason. The regularities, laws, and principles of the universe, being ideas derived by reason, are available to qualified, inquiring minds. Furthermore, it is important for men to know the laws of reality. Human life is often, to be sure, not harmonious or structured; indeed, it often has the opposite characteristics. To become meaningful, to become lawful and good, life and society must be directed and ordered so as to mirror the objective structure of the universe. The microcosm or little world within man must reflect the order of the macrocosm without, and the instrument of this reflection is reason.

Early and medieval Christianity; whose philosophical expression is also included within classical realism, modified these Greek assumptions in the light of revelation and belief in a personal, creative God; yet the continuity is apparent. Superimposed on (or above) the Greek cosmos is a divine being, creator of all other being and the font of all order, law, and reason. Though above natural being (and hence above natural reason), however, God provided another means, namely faith and the church, by which men could reflect in their individual and social lives that order and level of being through which they achieve happiness, fulfillment, and a meaningful life.

The basic problem of social philosophy for the realist, then, is to determine the place of man and society alongside other beings in the cosmos, in the hierarchical totality of things. This problem depends in turn on that of being and its principles. For its exploration, the work of Aristotle is basic.

What is being? Aristotle noted that this question has many senses, and that the word being is used in many ways. But in its primary meaning, being refers to concrete, individual, existing things such as this desk, this tree, and this man. Aristotle introduced the word substance to refer to beings so understood: desks, trees, and men. Thus far, however, Aristotle did little more than ascribe a new name to things. Much more fundamental is the analysis of what it means to be a substance. Here Aristotle made four observations. First, every substance is made out of something. It derives from something as its constituent basis, as a desk is made of wood. That out of which any thing comes or is made is called its matter or *material cause*. Next, a thing is brought into existence by some power or agency, which is its *efficient cause*. Third, every thing is characterized as some kind or type of thing, that is, each thing has a distinctive nature which it shares with other things of the same class and which determines that it shall be just that thing and not something else. This is its *formal cause*. Last is the end or *final cause*. Each thing belongs to a kind or class and seeks to become fully and perfectly that kind. Such seeking is for the end which is the completion or perfection of the nature that makes the thing to be what it is. In fact, the very nature of anything is viewed by Aristotle as a system of capacities or forces of growth directed by the particular nature in question toward the end of completion and full realization of that nature.

This notion of nature and its realization leads to another pair of concepts of great significance for the realist. Viewed simply as a set of capacities tending toward an end, any particular nature is not yet fully being, for it lacks the full realization appropriate to its nature and is, therefore, only *potentially* that completed nature. If a thing does achieve its end, however, it becomes *actual,* that is, most fully a being of its kind. Thus, potentiality is to incomplete as actuality is to complete—the potential involving lack of being, the actual being complete being.

Two technical implications of these concepts must now be noted. The first is the doctrine that being and good are convertible terms. This means that any being, insofar as it is being (that is, has realized its nature), is good, and insofar as it falls short of such realization, it is less than good. For example, a horse is a good horse to the extent that it *is* a horse, that it has realized the nature appropriate to a horse. Or, a man is good as he most fully realizes human nature; he is not good if he fails to do so. To become good is for any thing to be most fully. The second implication of the concepts of potency and act is the doctrine of the hierarchy of being. This means that beings form an *order of being* by reference to the concepts of potency and act themselves. A thing that is more fully being is higher on the scale of being than a thing that is to some extent merely potential, that *is not yet*. The actual is thus prior to the potential. The potential is known by reference to the actual, and the potential is actualized by something actual. The not-yet-being becomes being only by the influence of being.

The concepts that have been sketched—substance, matter, form, end, potency, act, order, and good—are the instruments with which realists attempt to understand man's social existence and to direct it toward higher ends. Realists form one perspective in social philosophy by the context of their questions about man and society, by the metaphysical and sometimes religious background and terminology of their position, and from the authority of Aristotle. The next task is to turn to the literature in which these efforts toward understanding are given fuller statement.

Man and Society

The rather abstract discussion of the introduction may now be given more concrete illustration, for man and society, as beings, are understood by realists through the concepts originally developed by Aristotle. Man, first of all, is a being who has a distinctive nature, namely human nature, that determines the kind of being he is and defines the ends he must realize to become most fully a being. As any person realizes these ends, he achieves "well-being" or happiness. He achieves, in other words, his full being and therewith his good.

This individual human good can be specified more fully, for man is not only a being, he is also a living, animal being and a rational being. As he perfects his animal being with its various desires and appetites, he achieves the *moral virtues* such as courage and temperance, which are the habits of right function and realization in respect to desire;* and as he perfects his rational nature, he realizes such *intellectual virtues* as wisdom, prudence, and art. Happiness, Aristotle's ethical ideal, is human activity in accordance with virtue; and since his rational nature is unique to him, man is most perfectly fulfilled in the intellectual virtues and the life of contemplation.

Like all natures, human nature is thus a set of capacities tending toward the distinctively human ends of virtue and happiness. But the virtues are primarily *internal* principles of man's self-realization, and they are not in themselves completely sufficient for happiness. Men stand in need of society in order fully to realize their capacities. And since this need of external conditions is rooted in man's being, it follows that the state or society is natural. The proof of this, Aristotle said, is that an individual is not self-sufficing when isolated from others; rather, he is like a part in relation to the whole. "A social instinct is implanted in man by nature," and anyone unable to live in society or who has no need of it is either a beast or a god, but not a human being. Men, therefore, cannot be separated from society and the principles of justice and order upon which it depends; they are the parts, society is the whole. Society is the external support of self-realization, and in isolation, men are incapable of becoming rational animals.

It follows for the realist that the state† has a moral purpose: "every community is established with a view to some good"; and that, as the individual is to be viewed as a part in relation to the whole, the state is "organic" in structure. The state comes into existence in order that men might live, and it continues in existence for the sake of the good life. Though not itself a substance—states and societies do not have the unity of natural substances—the state has a nature and an end of its own; it is the actuality of less inclusive communities such as the family and the village. The nature of the state requires that it be a proper order under the ideal of justice, that it serve the good of the whole or the common good, that it function according to rules of reason or law, and that the system have a ruling part which acts in trust for the whole community.

These last assertions will be developed in later selections. The present section treats of the notions of man as a social animal and of society as an order under justice necessary to man's complete existence. The first selection is from Plato's *Republic*. Though Plato is a major source of realistic ideas, he does not belong

---

* The defining mark of "right function" is a mean between the extremes of excess and deficiency. This doctrine is developed below in connection with Aristotle's treatment of justice.

† The discussion here refers somewhat indiscriminately to either state or society. Most scholars agree that Greek and early medieval thought did not make a distinction between them in any modern way. As Aristotle writes on politics, his thought is directed toward the *polis* or city-state.

primarily to this perspective. In fact, his influence has been quite diverse and has been felt by many different philosophies. Nevertheless, the discussion of justice in the selection is a good introduction to social philosophy as well as to some of the elements of the realist's position. The general topic of the *Republic* is the concept of justice, which Plato views as the bond holding society together as well as a virtue necessary to individuals. This ideal, Plato teaches, is implicit in all societies; and the major task incumbent on political leaders is to arrange matters so that justice becomes explicit and fully realized.

The second selection is from Aristotle's *Politics*. The importance of this work can hardly be exaggerated. As G. H. Sabine has observed, "Until the sixteenth century it was scarcely possible to write a treatise on politics which . . . did not owe a debt to the *Politics*."‡ The pages of the text develop themes to which all later realists are indebted.

‡ *A History of Political Theory*, New York: Holt, Rinehart and Winston, Inc., 1961, p. 245.

PLATO   Society and the Good

[Socrates.] Well then, I will repeat the question which I put to you just now, that our inquiry may be carried out continuously; namely, what sort of a thing justice is compared with injustice. It was said, I think, that injustice is more powerful and stronger than justice: but now, seeing that justice is both wisdom and virtue, and injustice is ignorance, it may easily be shewn, I imagine, that justice is likewise stronger than injustice. No one can now fail to see this. But I do not wish to settle the question in that absolute way, Thrasymachus, but I would investigate it in the following manner: Should you admit that a city may be unjust, and that it may unjustly attempt to enslave other cities, and so succeed in so doing, and hold many in such slavery to itself?

[Thrasymachus.] Undoubtedly I should: and this will be more frequently done by the best city, that is, the one that is most completely unjust, than by any other.

I understand, I said, that this is your position. But the question which I wish to consider is, whether the city that becomes the mistress of another city, will have this power without the aid of justice, or whether justice will be indispensable to it.

If, as you said just now, justice is wisdom, justice must lend her aid; but if it is as I said[1] injustice must lend hers.

I am quite delighted to find, Thrasymachus, that you are not content merely to nod and shake your head, but give exceedingly good answers.

I do it to indulge you.

You are very good: but pray indulge me so far as to say, whether you think that either a city, or an army, or a band of thieves or robbers, or any other body of men, pursuing certain unjust ends in common, could succeed in any enter-

[1] Earlier in the dialogue, Thrasymachus defined justice as "the interest of the stronger." Socrates argued against and rejected this definition. Now he is arguing that, as wisdom and virtue, justice is actually the bond of strength in the community. *Ed.*

From *The Republic of Plato*, trans. J. L. Davies and D. J. Vaughan, London: Macmillan & Co., Ltd., 1895.

prize if they were to deal unjustly with one another?

Certainly not.

If they refrain from such conduct towards one another, will they not be more likely to succeed?

Yes, certainly.

Because, I presume, Thrasymachus, injustice breeds divisions and animosities and broils between man and man, while justice creates unanimity and friendship; does it not?

Be it so, he said, that I may not quarrel with you.

Truly I am very much obliged to you, my excellent friend: but pray tell me this;—if the working of injustice is to implant hatred wherever it exists, will not the presence of it, whether among freemen or slaves, cause them to hate one another, and to form parties, and disable them from acting together in concert?

Certainly.

Well, and if it exist in two persons, will they not quarrel and hate one another, and be enemies each to the other, and both to the just?

They will.

And supposing, my admirable friend, that injustice has taken up its residence in a single individual, will it lose its proper power, or retain it just the same?

We will say it retains it.

And does not its power appear to be of such a nature, as to make any subject in which it resides, whether it be city, or family, or army, or anything else whatsoever, unable to act unitedly, because of the divisions and quarrels it excites, and moreover hostile both to itself and to everything that opposes it, and to the just? Is it not so?

Certainly it is.

Then, if it appears in an individual also, it will produce all these its natural results: in the first place it will make

him unable to act because of inward strife and division; in the next place, it will make him an enemy to himself and to the just, will it not?

It will.

And the gods, my friend, are just?

We will suppose they are.

Then to the gods also will the unjust man be an enemy, and the just a friend.

Feast on your argument, said he, to your heart's content: I will not oppose you, or I shall give offence to the company.

Be so good, said I, as to make my entertainment complete by continuing to answer as you have now been doing. I am aware, indeed, that the just are shewn to be wiser, and better, and more able to act than the unjust, who are indeed, incapable of any combined action. Nay, we do not speak with entire accuracy when we say that any party of unjust men ever acted vigorously in concert together; for, had they been thoroughly unjust, they could not have kept their hands off each other. But it is obvious that there was some justice at work in them, which made them refrain at any rate from injuring, at one and the same moment, both their comrades and the objects of their attacks, and which enabled them to achieve what they did achieve; and that their injustice partly disabled them, even in the pursuit of their unjust ends, since those who are complete villains, and thoroughly unjust, are also thoroughly unable to act. I learn that all this is true, and that the doctrine which you at first propounded is not true. But whether the just also live a better life, and are happier than the unjust, is a question which we proposed to consider next, and which we now have to investigate. Now, for my part, I think it is already apparent, from what we have said, that they do: nevertheless, we must examine the point still more carefully. For we are debating no trivial question, but the manner in which a man ought to live.

Pray consider it.

I will. Tell me, do you think there is such a thing as a horse's function?

I do.

Would you, then, describe the function of a horse, or of anything else whatever, as that work, for the accomplishment of which it is either the sole or the best instrument?

I do not understand.

Look at it this way. Can you see with anything besides eyes?

Certainly not.

Can you hear with anything besides ears?

No.

Then should we not justly say that seeing and hearing are the functions of these organs?

Yes, certainly.

Again, you might cut off a vine-shoot with a carving knife, or chisel, or many other tools?

Undoubtedly.

But with no tool, I imagine, so well as with the pruning knife made for the purpose.

True.

Then shall we not define pruning to be the function of the pruning knife?

By all means.

Now then, I think, you will better understand what I wished to learn from you just now, when I asked whether the function of a thing is not that work for the accomplishment of which it is either the sole or the best instrument?

I do understand, and I believe that this is in every case the function of a thing.

Very well: do you not also think that everything which has an appointed function has also a proper *virtue?* Let us revert to the same in-stances; we say that the eyes have a function?

They have.

Then have the eyes a virtue also?

They have.

And the ears: did we assign them a function?

Yes.

Then have they a virtue also?

They have.

And is it the same with all other things?

The same.

Attend then: Do you suppose that the eyes could discharge their own function well if they had not their own proper virtue,—that virtue being replaced by a vice?

How could they? You mean, probably, if sight is replaced by blindness.

I mean, whatever their virtue be; for I am not come to that question yet. At present I am asking whether it is through their own peculiar virtue that things perform their proper functions well, and through their own peculiar vice that they perform them ill?

You cannot be wrong in that.

Then if the ears lose their own virtue, will they execute their functions ill?

Certainly.

May we include all other things under the same proposition?

I think we may.

Come, then, consider this point next. Has the soul any function which could not be executed by means of anything else whatsoever? For example, could we in justice assign superintendence and government, deliberation and the like, to anything but the soul, or should we pronounce them to be peculiar to it?

We could ascribe them to nothing else.

Again, shall we declare life to be a function of the soul?

Decidedly.

Do we not also maintain that the soul has a virtue?

We do.

Then can it ever so happen, Thrasymachus, that the soul will perform its functions well when destitute of its own peculiar virtue, or is that impossible?

Impossible.

Then a bad soul must needs exercise authority and superintendence ill, and a good soul must do all these things well.

Unquestionably.

Now did we not grant that justice was a virtue of the soul, and injustice a vice?

We did.

Consequently the just soul and the just man will live well, and the unjust man ill?

Apparently, according to your argument.

And you will allow that he who lives well is blessed and happy, and that he who lives otherwise is the reverse.

Unquestionably.

Consequently the just man is happy, and the unjust man miserable.

Let us suppose them to be so.

But surely it is not misery, but happiness, that is advantageous.

Undoubtedly.

Never then, my excellent Thrasy-machus, is injustice more advantageous than justice.

Well, Socrates, let this be your entertainment for the feast of Bendis.[2]

I have to thank *you* for it, Thrasymachus, because you recovered your temper, and left off being angry with me. Nevertheless, I have not been well entertained; but that was my own fault, and not yours: for as your gourmands seize upon every new dish as it goes round, and taste its contents before they have had a reasonable enjoyment of its predecessor, so I seem to myself to have left the question which we were at first examining, concerning the real nature of justice, before we had found out the answer to it, in order to rush to the inquiry whether this unknown thing is a vice and an ignorance, or a virtue and a wisdom; and again, when a new theory, that injustice is more profitable than justice, was subsequently started, I could not refrain from passing from the other to this, so that at present the result of our conversation is that I know nothing: for while I do not know what justice is, I am little likely to know whether it is in fact a virtue or not, or whether its owner is happy or unhappy.

[2] A festival honoring Bendis, a Thracian goddess. The *Republic* begins with a reference to Socrates' attendance at the occasion. *Ed.*

ARISTOTLE Man as Political Animal

Every state is a community of some kind, and every community is established with a view to some good; for mankind always act in order to obtain that which they think good. But, if all communities aim at some good, the state or political community, which is the highest of all, and which embraces all the rest, aims, and in a greater degree than any other, at the highest good.

Now there is an erroneous opinion that a statesman, king, householder, and master are the same, and that they differ, not in kind, but only in the number of their subjects. For example,

From Aristotle, *Politics,* trans. B. Jowett, Oxford: Clarendon Press, 1885.

the ruler over a few is called a master; over more, the manager of a household; over a still larger number, a statesman or king, as if there were no difference between a great household and a small state. The distinction which is made between the king and the statesman is as follows: When the government is personal, the ruler is a king; when, according to the principles of the political science, the citizens rule and are ruled in turn, then he is called a states-man.

But all this is a mistake; for governments differ in kind, as will be evident to any one who considers the matter according to the method which has hitherto guided us. As in other departments of science, so in politics, the compound should always be resolved into the simple elements or least parts of the whole. We must therefore look at the elements of which the state is composed, in order that we may see in what they differ from one another, and whether any scientific distinction can be drawn between the different kinds of rule.

He who thus considers things in their first growth and origin, whether a state or anything else, will obtain the clearest view of them. In the first place (1) there must be a union of those who cannot exist without each other; for example, of male and female, that the race may continue; and this is a union which is formed, not of deliberate purpose, but because, in common with other animals and with plants, mankind have a natural desire to leave behind them an image of themselves. And (2) there must be a union of natural ruler and subject, that both may be preserved. For he who can foresee with his mind is by nature intended to be lord and master, and he who can work with his body is a subject, and by nature

a slave; hence master and slave have the same interest. Nature, however, has distinguished between the female and the slave. For she is not niggardly, like the smith who fashions the Delphian knife for many uses; she makes each thing for a single use, and every instrument is best made when intended for one and not for many uses. But among barbarians no distinction is made between women and slaves, because there is no natural ruler among them: they are a community of slaves, male and female. Wherefore the poets say,—

"It is meet that Hellenes should rule over barbarians";

as if they thought that the barbarian and the slave were by nature one.

Out of these two relationships between man and woman, master and slave, the family first arises, and Hesiod is right when he says,—

"First house and wife and an ox for the plough,"

for the ox is the poor man's slave. The family is the association established by nature for the supply of men's every day wants, and the members of it are called by Charondas "companions of the cupboard" [ὁμοσιπύους], and by Epimenides the Cretan, "companions of the manager" [ὁμοκάπους]. But when several families are united, and the association aims at something more than the supply of daily needs, then comes into existence the village. And the most natural form of the village appears to be that of a colony from the family, composed of the children and grandchildren, who are said to be "suckled with the same milk." And this is the reason why Hellenic states were originally governed by kings; because the Hellenes were under royal rule before they came together, as the barbarians still are. Every family is ruled by the eldest, and therefore in the colonies of the family the kingly form of government prevailed because they were of the same blood. As Homer says [of the Cyclopes]:—

"Each one gives law to his children and to his wives."

For they lived dispersedly, as was the manner in ancient times. Wherefore men say that the Gods have a king, because they themselves either are or were in ancient times under the rule of a king. For they imagine, not only the forms of the Gods, but their ways of life to be like their own.

When several villages are united in a single community, perfect and large enough to be nearly or quite self-sufficing, the state comes into existence, originating in the bare needs of life, and continuing in existence for the sake of a good life. And therefore, if the earlier forms of society are natural, so is the state, for it is the end of them, and the [completed] nature is the end. For what each thing is when fully developed, we call its nature, whether we are speaking of a man, a horse, or a family. Besides, the final cause and end of a thing is the best, and to be self-sufficing is the end and the best.

Hence it is evident that the state is a creation of nature, and that man is by nature a political animal. And he who by nature and not by mere accident is without a state, is either above humanity, or below it; he is the

"Tribeless, lawless, heartless one,"

whom Homer denounces—the outcast who is a lover of war; he may be compared to a bird which flies alone.

Now the reason why man is more of a political animal than bees or any other gregarious animals is evident. Nature, as we often say, makes nothing in vain, and man is the only animal whom she has endowed with the gift of speech. And whereas mere sound is but an indication of pleasure or pain, and is therefore found in other animals (for their nature attains to the perception of pleasure and pain and the intimation of them to one another, and no further), the power of speech is intended to set forth the expedient and inexpedient, and likewise the just and the unjust. And it is a characteristic of man that he alone has any sense of good and evil, of just and unjust, and the association of living beings who have this sense makes a family and a state.

Thus the state is by nature clearly prior to the family and to the individual, since the whole is of necessity prior to the part; for example, if the whole body be destroyed, there will be no foot or hand, except in an equivocal sense, as we might speak of a stone hand; for when destroyed the hand will be no better. But things are defined by their working and power; and we ought not to say that they are the same when they are no longer the same, but only that they have the same name. The proof that the state is a creation of nature and prior to the individual is that the individual, when isolated, is not self-sufficing; and therefore he is like a part in relation to the whole. But he who is unable to live in society, or who has no need because he is sufficient for himself, must be either a beast or a god: he is no part of a state. A social instinct is implanted in all men by nature, and yet he who first founded the state was the greatest of benefactors. For man, when perfected, is the best of animals, but, when separated from law and justice, he is the worst of all; since armed injustice is the more dangerous, and he is equipped at birth with the arms of intelligence and with moral qualities which he may use for the worst ends. Wherefore, if he have not virtue, he is the most unholy and the most savage of animals, and the most full of lust and gluttony. But justice is the bond of men in states, and the administration of justice, which is the determination of what is just, is the principle of order in political society. . . .

A state exists for the sake of a good life, and not for the sake of life only: if life only were the object, slaves and brute animals might form a state, but they cannot, for they have no share in happiness or in a life of free choice. Nor does a state exist for the sake of alliance and security from injustice, nor yet for the sake of exchange and mutual intercourse; for then the Tyrrhenians and the Carthaginians, and all who have commercial treaties with one another, would be the citizens of one state. True, they have agreements about imports, and engagements that they will do no wrong to one another, and written articles of alliance. But there are no magistracies common to the contracting parties who will enforce their engagements; different states have each their own magistracies. Nor does one state take care that the citizens of the other are such as they ought to be, nor see that those who come under the terms of the treaty do no wrong or wickedness at all, but only that they do no injustice to one another. Whereas, those who care for good government take into consideration [the larger question of] virtue and vice in states. Whence it may be further inferred that virtue must be the serious care of a state which truly deserves the name: for [without this ethical end] the community becomes a mere alliance which differs only in place from alliances of which the members live apart; and law is only a convention, "a surety to one another of justice," as the sophist Lycophron says, and no real power to make the citizens good and just. . . .

Our conclusion, then, is that political society exists for the sake of noble actions, and not of mere companionship. And they who contribute most to such a society have a greater share in it than those who have the same or a greater freedom or nobility of birth but are inferior to them in political virtue; or than those who exceed them in wealth but are surpassed by them in virtue. . . .

Returning to the constitution itself, let us seek to determine out of what and what sort of elements the state which is to be happy and well-governed should be composed. There are two things in which all well-being consists, one of them is the choice of a right end and aim of action, and the other the discovery of the actions which are means towards it; for the means and the end may agree or disagree. Sometimes the right end is set before men, but in practice they fail to attain it; in other cases they are successful in all the means, but they propose to themselves a bad end, and sometimes they fail in both. Take, for example, the art of medicine; physicians do not always understand the nature of health, and also the means which they use may not effect the desired end. In all arts and sciences both the end and the means should be equally within our control.

The happiness and well-being which all men manifestly desire, some have the power of attaining, but to others, from some accident or defect of nature, the attainment of them is not granted; for a good life requires a supply of external goods, in a less degree when men are in a good state, in a greater degree when they are in a lower state. Others again, who possess the condition of happiness, so utterly wrong from the first in the pursuit of it. But since our object is to discover the best form of government, that, namely, under which a city will be best governed, and since the city is best governed which has the greatest opportunity of obtaining happiness, it is evident that we must clearly ascertain the nature of happiness.

We have said in the Ethics, if the arguments there adduced are of any value, that happiness is the realization and perfect exercise of virtue, and this not conditional, but absolute. And I used the term "conditional" to express that which is indispensable, and "absolute" to express that which is good in itself. Take the case of just actions; just punishments and chastisements do indeed spring from a good principle, but they are good only because we cannot do without them—it would be better that neither individuals nor states should need anything of the sort—but actions which aim at honour and advantage are absolutely the best. The conditional action is only the choice of a lesser evil; whereas these are the foundation and creation of good. A good man may make the best even of poverty and disease, and the other ills

of life; but he can only attain happiness under the opposite conditions. As we have already said in the Ethics, the good man is he to whom, because he is virtuous, the absolute good is his good. It is also plain that his use of other goods must be virtuous and in the absolute sense good. This makes men fancy that external goods are the cause of happiness, yet we might as well say that a brilliant performance on the lyre was to be attributed to the instrument and not to the skill of the performer.

It follows then from what has been said that some things the legislator must find ready to his hand in a state, others he must provide. And therefore we can only say: May our state be constituted in such a manner as to be blessed with the goods of which fortune disposes (for we acknowledge her power): whereas virtue and goodness in the state are not a matter of chance but the result of knowledge and purpose. A city can be virtuous only when the citizens who have a share in the government are virtuous, and in our state all the citizens share in the government; let us then enquire how a man becomes virtuous. For even if we could suppose all the citizens to be virtuous, and not each of them, yet the latter would be better, for in the virtue of each the virtue of all is involved.

Social and Political Values

Bishop of Hippo and Christian saint, Augustine (354–430) stands as a towering figure in the history of thought. Though much of his intellectual effort was directed toward the resolution of theological conflicts, he also thought deeply on social and political issues. One of his major works, *The City of God,* was written in response to criticisms of Christianity that followed the sacking of Rome by the Visigoths in 410, and it therefore dealt with basic social and political as well as religious matters.

Augustine's thoughts on society, like most realistic philosophy influenced by Christianity, may be characterized generally as a Christianization of the Greek approach to the theory of man and society. This transformation occurred by giving the Platonic notion of justice and the Aristotelian ideal of the good life a Christian context and development. As with the Greeks, Christian realists view the state in terms of moral purpose rather than formal authority and command; but unlike them, Christian realists hold that man's complete happiness or fulfillment includes, along with the natural, a supernatural end made possible for men by the theological virtues of faith, hope, and love. A Christian thus belongs to two societies, one natural, one supernatural—one temporal, one eternal.*

Yet the earthly city has an integrity, an end or purpose, of its own, with values and principles appropriate to its nature and mission. Though realists differ somewhat in the terminology they use, the principles of peace and justice as stated by Augustine are generally taken as defining the good for society. For Augustine peace is the bond that all men desire in their sociableness, "the orderly disposal of parts" in society under orderly command and authority. Justice is the principle of order that issues forth in peace, and its basic definition is "giving every one his due." Subordinate to these ideals and regulated or distributed by them are two other values, equality and liberty. Equality for realists has traditionally meant equality before God in the sense that every man possesses a soul, and liberty is the freedom to act rightly according to virtue.†

Augustine, and realists generally, assert that the state has "all the good on earth" since it is the highest of human institutions. The state must provide the necessities of life, as well as the opportunities for the good life. It is thus rooted in man's nature and needs,‡ and the values the state seeks to embody are values for the needs of man as the realist understands them.

---

* The relationship of these two ends became a problem for the entire Middle Ages, and the history of alternative views on this topic involves almost the whole history of the period.

† The student will want to study carefully the development of concepts of liberty and equality, both in realism and in other perspectives. Though the matter is subject to scholarly debate, there is some agreement that in these traditional sources one does not find modern conceptions of liberty and equality: not these values, but rather the common good is the highest social principle. Aristotle seemed to deny equality in his theory of "natural slavery," and whether spiritual equality has any political meaning is at least doubtful. Liberty in the sense of conscience, that is, the right to hold, profess, and live by the principles one chooses, first became a social ideal in the toleration controversies of the sixteenth and seventeenth centuries. Whether realistic principles are consistent with recent meanings of liberty and equality is also subject to debate. The student may consult, for example, the social writings of Jacques Maritain or Fr. John C. Murray for efforts made to develop realism in ways sympathetic to these meanings. Many later selections in the text will touch on these meanings.

‡ Some commentators see a difference between Augustine's view here and the more commonly held position of Aquinas. Augustine did hold that sin is the cause of servitude and the subjection of man to man, while Aquinas—following Aristotle more closely—argued that society is "natural" to man's nature. But this difference in explaining the origin of the state does not lead to great opposition between them in their understanding of the nature of the state and its values, where differences are more matters of emphasis than divergence.

ST. AUGUSTINE Peace and Justice

XII, 13. THE STATE OF THE TWO CITIES, THE HEAVENLY AND THE EARTHLY.

Two loves therefore, have given original to these two cities: self-love in contempt of God unto the earthly, love of God in contempt of one's self to the heavenly; the first seeks the glory of men, and the latter desires God only as the testimony of the conscience, the greatest glory. That glories in itself, and this in God. That exalts itself in self-glory: this says to God: "My glory and the lifter up of my head." That boasts of the ambitious conquerors, led by the lust of sovereignty: in this every one serves other in charity, both the rulers in counselling and the subjects in obeying. That loves worldly virtue in the potentates: this says unto God, "I will love Thee, O Lord, my strength." And the wise men of that, follow either the good things of the body, or mind, or both: living according to the flesh: and such as might know God, honoured Him not as God, nor were thankful but became vain in their own imaginations, and their foolish heart was darkened: for professing themselves to be wise, that is, extolling themselves proudly in their wisdom, they became fools: changing the glory of the incorruptible God to the likeness of the image of a corruptible man, and of birds and four-footed beasts and serpents: for they were the people's guides, or followers unto all those idolatries, and served the creature more than the Creator who is blessed for ever. But in this other, this heavenly city, there is no wisdom of man, but only the piety that serves the true God and expects a reward in the society of the holy angels, and men, that God may be all in all.

XIII, 4. OF THE CONFLICT AND PEACE OF THE EARTHLY CITY.

But the temporal, earthly city (temporal, for when it is condemned to perpetual pains it shall be no more a city) has all the good here upon earth, and therein takes that joy that such an object can afford. But because it is not a good that acquits the possessors of all troubles, therefore this city is divided in itself into wars, altercations, and appetites of bloody and deadly victories. For any part of it that wars against another, desires to be the world's conqueror, whereas indeed it is vice's slave. And if it conquer, it extols itself and so becomes its own destruction: but if we consider the condition of worldly affairs, and grieve at man's openness to adversity, rather than delight in the events of prosperity, thus is the victory deadly: for it cannot keep a sovereignty for ever where it got a victory for once.

Nor can we call the objects of this city's desires, good, it itself in its own human nature, far surmounting them. It desires an earthly peace, for very low ambitions, and seeks it by war, where if it subdue all resistance, it attains peace: which notwithstanding the other side, that fought so unfortunately for the same reasons, lack. This peace they seek by laborious war, and obtain (they think) by a glorious victory. And when they conquer that had the right cause, who will not congratulate their victory,

From St. Augustine, *The City of God,* trans. John Healey, 3 vols.; London: J. M. Dent & Sons, Ltd., 1893.

and be glad of their peace? Doubtless those are good, and God's good gifts. But if the things appertaining to that celestial and supernal city where the victory shall be everlasting, be neglected for those goods, and those goods desired as the only goods, or loved as if they were better than the other, misery must needs follow and increase that which is inherent before.

XV, 5. OF LIVING SOCIABLY WITH OUR NEIGHBOR: HOW FIT IT IS, AND YET HOW SUBJECT TO CROSSES.

We do worthily approve their enjoining a wise man to live in mutual society: for how should our Celestial City (the fifteenth book whereof we now have in hand) have ever come to its origin, development, or perfection, unless the saints live all in sociable union? But yet what is he that can recount all the miseries incident unto the societies of mortals? Hear what the comedian says, with a general applause: "I married a wife. O what misery wanted I then! I begat children: so there's one care more." And those inconveniences that Terence pins on the back of love as injuries, enmities, war, and peace again, do not all these lackey our morality continually? do not these foot sometimes into the friendliest affections? and does not all the world keep these examples in continual renovation as war, I mean injuries and enmities? And our peace is as uncertain, as we are ignorant of their hearts, with whom we hold it, and though we nigh know to-day what they would do, to-morrow we shall not. Who should be greater friends than those of one family? yet how many secret plots of malice lie even

amongst such, to expel security? their firmer peace becoming fouler malice: and being reputed most loyal, whereas it was only most craftily feigned: the far-spread contagion of this made Tully let this saying run out with his tears: "Treason is never so close carried, as when it lurks under the name of duty or affinity. An open foe is easily watched: but this your secret serpent both breeds and strikes ere ever you can discover it." Wherefore that which the Holy Scriptures says, "A man's foes are those of his own household," this we hear with great grief: for though a man have fortitude to endure it, or prevention to avoid it, yet if he be a good man, he must needs take great grief at the badness of those so near him; be it that they have been accustomed unto this viperous dissimulation of old, or have learnt it but of late. So, then, if a man's own private house afford him no shelter from these incursions, what shall the city do, which, as it is larger, so is it fuller of brabbles, and suits, and quarrels, and accusations, even if we grant the absence of seditions and civil contentions, which are too often present: and whereof the cities are in continual danger, when they are in their safest estate?

XV, 12. THAT THE BLOODIEST WAR'S CHIEF AIM IS PEACE: THE DESIRE OF WHICH IS NATURAL IN MAN.

Who will not confess this with me, who marks man's affairs, and the general form of nature? For joy and peace are desired alike of all men. The warrior would but conquer: war's aim is nothing but glorious peace: what is victory but a suppression of resistants, which being done, peace follows? So that peace is war's purpose, the scope of all military discipline, and the limit at which all just contentions level. All men seek peace by war, but none seek war by peace. For they that perturb the peace they live in, do it not for hate of it, but to shew their power in alteration of it. They would not disannul it, but they would have it as they like; and though they break into seditions from the rest, yet must they hold a peaceful force with their fellows that are engaged with them, or else they shall never effect what they intend. Even the thieves themselves that molest all the world besides them, are at peace amongst themselves. Admit one be so strong, or subtle that he will have no fellow, but plays all his parts of roguery alone, yet such as he can neither cut off, nor care to make known his deeds unto, with those he must needs hold a kind of peace. And at home, with his wife and family, there must he needs observe quietness, and questionless delights in their obedience unto him, which if they fail in, he chases, and chides and strikes, setting all in order by force if need be, or by cruelty: which he sees he cannot do, unless all the rest be subjected under one head, which is himself. And might he have the sway of a city, or province in such sort as he has that of his house, he would put off his thievish nature, and put on a king's, albeit his covetousness and malice remained unchanged. Thus then you see that all men desire to have peace with such as they would have live according to their liking. For those against whom they wage war, they would make their own if they could, and if they conquer them they give them such laws as they like. But let us imagine some such insociable fellow as the poet's fable records, calling him half-man, for his inhuman barbarism.

Now he although his kingdom lay in a lightless cave, and his villainies so rare that they gave him the great name of Cacus, which is, evil, though his wife never had good word of him, he never played with his children, nor ruled them in their manlier age, never spoke with friend, nor so much as with his father Vulcan (than whom he was far more happy in that he begat no such monster as Vulcan had in begetting him) though he never gave to any, but robbed and reaved all that he could grip from all manner of persons, yea and the persons themselves, yet in that horrid dungeon of his, whose floor and walls were always dank with the blood of new slaughters, he desired nothing but to rest in peace therein, without molestation. He desired also to be at peace with himself, and what he had, he enjoyed, he ruled over his own body, and to satisfy his own hungry nature that menaced the separation of soul and body, he fell to his robberies with celerity, and though he were barbarous and bloody, yet in all that, he had a care to provide for his life and safety: and therefore if he would have had that peace with others, which he had in the cave with himself alone, he would neither have been called half-man nor monster. But if it were his horrible shape and breathing of fire that made men avoid him, then was it not will, but necessity that made him live in that cave and play the thief for his living. But there was no such man, or if there were, he was not such as the poets feign him. For unless they had mightily belied Cacus, they should not sufficiently have commended Hercules. But, as I said, it is likely that there was no such man, no more than is truth in many other of their fictions: for the very wild beasts (part of whose brutishness they place in him), do preserve a peace each with other in their kind, begetting, breeding, and living together amongst themselves, being otherwise the insociable births of the deserts: I speak not here of sheep, deer, pigeons, starlings or bees, but of lions, foxes, eagles, and owls. For what tiger is there that does not purr over her young ones, and fawn upon them in their tenderness? What kite is there, though he fly solitarily about for his prey, but will seek his female, build his nest, sit his eggs, feed his young, and assist his mate in her motherly duty, all that in him lies? Far stronger are the bands that bind man unto society, and peace with all that are peaceable: the worst men of all do fight for their fellows' quietness, and would (if it lay in their power) reduce all into a distinct form of state, drawn by themselves, whereof they would be the heads, which could never be, but by a coherence either through fear or love. For herein is perverse pride an imitator of the goodness of God, having equality of others with itself under Him, and laying a yoke of obedience upon its fellows, under itself, instead of Him: thus hates it the just peace of God, and builds an unjust one for itself. Yet can it not but love peace, for no vice however unnatural, can pull nature up by the roots. But he that can discern between good and bad, and between order and confusion, may soon distinguish the godly peace from the wicked. Now that perverse confusion must be reformed by the better disposing of the thing wherein it is, if it be at all, as, for example: hang a man up with his head downwards, all his posture is confounded, that which should be lowest, having the highest place, and so contrary this confusion disturbs the flesh, and is troublesome to it. But it is the soul's peace with the body that causes the feeling of that disturbance. Now if the soul leave the body by the means of those troubles, yet as long as the body's form remains

it has a certain peace with itself, and in the very manner of hanging, shews that it desires to be placed in the peace of nature, the very weight, seeming to demand a place for rest, and though life be gone, yet very nature sways it unto that order wherein she placed it. For if the dead body be preserved from putrefaction by unguents, and embalmings, yet the peace of nature is kept, for the body's weight is applied thereby to an earthly sympathising site, and convenient place for it to rest in. But if it be not embalmed, but left to nature's dissolving, it is so long altered by ill-tasting vapours, until each part be wholly reduced to the particular natures of the elements, yet is not a tittle of the Creator's all-disposing law controlled: for if there grow out of this carcase, a many more living creatures, each body of these, serves the quantity of life that is in it, according to the same law of creation. And if that be devoured up, by other ravenous beasts or birds, it shall follow the ordinance of the same law, disposing all things congruently, into what form of nature soever it be changed.

XV, 13. OF THAT UNIVERSAL PEACE WHICH PERTURBANCES CAN SECLUDE FROM THE LAW OF NATURE, GOD'S JUST JUDGMENTS DISPOSING OF EVERY ONE ACCORDING TO HIS PROPER DESERT.

The body's peace therefore is an orderly disposal of the parts thereof: the unreasonable soul's, a good temperature of the appetites thereof: the reasonable soul's a true harmony between the knowledge, and the performance. That of body and soul alike, a temperate and undiseased habit of nature in the whole creature. The peace of mortal man with immortal God, is an orderly obedience unto His eternal law, performed in faith. Peace of man and man, is a mutual concord: peace of a family, an orderly rule and subjection amongst the parts thereof: peace of a city, an orderly command, and obedience amongst the citizens: peace of God's City a most orderly coherence in God, and fruition of God: peace of all things, is a well disposed order. For order, is a good disposition of discrepant parts, each in the fittest place, and therefore the miserable (as they are miserable), are out of order, wanting that peaceable and unperturbed state which order exacts. But because their own merits have incurred this misery, therefore even herein they are imposed in a certain set order howsoever. Being not conjoined with the blessed, but severed from them by the law of order, and being exposed to miseries, yet these are adapted unto the places wherein they are resident, and so are digested into some kind of methodical form, and consequently into some peaceful order. But this is their misery, that although that some little security wherein they live, may exempt them from present sorrows, yet are they not in that state which secludes sorrow for ever, and affords eternal security. And their misery is far greater if they want the peace of nature: and when they are offended, the part that grieves is the first disturber of their peace: for that which is neither offended, nor dissolved, preserves the peace of nature still. So then as one may possibly live without grief, but cannot possibly grieve unless he live: so may there be peace without any war or contention: but contention cannot be without some peace (not as it is contention, but), because the contenders do suffer and perform diverse things herein according to nature's pre-

script, which things could not consist, had they not some peaceful order amongst them. So that there may be a nature (you see) where no evil may have inherence, but to find a nature utterly void of goodness, is utterly impossible. For the very nature of the devils (considered as nature) is most excellent, but their own voluntary perverseness depraved it. The devil abode not in the truth, yet escaped he not the sentence of the truth: for he transgressed the peaceful law of order, yet could not avoid the powerful hand of the Orderer.

The good which God had bestowed on his nature, cleared him not from God's heavy judgment which allotted him to punishment. Yet does not God herein punish the good which Himself created, but the evil which the devil committed: nor did He take away his whole nature from him, but left him part, whereby to bewail the loss of the rest: which lamentation, testifies both what he had and what he has: for had he not some good left, he could not lament for what he had lost. For his guilt is the greater that having lost all his uprightness, should rejoice at the loss thereof. And he that is sick, if it benefit him nothing yet grieves at the loss of his health. For uprightness and health being both good in themselves, it behoves the losers of them to mourn, and not to rejoice, unless this loss be repaired with better recompence, as uprightness of mind is better than health of body: but far more reason has the sinner to lament in his suffering than to rejoice in his transgression. Therefore even as to rejoice at the loss of goodness in sinning, argues a depraved will: so likewise lament for the same loss, in suffering, proves a good nature. For he that bewails the loss of his natural peace, has his light from the remainder of that peace, which are left in him, keeping his nature and him in concord.

And in the last judgment, it is but reasonable that the wicked should deplore the loss of their natural goods, and feel God's hand justly heavy in depriving them of them, whom they scornfully respected not in the bestowing them upon them. Wherefore the high God, nature's wisest Creature, and most just Disposer, the Parent of the world's fairest wonder (mankind) bestowed divers good things upon him, which serve for this life only, as the worldly and temporal peace, kept by honest coherence and society: together with all the adjuncts of this peace, as the visible light, the spirable air; the potable water; and all the other necessaries of meat, drink, and clothing: but with this condition, that he that shall use them in their due manner, and reference unto human peace, shall be rewarded with gifts of far greater moment, namely with the peace of immortality, and with unshaded glory, and full fruition of God, and his brother, in the same God: but he that uses them amiss, shall neither partake of the former nor the latter.

XV, 14. OF THE LAW OF HEAVEN AND EARTH WHICH SWAYS HUMAN SOCIETY BY COUNSEL AND UNTO WHICH COUNSEL HUMAN SOCIETY IS OBEDIENT.

All temporal things are referred unto the benefit of the peace which is resident in the terrestrial city, by the members thereof: and unto the use of the eternal peace, by the citizens of the Heavenly society. Wherefore if we wanted reason, we should desire only an orderly state of body, and a good temperature of desires: nothing but fleshly ease, and

fulness of pleasure. For the peace of the body augments the quiet of the soul: and if it be awanting, it procures a disturbance even in brute beasts, because the emotions have not their true temperature.

Now both these combined add unto the peace of soul and body both, that is, unto the healthful order of life. For as all creatures shew how they desire their bodies' peace, in avoiding the causes of their hurt: and their souls', in following their appetites when need requires: so in flying of death; they make it as apparent how much they set by their peace of soul and body. But man having a reasonable soul, subjects all his actions common to animals, unto the peace of that, to work so both in his contemplation and action, that there may be a true consonance between them both, and this we call the peace of the reasonable soul. To this end he is to avoid molestation by grief, disturbance by desire, and dissolution by death, and to aim at profitable knowledge, whereunto his actions may be conformable. But lest his own infirmity, through the much desire to know, should draw him into any pestilent inconvenience of error, he must have a divine instruction, to whose directions and assistance, he is to assent with firm and free obedience. And because that during this life, "He is absent from the Lord, he walketh by faith, and not by sight," and therefore he refers all his peace of body, of soul, and of both, unto that peace which mortal man has with immortal God: to live in an orderly obedience under His eternal law, by faith.

Now God, our good Master, teaching us in the two great commandments the love of Him, and the love of our neighbour, to love three things, God, our neighbour, and ourselves, and seeing he that loves God, offends not in loving himself: it follows that he ought to counsel his neighbour to love God, and to provide for him in the love of God, sure he is commanded to love him, as his own self. So must he do for his wife, children, family, and all men besides: and wish likewise that his neighbor would do as much for him, in his need: thus shall he be settled in peace and orderly concord with all the world. The order whereof is, first, to do no man hurt, and secondly, to help all that he can. So that his own have the first place in his care, and those, his place and order in human society affords him more conveniency to benefit. Whereupon St. Paul says, "He that provideth not for his own, and, namely, for them that be of his household, denieth the faith, and is worse than an infidel." For this is the foundation of domestic peace, which is, an orderly rule, and subjection in the parts of the family, wherein the provisors are the commanders, as the husband over his wife; parents over their children, and masters over their servants: and they that are provided for, obey, as the wives do their husbands, children their parents, and servants their masters. But in the family of the faithful man, the heavenly pilgrim, there the commanders are indeed the servants of those they seem to command: ruling not in ambition, but being bound by careful duty: not in proud sovereignty, but in nourishing pity.

XV, 15. NATURE'S FREEDOM, AND BONDAGE, CAUSED BY SIN: IN WHICH MAN IS A SLAVE TO HIS OWN PASSIONS, THOUGH HE BE NOT BONDMAN TO ANY ONE BESIDES.

Thus has nature's order prescribed, and man by God was thus created. "Let them rule," saith He, "over the fishes of the sea, and the fowls of the air, and over every thing that creepeth upon the earth." He made him reasonable, and lord only over the unreasonable, not over man, but over beasts. Whereupon the first holy men were rather shepherds than kings, God shewing herein what both the order of the creation desired, and what the merit of sin exacted. For justly was the burden of servitude laid upon the back of transgression. And therefore in all the Scriptures we never read the word servant, until such time as that just man Noah laid it as a curse upon his offending son. So that it was guilt, and not nature that gave original unto that name. The Latin word *servus,* had the first derivation from hence: those that were taken in the wars, being in the hands of the conquerors to massacre or to preserve, if they saved them, then were they called *servi,* of *servo,* "to save." Nor was this effected beyond the desert of sin. For in the justest war, the sin upon one side causes it; and if the victory fall to the wicked (as sometimes it may) it is God's decree to humble the conquered, either reforming their sins herein, or punishing them. Witness that holy man of God, Daniel, who, being in captivity, confessed unto his Creator that his sins, and the sins of the people were the real causes of that captivity.

Sin therefore is the mother of servitude, and first cause of man's subjection to man: which notwithstanding comes not to pass but by the direction of the highest, in whom is no injustice, and who alone knows best how to proportionate his punishment unto man's offences: and he himself says: "Whosoever committeth sin is the servant of sin," and therefore many religious Christians are servants unto wicked masters, yet not unto freemen, for that which a man is addicted unto, the same is he slave unto. And it is a happier servitude to serve man than lust: for lust (to omit all the other passions) practises extreme tyranny upon the hearts of those that serve it, be it lust after sovereignty or fleshly lust. But in the peaceful orders of states, wherein one man is under another, as humility does benefit the servant, so does pride endamage the superior. But take a man as God created him at first, and so he is neither slave to man nor to sin. But penal servitude had the institution from that law which commands the conservation, and forbids the disturbance of nature's order: for if that law had not first been transgressed, penal servitude had never been enjoined.

Therefore the apostle warns servants to obey their masters and to serve them with cheerfulness, and good will: to the end that if they cannot be made free by their masters, they make their servitude a freedom to themselves, by serving them, not in deceitful fear, but in faithful love, until iniquity be overpassed, and all man's power and principality disannulled, and God only be all in all.

XV, 16. OF THE JUST LAW OF SOVEREIGNTY.

Wherefore although our righteous forefathers had servants in their families, and according to their temporal estates, made a distinction between their servants and their children, yet in matter of religion (the fountain whence all eternal good flows), they provided for all their household with an equal respect unto each member thereof. This, nature's order prescribed, and hence came the name of, "The Father of the family," a name which even the worst masters love to be called by. But such as merit that name truly, do care that all their families should continue in the service of God, as if they were all their own children,

desiring that they should all be placed in the household of heaven, where command is wholly unnecessary, because then they are past their charge, having attained immortality, which until they be installed in, the masters are to endure more labour in their government, than the servants in their service. If any be disobedient, and offend this just peace, he is forthwith to be corrected, with strokes, or some other convenient punishment, whereby he may be reingraffed into the peaceful stock from whence his disobedience has torn him. For as it is no good turn to help a man unto a smaller good by the loss of a greater: no more is it the part of innocence by pardoning a small offence, to let it grow unto a fouler. It is the duty of an innocent to hurt no man, but, withal, to curb sin in all he can, and to correct sin in whom he can, that the sinner's correction may be profitable to himself, and his example a terror unto others. Every family then being part of the city, every beginning having relation unto some end, and every part tending to the integrity of the whole, it follows apparently, that the family's peace adheres unto the city's, that is, the orderly command, and obedience in the family, has real reference to the orderly rule and subjection in the city. So that "the father of the family" may fetch his instructions from the city's government, whereby he may proportionate the peace of his private estate, by that of the common.

XV, 17. THE GROUNDS OF THE CONCORD AND DISCORD BETWEEN THE CITIES OF HEAVEN AND EARTH.

But they that live not according to faith, angle for all their peace in the sea of temporal profits: whereas the righteous live in full expectation of the glories to come, using the occurrences of this world, but as pilgrims, not to abandon their course towards God for mortal respects, but thereby to assist the infirmity of the corruptible flesh, and make it more able to encounter with toil and trouble. Wherefore the necessaries of this life are common, both to the faithful and the infidel, and to both their families: but the ends of their two usages thereof are far different.

The faithless, "worldly city" aims at earthly peace, and settles the self therein, only to have an uniformity of the citizens' wills in matters only pertaining to mortality. And the "Heavenly City," or rather that part thereof, which is as yet a pilgrim on earth and lives by faith, uses this peace also: as it should, it leaves this mortal life, wherein such a peace is requisite, and therefore lives (while it is here on earth) as if it were in captivity, and having received the promise of redemption, and divers spiritual gifts as seals thereof, it willingly obeys such laws of the "temporal city" as order the things pertaining to the sustenance of this mortal life, to the end that both the cities might observe a peace in such things as are pertinent hereunto. But because that the "earthly city" has some members whom the Holy Scriptures utterly disallow, and who standing either too well affected to the devils, or being deluded by them, believed that each thing had a peculiar deity over it, and belonged to the charge of a several god: as the body to one, the soul to another, and in the body itself the head to one, the neck to another, and so of every member: as likewise of the soul, one had the wit, another the learning, a third the wrath, a fourth the desire: as also in other necessaries or accidents belonging to man's life, the cattle, the corn, the wine, the oil, the woods, the monies, the navigation, the wars, the marriages, the generations, each being a several charge unto a particular power, whereas the citizens of the "Heavenly State" acknowledged but one only God, to whom that worship, which is called λατρεία was peculiarly and solely due; hence came it that the "two hierarchies" could not be combined in one religion, but must needs dissent herein, so that the good part was fain to bear the pride and persecution of the bad, had not their own multitude sometimes, and the providence of God continually stood for their protection.

This "celestial society" while it is here on earth, increases itself out of all languages, never respecting the temporal laws that are made against so good and religious a practice: yet not breaking, but observing their diversity in divers nations, all which do tend unto the preservation of earthly peace, if they oppose not the adoration of one only God. So that you see, the "Heavenly City" observes and respects this temporal peace here on earth, and the coherence of men's wills in honest morality, as far as it may with a safe conscience; yea, and so far desires it, making use of it for the attainment of the peace eternal: which is so truly worthy of that name, as that the orderly and uniform combination of men in the fruition of God, and of one another in God, is to be accounted the reasonable creature's only peace, which being once attained, mortality is banished, and life then is the true life indeed, nor is the carnal body any more an encumbrance to the soul, by corruptibility, but is now become spiritual, perfected and entirely subject unto the sovereignty of the will.

This peace is that unto which the pilgrim in faith refers the other which he has here in his pilgrimage, and then lives he according to faith, when all that he does for the obtaining hereof is by himself referred unto God, and his neighbour withal, because being a citizen, he must not be all for himself, but sociable in his life and actions.

XV, 21. WHETHER THE CITY OF ROME HAD EVER A TRUE COMMONWEALTH, ACCORDING TO SCIPIO'S DEFINITION OF A COMMONWEALTH, IN TULLY.

Now it is time to perform a promise which I passed in the second book of this work: and that was, to shew that Rome never had a true commonwealth as Scipio defines one in Tully's book *De Republicâ*. His definition was: a commonwealth is the estate of the people, *Respublica est res populi*. If this be true, Rome never had any, for it never had an estate of the people, which he defines the commonwealth by: for, he defines the people to be a multitude, united in one consent of law and profit: what he means by a consent of law, he shews himself: and shews thereby that a state cannot stand without justice: so that where true justice is wanting, there can be no law. For what law does, justice does, and what is done unjustly, is done unlawfully. For we may not imagine men's unjust decrees to be laws: all men defining law to arise out of the fountain of justice; and that that same unjust assertion of some, is utterly false: "That is law which is profitable unto the greatest." So then, where justice is not, there can be no society united in one consent of law, therefore no people, according to Scipio's definitions in Tully. If no people, then no estate of the people, but rather of a confused multitude, unworthy of a people's name. If then the commonwealth be an estate of the people, and that they be no people that are

not united in one consent of law: nor that a law, which is not grounded upon justice: then it must needs follow, that where no justice is, there no commonwealth is. Now then *ad propositum:* justice is a virtue distributing unto everyone his due. What justice is that then, that takes man from the true God, and gives him unto the condemned fiends? is this distribution of due? is he that takes away thy possessions, and gives them to one that has no claim to them, guilty of injustice, and is not he so likewise, that takes himself away from his Lord God, and gives himself to the service of the devil? There are wise and powerful disputations in those books, *De Republicâ*, for justice against injustice. Wherein, it having first been argued for injustice, against justice, and averred that a state could not stand without injustice; and this brought as a principal confirmation hereof, that it is injustice for man to rule over man, and yet if the city whose dominion is so large, should not observe this form of injustice, she could never keep the provinces under. Unto this it was answered on the behalf of justice, that this was a just course, it being profitable for such to serve, and for their good to wit, when the power to do hurt is taken from the wicked, they will carry themselves better being curbed, because they carried themselves so badly before they were curbed. To ·confirm this answer this notable example was alleged, as being fetched from nature itself: "If it were unjust to rule, why does God rule over man, the soul over the body, reason over lust, and all the mind's other vicious affections?" This example teaches plain that it is good for some to serve in particular, and it is good for all to serve God in general. And the mind serving God, is lawful Lord over the body: so is reason being subject unto God, over the lusts and other vices. Wherefore if man serve not God, what justice can be thought to be in him? seeing that if he serve not Him the soul has neither lawful sovereignty over the body, nor the reason over the affections: now if this justice cannot be found in one man, no more can it then in a whole multitude of such like men. Therefore amongst such there is not that consent of law which makes a multitude a people, whose estate makes a commonwealth: what need I speak of the profit, that is named in the definition of a people? for although that none live profitably that live wickedly, that serve not God but the devils (who are so much the more wicked in that they being most filthy creatures, dare exact sacrifices as if they were gods): yet I think that what I have said of the consent of law may serve to shew that they were no people whose estate might make a weal-public, having no justice amongst them. If they say they did not serve devils, but holy gods, what need we rehearse that here which we said so often before? Who is he that has read over this work unto this chapter, and yet doubts whether they were devils that the Romans worshipped or no? unless he be either senselessly thick-headed, or shamelessly contentious? But to leave the powers that they offered unto, take this place of holy writ for all: "He that sacrificeth unto gods, shall be rooted out, save unto one God alone." He that taught this in such threatening manner will have no gods sacrificed unto, be they good or be they bad.

State, Power, and Authority

It has been observed that society for the realist is a system of ends or purposes rooted in man's nature, where the lower serves the higher and the higher directs the lower. The entire hierarchical structure is controlled by the central values of peace and justice, and the good of the whole is the good of all, or the common good.

Realists make a number of inferences about power and authority from these premises. All power originates in being (for theists in the supreme being who is God*), is mediated through the people in community (human nature), and is entrusted to some ruler. The common good itself dictates that there be some head or ruling part upon whom the order and structure of society centers. Rulership is a trust for the whole community that seeks to lay the foundations of human happiness by maintaining peace and order. Furthermore, the moral purpose of government implies that authority must be limited and exercised only in accordance with law. Law, the subject of the next section, makes for legitimate government, and the common good makes for its necessity.

Thus, the basic realist view of government is that of a central authority which acts for the common good and which is morally justified by the fact that it is lawful. But what form should actual governments take? In his *Politics,* Aristotle distinguished monarchy, aristocracy, and polity as legitimate forms of government, and gave tyranny, oligarchy, and democracy as the parallel corruptions of

---

* See also *Romans* 13:1: "For there is no power but of God: the powers that be are ordained of God."

each.† This classification is based primarily on a quantitative principle: rule by one, by a few, or by many. Aristotle himself expressed a preference for a "mixed" government, though he recognized that the varying circumstances of different peoples might dictate different governmental forms. One-man rule allows for unity and decisiveness, the rule of an élite allows for the selection of the best abilities in the state, and the rule of polity or constitutional democracy allows for freedom and economic equality. Medieval realists on the whole preferred monarchy for they saw an analogy between God's rule of creation and the king's rule of his kingdom. Modern realists have generally argued for polity of some form or other. Important as the question of the form of government is—and it is important for the realist, since the aim of statecraft is to develop a form and ethos that will synthesize the historic conditions of a people with basic political values—it is nevertheless subordinate to questions of legitimacy through law and moral purpose.

The following two selections develop these views on government and authority primarily in a medieval context. John of Salisbury (c. 1120–1180) wrote after Pope Gelasius (492–496) had developed the doctrine of two authorities, one spiritual and one temporal. The conflicts between papacy and empire that continued through the Middle Ages were developing in John's time, and he generally sided with the papalists in these controversies. His position, however, allowed him to hold three important views. He believed that the authority of the papacy would provide a check on unjust and intemperate temporal rulers. He developed—quite independently of Aristotle's thought which he did not know—an organic conception of society. His famous analogy of society and the human body points out the dependence of parts on the whole, which is the essential feature of organic theories of the state. The analogy also points out the dependence of lower parts on the head, which is the principle of hierarchy. Finally, John inferred the right of tyrannicide. A king, he believed, is distinguished from a tyrant as law is from force, and tyrants may be slain if it becomes necessary to rid the body politic of their evil influence. In this doctrine John went far beyond other medieval thinkers, who generally denied the right of tyrannicide altogether or limited it only to subordinate officials, not to the people as a whole.

Historically, Marsilius of Padua (1275–1343) stands as a link between the medieval and modern periods as well as between realism and later developments in social philosophy. Following Aristotle, Marsilius defined the state as a kind of "living being" composed of parts that perform functions necessary to its life. The health of the social organism is expressed in the orderly working of its parts and in the peace that issues from such order. Such an idea has been met in preceding selections.

But Marsilius added a further and distinctive notion to this idea, for he taught that good governments rule for the benefit of the people *with their consent*. This doctrine was by no means discovered by Marsilius; it was commonly held from Greek and Roman days by philosophers and statesmen alike that the people are the source of authority. To be sure, such consent was not equivalent to the modern idea of "popular sovereignty." Rather, it was most frequently connected with

† "Democracy" for Greek thinkers did not have its modern meaning; it rather connoted to them "mob-rule." The legitimate forms are marked by the rule of law and the common good, the corruptions by the absence of these factors.

the notion of custom,‡ for kingship was believed to be both legitimate and based on consent if it existed for a relatively long time. While he did not discover this teaching, Marsilius cleared it of all encumbrances so that it could become a call to action. He also integrated this teaching and the process of election, another idea from Aristotle. Marsilius took election to be the most certain standard of government, and his full position is that the basis of authority is the will of the community as expressed in election.

Much of the writing of John and Marsilius must be seen in the light of the conflicts and problems of their day. To some extent also, Marsilius is a transitional figure§ who clearly expressed Aristotelian realism, and yet looked beyond the political forms of his day. Nevertheless, the writings of John and Marsilius contain major sources of understanding the state, power, and authority from a realistic point of view.

‡ Some authorities, in fact, hold that the ancient political distinction between "nature" and "convention" might better be expressed as "custom" and "convention."

§ The student may follow this on two points at least. Marsilius looks forward historically to positivist and utilitarian doctrines in his view that law is not derived from divine law, as St. Thomas Aquinas writes in the next section, but is rather the commands of the legislator enforceable in the courts. The practical meaning of this definition is that the teaching of priests has no proper power or (political) authority. Secondly, there is much in Marsilius that anticipates the modern secular state, such as his belief that in order to insure peace, the papacy must be denied authority in temporal affairs.

JOHN OF SALISBURY The Order of the Commonwealth

IV, 1. OF THE DIFFERENCE BETWEEN A PRINCE AND A TYRANT AND OF WHAT IS MEANT BY A PRINCE.

Between a tyrant and a prince there is this single or chief difference, that the latter obeys the law and rules the people by its dictates, accounting himself as but their servant. It is by virtue of the law that he makes good his claim to the foremost and chief place in the management of the affairs of the commonwealth and in the bearing of its burdens; and his elevation over others consists in this, that whereas private men are held responsible only for their private affairs, on the prince fall the burdens of the whole community. Wherefore deservedly there is conferred on him,

and gathered together in his hands, the power of all his subjects, to the end that he may be sufficient unto himself in seeking and bringing about the advantage of each individually, and of all; and to the end that the state of the human commonwealth may be ordered in the best possible manner, seeing that each and all are members one of another. Wherein we indeed but follow nature, the best guide of life; for nature has gathered together all the senses of her microcosm or little world, which is man, into the head, and has subjected all the members in obedience to it in such wise that they will all function properly so long as they follow the guidance of the head, and the head remains sane. Therefore the prince stands

From *The Statesman's Book of John of Salisbury,* trans. into English by John Dickinson. Copyright 1927, by Alfred A. Knopf, Inc. Reprinted by permission of Appleton-Century-Crofts. Division of Meredith Publishing Company.

on a pinnacle which is exalted and made splendid with all the great and high privileges which he deems necessary for himself. And rightly so, because nothing is more advantageous to the people than that the needs of the prince should be fully satisfied; since it is impossible that his will should be found opposed to justice. Therefore, according to the usual definition, the prince is the public power, and a kind of likeness on earth of the divine majesty. Beyond doubt a large share of the divine power is shown to be in princes by the fact that at their nod men bow their necks and for the most part offer up their heads to the axe to be struck off, and, as by a divine impulse, the prince is feared by each of those over whom he is set as an object of fear. And this I do not think could be, except as a result of the will of God. For all power is from the Lord God, and has been with Him always, and is from everlasting. The power which the prince has is therefore from God, for the power of God is never lost, nor severed from Him, but He merely exercises it through a subordinate hand, making all things teach His mercy or justice. "Who, therefore, resists the ruling power, resists the ordinance of God,"[1] in whose hand is the authority of conferring that power, and when He so desires, of withdrawing it again, or diminishing it. For it is not the ruler's own act when his will is turned to cruelty against his subjects, but it is rather the dispensation of God for His good pleasure to punish or chasten them. Thus during the Hunnish persecution, Attila, on being asked by the reverend bishop of a certain city who he was, replied, "I am Attila, the scourge of God." Whereupon it is written that the bishop adored him as representing the divine majesty. "Welcome,"

he said, "is the minister of God," and "Blessed is he that cometh in the name of the Lord," and with sighs and groans he unfastened the barred doors of the church, and admitted the persecutor through whom he attained straightway to the palm of martyrdom. For he dared not shut out the scourge of God, knowing that His beloved Son was scourged, and that the power of this scourge which had come upon himself was as nought except it came from God. If good men thus regard power as worthy of veneration even when it comes as a plague upon the elect, who should not venerate that power which is instituted by God for the punishment of evil-doers and for the reward of good men, and which is promptest in devotion and obedience to the laws? To quote the words of the Emperor, "it is indeed a saying worthy of the majesty of royalty that the prince acknowledges himself bound by the Laws."[2] For the authority of the prince depends upon the authority of justice and law; and truly it is a greater thing than imperial power for the prince to place his government under the laws, so as to deem himself entitled to do nought which is at variance with the equity of justice.

V, 6. CONCERNING THE PRINCE, WHO IS THE HEAD OF THE COMMONWEALTH, AND OF HIS ELECTION AND PRIVILEGES; AND CONCERNING THE RECOMPENSE OF VIRTUE AND GUILT: AND THAT BLESSED JOB SHOULD BE IMITATED; AND CONCERNING THE VIRTUES OF BLESSED JOB.

Following in the footsteps of our author, we come next to consider the

---

[1] *Rom.,* xiii., 2. *Tr.*

[2] Justin., *Cod.,* 1., 14, § 4. *Tr.*

members of the commonwealth. It has been said that the prince holds the place of the head, and is guided solely by the judgment of his own mind. And so, as has been said, he is placed by the divine governance at the apex of the commonwealth, and preferred above all others, sometimes through the secret ministry of God's providence, sometimes by the decision of His priests, and again it is the votes of the whole people which concur to place the ruler in authority. Wherefore we read in the Old Testament that Moyses, when about to ordain him who should have authority over the people, called together the whole synagogue to the end that he might be chosen in the presence of the people, so that afterwards no man might have ground for retraction, and no least scruple of uncertainty might remain to cloud his title. We read in the Book of Kings that Saul, when about to be made king, appeared before the face of the people, and was lifted up on their shoulders, above the whole people. Why so, I ask, if not because he that is to be over others ought in heart and countenance to show that he has strength sufficient to embrace as it were the breadth of the whole people in the arms of his good works, and to protect them, as being more learned, more holy, more prudent, and more excellent in every virtue? For the Lord said unto Moyses: "Take unto thee Jesus the son of Nave, a man in whom is the spirit of God, and lay thy hands upon him, and set him before Eleazer the priest, and let him give him commandments in the sight of the whole synagogue; and thou shalt give instructions concerning him in their presence, and shalt put of thy honor upon him that the children of Israel may hear and obey him."[3] Evidently we are here list-

---

[3] *Num.* xxvii, 18. *Tr.*

ening to the ordination of a prince of the people, described so clearly that it needs no explanation. If, however, you ask for one in yet plainer terms, I will explain it to you on the authority of the Lord if you will advise me at the proper time and place, and I will add the meaning of the robes and certain features of the ritual. But here is plainly no acclamation by the people, no argument or title founded upon ties of blood, no consideration accorded to family relationship. . . .

V, 11. OF THE EYES, EARS, AND TONGUE OF RULERS; AND OF THE OFFICE OF GOVERNOR; AND THAT A JUDGE SHOULD HAVE KNOWLEDGE OF THE LAW AND OF EQUITY, A WILL DISPOSED TOWARD GOOD, AND ADEQUATE POWER OF ENFORCEMENT, AND THAT HE SHOULD BE BOUND BY AN OATH TO KEEP THE LAWS AND SHOULD BE FREE FROM THE TAINT OF RECEIVING GIFTS.

Next in order comes the simile of eyes, ears, and tongue, which, as above-mentioned, is applied to provincial governors. A governor is one who presides over the administration of justice among the people of a province. He therefore should have knowledge of the just and the unjust, and should have the means and the will to enforce justice. For although the common lot of death ought not to be imputed to the physician, yet if tragic consequences are the result of his ignorance or lack of skill, they are deservedly charged to him. Furthermore if he knows the proper remedy and refuses to apply it, he is condemned not for ignorance but for wilful wrong. Condemnation results in either situation; though the punishment of ignorance is the milder of the two, except in cases where the ignorance has been brought about by negligence. For if ignorance is invincible, it does not lead to the death penalty but is excused by innate incapacity. So if a governor knows and wishes to do equity, but has not adequate power, the fault is not so much his own as it is the fault of the prince. It is, however, most certain that the duty of a judge and his religion should include the following things: he ought to have a knowledge of law, a will disposed toward good, and adequate power to enforce his decisions, and he should be bound by an oath to keep the laws so that he may know that it is not permissible for him to depart in any particular from the purity thereof. The book of Wisdom instructs us with regard to the wisdom of a judge: "A wise judge judges the people, and the rule of a prudent man shall stand firm. As is the judge of a people, so also are his ministers; and what manner of man is the ruler of a city, such likewise are they that dwell therein."[4] But it is also pointed out that power is necessary: "Seek not to be made a judge unless thou have power and strength to break down iniquities, lest perchance thou quail before the face of the powerful and in they obsequiousness lay a stone of stumbling for thyself. Sin not against the populace of a city, nor thrust thyself in among them, nor make thyself guilty of two sins, for not even in one shalt thou escape untouched. Be not cowardly in thine own spirit; despise not to pray and to give alms. Say not 'God will look with favor on the multitude of my gifts, and when I offer them to God the Most High, He will accept my offerings.' Laugh at no man in the bitterness of his soul; for it is all-seeing God alone who exalteth and bringeth low."[5] From these words the attentive reader will observe that a will disposed toward good is not less necessary to a judge than are knowledge and power; since he is held responsible not only for his own offences but for those of others, and, laboring under the double burden of both, he will not be accounted faithful before God merely because of the multitude of his gifts without cleanness of will also. Wherefore Plato says[6] well and pointedly (if men would but heed his words) that those who contend with one another for the prize of bearing public office act as if sailors in the face of a tempest were to fight over which of them should be helmsman of the ship. At such a turn of fortune the man does not exist, or only rarely, and he is a rash man indeed, who makes good his title to the magistracy without skill and strength. And in my own time, I have seen nought more lamentable than judges ignorant of the science of law and devoid of good-will, as is proved by their love of gifts and rewards, exercising the power which they have in the service of avarice or ostentation or advancing the fortunes of their own flesh and blood, and exempted from the necessity of swearing obedience to the laws. From this it is plain that the princes who have conferred regular jurisdiction on such judges are themselves either ignorant of law or else hold it in contempt. But, whatever we may say regarding legal learning or the power of enforcement, at least a judge ought to be an eminently religious man, and one who hates all injustice worse than death itself. . . .

---

[4] *Eccli.* x, 1–2. *Tr.*

[5] *Eccli.* vii., 6–12. *Tr.*

[6] Cicero, *De Off.*, i., 25, § 87, quoting Plato, *Rep.*, vi., 488B. *Tr.*

VI, 21. That the Common-wealth Should Be Ordered to the Pattern of Nature, and that Its Ordering Should Be Borrowed from the Bees.

In different fashion both Cicero and Plato have written of the commonwealth, the one discussing it as it ought to be, the other as it was instituted and handed down by the men of earlier times. But both laid down the same formula for the existing or projected body politic, namely that its life should imitate nature, which we have so often called the best guide of life. Otherwise it will deserve to be called not only anarchical, but rather bestial and brutal. What Nature's design is, is disclosed even by creatures which are devoid of reason. When Plutarch bids Trajan to borrow the pattern of civil life from the bees, he but follows Maro, most learned of poets, who sings "of the marvellous spectacle of tiny beings. . . ."[7]

VI, 25. Of the Cohesion and Mutual Dependence of the Head and Members of the Commonwealth; and that the Prince Is as It Were the Likeness of Deity; and of the Crime of Lèse Majesté, and of the Obligations of Fealty.

For myself, I am satisfied and persuaded that loyal shoulders should uphold the power of the ruler; and not only do I submit to his power patiently, but with pleasure, so long as it is exercised in subjection to God and follows His

ordinances. But on the other hand if it resists and opposes the divine commandments, and wishes to make me share in its war against God; then with unrestrained voice I answer back that God must be preferred before any man on earth. Therefore inferiors should cleave and cohere to their superiors, and all the limbs should be in subjection to the head; but always and only on condition that religion is kept inviolate. We read that Socrates framed a polity for a commonwealth and laid down precepts therefor which are said to flow from the purity of wisdom as from a natural fountain. And this one thing he emphasized above all else, that the more humble elements of the commonwealth should receive proportionately greater care and attention from those in higher station as part of their public duty. Read diligently again the "Instruction of Trajan," of which mention has been made above, and you will find these things discussed there at large.

Let it suffice at present to have said so much concerning the unity of head and members, adding only what we have already premised, namely that an injury to the head, as we have said above, is brought home to all the members, and that a wound unjustly inflicted on any member tends to the injury of the head. Furthermore whatsoever is attempted foully and with malice against the head, or corporate community, of the members, is a crime of the greatest gravity and nearest to sacrilege; for as the latter is an attempt against God, so the former is an attack upon the prince, who is admitted to be as it were the likeness of deity upon earth. And therefore it is called the crime of lèse majesté, for the reason that it is aimed against the likeness of Him who alone, as the famous

---

[7] Here follows a transcript of Virgil's *Fourth Georgic*, lines 153–218, on the political constitution of the bees. *Tr.*

Count Robert of Leicester, a man who modestly discharged the office of proconsul in the British lands, was wont to say, wears the truth of true and native majesty,—to wit if any one undertakes aught against the security of the prince or of the people, either directly or through another. In the punishment of such a man, all are treated as of equal rank and in like case; and generally it comes to pass that such men, with whom none have any commerce in life, are not even released by the kindness of death; but if they are convicted, then after death their memory is condemned and their goods are forfeited by their heirs. For where the wickedness of an offender lies as here in having taken most wicked counsel, for such an offence he is punished as it were in mind. And when once a man has committed such a crime, it is settled that he can neither legally alienate nor manumit, nor can his debtor lawfully discharge his debt to him.[8] Because of the greatness of this crime, even infamous persons who in other cases do not have the right of bringing accusations are here permitted to do so without any impediment, as well as soldiers, who may not maintain other actions. For those who are on guard to defend the peace are all the more properly admitted to bring this charge. Also slaves may lawfully inform against their masters and freedmen against their patrons. Nevertheless this accusation is not to be dealt with by judges as an opportunity for displaying their subservience to the prince's majesty, but solely on the basis of the truth. The person of the accused must be looked to, as to whether he could have done the act, and whether he actually did it, or whether he devised it, and whether, before he presumed so far, he was of sane mind. Nor ought a mere slip of the tongue to be drawn readily on to punishment; for although the foolhardy are deserving of punishment, still even such men should be spared if their offence is not one which flows directly from the letter of the law or which must be punished in accordance with the analogy of the law.[9] Women also are heard on a question of lèse majesté; for the conspiracy of Sergius Cathelina was disclosed by a woman, a certain Julia, who supplied Marcus Tully with information in proceeding against him.[10] Also, if necessity or utility recommends, torture is to be applied to those who are thought to be guilty of this crime, as well as to those by whose counsel and instigation they appear to have undertaken the alleged criminal act, so that the prescribed penalty may be brought home to all who were concerned or had knowledge therein.[11]

The acts are many which constitute the crime of lèse majesté, as for example if one conceives the death of the prince or magistrates, or has borne arms against his country, or, forsaking his prince, has deserted in a public war, or has incited or solicited the people to rebel against the commonwealth; or if by the act or criminal intent of any, the enemies of the people and commonwealth are aided with supplies, armor, weapons, money, or any thing else whatsoever, or if, from being friends, they are turned into enemies of the commonwealth; or if by the criminal intent or act of any, it comes to pass that pledges or money are given against the commonwealth, or the people of a foreign country are perverted from their obedience to the commonwealth; like-

---

[8] Justin., *Cod.*, ix, 8, 4–6. *Tr.*

[9] *Dig.* xviii, 4, 7. *Tr.*

[10] *Dig.* xlviii, 4, 8. *Tr.*

[11] Justin., *Cod.*, ix, 8, 4–6. *Tr.*

wise he commits the crime who effects the escape of one who after confessing his guilt in court has on this account been thrown into chains; and many other acts of this nature, which it would be too long or impossible to enumerate.[12]

But because the formula of fidelity or fealty ought herein above all else to be kept, there is language in the oath from which we can most conveniently learn a few of the acts which are not permitted. For a thing which is the opposite of something that is necessary is impossible, and by the same process of reasoning a thing which ought to be done is contradicted only by something that is not permitted. The formula of fealty, then, extracts the things which are inserted therein as being the necessary elements of loyalty, and expresses the latter by the words "sound," "safe," "honorable," "advantageous," "easy,"

[12] *Dig.* xlviii, 4, 1–4. *Tr.*

"possible."[13] If therefore, we are bound by fealty to anyone, we must not harm his soundness of body, or take from him the military resources upon which his safety depends, or presume to commit any act whereby his honor or advantage is diminished; neither is it lawful that that which is easy for him should be made difficult, or that which is possible impossible. Besides, one who holds a benefice from him whose liege man he is, owes to him aid and counsel in his undertakings; from which fact it is clearer than the sun how much is owed to the God of all, if so much is owed even to those to whom we are bound only by fealty.

[13] These six words are used to describe the elements of feudal obligation in the oldest extant document which informs us of the nature of such obligation,—a letter of Fulbert of Chartres to the Duke of Aquitaine, belonging to the first part of the eleventh century. The letter is translated in J. H. Robinson, "Readings in European History," vol. i, p. 184. See Luchaire, "Manuel des Institutions," p. 185. *Tr.*

MARSILIUS OF PADUA

IV. On the Final Cause of the State and of Its Civil Requirements, and the Differentiation in General of Its Parts.

The state, according to Aristotle in the *Politics,* Book I, Chapter 1, is "the perfect community having the full limit of self-sufficiency, which came into existence for the sake of living, but exists for the sake of living well."[1] This phrase of Aristotle—"came into exist-

[1] Aristotle *Politics* I. 2. 1252b 27. *Tr.*

The Ends of the State

ence for the sake of living, but exists for the sake of living well"—signifies the perfect final cause of the state, since those who live a civil life not only live, which beasts or slaves do too, but live well, having leisure for those liberal functions in which are exercised the virtues of both the practical and the theoretic soul.

2. Having thus determined the end of the state to be living and living well, we must treat first of living and its modes. For this, as we have said, is the purpose for the sake of which the state was established, and which necessitates

From Marsilius of Padua, *The Defender of Peace,* trans. Alan Gewirth, New York: Columbia University Press, 1956, Vol. II, pp. 12–14, 31–33, and 44–48. Used by permission of the publisher.

all the things which exist in the state and are done by the association of men in it. Let us therefore lay this down as the principle of all the things which are to be demonstrated here, a principle naturally held, believed, and freely granted by all: that all men not deformed or otherwise impeded naturally desire a sufficient life, and avoid and flee what is harmful thereto. This has been acknowledged not only with regard to every genus of animals, according to Tully in his treatise *On Duties,* Book I, Chapter III, where he says: "It is an original endowment which nature has bestowed upon every genus of living things, that it preserves itself, its body, and its life, that it avoids those things which seem harmful, and that it seeks and obtains all those things which are necessary for living."[2] This principle can also be clearly grasped by everyone through sense induction.

3. But the living and living well which are appropriate to men fall into two kinds, of which one is temporal or earthly, while the other is usually called eternal or heavenly. However, this latter kind of living, the eternal, the whole body of philosophers were unable to prove by demonstration, nor was it self-evident, and therefore they did not concern themselves with the means thereto. But as to the first kind of living and living well or good life, that is, the earthly, and its necessary means, this the glorious philosophers comprehended almost completely through demonstration. Hence for its attainment they concluded the necessity of the civil community, without which this sufficient life cannot be obtained. Thus the foremost of the philosophers, Aristotle, said in his *Politics,* Book I, Chapter 1: "All men are driven toward such an associa-

tion by a natural impulse."[3] Although sense experience teaches this, we wish to bring out more distinctly that cause of it which we have indicated, as follows: Man is born composed of contrary elements, because of whose contrary actions and passions some of his substance is continually being destroyed; moreover, he is born "bare and unprotected" from excess of the surrounding air and other elements, capable of suffering and of destruction, as has been said in the science of nature.[4] As a consequence, he needed arts of diverse genera and species to avoid the afore-mentioned harms. But since these arts can be exercised only by a large number of men, and can be had only through their association with one another, men had to assemble together in order to attain what was beneficial through these arts and to avoid what was harmful.[5]

4. But since among men thus assembled there arise disputes and quarrels which, if not regulated by a norm of justice, would cause men to fight and separate and thus finally would bring about the destruction of the state, there had to be established in this association a standard of justice and a guardian or maker thereof. And since this guardian has to restrain excessive wrongdoers as well as other individuals both within

---

[2] Cicero *De officiis* I. iv. 11. *Tr.*

[3] Aristotle *Politics* I. 2. 1253a 29. *Tr.*

[4] Aristotle *On the Parts of Animals* IV. 10. 687a 25. *Tr.*

[5] It will be noted that this paragraph proves the necessity of "society," just as the first sentence of paragraph 4 proves the necessity of government, so that the two paragraphs might be viewed as providing that man is, respectively, a "social" and a "political" animal, without any need for referring to a "contract" of society and of government, as was to be the case in the seventeenth century. However, Marsilius' proofs, with their emphasis on merely biological needs as generating society, and on the need for regulating disputes as generating government, are also departures from Aristotle. *Tr.*

and outside the state who disturb or attempt to oppress the community, the state had to have within it something by which to resist these. Again, since the community needs various conveniences, repairs, and protection of certain common things, and different things in time of peace and in time of war, it was necessary that there be in the community men to take care of such matters, in order that the common necessity might be relieved when it was expedient or needful. But beside the things which we have so far mentioned, which relieve only the necessities of the present life, there is something else which men associated in a civil community need for the status of the future world promised to the human race through God's supernatural revelation, and which is useful also for the status of the present life. This is the worship and honoring of God, and the giving of thanks both for benefits received in this world and for those to be received in the future one. For the teaching of these things and for the directing of men in them, the state had to designate certain teachers. The nature and qualities of all these and the other matters mentioned above will be treated in detail in the subsequent discussions.

5. Men, then, were assembled for the sake of the sufficient life, being able to seek out for themselves the necessaries enumerated above, and exchanging them with one another. This assemblage, thus perfect and having the limit of self-sufficiency, is called the state, whose final cause as well as that of its many parts has already been indicated by us in some measure, and will be more fully distinguished below. For since diverse things are necessary to men who desire a sufficient life, things which cannot be supplied by men of one order or office, there had to be diverse orders or offices of men in this association, exercising or supplying such diverse things which men need for sufficiency of life. But these diverse orders or offices of men are none other than the many and distinct parts of the state.

Let it suffice, then, to have covered thus in outline what the state is, why there came about such an association, and the number and division of its parts.

IX. On the Methods of Establishing a Kingly Monarchy, and Which Method Is the More Perfect; also on the Methods of Establishing the Other Kinds of Regime or Policy, both Temperate and Diseased.

5. To make clearer these concepts of Aristotle, and to summarize all the methods of establishing the other kinds of government, we shall say that every government is over either voluntary or involuntary subjects. The first is the genus of well-tempered governments, the second of diseased governments. Each of these genera is divided into three species or kinds. . . . And since one of the species of well-tempered government, and perhaps the more perfect, is kingly monarchy, let us resume our previous statements about its various kinds or methods, by saying that the king or monarch either is named by the election of the inhabitants or citizens, or duly obtains the rulership without their election. If without the election of the citizens, this is either because he or his ancestors first inhabited the region, or because he bought the land and jurisdiction, or acquired it by a just war or by some other lawful method, such as by gift made to him for some great

service. Each of these kinds of monarchy participates so much the more in true kingship, the more it is over voluntary subjects and according to law made for the common benefit of the subjects; and it savors so much the more of tyranny the more it departs from these features, that is, the consent of the subjects and law established for their common benefit. Hence it is written in the *Politics*, Book IV, Chapter 8: "These," that is monarchies, "were kingly because they were according to law, and ruled voluntary subjects; but they were tyrannical because they ruled despotically and in accordance with their," that is, the monarchs', "own judgment."[6] These two features, then, distinguish temperate from diseased government, as is apparent from the clear statement of Aristotle, but absolutely or in greater degree it is the consent of the subjects which is the distinguishing criterion. Now if the ruling monarch is elected by the inhabitants, it is either with all his posterity succeeding him or not. If the latter, this may be in several ways, as he is named either for his own lifetime alone, or for his own lifetime and that of one or more of his successors, or not for the whole lifetime either of himself or of any of his successors but only for some determinate period, such as one or two years, more or less. Again, he is named to exercise either every judicial office, or only one office such as leading the army.

6. The elected and the non-elected kingly monarchs agree in that each rules voluntary subjects. They differ, however, in that the non-elected kings rule less voluntary subjects, and by laws which are less politic for the common benefit, as we said before in the case of the barbarians. The elected kings, on the other hand, rule more voluntary subjects, and by laws which are more politic, in that they are made for the common benefit, as we have said.

7. From these considerations it is clear, and will be even more apparent in the sequel, that the elected kind of government is superior to the non-elected. This is also the view of Aristotle in that passage of the *Politics*, Book III, Chapter 8, which we cited above with reference to those who were made rulers in the heroic days.[7] Again, this method of establishing governments is more permanent in perfect communities. For at some time or other it becomes necessary to have recourse to this from among all the other methods of establishing governments, but not conversely. For example, if hereditary succession fails, or if for some reason the multitude cannot bear the excessive malice of that family's rule, they must then turn to the method of election, which can never fail so long as the generation of men does not fail. Moreover, by the method of election alone is the best ruler obtained. For it is expedient that the ruler be the best man in the polity, since he must regulate the civil acts of all the rest.

8. The method of establishing the other species of temperate government is usually election; in some cases the ruler is chosen by lot,[8] without subsequent hereditary succession. Diseased governments, on the other hand, are usually established by fraud or force or both.[9]

9. Which of the temperate governments is better, monarchy or one of the other two species, aristocracy or polity; and again, which of the monarchies is

---

[6] *Politics* IV. 10. 1295a 15. *Tr.*

[7] *Politics* III. 14. 1285b 2. *Tr.*

[8] Cf. *Politics* II. 6. 1266a 9; VI. 2. 1317b 21, 1318a 2. *Tr.*

[9] Cf. *Politics* V. 4. 1304b 8. *Tr.*

better, the elected or the non-elected; and moreover, which of the elected monarchies, that established with hereditary succession ensuing or that in which one man alone is named without such succession; which in turn is divided into the further alternatives of whether it is better to name the ruler for a whole lifetime, either of himself alone or of some of his successors also, or only for some determinate period, such as one or two years, more or less—in all these questions there is room for inquiry and reasonable doubt. It must be held without doubt, however, in accordance with the truth and the manifest view of Aristotle, that election is the more certain standard of government.

XII. ON THE DEMONSTRABLE EFFICIENT CAUSE OF HUMAN LAWS, AND ALSO ON THAT CAUSE WHICH CANNOT BE PROVED BY DEMONSTRATION: WHICH IS TO INQUIRE INTO THE LEGISLATOR.
WHENCE IT APPEARS ALSO THAT WHATEVER IS ESTABLISHED BY ELECTION DERIVES ITS AUTHORITY FROM ELECTION ALONE APART FROM ANY OTHER CONFIRMATION.

We must next discuss that efficient cause of the laws which is capable of demonstration. For I do not intend to deal here with that method of establishing laws which can be effected by the immediate act or oracle of God apart from the human will, or which has been so effected in the past. It was by this latter method, as we have said, that the Mosaic law was established; but I shall not deal with it here even insofar as it contains commands with regard to civil acts for the status of the present world. I shall discuss the establishment of only those laws and governments which emerge immediately from the decision of the human mind.

2. Let us say, to begin with, that it can pertain to any citizen to discover the law taken materially and in its third sense, as the science of civil justice and benefit. Such inquiry, however, can be carried on more appropriately and be completed better by those men who are able to have leisure, who are older and experienced in practical affairs, and who are called "prudent men,"[10] than by the mechanics who must bend all their efforts to acquiring the necessities of life. But it must be remembered that the true knowledge or discovery of the just and the beneficial, and of their opposites, is not law taken in its last and most proper sense, whereby it is the measure of human civil acts, unless there is given a coercive command as to its observance, or it is made by way of such a command, by someone through whose authority its transgressors must and can be punished. Hence, we must now say to whom belongs the authority to make such a command and to punish its transgressors. This, indeed, is to inquire into the legislator or the maker of the law.

3. Let us say, then, in accordance with the truth and the counsel of Aristotle in the Politics, Book III, Chapter 6,[11] that the legislator, or the primary and proper efficient cause of the law, is the people or the whole body of citizens, or the weightier part thereof, through its election or will expressed by words in the general assembly of the citizens, commanding or determining that something be done or omitted with

---

[10] This seems to refer both to Aristotle's conception of "prudence" (e.g., Nicomachean Ethics VI. 8. 1141b 23 ff.) and to the prudentes of the Italian communes. Tr.
[11] Politics III. 11. 1281a 39 ff. Tr.

regard to human civil acts, under a temporal pain or punishment. By the "weightier part" I mean to take into consideration the quantity and the quality of the persons in that community over which the law is made.[12] The aforesaid whole body of citizens or the weightier part thereof is the legislator regardless of whether it makes the law directly by itself or entrusts the making of it to some person or persons, who are not and cannot be the legislator in the absolute sense, but only in a relative sense and for a particular time and in accordance with the authority of the primary legislator. And I say further that the laws and anything else established through election must receive their necessary approval by that same primary authority and no other, whatever be the case with regard to certain ceremonies or solemnities, which are required not for the being of the matters elected but for their well-being, since the election would be no less valid even if these ceremonies were not performed. Moreover, by the same authority must the laws and other things established through election undergo addition, subtraction, complete change, interpretation, or suspension, insofar as the exigencies of time or place or other circumstances make any such action opportune for the common benefit. And by the same authority, also, must the laws be promulgated or proclaimed after their enactment, so that no citizen or alien who is delinquent in observing them may be excused because of ignorance.

4. A citizen I define in accordance with Aristotle in the *Politics,* Book III, Chapters 1, 3, and 7, as one who participates in the civil community in the government or the deliberative or judicial function according to his rank.[13] By this definition, children, slaves, aliens, and women are distinguished from citizens, although in different ways. For the sons of citizens are citizens in proximate potentiality, lacking only in years. The weightier part of the citizens should be viewed in accordance with the honorable custom of polities, or else it should be determined in accordance with the doctrine of Aristotle in the *Politics,* Book VI, Chapter 2.[14]

5. Having thus defined the citizen and the weightier part of the citizens, let us return to our proposed objective, namely, to demonstrate that the human authority to make laws belongs only to the whole body of the citizens or to the weightier part thereof. Our first proof is as follows. The absolutely primary human authority to make or establish human laws belongs only to those men from whom alone the best laws can emerge. But these are the whole body of the citizens, or the weightier part thereof, which represents that whole body; since it is difficult or impossible for all persons to agree upon one decision, because some men have a deformed nature, disagreeing with the common decision through singular malice or ignorance. The common benefit should not, however, be impeded or neglected because of the unreasonable protest or opposition of these men. The authority to make or establish laws, therefore, belongs only to the whole body of the citizens or to the weightier part thereof.

The first proposition of this demon-

---

[12] The words *personarum et qualitate* were omitted from a younger group of manuscripts and from early printed versions, thereby leading to a mistaken interpretation of Marsilius' position as purely majoritarian. *Tr.*

[13] *Politics* III. 1. 1275a 22, 1275b 19; III. 3. 1277b 33; III. 13. 1283b 42. *Tr.*

[14] *Politics* VI. 3–4. 1318a 3 ff. *Tr.*

stration is very close to self-evident, although its force and its ultimate certainty can be grasped from Chapter V of this discourse. The second proposition, that the best law is made only through the hearing and command of the entire multitude, I prove by assuming with Aristotle in the *Politics,* Book III, Chapter 7, that the best law is that which is made for the common benefit of citizens. As Aristotle said: "That is presumably right," that is, in the laws, "which is for the common benefit of the state and the citizens."[15] But that this is best achieved only by the whole body of the citizens or by the weightier part thereof, which is assumed to be the same thing, I show as follows: That at which the entire body of the citizens aims intellectually and emotionally is more certainly judged as to its truth and more diligently noted as to its common utility. For a defect in some proposed law can be better noted by the greater number than by any part thereof, since every whole, or at least every corporeal whole, is greater in mass and in virtue than any part of it taken separately. Moreover, the common utility of a law is better noted by the entire multitude, because no one knowingly harms himself. Anyone can look to see whether a proposed law leans toward the benefit of one or a few persons more than of the others or of the community, and can protest against it. Such, however, would not be the case were the law made by one or a few persons, considering their own private benefit rather than that of the community. This position is also supported by the arguments which we advanced in Chapter XI of this discourse with regard to the necessity of having laws.

6. Another argument to the principal

conclusion is as follows. The authority to make the law belongs only to those men whose making of it will cause the law to be better observed or observed at all. Only the whole body of the citizens are such men. To them, therefore, belongs the authority to make the law. The first proposition of this demonstration is very close to self-evident, for a law would be useless unless it were observed. Hence Aristotle said in the *Politics,* Book IV, Chapter 6: "Laws are not well ordered when they are well made but not obeyed."[16] He also said in Book VI, Chapter 5: "Nothing is accomplished by forming opinions about justice and not carrying them out."[17] The second proposition I prove as follows. That law is better observed by every citizen which each one seems to have imposed upon himself. But such is the law which is made through the hearing and command of the entire multitude of the citizens. The first proposition of this prosyllogism is almost self-evident; for since "the state is a community of free men," as is written in the *Politics,* Book III, Chapter 4,[18] every citizen must be free, and not undergo another's despotism, that is, slavish dominion. But this would not be the case if one or a few of the citizens by their own authority made the law over the whole body of citizens. For those who thus made the law would be despots over the others, and hence such a law, however good it was, would be endured only with reluctance, or not at all, by the rest of the citizens, the more ample part. Having suffered contempt, they would protest against it, and not having been called upon to make it, they would not observe it. On the other hand, a

---

15 *Politics* III. 13. 1283b 40. *Tr.*

16 *Politics* IV. 8. 1294a 3. *Tr.*
17 *Politics* VI. 8. 1322a 5. *Tr.*
18 *Politics* III. 6. 1279a 21. *Tr.*

law made by the hearing or consent of the whole multitude, even though it were less useful, would be readily observed and endured by every one of the citizens, because then each would seem to have set the law upon himself, and hence would have no protest against it, but would rather tolerate it with equanimity. The second proposition of the first syllogism I also prove in another way, as follows. The power to cause the laws to be observed belongs only to those men to whom belongs coercive force over the transgressors of the laws. But these men are the whole body of citizens or the weightier part thereof. Therefore, to them alone belongs the authority to make the laws.

7. The principal conclusion is also proved as follows. That practical matter whose proper establishment is of greatest importance for the common sufficiency of the citizens in this life, and whose poor establishment threatens harm for the community, must be established only by the whole body of the citizens. But such a matter is the law. Therefore, the establishment of the law pertains only to the whole body of the citizens. The major premise of this demonstration is almost self-evident, and is grounded in the immediate truths which were set forth in Chapters IV and V of this discourse. For men came together to the civil community in order to attain what was beneficial for sufficiency of life, and to avoid the opposite. Those matters, therefore, which can affect the benefit and harm of all ought to be known and heard by all, in order that they may be able to attain the beneficial and to avoid the opposite. Such matters are the laws, as was assumed in the minor premise. For in the laws being rightly made consists a large part of the whole common sufficiency of men, while under bad laws there arise unbearable slavery, oppression, and misery of the citizens, the final result of which is that the polity is destroyed.

Law and Rights

The pivot of realistic social philosophy is the doctrine of natural law, and the major text for its exposition is the "Treatise on Law" in St. Thomas Aquinas' *Summa Theologica*. A long tradition lay behind his work: Aristotle stated fundamental realistic assumptions about law and justice in his ethical and political writings, Cicero spelled out even more the belief in law as right reason embodied in the very structure of the universe, and Stoic lawyers of Rome continued to develop and amplify the position. Aquinas drew heavily on these many sources, yet much is original in his view of law. He is generally less dependent on Aristotle here than in other aspects of his social doctrine.

Aquinas (1226–1274) invites his reader to take a start, not with the individual and so-called individual rights, but rather with the cosmos, that is, with the conception of a world well-ordered and graded by rational principle. There is an order of being, under God who is the primal Being, in which man can participate through his rationality. The very being of God expresses itself in rationality and providential concern over creation, instructing rational creatures (man) by law and assisting them by grace. Aquinas calls this law of God eternal law; the other levels of law that will concern us are most properly law only as they reflect or participate in the eternal law itself.

But what is law? Aquinas defines it as a rule and measure of acts that induces or restrains a man's activity. He notes immediately, however, that reason is the source of all command, and he infers next that law pertains to reason. Law in fact is reason measuring actions. Thus, reason is the extrinsic principle of acts (virtue is their intrinsic principle), and rules not in accord with reason are not properly laws at all.

Three levels of law are specified in Aquinas' social philosophy.* The first and highest law, namely eternal law, has been mentioned above. Eternal law is imprinted on creatures; from it they derive their inclinations to their proper ends and acts. Since man participates in rationality, this imprinted law can be apprehended by him and thus is itself a law rooted in and appropriate to his nature. Aquinas calls it the natural law; the law that rules and measures actions with special reference to the nature of man. When considered simply as a being, man is directed to such ends as are common to all beings, such as self-preservation. When considered as an animal being, man is directed toward procreation and the education of offspring. As a human being, he is given, for example, the desire to know God.

The natural law, Aquinas teaches, is directed toward the common good and universal happiness. As with all law, it thus aims to lead men to that fulfillment of being or nature which is the good. Whatever is prescribed or prohibited by natural law is done so with reference to the attainment of the ends of human nature under the guidance of reason. Reason itself, Aquinas notes, is a reflection of being, and acts of virtue are dictates of reason. It therefore follows that, in this sense, natural law commands all the acts of virtue† and, since reason and man's being are everywhere and always the same, the natural law is identical for all men in its common principles and unchangeable in its concept except by addition.

Finally, Aquinas recognizes a third level of law, namely human law. Perfection in virtue, he argues, requires training and control, together with the restraints of force and fear. Laws, therefore, must be framed by human societies to achieve the order and peace needed for perfection. Human law is also needed to order the particular practices of societies that differ from one another, and even the particular conclusions of the natural law may differ from one people to another, according to Aquinas. But in all its detailed developments, human law is truly law only as it is derived from the natural law.

The theory of natural law has a central position in realist philosophy. It looks back, so to speak, to fundamental assumptions about being, man, nature, and the good. At the same time it looks forward, for natural law serves as the basis upon which realists make judgments on further problems in social philosophy such as

---

* A fourth type of law, divine law, is also explored by Aquinas. This law is primarily religious in character, in the sense that it is addressed to man's quest for salvation, and curbs and directs *interior* human acts.

† Though it does not command all virtuous acts considered in themselves. See this distinction in the selection below.

obligation and specific issues requiring political decision. The importance of this theory is reflected in realist writings to the present day.

ST. THOMAS AQUINAS   Treatise on Law

QUESTION XC.
OF THE ESSENCE OF LAW.

FIRST ARTICLE.
WHETHER LAW IS SOMETHING PERTAINING TO REASON?

We proceed thus to the First Article:—

Objection 1. It seems that law is not something pertaining to reason. For the Apostle says (Rom. vii. 23): *I see another law in my members,* etc. But nothing pertaining to reason is in the members; since the reason does not make use of a bodily organ. Therefore law is not something pertaining to reason.

Obj. 2. Further, in the reason there is nothing else but power, habit, and act. But law is not the power itself of reason. In like manner, neither is it a habit of reason: because the habits of reason are the intellectual virtues of which we have spoken above (Q. LVII.). Nor again is it an act of reason: because then law would cease, when the act of reason ceases, for instance, while we are asleep. Therefore law is nothing pertaining to reason.

Obj. 3. Further, the law moves those who are subject to it to act aright. But it belongs properly to the will to move to act, as is evident from what has been said above (Q. IX., A. 1). Therefore law pertains, not to the reason, but to the will; according to the words of the Jurist (*Lib.* i. *ff., De Const. Prin.*): *Whatsoever pleaseth the sovereign, has force of law.*

On the contrary, It belongs to the law to command and to forbid. But it belongs to reason to command, as stated above (Q. XVII., A. 1). Therefore law is something pertaining to reason.

I answer that, Law is a rule and measure of acts, whereby man is induced to act or is restrained from acting: for *lex* (law) is derived from *ligare* (to bind), because it binds one to act. Now the rule and measure of human acts is the reason, which is the first principle of human acts, as is evident from what has been stated above (Q. I., A. 1 *ad* 3); since it belongs to the reason to direct to the end, which is the first principle in all matters of action, according to the Philosopher (*Phys.* ii.). Now that which is the principle in any genus, is the rule and measure of that genus: for instance, unity in the genus of numbers, and the first movement in the genus of movements. Consequently it follows that law is something pertaining to reason.

Reply Obj. 1. Since law is a kind of rule and measure, it may be in something in two ways. First, as in that which measures and rules: and since this is proper to reason, it follows that, in this way, law is in the reason alone. —Secondly, as in that which is measured and ruled. In this way, law is in all

From *The "Summa Theologica" of St. Thomas Aquinas,* literally trans. by the Fathers of the English Dominican Province, New York: Benziger Brothers, Inc., London: Burns & Oates Ltd., 1911. Used by permission of the publishers.

those things that are inclined to something by reason of some law: so that any inclination arising from a law, may be called a law, not essentially but by participation as it were. And thus the inclination of the members to concupiscence is called *the law of the members.*

Reply Obj. 2. Just as, in external action, we may consider the work and the work done, for instance the work of building and the house built; so in the acts of reason, we may consider the act itself of reason, i.e., to understand and to reason, and something produced by this act. With regard to the speculative reason, this is first of all the definition; secondly, the proposition; thirdly, the syllogism or argument. And since also the practical reason makes use of a syllogism in respect of the work to be done, as stated above (Q. XIII., A. 3; Q. LXXVI., A. 1) and as the Philosopher teaches (*Ethic.* vii.); hence we find in the practical reason something that holds the same position in regard to operations, as, in the speculative intellect, the proposition holds in regard to conclusions. Suchlike universal propositions of the practical intellect that are directed to actions have the nature of law. And these propositions are sometimes under our actual consideration, while sometimes they are retained in the reason by means of a habit.

Reply Obj. 3. Reason has its power of moving from the will, as stated above (Q. XVII., A. 1): for it is due to the fact that one wills the end, that the reason issues its commands as regards things ordained to the end. But in order that the volition of what is commanded may have the nature of law, it needs to be in accord with some rule of reason. And in this sense is to be understood

the saying that the will of the sovereign has the force of law; otherwise the sovereign's will would savour of lawlessness rather than of law.

SECOND ARTICLE.
WHETHER THE LAW IS ALWAYS DIRECTED TO THE COMMON GOOD?

We proceed thus to the Second Article:—

Objection 1. It seems that the law is not always directed to the common good as to its end. For it belongs to law to command and to forbid. But commands are directed to certain individual goods. Therefore the end of the law is not always the common good.

Obj. 2. Further, the law directs man in his actions. But human actions are concerned with particular matters. Therefore the law is directed to some particular good.

Obj. 3. Further, Isidore says (*Etym.* ii.): *If the law is based on reason, whatever is based on reason will be a law.* But reason is the foundation not only of what is ordained to the common good, but also of that which is directed to private good. Therefore the law is not only directed to the good of all, but also to the private good of an individual.

On the contrary, Isidore says (*Etym.* v.) that *laws are enacted for no private profit, but for the common benefit of the citizens.*

I answer that, As stated above (A. 1), the law belongs to that which is a principle of human acts, because it is their rule and measure. Now as reason is a principle of human acts, so in reason itself there is something which is the principle in respect of all the rest: wherefore to this principle chiefly and mainly law must needs be referred.— Now the first principle in practical matters, which are the object of the practical reason, is the last end: and the last end of human life is bliss or happiness, as stated above (Q. II., A. 7; Q. III., A. 1). Consequently the law must needs regard principally the relationship to happiness. Moreover, since every part is ordained to the whole, as imperfect to perfect; and since one man is a part of the perfect community, the law must needs regard properly the relationship to universal happiness. Wherefore the Philosopher, in the above definition of legal matters mentions both happiness and the body politic: for he says (*Ethic.* v.) that we call those legal matters *just, which are adapted to produce and preserve happiness and its parts for the body politic:* since the state is a perfect community, as he says in *Polit.* i.

Now in every genus, that which belongs to it chiefly is the principle of the others, and the others belong to that genus in subordination to that thing: thus fire, which is chief among hot things, is the cause of heat in mixed bodies, and these are said to be hot in so far as they have a share of fire. Consequently, since the law is chiefly ordained to the common good, any other precept in regard to some individual work, must needs be devoid of the nature of a law, save in so far as it regards the common good. Therefore every law is ordained to the common good.

Reply Obj. 1. A command denotes an application of a law to matters regulated by the law. Now the order to the common good, at which the law aims, is applicable to particular ends. And in this way commands are given even concerning particular matters.

Reply Obj. 2. Actions are indeed concerned with particular matters: but those particular matters are referable to the common good, not as to a common genus or species, but as to a common final cause, according as the common good is said to be the common end.

Reply Obj. 3. Just as nothing stands firm with regard to the speculative reason except that which is traced back to the first indemonstrable principles, so nothing stands firm with regard to the practical reason, unless it be directed to the last end which is the common good: and whatever stands to reason in this sense, has the nature of a law.

QUESTION XCI.
OF THE VARIOUS KINDS OF LAW.

FIRST ARTICLE.
WHETHER THERE IS
AN ETERNAL LAW?

We proceed thus to the First Article:—

Objection 1. It seems that there is no eternal law. Because every law is imposed on someone. But there was not someone from eternity on whom a law could be imposed: since God alone was from eternity. Therefore no law is eternal.

Obj. 2. Further, promulgation is essential to law. But promulgation could not be from eternity: because there was no one to whom it could be promulgated from eternity. Therefore no law can be eternal.

Obj. 3. Further, a law implies order to an end. But nothing ordained to an end is eternal: for the last end alone is eternal. Therefore no law is eternal.

On the contrary, Augustine says (*De Lib. Arb.* i.): *That Law which is the Supreme Reason cannot be understood to be otherwise than unchangeable and eternal.*

I answer that, As stated above (Q. XC., A. 1 *ad* 2; AA. 3,4), a law is nothing else but a dictate of practical reason eminating from the ruler who governs a perfect community. Now it is evident, granted that the world is ruled by Divine Providence, as was stated in the First Part (Q. XXII., AA. 1, 2), that the whole community of the universe is governed by Divine Reason. Wherefore the very Idea of the government of things in God the Ruler of the universe, has the nature of a law. And since the Divine Reason's conception of things is not subject to time but is eternal, according to Prov. viii. 23, therefore it is that this kind of law must be called eternal.

Reply Obj. 1. Those things that are not in themselves, exist with God, inasmuch as they are foreknown and preordained by Him, according to Rom. iv. 17: *Who calls those things that are not, as those that are.* Accordingly the eternal concept of the Divine law bears the character of an eternal law, in so far as it is ordained by God to the government of things foreknown by Him.

Reply Obj. 2. Promulgation is made by word of mouth or in writing; and in both ways the eternal law is promulgated: because both the Divine Word and the writing of the Book of Life are eternal. But the promulgation cannot be from eternity on the part of the creature that hears or reads.

Reply Obj. 3. The law implies order to the end actively, in so far as it directs certain things to the end; but not passively,—that is to say, the law itself is not ordained to the end,—except accidentally, in a governor whose end is extrinsic to him, and to which end his law must needs be ordained. But the end of the Divine government is God Himself, and His law is not distinct from Himself. Wherefore the eternal law is not ordained to another end.

SECOND ARTICLE.
WHETHER THERE IS IN US
A NATURAL LAW?

We proceed thus to the Second Article:—

Objection 1. It seems that there is no natural law in us. Because man is governed sufficiently by the eternal law: for Augustine says (*De Lib. Arb.* i.) that *the eternal law is that by which it is right that all things should be most orderly.* But nature does not abound in superfluities as neither does she fail in necessaries. Therefore no law is natural to man.

Obj. 2. Further, by the law man is directed, in his acts, to the end, as stated above (Q. XC., A. 2). But the directing of human acts to their end is not a function of nature, as is the case in irrational creatures, which act for an end solely by their natural appetite; whereas man acts for an end by his reason and will. Therefore no law is natural to man.

Obj. 3. Further, the more a man is free, the less is he under the law. But man is freer than all the animals, on account of his free-will, with which he is endowed above all other animals. Since therefore other animals are not subject to a natural law, neither is man subject to a natural law.

On the contrary, The gloss on Rom. ii. 14: *When the Gentiles, who have not the law, do by nature those things that are of the law,* comments as follows: *Although they have no written law, yet they have the natural law, whereby each one knows, and is conscious of, what is good and what is evil.*

I answer that, As stated above (Q. XC., A. 1 *ad* 1), law, being a rule and measure, can be in a person in two ways: in one way, as in him that rules and measures; in another way, as in that which is ruled and measured, since a thing is ruled and measured, in so far as it partakes of the rule or measure. Wherefore, since all things subject to Divine providence are ruled and measured by the eternal law, as was stated above (A. 1); it is evident that all things partake somewhat of the eternal law, in so far as, namely, from its being imprinted on them, they derive their respective inclinations to their proper acts and ends. Now among all others, the rational creature is subject to Divine providence in the most excellent way, in so far as it partakes of a share of providence, by being provident both for itself and for others. Wherefore it has a share of the Eternal Reason, whereby it has a natural inclination to its proper act and end: and this participation of the eternal law in the rational creature is called the natural law. Hence the Psalmist after saying (Ps. iv. 6): *Offer up the sacrifice of justice,* as though someone asked what the works of justice are, adds: *Many say, Who showeth us good things?* in answer to which question he says: *The light of Thy countenance, O Lord, is signed upon us:* thus implying that the light of natural reason, whereby we discern what is good and what is evil, which is the function of the natural law, is nothing else than an imprint on us of the Divine light. It is therefore evident that the natural law is nothing else than the rational creature's participation of the eternal law.

Reply Obj. 1. This argument would hold, if the natural law were something different from the eternal law: whereas it is nothing but a participation thereof, as stated above.

Reply Obj. 2. Every act of reason and will in us is based on that which is according to nature, as stated above (Q. X., A. 1): for every act of reasoning is based on principles that are known naturally, and every act of appetite in respect of the means is derived from the natural appetite in respect of the last end. Accordingly the first direction of our acts to their end must needs be in virtue of the natural law.

Reply Obj. 3. Even irrational animals partake in their own way of the Eternal Reason, just as the rational creature does. But because the rational creature partakes thereof in an intellectual and rational manner, therefore the participation of the eternal law in the rational creature is properly called a law, since a law is something pertaining to reason, as stated above (Q. XC., A. 1). Irrational creatures, however, do not partake thereof in a rational manner, wherefore there is no participation of the eternal law in them, except by way of similitude.

THIRD ARTICLE.
WHETHER THERE IS
A HUMAN LAW?

We proceed thus to the Third Article:—

Objection 1. It seems that there is not a human law. For the natural law is a participation of the eternal law, as stated above (A. 2). Now through the eternal law *all things are most orderly,* as Augustine states (*De Lib. Arb.* i.). Therefore the natural law suffices for the ordering of all human affairs. Consequently there is no need for a human law.

Obj. 2. Further, a law bears the character of a measure, as stated above (Q. XC., A. 1). But human reason is not a measure of things, but vice versa (*cf. Metaph.* x.). Therefore no law can emanate from human reason.

Obj. 3. Further, a measure should be most certain, as stated in *Metaph.* x.

But the dictates of human reason in matters of conduct are uncertain, according to Wis. ix. 14: *The thoughts of mortal men are fearful, and our counsels uncertain.* Therefore no law can emanate from human reason.

On the contrary, Augustine (*De Lib. Arb.* 1.) distinguishes two kinds of law, the one eternal, the other temporal, which he calls human.

I answer that, As stated above (*Q. XC., A.* 1, *ad* 2), a law is a dictate of the practical reason. Now it is to be observed that the same procedure takes place in the practical and in the speculative reason: for each proceeds from principles to conclusions, as stated above (*ibid.*). Accordingly we conclude that just as, in the speculative reason, from naturally known indemonstrable principles, we draw the conclusions of the various sciences, the knowledge of which is not imparted to us by nature, but acquired by the efforts of reason, so too it is from the precepts of the natural law, as from general and indemonstrable principles, that the human reason needs to proceed to the more particular determination of certain matters. These particular determinations, devised by human reason, are called human laws, provided the other essential conditions of law be observed, as stated above (Q. XC., AA. 2, 3, 4). Wherefore Tully says in his *Rhetoric* (*De Invent. Rhet.* ii.) that *justice has its source in nature; thence certain things came into custom by reason of their utility; afterwards these things which emanated from nature and were approved by custom, were sanctioned by fear and reverence for the law.*

Reply Obj. 1. The human reason cannot have a full participation of the dictate of the Divine Reason, but according to its own mode, and imperfectly. Consequently, as on the part of the speculative reason, by a natural participation of Divine Wisdom, there is in us the knowledge of certain general principles, but not proper knowledge of each single truth, such as that contained in the Divine Wisdom; so too, on the part of the practical reason, man has a natural participation of the eternal law, according to certain general principles, but not as regards the particular determinations of individual cases, which are, however, contained in the eternal law. Hence the need for human reason to proceed further to sanction them by law.

Reply Obj. 2. Human reason is not, of itself, the rule of things: but the principles impressed on it by nature, are general rules and measures of all things relating to human conduct, whereof the natural reason is the rule and measure, although it is not the measure of things that are from nature.

Reply Obj. 3. The practical reason is concerned with practical matters, which are singular and contingent: but not with necessary things, with which the speculative reason is concerned. Wherefore human laws cannot have that inerrancy that belongs to the demonstrated conclusions of sciences. Nor is it necessary for every measure to be altogether unerring and certain, but according as it is possible in its own particular genus.

Question XCII.
Of the Effects of Law.

FIRST ARTICLE.
WHETHER AN EFFECT OF LAW IS TO MAKE MEN GOOD?

We proceed thus to the First Article:—

Objection 1. It seems that it is not an effect of law to make men good. For men are good through virtue, since virtue, as stated in *Ethic.* ii. is *that which makes its subject good.* But virtue is in man from God alone, because He it is Who *works it in us without us,* as we stated above (Q. LV., A. 4) in giving the definition of virtue. Therefore the law does not make men good.

Obj. 2. Further, Law does not profit a man unless he obeys it. But the very fact that a man obeys a law is due to his being good. Therefore in man goodness is presupposed to the law. Therefore the law does not make men good.

Obj. 3. Further, Law is ordained to the common good, as stated above (Q. XC., A. 2). But some behave well in things regarding the community, who behave ill in things regarding themselves. Therefore it is not the business of the law to make men good.

Obj. 4. Further, some laws are tyrannical, as the Philosopher says (*Polit.* iii.). But a tyrant does not intend the good of his subjects, but considers only his own profit. Therefore law does not make men good.

On the contrary, The Philosopher says (*Ethic.* ii.) that the *intention of every lawgiver is to make good citizens.*

I answer that, As stated above (Q. XC., A. 1 *ad* 2; AA. 3, 4), a law is nothing else than a dictate of reason in the ruler by whom his subjects are governed. Now the virtue of any subordinate thing consists in its being well subordinated to that by which it is regulated: thus we see that the virtue of the irascible and concupiscible faculties consists in their being obedient to reason; and accordingly *the virtue of every subject consists in his being well subjected to his ruler,* as the Philosopher says (*Polit.* i.). But every law aims at being obeyed by those who are subject to it. Consequently it is evident that the

proper effect of law is to lead its subjects to their proper virtue: and since virtue is *that which makes its subject good,* it follows that the proper effect of law is to make those to whom it is given, good, either simply or in some particular respect. For if the intention of the lawgiver is fixed on true good, which is the common good regulated according to Divine justice, it follows that the effect of the law is to make men good simply. If, however, the intention of the lawgiver is fixed on that which is not simply good, but useful or pleasurable to himself, or in opposition to Divine justice; then the law does not make men good simply, but in respect to that particular government. In this way good is found even in things that are bad of themselves: thus a man is called a good robber, because he works in a way that is adapted to his end.

Reply Obj. 1. Virtue is twofold, as explained above (Q. LXIII., A. 2), viz., acquired and infused. Now the fact of being accustomed to an action contributes to both, but in different ways; for it causes the acquired virtue; while it disposes to infused virtue, and preserves and fosters it when it already exists. And since law is given for the purpose of directing human acts; as far as human acts conduce to virtue, so far does law make men good. Wherefore the Philosopher says in the second book of the *Politics* (*Ethic.* ii.) that *lawgivers make men good by habituating them to good works.*

Reply Obj. 2. It is not always through perfect goodness of virtue that one obeys the law, but sometimes it is through fear of punishment, and sometimes from the mere dictate of reason, which is a beginning of virtue, as stated above (Q. LXIII., A. 1).

Reply Obj. 3. The goodness of any part is considered in comparison with the whole; hence Augustine says (*Conf.* iii.) that *unseemly is the part that harmonizes not with the whole*. Since then every man is a part of the state, it is impossible that a man be good, unless he be well proportionate to the common good: nor can the whole be well consistent unless its parts be proportionate to it. Consequently the common good of the state cannot flourish, unless the citizens be virtuous, at least those whose business it is to govern. But it is enough for the good of the community, that the other citizens be so far virtuous that they obey the commands of their rulers. Hence the Philosopher says (*Polit.* iii.) that *the virtue of a sovereign is the same as that of a good man, but the virtue of any common citizen is not the same as that of a good man*.

Reply Obj. 4. A tyrannical law, through not being according to reason, is not a law, absolutely speaking, but rather a perversion of law; and yet in so far as it is something in the nature of a law, it aims at the citizens being good. For all it has in the nature of a law consists in its being an ordinance made by a superior to his subjects, and aims at being obeyed by them, which is to make them good, not simply; but with respect to that particular government.

QUESTION XCIV.
OF THE NATURAL LAW.

THIRD ARTICLE.
WHETHER ALL ACTS
OF VIRTUE ARE PRESCRIBED
BY THE NATURAL LAW?

We proceed thus to the Third Article:—

Objection 1. It seems that not all acts of virtue are prescribed by the natural law. Because, as stated above (Q. XC., A. 2) it is essential to a law that it be ordained to the common good. But some acts of virtue are ordained to the private good of the individual, as is evident especially in regard to acts of temperance. Therefore not all acts of virtue are the subject of natural law.

Obj. 2. Further, every sin is opposed to some virtuous act. If therefore all acts of virtue are prescribed by the natural law, it seems to follow that all sins are against nature: whereas this applies to certain special sins.

Obj. 3. Further, those things which are according to nature are common to all. But acts of virtue are not common to all: since a thing is virtuous in one, and vicious in another. Therefore not all acts of virtue are prescribed by the natural law.

On the contrary, Damascene says (*De Fide Orthod.* iii.) that *virtues are natural*. Therefore virtuous acts also are a subject of the natural law.

I answer that, We may speak of virtuous acts in two ways: first, under the aspect of virtuous; secondly, as such and such acts considered in their proper species. If then we speak of acts of virtue, considered as virtuous, thus all virtuous acts belong to the natural law. For it has been stated (A. 2) that to the natural law belongs everything to which a man is inclined according to his nature. Now each thing is inclined naturally to an operation that is suitable to it according to its form: thus fire is inclined to give heat. Wherefore, since the rational soul is the proper form of man, there is in every man a natural inclination to act according to reason: and this is to act according to virtue. Consequently, considered thus, all acts of virtue are prescribed by the natural law: since each one's reason naturally dictates to him to act virtuously. But if we speak of virtuous acts, considered in themselves, i.e., in their proper species, thus not all virtuous acts are prescribed by the natural law: for many things are done virtuously, to which nature does not incline at first; but which, through the inquiry of reason, have been found by men to be conducive to well-living.

Reply Obj. 1.   Temperance is about the natural concupiscences of food, drink and sexual matters, which are indeed ordained to the natural common good, just as other matters of law are ordained to the moral common good.

Reply Obj. 2.   By human nature we may mean either that which is proper to man—and in this sense all sins, as being against reason, are also against nature, as Damascene states (*De Fide Orthod.* ii.): or we may mean that nature which is common to man and other animals; and in this sense, certain special sins are said to be against nature; thus contrary to sexual intercourse, which is natural to all animals, is unisexual lust, which has received the special name of the unnatural crime.

Reply Obj. 3.   This argument considers acts in themselves. For it is owing to the various conditions of men, that certain acts are virtuous for some, as being proportionate and becoming to them, while they are vicious for others, as being out of proportion to them.

FOURTH ARTICLE.
WHETHER THE NATURAL LAW IS THE SAME IN ALL MEN?

We proceed thus to the Fourth Article:—

Objection 1.   It seems that the natural law is not the same in all. For it is stated in the Decretals (*Dist.* i.) that *the natural law is that which is contained in the Law and the Gospel.* But this is not common to all men; because, as it is written (Rom. x. 16), *all do not obey the gospel.* Therefore the natural law is not the same in all men.

Obj. 2.   Further, *Things which are according to the law are said to be just,* as stated in *Ethic.* v. But it is stated in the same book that nothing is so universally just as not to be subject to change in regard to some men. Therefore even the natural law is not the same in all men.

Obj. 3.   Further, as stated above (AA. 2, 3), to the natural law belongs everything to which a man is inclined according to his nature. Now different men are naturally inclined to different things; some to the desire of pleasures, others to the desire of honours, and other men to other things. Therefore there is not one natural law for all.

On the contrary, Isidore says (*Etym.* v.): *The natural law is common to all nations.*

I answer that, As stated above (AA. 2, 3), to the natural law belongs those things to which a man is inclined naturally: and among these it is proper to man to be inclined to act according to reason. Now the process of reason is from the common to the proper, as stated in *Phys.* i. The speculative reason, however, is differently situated in this matter, from the practical reason. For, since the speculative reason is busied chiefly with necessary things, which cannot be otherwise than they are, its proper conclusions, like the universal principles, contain the truth without fail. The practical reason, on the other hand, is busied with contingent matters, about which human actions are concerned: and consequently, although there is necessity in the general principles, the more we descend to matters of detail, the more frequently we encounter defects. Accordingly then in speculative matters truth is the same in all men, both as to principles and as to conclusions: although the truth is not known to all as regards the conclusions, but only as regards the principles which are called common notions. But in matters of action, truth or practical rectitude is not the same for all, as to matters of detail, but only as to the general principles: and where there is the same rectitude in matters of detail, it is not equally known to all.

It is therefore evident that, as regards the general principles whether of speculative or of practical reason, truth or rectitude is the same for all, and is equally known by all. As to the proper conclusions of the speculative reason, the truth is the same for all, but is not equally known to all: thus it is true for all that the three angles of a triangle are together equal to two right angles, although it is not known to all. But as to the proper conclusions of the practical reason, neither is the truth or rectitude the same for all, nor, where it is the same, is it equally known by all. Thus it is right and true for all to act according to reason: and from this principle it follows as a proper conclusion, that goods entrusted to another should be restored to their owner. Now this is true for the majority of cases: but it may happen in a particular case that it would be injurious, and therefore unreasonable, to restore goods held in trust; for instance if they are claimed for the purpose of fighting against one's country. And this principle will be found to fail the more, according as we descend further into detail, *e.g.,* if one were to say that goods held in trust should be restored with such and such a guarantee, or in such and such a way; because the greater the number of conditions added, the greater the number of ways in which the principle may fail, so that it be not right to restore or not to restore.

Consequently we must say that the natural law, as to general principles, is the same for all, both as to rectitude and as to knowledge. But as to certain matters of detail, which are conclusions, as it were, of those general principles, it is the same for all in the majority of cases, both as to rectitude and as to knowledge; and yet in some few cases it may fail, both as to rectitude, by reason of certain obstacles (just as natures subject to generation and corruption fail in some few cases on account of some obstacle), and as to knowledge, since in some the reason is perverted by passion, or evil habit, or an evil disposition of nature; thus formerly, theft, although it is expressly contrary to the natural law, was not considered wrong among the Germans, as Julius Cæsar relates (*De Bello Gall.* vi.).

Reply Obj. 1. The meaning of the sentence quoted is not that whatever is contained in the Law and the Gospel belongs to the natural law, since they contain many things that are above nature; but that whatever belongs to the natural law is fully contained in them. Wherefore Gratian, after saying that *the natural law is what is contained in the Law and the Gospel,* adds at once, by way of example, *by which everyone is commanded to do to others as he would be done by.*

Reply Obj. 2. The saying of the Philosopher is to be understood of things that are naturally just, not as general principles, but as conclusions drawn from them, having rectitude in the majority of cases, but failing in a few.

Reply Obj. 3. As, in man, reason rules and commands the other powers, so all the natural inclinations belonging to the other powers must needs be directed according to reason. Wherefore it is universally right for all men, that all their inclinations should be directed according to reason.

FIFTH ARTICLE.
WHETHER THE NATURAL LAW CAN BE CHANGED?

We proceed thus to the Fifth Article:—

Objection 1. It seems that the natural law can be changed. Because on Ecclus. xvii. 9, *He gave them instructions, and the law of life,* the gloss says: *He wished the law of the letter to be written, in order to correct the law of nature.* But that which is corrected is changed. Therefore the natural law can be changed.

Obj. 2. Further, the slaying of the innocent, adultery, and theft are against the natural law. But we find these things changed by God: as when God commanded Abraham to slay his innocent son (Gen. xxii. 2); and when He ordered the Jews to borrow and purloin the vessels of the Egyptians (Exod. xii. 35); and when He commanded Osee to take to himself *a wife of fornications* (*Osee* i. 2). Therefore the natural law can be changed.

Obj. 3. Further, Isidore says (*Etym.* v.) that *the possession of all things in common, and universal freedom, are matters of natural law.* But these things are seen to be changed by human laws. Therefore it seems that the natural law is subject to change.

On the contrary, It is said in the Decretals (*Dist.* v.): *The natural law dates from the creation of the rational creature. It does not vary according to time, but remains unchangeable.*

I answer that, A change in the natural law may be understood in two ways. First, by way of addition. In this sense nothing hinders the natural law from being changed: since many things for the benefit of human life have been added over and above the natural law, both by the Divine law and by human laws.

Secondly, a change in the natural law may be understood by way of subtraction, so that what previously was according to the natural law, ceases to be so. In this sense, the natural law is altogether unchangeable in its first principles: but in its secondary principles, which, as we have said (A. 4), are certain detailed proximate conclusions drawn from the first principles, the natural law is not changed so that what it prescribes be not right in most cases. But it may be changed in some particular cases of rare occurrence, through some special causes hindering the observance of such precepts, as stated above (A. 4).

Reply Obj. 1. The written law is said to be given for the correction of the natural law, either because it supplies what was wanting to the natural law; or because the natural law was perverted in the hearts of some men, as to certain matters, so that they esteemed those things good which are naturally evil; which perversion stood in need of correction.

Reply Obj. 2. All men alike, both guilty and innocent, die the death of nature: which death of nature is inflicted by the power of God on account of original sin, according to 1 Kings ii. 6: *The Lord killeth and maketh alive.* Consequently, by the command of God, death can be inflicted on any man, guilty or innocent, without any injustice whatever.—In like manner adultery is intercourse with another's wife; who is allotted to him by the law emanating from God. Consequently intercourse with any woman, by the command of God, is neither adultery nor fornication.—The same applies to theft, which is the taking of another's property. For whatever is taken by the command of God, to Whom all things belong, is not taken against the will of its owner, whereas it is in this that theft consists.—Nor is it only in human things, that whatever is commanded by God is right; but also in natural things, whatever is done by God, is, in some way, natural, as stated in the First Part (Q. CV., A. 6 *ad* 1).

Reply Obj. 3. A thing is said to belong to the natural law in two ways. First, because nature inclines thereto: *e.g.*, that one should not do harm to another. Secondly, because nature did not bring in the contrary: thus we might say that for man to be naked is of the natural law, because nature did not give him clothes, but art invented them. In this sense, *the possession of all things in common and universal freedom* are said to be of the natural law, because, to wit, the distinction of possessions and slavery were not brought in by nature, but devised by human reason for the benefit of human life. Accordingly the law of nature was not changed in this respect, except by addition.

QUESTION XCV.
OF HUMAN LAW.

FIRST ARTICLE.
WHETHER IT WAS USEFUL FOR LAWS TO BE FRAMED BY MEN?

We proceed thus to the First Article:—

Objection 1. It seems that it was not useful for laws to be framed by men. Because the purpose of every law is that man be made good thereby, as stated above (Q. XCII., A. 1). But men are more to be induced to be good willingly by means of admonitions, than against their will, by means of laws. Therefore there was no need to frame laws.

Obj. 2. Further, As the Philosopher says (*Ethic.* v.), *men have recourse to a judge as to animate justice.* But animate justice is better than inanimate justice, which is contained in laws. Therefore it would have been better for the execution of justice to be entrusted to the decision of judges, than to frame laws in addition.

Obj. 3. Further, every law is framed for the direction of human actions, as is evident from what has been stated above (Q. XC., AA. 1, 2). But since human actions are about singulars, which are infinite in number, matters pertaining to the direction of human actions cannot be taken into sufficient consideration except by a wise man, who looks into each one of them. Therefore it would have been better for human acts to be directed by the judgment of wise men, than by the framing of laws. Therefore there was no need of human laws.

On the contrary, Isidore says (*Etym.* v.): *Laws were made that in fear thereof human audacity might be held in check, that innocence might be safeguarded in the midst of wickedness, and that the dread of punishment might prevent the wicked from doing harm.* But these things are most necessary to mankind. Therefore it was necessary that human laws should be made.

I answer that, As stated above (Q. LXIII., A. 1; Q. XCIV., A. 3), man has a natural aptitude for virtue; but the perfection of virtue must be acquired by man by means of some kind of training. Thus we observe that man is helped by industry in his necessities, for instance, in food and clothing. Certain beginnings of these he has from nature, viz., his reason and his hands; but he has not the full complement, as other animals have, to whom nature has given sufficiency of clothing and food. Now it is difficult to see how man could suffice for himself in the matter of this training: since the perfection of virtue consists chiefly in withdrawing man from undue pleasures, to which above all man is inclined, and especially the young, who are more capable of being trained. Consequently a man needs to receive this training from another, whereby to arrive at the perfection of virtue. And as to those young people who are inclined to acts of virtue, by their good natural disposition, or by custom, or rather by the gift of God, paternal training suffices, which is by admonitions. But since some are found to be depraved, and prone to vice, and not easily amenable to words, it was necessary for such to be restrained from evil by force and fear, in order that, at least, they might desist from evil-doing, and leave others in peace, and that they themselves, by being habituated in this way, might be brought to do willingly what hitherto they did from fear, and thus become virtuous. Now this kind of training, which compels through fear of punishment, is the discipline of laws. Therefore, in order that man might have peace and virtue, it was necessary for laws to be framed: for, as the Philosopher says (*Polit.* i.), *as man is the most noble of animals if he be perfect in virtue, so is he the lowest of all, if he be severed from law and righteousness;* because man can use his reason to devise means of satisfying his lusts and evil passions, which other animals are unable to do.

Reply Obj. 1. Men who are well disposed are led willingly to virtue by being admonished better than by coercion: but men who are evilly disposed are not led to virtue unless they are compelled.

Reply Obj. 2. As the Philosopher says (*Rhet.* i.), *it is better that all things be regulated by law, than left to be decided by judges:* and this for three reasons. First, because it is easier to find a few wise men competent to frame right laws, than to find the many who would be necessary to judge aright of each single case.—Secondly, because those who make laws consider long beforehand what laws to make; whereas judgment on each single case has to be pronounced as soon as it arises: and it is easier for man to see what is right, by taking many instances into consideration, than by considering one solitary fact.—Thirdly, because lawgivers judge in the abstract and of future events; whereas those who sit in judgment judge of things present, towards which they are affected by love, hatred, or some kind of cupidity; wherefore their judgment is perverted.

Since then the animated justice of the judge is not found in every man, and since it can be deflected, therefore it was necessary, whenever possible, for the law to determine how to judge, and for very few matters to be left to the decision of men.

Reply Obj. 3. Certain individual facts which cannot be covered by the law *have necessarily to be committed to judges,* as the Philosopher says in the same passage: for instance, *concerning something that has happened or not happened,* and the like.

SECOND ARTICLE.
WHETHER EVERY HUMAN LAW IS DERIVED FROM THE NATURAL LAW?

We proceed thus to the Second Article:—

Objection 1. It seems that not every human law is derived from the natural law. For the Philosopher says

(*Ethic.* v.) that *the legal just is that which originally was a matter of indifference.* But those things which arise from the natural law are not matters of indifference. Therefore the enactments of human laws are not all derived from the natural law.

Obj. 2. Further, positive law is contrasted with natural law, as stated by Isidore (*Etym.* v.) and the Philosopher (*Ethic.* v.). But those things which flow as conclusions from the general principles of the natural law belong to the natural law, as stated above (Q. XCIV., A. 4). Therefore that which is established by human law does not belong to the natural law.

Obj. 3. Further, the law of nature is the same for all; since the Philosopher says (*Ethic.* v.) that *the natural just is that which is equally valid everywhere.* If therefore human laws were derived from the natural law, it would follow that they too are the same for all: which is clearly false.

Obj. 4. Further, it is possible to give a reason for things which are derived from the natural law. But *it is not possible to give the reason for all the legal enactments of the lawgivers* (*Pandect. Justin.* Lib. I., Tit. III., Art V., *De legibus,* etc.). Therefore not all human laws are derived from the natural law.

On the contrary, Tully says (*Rhetor.* ii.): *Things which emanated from nature and were approved by custom, were sanctioned by fear and reverence for the laws.*

I answer that, As Augustine says (*De Lib. Arb.* i.), *that which is not just seems to be no law at all:* wherefore the force of a law depends on the extent of its justice. Now in human affairs a thing is said to be just, from being right, according to the rule of reason. But the first rule of reason is the law of nature,

as is clear from what has been stated above (Q. XCI., A. 2 *ad* 2). Consequently every human law has just so much of the nature of law, as it is derived from the law of nature. But if in any point it deflects from the law of nature, it is no longer a law but a perversion of law.

But it must be noted that something may be derived from the natural law in two ways: first, as a conclusion from premisses, secondly, by way of determination of certain generalities. The first way is like to that by which in sciences, demonstrated conclusions are drawn from the principles: while the second mode is likened to that whereby, in the arts, general forms are particularized as to details: thus the craftsman needs to determine the general form of a house to some particular shape. Some things are therefore derived from the general principles of the natural law, by way of conclusions; *e.g.,* that *one must not kill* may be derived as a conclusion from the principle that *one should do harm to no man:* while some are derived therefrom by way of determination; *e.g.,* the law of nature has it that the evil-doer should be punished; but that he be punished in this or that way, is a determination of the law of nature.

Accordingly both modes of derivation are found in the human law. But those things which are derived in the first way, are contained in human law not as emanating therefrom exclusively, but have some force from the natural law also. But those things which are derived in the second way, have no other force than that of human law.

Reply Obj. 1. The Philosopher is speaking of those enactments which are by way of determination or specification of the precepts of the natural law.

Reply Obj. 2. This argument avails

for those things that are derived from the natural law, by way of conclusions.

Reply Obj. 3. The general principles of the natural law cannot be applied to all men in the same way on account of the great variety of human affairs: and hence arises the diversity of positive laws among various people.

Reply Obj. 4. These words of the Jurist are to be understood as referring to decisions of rulers in determining particular points of the natural law: on which determinations the judgment of expert and prudent men is based as on its principles; in so far, to wit, as they see at once what is the best thing to decide.

Hence the Philosopher says (*Ethic.* vi.) that in such matters, *we ought to pay as much attention to the undemonstrated sayings and opinions of persons who surpass us in experience, age and prudence, as to their demonstrations.*

QUESTION XCVI.
OF THE POWER OF HUMAN LAW.

THIRD ARTICLE.
WHETHER HUMAN LAW PRESCRIBES ACTS OF ALL THE VIRTUES?

We proceed thus to the Third Article:—

Objection 1. It seems that human law does not prescribe acts of all the virtues. For vicious acts are contrary to acts of virtue. But human law does not prohibit all vices, as stated above (A. 2). Therefore neither does it prescribe all acts of virtue.

Obj. 2. Further, a virtuous act proceeds from a virtue. But virtue is the end of law; so that whatever is from a virtue, cannot come under a precept of law. Therefore human law does not prescribe all acts of virtue.

Obj. 3. Further, law is ordained to the common good, as stated above (Q. XC., A. 2). But some acts of virtue are ordained, not only to the common good, but to private good. Therefore the law does not prescribe all acts of virtue.

On the contrary, The Philosopher says (*Ethic.* v.) that the law *prescribes the performance of the acts of a brave man, . . . and the acts of the temperate man, . . . and the acts of the meek man: and in like manner as regards the other virtues and vices, prescribing the former, forbidding the latter.*

I answer that, The species of virtues are distinguished by their objects, as explained above (Q. LIV., A. 2; Q. LX., A. 1; Q. LXII., A. 2). Now all the objects of virtues can be referred either to the private good of an individual, or to the common good of the multitude: thus matters of fortitude may be achieved either for the safety of the state, or for upholding the rights of a friend, and in like manner with the other virtues. But law, as stated above (Q. XC., A. 2) is ordained to the common good. Wherefore there is no virtue whose acts cannot be prescribed by the law. Nevertheless human law does not prescribe concerning all the acts of every virtue: but only in regard to those that are ordained to the common good, —either immediately, as when certain things are done directly for the common good,—or mediately, as when a lawgiver prescribes certain things pertaining to good order, whereby the citizens are directed in the upholding of the common good of justice and peace.

Reply Obj. 1. Human law does not forbid all vicious acts, by the obligation of a precept, as neither does it prescribe all acts of virtue. But it forbids certain acts of each vice, just as it prescribes some acts of each virtue.

Reply Obj. 2. An act is said to be an act of virtue in two ways. First, from the fact that a man does something virtuous; thus the act of justice is to do what is right, and an act of fortitude is to do brave things: and in this way law prescribes certain acts of virtue.— Secondly an act of virtue is when a man does a virtuous thing in a way in which a virtuous man does it. Such an act always proceeds from virtue: and it does not come under a precept of law, but is the end at which every lawgiver aims.

Reply Obj. 3. There is no virtue whose act is not ordainable to the common good, as stated above, either mediately or immediately.

Political Obligation

The problem of political obligation as understood in the modern world is in many ways a new problem. The philosophic assumptions of realism as well as the social conditions of the Greek city-state and medieval feudalism did not lead to the formulation of distinct questions regarding the grounds of political obligation. These questions had to wait the great change between the Middle Ages and the modern era, and the latter age developed a concept of central and supreme sovereign within the state to whom every person owes allegiance.

But the emphasis must be on "distinct questions," for there is certainly implicit in realist writing, traditional and contemporary alike, a theory of political obligation. By nature man is a social animal because society is necessary to his very being, both in making life possible and the good life available. The obligations to live in society and to accept the conditions necessary to the existence of society such as order, authority, and government thus derive from man's very being and his need to fulfill that being.

The need for society is a fact of man's nature. What gives it moral legitimacy? Why should men feel obliged to accept regulation and authority? Because, realists answer, the fulfillment of man's being is itself a moral obligation and because society, when directed toward the common good and ordered by natural law, serves as the external ground and support of that fulfillment. The basis of political obligation is the nature of man; the state has its roots in social experience which shows that a governing authority is necessary for order; and natural law determines the legitimacy and scope of political authority: these assertions are the core of the realistic understanding of the political obligation that every citizen has to the state. But these same assumptions imply that the state, in turn, has obligations to its citizens. The ideas of natural law, justice, and the common good mean that government must be directed by reference to duties and limitations. Law and the common good are, for realists, the grounds on which political relations are secured, comprehended, and made legitimate and obligatory.

Realists thus view society as ordered interactions between governed and governor, teleologically directed toward man's happiness. Should an individual citizen violate the common good by breaking law, thereby destroying these relations, the state properly has the right to judge and punish, even to restrain the offender, so as to maintain order. On the question of transgressions by the state, however, realists have differed widely. John of Salisbury, as was observed above, taught a doctrine of tyrannicide, but his views are not generally shared by other realists. Aquinas is perhaps more representative of medieval realism in his denial that the people as a whole have the right to depose a tyrant. This right falls only to those who share in political authority such as lesser officials of the realm. Through the centuries since Aquinas, realists have tended to waver between these two views.

In brief form, the selection from Aquinas gives a realistic interpretation of society and government in which the meaning of political obligation can be found. Society is naturally necessary to man but, like the ship that needs the helmsman to arrive at a port, men and society need guidance in order to attain their ends. Therefore, Aquinas infers that government and authority are necessary in society. The common good, apprehended by man's reason, unites and directs society and makes government right. In being right or legitimate, government deserves, as well as demands, the obedience of its citizens.

The second selection is from the political writings of the great medieval poet, Dante (1265–1321). He promoted the ideal of universal empire (an ideal not expressed by Aquinas) and asserted that the authority of the empire derives from God directly rather than through the papacy. For these purposes, he looked beyond feudalism and medieval understandings of the relationship of church and temporal authority. Yet Dante's thought remains rather thoroughly enmeshed in Aristotelian principles. Government, he wrote, must be understood by reference to ends or purposes, and if there is no universal, inclusive end, particular ends are groundless and irrational. A universal end for man thus requires a universal empire. Furthermore, mankind is ordered for a distinct function, namely the exercise of his power of intellect. To pursue this function, man must live in peace. Empire and peace are the two demands on government that Dante saw issuing from man's nature. And, as these demands do derive from his very being, man is obliged to government as a condition of his self-realization.

ST. THOMAS AQUINAS   The Need for a Political Order

Our first task must be to explain how the term king is to be understood. Now whenever a certain end has been decided upon, but the means for arriving thereat are still open to choice, some one must provide direction if that end is to be expeditiously attained. A ship, for instance, will sail first on one course and then on another, according to the winds it encounters, and it would never reach its destination but for the skill of the helmsman who steers it to port. In the same way man, who acts by intelligence, has a destiny to which all his life and activities are directed; for it is clearly the nature of intelligent beings to act with some end in view. Yet the diversity of human interests and pursuits makes it

From St. Thomas Aquinas, "On Princely Government," *Selected Political Writings*, trans. J. G. Dawson, Oxford: Basil Blackwell and Mott Ltd., 1948. Used by permission of the publisher.

equally clear that there are many courses open to men when seeking the end they desire. Man, then, needs guidance for attaining his ends. Now, every man is endowed with reason, and it is by the light of reason that his actions are directed to their end. So if it befitted man to live a solitary life, after the fashion of many other animals, he would need no other guide, but each would be a king unto himself, under God, the King of kings, and would have the full ordering of his own actions by the light of God-given reason. When we consider all that is necessary to human life, however, it becomes clear that man is naturally a social and political animal, destined more than all other animals to live in community. Other animals have their food provided for them by nature, and a natural coat of hair. They are also given the means of defence, be it teeth, horns, claws, or at least speed in flight. Man, on the other hand, is not so provided, but having instead the power to reason must fashion such things for himself. Even so, one man alone would not be able to furnish himself with all that is necessary, for no one man's resources are adequate to the fullness of human life. For this reason the companionship of his fellows is naturally necessary to man.

Furthermore: other animals have a natural instinct for what is useful or hurtful to them; the sheep, for instance, instinctively senses an enemy in the wolf. Some animals even appear to have an instinctive knowledge of the medical properties of certain herbs and of other things necessary to their existence. Man, on the other hand has a natural knowledge of life's necessities only in a general way. Being gifted with reason, he must use it to pass from such universal principles to the knowledge of what in particular concerns his wellbeing. Reasoning thus, however, no one man could attain all necessary knowledge. Instead, nature has destined him to live in society, so that dividing the labour with his fellows each may devote himself to some branch of the sciences, one following medicine, another some other science, and so forth. This is further evident from the fact that men alone have the power of speech which enables them to convey the full content of their thoughts to one another. Other animals show their feelings it is true, but only in a general way, as when a dog betrays its anger by barking and other animals in different ways. Man, then, is more able to communicate with his kind than any other animal, even those which appear to be the most gregarious, such as cranes, ants or bees. Solomon had this in mind when he said (*Ecclesiastes,* IV, 9): "It is better for two to live together than solitary, for they gain by mutual companionship." The fellowship of society being thus natural and necessary to man, it follows with equal necessity that there must be some principle of government within the society. For if a great number of people were to live, each intent only upon his own interests, such a community would surely disintegrate unless there were one of its number to have a care for the common good: just as the body of a man or of any other animal would disintegrate were there not in the body itself a single controlling force, sustaining the general vitality of all the members. As Solomon tells us (*Prov.* XI, 14): "Where there is no ruler the people shall be scattered." This conclusion is quite reasonable; for the particular interest and the common good are not identical. We differ in our particular interests and it is the common good that unites the community. But matters which differ thus are the products of different causes. So, in addition to the motives of interest proper to each individual there must be some principle productive of the good of the many. For this reason, whenever there is an ordered unity arising out of a diversity of elements there is to be found some such controlling influence. In the material universe, for example, there is a certain order of divine providence under which all bodies are controlled by the first or heavenly body. Similarly all material bodies are controlled by rational creatures. In each man it is the soul which controls the body, and within the soul itself reason controls the faculties of passion and desire. Lastly, among the members of the body itself one is the principle, moving all the others: some say it is the heart, but others the head. So in all multiplicity there must be some controlling principle.

When matters are thus ordered to some end it can sometimes happen that such direction takes place either aright or wrongly. So political rule is sometimes just and sometimes unjust. Now anything is directed aright when it is brought to an end which befits it, but wrongly when it is brought to an end which is not so fitting. The object of a community of free men differs, for instance, from that of a community of slaves. For a free man is one who is master of his own actions, but a slave owes all that he is to another. If, then, a community of free men is administered by the ruler for the common good, such government will be just and fitting to free men. If, on the other hand, the community is directed in the particular interest of the ruler and not for the common good, this is a perversion of government and no longer just. Such rulers were warned by God, speaking through *Ezechiel* (XXXIV, 2), when he said: "Woe to those shepherds who fatten themselves (because they seek only their own comfort): is it not the duty of the shepherd to pasture his sheep?" Shepherds must care for the good of the flock, and all who are in authority for the good of those entrusted to them.

When government is unjustly exercised by one man who seeks personal profit from his position instead of the good of the community subject to him, such a ruler is called a tyrant. This word is derived from the idea of force, since a tyrant forcibly oppresses the people instead of ruling justly. The ancients were in the habit of calling all powerful chieftains tyrants. If, on the other hand, unjust government is exercised, not by one man alone, but by several banded together in a clique, such a state of affairs is called an oligarchy or rule by the few. This can happen when a few rich men take advantage of their wealth to oppress the rest of the people; and such government differs from tyranny only in the fact that the oppressors are many. Finally, unjust government can be exercised by a great number, and it is then called a democracy: such is mob rule when the common folk take advantage of their numbers to oppress the rich. In such a case the entire community becomes a sort of tyrant.

Similarly we must distinguish the various types of just rule. If the administration is carried out by some large section of the community, it is commonly called a polity: as for instance when an army rules in a province or a city. If, however, the administration falls to a few but virtuous men, it is called an aristocracy: that is rule by the best; and on account of this they are called aristocrats. Finally, if just government is exercised by one man alone, such a person is rightly called a king. So the Lord, speaking through *Ezechiel* (XXXVII, 24), said: "My servant David shall be king over all; he shall be the sole shepherd of them all." So it is quite clear that it is of the nature of kingship that there should be one to rule and that he should do so with a view to the common good without seeking private gain.

We have already seen that a communal life is proper to man because he would not be able to provide all that is necessary to life out of his own resources if he were to live like a hermit. So it follows that a communal society is the more perfect to the extent that it is sufficient in providing for life's necessities. There is indeed a certain sufficiency in the family of one household, so far as the elementary necessities of nutrition and procreation and such like

are concerned. Similarly in one locality you may find all that is necessary for a particular trade or calling. In a city, however, there is a perfect community, providing all that is necessary for the fullness of life; and in a province we have an even better example, because in this case there is added the mutual assistance of allies against hostile attack. Whoever, then, rules a perfect community, be it a city or a province; is rightly called a king. The head of a household, on the other hand, is not called king but father. Even so there is a certain similarity about the two cases, and kings are sometimes called the fathers of their people.

From what we have said, then, it is clear that a king is one who rules the people of a city or a province for their common good. So Solomon declared (*Ecclesiastes,* V, 8), "The king commands over all the lands which are subject to him."

DANTE ALIGHIERI   Universal Government

I, 2. To What End Does Government Exist among All Men?

1. First, we must ascertain what temporal Monarchy is in its idea, as I may say, and in its purpose. Temporal Monarchy, called also the Empire, we defined as a single Principality extending over all peoples in time, or in those things and over those things which are measured by time. Concerning it three main questions arise. First, we may ask and seek to prove whether it is necessary for the well-being of the world; secondly, whether the Roman people

rightfully appropriated the office of Monarchy; and thirdly, whether the authority of Monarchy derives from God directly, or from another, a minister or vicar of God.

2. But as every truth which is not a first principle is manifested by the truth of some first principle, it is necessary in every investigation to know the first principle to which we may return, in analysis, for the proof of all propositions which are subsequently assumed. And as the present treatise is an investigation, we must before all else search out a basic principle, on the validity of

From Dante, *De Monarchia,* trans. Aurelia Henry, Boston: Houghton Mifflin Co., 1904.

which will depend whatever follows. Be it known, therefore, that certain things exist which are not at all subject to our control, and which we can merely speculate upon, but cannot cause to be or to do: such are mathematics, physics, and divinity. On the other hand, certain things exist which are subject to our control, and which are matter not only for speculation, but for execution. In these things the action is not performed for the sake of the speculation, but the latter for the sake of the former, because in them action is the end. Since the matter under consideration is governmental, nay, is the very source and first principle of right governments, and since everything governmental is subject to our control, it is clear that our present theme is primarily adapted for action rather than for speculation. Again, since the first principle and cause of all actions is their ultimate end, and since the ultimate end first puts the agent in motion, it follows that the entire procedure of the means toward an end must derive from the end itself. For the manner of cutting wood to build a house will be other than that of cutting wood to build a ship. So if there exists an end for universal government among men, that end will be the basic principle through which all things to be proved hereafter may be demonstrated satisfactorily. But to believe that there is an end for this government and for that government, and that there is no single end common to all, would indeed be irrational.

I, 3. To Actualize
THE WHOLE CAPACITY OF
THE POSSIBLE INTELLECT
IN SPECULATION AND ACTION.

1. We must now determine what is the end of human society as a whole, and having determined that, we shall have accomplished more than half of our labor, according to the Philosopher in his writings *to Nicomachus*. In order to discern the point in question more clearly, observe that as Nature fashions the thumb for one purpose, the whole hand for another, then the arm for a purpose differing from both, and the entire man for one differing from all, so she creates for one end the individual, for another the family, for another the village, for still another end the city, for another the kingdom, and finally for an ultimate end, by means of His art which is Nature, the Eternal God brings into being the human race in its totality. And this last is what we are in search of as the directive first principle of our investigation.

2. In beginning, then, let it be recognized that God and Nature make nothing in vain; but that whatever comes into being comes with a definite function. For, according to the intention of the creator, as creator, the ultimate end of a created being is not the being itself but its proper function. Wherefore a proper function exists not for the sake of the being, but contrariwise. There is, then, some distinct function for which humanity as a whole is ordained, a function which neither an individual nor a household, neither a village, nor a city, nor a particular kingdom, has power to perform. What this function is will be evident if we point out the distinctive capacity of humanity as a whole. I say, therefore, that no faculty shared by many things diverse in species is the differentiating characteristic of any one of them. For since the differentiating characteristic determines species, it would follow that one essence would be specific to many species, which is impossible. So the differentiating characteristic in man is not simple existence,

for that is shared by the elements; nor existence in combination, for that is met with in minerals; nor existence animate, for that is found in plants; nor existence intelligent, for that is participated in by the brutes; but the characteristic competent to man alone, and to none other above or below him, is existence intelligent through the possible intellect. Although other beings possess intellect, it is not intellect distinguished by potentiality, as is man's. Such beings are intelligent species in a limited sense, and their existence is no other than the uninterrupted act of understanding; they would otherwise not be eternal. It is evident, therefore, that the differentiating characteristic of humanity is a distinctive capacity or power of intellect.

3. And since this capacity as a whole cannot be reduced to action at one time through one man, or through any one of the societies discriminated above, multiplicity is necessary in the human race in order to actualize its capacity in entirety. Likewise multiplicity is necessary in creatable things in order to exercise continually the capacity of primal matter. Were it not so, we should be granting the existence of unactualized potentiality, which is impossible. With this belief Averroës[1] accords in his commentary on the treatise *concerning the Soul*. Further, the intellectual capacity of which I speak has reference not only to universal forms or species, but, by a sort of extension, to particular ones. Wherefore it is a common saying that the speculative intellect becomes by extension the practical, whose end is to do

and to make. I speak of things to be done, which are controlled by political sagacity, and things to be made, which are controlled by art, because they are all handmaids of speculation, that supreme end for which the Primal Good brought into being the human race. From this now grows clear the saying in the *Politics* that "the vigorous in intellect naturally govern other men."

I, 4. To Attain This End Humanity Requires Universal Peace.

1. It has now been satisfactorily explained that the proper function of the human race, taken in the aggregate, is to actualize continually the entire capacity of the possible intellect, primarily in speculation, then, through its extension and for its sake, secondarily in action. And since it is true that whatever modifies a part modifies the whole, and that the individual man seated in quiet grows perfect in knowledge and wisdom, it is plain that amid the calm and tranquillity of peace the human race accomplishes most freely and easily its given work. How nearly divine this function is revealed in the words, "Thou hast made him a little lower than the angels."[2] Whence it is manifest that universal peace is the best of those things which are ordained for our beatitude. And hence to the shepherds sounded from on high the message not of riches, nor pleasures, nor honors, nor length of life, nor health, nor beauty; but the message of peace. For the heavenly host said, "Glory to God in the highest, and on earth peace among men in whom he is well pleased."[3] Like-

---

[1] Averroës was an Arabian philosopher of the twelfth century, and author of the famous commentary upon Aristotle here alluded to. He is mentioned in *Conv.* 4. 13. 3, and placed among the great thinkers in Limbo, *Inf.* 4. 144. *Tr.*

[2] *Ps.* 8. 6; cf. *Heb.* 2. 7. *Tr.*

[3] *Luke* 2. 14. *Tr.*

wise, "Peace be unto you"[4] was the salutation of the Saviour of men. It befitted the supreme Saviour to utter the supreme salutation. It is evident to all that the disciples desired to preserve this custom; and Paul likewise in his words of greeting.[5]

2. From these things which have been expounded we perceive through what better, nay, through what best means the human race may fulfill its proper office. Consequently we perceive the nearest way through which may be reached that universal peace toward which all our efforts are directed as their ultimate end, and which is to be assumed as the basic principle of subsequent reasoning. This principle was necessary, we have said, as a predetermined formula, into which, as into a most manifest truth, must be resolved all things needing to be proved.

I, 5. WHEN SEVERAL THINGS ARE ORDAINED FOR ONE END, ONE MUST RULE AND THE OTHERS OBEY.

1. Resuming what was said in the beginning, I repeat, there are three main questions asked and debated in regard to temporal Monarchy, which is more commonly termed the Empire, and it is my purpose to make inquiry concerning these in the order cited, according to the principle now enunciated. And so let the first question be whether temporal Monarchy is necessary for the well-being of the world. The necessity of temporal Monarchy can be gainsaid with no force of reason or authority, and can be proved by the most powerful and patent arguments, of which the

first is taken on the testimony of the Philosopher in the *Politics*. There this venerable authority asserts that when several things are ordained for one end, one of them must regulate or rule, and the others submit to regulation or rule. This, indeed, not only because of the author's glorious name, but because of inductive reasoning, demands credence.

2. If we consider the individual man, we shall see that this applies to him, for, when all his faculties are ordered for his happiness, the intellectual faculty itself is regulator and ruler of all others; in no way else can man attain to happiness. If we consider the household, whose end is to teach its members to live rightly, there is need for one called the *pater-familias,* or for some one holding his place, to direct and govern, according to the Philosopher when he says, "Every household is ruled by its eldest." It is for him, as Homer says, to guide and make laws for those dwelling with him. From this arises the proverbial curse, "May you have an equal in your house." If we consider the village, whose aim is adequate protection of persons and property, there is again needed for governing the rest either one chosen for them by another, or one risen to prëeminence from among themselves by their consent; otherwise, they not only obtain no mutual support, but sometimes the whole community is destroyed by many striving for first place. Again, if we consider the city, whose end is to insure comfort and sufficiency in life, there is need for undivided rule in rightly directed governments, and in those wrongly directed as well; else the end of civil life is missed, and the city ceases to be what it was. Finally, if we consider the individual kingdom, whose end is that of the city with greater promise

---

4 *Luke* 24. 36; *John* 20. 21, 26. *Tr.*
5 *Rom.* 1. 7. *Tr.*

of tranquillity, there must be one king to direct and govern. If not, not only the inhabitants of the kingdom fail of their end, but the kingdom lapses into ruin, in agreement with that word of infallible truth, "Every kingdom divided against itself is brought to desolation."[6] If, then, this is true of these instances, and of all things ordained for a single end, it is true of the statement assumed above.

3. We are now agreed that the whole human race is ordered for one end, as already shown. It is meet, therefore, that the leader and lord be one, and that he be called Monarch, or Emperor. Thus it becomes obvious that for the well-being of the world there is needed a Monarchy, or Empire.

III, 16. THE AUTHORITY OF THE EMPIRE DERIVES FROM GOD DIRECTLY.

1. Although by the method of reduction to absurdity it has been shown in the foregoing chapter that the authority of Empire has not its source in the Chief Pontiff, yet it has not been fully proved, save by an inference, that its immediate source is God, seeing that if the authority does not depend on the Vicar of God, we conclude that it depends on God Himself. For a perfect demonstration of the proposition we must prove directly that the Emperor, or Monarch, of the world has immediate relationship to the Prince of the universe, who is God.

2. In order to realize this, it must be understood that man alone of all beings holds the middle place between corruptibility and incorruptibility, and is therefore rightly compared by philosophers to the horizon which lies be-

tween the two hemispheres. Man may be considered with regard to either of his essential parts, body or soul. If considered in regard to the body alone, he is perishable; if in regard to the soul alone, he is imperishable. So the Philosopher spoke well of its incorruptibility when he said in the second book *on the Soul,* "And this only can be separated as a thing eternal from that which perishes."

3. If man holds a middle place between the perishable and imperishable, then, inasmuch as every mean shares the nature of the extremes, man must share both natures. And inasmuch as every nature is ordained for a certain ultimate end, it follows that there exists for man a twofold end, in order that as he alone of all beings partakes of the perishable and the imperishable, so he alone of all beings should be ordained for two ultimate ends. One end is for that in him which is perishable, the other for that which is imperishable.

4. Ineffable Providence has thus designed two ends to be contemplated of man: first, the happiness of this life, which consists in the activity of his natural powers, and is prefigured by the terrestrial Paradise; and then the blessedness of life everlasting, which consists in the enjoyment of the countenance of God, to which man's natural powers may not attain unless aided by divine light, and which may be symbolized by the celestial Paradise.

5. To these states of blessedness, just as to diverse conclusions, man must come by diverse means. To the former we come by the teachings of philosophy, obeying them by acting in conformity with the moral and intellectual virtues; to the latter through spiritual teachings which transcend human reason, and

---

[6] *Luke* 11. 17. *Tr.*

which we obey by acting in conformity with the theological virtues, Faith, Hope, and Charity. Now the former end and means are made known to us by human reason, which the philosophers have wholly explained to us; and the latter by the Holy Spirit, which has revealed to us supernatural but essential truth through the Prophets and Sacred Writers, through Jesus Christ, the coeternal Son of God, and through His disciples. Nevertheless, human passion would cast all these behind, were not men, like horses astray in their brutishness, held to the road by bit and rein.

6. Wherefore a twofold directive agent was necessary to man, in accordance with the twofold end; the Supreme Pontiff to lead the human race to life eternal by means of revelation, and the Emperor to guide it to temporal felicity by means of philosophic instruction. And since none or few—and these with exceeding difficulty—could attain this port, were not the waves of seductive desire calmed, and mankind made free to rest in the tranquillity of peace, therefore this is the goal which he whom we call the guardian of the earth and Roman Prince should most urgently seek; then would it be possible for life on this mortal threshing-floor to pass in freedom and peace. The order of the world follows the order inherent in the revolution of the heavens. To attain this order it is necessary that instruction productive of liberality and peace should be applied by the guardian of the realm, in due place and time, as dispensed by Him who is the ever present Watcher of the whole order of the heavens. And He alone foreordained this order, that by it in His providence He might link together all things, each in its own place.

7. If this is so, and there is none higher than He, only God elects and only God confirms. Whence we may further conclude that neither those who are now, nor those who in any way whatsoever have been, called Electors have the right to be so called; rather should they be entitled heralds of divine providence. Whence it is that those in whom is vested the dignity of proclamation suffer dissension among themselves at times, when, all or part of them being shadowed by the clouds of passion, they discern not the face of God's dispensation.

8. It is established, then, that the authority of temporal Monarchy descends without mediation from the fountain of universal authority. And this fountain, one in its purity of source, flows into multifarious channels out of the abundance of its excellence.

9. Methinks I have now approached close enough to the goal I had set myself, for I have taken the kernels of truth from the husks of falsehood, in that question which asked whether the office of Monarchy was essential to the welfare of the world, and in the next which made inquiry whether the Roman people rightfully appropriated the Empire, and in the last which sought whether the authority of the Monarch derived from God immediately, or from some other. But the truth of this final question must not be restricted to mean that the Roman Prince shall not be subject in some degree to the Roman Pontiff, for felicity that is mortal is ordered in a measure after felicity that is immortal. Wherefore let Caesar honor Peter as a first-born son should honor his father, so that, refulgent with the light of paternal grace, he may illumine with greater radiance the earthly sphere over which he has been set by Him who alone is Ruler of all things spiritual and temporal.

The Ideal of Justice

Greek philosophers gave attention to the nature of society and to the ideal of justice that should govern it. Heraclitus (536–470) wrote of parallels between the law of the world and the law of society. Possibly this thought also occurred to Anaximander (sixth century), one of his predecessors. The school of Pythagoras (572–497) went further in articulating the meaning of justice. Justice, they said, is a number multiplied by itself, that is, a square number. A square number is a perfect harmony because it is composed of equal parts. It follows, therefore, that justice is related to a conception of the state based on equal parts. The Pythagoreans also defined justice as requital, for it is the measure between aggressor and loser in acts of injustice.

Influenced by the Pythagoreans, Plato articulated further the ideal of justice in terms of harmony and measure. As was seen in the first selection, Plato believed that justice and law are the common spiritual substance of a society that bring and hold it together. He understood justice in terms of an adjustment that gives the parts or factors forming a society their proper place, for the justice of a society is the citizen's sense of the duties of his station in that society. From his station, the citizen discharges his appropriate function in public action. While this conception of justice is a principle of social ethics that gives coherence to the community as a whole, it served Plato as an ideal of individual ethics as well. In fact, Plato quite deliberately compared society and the individual, holding that both are made of parts or elements, that both demand meaningful unification, and that both ought to be ordered by reason in the light of the ideal of justice.

The dominant philosophical trend of Greece to which these allusions refer provides the background for Aristotle's more detailed treatment of justice.* Justice, he writes, is fairness in human action, and fairness is a mean between the extremes of excess and deficiency, of too much and too little.† Justice therefore is a mean; it involves the fair or equal and, as justice involves persons and their relations, it is relative to certain persons.

These references to fairness, equality, and the mean indicate that Aristotle understands justice as the principle of coherence and order in society. As he specifies two conceptions of justice in the selection, his emphasis on rational order is even more apparent, for he relates justice to mathematical principles. Distributive or social justice is based on the notion of geometrical proportion: it is defined as a mean between the violations of proportion. Corrective justice, which seeks to restore equality by imposing penalties, is based on arithmetical proportion, and is a mean between the extremes of "profit" and "loss." All actions involving injustice

---

* Though much of Greek thought was realistic, in part or by way of anticipation, the student should not infer that realism was the sole position in the philosophy of that time. Quite the opposite is the case, for the adventurous Greek mind touched on many of the chief alternatives in social philosophy.

† Aristotle also used the idea of the mean to define the moral virtues. Courage, for example, is the mean between the excesses of foolhardiness on the one hand, and cowardice on the other.

damage or destroy the coherence of society because they aim at the destructive extreme.

The influence of Aristotle's discussion of justice on philosophy generally and on later theories of realism in particular can hardly be exaggerated. There have been, it is true, additions and modifications of the doctrine, but Aristotle gave it its fundamental meaning and direction. Realistic assumptions about man and society, as they have been suggested in previous selections, provide the context in which the ideal of justice takes on its full meaning: happiness as the fulfillment of man's being, society as a moral and educational organism, and order and authority as conditions of happiness. Perhaps most basic of all, however, is the realist's belief that, though men come to recognize the need of society out of a variety of motives, "the ultimate bond of human society is reason."‡

‡ Etienne Gilson, *The Christian Philosophy of St. Thomas Aquinas,* trans. L. K. Shook, New York: Random House, Inc., 1956, p. 327.

ARISTOTLE   Justice as a Mean

As the person who is unjust is unfair, and the thing which is unjust is unfair, it is clear that there is a certain mean in respect of unfairness, or inequality. This mean is that which is fair or equal; for whatever be the nature of an action that admits of excess or defect, it admits also of fairness or equality.

If then that which is unjust is unfair, that which is just is fair, as indeed every one sees without argument.

But since that which is fair or equal is a mean between two extremes, that which is just will in a certain sense be a mean. But fairness or equality implies two persons or things at least. It follows therefore that that which is just is a mean, that it is fair or equal and that it is relative to certain persons. It follows also that, inasmuch as it is a mean, it is a mean between certain extremes, viz. excess and defect, and that inasmuch as it is just, it is relative to certain persons. But, if so, then that which is just must imply four terms at least; for the persons relatively to whom it is just are two, and the things in which it consists are two likewise. Also, if the persons are equal, the things will be equal; for as one thing is to the other thing, so is one person to the other person. For if the persons are not equal, they will not have equal shares; in fact the source of battles and complaints is either that people who are equal have unequal shares, or that people who are not equal have equal shares, distributed to them. The same truth is clearly seen from the principle of merit; for everybody admits that justice in distributions is determined by merit of some sort; only people do not all understand the same thing by merit. The democrats understand freedom, the oligarchs wealth or nobility, and the aristocrats virtue.

Justice then is a sort of proportion; for proportion is not peculiar to abstract quantity, but belongs to quantity generally, proportion being equality of ratios and implying four terms at least.

Now it is plain that discrete propor-

From Aristotle, *The Nicomachean Ethics,* trans. J. E. Welldon, London: Macmillan & Co., Ltd., 1902.

tion implies four terms; but the same is true of continuous proportion; for in continuous proportion one of the terms is used as two, and is repeated. Thus as *A* is to *B,* so is *B* to *C;* here *B* is repeated; consequently if *B* be set down twice, the terms of the proportion will be four.

That which is just then requires four terms at least, and an equality of ratio between them, the persons and the things being similarly divided. As then the term *A* is to the term *B,* so will *C* be to *D,* and consequently *alternando* as *A* is to *C,* so will *B* be to *D*. The whole therefore will bear the same ratio to the whole i.e. *A + C will be to B + D as A is to B or C to D;* but this is the combination which the distribution effects, and, if the terms be thus united, it is a just combination.

The conjunction therefore of *A* with *C* and of *B* with *D* is what is just in distribution, and this justice is a mean between the violations of proportion; for that which is proportionate is a mean, and that which is just is proportionate. Mathematicians call this kind of proportion geometrical; for in geometrical proportion the whole is to the whole as each of the separate terms is to each. But this proportion is not continuous, as no one arithmetical term can stand both for person and for thing.

That which is just then in this sense is that which is proportionate, and that which is unjust is that which is disproportionate. It follows that this disproportion may take the form either of excess or defect; and this is actually the case, for the author of the injustice has too much, and the victim has too little, of the good. In regard to evil the contrary is the case; for the lesser evil in comparison with the greater counts as a good, as the lesser evil is more desirable than the greater, and that which is de-

sirable is a good, and that which is more desirable is a greater good.

This then, is one form of justice *i.e. of particular justice.*

The remaining form of justice is the corrective, which occurs in private transactions whether voluntary or involuntary.

This justice is different in kind from the former. For distributive justice in dealing with the public funds invariably follows the proportion which has been described, *i.e. geometrical proportion,* as even if the distribution be made *to two or more people* out of the public funds, it will be in accordance with the ratio of the contributions which they have severally made. Also the injustice which is opposite to this form of justice is the violation of *geometrical* proportion. But the justice which exists in private transactions, although in a sense it is fair or equal, and the corresponding injustice is unfair or unequal, follows not geometrical but arithmetical proportion. For it makes no difference here whether it be a virtuous man who defrauded a bad man, or a bad man who defrauded a virtuous man, or whether it be a virtuous or a bad man who committed adultery; the law looks only to the degree of the injury, it treats the parties as equal, and asks only if one is the author and the other the victim of injustice or if the one inflicted and the other has sustained an injury. Injustice then in this sense is unfair or unequal, and the endeavour of the judge is to equalize it; for even when one person deals a blow and the other receives it, or one person kills and the other is killed, the suffering and the action are divided into unequal parts, and it is the effort of the judge to restore equality by the penalty which he inflicts, as the penalty is so much subtracted from the profit. For the term "profit" is applied generally to such cases, although it is sometimes not strictly appropriate; thus we speak of the "profit" of one who inflicts a blow, or the "loss" of one who suffers it, but it is when the suffering is assessed *in a court of law* that the prosecutor gets profit, and the guilty person loss. That which is fair or equal then is the mean between excess and defect. But profit and loss are excess and defect, although in opposite senses, the excess of good and the defect of evil being profit, and the excess of evil and the defect of good being loss. The mean between them, is, as we said, the equal, which we call just. Hence corrective justice will be the mean between profit and loss.

This is the reason why, when people dispute, they have recourse to a judge (δικαστής) and to go to a judge is to go to what is just; for the judge professes to be a sort of personification of justice.

Again, people look for the mean in a judge, and sometimes give judges the name of "mediators," which implies that, if they attain the mean, they will attain what is just. That which is just then is, in a sense, a mean, as the judge is a mean. . . .

The nature of the just and the unjust has now been described. The definitions which have been given make it clear that just conduct is a mean between committing and suffering injustice; for to commit injustice is to have too much, and to suffer it is to have too little. But justice is a mean state, not in the same sense as the virtues already described, but rather as aiming at the mean, while injustice aims at the extremes. . . .

Justice, as between masters and slaves, or between fathers and children, is not the same as political justice, *i.e. justice between citizen and citizen,* although it resembles it, for a man cannot commit injustice in an absolute *or*

strict sense against what is his own; but his property and his children, until they reach a certain age and become independent, are, as it were, parts of himself, and nobody deliberately chooses to hurt himself; hence injustice to oneself is an impossibility. It follows that political justice and injustice are also impossible *in the relation of a master to slaves or of a father to children;* for they depend, as we said, upon law, and exist only where law has a natural existence i.e. among people who, as we saw, enjoy equality of rule and subjection. There is more scope then for justice in relation to a wife than in relation to children and property, for this, *i.e. justice in the relation of husband and wife,* is domestic justice, although this again is different from political justice.

Political justice is partly natural and partly conventional.

The part which is natural is that which has the same authority everywhere, and is independent of opinion; that which is conventional is such that it does not matter in the first instance whether it takes one form or another, it only matters when it has been laid down, e.g. that the ransom of a prisoner should be a mina, or that a goat, and not two sheep, should be offered in sacrifice, and all legislative enactments which are made in particular cases, as the sacrifice in honour of Brasidas at Amphipolis, and the provisions of an Act of Parliament.

It is the opinion of some people that all the rules of justice are conventional, because that which is natural is immutable and has the same authority everywhere, as fire burns equally here and in Persia, but they see the rules of justice continually altering.

But this is not altogether true, although it is true to some extent. Among the gods indeed it is probably not true at all; but in this world, although there is such a thing as natural justice, still all justice is variable. Nevertheless there is a justice which is, as well as a justice which is not, natural.

Within the sphere of the contingent it is easy to see what kind of thing it is that is natural, and what kind that is not natural but legal and conventional, both kinds being similarly variable. The same distinction will apply to other cases; thus the right hand is naturally stronger than the left, although there is nobody who may not acquire the power of using both hands alike.

Such rules of justice as depend on convention and convenience may be compared to standard measures; for the measures of wine and corn are not everywhere equal, but are larger where people buy and smaller where they sell. Similarly, such rules of justice as exist not by nature, but by the will of Man, are not everywhere the same, as polities themselves are not everywhere the same, although there is everywhere only one naturally perfect polity.

But every rule of justice or law stands *to individual actions* in the relation of the universal to particulars; for while actions are numerous, every such rule is one, as being universal.

There is a difference between an act of injustice and that which is unjust, between an act of justice and that which is just. A thing is unjust by nature, or by ordinance; but this very thing, when it is done, is an act of injustice, although, before it is done, it is only unjust. The same is true of an act of justice. But the several kinds of acts of justice, or injustice, their number, and their sphere, will form subjects of investigation hereafter.

Such being the things which are just and unjust, a person may be said to act justly or unjustly when he does them

voluntarily. When he does them involuntarily, he does not act justly or unjustly, except in an accidental sense, i.e. he does what is accidentally just or unjust.

The definition of an act of justice or injustice depends upon its voluntary or involuntary character; for when it is voluntary, it is open to censure, and it is then also an act of injustice. It will be unjust then in a sense, but will not amount to an act of injustice, if it lacks voluntariness.

By a voluntary action I mean, as has been already said, such an action as is in a person's power, and is performed by him knowingly, and not in ignorance of the person to whom he does it, or of the instrument with which he does it, or of the result, e.g. of the person whom he strikes, and the instrument with which he strikes, and the effect of his blow; and not only so, but he must not perform it accidentally or under compulsion; for if a person e.g. were to seize his hand and strike somebody else with it, it would not be a voluntary action, as not being in his own power. Again, it is possible that the person struck may be his father, and that he may know him to be a man or some one who is present, but may not know him to be his father. The same sort of distinction must be made in regard to the effect and to the action generally. If an action is done in ignorance, or, although not done in ignorance, is not in a person's power, or if he is compelled to do it, it is involuntary; for there are many things in the course of nature which we both do and suffer with full knowledge but which are not either voluntary or involuntary, as e.g. growing old or dying.

The accidental character may belong equally to just and unjust actions. Thus a person may restore a deposit involuntarily and from motives of fear; but in that case it is not right to say that he does what is just or that his conduct is just, except accidentally. Similarly, if a person under compulsion and involuntarily refuses to restore a deposit, he must be said to be unjust and to do what is unjust accidentally.

Voluntary actions we perform either with or without deliberate purpose—with it, if we perform them after previous deliberation, and without it, if without such deliberation.

There are three ways in which people may hurt each other in society. An action done in ignorance is called a mistake, when the person affected, or the thing done, or the instrument, or the effect, is not such as the agent supposed. For instance, he supposed that he would not hit or would not hit with the particular instrument or would not hit the particular person, or that the blow would not have the particular effect; but the effect proved different from his expectation, e.g. it was his intention to prick a person and not to wound him,

or the person was different, or the instrument.

Now when the hurt done is contrary to expectation, it is a mishap; but when, although it is not contrary to expectation, it does not imply malice, it is a mistake; for a person makes a mistake, when the original culpability lies in himself, but he meets with a mishap, when it lies outside himself. When a person acts with knowledge, but without deliberation, it is an act of injustice, as in all human actions which arise from anger and other necessary or natural emotions; for in doing such hurt, and making such mistakes we are unjust, and they are acts of injustice, but it does not follow that we are at once unjust or vicious, as the hurt is not the consequence of vice.

But when the action is the result of deliberate purpose, the agent is unjust and wicked. Hence it is rightly held that such actions as arise from anger are not done of malice prepense; for it is not he who acts in anger, but he who provoked the anger, that begins the quarrel.

SECTION TWO

Positivism

It is often pointed out that the word positivism has been used in two ways: to name a particular philosophy and to stand for a distinctive, but rather common, temper of mind. In its first meaning, positivism is associated with the eccentric yet influential French philosopher, Auguste Comte, who was the first thinker to use the word for a philosophical position. This use is connected with his famous "law" of social growth and with the evaluation of different modes of knowledge implicit in it.

All history, Comte taught, passes through three different ascending levels.* The most primitive is the *theological,* where men attempt to explain natural phenomena by appealing to spiritual, anthropomorphic beings. The second stage, the *metaphysical,* depersonalizes these beings so that they become forces and essences. The third level is the *positive,* where explanation proceeds by scientific description. Correlative with these stages in knowledge are different organizations of society and the highest of these, according to Comte, is that which is based firmly on science and scientific discoveries.†

Comte's philosophy leads to and is included in the second meaning of positivism as a special temper of mind. Most broadly put, this attitude involves a "tough-minded" orientation toward facts and natural phenomena. It holds that thought should confine itself to the data of experience and reject all transcendent metaphysical and abstract speculation. So understood, positivism has been a recurring position in the history of thought, represented by a stream of philosophers from the Sophists of ancient Greece to contemporary analytic positivists. But also so understood, the term may be so broad that the student will find it of little or no

---

* Comte refers to this law in many places, among them, for example, *The Positive Philosophy,* trans. Harriet Martineau, New York, 1855.

† Comte's views on these matters are treated further below.

value since it will apply to many quite divergent philosophies, and its meaning for social philosophy will be vague, if not completely lost. While taking the fact-orientation of the positivist as a starting point, therefore, one must specify the themes of positivism more closely in order to make the term a useful classificatory device. This can be done by examining more carefully typical positivist theories of *knowledge,* of *value,* and of *society.*

1. Positivism in the more technical sense may be characterized, first, by its claim that science provides man with the clearest possible ideal of knowledge. Rejecting theological, metaphysical, and speculative methods, the positivist argues that phenomena—social as well as natural—are to be explained by scientific laws, not by ends, final causes or transcendent grounds. Speculation is to be replaced by science, wisdom becomes control through science, and philosophy, in its traditional sense, is judged to be a meaningless, if not a dangerous illusion.

These assertions are perhaps clear enough, but the student should watch for several refinements of them. It must be noted that, except for a few sporadic anticipations (Machiavelli is an example in social thought), positivism arose with the scientific revolution of the seventeenth century. Historians usually place the rise of modern science in that century (only organic chemistry had to await a later date), and the century's philosophers such as Bacon, Descartes, Leibniz, and Locke articulated the methods and assumptions on which science rests.

Next, the student should watch for various conceptions of science and for their distinctive elements. Different men during different times have practiced science diversely, and they have also interpreted and applied science in quite divergent ways. Hobbes, for example, viewed science as a deductive procedure that begins with adequate definitions and proceeds by demonstration of derived consequences. Saint-Simon, Comte, and the "scientific socialists" of the nineteenth century understood science to be the formulation of descriptive generalizations (laws) derived from uninterpreted and unbiased observation. Modern science has yet another emphasis, employing chiefly, though not solely, the hypothesis that may be described briefly as "hypothetical-deductive." To understand a social philosopher who takes science to be his model or ideal of knowledge, it is necessary to grasp something of his conception of science.

Another caution concerns the relation of science to philosophy in different philosophic perspectives. Positivists are not alone in attempting to relate science to philosophy; modern philosophers of all persuasions face this problem. Positivists are not alone either in seeking to *base* philosophy on science; in their own ways, utilitarians, Marxists, and pragmatists do the same.‡ The main point is that the embrace of science is a fundamental element in positivism, though it is not alone the principal characteristic.

2. Consistent with its orientation toward fact, positivism rejects all attempts to understand value in metaphysical and nonempirical ways. Statements about the convertibility of being and good and about the rational order of value are examples of speculative assertions that the positivist finds to be nonsense. Not that the posi-

---

‡ The differences are important however. Positivists generally have been influenced by the procedures of physics, pragmatists by biology, utilitarians seek to give morals and legislation a scientific status, and Marxists offer a scientific law of history.

tivist thinks values are unimportant to men; he believes that value must be understood within the context of human life and in ways susceptible to scientific treatment. Positivists have often defined value in a noncognitive yet empirical way—as need or interest, for example—and have analyzed rules of value as imperatives or commands to men to behave in certain ways. Even for positivists like Comte, who write about developing a "science of value," the emphasis is on observable needs and on generalizations regarding the means for satisfying these needs.

3. This noncognitive yet empirical understanding of value may be amplified and illustrated by reference to society. The starting point of this approach is not man's moral needs such as the realization of virtue, but needs in the form of desires and interests. At times these needs have been viewed in terms of self-assertion (Machiavelli) and security (Hobbes), at other times in terms of a variety of satisfactions of wants (Comte). But the main effort of positivists is to look empirically at human nature and social conduct in order to isolate the basic needs of individuals living together in the context of cooperation and mutual dependence. In this context human beings also develop rules and standards governing their associative lives, and positivists believe that these too are subject to scientific investigation. Thus, to illustrate: moral value, which involves relations of persons to each other, may be understood empirically as obedience to positive law or custom, and justice is found in the concrete workings of society and government rather than in the realm of transcendental ideals.

These assertions, then, serve as an introduction to positivist thought: the primacy of science and the rejection of metaphysics, an empirical theory of value, and an understanding of man and society in terms of human needs and interests. Their fuller meaning and implications for social philosophy are developed in the selections that follow.

Man and Society

Thomas Hobbes (1588–1679) is the first great thinker to attempt to bring political philosophy into relationship with a modern system of ideas. Scorning Aristotle's "essences" and definitions based on purposes, he sought to accomplish in political theory what scientists were achieving in physics and cosmology. While his view of science has been out of date for a long time, he did produce something of a "science of politics."

Hobbes attempted to explain man and society solely in terms of self-interest, without reference to transcendent sanctions or metaphysical notions like the common good. Realists and other natural law theorists argue that society must preserve the basic moral conditions of civilized life, and that these conditions are determined by reference to ends or purposes. Hobbes asserts that causes, not ends, control human life, and that a scientific account of causes will lead to an understanding of society. Thus rejecting final causes, Hobbes proceeds in Cartesian* fashion to frame clear and real definitions and to develop their implications deductively.

Considered in themselves and apart from society (the state of nature), men are fundamentally equal. In matters of strength, of ability, and of hope for attaining their own ends, there is no basic difference among them that requires special attention in political theory. The last matter especially, namely hope, which is shared by all men, is the source of the misery pervading the natural state of man; from it arises the desire of domination over others to secure one's own interests. Men quarrel or "war" with each other from motives of competition, diffidence, and glory; the natural condition of men is thus a state of war of man against man. Life is solitary, poor, nasty, brutish, and short.

What men desire, Hobbes is saying, is what they call good, and happiness is success in getting what is desired. And since all men are equal and motivated in the same way, each man finds that his hopes, values, and happiness are threatened and insecure. The state of nature does not offer hope for security. Since there is no law, there is no common power that all men fear and obey, and there are no constraining notions of morality or justice. Hobbes uses the traditional terms, natural right and natural law, of the state of nature, but he empties them of all traditional meaning. Natural right is the liberty of each man to use his power to preserve himself, and natural laws are rules of conduct given by reason for the sake of one's own interests. In neither case, however, does Hobbes intend to write of moral principles. He believes he is describing the condition of man and the causes that account for his behavior.

Since man's natural condition is one of misery, Hobbes infers that it is in man's interest to form societies and governments. The need for security leads to a demand for common power, and since the state of nature is essentially without effective power and obligation, even a modest need for security leads to an endless need of power. Therefore, men consent to the creation of a sovereign power who can secure their interests by removing the threats to them in the state of nature. Further, Hobbes argues, wherever power is effective, it is to man's advantage to submit to it. The "social contract" is kept because it is in the interest of every man; rules limiting obedience to government are never in the interest of man. To submit to power is to consent to it, and consent creates the duty of obedience in the sense that the ruler who maintains such security—since men have more to gain than lose by submission to him—acquires the right of command. With command comes law and with law justice, morality, and civilization.

For Hobbes, sovereign power is the only basis for an effective society and government.† To be sure, men are not naturally inclined to society; they have to be prepared for it by education. Yet sovereignty, justice, and honesty, and indeed all political behavior, are but refined forms of egoism, for they have been defined by Hobbes entirely in terms of self-interest. Beyond separate self-interests, Hobbes

---

* René Descartes (1596–1650), French philosopher and one of the developers of the theory of scientific method. Incidentally, it may be noted that Spinoza applied the Cartesian method morally, Hobbes in a nonmoral fashion.

† For Hobbes, society and government finally mean the same thing. Any distinction between them, as any between law and morals, is confusion.

admits no explanatory principles. Society itself is an "artificial" body, for the word itself refers only to the fact that human beings find it individually advantageous to exchange goods and services and to submit to control.

THOMAS HOBBES The Need for Security

OF THE NATURAL CONDITION OF MANKIND AS CONCERNING THEIR FELICITY, AND MISERY.

Nature hath made men so equal, in the faculties of the body, and mind; as that though there be found one man sometimes manifestly stronger in body, or of quicker mind than another; yet when all is reckoned together, the difference between man, and man, is not so considerable, as that one man can thereupon claim to himself any benefit, to which another may not pretend, as well as he. For as to the strength of body, the weakest has strength enough to kill the strongest, either by secret machination, or by confederacy with others, that are in the same danger with himself.

And as to the faculties of the mind, setting aside the arts grounded upon words, and especially that skill of proceeding upon general, and infallible rules, called science; which very few have, and but in few things; as being not a native faculty, born with us; nor attained, as prudence, while we look after somewhat else, I find yet a greater equality amongst men, than that of strength. For prudence, is but experience; which equal time, equally bestows on all men, in those things they equally apply themselves unto. That which may perhaps make such equality incredible, is but a vain conceit of one's own wisdom, which almost all men think they have in a greater degree, than the vulgar; that is, than all men but themselves, and a few others, whom by fame, or for concurring with themselves, they approve. For such is the nature of men, that howsoever they may acknowledge many others to be more witty, or more eloquent, or more learned; yet they will hardly believe there be many so wise as themselves; for they see their own wit at hand, and other men's at a distance. But this proveth rather that men are in that point equal, than unequal. For there is not ordinarily a greater sign of the equal distribution of any thing, than that every man is contented with his share.

From this equality of ability, ariseth equality of hope in the attaining of our ends. And therefore if any two men desire the same thing, which nevertheless they cannot both enjoy, they become enemies; and in the way to their end, which is principally their own conservation, and sometimes their delectation only, endeavour to destroy, or subdue one another. And from hence it comes to pass, that where an invader hath no more to fear, than another man's single power; if one plant, sow, build, or possess a convenient seat, others may probably be expected to come prepared with forces united, to dispossess, and deprive him, not only of the fruit of his labour, but also of his life, or liberty. And the

From Thomas Hobbes, *Leviathan*, in *The English Works of Thomas Hobbes*, ed. William Molesworth, London: John Bohn, 1849.

invader again is in the like danger of another.

And from this diffidence of one another, there is no way for any man to secure himself, so reasonable, as anticipation; that is, by force, or wiles, to master the persons of all men he can, so long, till he see no other power great enough to endanger him: and this is no more than his own conservation requireth, and is generally allowed. Also because there be some, that taking pleasure in contemplating their own power in the acts of conquest, which they pursue farther than their security requires; if others, that otherwise would be glad to be at ease within modest bounds, should not by invasion increase their power, they would not be able, long time, by standing only on their defence, to subsist. And by consequence, such augmentation of dominion over men being necessary to a man's conservation, it ought to be allowed him.

Again, men have no pleasure, but on the contrary a great deal of grief, in keeping company, where there is no power able to over-awe them all. For every man looketh that his companion should value him, at the same rate he sets upon himself: and upon all signs of contempt, or undervaluing, naturally endeavours, as far as he dares, (which amongst them that have no common power to keep them in quiet, is far enough to make them destroy each other), to extort a greater value from his contemners, by damage; and from others, by the example.

So that in the nature of man, we find three principal causes of quarrel. First, competition; secondly, diffidence; thirdly, glory.

The first, maketh men invade for gain; the second, for safety; and the third, for reputation. The first use vio-

lence, to make themselves masters of other men's persons, wives, children, and cattle; the second, to defend them; the third, for trifles, as a word, a smile, a different opinion, and any other sign of undervalue, either direct in their persons, or by reflection in their kindred, their friends, their nation, their profession, or their name.

Hereby it is manifest, that during the time men live without a common power to keep them all in awe, they are in that condition which is called war; and such a war, as is of every man, against every man. For WAR, consisteth not in battle only, or the act of fighting; but in a tract of time, wherein the will to contend by battle is sufficiently known: and therefore the notion of *time*, is to be considered in the nature of war; as it is in the nature of weather. For as the nature of foul weather, lieth not in a shower or two of rain; but in an inclination thereto of many days together: so the nature of war, consisteth not in actual fighting; but in the known disposition thereto, during all the time there is no assurance to the contrary. All other time is PEACE.

Whatsoever therefore is consequent to a time of war, where every man is enemy to every man; the same is consequent to the time, wherein men live without other security, than what their own strength, and their own invention shall furnish them withal. In such condition, there is no place for industry; because the fruit thereof is uncertain: and consequently no culture of the earth; no navigation, nor use of the commodities that may be imported by sea; no commodious building; no instruments of moving, and removing, such things as require much force; no knowledge of the face of the earth; no account of time; no arts; no letters; no society; and which is worst of all, continual fear, and danger of violent death; and the life of man, solitary, poor, nasty, brutish, and short.

It may seem strange to some man, that has not well weighed these things; that nature should thus dissociate, and render men apt to invade, and destroy one another: and he may therefore, not trusting to this inference, made from the passions, desire perhaps to have the same confirmed by experience. Let him therefore consider with himself, when taking a journey, he arms himself, and seeks to go well accompanied; when going to sleep, he locks his doors; when even in his house he locks his chests; and this when he knows there be laws, and public officers, armed, to revenge all injuries shall be done him; what opinion he has of his fellow-subjects, when he rides armed; of his fellow citizens, when he locks his doors; and of his children, and servants, when he locks his chests. Does he not there as much accuse mankind by his actions, as I do by my words? But neither of us accuse man's nature in it. The desires, and other passions of man, are in themselves no sin. No more are the actions, that proceed from those passions, till they know a law that forbids them: which till laws be made they cannot know: nor can any law be made, till they have agreed upon the person that shall make it.

It may peradventure be thought, there was never such a time, nor condition of war as this; and I believe it was never generally so, over all the world: but there are many places, where they live so now. For the savage people in many places of America, except the government of small families, the concord whereof dependeth on natural lust, have no government at all; and live at this day in that brutish manner, as I said before. Howsoever, it may be perceived what manner of life there would be, where there were no common power to fear, by the manner of life, which men that have formerly lived under a peaceful government, use to degenerate into, in a civil war.

But though there had never been any time, wherein particular men were in a condition of war one against another; yet in all times, kings, and persons of sovereign authority, because of their independency, are in continual jealousies, and in the state and posture of gladiators; having their weapons pointing, and their eyes fixed on one another; that is, their forts, garrisons, and guns upon the frontiers of their kingdoms; and continual spies upon their neighbours; which is a posture of war. But because they uphold thereby, the industry of their subjects; there does not follow from it, that misery, which accompanies the liberty of particular men.

To this war of every man, against every man, this also is consequent; that nothing can be unjust. The notions of right and wrong, justice and injustice have there no place. Where there is no common power, there is no law: where no law, no injustice. Force, and fraud, are in war the two cardinal virtues. Justice, and injustice are none of the faculties neither of the body, nor mind. If they were, they might be in a man that were alone in the world, as well as his senses, and passions. They are qualities, that relate to men in society, not in solitude. It is consequent also to the same condition, that there be no propriety, no dominion, no *mine* and *thine* distinct; but only that to be every man's, that he can get; and for so long, as he can keep it. And thus much for the ill condition, which man by mere nature is actually placed in; though with a possibility to come out of it, consisting partly in the passions, partly in his reason.

The passions that incline men to peace, are fear of death; desire of such things as are necessary to commodious living; and a hope by their industry to obtain them. And reason suggesteth convenient articles of peace, upon which men may be drawn to agreement. These articles, are they, which otherwise are called the Laws of Nature: whereof I shall speak more particularly, in the two following chapters.

Of the First and Second Natural Laws, and of Contracts.

The Right of Nature, which writers commonly call *jus naturale,* is the liberty each man hath, to use his own power, as he will himself, for the preservation of his own nature; that is to say, of his own life; and consequently, of doing any thing, which in his own judgment, and reason, he shall conceive to be the aptest means thereunto.

By Liberty, is understood, according to the proper signification of the word, the absence of external impediments: which impediments, may oft take away part of a man's power to do what he would; but cannot hinder him from using the power left him, according as his judgment, and reason shall dictate to him.

A Law of Nature, lex naturalis, is a precept or general rule, found out by reason, by which a man is forbidden to do that, which is destructive of his life, or taketh away the means of preserving the same; and to omit that, by which he thinketh it may be best preserved. For though they that speak of this subject, use to confound *jus,* and *lex, right* and *law:* yet they ought to be distinguished; because RIGHT, consisteth in liberty to do, or to forbear; whereas LAW, determineth, and bindeth to one of them: so that law, and right, differ as much, as obligation, and liberty; which is one and the same matter are inconsistent.

And because the condition of man, as hath been declared in the precedent chapter, is a condition of war of every one against every one; in which case every one is governed by his own reason; and there is nothing he can make use of, that may not be a help unto him, in preserving his life against his enemies; it followeth, that in such a condition, every man has a right to every thing; even to one another's body. And therefore, as long as this natural right of every man to every thing endureth, there can be no security to any man, how strong or wise soever he be, of living out the time, which nature ordinarily alloweth men to live. And consequently it is a precept, or general rule of reason, *that every man, ought to endeavour peace, as far as he has hope of obtaining it; and when he cannot obtain it, that he may seek, and use, all helps, and advantages of war.* The first branch of which rule, containeth the first, and fundamental law of nature; which is, *to seek peace, and follow it.* The second, the sum of the right of nature; which is, *by all means we can, to defend ourselves.*

From this fundamental law of nature, by which men are commanded to endeavour peace, is derived this second law; *that a man be willing, when others are so too, as far-forth, as for peace, and defence of himself he shall think it necessary, to lay down this right to all things; and be contented with so much liberty against other men, as he would allow other men against himself.* For as long as every man holdeth this right, of doing any thing he liketh; so long are all men in the condition of war. But if other men will not lay down their right, as well as he; then there is no reason for any one, to divest himself of his: for that were to expose himself to prey, which no man is bound to, rather than to dispose himself to peace. This is that law of the Gospel; *whatsoever you require that others should do to you, that do ye to them.* And that law of all men, *quod tibi fieri non vis, alteri ne feceris.* . . .

Of the Causes, Generation, and Definition of a Commonwealth.

The final cause, end, or design of men, who naturally love liberty, and dominion over others, in the introduction of that restraint upon themselves, in which we see them live in commonwealths, is the foresight of their own preservation, and of a more contented life thereby; that is to say, of getting themselves out from that miserable condition of war, which is necessarily consequent, as hath been shown in chapter XIII, to the natural passions of men, when there is no visible power to keep them in awe, and tie them by fear of punishment to the performance of their covenants, and observation of those laws of nature set down in the fourteenth and fifteenth chapters.

For the laws of nature, as *justice, equity, modesty, mercy,* and, in sum, *doing to others, as we would be done to,* of themselves, without the terror of some power, to cause them to be observed, are contrary to our natural passions, that carry us to partiality, pride, revenge, and the like. And covenants, without the sword, are but words, and of no strength to secure a man at all. Therefore notwithstanding the laws of nature, which every one hath then kept, when he has the will to keep them, when he can do it safely, if there be no power erected, or not great enough for our security; every man will, and may lawfully rely on his own strength and art, for caution against all other men. And in all places, where men have lived by small families, to rob and spoil one another, has been a trade, and so far from being reputed against the law of nature, that the greater spoils they gained, the greater was their honour; and men observed no other laws therein, but the laws of honour; that is, to abstain from cruelty, leaving to men their lives, and instruments of husbandry. And as small families did then; so now do cities and kingdoms which are but greater families, for their own security, enlarge their dominions, upon all pretences of danger, and fear of invasion, or assistance that may be given to invaders, and endeavour as much as they can, to subdue, or weaken their neighbours, by open force, and secret arts, for want of other caution, justly; and are remembered for it in after ages with honour.

Nor is it the joining together of a small number of men, that gives them this security; because in small numbers, small additions on the one side or the other, make the advantage of strength so great, as is sufficient to carry the victory; and therefore gives encouragement to an invasion. The multitude sufficient to confide in for our security, is not determined by any certain number, but by comparison with the enemy we fear; and is then sufficient, when the odds of the enemy is not of so visible and conspicuous moment, to determine the event of war, as to move him to attempt.

And be there never so great a multitude; yet if their actions be directed according to their particular judgments, and particular appetites, they can expect thereby no defence, nor protection, neither against a common enemy, nor against the injuries of one another. For being distracted in opinions concerning the best use and application of their strength, they do not help but hinder one another; and reduce their strength by mutual opposition to nothing: whereby they are easily, not only subdued by a very few that agree together; but also when there is no common enemy, they make war upon each other, for their particular interests. For if we could suppose a great multitude of men to consent in the observation of justice, and other laws of nature, without a common power to keep them all in awe; we might as well suppose all mankind to do the same; and then there neither would be, nor need to be any civil government, or commonwealth at all; because there would be peace without subjection.

Nor is it enough for the security, which men desire should last all the time of their life, that they be governed, and directed by one judgment, for a limited time; as in one battle, or one war. For though they obtain a victory by their unanimous endeavour against a foreign enemy; yet afterwards, when either they have no common enemy, or he that by one part is held for an enemy, is by another part held for a friend, they must needs by the difference of their interests dissolve, and fall again into a war amongst themselves.

It is true, that certain living creatures, as bees, and ants, live sociably one with another, which are therefore by Aristotle numbered amongst political creatures; and yet have no other direc-

tion, than their particular judgments and appetites; nor speech, whereby one of them can signify to another, what he thinks expedient for the common benefit: and therefore some man may perhaps desire to know, why mankind cannot do the same. To which I answer,

First, that men are continually in competition for honour and dignity, which these creatures are not; and consequently amongst men there ariseth on that ground, envy and hatred, and finally war; but amongst these not so.

Secondly, that amongst these creatures, the common good differeth not from the private; and being by nature inclined to their private, they procure thereby the common benefit. But man, whose joy consisteth in comparing himself with other men, can relish nothing but what is eminent.

Thirdly, that these creatures, having not, as man, the use of reason, do not see, nor think they see any fault, in the administration of their common business; whereas amongst men, there are very many, that think themselves wiser, and abler to govern the public, better than the rest; and these strive to reform and innovate, one this way, another that way; and thereby bring it into distraction and civil war.

Fourthly, that these creatures, though they have some use of voice, in making known to one another their desires, and other affections; yet they want that art of words, by which some men can represent to others, that which is good, in the likeness of evil; and evil, in the likeness of good; and augment, or diminish the apparent greatness of good and evil; discontenting men, and troubling their peace at their pleasure.

Fifthly, irrational creatures cannot distinguish between *injury*, and *dam-*

age; and therefore as long as they be at ease, they are not offended with their fellows: whereas man is then most troublesome, when he is most at ease: for then it is that he loves to shew his wisdom, and control the actions of them that govern the commonwealth.

Lastly, the agreement of these creatures is natural; that of men, is by covenant only, which is artificial: and therefore it is no wonder if there be somewhat else required, besides covenant, to make their agreement constant and lasting; which is a common power, to keep them in awe, and to direct their actions to the common benefit.

The only way to erect such a common power, as may be able to defend them from the invasion of foreigners, and the injuries of one another, and thereby to secure them in such sort, as that by their own industry, and by the fruits of the earth, they may nourish themselves and live contentedly; is, to confer all their power and strength upon one man, or upon one assembly of men, that may reduce all their wills, by plurality of voices, unto one will: which is as much as to say, to appoint one man, or assembly of men, to bear their person; and every one to own, and acknowledge himself to be author of whatsoever he that so beareth their person, shall act, or cause to be acted, in those things which concern the common peace and safety; and therein to submit their wills, every one to his will, and their judgments, to his judgment. This is more than consent, or concord; it is a real unity of them all, in one and the same person, made by covenant of every man with every man, in such manner, as if every man should say to every man, *I authorise and give up my right of governing myself, to this man, or to this assembly of men, on this condition, that thou give up thy right to him, and authorize all his actions in like manner.* This done, the multitude so united in one person, is called a COMMONWEALTH, in Latin CIVITAS. This is the generation of the great LEVIATHAN, or rather, to speak more reverently, of that *mortal god,* to which we owe under the *immortal God,* our peace and defence. For by this authority, given him by every particular man in the commonwealth, he hath the use of so much power and strength conferred on him, that by terror thereof, he is enabled to perform the wills of them all, to peace at home, and mutual aid against their enemies abroad. And in him consisteth the essence of the commonwealth; which, to define it, is *one person, of whose acts a great multitude, by mutual covenants one with another, have made themselves every one the author, to the end he may use the strength and means of them all, as he shall think expedient, for their peace and common defence.*

And he that carrieth this person, is called SOVEREIGN, and said to have *sovereign power;* and every one besides, his SUBJECT.

The attaining to this sovereign power, is by two ways. One, by natural force; as when a man maketh his children, to submit themselves, and their children to his government, as being able to destroy them if they refuse; or by war subdueth his enemies to his will, giving them their lives on that condition. The other, is when men agree amongst themselves, to submit to some man, or assembly of men, voluntarily, on confidence to be protected by him against all others. This latter, may be called a political commonwealth, or commonwealth by *institution;* and the former, a commonwealth by *acquisition.*

Social and Political Values

What can men do who, without reference to theology and metaphysics, want to explain society and its values as a complex structure adopted to men's needs? As we have seen, Hobbes's answer was in terms of science, understood primarily as a matter of definition and deduction. By the end of the eighteenth century, how-ever, there was a developing realization that science relies on observation and in-duction rather than deduction. Hence arose the necessity for those influenced by the general positivist temper to rethink the meanings of science, philosophy, and social value.

One important source of this reexamination and construction is the work of Saint-Simon and his followers. Comte de Saint-Simon (1760–1825) maintained the positivist conviction that everything happens according to laws that can be known by observation and experiment. The Saint-Simonians held that a scientific explanation of society could be found by postulating a law of historical change on the basis of induction. This they did, Comte offering his famous law of three stages,* and Saint-Simon himself devising a principle of the alternation of organic and critical periods of history. Such "laws" of history provided the Saint-Simonians with an explanation of historical process, an understanding of the goal of historical movement, and a grasp of the values that society is gradually seeking to embody.

According to Bazard,† who gave the lectures from which the following selection is taken, the facts of history have been collected and classified, and it is necessary for men to know the law and the goal of history. The law is one of progress from organic to critical periods of social organization, and back to organic ones; the goal of history is an organic period of universal association. An organic society is one whose purposes are clearly defined for all its members and which, therefore, is harmonious and unified. A critical period, which involves criticism and destruc-tion of forms of order leads to anarchy and egoism. The recurring cycle of organic and critical stages tends ultimately toward an organic society which, unlike such societies in the past, will be universal and based on science.

The world, the Saint-Simonians said, is on the threshold of a new organic age. The developing industrial society will become organic when it is given a positive purpose, by which is meant not just a common notion of justice but a general sharing in a common enterprise. That enterprise, to be accomplished when society is scientifically organized, is the multiplication and satisfaction of human wants. That is, society should be taken over by industrialists who, supported by scientists and artists, would manage its resources as means to human satisfactions. Govern-ment would become primarily the seat of administration rather than the center of organized force (many early socialists felt that if their reforms were adopted, the

---

* See the introduction to positivism above. Comte remained a disciple of Saint-Simon for a while, but later broke with the master.

† Amand Bazard (1791–1832), French socialist and free interpreter of Saint-Simon. The differences between their positions are not important for present purposes.

need for force to maintain order would greatly diminish), it would be in the hands of experts, and it would be directed, even made possible, by scientific knowledge and techniques. So understood, universal association is the final goal of history, not as some static state of perfection, but as a society organized directly for progress. The law of history is in fact also a law of progress: the evidence for progress is empirical, and the reason for progress is causal.‡

Thus the Saint-Simonians held satisfaction through science rather than through liberty or equality to be the primary social value. Impressed more by how science affects man's conception of his world than by particular developments, they defined philosophy as a kind of compendium of the sciences, including the new science of sociology that they as well as Comte had promoted. They believed that philosophy so conceived would do for an industrial society what theology had done for feudal society, namely to give it a cosmology intimately connected with a morality suitable for the age. Philosophy, society, morality—even man's very nature—are all under the control and spirit of the scientific enterprise and the values it contains or discovers.

‡ The Saint-Simonians also generally coupled this belief with a theory of social determinism, for they held that the way men behave is determined by their society and culture.

THE SAINT-SIMONIANS   Order, Peace, and Association
Amand Bazard

Must we not ask ourselves, when regarding the past and observing in detail the facts that tradition has transmitted to us, which thread will lead us into that immense labyrinth? All these facts, up to our time, have already been observed, classified, and named. The monuments of various civilizations have been described or are still standing. The books they have produced are available, translated with commentaries and explained. And finally the great men that moved these masses, the laws which these masses obeyed, the beliefs that filled their souls are there; all are living for him who loves mankind and who knows its destinies and applies himself to their realization.

Of what use are these facts to us if we do not know how to read from them clearly a wish, a desire, a sought for goal, never attained but which mankind is approaching ceaselessly, and toward which we ourselves shall help to guide her? Of what use are they if we do not know how to link them by a general conception which, embracing all, indicates to us the place each one of them should occupy in the sequence of the development of the human species? And what mighty genius will reveal this conception to us?

A man passionately concerned about mankind, who loved order but lived in the midst of a society in disorder, who burned with the desire to see his fellow-

From Bazard's lectures of 1828–1829, 3d and 4th Sessions, in *The Doctrine of Saint-Simon,* trans. George G. Iggers, Boston: Beacon Press, 1958. Used by permission of Professor Iggers.

men united and brethren at the very moment when everyone around him was struggling, warring, destroying each other; an eminently sympathetic man, a poet before being a scientist, came to give human science a new basis and new axioms. Saint-Simon said: "Order, peace, and love are for the future. The past has always loved, studied, and practiced war, hatred and antagonism. However, the human species marched ceaselessly towards its peaceful destiny, passing by successive steps from an imperfect order to a better order and from a weak and narrow association to a stronger and wider one. Each step mankind made was at first a crisis, for it had to deny its past and break violently the bonds which had been healthy in its childhood but which had become obstacles to its development."[1] With these words of our master, history takes on an altogether new character. The observer, the scientist, verifies that sublime inspiration of the genius by a new examination of the past. He studies how the savage's hut was replaced by the city, the city by the fatherland, the fatherland by mankind. In the long succession of centuries that preceded us, he observes which are the epochs in which men, belonging first to a family, then to a city, and later even to a fatherland, appeared bound by love to the destiny of their race, their fellow citizens, and their compatriots; and, on the other hand, those epochs in which the bonds of affections have been broken, and an order, formerly loved, has become oppressive and incompatible with the new

desires that move hearts. In the first epochs all efforts seemed to converge towards one goal; in the latter epochs everyone was isolated. In the former all the elements of the social body come together, combine, and organize; in the latter, dissolution and death seem nearer every day, until a seed of love comes to call the members of this body, weary from a terrible crisis, back to life and to unite them more strongly than ever.

Thus we are given the first extensive classification of the past. We can divide it into organic epochs in each of which a social order is developed, incomplete since it is not universal, provisional since it is not yet peaceful; and into critical epochs in which the former order is criticized, attacked, and destroyed; epochs which extend up to the moment when a new principle of order is revealed to the world.

Let us look at the epochs of civilization to which we are tied directly, and which are best known to us. To us, educated in Greek and Roman letters, sons of Christians, witnesses of the decline of Catholicism and even of the luke-warm reformation, two clearly pronounced critical epochs appear during the period of twenty-three centuries: the first separates polytheism from Christianity and extends from the appearance of the first Greek philosophers to the preaching of the Gospels; the second separates the Catholic doctrine from that of the future and includes the three centuries from Luther to our day. The corresponding organic periods are the one when Greek and Roman polytheism was in full vigor, which ends in the centuries of Pericles and Augustus; and the period when Catholicism and feudalism were at their greatest might and splendor, which came to an end as far as its religious side was concerned with Leo X

---

[1] This terminology is not Saint-Simon's, but that of the Saint-Simonians of 1829. The latter occasionally sought to give their doctrine a "religious" character through allusions to a supposed oral teaching of their master. Adopted from *Tr.'s* note.

and from the political point of view with Louis XIV.

What is man's destiny in relation to his fellow-man and in relation to the universe? These are the general terms of the dual problem which mankind has always posed. All organic epochs have been at least temporary solutions of these problems. But soon the progress achieved with the help of these solutions, and sheltered by social institutions based on these solutions, makes even them insufficient and new solutions are called for. The critical epochs, the moments of contest, of protest,[2] of expectation, and transition, follow—to fill the interval with doubt, with indifference concerning these great problems, with egoism, a necessary consequence of this doubt and indifference. Wherever these great social problems have been solved, there has been an organic epoch; when they have remained unsolved, there has been a critical period.

During organic periods, the goal of activity is clearly defined. We have said that all efforts are dedicated to achieving this goal, toward which man is continuously directed by education and legislation during his entire life. If general relations are fixed, individual relations are modeled on them and are also fixed. The goal that society intends to attain is revealed to all hearts and all intellects. It becomes easy to recognize the men of capacity most suited to further this trend, and the truly superior are, of course, in possession of power. Legitimacy, sovereignty, and authority exist in the real meaning of these words. Harmony rules in social relationships.

Man then sees the totality of phenomena administered by a providence and by a benevolent will. The very principle of human societies, the law which they obey, appears to him as an expression of this will. And this common belief is manifested by a cult which binds the strong to the weak, and the weak to the strong. It may be said that in this sense the character of the organic epoch is essentially religious.

The unity existing in the sphere of social relations is reflected in an order of facts which we should mention here, in particular, because of the importance attached to it today. We wish to speak of the sciences. The different special fields of which they are composed appear in the organic epoch only in a series of subdivisions of the general conception of the fundamental dogma. There really exists then an encyclopedia of the sciences, if we keep the true meaning of the word "encyclopedia," which is the connectedness of human knowledge.

The critical epochs offer a diametrically opposed picture. True, at their beginning one can observe co-operation determined by the generally felt need for destruction. But soon differences appear and become insurmountable. Everywhere anarchy manifests itself, and soon everyone is busy appropriating ruins of the structure which crumbles and is scattered until it is reduced to dust. The goal of social activity is completely ignored. The uncertainty in general relationships passes over into private ones. The true men of ability no longer are or can be appreciated. The legitimacy of the power of those who exercise it is contested. Governors and governed are at war; a similar war begins among particular interests, which daily acquire a more and more marked predominance over general interest.

---

[2] The underlining suggests that the Saint–Simonians meant Protestantism, whose critical spirit they rejected. *Tr.*

Egoism finally succeeds devotion as atheism replaces godliness.

Man has ceased to understand his relation to his fellow-men as well as the relation which unites his destiny with universal destiny. He passes from faith to doubt, from doubt to unbelief, or rather to the negation of the former faith, for that negation itself is a new faith. He believes in fatalism, as he believed in Providence. He loves and sings of disorder as he adored and extolled harmony.

In these epochs one sees a large number of systems appear that more or less win the sympathy of some factions of society and which divide society more and more while, almost unnoticed, the former doctrine and the old institutions continue to serve society as a link, or at least a barrier against excessive disorder.

The different systems of human knowledge no longer form a unity. Man's knowledge no longer constitutes dogma: the collection of the sciences no longer deserves the name encyclopedia, for the tomes containing them, however voluminous, are merely an aggregation lacking connection.

At such epochs, when all social ties have been broken, the masses experience only imperfectly the immense gap in moral activity. For them this gap is overcome by a surplus in spiritual or material activity without any sympathetic goal—without any inspiration of love. But the men of superior mind view the abyss with terror. The more the moral nothingness places bitter and bloody satire in their mouths, the more they are inspired by songs of sadness and despair. In such epochs a Juvenal appears, or a Persius, a Goethe, or a Byron.

In summary, the distinct characteristics of the organic epoch are unity and harmony in all spheres of human activity, while the critical epoch is distinguished by anarchy, confusion, and disorder in all directions. In the former, the totality of general ideas has until now been given the name "religion"; in the latter, they are formulated under the name "philosophy," a term which in this sense had only a destructive meaning in regard to the former beliefs. However, it may be observed that ideas destined to serve in later reorganization, too, adopt the name "philosophy" at their birth. In the organic epochs the highest manifestations of feelings bear the name "cult" in the most exact sense of this word; in the critical periods they take on the name "fine arts," an expression that comprehends the same critical thought in respect to cult that the term "philosophy" has in regard to religion. We have now determined the general characteristics of the organic and critical epochs. In all epochs of the same nature, whether organic or critical, whatever the time and place, men are always occupied in building during the former, and destroying during the latter. The differences that can be noticed between two organic epochs or two critical epochs depend solely on the nature of the object that is to be constructed or to be destroyed. The intensity of belief, and the extent of association give each epoch its distinctive expression. But an appraisal of the details distinguishing one epoch from another of the same nature is of little importance and can easily be made, once the characteristics common to every critical epoch and those pertaining to all organic epochs have been grasped. . . .

At our last meeting we showed you what the general characteristics of the organic and the critical epochs of the past were. You must have understood that this alternation of epochs of order and of disorder was the condition underlying social progress. It remains for us to make you understand how this continuous succession of seeming grandeur and apparent decline, commonly called the vicissitudes of mankind, is nothing but the regular series of efforts made by mankind to attain a final goal.

This goal is *universal association,* which is to say, the association of all men on the entire surface of the globe in all spheres of their relationships. But perhaps it will be said that association is only a means; that it is more important to determine the goal towards which mankind must travel. For anyone who would reflect on the strict meaning of the terms, it should be evident that the end and the means are expressed at the same time, at least in a general fashion, as we employ the terms here, and that *universal association* can be understood only through the combination of human forces into a peaceful direction.

Nevertheless, since the word "association" is being applied in our time only to narrow combinations that embrace but one type of interest, it seems necessary to distinguish among historical phenomena those that place mankind outside of association and those which by their development have brought mankind closer to association. In this way, one may understand the full scope of the terms "association" and "universal" as used by us.

From a viewpoint high enough to embrace at once the past and the future of mankind—terms inseparable from each other, since both are parts of one process and one cannot be judged without the other—one recognizes that society in its entire duration contains two distinct general states: a provisional one belonging to the past and a final one reserved for the future, the state of antagonism and the state of association. In the former, the different partial, coexisting aggregations consider themselves as reciprocal obstacles and feel for each other nothing but distrust and hatred. Each aspires only to destroy its rivals and subject them to its domination. On the other hand, in the state of association, the division of the human family into classes is presented as a division of labor, as a systematization of efforts to attain a common goal. Each particular aggregation sees its prosperity and growth bound up with the prosperity and growth of all other aggregations.

We certainly do not maintain that the march of mankind is subject to the action of two general laws, antagonism and association. The successive development of the human species recognizes only one single law, the uninterrupted progress of association. But precisely because there has been progress in regard to association, it is evident that while this progress was taking place facts must have emerged which to a greater or lesser degree were outside of association. We call this state of things antagonism, a state which, strictly speaking, expresses only a negation. It should, nevertheless, be studied apart if one wants clearly to appraise the differences between the first and the last stage of social development.

The further we go back into the past, the narrower and the more incomplete we find the sphere of association. The most confined circle, one which is thought of as necessarily having developed first, is the family. History has shown us societies which had no other bond. Today tribes on the globe[3] exist among whom association seems not to have spread beyond this limit. Finally,

---

[3] For example, Australia. *Tr.*

even among us in Europe certain peoples (for example, the clans of Scotland and the inhabitants of Corsica), which through particular circumstances have been isolated to a certain extent from the movement of civilization, still reveal in their social relationships traces of this primitive state.

The first progress that takes place in the development of association is the union of several families into a city. The second is that of several cities into a national body. The third is that of several nations, linked by a common belief, into a federation. We have already stated that mankind has remained at this last stage, which was realized by the Catholic association. And however immense this progress may be if one compares the social state that it created with those that preceded it, it must yet be recognized that the degree of association attained at this stage is still, from the dual standpoint of depth and extent, far from the one which it is to attain. Indeed, Christianity, whose principle and expansive force have long since been exhausted, embraced in its love and sanctified by its law only one of the modes of human existence, and did not succeed in establishing its rule—now failing—over more than a portion of mankind. . . .

To sum up: to the degree that the circle of association became wider, exploitation of man by man diminished, antagonism became less violent, and all human faculties were developed more and more in a peaceful direction.

This continuous tendency suffices to indicate the general character of the final state towards which mankind is traveling. In any case, a clear idea can be obtained of the universal association which is gradually becoming established only after, in a general way, the nature and relations of the different components of the social institution in that epoch are understood. This picture should appear from the course of our exposition.

But before continuing, we think it necessary to anticipate an objection that might be suggested by the word "final," with which we describe the state of universal association toward which the human species is advancing.

We do not want to say that mankind, once it has reached this state, will no longer have any progress to make. On the contrary, it will march faster than ever towards perfection. But this epoch will be final for mankind in the sense that it will have realized the political combination most favorable to progress. Man will always have to love and to know more and more and to assimilate the outside world more completely to himself. The fields of science and industry will gather daily more abundant harvests and will furnish man with new ways to express his love even more nobly. He will broaden the sphere of his intelligence, that of his physical power, and that of his sympathies, for the course of his progress is unlimited. But the social combination that will be most favorable to his moral, intellectual, and physical development, and in which every individual, whatever his birth, will be loved, honored, and rewarded according to his works, which is to say according to his efforts to improve the moral, intellectual, and physical existence of the masses, and consequently his own, and in which all will be ceaselessly moved to rise in this threefold direction, is not susceptible of perfection. In other words, the organization of the future will be final because only then will society be formed directly for progress.

State, Power, and Authority

Though fascinating and important to all political theorists, questions of power and authority have been particularly central for many positivists. The reason for this is not difficult to see, for while there are other possible candidates, power appears as the most striking observable fact about social organization. Whether one considers the structure and parts of government, the authority of law, or the effects of rule, one finds a factor common to them all. This, many positivists assert, is power. And since power and its effects are observable, an account of the state in terms of power will provide both a theory of social behavior and a social philosophy free of unempirical speculation.

Two classic examples of this approach are found in the writings of Machiavelli (1469–1527) and Bodin (1530–1596). One of the most representative men of the Italian Renaissance, Machiavelli warns his reader that he intends to say something useful about government, and that to this end he will go to the truth of the matter, not to imagination. "The manner in which we live," he writes, "and that in which we ought to live, are things so wide asunder, that he who quits the one to betake himself to the other is more likely to destroy than to save himself." Machiavelli's interest is in man in his political behavior; man is political not as a being capable of realizing his potentialities in society, but as a lover of power and reputation, as self-assertive in wishing to control others.

Machiavelli thus considers the state as many modern thinkers do. He does not view it as a hierarchy of magistrates whose authority is defined by custom or as a *polis* or a commonwealth aiming at the moral development of its citizens and preserving them from evil. Rather, the state is a human contrivance, morally neutral, organized for power, and centered in a single, all-controlling structure. Machiavelli rejects the idea common to many theories that there is an end for society for which power is a means. He makes power an end in itself, and suggests an autonomous system of "values" implied by this end. In relation to power, the good becomes efficiency (hence Machiavelli's oft-debated nonmoralism), and morality and justice, in their more ordinary meanings, are acquired by men only by living in a society. For Machiavelli morality and even religion are subservient to the rules of power, which override all other considerations. The advice of *The Prince* in the selection below is indoctrination into these rules of power.

Machiavelli's approach to politics cannot be called scientific in any modern sense, for he knew nothing of the experimental method or of disciplined classification of facts. But he certainly is positivist in spirit in his factual temper and his use of shrewd common sense. Perhaps the most striking feature of all, however, is his secularism, with its rather total absence of any moral framework for the state. This does not mean, of course, that Machiavelli had no preference for society. He believed that, for the preservation of liberty, popular government is best for a vigorous and healthy people, and he spoke of *virtu* as the energy of the patriotic and valuable citizen. Yet Machiavelli always believed that the first condition of order and liberty is the preservation or enlargement of power, and he was prepared, if necessary, to support even a tyrant to achieve the needed power.

The second selection presents the important discussion of sovereignty by the French theorist, Jean Bodin. By sovereignty Bodin means the perpetual, humanly unlimited, and unconditional right to make, interpret, and execute law; "the absolute and perpetual power in a commonwealth." Though he remained more medieval than Machiavelli with whom he is often compared, Bodin agreed that politics should be studied on the basis of experience, and that the state should be explained by itself rather than from some supposed metaphysical or divinely given order of the universe. Bodin also agreed with both Hobbes and Machiavelli that sovereign power is the only basis for effective government.

Bodin himself did not derive the notion of limitless power from the sovereign's supreme legal authority—others were to do this later. Sovereignty remained for him the unlimited power of making law, which he defined as the command of the sovereign touching all his subjects on general matters. Natural law, the law of succession, and the right to private property were limits on power accepted by Bodin. Unlike some positivists, Bodin was also interested in questions of the legitimacy of government, although he did not distinguish this moral issue from questions of fact. Nevertheless, the doctrine of sovereignty is historically a most influential conception, involving as it does the explicit rejection of medieval ideas about the limited authority of the state and of unempirical efforts to understand its functions.

NICCOLO MACHIAVELLI   The Exercise of Power

OF THE QUALITIES IN RESPECT OF WHICH MEN, AND MOST OF ALL PRINCES, ARE PRAISED OR BLAMED

It now remains for us to consider what ought to be the conduct and bearing of a Prince in relation to his subjects and friends. And since I know that many have written on this subject, I fear it may be thought presumptuous in me to write of it also; the more so, because in my treatment of it I depart from the views that others have taken.

But since it is my object to write what shall be useful to whosoever understands it, it seems to me better to follow the real truth of things than an imaginary view of them. For many Republics and Princedoms have been imagined that were never seen or known to exist in reality. And the manner in which we live, and that in which we ought to live, are things so wide asunder, that he who quits the one to betake himself to the other is more likely to destroy than to save himself; since any one who would act up to a perfect standard of goodness in everything, must be ruined among so many who are not good. It is essential, therefore, for a Prince who desires to maintain his position, to have learned how to be other than good, and to use or not to use his goodness as necessity requires.

Laying aside, therefore, all fanciful notions concerning a Prince, and con-

From Machiavelli's *The Prince,* trans. N. H. Thomson, New York: P. F. Collier & Son, 1910.

sidering those only that are true, I say
that all men when they are spoken of,
and Princes more than others from their
being set so high, are characterized by
some one of those qualities which attach
either praise or blame. Thus one is accounted liberal, another miserly (which
word I use, rather than *avaricious,* to
denote the man who is too sparing of
what is his own, *avarice* being the disposition to take wrongfully what is another's); one is generous, another
greedy; one cruel, another tender-
hearted; one is faithless, another true to
his word; one effeminate and cowardly,
another high-spirited and courageous;
one is courteous, another haughty; one
impure, another chaste; one simple, another crafty; one firm, another facile;
one grave, another frivolous; one de-
vout, another unbelieving; and the like.
Every one, I know, will admit that it
would be most laudable for a Prince to
be endowed with all of the above qualities that are reckoned good; but since it
is impossible for him to possess or constantly practise them all, the conditions
of human nature not allowing it, he
must be discreet enough to know how to
avoid the infamy of those vices that
would deprive him of his government,
and, if possible, be on his guard also
against those which might not deprive
him of it; though if he cannot wholly
restrain himself, he may with less scruple indulge in the latter. He need never
hesitate, however, to incur the reproach
of those vices without which his authority can hardly be preserved; for if he
well consider the whole matter, he will
find that there may be a line of conduct
having the appearance of virtue, to follow which would be his ruin, and that
there may be another course having the
appearance of vice, by following which
his safety and well-being are secured.

Of Cruelty and Clemency, and Whether It Is Better to Be Loved or Feared

Passing to the other qualities above
referred to, I say that every Prince
should desire to be accounted merciful
and not cruel. Nevertheless, he should
be on his guard against the abuse of this
quality of mercy. Cesare Borgia was reputed cruel, yet his cruelty restored
Romagna, united it, and brought it to
order and obedience; so that if we look
at things in their true light, it will be
seen that he was in reality far more
merciful than the people of Florence,
who, to avoid the imputation of cruelty,
suffered Pistoja to be torn to pieces by
factions.

A Prince should therefore disregard
the reproach of being thought cruel
where it enables him to keep his subjects united and obedient. For he who
quells disorder by a very few signal examples will in the end be more merciful
than he who from too great leniency permits things to take their course and so
to result in rapine and bloodshed; for
these hurt the whole State, whereas the
severities of the Prince injure individuals
only.

And for a new Prince, of all others,
it is impossible to escape a name for
cruelty, since new States are full of dangers. Wherefore Virgil, by the mouth of
Dido, excuses the harshness of her reign
on the plea that it was new, saying:—

"A fate unkind, and newness in my reign
Compel me thus to guard a wide domain."

Nevertheless, the new Prince should
not be too ready of belief, nor too easily
set in motion; nor should he himself be
the first to raise alarms; but should so
temper prudence with kindliness that
too great confidence in others shall not

throw him off his guard, nor groundless distrust render him insupportable.

And here comes in the question whether it is better to be loved rather than feared, or feared rather than loved. It might perhaps be answered that we should wish to be both; but since love and fear can hardly exist together, if we must choose between them, it is far safer to be feared than loved. For of men it may generally be affirmed that they are thankless, fickle, false, studious to avoid danger, greedy of gain, devoted to you while you are able to confer benefits upon them, and ready, as I said before, while danger is distant, to shed their blood, and sacrifice their property, their lives, and their children for you; but in the hour of need they turn against you. The Prince, therefore, who without otherwise securing himself builds wholly on their professions is undone. For the friendships which we buy with a price, and do not gain by greatness and nobility of character, though they be fairly earned are not made good, but fail us when we have occasion to use them.

Moreover, men are less careful how they offend him who makes himself loved than him who makes himself feared. For love is held by the tie of obligation, which, because men are a sorry breed, is broken on every whisper of private interest; but fear is bound by the apprehension of punishment which never relaxes its grasp.

Nevertheless a Prince should inspire fear in such a fashion that if he do not win love he may escape hate. For a man may very well be feared and yet not hated, and this will be the case so long as he does not meddle with the property or with the women of his citizens and subjects. And if constrained to put any to death, he should do so only when there is manifest cause or reasonable justification. But, above all, he must abstain from the property of others. For men will sooner forget the death of their father than the loss of their patrimony. Moreover, pretexts for confiscation are never to seek, and he who has once begun to live by rapine always finds reasons for taking what is not his; whereas reasons for shedding blood are fewer, and sooner exhausted.

But when a Prince is with his army, and has many soldiers under his command, he must needs disregard the reproach of cruelty, for without such a reputation in its Captain, no army can be held together or kept under any kind of control. Among other things remarkable in Hannibal this has been noted, that having a very great army, made up of men of many different nations and brought to fight in a foreign country, no dissension ever arose among the soldiers themselves, nor any mutiny against their leader, either in his good or in his evil fortunes. This we can only ascribe to the transcendent cruelty, which, joined with numberless great qualities, rendered him at once venerable and terrible in the eyes of his soldiers; for without this reputation for cruelty these other virtues would not have produced the like results. . . .

Returning to the question of being loved or feared, I sum up by saying, that since his being loved depends upon his subjects, while his being feared depends upon himself, a wise Prince should build on what is his own, and not on what rests with others. Only, as I have said, he must do his utmost to escape hatred.

How Princes Should Keep Faith

Every one understands how praiseworthy it is in a Prince to keep faith, and to live uprightly and not craftily.

Nevertheless, we see from what has taken place in our own days that Princes who have set little store by their word, but have known how to overreach men by their cunning, have accomplished great things, and in the end got the better of those who trusted to honest dealing.

Be it known, then, that there are two ways of contending, one in accordance with the laws, the other by force; the first of which is proper to men, the second to beasts. But since the first method is often ineffectual, it becomes necessary to resort to the second. A Prince should, therefore, understand how to use well both the man and the beast. And this lesson has been covertly taught by the ancient writers, who relate how Achilles and many others of these old Princes were given over to be brought up and trained by Chiron the Centaur; since the only meaning of their having for instructor one who was half man and half beast is, that it is necessary for a Prince to know how to use both natures, and that the one without the other has no stability.

But since a Prince should know how to use the beast's nature wisely, he ought of beasts to choose both the lion and the fox; for the lion cannot guard himself from the toils, nor the fox from wolves. He must therefore be a fox to discern toils, and a lion to drive off wolves.

To rely wholly on the lion is unwise; and for this reason a prudent Prince neither can nor ought to keep his word when to keep it is hurtful to him and the causes which led him to pledge it are removed. If all men were good, this would not be good advice, but since they are dishonest and do not keep faith with you, you, in return, need not keep faith with them; and no prince was ever at a loss for plausible reasons to cloak a breach of faith. Of this numberless recent instances could be given, and it might be shown how many solemn treaties and engagements have been rendered inoperative and idle through want of faith in Princes, and that he who was best known to play the fox has had the best success.

It is necessary, indeed, to put a good colour on this nature, and to be skilful in simulating and dissembling. But men are so simple, and governed so absolutely by their present needs, that he who wishes to deceive will never fail in finding willing dupes. One recent example I will not omit. Pope Alexander VI had no care or thought but how to deceive, and always found material to work on. No man ever had a more effective manner of asseverating, or made promises with more solemn protestations, or observed them less. And yet, because he understood this side of human nature, his frauds always succeeded.

It is not essential, then, that a Prince should have all the good qualities which I have enumerated above, but it is most essential that he should seem to have them; I will even venture to affirm that if he has and invariably practises them all, they are hurtful, whereas the appearance of having them is useful. Thus, it is well to seem merciful, faithful, humane, religious, and upright, and also to be so; but the mind should remain so balanced that were it needful not to be so, you should be able and know how to change to the contrary.

And you are to understand that a Prince, and most of all a new Prince, cannot observe all those rules of conduct in respect whereof men are accounted good, being often forced, in order to preserve his Princedom, to act in opposition to good faith, charity, humanity, and religion. He must therefore keep his mind ready to shift as the winds and tides of Fortune turn, and, as I have already said, he ought not to quit good courses if he can help it, but should know how to follow evil courses if he must.

A Prince should therefore be very careful that nothing ever escapes his lips which is not replete with the five qualities above named, so that to see and hear him, one would think him the embodiment of mercy, good faith, integrity, humanity, and religion. And there is no virtue which it is more necessary for him to seem to possess than this last; because men in general judge rather by the eye than by the hand, for every one can see but few can touch. Every one sees what you seem, but few know what you are, and these few dare not oppose themselves to the opinion of the many who have the majesty of the State to back them up.

Moreover, in the actions of all men, most of all of Princes, where there is no tribunal to which we can appeal, we look to results. Wherefore if a Prince succeeds in establishing and maintaining his authority, the means will always be judged honourable and be approved by every one. For the vulgar are always taken by appearances and by results, and the world is made up of the vulgar, the few only finding room when the many have no longer ground to stand on.

A certain Prince of our own days, whose name it is as well not to mention[1] is always preaching peace and good faith, although the mortal enemy of both; and both, had he practised them as he preaches them, would, oftener than once, have lost him his kingdom and authority.

---

[1] A later reference by Machiavelli suggests that he had Ferdinand and Isabella of Spain in mind here. *Ed.*

JEAN BODIN The Concept of Sovereignty

Sovereignty is that absolute and perpetual power vested in a commonwealth which in Latin is termed *majestas* . . . The term needs careful definition, because although it is the distinguishing mark of a commonwealth, and an understanding of its nature fundamental to any treatment of politics, no jurist or political philosopher has in fact attempted to define it. . . .

I have described it as *perpetual* because one can give absolute power to a person or group of persons for a period of time, but that time expired they become subjects once more. Therefore even while they enjoy power, they cannot properly be regarded as sovereign

rulers, but only as the lieutenants and agents of the sovereign ruler, till the moment comes when it pleases the prince or the people to revoke the gift. The true sovereign remains always seized of his power. Just as a feudal lord who grants lands to another retains his eminent domain over them, so the ruler who delegates authority to judge and command, whether it be for a short period, or during pleasure, remains seized of those rights of jurisdiction actually exercised by another in the form of a revocable grant, or precarious tenancy. For this reason the law requires the governor of a province, or the prince's lieutenant, to make a formal surrender

---

From Jean Bodin, *Six Books of the Commonwealth,* trans. M. J. Tooley, Oxford: Basil Blackwell & Mott, Ltd., 1955. Used by permission of the publisher.

of the authority committed to him, at the expiration of his term of office. In this respect there is no difference between the highest officer of state and his humblest subordinate. If it were otherwise, and the absolute authority delegated by the prince to a lieutenant was regarded as itself sovereign power, the latter could use it against his prince who would thereby forfeit his eminence, and the subject could command his lord, the servant his master. This is a manifest absurdity, considering that the sovereign is always excepted personally, as a matter of right, in all delegations of authority, however extensive. However much he gives there always remains a reserve of right in his own person, whereby he may command, or intervene by way of prevention, confirmation, evocation, or any other way he thinks fit, in all matters delegated to a subject, whether in virtue of an office or a commission. Any authority exercised in virtue of an office or a commission can be revoked, or made tenable for as long or short a period as the sovereign wills. . . .

A perpetual authority therefore must be understood to mean one that lasts for the lifetime of him who exercises it. If a sovereign magistrate is given office for one year, or for any other predetermined period, and continues to exercise the authority bestowed on him after the conclusion of his term, he does so either by consent or by force and violence. If he does so by force, it is manifest tyranny. The tyrant is a true sovereign for all that. The robber's possession by violence is true and natural possession although contrary to the law, for those who were formerly in possession have been disseized. But if the magistrate continues in office by consent, he is not a sovereign prince, seeing that he only exercises power on sufferance. Still less

is he a sovereign if the term of his office is not fixed, for in that case he has no more than a precarious commission. . . .

What bearing have these considerations on the case of the man to whom the people has given absolute power for the term of his natural life? One must distinguish. If such absolute power is given him simply and unconditionally, and not in virtue of some office or commission, nor in the form of a revocable grant, the recipient certainly is, and should be acknowledged to be, a sovereign. The people has renounced and alienated its sovereign power in order to invest him with it and put him in possession, and it thereby transfers to him all its powers, authority, and sovereign rights, just as does the man who gives to another possessory and proprietary rights over what he formerly owned. The civil law expresses this in the phrase "all power is conveyed to him and vested in him."

But if the people give such power for the term of his natural life to anyone as its official or lieutenant, or only gives the exercise of such power, in such a case he is not a sovereign, but simply an officer, lieutenant, regent, governor, or agent, and as such has the exercise only of a power inhering in another. When a magistrate institutes a perpetual lieutenant, even if he abandons all his rights of jurisdiction and leaves their exercise entirely to his lieutenant, the authority to command and to judge nevertheless does not reside in the lieutenant, nor the action and force of the law derive from him. If he exceeds his authority his acts have no validity, unless approved and confirmed by him from whom he draws his authority. For this reason King John, after his return from captivity in England, solemnly ratified all the acts of his son Charles, who had acted in his name as regent,

44788

in order, as was necessary, to regularize the position.

Whether then one exercises the power of another by commission, by institution, or by delegation, or whether such exercise is for a set term, or in perpetuity, such a power is not a sovereign power, even if there is no mention of such words as representative, lieutenant, governor, or regent, in the letters of appointment, or even if such powers are a consequence of the normal working of the laws of the country. In ancient times in Scotland, for instance, the law vested the entire governance of the realm in the next of kin, if the king should be a minor, on condition that everything that was done, was done in the king's name. But this law was later altered because of its inconvenient consequences.

Let us now turn to the other term of our definition and consider the force of the word *absolute*. The people or the magnates of a commonwealth can bestow simply and unconditionally upon someone of their choice a sovereign and perpetual power to dispose of their property and persons, to govern the state as he thinks fit, and to order the succession, in the same way that any proprietor, out of his liberality, can freely and unconditionally make a gift of his property to another. Such a form of gift, not being qualified in any way, is the only true gift, being at once unconditional and irrevocable. Gifts burdened with obligations and hedged with conditions are not true gifts. Similarly sovereign power given to a prince charged with conditions is neither properly sovereign, nor absolute, unless the conditions of appointment are only such as are inherent in the laws of God and of nature. . . .

If we insist however that absolute power means exemption from all law whatsoever, there is no prince in the world who can be regarded as sovereign, since all the princes of the earth are subject to the laws of God and of nature, and even to certain human laws common to all nations. On the other hand, it is possible for a subject who is neither a prince nor a ruler, to be exempted from all the laws, ordinances, and customs of the commonwealth. We have an example in Pompey the Great who was dispensed from the laws for five years, by express enactment of the Roman people, at the instance of the Tribune Gabinius . . . But notwithstanding such exemptions from the operations of the law, the subject remains under the authority of him who exercises sovereign power, and owes him obedience.

On the other hand it is the distinguishing mark of the sovereign that he cannot in any way be subject to the commands of another, for it is he who makes law for the subject, abrogates law already made, and amends obsolete law. No one who is subject either to the law or to some other person can do this. That is why it is laid down in the civil law that the prince is above the law, for the word *law* in Latin implies the command of him who is invested with sovereign power. Therefore we find in all statutes the phrase "notwithstanding all edicts and ordinances to the contrary that we have infringed, or do infringe by these present." This clause applies both to former acts of the prince himself, and to those of his predecessors. For all laws, ordinances, letters patent, privileges, and grants whatsoever issued by the prince, have force only during his own lifetime, and must be expressly, or at least tacitly, confirmed by the reigning prince who has cognizance of them . . . In proof of which, it is the custom of this realm for all corporations and corporate bodies to ask for the confirmation of their privileges, rights, and jurisdictions, on the accession of a new king. Even Parlements and high courts do this, as well as individual officers of the crown.

If the prince is not bound by the laws of his predecessors, still less can he be bound by his own laws. One may be subject to laws made by another, but it is impossible to bind oneself in any matter which is the subject of one's own free exercise of will. As the law says, "there can be no obligation in any matter which proceeds from the free will of the undertaker." It follows of necessity that the king cannot be subject to his own laws. Just as, according to the canonists, the Pope can never tie his own hands, so the sovereign prince cannot bind himself, even if he wishes. For this reason edicts and ordinances conclude with the formula "for such is our good pleasure," thus intimating that the laws of a sovereign prince, even when founded on truth and right reason, proceed simply from his own free will. . . .

Many have been led astray by confusing the laws of the prince with covenants entered into by him. This confusion has led some to call these covenants contractual laws. This is the term used in Aragon when the king issues an ordinance upon the petition of the Estates, and in return receives some aid or subsidy. It is claimed that he is strictly bound by these laws, even though he is not by any of his other enactments. It is however admitted that he may override even these when the purpose of their enactment no longer holds. All this is true enough, and well-founded in reason and authority. But no bribe or oath is required to bind a sovereign prince to keep a law which is in the interests of his subjects. The bare word of a prince should be as sacred as a divine pronouncement. It loses its force if he is ill-thought of as one who cannot be trusted except under oath, nor relied on to keep a promise unless paid to do so. Nevertheless it remains true in principle that the sovereign prince can set aside the laws which he has promised or sworn to observe, if they no longer satisfy the requirements of justice, and he may do this without the consent of his subjects. It should however be added that the abrogation must be express and explicit in its reference, and not just in the form of a general repudiation. But if on the other hand there is no just cause for breaking a law which the prince has promised to keep, the prince ought not to do so, and indeed cannot contravene it, though he is not bound to the same extent by the promises and covenants of his predecessors unless he succeeds by strict hereditary right.

A law and a covenant must therefore not be confused. A law proceeds from him who has sovereign power, and by it he binds the subject to obedience, but cannot bind himself. A covenant is a mutual undertaking between a prince and his subjects, equally binding on both parties, and neither can contravene it to the prejudice of the other, without his consent. The prince has no greater privilege than the subject in this matter. But in the case of laws, a prince is no longer bound by his promise to keep them when they cease to satisfy the claims of justice. Subjects however must keep their engagements to one another in all circumstances, unless the prince releases them from such obligations. Sovereign princes are not bound by oath to keep the laws of their predecessors. If they are so bound, they are not properly speaking sovereign. . . .

From all this it is clear that the principal mark of sovereign majesty and absolute powers is the right to impose laws generally on all subjects regardless of their consent . . . And if it is expedient that if he is to govern his state well, a sovereign prince must be above the law, it is even more expedient that the ruling class in an aristocracy should be so, and inevitable in a popular state. A monarch in a kingdom is set apart from his subjects, and the ruling class from the people in an aristocracy. There are therefore in each case two parties, those that rule on the one hand, and those that are ruled on the other. This is the cause of the disputes about sovereignty that arise in them, but cannot in a popular state . . . There the people, rulers and ruled, form a single body and so cannot bind themselves by their own laws. . . .

When edicts are ratified by Estates or Parlements, it is for the purpose of securing obedience to them, and not because otherwise a sovereign prince could not validly make law. As Theodosius said with reference to the consent of the Senate, "it is not a matter of necessity but of expediency." He also remarked that it was most becoming in a sovereign prince to keep his own laws, for this is what makes him feared and respected by his subjects, whereas nothing so undermines his authority as contempt for them. As a Roman Senator observed "it is more foolish and ill-judged to break your own laws than those of another." . . .

It remains to be determined whether the prince is bound by the covenants of his predecessors, and whether, if so, it is a derogation of his sovereign power . . . A distinction must be made between the ruler who succeeds because he is the natural heir of his predecessor, and the ruler who succeeds in virtue of the laws and customs of the realm. In the first case the heir is bound by the oaths and promises of his predecessors just as is any ordinary heir. In the second case he is not so bound even if he is sworn, for the oath of the predecessors does not bind the successor. He is bound however in all that tends to the benefit of the kingdom.

There are those who will say that there is no need of such distinctions since the prince is bound in any case by the law of nations, under which covenants are guaranteed. But I consider that these distinctions are necessary nevertheless, since the prince is bound as much by the law of nations, but no more, than by any of his own enactments. If the law of nations is iniquitous in any respect, he can disallow it within his own kingdom, and forbid his subjects to observe it, as was done in France in regard to slavery. He can do the same in relation to any other of its provisions, so long as he does nothing against the law of God. If justice is the end of the law, the law the work of the prince, and the prince the image of God, it follows of necessity that the law of the prince should be modelled on the law of God.

Law and Rights

The positivist approach to problems of law and jurisprudence is the same as that developed in the preceding selections of this part: positivists seek solutions to these problems by the methods of science, and the shift is from metaphysical methods to empirical ones. This general statement can be made more specific, however, for the adjective "positivistic" is and has been used to refer to a number of quite definite theses in jurisprudence.

Professor H. L. Hart has found that this usage applies to five propositions.* The first is that laws are the commands of a sovereign. As commands, laws are understood by the positivist as imperatives, not as descriptions of rules rooted in man's nature or as discoveries of an objective legal order. As commands of a sovereign, laws are specifically related to observable features in the governmental system—the sovereign himself, the courts, or some other department. Second is the contention that there is no necessary connection between law and morals, or between law as it is and law as it ought to be. Third is the conviction that the analysis or study of meaning of legal concepts is worth pursuing, and is to be distinguished from other inquiries of a historical or sociological kind. This thesis has become even more important in the writings of recent positivists. Fourth is the belief that the legal order is a "closed logical system" in which correct legal decisions can be deduced from predetermined legal rules. Last is the philosophic assertion that moral judgments cannot be taken as statements of fact, or be established by rational argument or evidence. This theory is often referred to as the "emotive theory of value."

Of these five points, the second is perhaps the most distinctive of a positivistic philosophy of law.† What it does in effect is to make systems of value or conceptions of natural law irrelevant to jurisprudence. The task of jurisprudence is the elaboration and clarification of law as it actually exists in the modern state.

One example of this approach is given in the selection from John Chipman Gray (1839–1915). The philosophy of law, Gray asserts, must start with the recognition of the truth that the law is not an ideal, but something that actually exists. "It is not that which is in accordance with religion, or nature, or morality, it is not that which it ought to be, but that which it is." On this basis, Gray defines the law itself as what judges lay down as rules of conduct: "the law consists of the rules recognized and acted on by the courts of justice." These rules are given to protect and advance human interests, and they ascribe certain rights to persons, elaborating this protection. Thus rights are also determined by judges, who settle on the facts and who provide the rules according to which legal consequences may be deduced from the facts.

---

* See H. L. Hart, "Positivism and the Separation of Law and Morals," *Harvard Law Review,* 71(1958), 601.

† The first is also important historically, for men like Machiavelli, Bodin, and Hobbes enunciated command theories of law, as did the utilitarian Austin. The so-called analytic jurisprudence owes something to all these men.

JOHN CHIPMAN GRAY   Law and Interest

Sec. 34. . . .   Human society is organized for the protection and advancement of human interests. The object of its organization is to insure the doing of certain things which individuals could not do, and to protect individuals in

---

From John Chipman Gray, *The Nature and Sources of Law,* New York: Columbia University Press, 1909.

the accomplishment of their wishes to an extent to which they could not protect themselves. Sometimes the real purpose of organization is to secure the interests of a very limited number of persons. But yet, such are the blessings of order, that any political organization, however small the number of persons intended to be benefited by it, is better for the rest than anarchy.

Sec. 35. To accomplish its purposes, the chief means employed by an organized society is to compel individuals to do or to forbear from doing particular things. Sometimes the society puts this compulsion in force of its own motion; and sometimes it puts it in force only on the motion of the individuals who are interested in having it exercised.

Sec. 36. The rights correlative to those duties which the society will enforce of its own motion are the legal rights of that society. The rights correlative to those duties which the society will enforce on the motion of an individual are that individual's legal rights. The acts and forbearances which an organized society commands in order to protect legal rights are the legal duties of the persons to whom those commands are directed.

Sec. 50. By the interests of a man is meant the things which he may desire. I shall not attempt to enumerate or classify the objects of human desire. The object may be the ownership or possession of a corporeal thing, as a book; it may be an act, as eating a dinner; it may be a relation, as marriage; and the desire may be a foolish or hurtful one. The eating of shrimp salad is an interest of mine, and, if I can pay for it, the law will protect that interest, and it is, therefore, a right of mine to eat shrimp salad which I have paid for, although I know that shrimp salad always gives me the colic.

Sec. 51. The legal rights of a man are the rights which are exercisable on his motion. A man has, therefore, no legal right as to those interests in the realizing of which he is protected only by other people exercising their rights. The fact that the State can punish the burglar who breaks into my house does not give *me* any right not to have my house broken into. Not that I am without a right not to have my house broken into. The law can protect my interest not to have a thing done in several ways: as in the first place, by allowing me to withstand the act by force; or secondly, by allowing me to limit the freedom of the person who wishes to do the act by placing obstacles in his way; or thirdly, by appealing to the courts to punish such person. The law may deny to a man this third mode of protecting his interest, but if it allows him the first and second, or either of them, he has a legal right. A system of law may, as the Common Law does, merge the tort in the felony, and refuse the householder an action against the burglar, but so long as he can withstand the burglar, even to killing, and can draw bolts and bars to keep him out, he has the right not to have his house entered. If, when I heard a burglar lifting the latch of my door, the State allowed me to use neither threats nor force to compel him to desist, and if the State also forbade me to turn any lock or push any bolt, or in any other way interfere to keep him on the outside, and if the only thing to prevent his coming in was the fact that the State could, if it would, hang him or send him to prison, then *I* should have no right not to have my house entered, whatever right the State might have.

Sec. 52. So the interests of brute animals may have legal protection. Very often, indeed, acts commanded or forbidden towards animals are not commanded or forbidden for the sake of the animals, but for the sake of men; but certain acts of cruelty, for instance, towards beasts, may be forbidden, at least conceivably, for the sake of the creatures themselves. Yet beasts have no legal rights, because it is not on their motion that this protection is called forth.

Sec. 53. The protection which society gives to a man's interests is either *direct* or *indirect*. Sometimes it protects them directly, as when its courts compel a man who is threatening to flood the land of a riparian proprietor upstream to take down his dam; sometimes indirectly, as by giving a man a right to have a wrong-doer compelled to make compensation. And the right to ask the courts for aid is not always a right to sue in them, but is often a right to be protected against suits brought by others. For instance, under a statute of limitations, if a debt remains unpaid for six years, the creditor cannot compel the debtor to pay it; that is, the debtor has a right to interpose the defence of the statute and thereby call upon the court to refuse its assistance to enforce the creditor's demand. So again, a householder has the right to eject by force a trespasser from his "castle." That is, if sued by the trespasser for assault, he can call upon the court to refuse the plaintiff its help. In other words, a man's legal rights include not only the power effectually to call for aid from an organized society against others, but also the power to call effectually upon the society to abstain from aiding others.

Sec. 54. Let us dwell for a moment more on the nature of the protection which society affords to a man's interests. In the *first* place, it may allow him to protect himself; this is self-help. *Secondly,* it may allow him to appeal to the courts to protect him, as by an injunction. *Thirdly,* it may allow him to appeal to the courts for compensation for injuries. In all three of these cases, the actual volition of the man himself is necessary. He must put up his own fists; he must bring his suit for an injunction or for damages in the courts. The State will not double up his fists for him, nor will it bring a suit for him in the courts. The right to these modes of protection is, therefore, his right.

Sec. 55. But there is a *fourth* method in which the State protects a man's interests, and that is the prevention of injury to them, not by the intervention of the courts, but by the intervention of administrative officers. My interest not to have my windows broken is protected not only by my power of appealing to the courts to prevent or compensate for the breaking, but also by the presence of the policeman on his beat. In this case you may say there is no actual volition on my part. I do not know that the integrity of my windows is threatened. Yet the stopping of the window breaking is really dependent upon my will, for if I tell the police to let the boys go ahead and break my windows, it will cease to interfere. What really happens in this case is that the State assumes a wish on my part (an assumption amply fortified by the ordinary attributes of human nature) that my windows should not be broken. Indeed, after all, in this fourth class of cases is there not an actual volition? Every man undoubtedly actually wishes that his property should be protected, and also that the State, through its administrative officers, should protect it, so that, even in this case, there may be said to be an actual volition and that, therefore, the man has a right. It should be noted that the State may, and probably often does, allow a man to commit to the State a larger power to protect his interests than it would allow him to exercise in his own person.

Sec. 56.   There is a *fifth* method by which the State protects a man's interests, and that is, by declaring that it will punish criminally acts against certain interests of individuals, and by punishing accordingly. The dread of punishment undoubtedly protects the interests of the individuals, but in this protection the volition of the individuals protected has no place, and it cannot be said that they have any *right* to this form of protection.

Sec. 191.   The Law of the State or of any organized body of men is composed of the rules which the courts, that is, the judicial organs of that body, lay down for the determination of legal rights and duties. The difference in this matter between contending schools of Jurisprudence arises largely from not distinguishing between the Law and the Sources of the Law. On the one hand, to affirm the existence of *nicht positivisches Recht,* that is, of Law which the courts do not follow, is declared to be an absurdity; and on the other hand, it is declared to be an absurdity to say that the Law of a great nation means the opinions of half-a-dozen old gentlemen, some of them, conceivably, of very limited intelligence. The truth is, each party is looking at but one side of the shield. If those half-a-dozen old gentlemen form the highest judicial tribunal of a country, then no rule or principle which they refuse to follow is Law in that country. However desirable, for instance, it may be that a man should be obliged to make gifts which he has

promised to make, yet if the courts of a country will not compel him to keep his promise, it is not the Law of that country that promises to make a gift are binding. On the other hand, those six men seek the rules which they follow not in their own whims, but they derive them from sources often of the most general and permanent character, to which they are directed, by the organized body to which they belong, to apply themselves. . . .

Sec. 222.   When the element of long time is introduced, the absurdity of the view of Law preëxistent to its declaration is obvious. What was the Law in the time of Richard Cœur de Lion on the liability of a telegraph company to the persons to whom a message was sent? It may be said that though the Law can preëxist its declaration, it is conceded that the Law with regard to a natural force cannot exist before the discovery of the force. Let us take, then, a transaction which might have occurred in the eleventh century: A sale of chattels, a sending to the vendee, his insolvency, and an order by the vendor to the carrier not to deliver. What was the Law on stoppage *in transitu* in the time of William the Conqueror?

Sec. 223.   The difficulty of believing in preëxisting Law is still greater when there is a change in the decision of the courts. In Massachusetts it was held in 1849, by the Supreme Judicial Court, that if a man hired a horse in Boston on a Sunday to drive to Nahant, and drove instead to Nantasket, the keeper of the livery stable had no right to sue him in trover for the conversion of the horse. But in 1871 this decision was overruled, and the right was given to the stable-keeper. Now, did stable-keepers have such rights, say, in 1845? If they did, then the court in 1849 did not discover the Law. If they did not, then the court in 1871 did not discover the Law.

Sec. 224. And this brings us to the reason why courts and jurists have so struggled to maintain the preëxistence of the Law, why the common run of writers speak of the judges as merely stating the Law, and why Mr. Carter, in an advance towards the truth, says of the judges that they are discoverers of the Law. That reason is the unwillingness to recognize the fact that the courts, with the consent of the State, have been constantly in the practice of applying in the decision of controversies, rules which were not in existence and were, therefore, not knowable by the parties when the causes of controversy occurred. It is the unwillingness to face the certain fact that courts are constantly making *ex post facto* Law.[1]

Sec. 225. The unwillingness is natural, particularly on the part of the courts, who do not desire to call attention to the fact that they are exercising a power which bears so unpopular a name, but it is not reasonable. Practically in its application to actual affairs, for most of the laity, the Law, except for a few crude notions of the equity involved in some of its general principles, is all *ex post facto*. When a man marries, or enters into a partnership, or buys a piece of land, or engages in any other transaction, he has the vaguest possible idea of the Law governing the situation, and with our complicated system of Jurisprudence, it is impossible it should be otherwise. If he delayed to make a contract or do an act until he understood exactly all the legal conse-

quences it involved, the contract would never be made or the act done. Now the Law of which a man has no knowledge is the same to him as if it did not exist.

Sec. 226. Again, the function of a judge is not mainly to declare the Law, but to maintain the peace by deciding controversies. Suppose a question comes up which has never been decided,— and such questions are more frequent than persons not lawyers generally suppose,—the judge must decide the case somehow; he will properly wish to decide it not on whim, but on principle, and he lays down some rule which meets acceptance with the courts, and future cases are decided in the same way. That rule is the Law, and yet the rights and duties of the parties were not known and were not knowable by them. That is the way parties are treated and have to be treated by the courts; it is solemn juggling to say that the Law, undiscovered and undiscoverable, and which is finally determined in opposite ways in two communities separated only by an artificial boundary, has existed in both communities from all eternity. . . .

Sec. 231. To sum up. The State exists for the protection and forwarding of human interests, mainly through the medium of rights and duties. If every member of the State knew perfectly his own rights and duties, and the rights and duties of everybody else, the State would need no judicial organs; administrative organs would suffice. But there is no such universal knowledge. To determine, in actual life, what are the rights and duties of the State and of its citizens, the State needs and establishes judicial organs, the judges. To determine rights and duties, the judges settle what facts exist, and also lay down rules according to which they deduce legal consequences from facts. These rules are the Law.

---

[1] Technically the term "*ex post facto* Law" is confined with us to statutes creating crimes or punishments. I use the term here in its broader sense of retroactive Law.

Political Obligation

A positivist theory of political obligation is given in the following selection by Auguste Comte (1798–1857). Many of Comte's ideas such as his law of three stages and his social determinism have been presented in preceding introductory material. Comte also shared many ideas with Saint-Simon, whose follower he was for a time. His theory of obligation is developed within the context of these conceptions.

Basically Comte's view is that as knowledge increases, the need for spiritual authority in society will be felt and met. That is, the progress of science will so affect men that the authority needed to assure the use of knowledge for their own good will rise among them. (It will be remembered that Comte and Sainte-Simon believed that the influence of science is socially important more in relation to a changed vision of man and his place in the world than as a result of particular discoveries.) The recognition of this need is part of what Comte calls positive morality.

Positive morality is of course to be based on Comte's positive philosophy. Through education, good habits will be developed among the members of society that will establish the universal obligations of civilized men. Since education is also based on the positive philosophy, the obligations rooted in the social sentiment will be most fully developed, for positivism alone adequately comprehends human nature. Among the consequences of this development, Comte infers, will be the establishment of social subordination or hierarchy based on the same principles as biological classification. The highest level will be the speculative (scientific and artistic) and the practical (industrial) classes;* other social classes will be ordered beneath them. When the gradation is established, it will be preserved from confusion by the consciousness that each order is subordinate to the grade above it as a condition of its superiority to those below it. A second consequence is that "the most important object of this regenerated polity will be the substitution of Duties for Rights." Since no supernatural claims are admissible in positivist society, the idea of right will in fact disappear—it is a "metaphysical" notion. Everyone will thus have duties, but rights in the ordinary sense will be claimed by no one.

Although Comte with the Saint-Simonians valued happiness more than freedom and insisted on a rule of a knowledgeable elite, he nevertheless felt that the spiritual power must be "popular." This it will be, he thought, through its impartial concern for the lower classes. The spiritual authority is obligated to secure education and employment for all members of society, just as they in turn recognize their subordination to spiritual authority. Comte thus answers the questions

---

* Comte's rather elaborate presentation of his "Religion of Humanity" with its priests and rituals is an interesting, if eccentric, proposal. Hostile critics view it as nonsense; friendly critics find Comte attempting, even if inadequately, to find ways to satisfy man's emotional needs. The matter does not fall within the concern of this section, however.

of the obligation of ruler to ruled and of ruled to ruler in terms of the goal of human satisfactions made possible by the universal application of scientific knowledge.

AUGUSTE COMTE   The Social Sentiment

Under this system of general education, Morality will be immovably based upon positive philosophy as a whole. Human nature being one of the branches of positive knowledge, it will be understood how childhood is to be trained in good habits, by means of the best prepossessions; and how those habits and views are afterwards to be rationalized, so as solidly to establish the universal obligations of civilized Man,—duties personal, domestic, and social, with the modifications that will be required by changes in civilization. We have seen how all connection between theological faith and morality has long been recognized as arbitrary; and any such degree of theological unity as is necessary for affording a basis to morality, would now suppose a vast system of hypocrisy, which, if it were possible, would be fatal to the very morality it proposed to sustain. In the present state of the most advanced portion of the human race, the positive spirit is certainly the only one which, duly systematized, can at once generate universal moral convictions and permit the rise of a spiritual authority independent enough to regulate its social application. At the same time, the social sentiment, as a part of morals, can be fully developed only by the positive philosophy, because it alone contemplates and understands the whole of human nature. The social sentiment has hitherto been cultivated only in an indirect and even contradictory manner, under the theological philosophy first, which gave a character of exorbitant selfishness to all moral acts; and then under the metaphysical, which bases morality on self-interest. Human faculties, affective as well as intellectual, can be developed only by habitual exercise; and positive morality, which teaches the habitual practice of goodness without any other certain recompense than internal satisfaction, must be much more favourable to the growth of the benevolent affections than any doctrine which attaches devotedness itself to personal considerations,—the admission of which allows no fair play to the claims of our generous instincts. It will be long before habit, sustained by powerful interests, will permit the systematizing of morality without religious intervention; and when it is done, it will be by the fulfilment itself silencing all controversy; and this is why no other part of the great philosophical task can be nearly so important in determining the regeneration of modern society. Humanity must be regarded as still in a state of infancy while its laws of conduct are derived from extraordinary fictions, and not from a wise estimate of its own nature and condition. . . . .

The difference of social character between this authority and the Catholic sway is easily pointed out, and important to be understood. All spiritual authority must rest on free and perfect confidence and assent, such as are accorded to intellectual and moral su-

From *The Positive Philosophy of Auguste Comte,* trans. Harriet Martineau, London: Kegan Paul, Trench, Trübner and Co., Ltd., 1893.

periority; and they imply an agreement and sympathy in a common primary doctrine, regulating the exercise and the conditions of the relation, which is dissolved when the doctrine is disbelieved. The theological faith was connected with some revelation in which the believer had no share; and it must therefore be wholly different from the positive faith, which follows upon demonstration, open to universal examination, under due conditions. Thus, the positive authority is essentially relative, like the spirit of the corresponding philosophy: and as no individual can know everything and judge of everything, the confidence enjoyed by the most eminent thinker is analogous to that which, in a limited degree, he accords in turn to the humblest intelligence, on certain subjects best understood by the latter. The absolute power of man over man, which was so dreadful and irresistible in former ages, is gone for ever, together with the mental condition which gave rise to it: but, though the positive faith can never be so intense as the theological, its unsystematic action during the last three centuries proves that it can spontaneously occasion a sufficient agreement on subjects that have been duly explored. We see, by the universal admission of the chief scientific truths, notwithstanding their opposition to religious notions, how irresistible will be the sway of the logical force of genuine demonstration when human reason attains maturity; and especially when its extension to moral and social considerations shall have imparted to it its full energy. There will be a sufficient harmony between the need and the power of a regular discipline of minds,—at all events, when the theologico-metaphysical system, with all its disturbing influences, has died out. These considerations may serve to dissipate the theocratic uneasiness that naturally arises on the mere mention of any spiritual reorganization,—the philosophical nature of the new government wholly precluding such usurpations as those which were perpetrated by theological authority. Nevertheless, we must not suppose, on the other hand, that the positive system will admit of no abuses. The infirmity of our mental and moral nature will remain; and the social superintendence which will be natural will be also needful. We have only too much reason to know that true science is compatible with charlatanism, and that *savans* are quite as much disposed to oppression as the priests ever were, though happily they have not the same means and opportunity. The remedy lies in the critical social spirit, which was introduced with the Catholic system, and which must attend again upon the separation of the two powers. Its disastrous exaggeration in our day is no evidence against its future efficacy, when it shall have been duly subordinated to the organic spirit, and applied to restrain the abuses of the new system. The universal propagation of sound knowledge will check false pretension to a great extent: but there will also be need of the social criticism which will arise from the very constitution of the spiritual authority,—based as it must be on principles which may be at all times appealed to, as tests of capacity and morality. If, under the Catholic constitution, the meanest disciple might remonstrate against any authority, spiritual or temporal, which had infringed ordinary obligations, much more must such a liberty exist under the positive system, which excludes no subject whatever from discussion, under fitting conditions,—to say nothing of the greater precision and indisputableness of moral prescriptions under the positive system.

I have exhibited the nature and character of the spiritual reorganization which must result from the preparation of past ages. It is not possible to perform the same office in regard to the temporal system, because it must issue from the other; and it is impossible for any one to foresee more than the general principle and spirit which will regulate the classification of society. Of that principle and spirit I may briefly speak; but it would be countenancing the empiricism of the present day to enter into detail, which must be altogether premature. First, we must discard the distinction between public and private functions,—a distinction which could never be more than temporary, and which it is impossible to refer to any rational principle. The separation was never contemplated till the industrial system succeeded to that of personal bondage: and then the distinction referred to the old system, on the one hand, with its normal functions; and, on the other, to the new system, with its partial and empirical operations, which were not perceived to have any tendency towards a new economy. Thenceforward the conception represents our view of the whole past, in its negative and its positive progression; and it assumed its present preponderance when the final crisis began, when public professions, spiritual and temporal, dissolved, as an extension took place of functions which were formerly private. The distinction will endure till the primary conception of the new system shall have taught all men that there is a public utility in the humblest office of co-operation, no less truly than in the loftiest function of government. Other men would feel, if their labour were but systematized, as the private soldier feels in the discharge of his humblest duty, the dignity of public service, and the honour of a share in the action of the general economy. Thus, the abolition of this distinction depends on the universal regeneration of modern ideas and manners. We have thus to discard altogether the notion of private functions, as belonging to a transitory system, and to consider all as alike social, after having put out of the question whatever functions have to be eliminated; that is, the theological and metaphysical offices which will then have expired. The modern economy thus presenting only homogeneous elements, it becames possible to form a conception of the classification that is to ensue. The elevation of private professions to the dignity of public functions need occasion no essential change in the manner of their discharge; but it will make all the difference in the world in their general spirit, and not a little in their ordinary conditions. While on the one hand there will be a universal personal sense of social value, there will be on the other hand an admission of the necessity of systematic discipline, incompatible with a private career, but guaranteeing the obligations belonging to each function. This one change will be a universal symptom of modern regeneration.

The co-ordinating principle must be the same that I have applied in establishing the hierarchy of the sciences,—that of the degree of generality and simplicity of the subject, according to the nature of the phenomena. The same principle was tested in its application in the interior of each science; and when we were applying it in biology, we found it assuming a more active character, indicating its social destination. Transferred from ideas and phenomena to actual beings, it became the principle of zoological classification. We then found it to be the basis of social statics; and our dynamical inquiry showed us that it has determined all the elementary evolutions of modern social practice. It must thus be regarded as the law of all hierarchies; and its successive coincidences are explained by the necessary universality of logical laws. It will always be found working identically in every system which consists of homogeneous elements, subjecting all orders of activity to their due classification, according to their respective degrees of abstractness and generality. This was the principle of classification in old societies; and we see vestiges of it yet in the military organization, where the very terms of office indicate that the less general are subordinated to the more general functions. It needs no proof then, that, in a regenerated society, homogeneous in its elements, the change that will take place will be found to be in the elements, and not in their classification; for such classification as has taken place during the modern transition has been all in accordance with the principle. The only difficulty therefore lies in estimating the degrees of generality inherent in the various functions of the positive organism: and this very task has been almost entirely accomplished at the beginning of the last chapter, while the rest of the necessary material is furnished by the preceding part of the Work; so that I have only to combine these different particulars to create a rational conception of the final economy.

The idea of social subordination is common to the old and the new philosophy, opposite as are their points of view, and transitory as is the one view in comparison with the other. The old philosophy, explaining everything by the human type, saw everywhere a hierarchy regulated in imitation of the social classification. The new philosophy, studying Man in connection with the universe at large, finds this classification to be simply a protraction of the biological hierarchy. But science and theology, considering Man each in its own way,—the one as the first of animals, and the other as the lowest of angels,—lead to a very similar conclusion. The office of positive philosophy in this case is to substantiate the common notion of social subordination by connecting it with the principle which forms all hierarchies.

The highest rank is held, according to that principle, by the speculative class. When the separation of the two powers first took place under monotheism, the legal superiority of the clergy to all other orders was by no means owing only or chiefly to their religious character. It was more on account of their speculative character; and the continued growth of the tendency, amidst the decay of religious influences, shows that it is more disinterested than is commonly supposed, and testifies to the disposition of human reason to place the highest value on the most general conceptions. When the speculative class shall have overcome its dispersive tendencies, and returned to unity of principle amidst its diversity of employments, it will obtain the eminent position for which it is destined, and of which its present situation can scarcely afford any idea. While the speculative class is thus superior in dignity, the active class will be superior in express and immediate power, the division answering to the two opposite ways of classifying men, by capacity and by power. The same principle determines the next subdivision of each class, before pointed out in another connection. The speculative class divides itself, according to the direction taken by the contemplative spirit, into the scientific or philosophical (which we know to be ultimately one), and the æsthetic or poetic. Alike as these two classes are in their distinction from the active, they so differ from each other as to require division on the same principle as runs throughout. Whatever may be the ultimate importance and eminent function of the fine arts, the æsthetic point of view can never compare in generality and abstractness with the scientific or philosophical. The one is concerned with the fundamental conceptions which must direct the universal action of human reason; whereas the other is concerned only with the faculties of expression, which must ever hold a secondary place. As for the other leading class, the active or practical, which comprehends the vast majority, its more complete and marked development has already settled the point of its divisions; so that, in regard to them, the theory has only to rationalize the distinctions sanctioned by spontaneous usage. Industrial action is divided into production and transmission of products; the second of which is obviously superior to the first in regard to the abstractness of the work and the generality of the relations. Further division seems to be indicated according as production relates to the mere formation of materials or their working up; and as the transmission is of the products themselves, or of their representative signs, the generality being greater in the second particulars than in the first. Thus we find the industrial hierarchy formed, the bankers being in the first rank; then the merchants; then the manufacturers; and finally the agriculturists; the labours of the latter being more concrete, and their relations more special, than those of the other three classes. It would be out of place to proceed here to further subdivisions. They will be determined by the same principle when the progress of reorganization is sufficiently advanced; and I may observe that when that time comes, the most

concrete producers, the labourers, whose collisions with their employers are now the most dangerous feature of our industrial state, will be convinced that the position of the capitalist is owing, not to any abuse of strength or wealth, but to the more abstract and general character of his function. The action and responsibility of the operative are less extensive than those of the employer; and the subordination of the one to the other is therefore as little arbitrary and mutable as any other social gradation.

When the gradation is once established, it will be preserved from question and confusion, not only by the clearness of its principle, but by the consciousness in each order that its own subordination to the one above it is the condition of its superiority to those below it; and the lowest of all is not without its own special privileges. The abuses attending all inequality will be restrained, not only by the fundamental education common to all, but by the more extended and severe moral obligations which press upon members of society, in proportion to the generality of their functions. Again, in proportion as social occupations are particular and concrete, their utility is direct, incontestable, and assured, and the existence of the workers is more independent, and their responsibility more restricted,— corresponding as their labours do to the most indispensable wants. Thus, if the higher ranks are dignified by a more eminent and difficult co-operation, the lower have a more certain and urgent function: and the last could provisionally exist by themselves, without perverting their essential character; whereas the others could not. This difference is not only a guarantee of social harmony, but it is favourable to private happiness, which, when the primary wants are securely provided for, depends mainly on the small amount of habitual solicitude: and thus, the lowest classes really are privileged in that freedom from care, and that thoughtlessness, which would be a serious fault in the higher classes, but are natural to them. . . .

What I have said of the public character of all social offices under the new organization relates only to their social aspect, and not at all to the mode of their fulfilment. In fact, the more the individual is improved by education, the more freely may the execution of public operations be confided to private industry. The less general and more actual labours,—those which belong to the practical order,—may be safely delivered over to the natural action of individual minds; and, while the prerogative of the central authority is carefully preserved, there will be entire freedom from any regulating spirit which could impede spontaneous activity, on which progression directly depends. In the speculative case, however, the social efficacy is too indirect, too remote, and therefore too little felt by the multitude to depend altogether on private estimation for aid: and public munificence should protect labours of this kind, the political character of these functions becoming manifest, in proportion as they are more general and abstract. This is the only way in which there can be any distinction between public and private professions; and the distinction will not affect the idea of a common social destination.

It can hardly be necessary to point out that there will be perfect freedom in the formation of the respective classes of the positive hierarchy. The direct effect of a universal education is to place every one in the situation best adapted to his abilities, whatever his birth may have been. This is a liberty which depends more on general manners than on

political institutions; and it depends upon two conditions,—that access to every social career should remain open to the capable; and that there should be some means of excluding the unworthy. When order is once completely established, such changes will become exceptional; because it is natural for professions to be hereditary. Few have a determinate vocation, and few social employments require such a vocation; so that the disposition to domestic imitation will have its way; whereas, the quality of the universal education and the state of social manners will be safeguards against this hereditary tendency assuming any oppressive form. There is no room for apprehension of any restoration of the system of castes. Caste can have none but a theological foundation; and we have long passed out of the last social phase that is compatible with it; and its remaining traces are, as I have shown, fast disappearing from amidst the advanced civilization of Western Europe.

It remains for me to point out the connection between such an organization and the just claims of the lower classes: and for this purpose I must ascertain the influence of such a connection, both upon the mass of the people and upon the speculative class.

Any spiritual power must be, by its very nature, popular; for its function is to set up morality to guide the social movement, and its closest relations therefore must be with the most numerous classes, who most need its protection. The Catholic Church was obviously doomed to decay when it forsook its task of enlightening and protecting the people, and inclined to aristocratic interests: and in the same way, the inherent nullity of Protestantism appeared in the impotence of its puny authorities to protect the lower classes: and in the same way again, we recognize the empiricism and selfishness which spoil the speculative elements of our modern society in the strange aristocratic tendencies of so many *savans* and artists, who forget their own humble origin, and disdain to apply to the instruction and protection of the people the influence they have acquired,—preferring indeed to use it in confirmation of their own oppressive pretensions. There must be, in the normal state of the final economy, a strong sympathy between the speculative class and the multitude, from their analogous relation to the possessors of the chief temporal power, from their somewhat similar practical situation, and from their equivalent habits of material improvidence. Yet more important is the popular efficacy of the speculative authority, on account both of its educational function and of its regular intervention as moderator in social conflicts, through its habitual elevation of views and generosity of disposition. Without at all quitting its attitude of impartiality, its chief care will always be directed towards the humbler classes, who, on the one hand, are much the most in need of a public education such as their private means cannot attain; and, on the other hand, are much more exposed to constant injury. Even now, vast benefit would ensue if, in preparation for the system to come, positive knowledge and philosophy were sedulously brought within reach of the people. In the educational direction, the intellectual expansion would be much greater than is now easily believed: and the advantage in the other respect, in protecting them from collision with the governing classes, would be no less evident. The positive philosophy would teach them the real value of the political institutions from which they are apt to hope so much,

and convince them of the superiority of moral over political solutions. All evils and all pretexts derived from social disturbance would thus be obviated: quacks and dreamers would lose their vocation; and no excuse would be left for delay in social reform. When it is seen why wealth must chiefly abound among the industrial leaders, the positive philosophy will show that it is of small importance to popular interests in what hands capital is deposited, if its employment is duly useful to society at large: and that condition depends much more on moral than on political methods. No jealous legal provision against the selfish use of wealth, and no mischievous intervention, paralysing social activity by political prohibition, can be nearly so effectual as general reprobation, grounded on an ascertained principle, under the reign of positive morality. The new philosophical action would either obviate or repress all the dangers which attend the institution of property, and correct popular tendencies by a wise analysis of social difficulties, and a salutary conversion of questions of right into questions of duty.—In its impartiality it will make the superior classes participate in the lesson, proving to them the great moral obligations inherent in their position; so that, for instance, in this matter of property, the rich will morally consider themselves the depositories of the wealth of society, the use of which will not involve any political responsibility (except in extreme cases), but should lie under a moral supervision, necessarily open to all, from the indisputableness of its principle, and of which the spiritual authority is the natural organ. Since the abolition of personal servitude, the lowest class has never been really incorporated with the social system: the power of capital, once a means of emancipation, and then of independence, has become exorbitant in daily transactions, however just is its influence through its generality and superior responsibility. In short, this philosophy will show that industrial relations, instead of being left to a dangerous empiricism and an oppressive antagonism, must be systematized according to moral laws. The duty to the lower classes will not consist in almsgiving, which can never be more than a secondary resource, nor made reconcilable with any high social destination, in the present advanced state of human condition and dignity. The obligation will be to procure for all, suitable education and employment,— the only conditions that the lower classes can justly demand. Without entering on the perplexed subject of wages, it is enough to say that their settlement will be largely influenced by the same agency. We need not inquire whether any political institutions will in course of time embody social securities of this kind: it is enough that the principle will remain eminently moral, in as far as it will be efficacious and harmonizing.

Such will be the effect on society of the philosophical preparation for the new system. It is very observable that the reciprocal action on philosophy will be no less beneficial. In such a combination, the people will give to the philosophers more than they will have received from them. The popular adhesion will be the safeguard of the spiritual power against aggression from the temporal, such as will be instigated by human passions under the positive system, as under every other, notwithstanding its milder practical activity, and the increased sway of reason over conduct. On the one hand, the rich men may show their pride of wealth on occasion of the material dependence of the speculative class; and these again may manifest the disdain which men of theory are wont to feel towards men of practice: and then will the people become the regulators of their conflicts, more even than in the Middle Ages, being indebted to the one power for education and moral influence, and to the other for employment and material assistance; and always holding the balance between them, as of old.

The Ideal of Justice

It remains now to follow the implications of positivism for the ideal of justice. Among the various themes of positivism that have been surveyed in preceding selections is the conviction that explanations of social phenomena and realities must be made without recourse to transcendent or metaphysical notions. Values are not unimportant to the positivist, but he insists that they be understood within the context of human life. In society men develop rules and standards to govern the concrete relations of their lives, and their ideal conception of these relationships is their conception of justice.

Heir of Comte and important contributor to sociological research, Lucien Lévy-Bruhl (1857–1939) is a somewhat more recent spokesman for positivism's view of justice. His position in the following selection may be divided into three parts.

First is his rejection of alternative views, particularly of natural law theories of ethics and justice. Even if these theories are presented in pseudoscientific form (as Lévy-Bruhl believes the theory of Buckle's is), their fundamental falseness is apparent in the light of an elementary knowledge of sociology. Sociological data show that the formulas of justice come from the social realities existing at each epoch in the history of a society, and that progress or change in ideals of justice is not attributable to some conception of justice preexisting innately and universally in the minds of men.

The second part of Lévy-Bruhl's position is his constructive analysis of justice as a rule or ideal in society. He bases this analysis on his "law of solidarity of the social series" which, among other things, refers to the ways in which the various elements of a society such as its economic basis, its law, its beliefs, and its conscience intermingle and affect one another. This law also refers to the effects of the synthesis of reactions that the consciousness of an individual exercises upon other individuals. To remain stable, societies must relate, and to some extent integrate, these elements and experiences in a commonly held value system. Present in the value system are many ideal conceptions, including justice, which relate the members of societies in their respective duties and obligations toward one another. Lévy-Bruhl in fact develops his positivistic theory of value as a fundamental condition of social solidarity, for it allows him to view the various aspects of a society in their lived interrelationships rather than as a priori elaborations of "foreign" moral norms.

The third part of Lévy-Bruhl's statement is his admonition to societies to follow the positivist endorsement of science. "To be truly rational, our action on social reality ought not to be guided by an abstract ideal . . . but by the results of science." Science will determine how the obligations of conscience are established, strengthened, and related to social life, and how they can be modified to produce progress.

LUCIEN LÉVY-BRUHL   Justice and Social Reality

Buckle[1] maintained, supporting his argument by a large number of facts, that the progress of human societies depended chiefly on the discovery of new scientific truths, and in no way on the discovery of ethical truths, since they were transmitted from generation to generation, and even from civiliza-

[1] Henry Thomas Buckle (1821–62), English historian and author of *History of Civilization,* a volume developing the view discussed here by Lévy–Bruhl. *Ed.*

tion to civilization, always alike by their formulae, if not in their applications. According to him as far back as history permits us to go, we find societies already in possession of the fundamental principles of ethics although entirely ignorant of the sciences of nature. That conception is not new. The ancient philosophers, especially the stoics, had already made it a commonplace. It is in opposition to what we have tried to

From Lucien Lévy-Bruhl, *Ethics and Moral Science,* trans. Elizabeth Lee, London: Archibald Constable and Co., Ltd., 1905. Used by permission of Constable Publishers, London.

establish, for, at bottom it is only a slightly different expression of the belief in a natural law and in natural ethics. We may then, if we desire, consider it refuted by what precedes it. As, however, it claims to rest on observation, it will not perhaps be useless to criticize it in itself and to examine the value and bearing of the facts which it invokes.

Those facts are, in general, borrowed from civilizations which in comparison with those that are more familiar appear far remote in time and consequently relatively primitive: Egypt, Assyria, Babylon (three or four thousand years before Christ). A certain number of texts exist which testify that there was a conscience at that period, open to the idea of justice and to respect for the rights of others, and also to the duty of assisting others and of protecting the weak. But those civilizations, however remote they seem to us, were already very complex, highly developed, remarkably differentiated from the social point of view, and of an elevated type in organization. We do not know absolutely what space of time separated them from a condition analogous to that in which the inferior societies of Africa, America and Australia are at the present time; but we shall not be greatly in error if we conclude it to be very considerable. The alleged facts would tend to prove that wherever human societies have reached a high degree of civilization, the ethical relations of men between themselves testify to it. The contrary would indeed be surprising; and the same statement may be made in regard to their economic relations, their art, language and religion. It is an immediate consequence of the solidarity which unites the different fundamental series of social phenomena. The solidarity, doubtless, is not always equally apparent and intercurring causes may favour or retard the development of this or that series; but in a general way, and if we are careful to take into account the perturbations which may arise from the most diverse causes, the law is verified.

Consequently, by reason of the same law, it would be most unlikely that the conscience would be greatly differentiated and be master of itself in a society in which civilization was still low and savage. How is it that one single social series will evolve in isolation to a high degree of complexity and differentiation, while others remain at a much lower stage? How is it to be imagined that with a dull mentality, not yet admitting of abstract thought or generalization, in the absence of an advanced division of labour, of a clearly defined feeling of the opposition possible between the individual and the group, subtle ideas like those of reparative and distributive justice, individual responsibility, respect for law could, I will not say be expressed, but be formed?

To suppose so would be to grant the hypothesis of a special revelation; and it was exactly that hypothesis which we found when we reached the deepest root of the idea of "natural ethics." But we also saw that the hypothesis was not supported by the facts. Doubtless wherever human groups exist, relations also exist between their members which may be described as ethical, that is, acts permitted or forbidden beyond those (small in number) which are indifferent, are to be found as well as feelings of blame, admiration, reprobation, esteem for the perpetrators of the acts. But there is a long distance between those facts and the conscious and considered knowledge of "ethical truths," and especially of truths comparable to those which play so large a part in civilized societies. In the societies called primitive, the presence of an individual conscience possessing those truths itself, would be a sort of miracle. So far as we know that miracle nowhere occurs.

Besides, even in more elevated societies the external resemblance of the formulae should not hide from us the internal difference of the "ethical truths" they express. For instance, it is frequently stated that the essential rules of justice were as well known in the most remote civilized antiquity as in our own time: *Neminem laedere; suum cuique tribuere*. Perhaps: but all that may be legitimately concluded is, that since the days of that remote antiquity language has permitted an abstract expression of the essential ethical relations. The resemblance stops there. It lies only in generality and abstraction of the formula. If there was also resemblance in its signification the meaning of the terms would be almost the same in different civilizations. Now that is not at all the case. How is *neminem* to be understood? To what acts may *laedere* be applied? In half civilized societies, the stranger is not included in *neminem*. The boat cast up by the storm on a foreign shore is pillaged, the men who sailed it murdered, or brought into slavery, without anyone finding an infraction of the rule *neminem laedere*. Such examples abound not only in the past but with us, and in our day. The manner in which the natives of even civilized colonies, like the Annamites, are generally treated by Europeans, shows that "ethical truths" suffer a singular eclipse outside the land of their origin. Similarly for the rule *suum cuiqui tribuere*. How is *suum* defined? In a society where caste exists, justice consists in treating everyone according to his caste, the Brahmin as a Brahmin, the paria as a paria; with a number of half civilized races, it consists in regarding

female children as an importunate charge, and women as beasts of burden; in feudal society it consisted in regarding the villain as liable to taxation and statute labour at pleasure. Even in more developed societies, certain applications of the formula of justice call forth protestation from a smaller number of consciences, while others are not disturbed by them. The manufacturer who considers that he is not making sufficient profit may close his mill from one day to the next and consider that he "is wronging no one," since he paid his workmen, now unemployed, for the work done by them up to that day. In the middle of the nineteenth century at the time of the rapid development of manufactures in England, and of the horrible sacrifice of women and children working sixteen or eighteen hours a day in the factories, it does not seem that the masters were conscious of violating the rule of justice; *suum cuique tribuere*. Did they not pay suitable wages?

Those formulae, taken in the abstract, do not possess the power attributed to them of expressing at all times and in all lands the eternal essence of justice. Considered in themselves they are empty. They only receive their signification and their ethical value from their content, which is not provided *a priori* by a sort of ethical intuition nor by an immediate estimation of general utility.[2] It comes to them from the social reality existing at each epoch, and which imposes on every individual the manner in which he ought to behave in a given case. Thus they represent the expressions of ethics of such or such society at a particular time, and not expressions of "ethical truth" in itself. They say

[2] This reference is to a doctrine of Utilitarianism, a position to be examined in Section Four. *Ed.*

equally to the Egyptian, contemporary with the earliest dynasties, to the Assyrian of the time of Sargon, to the Greek of the time of Thucydides, to the baron and prelate of the eleventh century: "You must be just and render to each man his own." But these cases and others that might be put forward, have nothing in common except the formula bidding men conform to definite rules of action under penalty of social punishments, precise or vague, which are echoed in every individual conscience.

The effective progress of social justice cannot then be attributed to a pre-existing conception of justice in men's minds as its decisive or even principal cause. Undoubtedly when progress in morals or in laws is realized, it was demanded, for a long, and sometimes for a very long time, by a certain number of consciences. But why do those consciences feel the need of it? It is not a fresh result drawn from the formula of justice known before, for why should the result be felt at that particular moment, and not have been perceived sooner? The deduction then is merely apparent. The actual fact of which it is the abstract manifestation is, most often, a profound modification produced in another series of social phenomena, and almost always in the economic series. Thus slavery and serfdom, after being regarded as normal phenomena, as excellent institutions necessary to the social order, were gradually eliminated by the economic transformation of European societies, and excluded from what is right by the conscience and condemned in the name of morality. It is thus that the condition of the proletariat under the rule of the modern capitalist, after being long regarded by economists as normal, inevitable and even in a certain sense, providential, is regarded quite differently now that the proletariat, hav-

ing become conscious of its strength, exacts and obtains more humane conditions of life. The common conscience begins to acknowledge that the claims of the proletariat are just. The economic transformation once begun, the idea of the necessity of realizing a better justice will doubtless help immensely in quickening the movement. But the idea itself would never have been born, and would certainly not have been developed, or have acquired strength enough to obtain millions of adherents, if the whole of the conditions in which society found itself had not caused it to arise. Just as historical materialism is difficult to maintain if it claims to subordinate all evolution of society to its economic life, so is it true that no series of social phenomena, ethical and juridical phenomena no more than the rest, are developed independently of the other series.

Justice and more generally ethics should be conceived as a "becoming." There is nothing a priori to authorize the affirmation that becoming is a progress and an uninterrupted progress. To admit that postulate would be to return to the idea of a natural ethics. It would merely take a different form. Instead of supposing that justice was revealed directly in the conscience of every man coming into the world, we should imagine that it was revealed successively in the historical evolution of civilized societies. But the hypothesis, although thus projected into time, would not change its character. It would remain at bottom teleological, religious, and anthropocentric. From the scientific point of view the study of the facts does not prove that the evolution of human societies, not even of higher societies, is such that each series of phenomena, and all together, only vary in the sense of "better." On the contrary, it shows that a multitude of causes, internal and external, may check the development of one or several series, or cause it or them to deviate, and consequently all the others. If we consider the successive conditions of a portion of the ancient world (Spain, Italy, and Gaul) between the first century of the Christian era and the twelfth, it is difficult to assert that the progress towards better conditions has been uninterrupted. No matter from what point of view we regard it (economic, intellectual, moral, political, or any other), it is incontestable that the change, in the whole mass, was rather a retrogression than a progress. For by reason of the law of solidarity of the social series, a change for the worse in social relations from the ethical point of view and a corresponding obscuration of the conscience and the idea, was produced simultaneously. That is exactly what happened. Arabian civilization, that of India, of China, furnishes analogous examples.

Thus the variable content of "ethical truths" does not, even among the most civilized peoples, undergo an uninterrupted process of purification. It evolves parallel to the general evolution of the society. It loses its old elements and demands new ones. Sometimes from one point of view it loses what it would have been better to keep, or keeps what would have been better lost. In fact, it acquires what it would have been better for it not to have incorporated. The ever possible eventuality could only be excluded by the care of an omnipotent Providence who guided social evolution: it is perfectly compatible with the principle of the conditions of existence. Consequently, the conscience of a given time, in relation to the whole mass of the social reality of that time, will never provide the general formula of justice with a content that will be worthy of the respect demanded for it in all its parts.

By what it prescribes, by what it forbids, and even by what it never dreams of prescribing or forbidding, it necessarily retains more or less important traces of what may be called the social superstition and ignorance of that epoch. Superstition—in the etymological sense of the word—whenever it is a question of the distinction of classes, of old-established obligations, or interdictions, is now under the sway of the prevailing ideas and beliefs, now rejected by the conscience, but it nevertheless persists. Ignorance is insufficiently warned by facts, and our justice remains indifferent to the budding laws that have not as yet the strength to impose themselves.

It is futile to imagine that the waving of a magic wand will rid us of that superstition and ignorance. So far as ignorance is concerned, the impossibility is manifest. How could we learn the modifications of justice that will be exacted by changes still in the distance, and scarcely traced by the whole mass of social conditions, when very often we do not even discern those which are quite near us, and more than half accomplished? And that proves once again how chimerical is the idea of a justice absolute and immutable in itself; for at every new period of social life justice assumes a form that preceding periods could not foresee, and which would never be realized if the evolution of society was different. For instance, we can quite well imagine that the rule of capitalist production had not been set up in Western Europe; in that case a large part of what social justice now demands would never have been conceived. Similarly, whatever the greater number of liberal and socialistic economists may say, we are now in profound ignorance of the social rule which will take the place of ours in a more or less distant future, and consequently of the modifications that the content of "ethical truths" will undergo. We can only slightly remedy our ignorance. We can only (but even that is not to be neglected) make as complete and as objective a study as possible of the present ethical reality. We can determine the meaning, the power, the character, socially useful or harmful, of the different tendencies that are struggling with each other, of the laws which are in jeopardy, of the laws that are coming into being. Thus we may render the transitions less difficult to men's minds, less painful in the facts, and help to secure that the evolution of our society —if it is too ambitious to talk of the evolution of humanity—may take as much as possible the form of progress and of pacific progress.

As to "superstitions" (in the sense we gave the word just now), we can only weaken them very gradually, especially the oldest of them, which, being transmitted from generation to generation, ended by acquiring a power comparable to that of instinct. There should, too, be no illusion as regards the word "superstition" or "survival." We do not regard it as the eighteenth century philosophers did, who, in the name of a rational abstract ideal, pitilessly condemned all the traditions that could not be reconciled with that ideal. To imitate them would be to recognize "natural ethics," the existence of which seemed evident to them, and which seems to us incompatible with the reality of facts. It is not for us to undertake a rational crusade against the "superstitions" which still live in our conscience. It is true that all or nearly all is superstition since everything is a heritage of the past, and of a past that sometimes goes back beyond history. It matters little that the beliefs that are at the root of a custom are ill-founded, that the reasons which have led to such an interdiction have no longer any meaning in our eyes. If that custom or that interdiction has had a favourable influence on the progress of society, if it is so closely mingled with its life that it cannot be torn away without destroying the whole, in the name of what principle should we undertake to uproot it? To be truly rational, our action on social reality ought to be guided not by an abstract ideal—which claims to have an absolute value and merely expresses the exactions of the conscience to-day—but by the results of science. When science has determined for each of the obligations of the conscience, how it was established, strengthened, imposed, what effect it has produced, and what part it still plays in social life, we shall know in what degree it is expedient—and possible—to modify it. That will be the work of "the rational art" that we conceive to be the methodical application of the results obtained by ethical speculation become scientific.

Liberalism

Our third perspective in social philosophy involves a terminological problem. On the one hand, many of the themes and positions taken by its representatives are shared by thinkers of other philosophic schools. On the other hand, while there is a common core of ideas about society and government among them, there is also a rather wide divergence of views in other areas such as religion and metaphysics. Creating even further difficulty is the fact that while there is good historical ground for using the term liberalism regarding this group—many historians have said that John Locke's views are the very soul of liberalism—there are also good reasons for using the same term when referring to many utilitarians in the nineteenth century and to certain socialist positions in the twentieth century. In actual practice, liberalism seems to be used to denote positions covering a range from those centering on the interests of the middle class to the culmination of the whole Western political tradition. One could perhaps speak of a classical liberalism, although it may confuse this perspective with anticipations of liberalism in Greek and Roman thought; or perhaps of Enlightenment liberalism, although this might suggest that all Enlightenment social philosophers were liberals, which would be misleading also. Thus, it seems necessary to be somewhat arbitrary in the matter of names. Liberalism will be used in this book to refer to a scheme of ideas in social philosophy that, historically, did arise during the time of the Enlightenment (though many of its conceptions have been influential to the present day) and that presents a distinctive perspective in social philosophy.

More important than the matter of names, however, are the chief ideas of the liberal position. Perhaps the best starting point in discussing them is the liberal's belief that there are moral rules that men ought to obey simply because they are men. Unlike Hobbes, for example, the liberal asserts that men are by nature moral beings and that although society does enter into the development of human nature, there are rules men ought to obey because men have certain given capacities. As Locke put it, the "keeping of faith belongs to men as men and not as members of society."

The recognition of man as a moral being may suggest that the liberal is returning to some of the themes of classical realism. While the early liberals were influenced by medieval thought, their chief inspiration came from the ancient school of Stoicism. In fact, one of the defining characteristics of liberalism is its acceptance of Stoic values and of a number of ideas associated with them.

Flourishing from the third century B.C. to the fifth century A.D., Stoicism was primarily an ethical doctrine. Moral life was understood in terms of control of the emotions and passions by reason. Human beings, as the Stoics saw them, constantly experience unhappiness and misery for lack of this control; they become emotionally involved with things and persons to such a degree that these objects cannot support the involvement. An example or two from Epictetus (60–110), one of the greatest Stoics, may explain this point. "If you are fond of a jug," he wrote, "say you are fond of a jug; then you will not be disturbed if it is broken. If you kiss your child or your wife, say to yourself that you are kissing a human being, for then if death strikes it, you will not be disturbed."

The Stoic offered two maxims of advice in order to prevent this disturbance. He said that men should live "according to nature"; through their rational powers they should recognize and understand the natures of things—jugs and human beings—and the laws that govern them. An earthen thing must not be confused with a living being, nor a finite being confused with an infinite one. Secondly, the Stoic said that men should live in "independence of externals." Some matters lie within man's power, others do not. In man's power is his will; and so he is free to act or not to act, to get or to avoid. Not in man's power, however, are the natures of things and the laws that govern them.* Thus not only right reason but right will or virtue was involved in the Stoic's search for the good life. The Stoic sage who achieved this goal experienced the tranquillity and freedom that are the marks of a completed and fulfilled human life.

Stoicism also developed a rather complete metaphysical context for its ethical teachings. Since the universe acts in accordance with causal laws, it may be considered rational; and since it is rational, it is also divine. But men are also rational beings, and they therefore share in the divinity of the universe. Reason is a spark of the divine in men, and is the basis of individual rights and dignity. And, since all men are rational beings, they are and must be treated as equals. Unlike many of their contemporaries, Stoics held that even those who are slaves under positive law are equal to free men and have rights before the law of nature. The equality of men implies the brotherhood of men, and the universal law of the universe making men brothers means that men are citizens of the cosmos—cosmopolitans—before they are Greek or Roman.

Through these ideas, Stoicism exerted an extensive influence on political theory. It produced a new moral sanction for politics outside the Greek polis, and it taught the doctrine of a pervading natural law, rooted in the order of nature

---

* Stoic metaphysics was in fact deterministic: all things in nature happen by causal necessity.

and moral in content. Its emphasis was on the individual and his rights, and it based its appeal and sanction on reason. Most fundamental of all was its postulate that values inhere ultimately in the satisfactions and realizations of personality.

As liberalism developed in the seventeenth and eighteenth centuries, it accepted this inheritance from Stoicism and built upon it. Like Stoicism, liberalism sought to produce new moral sanctions for politics outside the medieval world and in the face of what it took to be the nonmoralism of positivism. It too appealed to natural law to answer questions of obligation, rights, and morality; it stressed individualism and individual rights; it sought to justify its position by an appeal to reason. To this cluster of ideas, however, must be added two further conceptions, namely limited government and the centrality of freedom. Liberalism in all its forms is marked by a distrust of government; power and authority must be limited by the ends they serve, for they are but means to an end. This is to be judged by reference to their purpose as well as by the regularities of the natural law that define mutual obligations and duties.

Liberals have generally adhered to some form of democratic government as that being best suited to their convictions that coercion is justified, not for national greatness, nor to enable men to attain virtue, nor for the sake of heaven, nor in the service of a common good transcending individual rights, but only because government is needed to secure the proper ends for individuals. That proper end, as liberals see it, is freedom. This political ideal is of course common to many philosophies; but liberalism gives it both a central importance and an individualistic meaning. Freedom is each man's right to live as seems good to him, provided he respects the same right in others. From this understanding of freedom come the correlative ideals of toleration and freedom of conscience, which are the special marks of the liberal's concern with freedom.

The philosophic judgments of liberalism thus involve an acceptance of Stoic values, especially individualism, moralism, and reason, a recommendation that government be limited in scope and authority, and a postulation of the ideal of freedom as the consummate political value. Having many spokesmen of its principles, liberalism developed into and remains one of the major alternatives in Western political philosophy.

Man and Society

Unlike the Hobbesian, positivistic assertion that morality is consequent upon and derived from society, the liberal is convinced that man is by nature a moral being. Society may enter into and form man's conscience, and it may even be taken as a necessary condition for any realization of man's capacities for moral behavior, but fundamental to liberalism are the two convictions that man is naturally a moral agent and that there are independent rules or laws that man must follow to realize himself as such an agent. "Obligations cease not in the state of nature."

The expression state of nature is common (though not universal) in the writings of liberals. Among the many uses to which it is put* is that of understanding man's moral capacities. In the state of nature—that is, apart from society (the state of nature need not be considered a historical state at all, though it was by some liberals)—men are reasonable and moral, active in the pursuit of certain values, and guided by rational moral norms. In that state they also are, to some extent, weak and defenseless; the need for association in society under government arises from this weakness.

The details of such a position were given their first philosophically important statement by John Locke (1632–1704), who was led to many of his assertions about man and society by his reflections on the problem of knowledge. As an empiricist, Locke took the basic elements of knowledge to be simple sensory experiences—his own list included yellow, white, heat, cold, soft, hard, bitter, sweet. When these simple ideas are compounded, they produce complex ideas, and when complex ideas are taken to represent particular existing things, they are ideas of substances. To put this theory another way: it is the combination of qualities such as color, odor, and shape that results in the idea of a thing. Since these qualities cannot be believed to be floating about with no binding principle that accounts for their togetherness, a substance is postulated as their substratum. This substratum fulfills the need of providing unity of qualities, even though the real essence of substance is unknowable.

The idea of a mental or spiritual substance arises in much the same way. Corresponding to the qualities that result in the idea of a thing are experiences such as doubting, fearing, and feeling. These too cannot exist "unattached" or of themselves, and hence an immaterial mental substratum must exist to support them.

By supposing a substance wherein thinking, knowing, doubting, and a power of moving, etc. do subsist, we have as clear a notion of the substance of spirit, as we have of body, the one being supposed to be (without knowing what it is) the substratum of those simple ideas we have from without, and the other supposed (with a like ignorance of what it is) to be the substratum to those operations we experiment in ourselves within.

Thus, Locke's theory of knowledge was the basis of his understanding of man as mental substance. It meant, as Locke inferred, that there is a new view of the state of nature and a new content for the "law of reason." A person is mental substance: one's rights, even one's own body, is now his "property." Religion is concerned properly only with this substance: hence toleration, not theocracy; democracy, not divine right. There is no natural relation among these substances (as, for example, the natural spatial relation among physical substances), hence "hierarchies" or political aristocracies are neither natural nor in the nature of things. No authority can grasp the essentially unknowable mental substance; hence men must submit to authority only as they agree to do so, and in all cases each

---

* Discussion here is limited to the meaning of the state of nature in relation to man's moral nature and the origins of society; later sections touch upon other problems such as government, law, and obligation where the concept is also important.

man is the best judge of himself. All social relations are conventions, including the relation of law, and conventions have authority solely through the consent of the related.

On the basis of this view of man, Locke states in his social philosophy that in the state of nature men are equally and perfectly free to order themselves and their possessions as they think fit. This freedom and equality are governed by a law of nature that obliges everyone to respect the freedom of self-determination in others, binding persons by the natural law to treat others as equals. In addition to refraining from interference with the rights of others, men in the state of nature have the right to punish transgressors of their rights "as calm reason and conscience dictate." The law of nature is thus a law of freedom. It is supported not by custom or tradition but by reason, which defines the rights and duties that constitute and sustain freedom.

Yet men find it necessary to give up their natural freedom and form a society. This they do because they find that the enjoyment of their natural rights in the state of nature is uncertain. The state of nature lacks (1) a settled, known law, (2) impartial judges, and (3) the power to enforce decisions and prevent infractions. Hence, men are driven to enter into a "social contract" where they give up their power of punishing transgressors and of doing whatever they think fit for their preservation in exchange for the collective and stronger action of society and government.† Through the social compact men agree to live in the bonds of civil society. The compact creates one body that acts by the consent of the majority, and by agreeing to the compact, individuals place themselves under the obligation to submit to the determinations of the majority.

Thus the existence of society and the authority of government arise for Locke out of men's freely given consent,‡ not out of their needs. To be sure, men need society and government, but it does not follow that because they need society, they cannot take care of themselves. The "one body" that men create is a device of human wisdom to meet their needs as rational and moral beings; since they are the only adequate judges of their needs, they take care of themselves by establishing a civil society. The authority men so establish is strictly derivative from their act, and the power of the commonwealth is a trust, limited by the ends it serves and the judgments citizens make of it. The end of the commonwealth is to secure and preserve property—"life, liberty, and estate"—or, since property for Locke is synonymous with individual rights,§ the end of civil society may be said to be the preservation of freedom. In matters pertaining to rights, but in none other, government must use force. The right of rebellion is the ultimate sanction against all abuse of power.

Natural rights and law, moralism, society as derivative, and government as limited are the themes of the liberal's understanding of man and society. The following pages from Locke are their *locus classicus*.

---

† Whether the compact is social or governmental is unclear in Locke. Althusius and Pufendorf made it clearer by proposing two contracts, one for society, a second for government.
‡ This key doctrine is explored in the section on "Political Obligation."
§ Generally, that is. Locke does occasionally speak of property in the restricted sense, thus becoming at times a spokesman of Whiggism.

JOHN LOCKE   The State of Nature

II. OF THE STATE OF NATURE

4. To understand political power right, and derive it from its original, we must consider what state all men are naturally in, and that is, a state of perfect freedom to order their actions and dispose of their possessions and persons, as they think fit, within the bounds of the law of nature; without asking leave, or depending upon the will of any other man.

A state also of equality, wherein all the power and jurisdiction is reciprocal, no one having more than another; there being nothing more evident, than that creatures of the same species and rank, promiscuously born to all the same advantages of nature, and the use of the same faculties, should also be equal one amongst another without subordination or subjection; unless the lord and master of them all should, by any manifest declaration of his will, set one above another, and confer on him, by an evident and clear appointment, an undoubted right to dominion and sovereignty.

6. But though this be a state of liberty, yet it is not a state of licence: though man in that state have an uncontrolable liberty to dispose of his person or possessions, yet he has not liberty to destroy himself, or so much as any creature in his possession, but where some nobler use than its bare preservation calls for it. The state of nature has a law of nature to govern it, which obliges every one: and reason, which is that law, teaches all mankind,

who will but consult it, that being all equal and independent, no one ought to harm another in his life, health, liberty, or possessions: for men being all the workmanship of one omnipotent and infinitely wise Maker; all the servants of one sovereign master, sent into the world by his order, and about his business; they are his property, whose workmanship they are, made to last during his, not another's pleasure: and being furnished with like faculties, sharing all in one community of nature, there cannot be supposed any such subordination among us, that may authorize us to destroy another, as if we were made for one another's uses, as the inferior ranks of creatures are for ours. Every one, as he is bound to preserve himself, and not to quit his station wilfully, so by the like reason, when his own preservation comes not in competition, ought he, as much as he can, to preserve the rest of mankind, and may not, unless it be to do justice to an offender, take away or impair the life, or what tends to the preservation of life, the liberty, health, limb, or goods of another.

7. And that all men may be restrained from invading others rights, and from doing hurt to one another, and the law of nature be observed, which willeth the peace and preservation of all mankind, the execution of the law of nature is, in that state, put into every man's hands, whereby every one has a right to punish the transgressors of that law to such a degree as may hinder its violation: for the law of nature would, as all other laws that concern men in this

From John Locke, "Two Treatises on Government," in *The Works of John Locke,* London: C. and J. Rivington and others, 1824.

world, be in vain, if there were nobody that in the state of nature had a power to execute that law, and thereby preserve the innocent and restrain offenders. And if any one in the state of nature may punish another for any evil he has done, every one may do so: for in that state of perfect equality, where naturally there is no superiority or jurisdiction of one over another, what any may do in prosecution of that law, every one must needs have a right to do.

8. And thus, in the state of nature, "one man comes by a power over another"; but yet no absolute or arbitrary power, to use a criminal, when he has got him in his hands, according to the passionate heats, or boundless extravagancy of his own will; but only to retribute to him, so far as calm reason and conscience dictate, what is proportionate to his transgression; which is so much as may serve for reparation and restraint: for these two are the only reasons, why one man may lawfully do harm to another, which is that we call punishment. In transgressing the law of nature, the offender declares himself to live by another rule than that of reason and common equity, which is that measure God has set to the actions of men, for their mutual security; and so he becomes dangerous to mankind, the tye, which is to secure them from injury and violence, being slighted and broken by him. Which being a trespass against the whole species, and the peace and safety of it, provided for by the law of nature; every man upon this score, by the right he hath to preserve mankind in general, may restrain, or, where it is necessary, destroy things noxious to them, and so may bring such evil on any one, who hath transgressed that law, as may make him repent the doing of it, and thereby deter him, and by his example others, from doing the like mis-chief. And in this case, and upon this ground, "every man hath a right to punish the offender, and be executioner of the law of nature."

11. From these two distinct rights, the one of punishing the crime for restraint, and preventing the like offence, which right of punishing is in every body; the other of taking reparation, which belongs only to the injured party; comes it to pass that the magistrate, who by being magistrate hath the common right of punishing put into his hands, can often, where the public good demands not the execution of the law, remit the punishment of criminal offences by his own authority, but yet cannot remit the satisfaction due to any private man for the damage he has received. That, he who has suffered the damage has a right to demand in his own name, and he alone can remit: the damnified person has this power of appropriating to himself the goods or service of the offender, by right of self-preservation, as every man has a power to punish the crime, to prevent its being committed again, "by the right he has of preserving all mankind"; and doing all reasonable things he can in order to that end: and thus it is, that every man, in the state of nature, has a power to kill a murderer, both to deter others from doing the like injury, which no reparation can compensate, by the example of the punishment that attends it from every body; and also to secure men from the attempts of a criminal, who having renounced reason, the common rule and measure God hath given to mankind, hath, by the unjust violence and slaughter he hath committed upon one, declared war against all mankind; and therefore may be destroyed as a lion or a tiger, one of those wild savage beasts, with whom men can have no society nor security: and upon this is

grounded that great law of nature, "Whoso sheddeth man's blood, by man shall his blood be shed." And Cain was so fully convinced, that every one had a right to destroy such a criminal, that after the murder of his brother, he cries out, "Every one that findeth me, shall slay me"; so plain was it writ in the hearts of mankind.

12. By the same reason may a man in the state of nature punish the lesser breaches of that law. It will perhaps be demanded, with death? I answer, each transgression may be punished to that degree, and with so much severity, as will suffice to make it an ill bargain to the offender, give him cause to repent, and terrify others from doing the like. Every offence, that can be committed in the state of nature, may in the state of nature be also punished equally, and as far forth, as it may in a commonwealth: for though it would be beside my present purpose, to enter here into the particulars of the law of nature, or its measures of punishment, yet it is certain there is such a law, and that too as intelligible and plain to a rational creature, and a studier of that law, as the positive laws of commonwealth: nay, possibly plainer, as much as reason is easier to be understood, than the fancies and intricate contrivances of men, following contrary and hidden interests put into words; for so truly are a great part of the municipal laws of countries, which are only so far right, as they are founded on the law of nature, by which they are to be regulated and interpreted.

VIII. OF THE BEGINNING OF POLITICAL SOCIETIES

95. Men being, as has been said, by nature, all free, equal, and independent, no one can be put out of this estate, and subjected to the political power of an-other, without his own consent. The only way, whereby any one divests himself of his natural liberty, and puts on the bonds of civil society, is by agreeing with other men to join and unite into a community, for their comfortable, safe, and peaceable living one amongst another, in a secure enjoyment of their properties, and a greater security against any, that are not of it. This any number of men may do, because it injures not the freedom of the rest; they are left as they were in the liberty of the state of nature. When any number of men have so consented to make one community or government, they are thereby presently incorporated, and make one body politic, wherein the majority have a right to act and conclude the rest.

96. For when any number of men have, by the consent of every individual, made a community, they have thereby made that community one body, with a power to act as one body, which is only by the will and determination of the majority: for that which acts any community, being only the consent of the individuals of it, and it being necessary to that which is one body to move one way; it is necessary the body should move that way whither the greater force carries it, which is the consent of the majority: or else it is impossible it should act or continue one body, one community, which the consent of every individual that united into it, agreed that it should; and so every one is bound by that consent to be concluded by the majority. And therefore we see, that in assemblies, impowered to act by positive laws, where no number is set by that positive law which impowers them, the act of the majority passes for the act of the whole, and of course determines; as having, by the law of nature and reason, the power of the whole.

97. And thus every man, by consent-

ing with others to make one body politic under one government, puts himself under an obligation, to every one of that society, to submit to the determination of the majority, and to be concluded by it; or else this original compact, whereby he with others incorporate into one society, would signify nothing, and be no compact, if he be left free, and under no other ties than he was in before in the state of nature. For what appearance would there be of any compact? what new engagement if he were no farther tied by any decrees of the society, than he himself thought fit, and did actually consent to? This would be still as great a liberty, as he himself had before his compact, or any one else in the state of nature hath, who may submit himself, and consent to any acts of it if he thinks fit.

98. For if the consent of the majority shall not, in reason, be received as the act of the whole, and conclude every individual; nothing but the consent of every individual can make any thing to be the act of the whole: but such a consent is next to impossible ever to be had, if we consider the infirmities of health, and avocations of business, which in a number, though much less than that of a commonwealth, will necessarily keep many away from the public assembly. To which if we add the variety of opinions, and contrariety of interest, which unavoidably happen in all collections of men, the coming into society upon such terms would be only like Cato's coming into the theatre, only to go out again. Such a constitution as this would make the mighty leviathan of a shorter duration, than the feeblest creatures, and not let it outlast the day it was born in: which cannot be supposed, till we can think, that rational creatures should desire and constitute societies only to be dissolved; for where

the majority cannot conclude the rest, there they cannot act as one body, and consequently will be immediately dissolved again.

99. Whosoever therefore out of a state of nature unite into a community, must be understood to give up all the power, necessary to the ends for which they unite into society, to the majority of the community, unless they expressly agreed in any number greater than the majority. And this is done by barely agreeing to unite into one political society, which is all the compact that is, or needs be, between the individuals, that enter into, or make up a commonwealth. And thus that, which begins and actually constitutes any political society, is nothing, but the consent of any number of freemen capable of a majority, to unite and incorporate into such a society. And this is that, and that only, which did, or could give beginning to any lawful government in the world.

105. I will not deny, that if we look back as far as history will direct us, towards the original of commonwealths, we shall generally find them under the government and administration of one man. And I am also apt to believe, that where a family was numerous enough to subsist by itself, and continued entire together, without mixing with others, as it often happens, where there is much land, and few people, the government commonly began in the father; for the father having, by the law of nature, the same power with every man else to punish, as he thought fit, any offences against that law, might thereby punish his transgressing children, even when they were men, and out of their pupilage; and they were very likely to submit to his punishment, and all join with him against the offender, in their turns, giving him thereby power to execute his sentence against any transgression, and

so in effect make him the law maker, and governour over all that remained in conjunction with his family. He was fittest to be trusted; paternal affection secured their property and interest under his care; and the custom of obeying him, in their childhood, made it easier to submit to him, rather than to any other. If, therefore, they must have one to rule them, as government is hardly to be avoided amongst men that live together; who so likely to be the man as he that was their common father; unless negligence, cruelty, or any other defect of mind or body made him unfit for it? But when either the father died, and left his next heir, for want of age, wisdom, courage, or any other qualities, less fit for rule; or where several families met, and consented to continue together; there, it is not to be doubted, but they used their natural freedom to set up him whom they judged the ablest, and most likely to rule well over them. Conformable hereunto we find the people of America, who (living out of the reach of the conquering swords, and spreading domination of the two great empires of Peru and Mexico) enjoyed their own natural freedom, though, *cæteris paribus,* they commonly prefer the heir of their deceased king; yet, if they find him any way weak, or incapable, they pass him by, and set up the stoutest and bravest man for their ruler.

XI. OF THE ENDS OF POLITICAL SOCIETY AND GOVERNMENT

123. If man in the state of nature be so free, as has been said; if he be absolute lord of his own person and possessions, equal to the greatest, and subject to nobody, why will he part with his freedom? why will he give up his empire, and subject himself to the dominion and control of any other power? To which it is obvious to answer, that though in the state of nature he hath such a right, yet the enjoyment of it is very uncertain, and constantly exposed to the invasion of others; for all being kings as much as he, every man his equal, and the greater part no strict observers of equity and justice, the enjoyment of the property he has in this state is very unsafe, very unsecure. This makes him willing to quit a condition, which, however free, is full of fears and continual dangers: and it is not without reason, that he seeks out, and is willing to join in society with others, who are already united, or have a mind to unit, for the mutual preservation of their lives, liberties, and estates, which I call by the general name, property.

124. The great and chief end, therefore, of men's uniting into commonwealths, and putting themselves under government, is the preservation of their property. To which in the state of nature there are many things wanting.

First, There wants an established, settled, known law, received and allowed by common consent to be the standard of right and wrong, and the common measure to decide all controversies between them: for though the law of nature be plain and intelligible to all rational creatures; yet men being biassed by their interest, as well as ignorant for want of studying it, are not apt to allow of it as a law binding to them in the application of it to their particular cases.

125. Secondly, In the state of nature there wants a known and indifferent judge, with authority to determine all differences according to the established law: for every one in that state being both judge and executioner of the law of nature, men being partial to them-

selves, passion and revenge is very apt to carry them too far, and with too much heat, in their own cases; as well as negligence, and unconcernedness, to make them too remiss in other men's.

126. Thirdly, In the state of nature, there often wants power to back and support the sentence when right, and to give it due execution. They who by any injustice offend, will seldom fail, where they are able, by force to make good their injustice; such resistance many times makes the punishment dangerous, and frequently destructive, to those who attempt it.

127. Thus mankind, notwithstanding all the privileges of the state of nature, being but in an ill condition, while they remain in it, are quickly driven into society. Hence it comes to pass that we seldom find any number of men live any time together in this state. The inconveniencies that they are therein exposed to, by the irregular and uncertain exercise of the power every man has of punishing the transgressions of others, make them take sanctuary under the established laws of government, and therein seek the preservation of their property. It is this makes them so willingly give up every one his single power of punishing, to be exercised by such alone, as shall be appointed to it amongst them; and by such rules as the community, or those authorized by them to that purpose, shall agree on. And in this we have the original right of both the legislative and executive power, as well as of the governments and societies themselves.

128. For in the state of nature, to omit the liberty he has of innocent delights, a man has two powers.

The first is to do whatsoever he thinks fit for the preservation of himself and others within the permission of the law of nature: by which law, common to them all, he and all the rest of mankind are one community, make up one society, distinct from all other creatures. And, were it not for the corruption and viciousness of degenerate men, there would be no need of any other; no necessity that men should separate from this great and natural community, and by positive agreements combine into smaller and divided associations.

The other power a man has in the state of nature, is the power to punish the crimes committed against that law. Both these he gives up, when he joins in a private, if I may so call it, or particular politic society, and incorporates into any commonwealth, separate from the rest of mankind.

129. The first power, viz. "of doing whatsoever he thought fit for the preservation of himself," and the rest of mankind, he gives up to be regulated by laws made by the society, so far forth as the preservation of himself and the rest of that society shall require; which laws of the society in many things confine the liberty he had by the law of nature.

130. Secondly, The power of punishing he wholly gives up, and engages his natural force, (which he might before employ in the execution of the law of nature, by his own single authority, as he thought fit) to assist the executive power of the society, as the law thereof shall require: for being now in a new state, wherein he is to enjoy many conveniencies, from the labour, assistance, and society of others in the same community, as well as protection from its whole strength; he is to part also, with as much of his natural liberty, in providing for himself, as the good, prosperity, and safety of the society shall require; which is not only necessary, but just, since the other members of the society do the like.

131. But though men, when they enter into society, give up the equality, liberty, and executive power they had in the state of nature, into the hands of the society, to be so far disposed of by the legislative, as the good of the society shall require; yet it being only with an intention in every one the better to preserve himself, his liberty and property; (for no rational creature can be supposed to change his condition with an intention to be worse) the power of the society, or legislative constituted by them, can never be supposed to extend farther, than the common good; but is obliged to secure every one's property, by providing against those three defects above mentioned, that made the state of nature so unsafe and uneasy. And so whoever has the legislative or supreme power of any commonwealth, is bound to govern by established standing laws, promulgated and known to the people, and not by extemporary decrees; by indifferent and upright judges, who are to decide controversies by those laws; and to employ the force of the community at home, only in the execution of such laws; or abroad to prevent or redress foreign injuries, and secure the community from inroads and invasion. And all this to be directed to no other end, but the peace, safety, and public good of the people.

Social and Political Values

Little mention can be made of any aspect of liberalism without touching on its values and ideals, for moralism pervades its treatment of all important social and political questions. It is important, nevertheless, to bring these values forward for explicit treatment. The writings of Montesquieu (1689–1755) and the Declaration of Independence, written in 1776, serve this purpose.

Montesquieu's major work, *The Spirit of the Laws,* is a wide-ranging and diffuse book that occasionally states doctrines that are difficult to classify. As the title indicates, the study seeks to uncover the *spirit* of laws, an effort that took Montesquieu into many aspects of history as well as into the gradually expanding, yet still infant, science of comparative anthropology. The relative simplicity of the available data allowed Montesquieu to make generalizations and classifications that a more recent writer would be embarrassed to develop. Yet his penetrating insights and superior style save the work from oblivion and indeed make it still valuable to the student today.

The spirit of the laws of a society depends on many factors—environment, forms of government, values held by citizens—and Montesquieu explores them all in the light of the evidence he has. While his method seems factual and empirical, he nevertheless has his own preferences and values, and he is not adverse to expressing them or judging situations by them. As with Locke and other liberals, Montesquieu's chief concern is with freedom and equality. Liberty, he says, "can consist only in doing what we ought to will, and in not being constrained to do what we ought not to do." This may seem to be a more authoritarian definition than Locke's "right to live as seems good to the individual" until it is remembered that Montesquieu gives his definition an individualistic setting. For liberals generally, liberty is not a matter of being consistent with the common good as in realism; nor as with Hobbes, the right to do what the laws do not forbid; nor as in Machiavelli, the right to participate in government; nor as Bodin, the security of external possessions and family rights: liberty is essentially the right of self-determination limited only by respect for the same right of others.

Montesquieu finds that *virtue* is the essential principle of democracies, but the "natural place of virtue is near to liberty." With other liberals, he is interested in equality as a condition of freedom (note his assertions that when the spirit of equality is either extinct or extreme, the principle of democracy is corrupt) and in the structure of governmental organization as a preserver of freedom. The latter problem of Montesquieu and other liberals is treated in the next section.

The second document is the Declaration of Independence. This historically important state paper is an almost perfect brief summary of the fundamental assumptions of liberalism as the American Enlightenment sought to express them. Confidence in the beneficent order of Nature, as Montesquieu would put it, is manifest in the appeal of the first paragraph to "the separate and equal station to which the Laws of Nature and of Nature's God entitle them." The criterion used in the second paragraph is self-evidence, a rationalistic, almost mathematical principle. This itself is significant, for by its use of self-evidence, the Declaration is rejecting many of the traditional sanctions of political values such as metaphysics and theology. Men are created equal or, as Locke wrote, "Princes indeed are born superior unto other men in power, but in nature equal." Men are as well endowed with "certain unalienable Rights," and they institute governments to secure them. Perhaps the most important word in the entire document is "deriving," for the just powers of government derive from the consent of the governed. Government is an agency serving human rights, and "whenever any Form of Government becomes destructive of these ends, it is the Right of the People to alter or to abolish it, and to institute new Government." The remainder of the Declaration presents detailed charges against invasions by the British crown on the rights of the people.

These ideals and principles—equality, rights, life, liberty, happiness, consent—are the traditional liberal values. They are also matters of reason, for the liberals of the day drew the implication from Sir Isaac Newton's work that the method of reason should be used to reach secure conclusions in moral and political affairs. Regularities and certainties are available to open eyes and inquiring minds; and the values that should govern the affairs of men are among those certainties.

BARON DE MONTESQUIEU Liberty, Equality, and the Republic

OF THE PRINCIPLE
OF DEMOCRACY

There is no great share of probity necessary to support a monarchical or despotic government. The force of laws in one, and the prince's arm in the other, are sufficient to direct and maintain the whole. But in a popular state, one spring more is necessary, namely, virtue.

From Montesquieu, *The Spirit of Laws,* trans. Thomas Nagent, New York: Colonial Press, 1900.

What I have here advanced is confirmed by the unanimous testimony of historians, and is extremely agreeable to the nature of things. For it is clear that in a monarchy, where he who commands the execution of the laws generally thinks himself above them, there is less need of virtue than in a popular government, where the person intrusted with the execution of the laws is sensible of his being subject to their direction.

Clear is it also that a monarch who, through bad advice or indolence, ceases to enforce the execution of the laws, may easily repair the evil; he has only to follow other advice, or to shake off this indolence. But when, in a popular government, there is a suspension of the laws, as this can proceed only from the corruption of the republic, the state is certainly undone.

A very droll spectacle it was in the last century to behold the impotent efforts of the English towards the establishment of democracy. As they who had a share in the direction of public affairs were void of virtue; as their ambition was inflamed by the success of the most daring of their members,[1] as the prevailing parties were successively animated by the spirit of faction, the government was continually changing: the people, amazed at so many revolutions, in vain attempted to erect a commonwealth. At length, when the country had undergone the most violent shocks, they were obliged to have recourse to the very government which they had so wantonly proscribed.

When Sylla thought of restoring Rome to her liberty, this unhappy city was incapable of receiving that blessing. She had only the feeble remains of virtue, which were continually diminishing. Instead of being roused from her lethargy by Cæsar, Tiberius, Caius Claudius, Nero, and Domitian, she riveted every day her chains; if she struck some blows, her aim was at the tyrant, not at the tyranny.

The politic Greeks, who lived under a popular government, knew no other support than virtue. The modern inhabitants of that country are entirely taken up with manufacture, commerce, finances, opulence, and luxury.

When virtue is banished, ambition invades the minds of those who are disposed to receive it, and avarice possesses the whole community. The objects of their desires are changed; what they were fond of before has become indifferent; they were free while under the restraint of laws, but they would fain now be free to act against law; and as each citizen is like a slave who has run away from his master, that which was a maxim of equity he calls rigor; that which was a rule of action he styles constraint; and to precaution he gives the name of fear. Frugality, and not the thirst of gain, now passes for avarice. Formerly the wealth of individuals constituted the public treasure; but now this has become the patrimony of private persons. The members of the commonwealth riot on the public spoils, and its strength is only the power of a few, and the license of many.

Athens was possessed of the same number of forces when she triumphed so gloriously as when with such infamy she was enslaved. She had twenty thousand citizens, when she defended the Greeks against the Persians, when she contended for empire with Sparta, and invaded Sicily. She had twenty thousand when Demetrius Phalereus numbered them, as slaves are told by the head in

---

[1] The reference is to Cromwell. *Ed.*

a market-place. When Philip attempted to lord it over Greece, and appeared at the gates of Athens, she had even then lost nothing but time. We may see in Demosthenes how difficult it was to awaken her; she dreaded Philip, not as the enemy of her liberty, but of her pleasures. This famous city, which had withstood so many defeats, and having been so often destroyed had as often risen out of her ashes, was overthrown at Chæronea, and at one blow deprived of all hopes of resource. What does it avail her that Philip sends back her prisoners, if he does not return her men? It was ever after as easy to triumph over the forces of Athens as it had been difficult to subdue her virtue.

How was it possible for Carthage to maintain her ground? When Hannibal, upon his being made prætor, endeavored to hinder the magistrates from plundering the republic, did not they complain of him to the Romans? Wretches, who would fain be citizens without a city, and be beholden for their riches to their very destroyers! Rome soon insisted upon having three hundred of their principal citizens as hostages; she obliged them next to surrender their arms and ships; and then she declared war. From the desperate efforts of this defenceless city, one may judge of what she might have performed in her full vigor, and assisted by virtue.

OF THE PRINCIPLE OF ARISTOCRACY

As virtue is necessary in a popular government, it is requisite also in an aristocracy. True it is that in the latter it is not so absolutely requisite.

The people, who in respect to the nobility are the same as the subjects with regard to a monarch, are restrained by their laws. They have, therefore, less

occasion for virtue than the people in a democracy. But how are the nobility to be restrained? They who are to execute the laws against their colleagues will immediately perceive that they are therefore necessary in this body, from the very nature of the constitution.

An aristocratic government has an inherent vigor, unknown to democracy. The nobles form a body, who by their prerogative, and for their own particular interest, restrain the people; it is sufficient that there are laws in being to see them executed.

But easy as it may be for the body of the nobles to restrain the people, it is difficult to restrain themselves. Such is the nature of this constitution, that it seems to subject the very same persons to the power of the laws, and at the same time to exempt them.

Now such a body as this can restrain itself only in two ways; either by a very eminent virtue, which puts the nobility in some measure on a level with the people, and may be the means of forming a great republic; or by an inferior virtue, which puts them at least upon a level with one another, and upon this their preservation depends.

Moderation is therefore the very soul of this government; a moderation, I mean, founded on virtue, not that which proceeds from indolence and pusillanimity.

OF THE CORRUPTION OF THE PRINCIPLES OF DEMOCRACY

The principle of democracy is corrupted not only when the spirit of equality is extinct, but likewise when they fall into a spirit of extreme equality, and when each citizen would fain be upon a level with those whom he has chosen to command him. Then the people, incapable of bearing the very power they have delegated, want to manage everything themselves, to debate for the senate, to execute for the magistrate, and to decide for the judges.

When this is the case, virtue can no longer subsist in the republic. The people are desirous of exercising the functions of the magistrates, who cease to be revered. The deliberations of the senate are slighted; all respect is then laid aside for the senators, and consequently for old age. If there is no more respect for old age, there will be none presently for parents; deference to husbands will be likewise thrown off, and submission to masters. This license will soon become general, and the trouble of command be as fatiguing as that of obedience. Wives, children, slaves will shake off all subjection. No longer will there be any such thing as manners, order, or virtue.

We find in Xenophon's Banquet a very lively description of a republic in which the people abused their equality. Each guest gives in his turn the reason why he is satisfied. "Content I am," says Chamides, "because of my poverty. When I was rich, I was obliged to pay my court to informers, knowing I was more liable to be hurt by them than capable of doing them harm. The republic constantly demanded some new tax of me; and I could not decline paying. Since I have grown poor, I have acquired authority; nobody threatens me; I rather threaten others. I can go or stay where I please. The rich already rise from their seats and give me the way. I am a king, I was before a slave: I paid taxes to the republic, now it maintains me: I am no longer afraid of losing: but I hope to acquire."

The people fall into this misfortune, when those in whom they confide, desirous of concealing their own corruption, endeavor to corrupt them. To disguise their own ambition, they speak to them only of the grandeur of the state; to conceal their own avarice, they incessantly flatter theirs.

The corruption will increase among the corruptors, and likewise among those who are already corrupted. The people will divide the public money among themselves, and, having added the administration of affairs to their indolence, will be for blending their poverty with the amusements of luxury. But with their indolence and luxury, nothing but the public treasure will be able to satisfy their demands.

We must not be surprised to see their suffrages given for money. It is impossible to make great largesses to the people without great extortion: and to compass this, the state must be subverted. The greater the advantages they seem to derive from their liberty, the nearer they approach towards the critical moment of losing it. Petty tyrants arise who have all the vices of a single tyrant. The small remains of liberty soon become insupportable; a single tyrant starts up, and the people are stripped of every thing, even of the profits of their corruption.

Democracy has, therefore, two excesses to avoid—the spirit of inequality, which leads to aristocracy or monarchy, and the spirit of extreme equality, which leads to despotic power, as the latter is completed by conquest.

True it is, that those who corrupted the Greek republics did not always become tyrants. This was because they had a greater passion for eloquence than for the military art. Besides there reigned an implacable hatred in the breasts of the Greeks against those who subverted a republican government; and for this reason anarchy degenerated into annihilation, instead of being changed into tyranny.

But Syracuse being situated in the midst of a great number of petty states, whose government had been changed from oligarchy to tyranny, and being governed by a senate scarcely ever mentioned in history, underwent such miseries as are the consequence of a more than ordinary corruption. This city, ever a prey to licentiousness, or oppression, equally laboring under the sudden and alternate succession of liberty and servitude, and notwithstanding her external strength, constantly determined to a revolution by the least foreign power— this city, I say, had in her bosom an immense multitude of people, whose fate it was to have always this cruel alternative, either of choosing a tyrant to govern them, or of acting the tyrant themselves.

Of the Spirit of Extreme Equality

As distant as heaven is from earth, so is the true spirit of equality from that of extreme equality. The former does not imply that everybody should command, or that no one should be commanded, but that we obey or command our equals. It endeavors not to shake off the authority of a master, but that its masters should be none but its equals.

In the state of nature, indeed, all men are born equal, but they cannot continue in this equality. Society makes them lose it, and they recover it only by the protection of the laws.

Such is the difference between a well-regulated democracy and one that is not so, that in the former men are equal only as citizens, but in the latter they are equal also as magistrates, as senators, as judges, as fathers, as husbands, or as masters.

The natural place of virtue is near to liberty; but it is not nearer to excessive liberty than to servitude.

In What Manner Republics Provide for Their Safety

If a republic be small, it is destroyed by a foreign force; if it be large, it is ruined by an internal imperfection.

To this twofold inconvenience democracies and aristocracies are equally liable, whether they be good or bad. The evil is in the very thing itself, and no form can redress it.

It is, therefore, very probable that mankind would have been, at length, obliged to live constantly under the government of a single person, had they not contrived a kind of constitution that has all the internal advantages of a republican, together with the external force of a monarchical, government. I mean a confederate republic.

This form of government is a convention by which several petty states agree to become members of a larger one, which they intend to establish. It is a kind of assemblage of societies, that constitute a new one, capable of increasing by means of further associations, till they arrive at such a degree of power as to be able to provide for the security of the whole body.

It was these associations that so long contributed to the prosperity of Greece. By these the Romans attacked the whole globe, and by these alone the whole globe withstood them; for when Rome had arrived at her highest pitch of grandeur, it was the associations beyond the Danube and the Rhine—associations formed by the terror of her arms—that enabled the barbarians to resist her.

Hence it proceeds that Holland, Germany, and the Swiss cantons are considered in Europe as perpetual republics.

The associations of cities were formerly more necessary than in our times. A weak, defenceless town was exposed to greater danger. By conquest it was deprived not only of the executive and legislative power, as at present, but, moreover, of all human property.

A republic of this kind, able to withstand an external force, may support itself without any internal corruption; the form of this society prevents all manner of inconveniences.

If a single member should attempt to usurp the supreme power, he could not be supposed to have an equal authority and credit in all the confederate states. Were he to have too great an influence over one, this would alarm the rest; were he to subdue a part, that which would still remain free might oppose him with forces independent of those which he had usurped, and overpower him before he could be settled in his usurpation.

Should a popular insurrection happen in one of the confederate states, the others are able to quell it. Should abuses creep into one part, they are reformed by those that remain sound. The state may be destroyed on one side, and not on the other; the confederacy may be dissolved, and the confederates preserve their sovereignty.

As this government is composed of petty republics, it enjoys the internal happiness of each; and with regard to its external situation, by means of the association, it possesses all the advantages of large monarchies.

DIFFERENT SIGNIFICATIONS OF THE WORD LIBERTY

There is no word that admits of more various significations, and has made more varied impressions on the human mind, than that of liberty. Some have taken it as a means of deposing a person on whom they had conferred a tyrannical authority; others for the power of choosing a superior whom they are obliged to obey; others for the right of bearing arms, and of being thereby enabled to use violence; others, in fine, for the privilege of being governed by a native of their own country, or by their own laws. A certain nation for a long time thought liberty consisted in the privilege of wearing a long beard. Some have annexed this name to one form of government exclusive of others: those who had a republican taste applied it to this species of polity; those who liked a monarchical state gave it to monarchy. Thus they have all applied the name of liberty to the government most suitable to their own customs and inclinations: and as in republics the people have not so constant and so present a view of the causes of their misery, and as the magistrates seem to act only in conformity to the laws, hence liberty is generally said to reside in republics, and to be banished from monarchies. In fine, as in democracies the people seem to act almost as they please, this sort of government has been deemed the most free, and the power of the people has been confounded with their liberty.

IN WHAT LIBERTY CONSISTS

It is true that in democracies the people seem to act as they please; but political liberty does not consist in an unlimited freedom. In governments, that is, in societies directed by laws, liberty can consist only in the power of doing what we ought to will, and in not being constrained to do what we ought not to will.

We must have continually present to our minds the difference between independence and liberty. Liberty is a right of doing whatever the laws permit, and if a citizen could do what they forbid he would be no longer possessed of liberty, because all his fellow-citizens would have the same power.

THE SAME SUBJECT CONTINUED

Democratic and aristocratic states are not in their own nature free. Political liberty is to be found only in moderate governments; and even in these it is not always found. It is there only when there is no abuse of power. But constant experience shows us that every man invested with power is apt to abuse it, and to carry his authority as far as it will go. Is it not strange, though true, to say that virtue itself has need of limits?

To prevent this abuse, it is necessary from the very nature of things that power should be a check to power. A government may be so constituted as no man shall be compelled to do things to which the law does not oblige him, nor forced to abstain from things which the law permits.

THE DECLARATION OF INDEPENDENCE

The Pursuit of Happiness

IN CONGRESS, JULY 4, 1776, THE UNANIMOUS DECLARATION OF THE THIRTEEN UNITED STATES OF AMERICA

When in the Course of human events, it becomes necessary for one people to dissolve the political bands which have connected them with another, and to assume among the Powers of the earth the separate and equal station to which the Laws of Nature and of Nature's God entitle them, a decent respect to the opinions of mankind requires that they should declare the causes which impel them to the separation.

We hold these truths to be self-evident, that all men are created equal, that they are endowed by their Creator with certain unalienable Rights, that among these are Life, Liberty and the pursuit of Happiness. That to secure these rights, governments are instituted among Men, deriving their just powers from the consent of the governed. That whenever any Form of Government becomes destructive of these ends, it is the Right of the People to alter or to abolish it, and to institute new Government, laying its foundation on such principles and organizing its powers in such form, as to them shall seem most likely to effect their Safety and Happiness. Prudence, indeed, will dictate that Governments long established should not be changed for light and transient causes; and accordingly all experience hath shown, that mankind are more disposed to suffer, while evils are sufferable, than to right themselves by abolishing the forms to which they are accustomed. But when a long train of abuses and usurpations, pursuing invariably the same Object evinces a design to reduce them under absolute Despotism, it is their right, it is their duty, to throw off such Government,

From *The Constitutions of the United States,* Winchester, Virginia, 1811.

and to provide new Guards for their future security. Such has been the patient sufferance of these Colonies; and such is now the necessity which constrains them to alter their former Systems of Government. The history of the present King of Great Britain is a history of repeated injuries and usurpations, all having in direct object the establishment of an absolute Tyranny over these States. To prove this, let Facts be submitted to a candid world.

He has refused his Assent to Laws, the most wholesome and necessary for the public good.

He has forbidden his Governors to pass Laws of immediate and pressing importance, unless suspended in their operation till his Assent should be obtained; and when so suspected, he has utterly neglected to attend to them.

He has refused to pass other Laws for the accommodation of large districts of people, unless those people would relinquish the right of Representation in the Legislature, a right inestimable to them and formidable to tyrants only.

He has called together legislative bodies at places unusual, uncomfortable, and distant from the depository of their Public Records, for the sole purpose of fatiguing them into compliance with his measures.

He has dissolved Representative Houses repeatedly, for opposing with manly firmness his invasions on the rights of the people.

He has refused for a long time, after such dissolutions, to cause others to be elected, whereby the Legislative Powers, incapable of Annihilation, have returned to the People at large for their exercise; the State remaining in the mean time exposed to all the dangers of invasion from without, and convulsions within.

He has endeavored to prevent the population of these States; for that purpose obstructing the Laws of Naturalization of Foreigners; refusing to pass others to encourage their migration hither; and raising the conditions of new Appropriations of Lands.

He has obstructed the Administrations of Justice, by refusing his Assent to Laws for establishing Judiciary Powers.

He has made Judges dependent on his Will alone, for the tenure of their offices, and the amount and payment of their salaries.

He has erected a multitude of New Offices, and sent hither swarms of Officers to harass our People, and eat out their substance.

He has kept among us, in times of peace, Standing Armies without the Consent of our Legislature.

He has affected to render the Military independent of and superior to the Civil Power.

He has combined with others to subject us to a jurisdiction foreign to our constitution, and unacknowledged by our laws; giving his Assent to their acts of pretended legislation:

For quartering large bodies of armed troops among us:

For protecting them, by a mock Trial, from Punishment for any Murders which they should commit on the Inhabitants of these States:

For cutting off our Trade with all parts of the world:

For imposing taxes on us without our Consent:

For depriving us in many cases, of the benefits of Trial by Jury:

For transporting us beyond Seas to be tried for pretended offenses:

For abolishing the free System of English Laws in a neighbouring Province, establishing therein an Arbitrary government, and enlarging its Boundaries so as to render it at once an example and fit instrument for introducing the same absolute rule into these Colonies:

For taking away our Charters, abolishing our most valuable Laws, and altering fundamentally the Forms of our Governments:

For suspending our own Legislature, and declaring themselves invested with Power to legislate for us in all cases whatsoever.

He has abdicated Government here, by declaring us out of his Protection and waging War against us.

He has plundered our seas, ravaged our Coasts, burnt our towns, and destroyed the lives of our people.

He is at this time transporting large armies of foreign mercenaries to compleat the works of death, desolation and tyranny, already begun with circumstances of Cruelty & perfidy scarcely paralleled in the most barbarous ages, and totally unworthy the Head of a civilized nation.

He has constrained our fellow Citizens taken Captive on the high Seas to bear Arms against their Country, to become the executioners of their friends and Brethren, or to fall themselves by their Hands.

He has excited domestic insurrections amongst us, and has endeavored to bring on the inhabitants of our frontiers, the merciless Indian Savages, whose known rule of warfare, is an undistinguished destruction of all ages, sexes and conditions.

In every stage of these Oppressions We have Petitioned for Redress in the most humble terms: Our repeated Petitions have been answered only by repeated injury. A Prince, whose character is thus marked by every act which may define a Tyrant, is unfit to be the ruler of a free People.

Nor have We been wanting in attention to our British brethren. We have warned them from time to time of attempts by their legislature to extend an unwarrantable jurisdiction over us. We have reminded them of the circumstances of our emigration and settlement here. We have appealed to their native justice and magnanimity, and we have conjured them by the ties of our common kindred to disavow these usurpations, which, would inevitably interrupt our connections and correspondence. They too have been deaf to the voice of justice and of consanguinity. We must, therefore, acquiesce in the necessity, which denounces our Separation, and hold them, as we hold the rest of mankind, Enemies in War, in Peace Friends.

We, therefore, the Representatives of the united States of America, in General Congress, Assembled, appealing to the Supreme Judge of the World for the rectitude of our intentions, do, in the Name, and by Authority of the good People of these Colonies, solemnly Publish and declare, That these United Colonies are, and of right ought to be Free and Independent States; that they are Absolved from all Allegiance to the British Crown, and that all political connection between them and the State of Great Britain, is and ought to be totally dissolved; and that as Free and Independent States, they have full Power to levy War, conclude Peace, contract Alliances, establish Commerce, and to do all other Acts and Things which Independent States may of right do: And for the support of this Declaration, with a firm reliance on the Protection of Divine Providence, we mutually pledge to each other our Lives, our Fortunes and our sacred Honor.

State, Power, and Authority

For liberals, the state with its power and authority is just and legitimate when it is organized for freedom, and a number of distinctive doctrines have been stated by liberals in developing this insight. The first is the theory of the social compact, which suggests that just government is established by individuals who, through an act of association, consent to a common authority as the agent of their rights.* The people are sovereign, authority is derived from and sanctioned by them, and—resting as it does on consent—the compact is revocable, limited, and conditional.

The writings of Jean Jacques Rousseau (1712–1778) provide one statement of this theory. Rousseau is a complex figure who is exceedingly difficult to classify firmly, for many strands run through his thought and not always consistently. Writing at the end of the Enlightenment and at the beginning of Romanticism, he reflects both movements. He praised the life of feeling, even to disparage reason, yet he believed that justice, for example, is a norm of reason. He seemed at times to find Locke and other liberals too individualistic, yet he believed that individuals have rights, and he defined sovereignty to include these rights. His theory sets up a notion of a general will that has been interpreted as a forerunner of totalitarian states and that paradoxically can force individuals to be free, but he also firmly asserted that justice can never be denied an individual on the pretext that government is serving the common good. Small wonder that there are different interpretations of Rousseau! Nevertheless, there are good grounds for including him in the liberal perspective, primarily for his love of freedom and of equality as a means to freedom.

Rousseau's problem is to explain how a just society can arise. He was convinced that the existing societies of his day were corrupt and enslaving: they made men dependent rather than free and—Stoic values lie behind this judgment—gave them false desires. He was also convinced that men are naturally good, and that the good society would be one that conformed to man's nature and to the freedom that is man's birthright. The problem of political subjection is thus primarily ethical and only secondarily a matter of law and power. Rousseau finds its solution in the social compact, which is an act where each person, in giving himself to all, gives himself to no one. A moral and collective body is established that is itself controlled by the general will. By this somewhat difficult notion Rousseau meant not simply the will of all or of the majority, but the will to justice, to impartiality, to the treatment of the good of others as equally important with one's own good.

The compact thus explains political obligation, for it is a personal act of each citizen. It establishes a moral authority dedicated to justice and it aims at freedom,

* The compact need not be thought of as an historical act: its point is ethical, since it is concerned with the nature of just government. It may be noted that the notion of a social contract is much older than liberalism, having been formulated by Lycophron in classical Greece.

for freedom is obedience to laws men prescribe to themselves. It maintains the consent of the governed and the sovereignty of the people, a sovereignty that is indivisible and inalienable. In all these particulars, Rousseau's theory is precisely the democracy liberals came to understand.

The second major doctrine of liberals is really a collection of ideas about the structure of government. The notions of derived authority and limited government are implicit in liberal values, and many liberal philosophers wrote about the structure that government should have if freedom is to be preserved. Montesquieu, with whom the principle of the separation of powers is especially associated, was an eloquent spokesman of the idea that power must be circumscribed in appropriate ways if freedom is to be preserved. Power, he thought, must be limited by power, and the basic branches of government check the possible abuses of each other. The separation of the judiciary prevents oppression in contempt of the law, and the separation of the legislative and executive branches prevents oppressions by means of the law. Closely related to the system of checks and balances is the principle of freedom discussed in the second selection from *The Federalist*. Different levels of government—local, regional, and national—must have separate and distinct exercises. And finally, liberals have also written of representative government as a scheme to maintain the people's control over the agency dealing with their interests.

JEAN JACQUES ROUSSEAU   The Social Compact

CHAPTER I.

SUBJECT OF THE FIRST BOOK

Man is born free, and everywhere he is in chains. Many a one believes himself the master of others, and yet he is a greater slave than they. How has this change come about? I do not know. What can render it legitimate? I believe that I can settle this question.

If I considered only force and the results that proceed from it, I should say that so long as a people is compelled to obey and does obey, it does well; but that, so soon as it can shake off the yoke and does shake it off, it does better; for, if men recover their freedom by virtue of the same right by which it was taken away, either they are justified in resuming it, or there was no justification for depriving them of it. But the social order is a sacred right which serves as a foundation for all others. This right, however, does not come from nature. It is therefore based on conventions. The question is to know what these conventions are. Before coming to that, I must establish what I have just laid down.

CHAPTER II.

PRIMITIVE SOCIETIES.

The earliest of all societies, and the only natural one, is the family; yet children remain attached to their father only so long as they have need of him for

From Rousseau, *The Social Contract, or Principles of Political Right,* trans. Henry J. Tozer, London: Swan Sonnenschein and Co., 1895.

their own preservation. As soon as this need ceases, the natural bond is dissolved. The children being freed from the obedience which they owed to their father, and the father from the cares which he owed to his children, become equally independent. If they remain united, it is no longer naturally but voluntarily; and the family itself is kept together only by convention.

This common liberty is a consequence of man's nature. His first law is to attend to his preservation, his first cares are those which he owes to himself; and as soon as he comes to years of discretion, being sole judge of the means adapted for his own preservation, he becomes his own master.

The family is, then, if you will, the primitive model of political societies; the chief is the analogue of the father, while the people represent the children; and all, being born free and equal, alienate their liberty only for their own advantage. The whole difference is that, in the family, the father's love for his children repays him for the care that he bestows upon them; while, in the State, the pleasure of ruling makes up for the chief's lack of love for his people.

Grotius denies that all human authority is established for the benefit of the government, and he cites slavery as an instance. His invariable mode of reasoning is to establish right by fact. A juster method might be employed, but none more favorable to tyrants.

It is doubtful then, according to Grotius, whether the human race belongs to a hundred men, or whether these hundred men belong to the human race; and he appears throughout his book to incline to the former opinion, which is also that of Hobbes. In this way we have mankind divided like herds of cattle, each of which has a master, who looks after it in order to devour it.

Just as a herdsman is superior in nature to his herd, so chiefs, who are the herdsmen of men, are superior in nature to their people. Thus, according to Philo's account, the Emperor Caligula reasoned, inferring truly enough from this analogy that kings are gods, or that men are brutes.

The reasoning of Caligula is tantamount to that of Hobbes and Grotius. Aristotle, before them all, had likewise said that men are not naturally equal, but that some are born for slavery and others for dominion.

Aristotle was right, but he mistook the effects for the cause. Every man born in slavery is born for slavery; nothing is more certain. Slaves lose everything in their bonds, even the desire to escape from them; they love their servitude as the companions of Ulysses loved their brutishness. If, then, there are slaves by nature, it is because there have been slaves contrary to nature. The first slaves were made such by force; their cowardice kept them in bondage.

I have said nothing about King Adam nor about Emperor Noah, the father of three great monarchs who shared the universe, like the children of Saturn with whom they are supposed to be identical. I hope that my moderation will give satisfaction; for, as I am a direct descendant of one of these princes, and perhaps of the eldest branch, how do I know whether, by examination of titles, I might not find myself the lawful king of the human race? Be that as it may, it cannot be denied that Adam was sovereign of the world, as Robinson was of his island, so long as he was its sole inhabitant; and it was an agreeable feature of that empire that the monarch, secure on his throne, had nothing to fear from rebellions, or wars, or conspirators.

CHAPTER III.

THE RIGHT OF THE STRONGEST.

The strongest man is never strong enough to be always master, unless he transforms his power into right, and obedience into duty. Hence the right of the strongest—a right apparently assumed in irony, and really established in principle. But will this phrase never be explained to us? Force is a physical power; I do not see what morality can result from its effects. To yield to force is an act of necessity, not of will; it is at most an act of prudence. In what sense can it be a duty?

Let us assume for a moment this pretended right. I say that nothing results from it but inexplicable nonsense; for if force constitutes right, the effect changes with the cause, and any force which overcomes the first succeeds to its rights. As soon as men can disobey with impunity, they may do so legitimately; and since the strongest is always in the right, the only thing is to act in such a way that one may be the strongest. But what sort of a right is it that perishes when force ceases? If it is necessary to obey by compulsion, there is no need to obey from duty; and if men are no longer forced to obey, obligation is at an end. We see, then, that this word *right* adds nothing to force; it here means nothing at all.

Obey the powers that be. If that means, Yield to force, the precept is good but superfluous; I reply that it will never be violated. All power comes from God, I admit; but every disease comes from him too; does it follow that we are prohibited from calling in a physician? If a brigand should surprise me in the recesses of a wood, am I bound not only to give up my purse when forced, but am I also morally bound to do so when

I might conceal it? For, in effect, the pistol which he holds is a superior force.

Let us agree, then, that might does not make right, and that we are bound to obey none but lawful authorities. Thus my original question ever recurs.

CHAPTER IV.

SLAVERY.

Since no man has any natural authority over his fellow-men, and since force is not the source of right, conventions remain as the basis of all lawful authority among men.

If an individual, says Grotius, can alienate his liberty and become the slave of a master, why should not a whole people be able to alienate theirs, and become subject to a king? In this there are many equivocal terms requiring explanation; but let us confine ourselves to the word *alienate*. To alienate is to give or sell. Now, a man who becomes another's slave does not give himself; he sells himself at the very least for his subsistence. But why does a nation sell itself? So far from a king supplying his subjects with their subsistence, he draws his from them; and, according to Rabelais, a king does not live on a little. Do subjects, then, give up their persons on condition that their property also shall be taken? I do not see what is left for them to keep.

It will be said that the despot secures to his subjects civil peace. Be it so; but what do they gain by that, if the wars which his ambition brings upon them, together with his insatiable greed and the vexations of his administration, harass them more than their own dissensions would? What do they gain by it if this tranquillity is itself one of their miseries? Men live tranquilly also in dungeons; is that enough to make them contented there? The Greeks confined in the cave of the Cyclops lived peacefully until their turn came to be devoured.

To say that a man gives himself for nothing is to say what is absurd and inconceivable; such an act is illegitimate and invalid, for the simple reason that he who performs it is not in his right mind. To say the same thing of a whole nation is to suppose a nation of fools; and madness does not confer rights.

Even if each person could alienate himself, he could not alienate his children; they are born free men; their liberty belongs to them, and no one has a right to dispose of it except themselves. Before they have come to years of discretion, the father can, in their name, stipulate conditions for their preservation and welfare, but not surrender them irrevocably and unconditionally; for such a gift is contrary to the ends of nature, and exceeds the rights of paternity. In order, then, that an arbitrary government might be legitimate, it would be necessary that the people in each generation should have the option of accepting or rejecting it; but in that case such a government would no longer be arbitrary.

To renounce one's liberty is to renounce one's quality as a man, the rights and also the duties of humanity. For him who renounces everything there is no possible compensation. Such a renunciation is incompatible with man's nature, for to take away all freedom from his will is to take away all morality from his actions. In short, a convention which stipulates absolute authority on the one side and unlimited obedience on the other is vain and contradictory. Is it not clear that we are under no obligations whatsoever towards a man from whom we have a right to demand everything? And does not this single condition, without equivalent, without exchange, involve the nullity of the act? For what right would my slave have against me, since all that he has belongs to me? His rights being mine, this right of me against myself is a meaningless phrase. . . .

CHAPTER VI.

THE SOCIAL PACT.

I assume that men have reached a point at which the obstacles that endanger their preservation in the state of nature overcomes by their resistance the forces which each individual can exert with a view to maintaining himself in that state. Then this primitive condition can no longer subsist, and the human race would perish unless it changed its mode of existence.

Now, as men cannot create any new forces, but only combine and direct those that exist, they have no other means of self-preservation than to form by aggregation a sum of forces which may overcome the resistance, to put them in action by a single motive power, and to make them work in concert.

This sum of forces can be produced only by the combination of many; but the strength and freedom of each man being the chief instruments of his preservation, how can he pledge them without injuring himself, and without neglecting the cares which he owes to himself? This difficulty, applied to my subject, may be expressed in these terms:—

"To find a form of association which may defend and protect with the whole force of the community the person and property of every associate, and by means of which each, coalescing with all, may nevertheless obey only himself, and remain as free as before." Such is the fundamental problem of which the social contract furnishes the solution.

The clauses of this contract are so determined by the nature of the act that the slightest modification would render them vain and ineffectual; so that, although they have never perhaps been formally enunciated, they are everywhere the same, everywhere tacitly admitted and recognised, until the social pact being violated, each man regains his original rights and recovers his natural liberty, whilst losing the conventional liberty for which he renounced it.

These clauses, rightly understood, are reducible to one only, viz. the total alienation to the whole community of each associate with all his rights; for, in the first place, since each gives himself up entirely, the conditions are equal for all; and, the conditions being equal for all, no one has any interest in making them burdensome to others.

Further, the alienation being made without reserve, the union is as perfect as it can be, and an individual associate can no longer claim anything; for, if any rights were left to individuals, since there would be no common superior who could judge between them and the public, each, being on some point his own judge, would soon claim to be so on all; the state of nature would still subsist, and the association would necessarily become tyrannical or useless.

In short, each giving himself to all, gives himself to nobody; and as there is not one associate over whom we do not acquire the same rights which we concede to him over ourselves, we gain the equivalent of all that we lose, and more power to preserve what we have.

If, then, we set aside what is not of the essence of the social contract, we shall find that it is reducible to the following terms: "Each of us puts in common his person and his whole power under the supreme direction of the general will; and in return we receive every member as an indivisible part of the whole."

Forthwith, instead of the individual personalities of all the contracting parties, this act of association produces a moral and collective body, which is composed of as many members as the assembly has voices, and which receives from this same act its unity, its common self (*moi*), its life, and its will. This public person, which is thus formed by the union of all the individual members, formerly took the name of *city,* and now takes that of *republic* or *body politic*, which is called by its members *State* when it is passive, *sovereign* when it is active, *power* when it is compared to similar bodies. With regard to the associates, they take collectively the name of *people,* and are called individually *citizens*, as participating in the sovereign power, and *subjects,* as subjected to the laws of the State. But these terms are often confused and are mistaken one for another; it is sufficient to know how to distinguish them when they are used with complete precision.

CHAPTER VII.

THE SOVEREIGN.

We see from this formula that the act of association contains a reciprocal engagement between the public and individuals, and that every individual, contracting so to speak with himself, is engaged in a double relation, viz. as a member of the sovereign towards individuals, and as a member of the State towards the sovereign. But we cannot apply here the maxim of civil law that no one is bound by engagements made with himself; for there is a great difference between being bound to oneself and to a whole of which one forms part.

We must further observe that the public resolution which can bind all subjects to the sovereign in consequence of the two different relations under which each of them is regarded cannot, for a contrary reason, bind the sovereign to itself; and that accordingly it is contrary to the nature of the body politic for the sovereign to impose on itself a law which it cannot transgress. As it can only be considered under one and the same relation, it is in the position of an individual contracting with himself; whence we see that there is not, nor can be, any kind of fundamental law binding upon the body of the people, not even the social contract. This does not imply that such a body cannot perfectly well enter into engagements with others in what does not derogate from this contract; for, with regard to foreigners, it becomes a simple being, an individual.

But the body politic or sovereign, deriving its existence only from the sanctity of the contract, can never bind itself, even to others, in anything that derogates from the original act, such as alienation of some portion of itself, or submission to another sovereign. To violate the act by which it exists would be to annihilate itself; and what is nothing produces nothing.

So soon as the multitude is thus united in one body, it is impossible to injure one of the members without attacking the body, still less to injure the body without the members feeling the effects. Thus duty and interest alike oblige the two contracting parties to give mutual assistance; and the men themselves should seek to combine in this twofold relationship all the advantages which are attendant on it.

Now, the sovereign, being formed only of the individuals that compose it, neither has nor can have any interest contrary to theirs; consequently the sovereign power needs no guarantee towards its subjects, because it is impossible that the body should wish to injure all its members; and we shall see hereafter that it can injure no one as an individual. The sovereign, for the simple reason that it is so, is always everything that it ought to be.

But this is not the case as regards the relation of subjects to the sovereign, which, notwithstanding the common interest, would have no security for the performance of their engagements, unless it found means to ensure their fidelity.

Indeed, every individual may, as a man, have a particular will contrary to, or divergent from, the general will which he has as a citizen; his private interest may prompt him quite differently from the common interest; his absolute and naturally independent existence may make him regard what he owes to the common cause as a gratuitous contribution, the loss of which will be less harmful to others than the payment of it will be burdensome to him; and, regarding the moral person that constitutes the State as an imaginary being because it is not a man, he would be willing to enjoy the rights of a citizen without being willing to fulfil the duties of a subject. The progress of such injustice would bring the ruin of the body politic.

In order, then, that the social pact may not be a vain formulary, it tacitly includes this engagement, which can alone give force to the others,—that whoever refuses to obey the general will shall be constrained to do so by the whole body; which means nothing else than that he shall be forced to be free; for such is the condition which, uniting every citizen to his native land, guarantees him from all personal dependence, a condition that ensures the control and working of the political machine, and alone renders legitimate civil engagements, which, without it, would be absurd and tyrannical, and subject to the most enormous abuses.

CHAPTER VIII.

THE CIVIL STATE.

The passage from the state of nature to the civil state produces in man a very remarkable change, by substituting in his conduct justice for instinct, and by giving his actions the moral quality that they previously lacked. It is only when the voice of duty succeeds physical impulse, and law succeeds appetite, that man, who till then had regarded only himself, sees that he is obliged to act on other principles, and to consult his reason before listening to his inclinations. Although, in this state, he is deprived of many advantages that he derives from nature, he acquires equally great ones in return; his faculties are exercised and developed; his ideas are expanded; his feelings are ennobled; his whole soul is exalted to such a degree that, if the abuses of this new condition did not often degrade him below that from which he has emerged, he ought to bless without ceasing the happy moment that released him from it for ever, and transformed him from a stupid and ignorant animal into an intelligent being and a man.

Let us reduce this whole balance to terms easy to compare. What man loses by the social contract is his natural liberty and an unlimited right to anything which tempts him and which he is able to attain; what he gains is civil liberty and property in all that he possesses. In order that we may not be mistaken about these compensations, we must clearly distinguish natural liberty, which is limited only by the powers of the individual, from civil liberty, which is limited by the general will; and possession, which is nothing but the result of force or the right of first occupancy, from property, which can be based only on a positive title.

Besides the preceding, we might add to the acquisitions of the civil state moral freedom, which alone renders man truly master of himself; for the impulse of mere appetite is slavery, while obedience to a self-prescribed law is liberty. But I have already said too much on this head, and the philosophical meaning of the term *liberty* does not belong to my present subject.

CHAPTER VI.

THE LAW.

By the social compact we have given existence and life to the body politic; the question now is to endow it with movement and will by legislation. For the original act by which this body is formed and consolidated determines nothing in addition as to what it must do for its own preservation.

What is right and conformable to order is such by the nature of things, and independently of human conventions. All justice comes from God, he alone is the source of it; but could we receive it directly from so lofty a source, we should need neither government nor laws. Without doubt there is a universal justice emanating from reason alone; but this justice, in order to be admitted among us, should be reciprocal. Regarding things from a human standpoint, the laws of justice are inoperative among men for want of a natural sanction; they only bring good to the wicked and evil to the just when the latter observe them with every one, and no one observes them in return. Conventions and laws, then, are necessary to couple rights with duties and apply justice to its object. In the state of nature, where everything is in common, I owe nothing to those to whom I have promised nothing; I recognize as belonging to others only what is useless to me. This is not the case in the civil state, in which all rights are determined by law.

But then, finally, what is a law? So long as men are content to attach to this word only metaphysical ideas, they will continue to argue without being understood; and when they have stated what a law of nature is, they will know no better what a law of the State is.

I have already said that there is no general will with reference to a particular object. In fact, this particular object is either in the State or outside of it. If it is outside the State, a will which is foreign to it is not general in relation to it; and if it is within the State, it forms part of it; then there is formed between the whole and its part a relation which makes of it two separate beings, of which the part is one, and the whole, less this same part, is the other. But the whole less one part is not the whole, and so long as the relation subsists, there is no longer any whole, but two unequal parts; whence it follows that the will of the one is no longer general in relation to the other.

But when the whole people decree concerning the whole people, they consider themselves alone; and if a relation is then constituted, it is between the whole object under one point of view and the whole object under another point of view, without any division at all. Then the matter respecting which they decree is general like the will that decrees. It is this act that I call a law.

When I say that the object of the laws is always general, I mean that the law considers subjects collectively, and ac-

tions as abstract, never a man as an individual nor a particular action. Thus the law may indeed decree that there shall be privileges, but cannot confer them on any person by name; the law can create several classes of citizens, and even assign the qualifications which shall entitle them to rank in these classes, but it cannot nominate such and such persons to be admitted to them; it can establish a royal government and a hereditary succession, but cannot elect a king or appoint a royal family; in a word, no function which has reference to an individual object appertains to the legislative power.

From this standpoint we see immediately that it is no longer necessary to ask whose office it is to make laws, since they are acts of the general will; nor whether the prince is above the laws, since he is a member of the State; nor whether the law can be unjust, since no one is unjust to himself; nor how we are free and yet subject to the laws, since the laws are only registers of our wills.

We see, further, that since the law combines the universality of the will with the universality of the object, whatever any man prescribes on his own authority is not a law; and whatever the sovereign itself prescribes respecting a particular object is not a law, but a decree, not an act of sovereignty, but of magistracy.

I therefore call any State a republic which is governed by laws, under whatever form of administration it may be; for then only does the public interest predominate and the commonwealth count for something. Every legitimate government is republican; I will explain hereafter what government is.

Laws are properly only the conditions of civil association. The people, being subjected to the laws, should be the authors of them; it concerns only the associates to determine the conditions of association. But how will they be determined? Will it be by a common agreement, by a sudden inspiration? Has the body politic an organ for expressing its will? Who will give it the foresight necessary to frame its acts and publish them at the outset? Or how shall it declare them in the hour of need? How would a blind multitude, which often knows not what it wishes because it rarely knows what is good for it, execute of itself an enterprise so great, so difficult, as a system of legislation? Of themselves, the people always desire what is good, but do not always discern it. The general will is always right, but the judgment which guides it is not always enlightened. It must be made to see objects as they are, sometimes as they ought to appear; it must be shown the good path that it is seeking, and guarded from the seduction of private interests; it must be made to observe closely times and places, and to balance the attraction of immediate and palpable advantages against the danger of remote and concealed evils. Individuals see the good which they erect; the public desire the good which they do not see. All alike have need of guides. The former must be compelled to conform their wills to their reason; the people must be taught to know what they require. Then from the public enlightenment results the union of the understanding and the will in the social body; and from that the close co-operation of the parts, and, lastly, the maximum power of the whole. Hence arises the need of a legislator.

FEDERALIST LI   The Separation of Powers
Alexander Hamilton

TO THE PEOPLE OF
THE STATE OF NEW YORK:

To what expedient, then, shall we finally resort, for maintaining in practice the necessary partition of power among the several departments, as laid down in the Constitution? The only answer that can be given is, that as all these exterior provisions are found to be inadequate, the defect must be supplied, by so contriving the interior structure of the government as that its several constituent parts may, by their mutual relations, be the means of keeping each other in their proper places. Without presuming to undertake a full develop-ment of this important idea, I will hazard a few general observations, which may perhaps place it in a clearer light, and enable us to form a more correct judgment of the principles and structure of the government planned by the convention.

In order to lay a due foundation for that separate and distinct exercise of the different powers of government, which to a certain extent is admitted on all hands to be essential to the preservation of liberty, it is evident that each department should have a will of its own; and consequently should be so constituted that the members of each

From the New York *Packet,* Friday, February 8, 1788, which appears in the *Universal Classics Library,* Washington: M. Walter Dunne, 1901.

should have as little agency as possible in the appointment of the members of the others. Were this principle rigorously adhered to, it would require that all the appointments for the supreme executive, legislative, and judiciary magistracies should be drawn from the same fountain of authority, the people, through channels having no communication whatever with one another. Perhaps such a plan of constructing the several departments would be less difficult in practice than it may in contemplation appear. Some difficulties, however, and some additional expense would attend the execution of it. Some deviations, therefore, from the principle must be admitted. In the constitution of the judiciary department in particular, it might be inexpedient to insist rigorously on the principle: first, because peculiar qualifications being essential in the members, the primary consideration ought to be to select that mode of choice which best secures these qualifications; secondly, because the permanent tenure by which the appointments are held in that department, must soon destroy all sense of dependence on the authority conferring them.

It is equally evident, that the members of each department should be as little dependent as possible on those of the others, for the emoluments annexed to their offices. Were the executive magistrate, or the judges, not independent of the legislature in this particular, their independence in every other would be merely nominal.

But the great security against a gradual concentration of the several powers in the same department, consists in giving to those who administer each department the necessary constitutional means and personal motives to resist encroachment of the others. The pro-vision for defense must in this, as in all other cases, be made commensurate to the danger of attack. Ambition must be made to counteract ambition. The interest of the man must be connected with the constitutional rights of the place. It may be a reflection on human nature, that such devices should be necessary to control the abuses of government. But what is government itself, but the greatest of all reflections on human nature? If men were angels, no government would be necessary. If angels were to govern men, neither external nor internal controls on government would be necessary. In framing a government which is to be administered by men over men, the great difficulty lies in this: you must first enable the government to control the governed; and in the next place oblige it to control itself. A dependence on the people is, no doubt, the primary control on the government; but experience has taught mankind the necessity of auxiliary precautions.

This policy of supplying, by opposite and rival interests, the defect of better motives, might be traced through the whole system of human affairs, private as well as public. We see it particularly displayed in all the subordinate distributions of power, where the constant aim is to divide and arrange the several offices in such a manner as that each may be a check on the other—that the private interest of every individual may be a sentinel over the public rights. These inventions of prudence cannot be less requisite in the distribution of the supreme powers of the State.

But it is not possible to give to each department an equal power of self-defense. In republican government, the legislative authority necessarily predominates. The remedy for this inconveniency is to divide the legislature into different branches; and to render them, by different modes of election and different principles of action, as little connected with each other as the nature of their common functions and their common dependences on the society will admit. It may even be necessary to guard against dangerous encroachments by still further precautions. As the weight of the legislative authority requires that it should be thus divided, the weakness of the executive may require, on the other hand, that it should be fortified. An absolute negative on the legislature appears, at first view, to be the natural defense with which the executive magistrate should be armed. But perhaps it would be neither altogether safe nor alone sufficient. On ordinary occasions it might not be exerted with the requisite firmness, and on extraordinary occasions it might be perfidiously abused. May not this defect of an absolute negative be supplied by some qualified connection between this weaker department and the weaker branch of the strongest department, by which the latter may be led to support the constitutional rights of the former, without being too much detached from the rights of its own department?

If the principles on which these observations are founded be just, as I persuade myself they are, and they be applied as a criterion to the several State constitutions, and to the federal Constitution it will be found that if the latter does not perfectly correspond with them, the former are infinitely less able to bear such a test.

There are, moreover, two considerations particularly applicable to the federal system of America, which place that system in a very interesting point of view.

First. In a single republic, all the power surrendered by the people is submitted to the administration of a single government; and the usurpations are guarded against by a division of the government into distinct and separate departments. In the compound republic of America, the power surrendered by the people is first divided between two distinct governments, and then the portion allotted to each subdivided among distinct and separate departments. Hence a double security arises to the rights of the people. The different governments will control each other, at the same time that each will be controlled by itself.

Second. It is of great importance in a republic not only to guard the society against the oppression of its rulers, but to guard one part of the society against the injustice of the other part. Different interests necessarily exist in different classes of citizens. If a majority be united by a common interest, the rights of the minority will be insecure. There are but two methods of providing against this evil: the one by creating a will in the community independent of the majority—that is, of the society itself; the other, by comprehending in the society so many separate descriptions of citizens as will render an unjust combination of a majority of the whole very improbable, if not impracticable. The first method prevails in all governments possessing an hereditary or self-appointed authority. This, at best, is but a precarious security; because a power independent of the society may as well espouse the unjust views of the major, as the rightful interests of the minority party, and may possibly be turned against both parties. The second method will be exemplified in the federal republic of the United States. Whilst all authority in it will be derived from and dependent on the society, the society itself will be broken into so many parts, interests, and classes of citizens, that the rights of individuals, or of the minority, will be in little danger from interested combinations of the majority. In a free government the security for civil rights must be the same as that for religious rights. It consists in the one case in the multiplicity of interests, and in the other in the multiplicity of sects. The degree of security in both cases will depend on the number of interests and sects; and this may be presumed to depend on the extent of country and number of people comprehended under the same government. This view of the subject must particularly recommend a proper federal system to all the sincere and considerate friends of republican government, since it shows that in exact proportion as the territory of the Union may be formed into more circumscribed Confederacies, or States oppressive combinations of a majority will be facilitated: the best security, under the republican forms, for the rights of every class of citizens, will be diminished; and consequently the stability and independence of some member of the government, the only other security, must be proportionately increased. Justice is the end of government. It is the end of civil society. It ever has been and ever will be pursued until it be obtained, or until liberty be lost in the pursuit. In a society under the forms of which the stronger faction can readily unite and oppress the weaker, anarchy may as truly be said to reign as in a state of nature, where the weaker individual is not secured against the violence of the stronger; and as, in the latter state, even the stronger individuals are prompted, by the uncertainty of their condition, to submit to a government which may protect the weak as well as themselves; so, in the former state, will the more powerful factions or parties be gradually induced, by a like motive, to wish for a government which will protect all parties, the weaker as well as the more powerful. It can be little doubted that if the State of Rhode Island was separated from the Confederacy and left to itself, the insecurity of rights under the popular form of government within such narrow limits would be displayed by such reiterated oppressions of factious majorities that some power altogether independent of the people would soon be called for by the voice of the very factions whose misrule had proved the necessity of it. In the extended republic of the United States, and among the great variety of interests, parties, and sects which it embraces, a coalition of a majority of the whole society could seldom take place on any other principles than those of justice and the general good; whilst there being thus less danger to a minor from the will of a major party, there must be less pretext, also, to provide for the security of the former, by introducing into the government a will not dependent on the latter, or, in other words, a will independent of the society itself. It is no less certain than it is important, notwithstanding the contrary opinions which have been entertained, that the larger the society, provided it lie within a practical sphere, the more duly capable it will be of self-government. And happily for the *republican cause,* the practicable sphere may be carried to a very good extent, by a judicious modification and mixture of the *federal principle.*

Publius.

Law and Rights

Natural rights and natural law have already emerged in preceding discussions of liberalism, and they are indeed central concepts for the position. Like many political ideas, however, they have had a longer history. Plato and Aristotle mention natural law, the Stoics held firmly to a law based on the nature of things, and Aquinas, as we have seen, made the natural law one of the main features of his philosophy of law. On the whole, liberalism is in this same tradition, differing from it not so much in the content as in the method of establishing and knowing the natural law.

Natural law may be defined as the expression, in the form of law, of an order essential to man that he is obliged to realize and obey. The function of the doctrine is to posit an objective moral principle for the right ordering of man and society. Thus understood, the definition applies generally to natural law positions, including realism. Liberals, however, develop the theory further with particular reference to their individualism and their rationalism. Positing a state of nature and the derivative status of authority, liberals see the natural law as an order necessary for individual development and happiness, and natural rights as specifications of the conditions for developing human capacities that a right order would respect. Although Locke's influential theory of man as mental substance has been stated earlier, it should be further noted that the "nature" of man upon which the natural law rests is not so much an empirical datum as an obligation (this is why the nature of man is expressed in the form of a duty or a law). Man is a datum in experience through his capabilities such as reason and freedom; his function is to develop and exercise these capabilities in conformity with the law of his nature.

Individualistic in emphasis, the liberals' doctrine of natural law is also rationalistic. It substitutes the authority of reason for the spiritual authority of divine law and for the positivists' authority of force. Moral ideas, liberals generally hold, are based on relations of congruity (in this regard, they are like mathematics); they are formed by the mind, and can conform to the objective order prescribed by the "Divine Legislator." Even further, moral ideas can be demonstrated, for they have relations of "connection and agreement" (Locke) that can be discovered by the inspection of the mind. By deduction, therefore, men can possess moral and political truth in a "self-evident" way, as the Declaration of Independence puts it.

By his establishment of a theory of government and law through reason, Hugo Grotius (1583–1645) is the founder of an independent and purely rationalistic system of natural law and natural right. In his major work on the rights of war and peace, he sought to prove that a "law of nations" governing the relations of sovereign states exists and is rooted not in positive law but in natural law. Within the context of this aim, Grotius defines a right as a moral quality annexed to a person and a natural right as a dictate of right reason. Natural rights indicate things that are binding or unlawful in themselves; like the mathematical relation that twice two is four, natural rights refer to an objective order that is eternally and universally valid and that cannot be changed even by God himself. Also like mathematical relations, the order of natural rights involves moral regularities that are available to and can be known by any reasonable mind. Natural rights and law thus constitute an autonomous domain, for their validity is independent of positions or conclusions held in metaphysics or religion. Grotius was one of the first to cut the cord of dependence of legal theory and to attempt to make it a separate science.

HUGO GROTIUS Natural Right

III. As the Rights of War is the title, by which this treatise is distinguished, the first inquiry, as it has been already observed, is, whether any war be just, and, in the next place, what constitutes the justice of that war. For, in this place, right signifies nothing more than what is just, and that, more in a negative than a positive sense; so that *right* is that, which is not unjust. Now any thing is unjust, which is repugnant to the nature of society, established among rational creatures. Thus for instance, to deprive another of what belongs to him, merely for one's own advantage, is repugnant to the law of nature, as Cicero observes in the fifth Chapter of his third book of offices; and, by way of proof, he says that, if the practice were general, all society and intercourse among men must be overturned. Florentinus, the Lawyer, maintains that it is impious for one man to form designs against another, as nature has established a degree of kindred amongst us. On this subject, Seneca remarks that, as all the members of the human body agree among themselves, because the preservation of each conduces to the welfare of the whole, so men should forbear from mutual injuries, as they were born for society, which cannot subsist unless all the parts of it are defended by mutual forbearance and good will. But as there is one kind of social tie founded upon an equality, for instance, among brothers, citizens, friends, allies, and another on pre-eminence, as Aristotle styles it, subsisting between parents and children, masters and servants, sovereigns and subjects, God and men. So justice takes place either amongst equals, or between the governing and the governed parties, notwithstanding their difference of rank. The former of these, if I am not mistaken, may be called the right of equality, and the latter the right of superiority.

IV. There is another signification of the word *right*, different from this, but yet arising from it, which relates directly to the person. In which sense, *right* is a moral quality annexed to the person, justly entitling him to possess some particular privilege, or to perform some particular act. This right is annexed to the person, although it sometimes follows the things, as the services of lands, which are called *real rights,* in opposition to those merely *personal.* Not because these rights are not annexed to persons, but the distinction is made, because they belong to the per-

From Hugo Grotius, *The Rights of War and Peace,* trans. A. C. Campbell, Washington: M. Walter Dunne, 1901.

sons only who possess some particular things. This moral quality, when perfect is called a *faculty;* when imperfect, an *aptitude.* The former answers to the *act,* and the latter to the *power,* when we speak of natural things.

V. Civilians call a faculty that Right, which every man has to his own; but we shall hereafter, taking it in its strict and proper sense, call it a right. This right comprehends the power, that we have over ourselves, which is called liberty, and the power, that we have over others, as that of a father over his children, and of a master over his slaves. It likewise comprehends property, which is either complete or imperfect; of the latter kind is the use or possession of any thing without the property, or power of alienating it, or pledges detained by the creditors till payment be made. There is a third signification, which implies the power of demanding what is due, to which the obligation upon the party indebted, to discharge what is owing, corresponds.

VI. Right, strictly taken, is again twofold, the one, *private,* established for the advantage of each individual, the other, *superior,* as involving the claims, which the state has upon individuals, and their property, for the public good. Thus the Regal authority is above that of a father and a master, and the Sovereign has a greater right over the property of his subjects, where the public good is concerned, than the owners themselves have. And when the exigencies of the state require a supply, every man is more obliged to contribute towards it, than to satisfy his creditors.

VII. Aristotle distinguishes aptitude or capacity, by the name of worth or merit, and Michael of Ephesus, gives the epithet of *suitable* or *becoming* to the equality established by this rule of merit.

IX.[1] There is also a third signification of the word Right, which has the same meaning as Law, taken in its most extensive sense, to denote a rule of moral action, obliging us to do what is proper. We say *obliging* us. For the best counsels or precepts, if they lay us under no obligation to obey them, cannot come under the denomination of law or right. Now as to permission,[2] it is no act of the law, but only the silence of the law, it however prohibits any one from impeding another in doing what the law permits. But we have said, the law obliges us to do what is proper, not simply what is just; because, under this notion, right belongs to the substance not only of justice, as we have explained it, but of all other virtues. Yet from giving the name of a *right* to that, which is *proper,* a more general acceptance of the word justice has been derived. The best division of right, in this general meaning, is to be found in Aristotle, who, defining one kind to be natural, and the other voluntary, calls it a *lawful right* in the strictest sense of the word law; and some times an instituted right. The same difference is found among the Hebrews, who, by way of distinction, in speaking, call that natural right, *precepts,* and the voluntary right,

---

[1] The eighth Section is omitted, the greater part of it consisting of verbal criticism upon Aristotle's notions of geometrical and arithmetical justice; a discussion no way conducive to that clearness and simplicity, so necessary to every didactic treatise. *Tr.*

[2] The law, by its silence, permits those acts, which it does not prohibit. Thus many acts, if they are not evil in themselves, are no offence, till the law has made them such. Of this kind are many acts, such as exporting gold, or importing certain articles of trade; doing certain actions, or following certain callings, without the requisite qualifications, which are made punishable offences by the Statute-Law. Those actions, before the prohibition was enjoined by the law, came under the class of what Grotius calls permissions. *Tr.*

statutes: the former of which the Septuagint call δικαώματα, and the latter ἐντολὰς.

X. Natural right is the dictate of right reason, shewing the moral turpitude, or moral necessity,[3] of any act from its agreement or disagreement with a rational nature, and consequently that such an act is either forbidden or commanded by God, the author of nature. The actions, upon which such a dictate is given, are either binding or unlawful in themselves, and therefore necessarily understood to be commanded or forbidden by God. This mark distinguishes natural right, not only from human law, but from the law, which God himself has been pleased to reveal, called, by some, the voluntary divine right, which does not command or forbid things in themselves either binding or unlawful, but makes them unlawful by its prohibition, and binding by its command. But, to understand natural right, we must observe that some things are said to belong to that right, not properly, but, as the schoolmen say, by way of accommodation. These are not repugnant to natural right, as we have already observed that those things are called *just,* in which there is no injustice. Some times also, by a wrong use of the word, those things which reason shews to be proper, or better than things of an opposite kind, although not binding, are said to belong to natural right.

We must farther remark, that natural right relates not only to those things that exist independent of the human will, but to many things, which necessarily follow the exercise of that will. Thus property, as now in use, was at first a creature of the human will. But, after it was established, one man was prohibited by the law of nature from seizing the property of another against his will. Wherefore, Paulus the Lawyer said, that theft is expressly forbidden by the law of nature. Ulpian condemns it as infamous in its own nature; to whose authority that of Euripides may be added, as may be seen in the verses of Helena:

"For God himself hates violence, and will not have us to grow rich by rapine, but by lawful gains. That abundance, which is the fruit of unrighteousness, is an abomination. The air is common to men, the earth also, where every man, in the ample enjoyment of his possession, must refrain from doing violence or injury to that of another."

Now the Law of Nature is so unalterable, that it cannot be changed even by God himself. For although the power of God is infinite, yet there are some things, to which it does not extend. Because the things so expressed would have no true meaning, but imply a contradiction. Thus two and two must make four, nor is it possible to be otherwise; nor, again, can what is really evil not be evil. And this is Aristotle's meaning, when he says, that some things are no sooner named, than we discover their evil nature. For as the substance of things in their nature and existence depends upon nothing but themselves; so there are qualities inseparably connected with their being and essence. Of this kind is the evil of certain actions, compared with the nature of a reasonable being. Therefore God himself suffers his actions to be judged by this rule, as may be seen in the xviiith chap. of Gen. 25. Isa. v. 3. Ezek. xviii. 25. Jer. ii. 9. Mich. vi. 2. Rom. ii. 6., iii. 6. Yet it sometimes happens that, in those cases, which are decided by the law of nature, the undiscerning are imposed

---

[3] By moral necessity is meant nothing more than that the Laws of Nature must always bind us. *Tr.*

upon by an appearance of change. Whereas in reality there is no change in the unalterable law of nature, but only in the things appointed by it, and which are liable to variation. For example, if a creditor forgive me the debt, which I owe him, I am no longer bound to pay it, not because the law of nature has ceased to command the payment of a just debt, but because my debt, by a release, has ceased to be a debt. On this topic, Arrian in Epictetus argues rightly, that the borrowing of money is not the only requisite to make a debt, but there must be the additional circumstance of the loan remaining undischarged. Thus if God should command the life, or property of any one to be taken away, the act would not authorize murder or robbery, words which always include a crime. But that cannot be murder or robbery, which is done by the express command of Him, who is the sovereign Lord of our lives and of all things. There are also some things allowed by the law of nature, not absolutely, but according to a certain state of affairs. Thus, by the law of nature, before property was introduced, every one had a right to the use of whatever he found unoccupied; and, before laws were enacted, to avenge his personal injuries by force.

XI. The distinction found in the books of the Roman Law, assigning one unchangeable right to brutes in common with man, which in a more limited sense they call the law of nature, and appropriating another to men, which they frequently call the Law of Nations, is scarcely of any real use. For no beings, except those that can form general maxims, are capable of possessing a right, which Hesiod has placed in a clear point of view, observing "that the supreme Being has appointed laws for men; but permitted wild beasts, fishes, and birds to devour each other for food." For they have nothing like justice, the best gift, bestowed upon men.

Cicero, in his first book of offices, says, we do not talk of the justice of horses or lions. In conformity to which, Plutarch, in the life of Cato the elder, observes, that we are formed by nature to use law and justice towards men only. In addition to the above, Lactantius may be cited, who, in his fifth book, says that in all animals devoid of reason we see a natural bias of self-love. For they hurt others to benefit themselves; because they do not know the evil of doing wilful hurt. But it is not so with man, who, possessing the knowledge of good and evil, refrains, even with inconvenience to himself, from doing hurt. Polybius, relating the manner in which men first entered into society, concludes, that the injuries done to parents or benefactors inevitably provoke the indignation of mankind, giving an additional reason, that as understanding and reflection form the great difference between men and other animals, it is evident they cannot transgress the bounds of that difference like other animals, without exciting universal abhorrence of their conduct. But if ever justice is attributed to brutes, it is done improperly, from some shadow and trace of reason they may possess. But it is not material to the nature of right, whether the actions appointed by the law of nature, such as the care of our offspring, are common to us with other animals or not, or, like the worship of God, are peculiar to man.

XIII. It has been already remarked, that there is another kind of right, which is the voluntary right, deriving its origin from the will, and is either human or divine.

XIV. We will begin with the human as more generally known. Now this is either a civil right, or a right more or less extensive than the civil right. The civil right is that which is derived from the civil power. The civil power is the sovereign power of the state. A state is a perfect body of free men, united together in order to enjoy common rights and advantages. The less extensive right, and not derived from the civil power itself, although subject to it, is various, comprehending the authority of parents over children, masters over servants, and the like. But the law of nations is a more extensive right, deriving its authority from the consent of all, or at least of many nations.

It was proper to add *many*, because scarce any right can be found common to all nations, except the law of nature, which itself too is generally called the law of nations. Nay, frequently in one part of the world, that is held for the law of nations, which is not so in another. Now this law of nations is proved in the same manner as the unwritten civil law, and that is by the continual experience and testimony of the Sages of the Law. For this law, as Dio Chrysostom well observes, is the discoveries made by experience and time. And in this we derive great advantage from the writings of eminent historians.

XV. The very meaning of the words divine voluntary right, shows that it springs from the divine will, by which it is distinguished from natural law, which, it has already been observed, is called divine also. This law admits of what Anaxarchus said, as Plutarch relates in the life of Alexander, though without sufficient accuracy, that God does not will a thing, because it is just, but that it is just, or binding, because God wills it. Now this law was given either to mankind in general, or to one particular people. We find three periods, at which it was given by God to the human race, the first of which was immediately after the creation of man, the second upon the restoration of mankind after the flood, and the third upon that more glorious restoration through Jesus Christ. These three laws undoubtedly bind all men, as soon as they come to a sufficient knowledge of them.

Political Obligation

Among the many doctrines of liberalism, none is more fundamental than the theory of the nature and limits of political obligation. Questions as to what makes a government legitimate, why citizens are obliged to obey laws, and whether governments ought to respect limits of their authority are all involved. The chief notion by which these questions are answered, namely the consent of the governed, has been mentioned and utilized in discussions of many of the topics in preceding selections. Both the state of nature and the social compact, however artificial they may seem, are intimately connected with the idea of a limited government based on the consent of its citizens.

John Locke, the major philosophic spokesman of this idea, used it to answer what for him was the central political question, namely the legitimacy of government. Consent, he argues, is the only possible basis of just subjection to authority. To be sure, Locke finds it necessary to use "consent" in a variety of ways—sometimes he means voluntary agreement, at other times a personal and deliberate act of choice. He also has to distinguish between express and tacit consent. The former, occurring when one takes up citizenship in a country, for example, is clear enough. Tacit consent to a government is merely implicit, but it is given, Locke believes, simply if a man has possessions. His argument for this is that the act of assent to the social compact places all property under the regulation of government, and therefore to possess property is to agree to that regulation. Difficult as some aspects of this doctrine of tacit consent may be, the principle that Locke is seeking to uphold by it is that every obligation must be laid on oneself voluntarily. Governments are thus legitimate when they rest on consent.

Though Locke is not interested in developing a theory of government in all its details, and does not do so, there is one implication that he does specify as following from the idea of consent. This is the supremacy of the legislative function of government, which is given by the people and which is sacred and unalterable when so given. All obligation, he writes, terminates in this supreme power. Thus, the question of why citizens are obliged to obey government is answered again by Locke: it is because government is basically their own act and preference.

But does government have obligations to its citizens that constitute limits for it? Locke answers with an emphatic yes. The authority of government is limited by the nature of the end it serves—the preservation of life, liberty, and property. When government does this, it may use force, and the obligation to obey is direct and complete. Government may not use force in other matters such as religion, for it has not been entrusted to concern itself with them. If the state should transgress beyond its limits, a trust is broken, the contract becomes void, and the people may institute a new agency for their rights.

In the selection Locke specifies some of the ways that government must act to be true to its proper end as, for example, rule by known laws. These too follow from Locke's conception of the purpose of government. But his fundamental assumptions about contract and consent are the heart of his position. People are obliged to obey government as the agent and protector of their rights, and government is obliged to serve its citizens because its very existence is derivative from them. Government and rights are two sides of the same coin, held together by the doctrine of consent.

JOHN LOCKE   Consent of the Governed

OF CONSENT.

119. Every man being, as has been showed, naturally free, and nothing being able to put him into subjection to any earthly power, but only his own consent; it is to be considered, what shall be understood to be a sufficient declaration of a man's consent, to make him subject to the laws of any government. There is a common distinction of an express and a tacit consent, which will concern our present case. Nobody doubts but an express consent, of any

From John Locke, "Two Treatises on Government," in *The Works of John Locke,* London: C. and J. Rivington and Others, 1824.

man entering into any society, makes him a perfect member of that society, a subject of that government. The difficulty is, what ought to be looked upon as a tacit consent, and how far it binds, i.e. how far any one shall be looked upon to have consented, and thereby submitted to any government, where he has made no expressions of it at all. And to this I say, that every man, that hath any possessions, or enjoyment of any part of the dominions of any government, doth thereby give his tacit consent, and is as far forth obliged to obedience to the laws of that government, during such enjoyment, as any one under it; whether this his possession be of land, to him and his heirs for ever, or a lodging only for a week; or whether it be barely travelling freely on the highway: and, in effect, it reaches as far as the very being of any one within the territories of that government.

120. To understand this the better, it is fit to consider, that every man, when he at first incorporates himself into any commonwealth, he, by his uniting himself thereunto, annexes also, and submits to the community, those possessions which he has, or shall acquire, that do not already belong to any other government: for it would be a direct contradiction, for any one to enter into society with others for the securing and regulating of property, and yet to suppose, his land, whose property is to be regulated by the laws of the society, should be exempt from the jurisdiction of that government, to which he himself, the proprietor of the land, is a subject. By the same act therefore, whereby any one unites his person, which was before free, to any commonwealth; by the same he unites his posessions, which were before free, to it also: and they become, both of them, person and possession, subject to the government and dominion of that commonwealth, as long as it hath a being. Whoever therefore, from thenceforth, by inheritance, purchase, permission, or otherways, enjoys any part of the land so annexed to, and under the government of that commonwealth, must take it with the condition it is under; that is, of submitting to the government of the commonwealth, under whose jurisdiction it is, as far forth as any subject of it.

121. But since the government has a direct jurisdiction only over the land, and reaches the possessor of it (before he has actually incorporated himself in the society), only as he dwells upon, and enjoys that; the obligation any one is under, by virtue of such enjoyment, to "submit to the government, begins and ends with the enjoyment": so that whenever the owner, who has given nothing but such a tacit consent to the government, will, by donation, sale, or otherwise, quit the said possession, he is at liberty to go and incorporate himself into any other commonwealth; or to agree with others to begin a new one, in *vacuis locis,* in any part of the world they can find free and unpossessed: whereas he, that has once, by actual agreement, and any express declaration, given his consent to be of any commonwealth, is perpetually and indispensably obliged to be, and remain unalterably a subject to it, and can never be again in the liberty of the state of nature; unless, by any calamity, the government he was under comes to be dissolved, or else by some public act cuts him off from being any longer a member of it.

122. But submitting to the laws of any country, living quietly, and enjoying privileges and protection under them, makes not a man a member of that society: this is only a local protec-

tion and homage due to and from all those, who, not being in a state of war, come within the territories belonging to any government, to all parts whereof the force of its laws extends. But this no more makes a man a member of that society, a perpetual subject of that commonwealth, than it would make a man a subject to another, in whose family he found it convenient to abide for some time, though, whilst he continued in it, he were obliged to comply with the laws, and submit to the government he found there. And thus we see, that foreigners, by living all their lives under another government, and enjoying the privileges and protection of it, though they are bound, even in conscience, to submit to its administration, as far forth as any denison; yet do not thereby come to be subjects or members of that commonwealth. Nothing can make any man so, but his actually entering into it by positive engagement, and express promise and compact. This is that, which I think, concerning the beginning of political societies, and that consent which makes any one a member of any commonwealth.

XI. OF THE EXTENT OF THE LEGISLATIVE POWER.

134. The great end of men's entering into society being the enjoyment of their properties in peace and safety, and the great instrument and means of that being the laws established in that society; the first and fundamental positive law of all commonwealths is the establishing of the legislative power; as the first and fundamental natural law, which is to govern even the legislative itself, is the preservation of the society, and (as far as will consist with the public good) of every person in it. This legislative is not only the supreme power of the common-wealth, but sacred and unalterable in the hands where the community have once placed it; nor can any edict of any body else, in what form soever conceived, or by what power soever backed, have the force and obligation of a law, which has not its sanction from that legislative which the public has chosen and appointed; for without this the law could not have that, which is absolutely necessary to its being a law,[1] the consent of the society; over whom nobody can have a power to make laws, but by their own consent, and by authority received from them. And therefore all the obedience, which by the most solemn ties any one can be obliged to pay, ultimately terminates in this supreme power, and is directed by those laws which it enacts; nor can any oaths to any foreign power whatsoever, or any domestic subordinate power, discharge any member of the society from his obedience to the legislative, acting pursuant to their trust; nor oblige him to any obedience contrary to the laws so enacted, or farther than they do allow; it being ridiculous to imagine

---

[1] "The lawful power of making laws to command whole politic societies of men, belonging so properly unto the same entire societies, that for any prince or potentate of what kind soever upon earth, to exercise the same of himself, and not by express commission immediately and personally received from God, or else by authority derived at the first from their consent, upon persons they impose laws; it is no better than mere tyranny. Laws they are not therefore which public approbation hath not made so." Hooker's Eccl. Pol. l. i. sect. 10.

"Of this point therefore we are to note, that sith men naturally have no full and perfect power to command whole politic multitudes of men, therefore utterly without our consent, we could in such sort be at no man's commandment living. And to be commanded we do consent, when that society, whereof we be a part, hath at any time before consented, without revoking the same by the like universal agreement.

"Laws therefore human, of what kind soever, are available by consent." *Ibid*.

one can be tied ultimately to obey any power in the society, which is not supreme.

135. Though the legislative, whether placed in one or more, whether it be always in being, or only by intervals, though it be the supreme power in every commonwealth; yet,

First, It is not, nor can possibly be absolutely arbitrary over the lives and fortunes of the people: for it being but the joint power of every member of the society given up to that person, or assembly, which is legislator; it can be no more than those persons had in a state of nature before they entered into society, and gave up to the community: for nobody can transfer to another more power than he has in himself; and nobody has an absolute arbitrary power over himself, or over any other, to destroy his own life, or take away the life or property of another. A man, as has been proved, cannot subject himself to the arbitrary power of another; and having in the state of nature no arbitrary power over the life, liberty, or possession of another, but only so much as the law of nature gave him for the preservation of himself and the rest of mankind; this is all he doth, or can give up to the commonwealth, and by it to the legislative power, so that the legislative can have no more than this. Their power, in the utmost bounds of it, is limited to the public good of the society. It is a power, that hath no other end but preservation, and therefore can never[2]

have a right to destroy, enslave or designedly to impoverish the subjects. The obligations of the law of nature cease not in society, but only in many cases are drawn closer, and have by human laws known penalties annexed to them, to enforce their observation. Thus the law of nature stands as an eternal rule to all men, legislators as well as others. The rules that they make for other men's actions, must, as well as their own and other men's actions, be conformable to the laws of nature, i.e. to the will of God, of which that is a declaration; and the "fundamental law of nature being the preservation of mankind," no human sanction can be good or valid against it.

136. Secondly,[3] The legislative or supreme authority cannot assume to itself a power to rule, by extemporary, arbitrary decrees; but is bound to dispense justice, and to decide the rights of the subject, by promulgated, standing laws, and known authorised judges. For the law of nature being unwritten, and

---

[2] "Two foundations there are which bear up public societies; the one a natural inclination, whereby all men desire sociable life and fellowship; the other an order, expressly or secretly agreed upon, touching the manner of their union in living together: the latter is that which we call the law of a commonweal, the very soul of a politic body, the parts whereof are by law animated, held together, and set on work in such actions as the common good requireth. Laws politic, ordained for external order and regiment amongst men, are never framed as they should be, unless presuming the will of man to be inwardly obstinate, rebellious, and averse from all obedience to the sacred laws of his nature; in a word, unless presuming man to be, in regard of his depraved mind, little better than a wild beast, they do accordingly provide, notwithstanding, so to frame his outward actions, that they be no hindrance unto the common good, for which societies are instituted. Unless they do this, they are not perfect." Hooker's Eccl. Pol. l. i. sect. 10.

[3] "Human laws are measures in respect of men whose actions they must direct, howbeit such measures they are as have also their higher rules to be measured by, which rules are two, the law of God, and the law of nature; so that laws human must be made according to the general laws of nature, and without contradiction to any positive law of scripture, otherwise they are ill made." Hooker's Eccl. Pol. l. iii. sect. 9.

"To constrain men to any thing inconvenient doth seem unreasonable." *Ibid.* l. i. sect. 10.

so no-where to be found, but in the minds of men; they who through passion, or interest, shall miscite, or misapply it, cannot so easily be convinced of their mistake, where there is no established judge: and so it serves not, as it ought, to determine the rights, and fence the properties of those that live under it; especially where every one is judge, interpreter, and executioner of it too, and that in his own case: and he that has right on his side, having ordinarily but his own single strength, hath not force enough to defend himself from injuries, or to punish delinquents. To avoid these inconveniences, which disorder men's properties in the state of nature, men unite into societies, that they may have the united strength of the whole society to secure and defend their properties, and may have standing rules to bound it, by which every one may know what is his. To this end it is that men give up all their natural power to the society which they enter into, and the community put the legislative power into such hands as they think fit: with this trust, that they shall be governed by declared laws, or else their peace, quiet, and property will still be at the same uncertainty, as it was in the state of nature.

137. Absolute arbitrary power, or governing without settled standing laws, can neither of them consist with the ends of society and government, which men would not quit the freedom of the state of nature for, and tie themselves up under, were it not to preserve their lives, liberties, and fortunes, and by stated rules of right and property to secure their peace and quiet. It cannot be supposed that they should intend, had they a power so to do, to give to any one, or more, an absolute arbitrary power over their persons and estates, and put a force into the magistrate's hand to execute his unlimited will arbitrarily upon them. This were to put themselves into a worse condition than the state of nature, wherein they had a liberty to defend their right against the injuries of others, and were upon equal terms of force to maintain it, whether invaded by a single man, or many in combination. Whereas by supposing they have given up themselves to the absolute arbitrary power and will of a legislator, they have disarmed themselves, and armed him, to make a prey of them when he pleases; he being in a much worse condition, who is exposed to the arbitrary power of one man, who has the command of 100,000, than he that is exposed to the arbitrary power of 100,000 single men; nobody being secure, that his will, who has such a command, is better than that of other men, though his force be 100,000 times stronger. And therefore, whatever form the commonwealth is under, the ruling power ought to govern by declared and received laws, and not by extemporary dictates and undetermined resolutions: for then mankind will be in a far worse condition than in the state of nature, if they shall have armed one or a few men with the joint power of a multitude, to force them to obey at pleasure the exorbitant and unlimited degrees of their sudden thoughts, or unrestrained, and till that moment unknown wills, without having any measures set down which may guide and justify their actions; for all the power the government has, being only for the good of the society, as it ought not to be arbitrary and at pleasure, so it ought to be exercised by established and promulgated laws; that both the people may know their duty, and be safe and secure within the limits of the law; and the rulers too kept within

their bounds, and not be tempted, by the power they have in their hands, to employ it to such purposes, and by such measures, as they would not have known, and own not willingly.

138. Thirdly, The supreme power cannot take from any man part of his property without his own consent, for the preservation of property being the end of government, and that for which men enter into society, it necessarily supposes and requires, that the people should have property, without which they must be supposed to lose that, by entering into society, which was the end for which they entered into it; too gross an absurdity for any man to own. Men therefore in society having property, they have such right to the goods, which by the law of the community are their's, that no body hath a right to take their substances or any part of it from them, without their own consent; without this they have no property at all; for I have truly no property in that, which another can by right take from me, when he pleases, against my consent. Hence it is a mistake to think, that the supreme or legislative power of any commonwealth can do what it will, and dispose of the estates of the subject arbitrarily, or take any part of them at pleasure. This is not much to be feared in governments where the legislative consists, wholly or in part, in assemblies which are variable, whose members, upon the dissolution of the assembly, are subjects under the common laws of their country, equally with the rest. But in governments, where the legislative is in one lasting assembly always in being, or in one man, as in absolute monarchies, there is danger still, that they will think themselves to have a distinct interest from the rest of the community; and so will be apt to increase their own riches and power, by taking what they think fit from the people: for a man's property is not at all secure, though there be good and equitable laws to set the bounds of it between him and his fellow-subjects, if he who commands those subjects, have power to take from any private man, what part he pleases of his property, and use and dispose of it as he thinks good.

141. Fourthly, The legislative cannot transfer the power of making laws to any other hands: for it being but a delegated power from the people, they who have it cannot pass it over to others. The people alone can appoint the form of the commonwealth, which is by constituting the legislative, and appointing in whose hands that shall be. And when the people have said, we will submit to rules, and be governed by laws made by such men, and in such forms, nobody else can say other men shall make laws for them; nor can the people be bound by any laws, but such as are enacted by those whom they have chosen, and authorized to make laws for them. The power of the legislative being derived from the people by a positive voluntary grant and institution, can be no other than what that positive grant conveyed, which being only to make laws, and not to make legislators, the legislative can have no power to transfer their authority of making laws and place it in other hands.

142. These are the bounds which the trust, that is put in them by the society and the law of God and nature, have set to the legislative power of every commonwealth, in all forms of government.

First, They are to govern by promulgated established laws, not to be varied in particular cases, but to have one rule for rich and poor, for the favorite at court, and the countryman at plough.

Secondly, These laws also ought to be

designed for no other end ultimately, but the good of the people.

Thirdly, They must not raise taxes on the property of the people, without the consent of the people, given by themselves or their deputies. And this properly concerns only such governments where the legislative is always in being, or at least where the people have not reserved any part of the legislative to deputies, to be from time to time chosen by themselves.

Fourthly, The legislative neither must nor can transfer the power of making laws to any body else, or place it any where, but where the people have.

The Ideal of Justice

The methodological and philosophical grounds of traditional liberalism's views of rights, law, and justice have been outlined above. Placing its trust in an objective moral order and in the power of reason to apprehend it, liberalism understands justice as that rational order where the law of nature is obeyed and the nature of man realized. The natural law, justice, and reason are nearly synonymous, and all three have an objective, universal meaning for the liberal.

Unlike Hobbes, the liberal denies that consent and compact bring justice into being; rather, the compact is founded on justice. Unlike utilitarianism, to which we shall come next in our study, liberalism denies that justice and freedom are externally related merely as means to end, and accordingly, the latter theory asserts that justice is the order of freedom or the realization of freedom itself. As a good and rational order, justice is that structure in which individuals are protected and encouraged in their right to the things of this world—life, liberty, and estate.

The writings of Samuel Pufendorf (1632–1694) present such a liberal, rationalistic interpretation of justice. Influenced by, and perhaps less original than, Grotius, the *De jure naturae et gentium* remained a widely studied work for over a century after its publication. In it, Pufendorf attempts to explain all human authority as the effect or consequence of contract, and he appeals explicitly to this notion in his discussions of distributive and commutative justice. Contractual arrangements are themselves matters of order and reason—a fact that places Pufendorf clearly within the liberal perspective.

Reflecting an old definition, he says that the justice of persons is to give everyone his due. To this conception is added a notion called justice of actions, which is the right application of actions to a person. Commutative justice is what is done as a result of obligations arising from mutual agreements among persons, and distributive justice is what is done between society and individuals, either that individuals may become members of the society or that society will accept individuals as its members. The ideal of justice thus seeks to regulate the actions of men and society to institute and to maintain a rational order wherein human nature is realized and the goals of security, tranquillity, and freedom are won.

SAMUEL PUFENDORF   Justice and Right Action

6. Let us now discuss justice, regarding which it should be noted, first of all, that the meaning, in which it is attributed to persons, is very different from that whereby it signifies an attribute of actions. For when we use it in describing persons, to be just means that one delights in acting justly, that he applies himself to justice, or that he tries in every thing to do what is just. And to be unjust means to neglect justice, or feel that it should be measured not by a man's obligation, but by his convenience. And for this reason many actions of a just man can be unjust, and of an unjust man just. A man should, therefore, be called just, who does just, who does just things in obedience to law, and unjust things only because of his weakness; he should be called unjust who does just things because of the penalty attached to the law, and unjust things because of his evil nature, or in order to secure glory or some other advantage. Hobbes, *De Cive,* chap. lll, ¶ 5. The words of Pliny, *Panegyric* [lvi], are based on such a definition: "Even bad men do many praiseworthy things; only the best of men deserves praise in his own person." Compare the statement of Philemon in Stobaeus [*Anthology,* III] ix [21]:

He is a just man, not the one who *does* no wrong, but he who, when he *may* do wrong, is unwilling to do so; not the one who refrains from taking little things, but he who is strong to refuse to take the great things, although he might seize and possess them without risk of harm; no, not even the one who observes all these requirements, but he who has a sincere and genuine character and wishes to be, and not to seem, just.

Archytas [in Stobaeus, *Anthology,* III. i. 114]:

Just as a man who has been guilty in some particular circumstances of a lack of self-restraint, or of injustice, or cowardice, is not to be classified among wicked men; no more is he to be classified among good men, on the basis of a single successful performance. [. . .] But the correct judgement is that drawn not from a single occasion but from a man's entire life.

Another illustration is the censure passed by Agathias, Bk. V [v], on the inhabitants of Byzantium, who were terrified by a severe earthquake and vied with one another in good deeds:

All this was done for a limited time. so long as their fear was fresh and strong. As soon, however, as the evil began to abate and come to an end, most of them made haste to return to their former habits. Now such a sudden impulse of the mind cannot properly be called justice, nor substantial and effective piety, such as is commonly formed in men by right opinion and constant application, but rather a reckless contrivance and cheating bargain-counter device, instituted to escape and avoid a momentary danger. Good deeds that come of necessity we experience only so long as the fear lasts.

It is clear from this that the definition of justice commonly used by the Roman Jurisconsults, namely, that it was a "constant and abiding desire to give every one his due," applies only to the justice of persons, and not of actions. This circumstance, I feel, is very unsatisfactory, since jurisprudence is chiefly concerned with justice of action, and

From Samuel Pufendorf, *De jure naturae et gentium,* trans. C. H. Olfather and W. A. Olfather, Oxford: The Clarendon Press, 1934. Used by permission of the publisher.

takes cognizance of justice of persons only in passing, and in a few particulars.

7. Now justice of actions differs from goodness of actions mainly in this, that goodness denotes simply an agreement with law, while justice includes further a relation to those towards whom the action is performed. Consequently, in our opinion, an action is called just which is applied from previous choice to the person to whom it is owed, and therefore, on this definition, justice will be the right application of actions to a person. It is our decision to make a division of it primarily on the ground of the matter which is owed, or which is applied to another as from an obligation.

We note, by way of introduction, that some actions can be called pure and some mixed. The former are performed, on the motion of some power which is applied to an object for a definite reason; such are an exhibition of honour, acts of respect, affection, aversion, consolation, praise, reproach, &c., the effect of all such being that the object is affected, or is thought to be affected, by the action in a certain way, leading either to satisfaction or dissatisfaction. But the latter are connected with the transfer of some advantage or disadvantage for the person towards whom they are said to be exercised, and so their effect consists mainly of some operation, whereby the person or property of some man is actually bettered or injured. Again, there are actions which are concerned with business, and are valued at a certain rate; while upon certain others men usually set no value. The distinction between these two kinds of actions will be discussed at length below.

It should be observed, in conclusion, that some things are due us by a perfect, others by an imperfect right. When what is due us on the former score is not voluntarily given, it is the right of those in enjoyment of natural liberty to resort to violence and war in forcing another to furnish it, or, if we live within the same state, an action against him at law is allowed; but what is due on the latter score cannot be claimed by war or extorted by a threat of the law. Writers frequently designate a perfect right by the additional words, "his own," as they say, for example, a man demands this by *his own* [*suo*] *right*. But the reason why some things are due us perfectly and others imperfectly, is because among those who live in a state of mutual natural law there is a diversity in the rules of this law, some of which conduce to the mere existence of society, others to an improved existence. And since it is less necessary that the latter be observed towards another than the former, it is, therefore, reasonable that the former can be exacted more rigorously than the latter, for it is foolish to prescribe a medicine far more troublesome and dangerous than the disease. There is, furthermore, in the case of the former usually an agreement, but not in the latter, and so, since the latter are left to a man's sense of decency and conscience, it would be inconsistent to extort them from another by force, unless a grave necessity happens to arise. In civil states this distinction arises from their civil laws, which either allow or deny an action, although in most instances states have followed in the footsteps of natural law, except where their own reasons persuaded them to take another course.

8. When, therefore, actions or things are extended to another, which are due him only by an imperfect right, or when actions are performed for another which

have no relation to business, it is usually said that universal justice is observed; as when one comes to the aid of a man with counsel, goods, or personal assistance, and performs a service of piety, respect, gratitude, kindness, or generosity, for those to whom he was obligated to perform the same. The only concern of this kind of justice is that one should furnish what is due another, without observing whether the service furnished is equal to, or less than, that which was the reason for the obligation. Thus an office of gratitude is fulfilled if as much is shown as one's faculties permit, although the kindness done may have far surpassed that measure. But when acts which concern business relations are performed for another, or acts by which something is transferred to another to which he had a perfect right, that is called particular justice.

9. Now this perfect right arises either for individuals from an agreement, tacit or expressed, made with some society to the end that they may become members of it; or for a society from the same agreement with individuals, that it will join them to it as members; or it arises from any kind of an agreement with any number of individuals about things and actions which concern business enterprises. When those things are fulfilled, which are due for the reasons given just above, from the agreement of a society with a member, or of a member with a society, it is called distributive justice. For whenever a person is received into a society an express or tacit agreement is entered into between the society and the member to be received, by which the society undertakes to give him a *pro rata* share of the goods which belong to the society as such, and the member, on his part, promises to undertake to bear his just share of the burdens

which make for the preservation of the society as such. The determination of the proportionate share of the goods to go to the member is made on an estimate of his labour, or of the amount of his expense in the service of the society as such, in proportion to the labours or expenses of the other members of the society. On the other hand, the determination of the proportionate share of the duties falling to the member is made on an estimate of the advantages which he receives from the society, in proportion to the advantages received by the rest of the members of the society. And so, since one member usually contributes more to the preservation of a society than another, and one usually derives more advantage from it than another, the reason is clear, why, in a society of many members, and where an inequality exists among them, a comparative equality must be observed in distributive justice. And this consists in maintaining a clear ratio between the worth or merit of one, compared with the worth of another, and his reward, as compared with the reward of the other. For, as Philo Judaeus says, *On Monarchy* [ii. 13]: "For it is an unequal measure to give equal honour to persons who are unequal in rank." (Y.) Arrian, *Epictetus,* Bk. III, chap. xvii: "It is a law of nature for the better to have the advantage of the worse in that which he is better." (M.) So, for example, if six rewards are to be distributed between Gaius, Seius, and Titius, if the desert of Titius is threefold that of Gaius, and twofold that of Seius, Titius should have three, Seius two, and Gaius one. Nor does this equality require that a person's reward shall exactly equal his desert, but it is enough if the proportion of the worth of one member to the worth of another should be observed in the portion he shall have of the common good, compared with the portion of the other. And the same rule should be applied in imposing tasks.

But what Hobbes, *De Cive,* chap. iii, ¶ 6, says in order to overthrow this respective equality which is observed in this kind of justice, namely, that I can distribute of my own more to him who deserves less, and give less to him who deserves more, provided I give what I have agreed upon, while he offers as proof the words of our Saviour, in *Matthew,* xx. 13, certainly has nothing to do with the case. For in the passage which he cites, it is shown that a man does not sin against commutative justice (which governs a contract of hiring, leasing), if, in his generosity, he gives some a higher wage than is due them, or if, in a spirit of liberality, which is allowable in universal justice, he adds somewhat to the wage which is due by virtue of commutative justice; provided, of course, he does not fail to give the rest the wage which they had agreed to. But what has that to do with our distributive justice, which demands that a fair share shall be apportioned of a thing to which several have a right, that is perfect, but unequal, in regard to quantity? And the word *distributive,* used in the passage cited, by no means indicates that the instance was concerned with distributive justice, but merely that there were many workmen to each of whom a wage had to be given by commutative justice. . . .

10. But whatever be done that is owed by virtue of a mutual agreement, in cases concerning things and arts connected with business, that is called commutative justice. Since such agreements have as their object that, in return for my contribution or act in the business transaction, I shall receive from another an equivalent contribution or act, or one that at least seems so to me, the reason is plain why this form of justice requires a simple equality which is commonly called an arithmetical proportion, yet scarcely such in the eyes of mathematicians, although Plutarch, *On the Love of Brothers* [xii], uses the term arithmetical proportion in this popular sense. Therefore, the thing or act concerned with business should correspond exactly, so far as its moral worth is concerned, with the other which is given or furnished in consideration of it. For a little later I shall discuss at length the objection of Hobbes, *De Cive,* chap. iii, ¶ 6: "If we sell our merchandise for as much as we can get, no injustice is done the buyer, since he wanted and asked for it. . . ."

14. Now that the character of justice has been established, it is easy to define injustice and its various kinds. An action is, therefore, unjust, which is performed with evil intent upon a person to whom a different action was due, or which denies a person something which was due him. It is, indeed, injustice to do a man some evil which we had no right to do, or to deny, or take from a man some good thing which was due him, for the nature of good is such that it can be done for some one without cause, provided a third party suffers no injury thereby; of evil such that we can without injury avoid punishing a man as he merits, provided others suffer no damage thereby. Hence an unjust act either does to a man what should not have been done, or takes from him what should not have been taken, or denies to him what should have been given him, for even the denial or omission of an obligated action is considered in moral matters an action.

15. Now an unjust act, which is done from choice, and infringes upon the perfect right of another is commonly designated by the one word, *injury*. That this term may be clear, it should be borne in mind that an injury may be done to a man in three ways: first, by denying to him what by right he should have (M. Antoninus [Aurelius], Bk. IX, ¶ 5: "There is often an injustice of omission as well as of commission." (H.); second, by taking from him that which he already possesses; and third, by doing him some evil, which one had no right to do. Regarding the first kind of injury it should be observed that something is owed a man, either by the mere law of nature, such as deeds of humanity, beneficence, and gratitude, to which, however, he has no perfect right; or by a covenant, which is, in turn, either particular, or such as is expressed in our obligation to civil law, which binds us to do for others what the laws require. When things of the latter kind are denied a man, it is properly called an injury, but not so in the other case, although they constitute an offence against the law of nature. Nor can the law of nature compel a man to observe its obligations, especially when no supreme power lies in it, unless a strict necessity happens to arise, since, indeed, the character of nature's offices requires that they be rendered without compulsion or fear of punishment. And to this extent, therefore, the statement of Hobbes is true, that: "An injury can be done only to the person with whom there is a covenant." But when some evil is wrought upon a man who has given neither consent nor cause, by taking from him something which he already had, or by inflicting some positive injury, it is certainly always an injury, whether there be a covenant or not,

for nature gives every man the right that he be done no harm by another unless he has already been in the wrong, and no man unprovoked may hurt another, further than the due exercise of government shall require. We add the word "unprovoked," because the condition, τὸ πρότερον, namely, that it be first, is required in order to make an action an injury. Aristotle, *Nicomachean Ethics*, Bk. V, chap. xv: "A man who retaliates because of wrong done to him, and retaliates on the same scale, is not regarded as acting unjustly." (W.)

16. A further requirement for a real injury is, that it proceed from previous choice and determination to hurt or injure another. The mishaps, therefore, which occur by mere chance, through an ignorant and unwilling agent, do not come under the head of injuries; as, for instance, when a soldier, while practising with a javelin in his regular grounds, happens to hit a passer-by, or when a man trimming his trees on his own property, unexpectedly lets fall a branch on a person who had no right to be there. Antiphon, *Orations*, VII [3 в], employs the following defence for a man who hit a boy with his javelin:

He was not doing anything that was forbidden, but he was following instructions; he was hurling the javelin not among persons who were taking exercise, but he was in his proper place among the javelin-throwers; neither did he miss the mark and shoot among persons who were some distance away. And yet, although he was doing correctly just what he intended to, he was not the agent of an involuntary act, but the victim, in that he was prevented from succeeding in achieving his purpose.

The same point is covered by Aristotle, *Nicomachean Ethics*, Bk. V, chap. x: "The definition of an act of justice or injustice depends upon its voluntary or involuntary character." And further:

"When the hurt is done contrary to expectation, it is a mishap; but when, although it is not contrary to expectation, it does not imply malice, it is a mistake." (W.) Michael of Ephesus makes the following comments on this passage [*On the Nicomachean Ethics, Commentaria in Aristotelem,* vol. XX-III c, p. 53, 8 ff.]:

Of hurts some arise from ignorance and are involuntary, others with our knowledge and are voluntary. Of those which arise from ignorance some are unforeseen and surprising, others are involuntary, indeed, but not unforeseen and surprising. Now after saying that hurts arising from ignorance fall under the general designation of errors, Aristotle goes on to make a sub-division, and asserts that those which come about unforeseen we ought to call misfortunes, and those which do not come about unforeseen ought to be called errors, using the same name for them as for the whole class. Those which come about unforeseen, would be the rare and unexpected; for example, if some one should open the door suddenly, and his father who was standing nearby be hit, or if some one were shooting with bow and arrow in a spot which no one ordinarily traversed, and suddenly a person who was passing through by some accident, was hit by the missile. For such events are unforeseen and unexpected. [. . .] But actions which are not, indeed, unforeseen, but where the agent is ignorant, ought to be called errors. For the man who casts a javelin along a road, or in a spot where it is perfectly possible that people may be, and strikes somebody, has committed an error, and such hurts are called errors. For, says Aristotle, a man commits an error when the moving cause of the fault rests with him; and it rests with him in this instance, in so far as he was casting his javelin into a place which people habitually passed through.

A trespass, ἁμάρτημα, of this kind is properly called by the Jurisconsults a fault [*culpa*] which they define as something committed through carelessness and awkwardness, when a man neglects and fails to know, what he should and

could have known and observed. They give it three degrees, according as we can conceive of three degrees in proper care, the failure to observe which is fault. There is, first, the care common to all men, not sharpened by a keen mind or attentiveness, but arising, as it were, from common sense. Then there is the care of a more educated man, beyond common care, exercised by any one in his personal affairs, which nature requires of each man according to his wit and capacity. And there is, finally, a most exact care, which is observed by only the most careful householder in his affairs. To the last is commonly opposed what is called a very light [*levissima*] fault, to the second a light [*levis*], and to the first a serious [*lata*] fault. Regarding serious fault, they observe that it is equivalent to deceit in contracts and similar affairs, and when the case concerns the reparation of damage, but not in crimes, although in such it only lessens, but does not remove the offence. The effect of light and very light fault they show in general, when they discuss engagements in contracts.

Now when a man, through violent passion and an only partial intent, is driven to hurt another, such a hurt cannot escape the brand of injury, although the man may not at once be called unjust, because of inflicting it. Aristotle concludes, therefore, *Nicomachean Ethics,* Bk. V, chap. x:

When a person acts with knowledge, but without deliberation, it is an act of injustice, as in all human actions which arise from anger and other necessary or natural emotions; for in doing such hurt, and making such mistakes, we are unjust, and they are acts of injustice, but it does not follow that we are at once unjust or vicious, as the hurt is not the consequence of vice. But when the action is the result of deliberate purpose, the agent is unjust and wicked.

Hence it is rightly held that such actions as arise from anger are not done of malice prepense; for it is not he who acts in anger, but he who provoked the anger, that begins the quarrel. (W.)

17. Finally, an action to be called an injury must be done to one against his will, for it is a well-worn dictum that an injury cannot be done a man who wills it [*volenti non fieri iniuriam*]. Aristotle, *Nicomachean Ethics,* Bk. V, chap. xi: "Thus a person may be hurt, and may suffer what is unjust, voluntarily, but he cannot be the voluntary victim of injustice." (W.) The reason for this is, because the good of which I deprive another at his wish, or the obligation which I do not fulfil at his wish, is considered a present from him to me. Who will say that I have committed an injury, when I have only accepted what is given me? Nor can what a man wishes to have brought upon himself be held an evil, since, indeed, an evil necessarily involves an abhorrence on the part of the will, it being understood, of course, that the man enjoys the full use of his reason, and has not been completely carried away by some violent passion. Add Ant. Matthaeus, *De Criminibus Prolegomena,* chap. iii, ¶ 2–3. The definition of Hobbes, *De Cive,* chap. iii, ¶ 7, suffers from the difficulty that, under his theory, an injury can only arise from the violation of an agreement. And Aristotle draws the conclusion, *Nicomachean Ethics,* Bk. V, chap. xv, that the man who has been so angered as to commit suicide, has wrought an injury not upon himself, but upon the state, which he has deprived of the services of a general, soldier, workman, or some servant of this nature. And so a state which has been injured by such a man used to punish him by attaching some disgrace to his corpse or his memory. Add Michael of Ephesus, on Aristotle, *Nicomachean Ethics,* Bk. V, chap. xv. Although the statement of Aristotle, *loc. cit.,* that "the law does not allow κελεύει [suicide], and whatever it does not allow it forbids," is false, unless the verb κελεύειν (command) be taken in the sense of "permit."

Utilitarianism

Utilitarians expound the theory that moral and political decisions are justified by their utility, that is, by their conduciveness to "the greatest good of the greatest number." The movement was largely English and, in the opinion of some writers, it was considered the most important contribution of English thought to ethics. (Utilitarian schools also flourished in France and, to a lesser extent, in America.) Founded by Richard Cumberland in his book, *De legibus naturae* (1672), utilitarianism reached full expression in David Hume's *A Treatise of Human Nature* (1739). Afterwards, the writings of the Benthamites dominated utilitarian thought, beginning with Jeremy Bentham's *A Fragment on Government* (1776) and ending with James Mill's *A Fragment on Mackintosh* (1835). Its most influential expression is given in John Stuart Mill's *Utilitarianism* (1861), and its most completely developed statement is in Henry Sidgwick's *Methods of Ethics* (1874).

"I am an adherent of the *Principle of Utility*," wrote Bentham.

when I measure my approval or disapproval of any act, public or private, by its tendency to produce pains and pleasures; when I use the terms *just, unjust, moral, immoral, good, bad,* as comprehensive terms which embrace the idea of certain pains and certain pleasures, and have no other meaning whatsoever.

This quotation gives the general features of utilitarian moral theories. First, utilitarianism is hedonistic (from the Greek *hedone,* pleasure). Good means pleasure, evil means pain, and thus the greatest good and happiness mean the sum total of pleasures. Secondly, utilitarians teach directly and simply that of the various possibilities open to men, they ought to choose that which will produce the greatest happiness (pleasure) for the greatest number of persons. The determination of moral acts is made in terms of the consequences they produce. In ethical terminology, utilitarianism is a *teleological* ethics because of this emphasis on consequences and because the idea of "right" is defined and understood through relation to the good: what is right is what produces good. Teleological ethical theories stand opposed to *deontological* theories that hold men ought to do what is inherently right as determined by a direct consideration of actions or by reference to some general formal principle.* Bentham suggests that other moral terms like just have no meaning except in relation to pleasure and pain.

What sort of proof do utilitarians offer for this assertion as well as for the principle of utility itself? Bentham states† that utilitarianism is "self-referentially" true, for "when a man attempts to combat the principle of utility, it is with reasons drawn, without his being aware of it, from that very principle itself." Different in emphasis, though not completely dissimilar, is John Stuart Mill's discussion "Of What Sort of Proof the Principle of Utility Is Susceptible."‡ The only proof that an object is visible, he wrote, is that people actually see it. And in like manner, the sole evidence that anything is desirable is that people do actually desire it. "No reason can be given why the general happiness is desirable except that each person, so far as he believes it to be attainable, desires his own happiness."

Finally, the quotation from Bentham reflecting the antimetaphysical import of utilitarianism, suggests that apart from pleasure and pain, moral terms "have no other meaning whatsoever." As he also put it elsewhere, "Take away pleasures and pains [and] not only happiness, but justice and duty and obligation . . . are so many empty words." There are to be no metaphysical notions or "fictions" in ethics—pleasure and pain have empirical reference. There are objective standards, for ethical and political decisions are justified by their conduciveness to the greatest happiness for the greatest number. Utilitarianism thus proposes to build a system that will stand without the scaffolding of such ideas as natural law and right reason. As a philosophic movement, it reflects the expansion of scientific knowledge and philosophical criticism, which led to a fading of the authority of transcendent notions embodied in abstract reason for many thinkers.

The philosophic criticism alluded to is primarily that of David Hume (1711–1776), who was himself one of the great utilitarians. Hume's discussion of knowledge and reason has affected the whole course of political philosophy. He subjects the concept of reason used by natural law theorists to careful analysis, and finds it to involve a confusion of four ideas. The first is that any mere comparison of ideas is not related to fact. It is necessary to distinguish between mathematical certainty and empirical probability, between "relations of ideas" and "matters of fact." Relations of ideas such as logical and mathematical truths do give certainty, but Hume argues that they never can give men knowledge of fact. One way he tries to show this is by pointing out that the contradictory of any matter of fact is always possible—it is possible that the sun will not rise tomorrow, however hard it may be to believe—although the contradictory of a logical truth is always impossible. Perhaps his most famous use of this distinction relates to the analysis of causality. Cause and effect are two distinct events, and reasoning about

---

* Most historical theories of ethics actually contain both teleological and deontological elements; "pure" views are rare. In terms of theories thus far covered, utilitarianism is closest to a teleological theory, and the appeal to self-evidence in the Declaration of Independence approximates a deontological theory.

† *An Introduction to the Principles of Morals and Legislation,* Chapter 1.

‡ Chapter 4 of *Utilitarianism.*

them will not reveal any intrinsic causal relation between them. Only experience provides a basis for linking causes and effects. Further, if reason attempts to become "metaphysical" about causality, it falls into a logical circle. As Hume puts it,

We have said that all arguments concerning existence are founded on the relation of cause and effect; that our knowledge of that relation is derived entirely from experience; and that all our experimental conclusions proceed upon the supposition, that the future will be comformable to the past. To endeavor, therefore, the proof of this last supposition by probable arguments, or arguments regarding existence, must be evidently going in a circle, and taking that for granted which is the very point in question.

The second idea about which natural law theories are confused concerns knowledge based on experience, according to Hume. Such knowledge yields only probability of judgment, not certainty, and the probabilities achieved by knowledge are limited to experience. Consequently, reason has no valid transcendent use and metaphysical skepticism is the result. Next, Hume argues that reason does not dictate to men a way of acting; if anything is good, it is so by reference to their desires, inclinations, and approvals. Reason is morally neutral and merely "obeys the passions." It is good enough to give direction and planning for obvious ends and thus to be an instrument of limited practical control, but it is powerless to discern ultimate ends or to motivate men toward them. Last is the distinction between *is* and *ought* statements. The former refer to facts, the latter to judgments about values and ideals, and Hume asserts that no value judgment can be inferred from premises that are factual. Reason cannot derive an *ought* from an *is,* and if an *ought* is given in a conclusion, it is there either circularly (because it is also in a premise) or invalidly. The conclusion of a valid argument can contain nothing that is not contained in the premises.

In relation to many traditional philosophies, Hume's critique of reason is negative and destructive.§ Yet, for the most part, its implications were accepted by utilitarians, and his philosophy marks a turning point in philosophical theory. Reason no longer reflects absolute values; hence political thought must be interpreted in relative and human terms, with no religious or metaphysical explanation behind it. Morality is not founded on the "dictates of right reason," for reason dictates no values. The basis and authority of value judgments, individual and social, must be referred to their utility and ultimately to human motives and human propensities to action.

Man and Society

Utilitarians accept the main conclusions of Hume's destructive critique of reason which, when kept firmly in mind, results in a theory of society that may be more easily followed. These conclusions imply that a rational basis for society, including

---

§ Hume's work also influenced later positivism and much twentieth-century thought. There are many points of similarity between positivistic and utilitarian epistemologies; differences between them are mainly in ethical theory. See, for example, the remark by Lévy-Bruhl on p. 120.

natural law and rationalist ethics, is destroyed and that another foundation is required in its place. Utilitarians attempt to build this foundation by using a new account of human nature and moral experience and by the principle of utility. Again, David Hume provides a crucially significant doctrine of human nature for the utilitarian tradition.

Hume believes that man is better defined as a creature of passions, needs, and interests than as a rational being—important as the limited scope of reason is. Having denied that reason is anything but "the slave of the passions," Hume still must account for human action and motivation. Most central to his theory of society and one of the most important aspects of all human operations, is sympathy, which according to him involves pleasure and pain with respect to the experiences of other persons* and to which a number of functions are ascribed. Sympathy makes men susceptible to the feelings of others and accounts for the relative uniformity of taste and values in any group that gives it the cohesion of a community. Thus, the individual is not in isolation, and furthermore, he inevitably develops the sentiment of sympathy more fully by his association with others.

Moral action and judgment also have their roots in sympathy. Things or human qualities are not good or bad in themselves, nor could reason, in Hume's view, determine their goodness. Instead, the moral character of acts depends on how men feel about them and the rules that govern them. Moral qualities fall into two groups which Hume calls "natural" and "artificial" virtues. Natural virtues are those directly connected with sympathy and appear in personal conduct; artificial virtues rest on the different, though related, motive of enlightened self-love† and concern the social sphere, particularly in economic and state matters.

The conventions of morality (a term Hume uses that suggests the unprovable status of moral law) are developed with reference to men's permanent interest, and thus they arise out of men's needs. In like manner, society has its basis in the *advantage* of peace and order to mankind. Hume considers the social contract theory false both historically and logically‡ and maintains that it does not account for the origin of society. "Common interest and utility beget infallibly a standard of right and wrong," and no sanction of society and government beyond men's interests is demanded. Hume also denies that society and government, or the principles controlling them, should be called immutable and eternal for they are the result of human nature and its needs.

As the result of men's interests, society and the social virtues like justice that are founded on the grounds of association do not depend, as they do for Hobbes, on the power of government. In a sense, justice and other social virtues are prior to government, not consequent upon it. Men associate naturally and form governments out of their permanent interests, not because of fear and egoistic drives. Hume allows that if the circumstances are right, men will act justly even in the

---

* Sympathy is produced through the "association of ideas," a doctrine of Hume's psychology, with special reference to pleasure and pain.

† This is not Hobbes' universal selfishness, but it is men's permanent interest in government for their own virtue.

‡ Hume thinks it probable that government first arose out of quarrels. Utilitarian views on the social contract are discussed more fully in the sections "State, Power, and Authority" and "The Ideal of Justice" of this perspective.

absence of government. This implies finally, also against Hobbes, that the power of government depends on men's assent and obedience, rather than obedience depending on the power of government.

In summary, Hume teaches that association is natural to men, that the basis of moral distinctions is men's feelings, that men form governments to secure their long-range interests, that the advantage and utility of civilized society to individuals is the standard for judging particular social actions, and that certain social conventions, like justice, arise to serve and to increase the advantage of society to men.

DAVID HUME   Utility and Association

Had every man sufficient *sagacity* to perceive, at all times, the strong interest, which binds him to the observance of justice and equity, and *strength of mind* sufficient to persevere in a steady adherence to a general and a distant interest, in opposition to the allurements of present pleasure and advantage; there had never, in that case, been any such thing as government or political society, but each man, following his natural liberty, had lived in entire peace and harmony with all others. What need of positive law where natural justice is, of itself, a sufficient restraint? Why create magistrates, where there never arises any disorder or iniquity? Why abridge our native freedom, when, in every instance, the utmost exertion of it is found innocent and beneficial? It is evident, that, if government were totally useless, it never could have place, and that the SOLE foundation of the duty of ALLEGIANCE is the *advantage,* which it procures to society, by preserving peace and order among mankind.

When a number of political societies are erected, and maintain a great intercourse together, a new set of rules are immediately discovered to be *useful* in

that particular situation; and accordingly take place under the title of LAWS of NATIONS. Of this kind are, the sacredness of the person of ambassadors, abstaining from poisoned arms, quarter in war, with others of that kind, which are plainly calculated for the *advantage* of states and kingdoms, in their intercourse with each other.

The rules of justice, such as prevail among individuals, are not entirely suspended among political societies. All princes pretend a regard to the rights of other princes; and some, no doubt, without hypocrisy. Alliances and treaties are every day made between independent states, which would only be so much waste of parchment, if they were not found, by experience, to have *some* influence and authority. But here is the difference between kingdoms and individuals. Human nature cannot, by any means, subsist, without the association of individuals; and that association never could have place, were no regard paid to the laws of equity and justice. Disorder, confusion, the war of all against all, are the necessary consequences of such a licentious conduct. But nations can subsist without inter-

From David Hume, "An Enquiry Concerning the Principles of Morals," in *Essays Moral, Political and Literary,* eds. T. H. Green and T. H. Grose, London: Longmans, Green and Co., 1875.

course. They may even subsist, in some degree, under a general war. The observance of justice, though useful among them, is not guarded by so strong a necessity as among individuals; and the *moral obligation* holds proportion with the *usefulness*. All politicians will allow, and most philosophers, that REASONS of STATE may, in particular emergencies, dispense with the rules of justice, and invalidate any treaty or alliance, where the strict observance of it would be prejudicial, in a considerable degree, to either of the contracting parties. But nothing less than the most extreme necessity, it is confessed, can justify individuals in a breach of promise, or an invasion of the properties of others.

In a confederated commonwealth, such as the ACHÆAN republic of old, or the SWISS Cantons and United Provinces in modern times; as the league has here a peculiar *utility,* the conditions of union have a peculiar sacredness and authority, and a violation of them would be regarded as no less, or even as more criminal, than any private injury or injustice.

The long and helpless infancy of man requires the combination of parents for the subsistence of their young; and that combination requires the virtue of CHASTITY or fidelity to the marriage bed. Without such a *utility,* it will readily be owned, that such a virtue would never have been thought of.

An infidelity of this nature is much more *pernicious* in *women* than in *men.* Hence the laws of chastity are much stricter over the one sex than over the other.

These rules have all a reference to generation; and yet women past child-bearing are no more supposed to be exempted from them than those in the flower of their youth and beauty. *General rules* are often extended beyond the principle, whence they first arise; and this in all matters of taste and sentiment. It is a vulgar story at PARIS, that, during the rage of the MISSISSIPPI, a humpbacked fellow went every day into the RUE DE QUINCEMPOIX, where the stock-jobbers met in great crowds, and was well paid for allowing them to make use of his hump as a desk, in order to sign their contracts upon it. Would the fortune, which he raised by this expedient, make him a handsome fellow; though it be confessed, that personal beauty arises very much from ideas of utility? The imagination is influenced by associations of ideas; which, though they arise at first from the judgment, are not easily altered by every particular exception that occurs to us. To which we may add, in the present case of chastity, that the example of the old would be pernicious to the young; and that women, continually foreseeing that a certain time would bring them the liberty of indulgence, would naturally advance that period, and think more lightly of this whole duty, so requisite to society.

Those who live in the same family have such frequent opportunities of licence of this kind, that nothing could preserve purity of manners, were marriage allowed, among the nearest relations, or any intercourse of love between them ratified by law and custom. IN-CEST, therefore, being *pernicious* in a superior degree, has also a superior turpitude and moral deformity annexed to it.

What is the reason, why, by the ATHENIAN laws, one might marry a half-sister by the father, but not by the mother? Plainly this: The manners of the ATHENIANS were so reserved, that a man was never permitted to approach the women's apartment, even in the same family, unless where he visited his own mother. His step-mother and her children were as much shut up from him as the women of any other family, and there was as little danger of any criminal correspondence between them. Uncles and nieces, for a like reason, might marry at ATHENS; but neither these, nor half-brothers and sisters, could contract that alliance at ROME, where the intercourse was more open between the sexes. Public utility is the cause of all these variations.

To repeat, to a man's prejudice, any thing that escaped him in private conversation, or to make any such use of his private letters, is highly blamed. The free and social intercourse of minds much be extremely checked, where no such rules of fidelity are established.

Even in repeating stories, whence we can foresee no ill consequences to result, the giving of one's author is regarded as a piece of indiscretion, if not of immorality. These stories, in passing from hand to hand, and receiving all the usual variations, frequently come about to the persons concerned, and produce animosities and quarrels among people, whose intentions are the most innocent and inoffensive.

To pry into secrets, to open or even read the letters of others, to play the spy upon their words and looks and actions; what habits more inconvenient in society? What habits, of consequence, more blameable?

This principle is also the foundation of most of the laws of good manners; a kind of lesser morality, calculated for the ease of company and conversation. Too much or too little ceremony are both blamed, and every thing, which promotes ease, without an indecent familiarity, is useful and laudable.

Constancy in friendships, attachments, and familiarities, is commendable, and is requisite to support trust and good correspondence in society. But

in places of general, though casual concourse, where the pursuit of health and pleasure brings people promiscuously together, public conveniency has dispensed with this maxim; and custom there promotes an unreserved conversation for the time, by indulging the privilege of dropping afterwards every indifferent acquaintance, without breach of civility or good manners.

Even in societies, which are established on principles the most immoral, and the most destructive to the interests of the general society, there are required certain rules, which a species of false honour, as well as private interest, engages the members to observe. Robbers and pirates, it has often been remarked, could not maintain their pernicious confederacy, did they not establish a new distributive justice among themselves, and recall those laws of equity, which they have violated with the rest of mankind.

I hate a drinking companion, says the GREEK proverb, who never forgets. The follies of the last debauch should be buried in eternal oblivion, in order to give full scope to the follies of the next.

Among nations, where an immoral gallantry, if covered with a thin veil of mystery, is, in some degree, authorised by custom, there immediately arise a set of rules, calculated for the conveniency of that attachment. The famous court or parliament of love in PROVENCE formerly decided all difficult cases of this nature.

In societies for play, there are laws required for the conduct of the game; and these laws are different in each game. The foundation, I own, of such societies is frivolous; and the laws are, in a great measure, though not altogether, capricious and arbitrary. So far is there a material difference between them and the rules of justice, fidelity, and loyalty. The general societies of men are absolutely requisite for the subsistence of the species; and the public conveniency, which regulates morals, is inviolably established in the nature of man, and of the world, in which he lives. The comparison, therefore, in these respects, is very imperfect. We may only learn from it the necessity of rules, wherever men have any intercourse with each other.

They cannot even pass each other on the road without rules. Waggoners, coachmen, and postilions have principles, by which they give the way; and these are chiefly founded on mutual ease and convenience. Sometimes also they are arbitrary, at least dependent of a kind of capricious analogy, like many of the reasonings of lawyers.[1]

To carry the matter farther, we may observe, that it is impossible for men so much as to murder each other without statutes, and maxims, and an idea of justice and honour. War has its laws as well as peace; and even that sportive kind of war, carried on among wrestlers, boxers, cudgel-players, gladiators, is regulated by fixed principles. Common interest and utility beget infallibly a standard of right and wrong among the parties concerned. . . .

The more we converse with mankind, and the greater social intercourse we maintain, the more shall we be familiarized to these general preferences and distinctions, without which our conversation and discourse could scarcely be rendered intelligible to each other. Every man's interest is peculiar to himself, and the aversions and desires, which result from it, cannot be supposed to affect others in a like degree. General language, therefore, being formed for general use, must be moulded on some more general views, and must affix the epithets of praise or blame, in conformity to sentiments, which arise from the general interests of the community. And if these sentiments, in most men, be not so strong as those, which have a reference to private good; yet still they must make some distinction, even in persons the most depraved and selfish; and must attach the notion of good to a beneficent conduct, and of evil to the contrary. Sympathy, we shall allow, is much fainter than our concern for ourselves, and sympathy with persons remote from us, much fainter than that with persons near and contiguous; but for this very reason, it is necessary for us, in our calm judgments and discourse concerning the characters of men, to neglect all these differences, and render our sentiments more public and social. Besides, that we ourselves often change our situation in this particular, we every day meet with persons, who are in a situation different from us, and who could never converse with us, were we to remain constantly in that position and point of view, which is peculiar to ourselves. The intercourse of sentiments, therefore, in society and conversation, makes us form some general unalterable standard, by which we may approve or disapprove of characters and manners. And though the heart takes not part with those general notions, nor regulates all its love and hatred, by the universal, abstract differences of vice and virtue,

---

[1] That the lighter machine yield to the heavier, and, in machines of the same kind, that the empty yield to the loaded: this rule is founded on convenience. That those who are going to the capital take place of those who are coming from it; this seems to be founded on some idea of the dignity of the great city, and of the preference of the future to the past. From like reasons, among footwalkers, the right-hand intitles a man to the wall, and prevents jostling, which peaceable people find very disagreeable and inconvenient.

without regard to self, or the persons with whom we are more intimately connected; yet have these moral differences a considerable influence, and being sufficient, at least, for discourse, serve all our purposes in company, in the pulpit, on the theatre, and in the schools.[2]

Thus, in whatever light we take this subject, the merit, ascribed to the social virtues, appears still uniform, and arises chiefly from that regard, which the natural sentiment of benevolence engages us to pay to the interests of mankind and society. If we consider the principles of the human make, such as they appear to daily experience and observation, we must, *à priori,* conclude it impossible for such a creature as man to be totally indifferent to the well or ill-being of his fellow-creatures, and not readily, of himself, to pronounce, where nothing gives him any particular byass, that what promotes their happiness is good, what tends to their misery is evil, without any farther regard or consideration. Here then are the faint rudiments, at least, or out-lines, of a *general* distinction between actions; and in proportion as the humanity of the person is supposed to encrease, his connexion with those who are injured or benefited, and his lively conception of their misery or happiness; his consequent censure or approbation acquires proportionable vigour. There is no necessity, that a

---

[2] It is wisely ordained by nature, that private connexions should commonly prevail over universal views and considerations; otherwise our affections and actions would be dissipated and lost, for want of a proper limited object. Thus a small benefit done to ourselves, or our near friends, excites more lively sentiments of love and approbation than a great benefit done to a distant commonwealth: But still we know here, as in all the senses, to correct these inequalities by reflection, and retain a general standard of vice and virtue, founded chiefly on general usefulness.

generous action, barely mentioned in an old history or remote gazette, should communicate any strong feelings of applause and admiration. Virtue, placed at such a distance, is liked a fixed star, which, though to the eye of reason, it may appear as luminous as the sun in his meridian, is so infinitely removed, as to affect the senses, neither with light nor heat. Bring this virtue nearer, by our acquaintance or connexion with the persons, or even by an eloquent recital of the case; our hearts are immediately caught, our sympathy enlivened, and our cool approbation converted into the warmest sentiments of friendship and regard. These seem necessary and infallible consequences of the general principles of human nature, as discovered in common life and practice.

Again; reverse these views and reasonings: Consider the matter *à posteriori;* and weighing the consequences, enquire if the merit of social virtue be not, in a great measure, derived from the feelings of humanity, with which it affects the spectators. It appears to be matter of fact, that the circumstance of *utility,* in all subjects, is a source of praise and approbation: That it is constantly appealed to in all moral decisions concerning the merit and demerit of actions: That it is the *sole* source of that high regard paid to justice, fidelity, honour, allegiance, and chastity: That it is inseparable from all the other social virtues, humanity, generosity, charity, affability, lenity, mercy, and moderation: And, in a word, that it is a foundation of the chief part of morals, which has a reference to mankind and our fellow-creatures.

It appears also, that, in our general approbation of characters and manners, the useful tendency of the social virtues moves us not by any regards to self-interest, but has an influence much more universal and extensive. It appears, that a tendency to public good, and to the promoting of peace, harmony, and order in society, does always, by affecting the benevolent principles of our frame, engage us on the side of the social virtues. And it appears, as an additional confirmation, that these principles of humanity and sympathy enter so deeply into all our sentiments, and have so powerful an influence, as may enable them to excite the strongest censure and applause. The present theory is the simple result of all these inferences, each of which seems founded on uniform experience and observation.

Were it doubtful, whether there were any such principle in our nature as humanity or a concern for others, yet when we see, in numberless instances, that whatever has a tendency to promote the interests of society, is so highly approved of, we ought thence to learn the force of the benevolent principle; since it is impossible for any thing to please as means to an end, where the end is totally indifferent. On the other hand, were it doubtful, whether there were, implanted in our nature, any general principle of moral blame and approbation, yet when we see, in numberless instances, the influence of humanity, we ought thence to conclude, that it is impossible, but that every thing, which promotes the interest of society, must communicate pleasure, and what is pernicious give uneasiness. But when these different reflections and observations concur in establishing the same conclusion, must they not bestow an undisputed evidence upon it?

Social and Political Values

The commonly used phrase, "the greatest happiness of the greatest number," interpreted in hedonistic terms, provides a succinct statement of the values to which society and government are to be dedicated for the utilitarian. It calls attention to the maximization of pleasure as a social goal, and it suggests the utilitarian's belief that the only proper meaning of the common good is found in the sum total of individual goods. Yet the phrase also contains some uncertainties, especially when related to the historically developing utilitarian ethical theory.

Two such ambiguities demand special attention. The first is, how to understand "the greatest number"? Is the reference of this expression purely quantitative or can pleasures differ in quality as well? While some of the first hedonists were unclear about this question, Bentham was not. He believed that pleasures differed only in quantitative ways such as their duration and extent, and that therefore "the greatest happiness" is a quantitative expression. Since pleasures vary only in this way, Bentham also suggested that they could be predicted and controlled by a quasi-mathematical technique he called the calculus of pleasures. (Prior to Bentham, utilitarianism had not been a "calculating" ethics.) Quantitative determinations of the pleasure or pain consequent upon choices or social policies can be made, and the right choice thereby will be determined for the individual or the legislator.

It is at this point that John Stuart Mill (1806–1873) made one of his chief modifications of utilitarianism, for Mill found it necessary to assert that pleasures differ in quality as well as in quantity. The pleasures of the mind are distinct in kind from those of the body: "it is better to be a human being dissatisfied than a pig satisfied; better to be Socrates dissatisfied than a fool satisfied." Competent judges, or those who have had education and experience, declare that some pleasures are qualitatively preferable to others, and Mill concluded that their testimony is true.

A second ambiguity is whether the happiness of the formula is that of individuals who follow only egoistic interests, or whether utilitarianism admits altruistic motives as well. Most utilitarians held a doctrine of psychological as well as ethical hedonism. In addition to defining the good in terms of pleasure, they believed men are *motivated* to seek pleasure and avoid pain. Psychological hedonism seems to imply—though in fact it does not necessitate—egoism, and many of the early hedonists did hold a theory of egoism. Hume, with his basic notion of sympathy, did not; Bentham was somewhat ambiguous on this point; but John Stuart Mill clearly rejected egoism for an altruistic hedonism. The utilitarian standard, he argued, "is not the agent's own happiness, but the greatest amount of happiness altogether." The standard requires, in fact, strict impartiality between one's own happiness and that of others, and the golden rule contains the complete spirit of the ethics of utility: "to do as you would be done by, and to love your neighbor as yourself, constitute the ideal perfection of utilitarian morality."

Thus while Mill accepts the greatest happiness formula with other utilitarians, his ethical doctrines of altruism and qualitatively distinct pleasures lead him to the recognition that certain things—chiefly, freedom and the cultivation of individuality—must be accepted as good in their own right. In the chapter immediately preceding that from which the selection is taken, Mill argues for the freedom of men to form and to express opinions, for freedom of thought, of private judgment, and of discussion. His argument takes two forms, one utilitarian and one that may be called "moral." Observing that mankind is not infallible and has not gained all possible knowledge, and that freedom of thought is a necessary condition for inquiry, Mill argues first that society must grant maximum freedom to individuals in order to further and to protect the pursuit of knowledge. His second argument asserts that the ideal of moral maturity implies that an individual order and judge his life in the light of his own ideas and experiences. Hence, if moral maturity is to be achieved by the members of a society, that society must allow men freedom as a condition of maturity and self-development.

The argument of the selection itself is that men must be free not only to form opinions but also to *act* on their own opinions, so long as they do not molest others. The reasons for the two freedoms are the same: men are not infallible, unity of opinion is not desirable unless it is the result of full and free comparison of opposite opinions, and diversity is not an evil but a positive good. These reasons lead Mill further, for they imply that in any society there should be both different opinions and different modes of living. It is desirable, then, that individuality and

varieties of character should assert themselves when they do not concern others.*
Human beings are more valuable as their individuality is cultivated, which means
that desires and impulses as well as opinions should be one's own. Freedom, self-
determination, individuality: these then are the chief social and political values
that Mill developed for the utilitarian tradition.

---

* Mill attempts to clarify this qualification by a distinction between actions that are private
and those that are public. He does not deny that the latter, involving acts that may affect
others without their consent, should be regulated by government; he does insist however
that government should protect and maintain the autonomy of private acts.

JOHN STUART MILL Individuality

Such being the reasons which make it imperative that human beings should be free to form opinions, and to express their opinions without reserve; and such the baneful consequences to the intellectual, and through that to the moral nature of man, unless this liberty is either conceded, or asserted in spite of prohibition; let us next examine whether the same reasons do not require that men should be free to act upon their opinions—to carry these out in their lives, without hindrance, either physical or moral, from their fellow-men, so long as it is at their own risk and peril. This last proviso is of course indispensable. No one pretends that actions should be as free as opinions. On the contrary, even opinions lose their immunity, when the circumstances in which they are expressed are such as to constitute their expression a positive instigation to some mischievous act. An opinion that corn-dealers are starvers of the poor, or that private property is robbery, ought to be unmolested when simply circulated through the press, but may justly incur punishment when delivered orally to an excited mob assembled before the house of a corn-dealer, or when handed about among the same mob in the form of a placard. Acts of whatever kind, which,

without justifiable cause, do harm to others, may be, and in the more important cases absolutely require to be, controlled by the unfavorable sentiments, and, when needful, by the active interference of mankind. The liberty of the individual must be thus far limited; he must not make himself a nuisance to other people. But if he refrains from molesting others in what concerns them, and merely acts according to his own inclination and judgment in things which concern himself, the same reasons which show that opinion should be free, prove also that he should be allowed, without molestation, to carry his opinions into practice at his own cost. That mankind are not infallible; that their truths, for the most part, are only half-truths; that unity of opinion, unless resulting from the fullest and freest comparison of opposite opinions, is not desirable, and diversity not an evil, but a good, until mankind are much more capable than at present of recognizing all sides of the truth, are principles applicable to men's modes of action, not less than to their opinions. As it is useful that while mankind are imperfect there should be different opinions, so is it that there should be different experiments of living; that free scope should be given to varieties

---

From John Stuart Mill, *On Liberty,* New York: P. F. Collier and Son, 1909.

of character, short of injury to others; and that the worth of different modes of life should be proved practically, when any one thinks fit to try them. It is desirable, in short, that in things which do not primarily concern others, individuality should assert itself. Where, not the person's own character, but the traditions of customs of other people are the rule of conduct, there is wanting one of the principal ingredients of human happiness, and quite the chief ingredient of individual and social progress. . . .

He who lets the world, or his own portion of it, choose his plan of life for him, has no need of any other faculty than the ape-like one of imitation. He who chooses his plan for himself, employs all his faculties. He must use observation to see, reasoning and judgment to foresee, activity to gather materials for decision, discrimination to decide, and when he has decided, firmness and self-control to hold to his deliberate decision. And these qualities he requires and exercises exactly in proportion as the part of his conduct which he determines according to his own judgment and feelings is a large one. It is possible that he might be guided in some good path, and kept out of harm's way, without any of these things. But what will be his comparative worth as a human being? It really is of importance, not only what men do, but also what manner of men they are that do it. Among the works of man, which human life is rightly employed in perfecting and beautifying, the first in importance surely is man himself. Supposing it were possible to get houses built, corn grown, battles fought, causes tried, and even churches erected and prayers said, by machinery—by automatons in human form—it would be a considerable loss to exchange for these automatons even the men and women who at present in-

habit the more civilized parts of the world, and who assuredly are but starved specimens of what nature can and will produce. Human nature is not a machine to be built after a model, and set to do exactly the work prescribed for it, but a tree, which requires to grow and develop itself on all sides, according to the tendency of the inward forces which make it a living thing.

It will probably be conceded that it is desirable people should exercise their understandings, and that an intelligent following of custom, or even occasionally an intelligent deviation from custom, is better than a blind and simply mechanical adhesion to it. To a certain extent it is admitted, that our understanding should be our own: but there is not the same willingness to admit that our desires and impulses should be our own likewise; or that to possess impulses of our own, and of any strength, is anything but a peril and a snare. Yet desires and impulses are as much a part of a perfect human being, as beliefs and restraints: and strong impulses are only perilous when not properly balanced; when one set of aims and inclinations is developed into strength, while others, which ought to coexist with them, remain weak and inactive. It is not because men's desires are strong that they act ill; it is because their consciences are weak. There is no natural connection between strong impulses and a weak conscience. The natural connection is the other way. To say that one person's desires and feelings are stronger and more various than those of another, is merely to say that he has more of the raw material of human nature, and is therefore capable, perhaps of more evil, but certainly of more good. Strong impulses are but another name for energy. Energy may be turned to bad uses; but more good may always be made of an energetic nature, than of an indolent and impassive one. Those who have most natural feeling, are always those whose cultivated feelings may be made the strongest. The same strong susceptibilities which make the personal impulses vivid and powerful, are also the source from whence are generated the most passionate love of virtue, and the sternest self-control. It is through the cultivation of these, that society both does its duty and protects its interests: not by rejecting the stuff of which heroes are made, because it knows not how to make them. A person whose desires and impulses are his own —are the expression of his own nature, as it has been developed and modified by his own culture—is said to have a character. One whose desires and impulses are not his own, has no character, no more than a steam-engine has a character. If, in addition to being his own, his impulses are strong, and are under the government of a strong will, he has an energetic character. Whoever thinks that individuality of desires and impulses should not be encouraged to unfold itself, must maintain that society has no need of strong natures—is not the better for containing many persons who have much character—and that a high general average of energy is not desirable. . . .

It is not by wearing down into uniformity all that is individual in themselves, but by cultivating it and calling it forth, within the limits imposed by the rights and interests of others, that human beings become a noble and beautiful object of contemplation; and as the works partake the character of those who do them, by the same process human life also becomes rich, diversified, and animating, furnishing more abundant aliment to high thoughts and elevating feelings, and strengthening the tie which binds every individual to the race, by making the race infinitely better worth belonging to. In proportion to the development of his individuality, each person becomes more valuable to himself, and is therefore capable of being more valuable to others. There is a greater fulness of life about his own existence, and when there is more life in the units there is more in the mass which is composed of them. As much compression as is necessary to prevent the stronger specimens of human nature from encroaching on the rights of others, cannot be dispensed with; but for this there is ample compensation even in the point of view of human development. The means of development which the individual loses by being prevented from gratifying his inclinations to the injury of others, are chiefly obtained at the expense of the development of other people. And even to himself there is a full equivalent in the better development of the social part of his nature, rendered possible by the restraint put upon the selfish part. To be held to rigid rules of justice for the sake of others, develops the feelings and capacities which have the good of others for their object. But to be restrained in things not affecting their good, by their mere displeasure, develops nothing valuable, except such force of character as may unfold itself in resisting the restraint. If acquiesced in, it dulls and blunts the whole nature. To give any fair play to the nature of each, it is essential that different persons should be allowed to lead different lives. In proportion as this latitude has been exercised in any age, has that age been noteworthy to posterity. Even despotism does not produce its worst effects, so long as Individuality exists under it; and whatever crushes individuality is despotism, by whatever name it may be called, and whether it professes to be enforcing the will of God or the injunctions of men.

Having said that Individuality is the same thing with development, and that it is only the cultivation of individuality which produces, or can produce, well-developed human beings, I might here close the argument: for what more or better can be said of any condition of human affairs, than that it brings human beings themselves nearer to the best thing they can be? or what worse can be said of any obstruction to good, than that it prevents this? Doubtless, however, these considerations will not suffice to convince those who most need convincing; and it is necessary further to show, that these developed human beings are of some use to the undeveloped—to point out to those who do not desire liberty, and would not avail themselves of it, that they may be in some intelligible manner rewarded for allowing other people to make use of it without hindrance.

In the first place, then, I would suggest that they might possibly learn something from them. It will not be denied by anybody, that originality is a valuable element in human affairs. There is always need of persons not only to discover new truths, and point out when what were once truths are true no longer, but also to commence new practices, and set the example of more enlightened conduct, and better taste and sense in human life. This cannot well be gainsaid by anybody who does not believe that the world has already attained perfection in all its ways and practices. It is true that this benefit is not capable of being rendered by everybody alike: there are but few persons, in comparison with the whole of mankind, whose experiments, if adopted by others, would be likely to be any improvement on established practice. But these few are the salt of the earth; without them, human life would become a stagnant pool. Not only is it they who introduce good things which did not before exist; it is they who keep the life in those which already existed. If there were nothing new to be done, would human intellect cease to be necessary? Would it be a reason why those who do the old things should forget why they are done, and do them like cattle, not like human beings? There is only too great a tendency in the best beliefs and practices to degenerate into the mechanical; and unless there were a succession of persons whose ever-recurring originality prevents the grounds of those beliefs and practices from becoming merely traditional, such dead matter would not resist the smallest shock from anything really alive, and there would be no reason why civilization should not die out, as in the Byzantine Empire. Persons of genius, it is true, are, and are always likely to be, a small minority; but in order to have them, it is necessary to preserve the soil in which they grow. Genius can only breathe freely in an *atmosphere* of freedom. Persons of genius are, *ex vi termini, more* individual than any other people—less capable, consequently, of fitting themselves, without hurtful compression, into any of the small number of moulds which society provides in order to save its members the trouble of forming their own character. If from timidity they consent to be forced into one of these moulds, and to let all that part of themselves which cannot expand under the pressure remain unexpanded, society will be little the better for their genius. If they are of a strong character, and break their fetters they become a mark for the society which has not succeeded in reducing them to commonplace, to point at with solemn warning as "wild," "erratic," and the like; much as if one should complain of the Niagara river for not flowing smoothly between its banks like a Dutch canal.

I insist thus emphatically on the importance of genius, and the necessity of allowing it to unfold itself freely both in thought and in practice, being well aware that no one will deny the position in theory, but knowing also that almost every one, in reality, is totally indifferent to it. People think genius a fine thing if it enables a man to write an exciting poem, or paint a picture. But in its true sense, that of originality in thought and action, though no one says that it is not a thing to be admired, nearly all, at heart, think they can do very well without it. Unhappily this is too natural to be wondered at. Originality is the one thing which unoriginal minds cannot feel the use of. They cannot see what it is to do for them: how should they? If they could see what it would do for them, it would not be originality. The first service which originality has to render them, is that of opening their eyes: which being once fully done, they would have a chance of being themselves original. Meanwhile, recollecting that nothing was ever yet done which some one was not the first to do, and that all good things which exist are the fruits of originality, let them be modest enough to believe that there is something still left for it to accomplish, and assure themselves that they are more in need of originality, the less they are conscious of the want.

In sober truth, whatever homage may be professed, or even paid, to real or supposed mental superiority, the general tendency of things throughout the world is to render mediocrity the ascendant power among mankind. In ancient history, in the Middle Ages, and in a diminishing degree through the long transition from feudality to the present time, the individual was a power in himself; and if he had either great talents or a high social position, he was a considerable power. At present individuals are lost in the crowd. In politics it is almost a triviality to say that public opinion now rules the world. The only power deserving the name is that of masses, and of governments while they make themselves the organ of the tendencies and instincts of masses. This is as true in the moral and social relations of private life as in public transactions. Those whose opinions go by the name of public opinion, are not always the same sort of public: in America, they are the whole white population; in England, chiefly the middle class. But they are always a mass, that is to say, collective mediocrity. And what is still greater novelty, the mass do not now take their opinions from dignitaries in Church or State, from ostensible leaders, or from books. Their thinking is done for them by men much like themselves, addressing them or speaking in their name, on the spur of the moment, through the newspapers. I am not complaining of all this. I do not assert that anything better is compatible, as a general rule, with the present low state of the human mind. But that does not hinder the government of mediocrity from being mediocre government. No government by a democracy or a numerous aristocracy, either in its political acts or in the opinions, qualities, and tone of mind which it fosters, ever did or could rise above mediocrity, except in so far as the sovereign Many have let themselves be guided (which in their best times they always have done) by the counsels and influence of a more highly gifted and instructed One or Few. The initiation of all wise or noble things, comes and must come from individuals; generally at first from some one individual. The honor and glory of the average man is that he is capable of following that initiative; that he can respond internally to wise and noble things, and be led to them with his eyes open. I am not countenancing the sort of "hero-worship" which applauds the strong man of genius for forcibly seizing on the government of the world and making it do his bidding in spite of itself. All he can claim is, freedom to point out the way. The power of compelling others into it, is not only inconsistent with the freedom and development of all the rest, but corrupting to the strong man himself. It does seem, however, that when the opinions of masses of merely average men are everywhere become or becoming the dominant power, the counterpoise and corrective to that tendency would be, the more and more pronounced individuality of those who stand on the higher eminences of thought. It is in these circumstances most especially, that exceptional individuals, instead of being deterred, should be encouraged in acting differently from the mass. In other times there was no advantage in their doing so, unless they acted not only differently, but better. In this age the mere example of non-conformity, the mere refusal to bend the knee to custom, is itself a service. Precisely because the tyranny of opinion is such as to make eccentricity a reproach, it is desirable, in order to break through that tyranny, that people should be eccentric. Eccentricity has always abounded when and where strength of character has abounded; and the amount of eccentricity in a society has generally been proportional to the amount of genius, mental vigor, and moral courage which it contained. That so few now dare to be eccentric, marks the chief danger of the time.

I have said that it is important to give the freest scope possible to uncustomary things, in order that it may in time appear which of these are fit to be converted into customs. But independence of action, and disregard of custom are not solely deserving of encouragement for the chance they afford that better modes of action, and customs more worthy of general adoption, may be struck out; nor is it only persons of decided mental superiority who have a just claim to carry on their lives in their own way. There is no reason that all human existences should be constructed on some one, or some small number of patterns. If a person possesses any tolerable amount of common sense and experience, his own mode of laying out his existence is the best, not because it is the best in itself, but because it is his own mode. Human beings are not like sheep; and even sheep are not undistinguishably alike. A man cannot get a coat or a pair of boots to fit him, unless they are either made to his measure, or he has a whole warehouseful to choose from: and is it easier to fit him with a life than with a coat, or are human beings more like one another in their whole physical and spiritual conformation than in the shape of their feet? If it were only that people have diversities of taste that is reason enough for not attempting to shape them all after one model. But different persons also require different conditions for their spiritual development; and can no more exist healthily in the same moral, than all the variety of plants can in the same physical atmosphere and climate. The same things which are helps to one person towards the cultivation of his higher nature, are hindrances to another. The same mode of life is a healthy excitement to one, keeping all his faculties of action and enjoyment in their best order, while to another it is a distracting burden, which suspends or crushes all internal life. Such are the differences among human beings in their sources of pleasure, their susceptibilities of pain, and the operation on them of different physical and moral agencies, that unless there is a corresponding diversity in their modes of life, they neither obtain their fair share of happiness, nor grow up to the mental, moral, and æsthetic stature of which their nature is capable. Why then should tolerance, as far as the public sentiment is concerned, extend only to tastes and modes of life which extort acquiescence by the multitude of their adherents? Nowhere (except in some monastic institutions) is diversity of taste entirely unrecognized; a person may without blame, either like or dislike rowing, or smoking, or music, or athletic exercises, or chess, or cards, or study, because both those who like each of these things, and those who dislike them, are too numerous to be put down. But the man, and still more the woman, who can be accused either of doing "what nobody does," or of not doing "what everybody does," is the subject of as much depreciatory remark as if he or she had committed some grave moral delinquency. Persons require to possess a title, or some other badge of rank, or the consideration of people of rank, to be able to indulge somewhat in the luxury of doing as they like without detriment to their estimation. To indulge somewhat, I repeat: for whoever allow themselves much of that indulgence, incur the risk of something worse than disparaging speeches—they are in peril of a commission *de lunatico,* and of having their property taken from them and given to their relations. . . .

The combination of all these causes forms so great a mass of influences hostile to Individuality, that it is not easy to see how it can stand its ground. It will do so with increasing difficulty, unless the intelligent part of the public can be made to feel its value—to see that it is good there should be differences, even though not for the better, even though, as it may appear to them, some should be for the worse. If the claims of Individuality are ever to be asserted, the time is now, while much is still wanting to complete the enforced assimilation. It is only in the earlier stages that any stand can be successfully made against the encroachment. The demand that all other people shall resemble ourselves, grows by what it feeds on. If resistance waits till life is reduced *nearly* to one uniform type, all deviations from that type will come to be considered impious, immoral, even monstrous and contrary to nature. Mankind speedily become unable to conceive diversity, when they have been for some time unaccustomed to see it.

State, Power, and Authority

Basing their social philosophy on the principle of utility, utilitarians find most of the doctrines of alternative social philosophies to be only "fictions," as Bentham (1748–1832) put it. The social contract, the community, the common good, the separation of powers—these and other notions fall under Bentham's judgment. He tried to describe the nature of political society in terms of interests and habits of obedience, and to understand the "advantage" of society to men in reference to empirical needs and men's desire to obey government.

Utilitarians have generally supported democracy and representative government. Their argument for democracy starts from the greatest happiness principle—it is the right of every man that his happiness shall not count for less than that of anyone else. This implication, together with the assumptions that every man considers own interests and that he is usually the best judge of them, leads to the principle of the sovereignty of the people. A society of any size, however, could not rule itself in the manner of "pure" democracies, and therefore it is necessary to have a representative scheme where it will be in the people's interest to choose representatives who are anxious to promote all the interests of the people.

Starting as they do from the utilitarian principle rather than natural rights or the common good, these arguments carry further implications about the nature of government. The community is only a "fictitious body" (Bentham), and the interest of the community is but the sum of the interests of those who compose it. Universal suffrage follows from the equal value of every man's happiness, and Bentham and Mill worked to achieve this goal as well as the rights of women. The complete sovereignty of the people meant for Bentham that the legislative branch of government should have but one chamber, and that "checks and balances" in government prevent the full working of democracy. His *Fragment* contains the first effective attack on the doctrine of the separation of powers since it was formulated by Polybius in ancient Greece. Because the satisfaction of human needs is the sole justification of government, Bentham argued that the power of government is effectively to be checked only by the interests of the community.

The selections present some of these utilitarian ideas on the state, power, and authority. Writing in opposition to Blackstone,* Bentham rejects (as did Hume before him) the fiction of the social contract as the basis of government. The doctrine is supposed to account for just government and for political obligation. In fact, it does neither. If the king be supposed the agent of the people's happiness, how can one determine, asks Bentham, whether he has acted against the people's happiness? There is nothing in the contract to decide this crucial issue. Shall it be decided on the question of whether the king rules according to law?—even though he might make laws against the people's happiness, or he might still rule by law but against happiness. The contract does not fare any better on obligation, for one may question why ought men to keep their promises. An intelligible answer would be that it is to men's advantage to keep them, but then there is no need to speak of obligations following from a contract. Utility alone provides the reason for the existence of authority.

Father of John Stuart Mill and ardent Benthamite, James Mill (1773–1836) interprets government as a means to the end of human happiness. The materials needed for happiness are scarce and depend on labor. Therefore, the power of protecting these materials is given to a small group of men, and this is government—a device for protecting men from one another, especially regarding greed for an-

---

* Sir William Blackstone (1723–1780), perhaps the most famous of English jurists. His *Commentaries* had a great influence in England and America.

other's property. Government implies power, which is defined by Mill as security in the conformity of the will of one man and the acts of other men. Power, however, is of such a nature that there is no limit to the desire to possess it. The existence of power, therefore, presents a problem that is resolved only by representative government with the right system of checks. And these checks are finally only the interests of the community itself.

JEREMY BENTHAM Utility and Government

XXXIX. A compact, then, it was said, was made by the King and People: the terms of it were to this effect:—The People, on their part, promised to the King a *general obedience:* the King, on his part, promised to *govern* the People in such a *particular* manner always, as should be *subservient* to their happiness. I insist not on the words: I undertake only for the sense; as far as an imaginary engagement, so loosely and so variously worded by those who have imagined it, is capable of any decided signification. Assuming, then, as a general rule, that promises, when made, ought to be observed; and, as a point of fact, that a promise to this effect in particular had been made by the party in question, men were more ready to deem themselves qualified to judge when it was such a promise was *broken,* than to decide directly and avowedly on the delicate question, when it was that a King acted so far in *opposition* to the happiness of his People, that it were better no longer to obey him.

XL. It is manifest, on a very little consideration, that nothing was gained by this manoeuvre after all: no difficulty removed by it. It was still necessary, and that as much as ever, that the question men studied to avoid should be determined, in order to determine the

question they thought to substitute in its room. It was still necessary to determine, whether the King in question had, or had not, acted so far in *opposition* to the happiness of his people, that it were better no longer to obey him; in order to determine, whether the promise he was supposed to have made, had or had not been broken. For what was the supposed purport of this promise? It was no other than what has just been mentioned.

XLI. Let it be said, that part at least of this promise was to govern in *subservience to Law:* that hereby a more precise rule was laid down for his conduct, by means of this supposal of a promise, than that other loose and general rule to govern in subservience to the *happiness of his people:* and that, by this means, it is the letter of the *Law* that forms the tenor of the rule.

Now true it is, that the governing in opposition to Law, is *one* way of governing in opposition to the happiness of the people: the natural effect of such a contempt of the Law being, if not actually to destroy, at least to threaten with destruction, all those rights and privileges that are founded on it: rights and privileges on the enjoyment of which that happiness depends. But still it is not this that can be safely taken

From Jeremy Bentham, "A Fragment on Government," in *The Works of Jeremy Bentham*, ed. John Bowring, Edinburgh: William Tait, 1843.

for the entire purport of the promise here in question: and that for several reasons. *First,* Because the most mischievous, and under certain constitutions the most feasible, method of governing in opposition to the happiness of the people, is, by setting the Law itself in opposition to their happiness. *Second,* Because it is a case very conceivable, that a King may, to a great degree, impair the happiness of his people without violating the letter of any single Law. *Third,* Because extraordinary occasions may now and then occur, in which the happiness of the people may be better promoted by acting, for the moment, in *opposition* to the Law, than in *subservience* to it. *Fourth,* Because it is not any single violation of the Law, as such, that can properly be taken for a breach of his part of the contract, so as to be understood to have released the people from the obligation of performing theirs. For, to quit the fiction, and resume the language of plain truth, it is scarce ever any single violation of the Law that, by being *submitted to,* can produce so much mischief as shall surpass the probable mischief of *resisting* it. If every single instance whatever of such a violation were to be deemed an entire dissolution of the contract, a man who reflects at all would scarce find any where, I believe, under the sun, that Government which he could allow to subsist for twenty years together. It is plain, therefore, that to pass any sound decision upon the question which the inventors of this fiction substituted instead of the true one, the latter was still necessary to be decided. All they gained by their contrivance was, the convenience of deciding it obliquely, as it were, and by a side wind; that is, in a crude and hasty way, without any direct and steady examination.

XLII. But, after all, for what *reason* is it, that men *ought* to keep their promises? The moment any intelligible reason is given, it is this: that it is for the *advantage* of society they should keep them; and if they do not, that as far as *punishment* will go, they should be *made* to keep them. It is for the advantage of the whole number that the promises of each individual should be kept: and, rather than they should not be kept, that such individuals as fail to keep them should be punished. If it be asked, how this appears? the answer is at hand:—Such is the benefit to gain, and mischief to avoid, by keeping them, as much more than compensates the mischief of so much punishment as is requisite to oblige men to it. Whether the dependence of *benefit* and *mischief* (that is, of *pleasure* and *pain*) upon men's conduct in this behalf, be as here stated, is a question of *fact,* to be decided, in the same manner that all other questions of fact are to be decided, by testimony, observation, and experience.

XLIII. This, then, and no other, being the *reason* why men should be made to keep their promises, viz. that it is for the advantage of society that they should, is a reason that may as well be given at once why *Kings,* on the one hand, in governing, should in general keep within established Laws, and (to speak universally) abstain from all such measures as tend to the unhappiness of their subjects: and, on the other hand, why *subjects* should obey Kings as long as they so conduct themselves, and no longer; why they should obey, in short, *so long as the probable mischiefs of obedience are less than the probable mischiefs of resistance:* why, in a word, taking the whole body together, it is their *duty* to obey just so long as it is their *interest,* and no longer. This being the case, what need of saying of the one, that *he* PROMISED so to *govern;*

of the other, that they PROMISED so to *obey,* when the fact is otherwise?

XLVII. But farther. Allow, for argument's sake, what we have disproved: allow that the obligation of a promise is independent of every other: allow that a promise is binding *propriâ vi:* Binding, then, on whom? On him certainly who makes it. Admit this: For what reason is the same individual promise to be binding on those who *never* made it? The King, *fifty years* ago, promised my *Great-Grandfather* to govern him according to Law: my Great-Grandfather, *fifty years ago,* promised the King to obey him according to Law. The King, *just now,* promised my *neighbour* to govern him according to Law: my neighbour, *just now,* promised the King to obey him according to Law. Be it so: What are these promises, all or any of them, to *me?* To make answer to this question, some other principle, it is manifest, must be resorted to, than that of the *intrinsic* obligation of promises upon those who make them.

XLVIII. Now this *other* principle that still recurs upon us, what other can it be than the *principle of* UTILITY? The principle which furnishes us with that *reason,* which alone depends not upon any higher reason, but which is itself the sole and all-sufficient reason for every point of practice whatsoever.

JAMES MILL   Power and
Representative Government

The question with respect to Government, is a question about the adaptation of means to an end. Notwithstanding the portion of discourse which has been bestowed upon this subject, it is surprising to find, upon a close inspection, how few of its principles are settled. The reason is, that the ends and means have not been analyzed; and it is only a general and undistinguishing conception of them which exists in the minds of the greater number of men. So long as either remain in this situation, they give rise to interminable disputes; more especially when the deliberation is subject, as in this case, to the strongest action of personal interest.

In a discourse, limited as the present, it would be obviously vain to attempt the accomplishment of such a task, as that of the analysis we have mentioned. The mode, however, in which the operation should be conducted, may perhaps be described, and evidence enough exhibited to show in what road we must travel to approach the point at which so many have vainly endeavoured to arrive.

The end of government has been described in a great variety of expressions. By Locke it was said to be "the public good"; by others it has been described as being "the greatest happiness of the greatest number." These, and equivalent expressions, are just; they are only defective in as much as the particular ideas which they embrace are indistinctly announced; and different combinations are by means of them raised in different minds, and even in

From James Mill's article on "Government," *Encyclopaedia Britannica,* Supplement to the 5th edition (1815–1818), Vol. 4.

the same mind on different occasions.

It is immediately obvious, that a wide and difficult field is opened, and that the whole science of human nature must be explored to lay a foundation for the science of government. To understand what is included in the happiness of the greatest number, we must understand what is included in the happiness of the individuals of whom it is composed.

That dissection of human nature which would be necessary to show, on proper evidence, the primary elements into which human happiness may be resolved, it is not compatible with the present design to undertake. We must content ourselves with assuming certain results.

We may allow, for example, in general terms, that the lot of every human being is determined by his pains and pleasures; and that his happiness corresponds with the degree in which his pleasures are great, and his pains are small.

Human pains and pleasures are derived from two sources. They are produced either by our fellow men, or by causes independent of other men.

We may assume it as another principle, that the concern of government is with the former of these two sources; and that its business is to increase to the utmost the pleasures, and diminish to the utmost the pains, which men derive from one another.

Of the laws of nature, on which the condition of man depends, that which is attended with the greatest number of consequences, is the necessity of labour for obtaining the means of subsistence, as well as the means of the greatest part of our pleasures. This is, no doubt, the primary cause of government; for, if nature had produced spontaneously all the objects which we desire, and in sufficient abundance for the desires of all, there would have been no source of dispute or of injury among men; nor would any man have possessed the means of ever acquiring authority over another.

The results are exceedingly different, when nature produces the objects of desire not in sufficient abundance for all. The source of dispute is then exhaustless; and every man has the means of acquiring authority over others, in proportion to the quantity of those objects which he is able to possess. In this case, the end to be obtained, through government as the means, would be, to make that distribution of the scanty materials of happiness which would insure the greatest sum of it in the members of the community taken altogether; and to prevent every individual, or combination of individuals, from interfering with that distribution, or making any man to have less than his share.

An element of great importance is taken into the calculation, when it is considered that most of the objects of desire, and even the means of subsistence, are the product of labour. The means of insuring labour must, in that case, be provided for as the foundation of all.

The means for the insuring of labour are of two sorts; the one made out of the matter of evil, the other made out of the matter of good. The first sort is commonly denominated force; and, under its application, the labourers are slaves. This mode of procuring labour we need not consider; for, if the end of government be to produce the greatest happiness of the number, that end cannot be attained by making the greatest number slaves.

The other mode of obtaining labour is by allurement, or the advantage which it brings. If we would obtain all the objects of desire in the greatest possible quantity, we must obtain labour in the greatest possible quantity; and, if we would obtain labour in the greatest possible quantity, we must raise the advantage attached to labour to the greatest possible height. It is impossible to attach to labour a greater degree of advantage than the whole of the product of labour. Why so? Because, if you give more to one man than the produce of his labour, you can do so only by taking it away from the produce of some other man's labour. The greatest possible happiness of society is, therefore, attained by insuring to every man the greatest possible quantity of the produce of his labour.

How is this to be accomplished? For it is obvious that every man who has not all the objects of his desire, has inducement to take them from any other man who is weaker than himself. And how is this to be prevented? One mode is sufficiently obvious; and it does not appear that there is any other. It is the union of a certain number of men, agreeing to protect one another; and the object is best accomplished when a great number of men combine together, and delegate to a small number the power necessary for protecting them all. This is government. And it thus appears, that it is for the sake of property that government exists. . . .

That one human being will desire to render the person and property of another subservient to his pleasure, notwithstanding the pain or loss of pleasure which it may occasion to that other individual, is the foundation of government. The desire of the object implies the desire of the power necessary to accomplish the object. The desire, therefore, of that power which is necessary to render the persons and properties of

human beings subservient to our pleasures, is a grand governing law of human nature.

What is implied in that desire of power? and what is the extent to which it carries the actions of men? are the questions which it is necessary to resolve, in order to discover the limit which nature has set to the desire of a king, or an aristocracy, to inflict evil upon the community for their own advantage.

Power is a means to an end. The end is every thing, without exception, which the human being calls pleasure, and the removal of pain. The grand instrument for attaining what a man likes, is the actions of other men. Power, in its most appropriate signification, therefore, means security for the conformity between the will of one man and the acts of other men. This, we presume, is not a proposition which will be disputed. The master has power over his servant, because when he wills him to do so and so, in other words, expresses a desire that he would do so and so, he possesses a kind of security that the actions of the man will correspond to his desire. The general commands his soldiers to perform certain operations, the king commands his subjects to act in a certain manner, and their power is complete or not complete, in proportion as the conformity is complete or not complete between the actions willed and the actions performed. The actions of other men, considered as means for the attainment of the objects of our desire, are perfect or imperfect, in proportion as they are or are not certainly and invariably correspondent to our will.—There is no limit, therefore, to the demand of security for the perfection of that correspondence. A man is never satisfied with a smaller degree if he can obtain a greater. And as there is no man whatsoever, whose acts, in some degree or another, in some way or another, more immediately or more remotely, may not have some influence as means to our ends, there is no man, the conformity of whose acts to our will we would not give something to secure. The demand, therefore, of power over the acts of other men is really boundless. It is boundless in two ways; boundless in the number of persons to whom we would extend it, and boundless in its degree over the actions of each.

It would be nugatory to say, with a view to explain away this important principle, that some human beings may be so remotely connected with our interests, as to make the desire of a conformity between our will and their actions evanescent. It is quite enough to assume, what nobody will deny, that our desire of that conformity is unlimited, in respect to all those men whose actions can be supposed to have any influence on our pains and pleasures. With respect to the rulers of a community, this at least is certain, that they have a desire for the uniformity between their will and the actions of every man in the community. And for our present purpose this is as wide a field as we need to embrace.

With respect to the community, then, we deem it an established truth, that the rulers, one, or a few, desire an exact uniformity between their will and the acts of every member of the community. It remains for us to inquire to what description of acts it is the nature of this desire to give existence.

There are two classes of means, by which the conformity between the will of one man and the acts of other men may be accomplished. The one is pleasure, the other pain.

With regard to securities of the pleas-urable sort for obtaining a conformity between one man's will and the acts of other men, it is evident, from experience, that when a man possesses a command over the objects of desire, he may, by imparting those objects to other men, insure to a great extent the conformity between his will and their actions. It follows, and is also matter of experience, that the greater the quantity of the objects of desire, which he may thus impart to other men, the greater is the number of men between whose actions and his own will he can insure a conformity. As it has been demonstrated that there is no limit to the number of men whose actions we desire to have conformable to our will, it follows, with equal evidence, that there is no limit to the command which there are motives for endeavouring to possess over the objects of desire.

It is, therefore, not true, that there is in the mind of a king, or in the minds of an aristocracy, any point of saturation with the objects of desire. The opinion, in examination of which we have gone through the preceding analysis, that a king or an aristocracy may be satiated with the objects of desire, and, after being satiated, leave to the members of the community the greater part of what belongs to them, is an opinion founded upon a partial and incomplete view of the laws of human nature.

We have next to consider the securities of the painful sort which may be employed for attaining conformity between the acts of one man and the will of another. We are of opinion, that the importance of this part of the subject has not been duly considered; and that the business of government will be ill understood, till its numerous consequences have been fully developed.

Pleasure appears to be a feeble instrument of obedience in comparison with pain. It is much more easy to despise pleasure than pain. Above all it is important to consider, that in this class of instruments is included the power of taking away life, and with it of taking away not only all the pleasures of reality, but, what goes so far beyond them, all the pleasures of hope. This class of securities is, therefore, incomparably the strongest. He who desires obedience to a high degree of exactness, cannot be satisfied with the power of giving pleasure, he must have the power of inflicting pain. He who desires it to the highest possible degree of exactness, must desire power of inflicting pain sufficient at least to insure that degree of exactness, that is, an unlimited power of inflicting pain; for, as there is no possible mark by which to distinguish what is sufficient and what is not, and as the human mind sets no bounds to its avidity for the securities of what it deems eminently good, it is sure to extend, beyond almost any limits, its desire of the power of giving pain to others.

So much with respect to the motive for having and holding power of inflicting pain upon others. It may, however, be said, that how inseparable a part soever of human nature it may appear to be to desire to possess unlimited power of inflicting pain upon others, it does not follow, that those who possess it will have a desire to make use of it. . . .

What then is to be done? For, according to this reasoning, we may be told that good government appears to be impossible. The people, as a body, cannot perform the business of government for themselves. If the powers of government are entrusted to one man, or a few men, and a monarchy, or governing aristocracy, is formed, the results are fatal.

And it appears that a combination of the simple forms is impossible.

Notwithstanding the certainty of these propositions, it is not yet proved that good government is impossible. For though it is perfectly true that, as the people cannot exercise the powers of government themselves, they must entrust them to some one individual, or set of individuals, and these individuals will, infallibly, have the strongest motives to make a bad use of them; it is nevertheless possible that checks may be found sufficient to prevent the bad use of them. The next subject of inquiry, then, is the doctrine of checks. It is sufficiently conformable to the established and new-fashioned opinions to say, that, upon the right constitution of checks, all goodness of government depends. To this proposition we fully subscribe. Nothing, therefore, can exceed the importance of correct conclusions upon this subject. After the developments which we have already made, it is hoped that the inquiry will be neither intricate nor unsatisfactory.

In the grand discovery of modern times, the system of representation, the solution of all the difficulties, both speculative and practical, will perhaps be found. If it cannot, we seem to be forced upon the extraordinary conclusion, that good government is impossible. For as there is no individual, or combination of individuals, except the community itself, who have not an interest in bad government, if entrusted with its powers; and as the community itself is incapable of exercising those powers, and must entrust them to some individual or combination of individuals, the conclusion is obvious. The community itself must check these individuals, or they will follow their interest, and produce bad government.

Law and Rights

The chief factors underlying a utilitarian theory of law have now been developed. The critique of ideas and the antimetaphysical temper of utilitarians destroyed the traditional notion that reason reflects a transcendent and eternal Law of Nature. Natural law and right reason are regarded ultimately as subjective fantasies created by the mind itself, with none of the objective validity that had ben claimed for them. There being no natural law and right, the utilitarian substitutes human conventions, which, based on the common experience of mankind, are adopted by men because it is in their interest to do so. The variety of human interests and the conflicts that might arise in the search for satisfaction lead men to place themselves under the power of government and to acknowledge it.

A theory of law based upon these factors is given in the selection from John Austin (1790–1859). Every positive law, Austin writes, is set by some sovereign individual or body whose purpose is to confer beneficent rights on individuals in ways conducive to their common happiness. As issued by a sovereign, law takes the form of a command, which is the expression of a desire coupled with the power to inflict pain if the desire is disregarded. The command produces an obligation of obedience because failure to obey may issue in evil (pain). Command and duty are in fact correlative terms, and when coupled with the notion of a sanction, all the elements needed for an understanding of law are present. And in so far as laws are what they ought to be, they are based on utility. Whether they are truly based on utility must be determined, Austin concludes, through observation and induction.*

Through these ideas, Austin became the founder of what is usually termed the school of analytic jurisprudence. This school seeks to develop a jurisprudence devoted to the analysis and "censure" (Bentham) of the law in the light of its contribution to the general happiness. The method it follows is generally the construction in clear and logical ways of a system of law based on firm foundations. Austin himself sought to do this in his definition of law as the command of a sovereign. Challenging both natural law theories and metaphysical idealisms, this definition makes sovereignty rather than any ideal of justice the essential element of law. Justice is related externally, not internally, to the definition.†

This last observation, together with Austin's emphasis on command and sovereignty, makes it imperative to contrast his views with those of the positivists, particu-

---

* Austin does write often as though the will of God is the ultimate test of laws, while utility is their proximate test. In fact, however, the former has no real juristic significance in Austin's theory as it did, for example, in medieval theories.

† An external relation is one that makes no difference to, or is not included in, its terms; an internal relation does affect the nature of the terms it relates. Austin suggests below that command, duty, and sanction are internally related: each term signifies the same notion, but each denotes a different part of that notion and connotes the rest. Anxious to define law as it is, however, he finds it related externally to justice. An unjust law is still a law, though a command without a sanction is not a law.

larly in regard to morality and power.‡ Utilitarians differ essentially from Hobbes, for example, in that they distinguish law and morals, and hold that moral rules are not laws. Laws are rules enforced by authority. But is this authority absolute? Utilitarians such as Austin (and Bentham before him) answer that the notion of legal sovereignty does indeed mean a legally unlimited right to make law. Yet complete legal sovereignty does not imply supreme and complete sovereignty, nor does it carry threats to liberty. No direct connection is posited between legal supremacy and obedience; the duties of subjects to rulers depend on how they rule. Effective sovereignty, as Hume had already pointed out, rests on a prelegal element, namely the habit of obedience from the bulk of society. Thus, on the one hand, the supreme legislative authority is limited both morally (since the rules of utility never collapse into the definition of law) and in fact (since authority rests on human habits); and on the other hand, in contrast to Montesquieu, the limitation of power by power does not exclude legal supremacy.

‡ Yet Austin's work has had tremendous influence on recent positivist schools. In part the reason is that Austin's theory of law is related externally to the principle of utility as to the ideal of justice. The theory can thus be separated from its context and used in the analytic, descriptive ways acceptable to positivists.

JOHN AUSTIN   Law as Command

Every *law* or *rule* (taken with the largest signification which can be given to the term *properly*) is a *command*. Or, rather, laws or rules, properly so called, are a *species* of commands.

Now, since the term *command* comprises the term *law,* the first is the simpler as well as the larger of the two. But, simple as it is, it admits of explanation. And, since it is the *key* to the sciences of jurisprudence and morals, its meaning should be analyzed with precision.

Accordingly, I shall endeavour, in the first instance, to analyze the meaning of "*command*": an analysis which is necessarily difficult and involves circumlocution in proportion as the term to be explained is simple.

If you express or intimate a wish that I shall do or forebear from some act, and if you will visit me with an evil in case I comply not with your wish, the *expression* or *intimation* of your wish is a command. A command is distinguished from other significations of desire, not by the style in which the desire is signified, but by the power and the purpose of the party commanding to inflict an evil or pain in case the desire be disregarded. If you cannot or will not harm me in case I comply not with your wish, the expression of your wish is not a command, although you utter your wish in imperative phrase. If you are able and willing to harm me in case I comply not with your wish, the expression of your wish amounts to a command, although you are prompted by a spirit of courtesy to utter it in the shape of a request. "*Preces erant, sed quibus contradici non posset.*" Such is

From John Austin, *Lectures on Jurisprudence,* ed. Robert Campbell, New York: Henry Holt and Co., 1873.

the language of Tacitus, when speaking of a petition by the soldiery to a son and lieutenant of Vespasian.

Being liable to evil from you if I comply not with a wish which you signify, I am *bound* or *obliged* by your command, or I lie under a *duty* to obey it.

Command and duty are, therefore, correlative terms: the meaning denoted by each being implied or supposed by the other. Wherever a duty lies, a command has been signified; and whenever a command is signified, a duty is imposed.

The evil which will probably be incurred in case a command be disobeyed or (to use an equivalent expression) in case a duty be broken, is frequently called a *sanction*. The command or the duty is said to be *sanctioned* by the chance of incurring the evil. Some sanctions are called punishments.

Paley,[1] in his analysis of the term *obligation,* lays much stress upon the *violence* of the motive to compliance. His meaning appears to be that, unless the motive to compliance be *violent* or *intense,* the expression of a wish is not a *command,* nor does it place the person to whom it is directed under a duty.

But in truth the magnitude of the eventual evil, and the magnitude of the chance of incurring it, are foreign to the matter in question. The greater the eventual evil, and the greater the chance of incurring it, the greater is the efficacy of the command, and the greater is the strength of the obligation. But where there is the smallest chance of incurring the smallest evil, the expression of a wish amounts to a command, and, therefore, imposes a duty. The sanc-

---

[1] The reference is to William Paley (1743–1805), an English churchman whose ethical writings develop a version of the utilitarian principle. *Ed.*

tion, if you will, is feeble or insufficient; but still there *is* a sanction, and, therefore, a duty and a command.

By Locke and Bentham, the term *sanction,* or *enforcement of obedience,* is applied to conditional good as well as to conditional evil: to reward as well as to punishment. But, with all my habitual veneration for these names, I think this extension of the term pregnant with confusion.

Rewards are, indisputably, *motives* to comply with the wishes of others. But to talk of commands and duties as *sanctioned* or *enforced* by rewards, is surely a wide departure from the established meaning of the terms. If *you* expressed a desire that *I* should render a service, and proffered a reward as the inducement to render it, *you* would scarcely be said to *command* the service, nor should *I,* in ordinary language, be *obliged* to render it.

If we put *reward* into the import of the term *sanction,* we must engage in a toilsome and probably unsuccessful struggle with the current of ordinary speech.

The ideas then comprehended by the term *command* are the following. (1) A wish or desire conceived by a rational being, that another rational being shall do or forbear. (2) An evil to proceed from the former, and to be incurred by the latter, in case the latter comply not with the wish. (3) An expression or intimation of the wish by words or other signs.

It appears from what has been premised, that *command, duty,* and *sanction* are inseparably connected terms: that each embraces the same ideas as the others, though each denotes those ideas in a peculiar order or series.

"A wish conceived by one, and expressed or intimated to another, with an evil to be inflicted and incurred in case the wish be disregarded," are signified directly and indirectly by each of the three expressions. Each is the name of the same complex notion. But they differ in this, that the word "*command*" points directly and prominently to the *wish* expressed by the one; the word "*duty*" to the chance of meeting the evil incurred by the other; the word "*sanction*" to the evil itself; each expression referring less directly and prominently to the remaining notions.

To those who are familiar with the language of logicians (language unrivalled for brevity, distinctness, and precision), I can express my meaning accurately in a breath.—Each of the three terms *signifies* the same notion; but each *denotes* a different part of that notion, and *connotes* the residue.

Commands are of two species. Some are *laws* or *rules*. The others have not acquired an appropriate name, nor is there any short expression which will mark them precisely. I must, therefore, note them as well as I can by the ambiguous and inexpressive name of "*occasional* or *particular* commands." The distinction may, I think, be stated in the following manner.

By every command, the party to whom it is directed is obliged to do or to forbear.

Now where it obliges *generally* to acts or forbearances of a class, a command is a law or rule. But where it obliges to a *specific* act or forbearance, or to acts or forbearances *specifically* or *individually,* a command is occasional or particular.

For instance, if you command your servant to go on a given errand, or *not* to leave your house on a given evening, or to rise at such an hour on such a morning, or to rise at that hour during the next week or month, the command is occasional or particular. For the act

or acts enjoined or forbidden are specifically determined or assigned.

But if you command him *simply* to rise at that hour, or to rise at that hour *always,* or *till further orders,* it may be said, with propriety, that you lay down a *rule* for the guidance of your servant's conduct. For no specific act is assigned by the command, but the command obliges him generally to acts of a determined class.

If a regiment be ordered to attack or defend a post, or to quell a riot, or to march from their present quarters, the command is occasional or particular. But an order to exercise daily till further orders would be called a *general* order, and *might* be called a *rule.*

If Parliament prohibited simply the exportation of corn, either for a given period or indefinitely, it would establish a law or rule: a *kind* or *sort* of acts being determined by the command, and acts of that kind or sort being *generally* forbidden. But an order issued by Parliament to meet an impending scarcity, and stopping the exportation of corn *then shipped and in port,* would not be a law or rule, though issued by the sovereign legislature. The order regarding exclusively a specified quantity of corn, the negative acts or forbearances, enjoined by the command, would be determined specifically or individually by the determinate nature of their subject.

Again: An act which is not an offence, according to the existing law, moves the sovereign to displeasure: and, though the authors of the act are legally innocent or unoffending, the sovereign commands that they shall be punished. As enjoining a specific punishment in that specific case, and as not enjoining generally acts or forbearances of a class, the order uttered by the sovereign is not a law or rule.

To conclude with an appropriate example, *judicial commands* are commonly occasional or particular, although the commands which they are calculated to enforce are commonly laws or rules.

For instance, the lawgiver commands that thieves shall be hanged. A specific theft and a specified thief being given, the judge commands that the thief shall be hanged, agreeably to the command of the lawgiver.

Now the lawgiver determines a class or description of acts; prohibits acts of the class generally and indefinitely; and commands, with the like generality, that punishment shall follow transgression. The command of the lawgiver is, therefore, a law or rule. But the command of the judge is occasional or particular. For he orders a specific punishment, as the consequence of a specific offence.

The distinction immediately above stated and illustrated does not indeed accurately square with established forms of speech. For instance an order by Parliament stopping the exportation of corn then in port, would very likely be called a law because it wears the form of law and is issued by the sovereign legislature. An act of attainder deliberately passed by a Parliament with the forms of legislation would probably be called a law, though a similar order made by a sovereign monarch without deliberation or ceremony would be styled an arbitrary command. And on the other hand there are many commands issued by way of delegated legislation which really are laws, although not called so by common language. Such are various Orders in Council, Orders issued by Public Departments, Schemes of the Charity Commissioners when duly laid before Parliament, Orders or "Rules" made under powers given in Acts of Parliament relating to Judicial Procedure or otherwise made in exer-cise of delegated legislative functions. . . .

A law, properly so called, is therefore a command which obliges a person or persons; and as distinguished from a particular or occasional command, obliges generally to acts or forbearances of a class.

Laws and other commands are said to proceed from *superiors* and to bind or oblige *inferiors*. I will, therefore, analyze the meaning of those correlative expressions; and will try to strip them of a certain mystery, by which that simple meaning appears to be obscured.

Superiority is often synonymous with *precedence* or *excellence:* as for instance when we talk of superiors in rank, wealth or virtue.

But, taken with the meaning wherein I here understand it, the term *superiority* signifies *might:* the power of affecting others with evil or pain, and of forcing them, through fear of that evil, to fashion their conduct to one's wishes.

For example, God is emphatically the *superior* of Man. For his power of affecting us with pain, and of forcing us to comply with his will, is unbounded and resistless.

To a limited extent, the Sovereign One or Number is the superior of the subject or citizen: the master, of the slave or servant: the father, of the child.

In short, whoever can *oblige* another to comply with his wishes, is the *superior* of that other, so far as the ability reaches: That other being, to the same extent, the inferior. . . .

In so far as law and morality are what they *ought* to be, legal and moral rules have been fashioned on the principle of utility, or obtained by observation and induction from the tendencies of human actions. But it is not necessary that all whom they bind should know or advert to the process through which they have been gotten. If all whom they bind keep or observe them, the ends to which they exist are sufficiently accomplished; although many of the persons who observe them are unable to perceive their ends, and ignorant of the method by which they have been constructed or of the proofs by which they are established.

According to the theory of utility, the science of Ethics or Deontology (or the science of Law and Morality, as they *should* be, or *ought* to be) rests upon observation and induction. The science has been formed, through a long succession of ages, by many and separate contributions from many and separate discoverers. No single mind could explore the whole of the field, though each of its numerous departments has been explored by numerous inquirers. . . .

In order to link this lecture with the preceding one, I will now restate in an abridged shape, the objection and the answer with which that lecture was occupied.

The objection may be put briefly, in the following manner.

If utility be the proximate test of positive law and morality, it is impossible that the rules of conduct *actually obtaining amongst mankind* should accord completely and correctly with the laws *established by the Deity.* The index to his will is imperfect and uncertain. His laws are signified obscurely to those upon whom they are binding, and are subject to inevitable and involuntary misconstruction.

For, *first,* positive law and morality, fashioned on the principle of utility, are gotten by observation and induction from the tendencies of human actions. And, these actions being infinitely various, and their effects being infinitely diversified, the work of classing them

and of collecting their effects completely, transcends the limited faculties of created and finite beings.

And, *secondly,* if utility be the proximate text of positive law and morality, the defects and errors of *popular* or *vulgar* ethics will scarcely admit of a remedy. For if ethical truth be matter of science, and not of immediate consciousness, most of the ethical maxims which govern the sentiments of the multitude must be taken, without examination, from human authority. And human authority upon such subjects seems to consist of conflicting maxims, taught under the influence of prejudice—the offspring of sinister interests.

Such is the objection.—The only answer of which the objection will admit, is suggested by the remarks which I offered in my last lecture, and which I here repeat in an inverted and compendious form.

In the *first* place, the *diffusion* of ethical science amongst the great bulk of mankind will gradually remove the obstacles which prevent or retard its *advancement.*

Secondly: Though the many must trust to authority for a number of subordinate truths, they are competent to examine the elements which are the ground-work of the science of ethics, and to infer the more momentous of the derivative practical consequences.

And, *thirdly,* as the science of ethics advances, and is cleared of obscurity and uncertainties, they who are debarred from opportunities of examining the science extensively will find an authority whereon they may rationally rely, in the unanimous or general agreement of searching and impartial inquirers. . . .

By the *general* or *public* good or happiness I mean the aggregate enjoyments of the individuals to whom I refer collectively by the words "*general*" or "*public*." These words "general," "public," and others such as "family," "country," "mankind," are concise expressions for a number of individual persons considered collectively or as a whole. If the good of those persons considered singly were sacrificed to the supposed good of the whole, the general good would be destroyed by the sacrifice. The general good would be sacrificed to the *name* of the general good:—an absurdity when broadly stated, but nevertheless a consequence to which some current notions, for example the notion of the *public good* current in the ancient republics, have inevitably tended.

Now (speaking generally) every individual is the best possible judge of his own interests: of what will affect himself with the greatest pleasures and pains. Compared with this intimate knowledge, his knowledge of the interests of others is vague conjecture.

If every individual neglected his own for the sake of pursuing and promoting the interests of others, the interests of every individual would be managed unskilfully; and the general or public good would diminish with the good of the individuals of whom that general or public is constituted or composed.

Consequently, the principle of general utility imperiously demands that each shall commonly attend to his own rather than to the interests of others: that he shall not habitually neglect that which he knows accurately in order that he may habitually pursue that which he knows imperfectly.

This is also the arrangement which the Author of man's nature manifestly intended. For our self-regarding affections are steadier and stronger than our social: the motives by which we are urged to pursue our peculiar good operate with more constancy, and com-

monly with more energy, than the motives by which we are solicited to pursue the good of our fellows.

The principle of general utility does not demand of us that we shall always or habitually intend the general good: but only that we shall never pursue our own peculiar good by means inconsistent with that paramount object.

For example: A man delves or spins to put money in his purse, and not with the purpose or thought of promoting the general well-being. But by delving or spinning, he adds to the sum of commodities: and promotes that general well-being, which is not, and ought not to be, his practical end. General utility is not his motive to action. But his action conforms to utility considered as the standard of conduct: and, when tried by the test of utility, deserves approbation.

Again: Of all pleasures, bodily or mental, the pleasures of mutual love, cemented by mutual esteem, are the most enduring and varied. They therefore contribute largely to swell the sum of human happiness. And for that reason, the well-wisher of the general good must consider them with much complacency. But he is far from maintaining that the general good ought to be the motive of the lover. It was never contended or conceived by a sound, orthodox utilitarian, that the lover should kiss his mistress with an eye to the common weal.

And by this last example, I am naturally conducted to this further consideration.

Even where utility requires that benevolence shall be our motive, it commonly requires that we shall be determined by partial rather than by general benevolence: by the love of family, rather than by sympathy with the wider circle of friends or acquaintance: by sympathy with friends or acquaintance, rather than by patriotism: by patriotism, or love of country, rather than by the larger humanity which embraces mankind.

In short, the principle of utility requires that we shall act with the utmost effect, to the end of producing good. And (speaking generally) we act most effectively to that end when our motive or inducement to conduct is the most urgent and steady, when the sphere wherein we act is the most restricted and the most familiar to us, and when the purpose which we directly pursue is the most determinate or precise. . . .

The proper purpose or end of a sovereign political government, or the purpose or end for which it ought to exist, is the greatest possible advancement of human happiness. To accomplish that end effectively, it commonly must labour directly and particularly to advance as far as is possible the weal of its own community. For the good of the universal society formed by mankind is the aggregate good of the particular societies into which mankind is divided: just as the happiness of any of those societies is the aggregate happiness of its single or individual members. And if every government consulted the weal of its own subjects, the probable tendency would clearly be to promote the general happiness of mankind. And it were easy to show, that the general and particular ends never or rarely conflict. An enlightened regard for the common happiness of nations, implies an enlightened patriotism; whilst the stupid and atrocious patriotism which looks exclusively to country, and would further the interests of country at the cost of all other communities, grossly misapprehends and frequently crosses the interests that are the object of its narrow concern. But

the topic which I now have suggested, belongs to the province of ethics, rather than the province of jurisprudence.[2] . . .

The definition of a positive law implicitly contained in the foregoing lectures, and which has been already stated by anticipation (p. 208 *supra*), may now be reiterated in terms which have been explained with an approach to precision. The essential difference which severs a positive law from a law not a positive law is this:—Every positive law

---

[2] The proper purpose or end of a sovereign political government is conceived inadequately or obscurely by most or many of the writers on political government and society.

Speaking generally and vaguely, it may be said that the proper end of government is to co-operate in advancing the happiness of mankind. This is the same as to say that the particular and determinate end is (in an enlightened manner, and therefore with due regard to the happiness of other communities) to advance as far as possible the weal of its own community. The writers in question mistake for the proper absolute end one or a few of the instrumental ends through which a government must accomplish that absolute end.

For example: It is said by many of the speculators on political government and society, that "the end of every government is to institute and protect property." And here I must remark, by the by, that the propounders of this absurdity give to the term "property" an extremely large and not very definite signification. They mean generally by the term "property," legal rights, or legal faculties: and they mean not particularly by the term "property," the legal rights, or legal faculties, which are denominated strictly "rights of property or dominion." Now the proper paramount purpose of a sovereign political government, is not the creation and protection of legal rights or faculties, or (in the terms of the proposition) the institution and protection of property. If that were the paramount purpose, the end might be the ·advancement of misery, rather than the advancement of happiness; since many of the legal rights which governments have created and protected (as the rights of masters, for example, to and against slaves), are generally pernicious, rather than generally useful. To advance as far as is possible the common happiness or weal, a government must confer on its subjects *beneficent* legal rights.

(or every law simply and strictly so called) is set, directly or circuitously, by a sovereign individual or body, to a member or members of the independent political society wherein its author is supreme. In other words, It is set, directly or circuitously, by a monarch or sovereign number, to a person or persons in a state of subjection to its author.

The definition, however, only approaches to a perfectly complete and perfectly exact definition. It is open to certain correctives which I will now briefly suggest.

Every law properly so called is set by a superior to an inferior or inferiors: it is set by a party armed with might, to a party or parties whom that might can reach. Now (speaking generally) a party who is liable to be reached by the might of the author of the law is a member of the independent community wherein the author is sovereign. In other words, a party who is amenable to a legal sanction is a subject of the author of the law to which the sanction is annexed. Although the positive law may affect to oblige strangers (or parties who are not members of that independent community), none but members of that independent community are virtually or truly bound by it. Besides, if the positive law of one independent community bound legally (and generally) the members of another, the other independent community would not be an independent community, but merely a subordinate community forming a limb of the first.

Speaking, then, generally, we may say that a positive law is set or directed exclusively to a subject or subjects of its author: or that a positive law is set or directed exclusively to a member or members of the community wherein its author is sovereign. But, in many cases,

the positive law of a given independent community imposes a duty on a *stranger:* on a party who is *not* a member of the given independent community, or is only a member to certain limited purposes. For such, in these cases, is the position of the stranger, that the imposition of the legal duty consists with the sovereignty of the government of which he is properly a subject. For example: A party not a member of a given independent community, but living within its territory and within the jurisdiction of its sovereign, is bound or obliged, to an extent which is limited by its positive law. Living within the territory, he is liable to be reached by the legal sanctions by which the law is enforced. And the legal duties imposed upon him by the law are consistent with the sovereignty of the foreign government of which he is properly a subject. For the duties are not imposed upon the foreign government itself, nor upon the members generally of the community subject to it, nor are they laid upon the obliged party as being one of its subjects, but as being a member, to certain limited purposes, of the community wherein he resides. Again: If a stranger not residing within the given community be the owner of land or moveables lying within its territory, the sanction of the law may reach him through the land or goods. For instance, if he be sued on an agreement, and judgment be given for the plaintiff, the tribunal may execute its judgment by resorting to the land or moveables, although the defendant's body is beyond the reach of its process. And this consists with the sovereignty of the government of which the stranger is properly a subject. In all the cases, therefore, which I now have noted and exemplified, the positive law of a given independent society may impose a duty on a stranger. By reason of the obstacles mentioned in the preceding paragraph, the binding virtue of the positive law cannot extend generally to members of foreign communities. But in the cases which I now have noted and exemplified those obstacles do not intervene.

The definition, therefore, of a positive law, which is assumed expressly or tacitly throughout the foregoing lectures, is not a perfectly complete and perfectly exact definition. In the cases noted and exemplified in the last paragraph, a positive law obliges legally, or a positive law is set or directed to, a *stranger* or *strangers:* that is to say, a person or persons *not* of the community wherein the author of the law is sovereign or supreme. Now, since the cases in question are omitted by that definition, the definition is too narrow, or is defective or inadequate: and to a corresponding extent the determination of the province of jurisprudence, which is attempted in these discourses, falls short of being a complete and exact determination.

But the truth of the positions and inferences contained in the preceding lectures is not, I believe, materially impaired by this omission and defect. And though the definition is not complete, it approaches nearly to completeness. Allowing for the omission of the anomalous cases in question, it is, I believe, an adequate definition of its subject.

Political Obligation

"The general obligation, which binds us to government," writes David Hume, "is the interest and necessities of society; and this obligation is very strong." Thus placing the basis of political obligation in men's general interests for peace and order, Hume speaks of what obliges men to obey government and of what obliges government to serve men by reference to human interests and to the principle of utility that judges them. He distinguishes two kinds of duties—natural and artificial. Natural duties such as love and pity, which involve feelings of approval, are based on "natural instinct." The second kind, sometimes called artificial by Hume, are performed from the sense of obligation arising from the necessities of society. So justice, fidelity, and allegiance become obligatory.

The obligation to society and authority is not a natural instinct, but rather a felt need for social order, and this felt need or interest is sufficient to explain allegiance; no other "fiction" is needed or helpful. The two great theories of authority of his day, hereditary succession and the social contract, are forcefully rejected by Hume. The latter is wanting, Hume finds, because the obligation to keep the promises of the contract is no more basic or more easily explained than obedience. They are both on the same level as artificial virtues, and one cannot be used to explain the other. Principles of succession are also wanting as theories of political obligation, since the fact of possessing authority, even for a long time, does not create the obligation to obey. Subjects obey a government, not because of a promise made by their ancestors, nor because a family has possessed the ruling power for generations, but because government is in their interest, and government could not be without obedience. Men approve of what makes for the common interest, they accept the obligations this seems to impose, and thus they make obedience and allegiance virtues.

These virtues are not absolute or unlimited: utilitarians are suspicious of power and absolutisms. Interestingly, while Hume rejects the contract theory, he does not deny the idea of consent. Consent for him is the acquiescence, grounded in knowledge, that government is in the public interest. This means, in effect, that power is the result of obedience, not that obedience is the effect of power, as Hobbes contends. Thus for Hume, consent explains what makes government possible; it is not a principle to explain the grounds of obligation. This is found rather in the interests of society and the principle of utility.

Since the power of government is limited by the motives of obedience that make government possible, it follows that if government is not in men's interest, they cease to obey. In fact, in such circumstances they would have a positive motive for resistance and reform. Resistance being admitted, Hume concludes, the only question can be the degree of necessity that can justify it and "render it lawful or commendable."

DAVID HUME   Allegiance and Interest

All *moral* duties may be divided into two kinds. The *first* are those, to which men are impelled by a natural instinct or immediate propensity, which operates on them, independent of all ideas of obligation, and of all views, either to public or private utility. Of this nature are, love of children, gratitude to benefactors, pity to the unfortunate. When we reflect on the advantage, which results to society from such humane instincts, we pay them the just tribute of moral approbation and esteem: But the person, actuated by them, feels their power and influence, antecedent to any such reflection.

The *second* kind of moral duties are such as are not supported by any original instinct of nature, but are performed entirely from a sense of obligation, when we consider the necessities of human society, and the impossibility of support-

ing it, if these duties were neglected. It is thus *justice* or a regard to the property of others, *fidelity* or the observance of promises, become obligatory, and acquire an authority over mankind. For as it is evident, that every man loves himself better than any other person, he is naturally impelled to extend his acquisitions as much as possible; and nothing can restrain him in this propensity, but reflection and experience, by which he learns the pernicious effects of that licence, and the total dissolution of society which must ensue from it. His original inclination, therefore, or instinct, is here checked and restrained by a subsequent judgment or observation.

The case is precisely the same with the political or civil duty of *allegiance,* as with the natural duties of justice and fidelity. Our primary instincts lead us, either to indulge ourselves in unlimited

From David Hume, "Of the Original Contract" and "Of Passive Obedience," in *Essays Moral, Political and Literary,* ed. T. H. Green and T. H. Grose, London: Longmans, Green and Co., 1875.

freedom, or to seek dominion over others: And it is reflection only, which engages us to sacrifice such strong passions to the interests of peace and public order. A small degree of experience and observation suffices to teach us, that society cannot possibly be maintained without the authority of magistrates, and that this authority must soon fall into contempt, where exact obedience is not paid to it. The observation of these general and obvious interests is the source of all allegiance, and of that moral obligation, which we attribute to it.

What necessity, therefore, is there to found the duty of *allegiance* or obedience to magistrates on that of *fidelity* or a regard to promises, and to suppose, that it is the consent of each individual, which subjects him to government; when it appears, that both allegiance and fidelity stand precisely on the same foundation, and are both submitted to by mankind, on account of the apparent interests and necessities of human society? We are bound to obey our sovereign, it is said; because we have given a tacit promise to that purpose. But why are we bound to observe our promise? It must here be asserted, that the commerce and intercourse of mankind, which are of such mighty advantage, can have no security where men pay no regard to their engagements. In like manner, may it be said, that men could not live at all in society, at least in a civilized society, without laws and magistrates and judges, to prevent the encroachments of the strong upon the weak, of the violent upon the just and equitable. The obligation to allegiance being of like force and authority with the obligation to fidelity, we gain nothing by resolving the one into the other. The general interests or necessities of society are sufficient to establish both.

If the reason be asked of that obedience, which we are bound to pay to government, I readily answer, *because society could not otherwise subsist:* And this answer is clear and intelligible to all mankind. Your answer is, *because we should keep our word.* But besides, that no body, till trained in a philosophical system, can either comprehend or relish this answer: Besides this, I say, you find yourself embarrassed, when it is asked, *why we are bound to keep our word?* Nor can you give any answer, but what would, immediately, without any circuit, have accounted for our obligation to allegiance.

But *to whom is allegiance due? And who is our lawful sovereign?* This question is often the most difficult of any, and liable to infinite discussions. When people are so happy, that they can answer, *Our present sovereign, who inherits, in a direct line, from ancestors, that have governed us for many ages;* this answer admits of no reply; even though historians, in tracing up to the remotest antiquity, the origin of that royal family, may find, as commonly happens, that its first authority was derived from usurpation and violence. It is confessed, that private justice, or the abstinence from the properties of others, is a most cardinal virtue: Yet reason tells us, that there is no property in durable objects, such as lands or houses, when carefully examined in passing from hand to hand, but must, in some period, have been founded on fraud and injustice. The necessities of human society, neither in private nor public life, will allow of such an accurate enquiry: And there is no virtue or moral duty, but what may, with facility, be refined away, if we indulge a false philosophy, in sifting and scrutinizing it, by every captious rule of logic, in every light or position, in which it may be placed.

The questions with regard to private

property have filled infinite volumes of law and philosophy, if in both we add the commentators to the original text; and in the end, we may safely pronounce, that many of the rules, there established, are uncertain, ambiguous, and arbitrary. The like opinion may be formed with regard to the succession and rights of princes and forms of government. Several cases, no doubt, occur, especially in the infancy of any constitution, which admit of no determination from the laws of justice and equity: And our historian RAPIN pretends, that the controversy between EDWARD the THIRD and PHILIP DE VALOIS was of this nature, and could be decided only by an appeal to heaven, that is, by war and violence.

Who shall tell me, whether GERMANICUS or DRUSUS ought to have succeeded to TIBERIUS, had he died, while they were both alive, without naming any of them for his successor? Ought the right of adoption to be received as equivalent to that of blood, in a nation, where it had the same effect in private families, and had already, in two instances, taken place in the public? Ought GERMANICUS to be esteemed the elder son because he was born before DRUSUS; or the younger, because he was adopted after the birth of his brother? Ought the right of the elder to be regarded in a nation, where he had no advantage in the succession of private families? Ought the ROMAN empire at that time to be deemed hereditary, because of two examples; or ought it, even so early, to be regarded as belonging to the stronger or to the present possessor, as being founded on so recent an usurpation?

COMMODUS mounted the throne after a pretty long succession of excellent emperors, who had acquired their title, not by birth, or public election, but by the fictitious rite of adoption. That bloody debauchee being murdered by a conspiracy suddenly formed between his wench and her gallant, who happened at that time to be *Prætorian Præfect;* these immediately deliberated about choosing a master to human kind, to speak in the style of those ages; and they cast their eyes on PERTINAX. Before the tyrant's death was known, the *Præfect* went secretly to that senator, who, on the appearance of the soldiers, imagined that his execution had been ordered by COMMODUS. He was immediately saluted emperor by the officer and his attendants; chearfully proclaimed by the populace; unwillingly submitted to by the guards; formally recognized by the senate; and passively received by the provinces and armies of the empire.

The discontent of the *Prætorian* bands broke out in a sudden sedition, which occasioned the murder of that excellent prince: And the world being now without a master and without government, the guards thought proper to set the empire formally to sale. JULIAN, the purchaser, was proclaimed by the soldiers, recognized by the senate, and submitted to by the people; and must also have been submitted to by the provinces, had not the envy of the legions begotten opposition and resistance. PESCENNIUS NIGER in SYRIA elected himself emperor, gained the tumultuary consent of his army, and was attended with the secret good-will of the senate and people of ROME. ALBINUS in BRITAIN found an equal right to set up his claim; but SEVERUS, who governed PANNONIA, prevailed in the end above both of them. That able politician and warrior, finding his own birth and dignity too much inferior to the imperial crown, professed, at first, an intention only of revenging the death of PERTINAX. He marched as general into ITALY; defeated JULIAN; and without our being able to fix any precise commencement even of the soldiers' consent, he was from necessity acknowledged emperor by the senate and people; and fully established in his violent authority by subduing NIGER and ALBINUS.

Inter hæc Gordianus CÆSAR (says CAPITOLINUS, speaking of another period) *sublatus a militibus,* Imperator *est appellatus, quia non erat alius in præsenti,* It is to be remarked, that GORDIAN was a boy of fourteen years of age.

Frequent instances of a like nature occur in the history of the emperors; in that of ALEXANDER'S successors; and of many other countries: Nor can anything be more unhappy than a despotic government of this kind; where the succession is disjoined and irregular, and must be determined, on every vacancy, by force or election. In a free government, the matter is often unavoidable, and is also much less dangerous. The interests of liberty may there frequently lead the people, in their own defence, to alter the succession of the crown. And the constitution, being compounded of parts, may still maintain a sufficient stability, by resting on the aristocratical or democratical members, though the monarchical be altered, from time to time, in order to accommodate it to the former.

In an absolute government, when there is no legal prince, who has a title to the throne, it may safely be determined to belong to the first occupant. Instances of this kind are but too frequent, especially in the eastern monarchies. When any race of princes expires, the will or destination of the last sovereign will be regarded as a title. Thus the edict of LEWIS the XIVth, who called the bastard princes to the succession in case of the failure of all the legitimate princes, would, in such an event, have some authority.[1] Thus the will of CHARLES the Second disposed of the whole SPANISH monarchy. The cession of the ancient proprietor, especially when joined to conquest, is likewise deemed a good title. The general obligation, which binds us to government, is the interest and necessities of society; and this obligation is very strong. The determination of it to this or that particular prince or form of government is frequently more uncertain and dubious. Present possession has considerable authority in these cases, and greater than in private property; because of the disorders which attend all revolutions and changes of government.

We shall only observe, before we conclude, that, though an appeal to general opinion may justly, in the speculative sciences of metaphysics, natural philos-

---

[1] It is remarkable, that, in the remonstrance of the duke of BOURBON and the legitimate princes, against this destination of LOUIS the XIVth, the doctrine of the *original contract* is insisted on, even in that absolute government. The FRENCH nation, say they, chusing HUGH CAPET and his posterity to rule over them and their posterity, where the former line fails, there is a tacit right reserved to choose a new royal family; and this right is invaded by calling the bastard princes to the throne, without the consent of the nation. But the Comte de BOULAINVILLIERS, who wrote in defence of the bastard princes, ridicules this notion of an original contract, especially when applied to HUGH CAPET; who mounted the throne, says he, by the same arts, which have ever been employed by all conquerors and usurpers. He got his title, indeed, recognized by the states after he had put himself in possession: But is this a choice or a contract? The Comte de BOULAINVILLIERS, we may observe, was a noted republican; but being a man of learning, and very conversant in history, he knew that the people were never almost consulted in these revolutions and new establishments, and that time alone bestowed right and authority on what was commonly at first founded on force and violence. *See État de la France,* Vol. III.

ophy, or astronomy, be deemed unfair and inconclusive, yet in all questions with regard to morals, as well as criticism, there is really no other standard, by which any controversy can ever be decided. And nothing is a clearer proof, that a theory of this kind is erroneous, than to find, that it leads to paradoxes, repugnant to the common sentiments of mankind, and to the practice and opinion of all nations and all ages. The doctrine, which founds all lawful government on an *original contract,* or consent of the people, is plainly of this kind; nor has the most noted of its partizans, in prosecution of it, scrupled to affirm, *that absolute monarchy is inconsistent with civil society, and so can be no form of civil government at all;* and *that the supreme power in a state cannot take from any man, by taxes and impositions, any part of his property, without his own consent or that of his representatives.* What authority any moral reasoning can have, which leads into opinions so wide of the general practice of mankind, in every place but this single kingdom, it is easy to determine.

The only passage I meet with in antiquity, where the obligation of obedience to government is ascribed to a promise, is in PLATO'S *Crito:* where SOCRATES refuses to escape from prison, because he had tacitly promised to obey the laws. Thus he builds a *tory* consequence of passive obedience, on a *whig* foundation of the original contract.

New discoveries are not to be expected in these matters. If scarce any man, till very lately, ever imagined that government was founded on compact, it is certain that it cannot, in general, have any such foundation.

The crime of rebellion among the ancients was commonly expressed by the terms νεωτερίζειν, *novas res moliri. . . .*

As the obligation to justice is founded entirely on the interests of society, which require mutual abstinence from property, in order to preserve peace among mankind; it is evident, that, when the execution of justice would be attended with very pernicious consequences, that virtue must be suspended, and give place to public utility, in such extraordinary and such pressing emergencies. The maxim, *fiat Justitia et ruat Cælum,* let justice be performed, though the universe be destroyed, is apparently false, and by sacrificing the end to the means, shews a preposterous idea of the subordination of duties. What governor of a town makes any scruple of burning the suburbs, when they facilitate the approaches of the enemy? Or what general abstains from plundering a neutral country, when the necessities of war require it, and he cannot otherwise subsist his army? The case is the same with the duty of allegiance; and common sense teaches us, that, as government binds us to obedience only on account of its tendency to public utility, that duty must always, in extraordinary cases, when public ruin would evidently attend obedience, yield to the primary and original obligation. *Salus populi suprema Lex,* the safety of the people is the supreme law. This maxim is agreeable to the sentiments of mankind in all ages: Nor is any one, when he reads of the insurrections against NERO or PHILIP the Second, so infatuated with party-systems, as not to wish success to the enterprize, and praise the undertakers. Even our high monarchical party, in spite of their sublime theory, are forced, in such cases, to judge, and feel, and approve, in conformity to the rest of mankind.

Resistance, therefore, being admitted in extraordinary emergencies, the question can only be among good reasoners, with regard to the degree of necessity, which can justify resistance, and render it lawful or commendable.

The Ideal of Justice

For their existence and comfort men depend on certain products of the earth. These cannot be used in common, however, without certain disputes arising, nor do natural products suffice unless they are improved by human labor. Yet no one works unless he will receive some benefits to himself. Therefore, certain rules arise implying a mutual recognition of rights and the institution of private property. Briefly, such is a general utilitarian account of the origin of the ideal of justice and of its relation to human interests. The notion of an essential Justice discoverable by Reason is abandoned; justice—with allegiance, modesty, and good manners—is treated as an "artificial" virtue in Hume's sense of the term. It is prior to government, it may be appealed to against government, but it is a social rather than an individual virtue because the desire for it arises as men live together. Government is not the maintainer of some eternal, transcendent ideal of justice. It is instead a device that makes it the immediate interest of some persons to promote the permanent interests of everyone.

Not merely useful, justice for many utilitarians has its character as a virtue determined *wholly* by its usefulness. It regulates property and rights to property—customary or conventional rights rather than natural ones—in the interest of their stability. (Other conventions have to do with legitimate authority, which rests on rules such as prescription and formal enactment.) Human interests and the utilitarian principle are thus sufficient to account for justice.

Most utilitarian writers have given attention to this problem, and some of the most widely read parts of Hume's and Mill's work have been their chapters on justice. The selection below has been taken from the treatment of justice by the last great utilitarian, Henry Sidgwick (1838–1900). Sidgwick's contributions to ethical utilitarianism are important and significant, for he seeks to show that utilitarianism can admit strictly moral judgments distinct from merely prudential ones. The moral "ought," for Sidgwick is an irreducible concept.

To develop and maintain this notion, Sidgwick introduces into ethics an intuitive and self-evident element that is cognizable by abstract intuition. He specifies this element in terms of three intuitive principles, corresponding to the virtues of prudence, benevolence, and justice. The principle of prudence is that one part of a given conscious experience is not to be regarded, other things being equal, as more important than any other equal part of the same experience. The principle of benevolence considers each person as morally bound to regard the good of any other person as much as he regards his own. The principle of justice postulates that it cannot be right for A to treat B in a manner in which it would be wrong for *B* to treat *A,* merely on the ground that they are two different persons.

The justice of which earlier utilitarians wrote, Sidgwick finds, is mainly a theory of order. And the need for order, he admits, is too obvious to require proof. Sidgwick also agrees that Utility is the principle guiding the meaning of justice. Justice as defined above is a notion more complex than order, and it contains many utilities. Those Sidgwick discusses include impartiality, just claims, normal expectations, and ideal justice, by which he means the distribution of good and evil according to desert and in relation to happiness. While intuitive principles enter into all his moral and political discussion, Sidgwick nevertheless remains a utilitarian because of his beliefs that pleasure is the only practical test of what is desirable, and that the principle of utility furnishes a common standard for understanding the different components of justice.

HENRY SIDGWICK Utility and Justice

"That Justice is useful to society," says Hume, "it would be a superfluous undertaking to prove": what he endeavours to show at some length is "that public utility is the *sole* origin of Justice": and the same question of origin has occupied the chief attention of J. S. Mill.[1] Here, however, we are not so much concerned with the growth of the sentiment of Justice from experiences of utility, as with the Utilitarian basis of the mature notion; while at the same time if the analysis previously given be correct, the Justice that is commonly demanded and inculcated is something more complex than these writers have recognised. What Hume (*e.g.*) means by Justice is rather what I should call Order, understood in its widest sense: the observance of the actual system of rules, whether strictly legal or customary, which bind together the different members of any society into an organic whole, checking malevolent or otherwise injurious impulses, distributing the different objects of men's clashing de-

sires, and exacting such positive services, customary or contractual, as are commonly recognised as matters of debt. And though there have rarely been wanting plausible empirical arguments for the revolutionary paradox quoted by Plato, that "laws are imposed in the interest of rulers," it remains true that the general conduciveness to social happiness of the habit of Order or Law-observance, is, as Hume says, too obvious to need proof; indeed it is of such paramount importance to a community, that even where particular laws are clearly injurious it is usually expedient to observe them, apart from any penalty which their breach might entail on the individual. We saw, however, that Common Sense sometimes bids us refuse obedience to bad laws, because "we ought to obey God rather than men" (though there seems to be no clear intuition as to the kind or degree of badness that justifies resistance); and further allows us, in special emergencies, to violate rules generally good, for "necessity has no law," and "salus populi suprema lex."

[1] *Utilitarianism,* chap. v.

From Henry Sidgwick, *The Methods of Ethics,* 6th edition, London: Macmillan & Co., Ltd., 1901.

These and similar common opinions seem at least to suggest that the limits of the duty of Law-observance are to be determined by utilitarian considerations. While, again, the Utilitarian view gets rid of the difficulties in which the attempt to define intuitively the truly legitimate source of legislative authority involved us; at the same time that it justifies to some extent each of the different views current as to the intrinsic legitimacy of governments. For, on the one hand, it finds the moral basis of any established political order primarily in its effects rather than its causes; so that, generally speaking, obedience will seem due to any *de facto* government that is not governing very badly. On the other hand, in so far as laws originating in a particular way are likely to be (1) better, or (2) more readily observed, it is a Utilitarian duty to aim at introducing this mode of origination: and thus in a certain stage of social development it may be right that (e.g.) a "representative system" should be popularly demanded, or possibly (in extreme cases) even introduced by force: while, again, there is expediency in maintaining an ancient mode of legislation, because men readily obey such: and loyalty to a dispossessed government may be on the whole expedient, even at the cost of some temporary suffering and disorder, in order that ambitious men may not find usurpation too easy. Here, as elsewhere, Utilitarianism at once supports the different reasons commonly put forward as absolute, and also brings them theoretically to a common measure, so that in any particular case we have a principle of decision between conflicting political arguments.

As was before said, this Law-observance, in so far at least as it affects the interests of other individuals, is what we frequently mean by Justice. It seems, however, that the notion of Justice, exhaustively analysed, includes several distinct elements combined in a somewhat complex manner: we have to inquire, therefore, what latent utilities are represented by each of these elements.

Now, first, a constant part of the notion, which appears in it even when the Just is not distinguished from the Legal, is impartiality or the negation of arbitrary inequality. This impartiality, as we saw (whether exhibited in the establishment or in the administration of laws), is merely a special application of the wider maxim that it cannot be right to treat two persons differently if their cases are similar in all material circumstances. And Utilitarianism, as we saw, admits this maxim no less than other systems of Ethics. At the same time, this negative criterion is clearly inadequate for the complete determination of what is just in laws, or in conduct generally; when we have admitted this, it still remains to ask, "What are the inequalities in laws, and in the distribution of pleasures and pains outside the sphere of law, which are not arbitrary and unreasonable? and to what general principles can they be reduced?"

Here in the first place we may explain, on utilitarian principles, why apparently arbitrary inequality in a certain part of the conduct of individuals is not regarded as injustice or even—in some cases—as in any way censurable. For freedom of action is an important source of happiness to the agents, and a socially useful stimulus to their energies: hence it is obviously expedient that a man's free choice in the distribution of wealth or kind services should not be restrained by the fear of legal penalties, or even of social disapprobation, beyond what the interests of others clearly require; and therefore, when distinctly recognised claims are satisfied, it is *pro tanto* expedient that the mere preferences of an individual should be treated by others as legitimate grounds for inequality in the distribution of his property or services. Nay, as we have before seen, it is within certain limits expedient that each individual should practically regard his own unreasoned impulses as reasonable grounds of action: as in the rendering of services prompted by such affections as are normally and properly spontaneous and unforced.

Passing to consider the general principles upon which "just claims" as commonly recognised appear to be based, we notice that the grounds of a number of such claims may be brought under the general head of "normal expectations"; but that the stringency of such obligations varies much in degree, according as the expectations are based upon definite engagements, or on some vague mutual understanding, or are merely such as an average man would form from past experience of the conduct of other men. In these latter cases Common Sense appeared to be somewhat perplexed as to the validity of the claims. But for the Utilitarian the difficulty has ceased to exist. He will hold any disappointment of expectations to be *pro tanto* an evil, but a greater evil in proportion to the previous security of the expectant individual, from the greater shock thus given to his reliance on the conduct of his fellow-men generally: and many times greater in proportion as the expectation is generally recognised as normal and reasonable, as in this case the shock extends to all who are in any way cognisant of his disappointment. The importance to mankind of being able to rely on each other's actions is so great, that in ordinary cases of absolutely definite engagements there is scarcely any advantage that can

counterbalance the harm done by violating them. Still, we found that several exceptions and qualifications to the rule of Good Faith were more or less distinctly recognised by Common Sense: and most of these have a utilitarian basis, which it does not need much penetration to discern. To begin, we may notice that the superficial view of the obligation of a promise which makes it depend on the assertion of the promiser, and not, as Utilitarians hold, on the expectations produced in the promisee, cannot fairly be attributed to Common Sense: which certainly condemns a breach of promise much more strongly when others have acted in reliance on it, than when its observance did not directly concern others, so that its breach involves for them only the indirect evil of a bad precedent,—as when a man breaks a pledge of total abstinence. We see, again, how the utilitarian reasons for keeping a promise are diminished by a material change of circumstances, for in that case the expectations disappointed by breaking it are at least not those which the promise originally created. It is obvious, too, that it is a disadvantage to the community that men should be able to rely on the performance of promises procured by fraud or unlawful force, so far as encouragement is thereby given to the use of fraud or force for this end.[2] We saw, again, that when the performance would be injurious to the promisee, Common Sense is disposed to admit that its obligation is superseded; and is at least doubtful whether the promise should be kept, even when it is only the promiser who would be injured, if the harm

---

[2] In the case of force, however, there is the counterbalancing consideration that the unlawful aggressor may be led to inflict worse injury on his victim, if he is unable to rely on the latter's promise.

be extreme;—both which qualifications are in harmony with Utilitarianism. And similarly for the other qualifications and exceptions: they all turn out to be as clearly utilitarian, as the general utility of keeping one's word is plain and manifest.

But further, the expediency of satisfying normal expectations, even when they are not based upon a definite contract, is undeniable; it will clearly conduce to the tranquillity of social existence, and to the settled and well-adjusted activity on which social happiness greatly depends, that such expectations should be as little as possible baulked. And here Utilitarianism relieves us of the difficulties which beset the common view of just conduct as something absolutely precise and definite. For in this vaguer region we cannot draw a sharp line between valid and invalid claims; "injustice" shades gradually off into mere "hardship." Hence the Utilitarian view that the disappointment of natural expectations is an evil, but an evil which must sometimes be incurred for the sake of a greater good, is that to which Common Sense is practically forced, though it is difficult to reconcile it with the theoretical absoluteness of Justice in the Intuitional view of Morality.

The gain of recognising the relativity of this obligation will be still more felt, when we consider what I distinguished as Ideal Justice, and examine the general conceptions of this which we find expressed or latent in current criticisms of the existing order of Society.

We have seen that there are two competing views of an ideally just social order—or perhaps we may say two extreme types between which the looser notions of ordinary men seem to fluctuate—which I called respectively Individualistic and Socialistic. According to

the former view an ideal system of Law ought to aim at Freedom, or perfect mutual non-interference of all the members of the community, as an absolute end. Now the general utilitarian reasons for leaving each rational adult free to seek happiness in his own way are obvious and striking: for, generally speaking, each is best qualified to provide for his own interests, since even when he does not know best what they are and how to attain them, he is at any rate most keenly concerned for them: and again, the consciousness of freedom and concomitant responsibility increases the average effective activity of men: and besides, the discomfort of constraint is directly an evil and *pro tanto* to be avoided. Still, we saw that the attempt to construct a consistent code of laws, taking Maximum Freedom (instead of Happiness) as an absolute end, must lead to startling paradoxes and insoluble puzzles: and in fact the practical interpretation of the notion "Freedom," and the limits within which its realisation has been actually sought, have always—even in the freest societies—been more or less consciously determined by considerations of expediency. So that we may fairly say that in so far as Common Sense has adopted the Individualistic ideal in politics, it has always been as subordinate to and limited by the Utilitarian first principle.

It seems, however, that what we commonly demand or long for, under the name of Ideal Justice, is not so much the realisation of Freedom, as the distribution of good and evil according to Desert: indeed it is as a means to this latter end that Freedom is often advocated; for it is said that if we protect men completely from mutual interference, each will reap the good and bad consequences of his own conduct, and so be happy or unhappy in proportion to his deserts. In particular, it has been widely held that if a free exchange of wealth and services is allowed, each individual will obtain from society, in money or other advantages, what his services are really worth. We saw, however, that the price which an individual obtains under a system of perfect free trade, for wealth or services exchanged by him, may for several reasons be not proportioned to the social utility of what he exchanges: and reflective Common Sense seems to admit this disproportion as to some extent legitimate, under the influence of utilitarian considerations correcting the unreflective utterances of moral sentiments.

To take a particular case: if a moral man were asked how far it is right to take advantage in bargaining of another's ignorance, probably his first impulse would be to condemn such a procedure altogether. But reflection, I think, would show him that such a censure would be too sweeping: that it would be contrary to Common Sense to "blame *A* for having, in negotiating with a stranger *B,* taken advantage of *B*'s ignorance of facts known to himself, provided that *A*'s superior knowledge had been obtained by a legitimate use of diligence and foresight, which *B* might have used with equal success. . . . What prevents us from censuring in this and similar cases is, I conceive, a more or less conscious apprehension of the indefinite loss to the wealth of the community that is likely to result from any effective social restrictions on the free pursuit and exercise" of economic knowledge. And for somewhat similar reasons of general expediency, if the question be raised whether it is fair for a class of persons to gain by the unfavourable economic situation of any class with which

they deal, Common Sense at least hesitates to censure such gains—at any rate when such unfavourable situation is due "to the gradual action of general causes, for the existence of which the persons who gain are not specially responsible."[3]

The general principle of "requiting good desert," so far as Common Sense really accepts it as practically applicable to the relations of men in society, is broadly in harmony with Utilitarianism; since we obviously encourage the production of general happiness by rewarding men for felicific conduct; only the Utilitarian scale of rewards will not be determined entirely by the magnitude of the services performed, but partly also by the difficulty of inducing men to perform them. But this latter element seems to be always taken into account (though perhaps unconsciously) by Common Sense: for, as we have been led to notice, we do not commonly recognise merit in right actions, if they are such as men are naturally inclined to perform rather too much than too little. Again, in cases where the Intuitional principle that ill-desert lies in wrong intention conflicts with the Utilitarian view of punishment as purely preventive, we find that in the actual administration of criminal justice, Common Sense is forced, however reluctantly, into practical agreement with Utilitarianism. Thus after a civil war it demands the execution of the most purely patriotic rebels; and after a railway accident it clamours for the severe punishment of unintentional neglects, which, except for their consequences, would have been regarded as very venial.

If, however, in any distribution of

[3] The quotations are from my *Principles of Political Economy,* Book iii. chap. ix, where these questions are discussed at somewhat greater length.

pleasures and privileges, or of pains and burdens, considerations of desert do not properly come in (*i.e.* if the good or evil to be distributed have no relation to any conduct on the part of the persons who are to receive either)—or if it is practically impossible to take such considerations into account—then Common Sense seems to fall back on simple equality as the principle of just apportionment.[4] And we have seen that the Utilitarian, in the case supposed, will reasonably accept Equality as the only mode of distribution that is not arbitrary; and it may be observed that this mode of apportioning the means of happiness is likely to produce more happiness on the whole, not only because men have a disinterested aversion to reason, but still more because they have an aversion to any kind of inferiority to others (which is much intensified when the inferiority seems unreasonable). This latter feeling is so strong that it often prevails in spite of obvious claims of desert; and it may

even be sometimes expedient that it should so prevail.

For, finally, it must be observed that Utilitarianism furnishes us with a common standard to which the different elements included in the notion of Justice may be reduced. Such a standard is imperatively required: as these different elements are continually liable to conflict with each other. The issue, for example, in practical politics between Conservatives and Reformers often represents such a conflict: the question is, whether we ought to do a certain violence to expectations arising naturally out of the existing social order, with the view of bringing about a distribution of the means of happiness more in accordance with ideal justice. Here, if my analysis of the common notion of Justice be sound, the attempt to extract from it a clear decision of such an issue must necessarily fail: as the conflict is, so to say, permanently latent in the very core of Common Sense. But the Utilitarian will merely use this notion of Justice as a guide to different kinds of utilities; and in so far as these are incompatible, he will balance one set of advantages against the other, and decide according to the preponderance.

---

[4] I have before observed that it is quite in harmony with Utilitarian principles to recognise a sphere of private conduct within which each individual may distribute his wealth and kind services as unequally as he chooses, without incurring censure as unjust.

Idealism

Like many terms used by philosophers, idealism has both a wider and a narrower meaning. Its wider meaning is the one usually used in ordinary speech, and refers to a concern for ideals and sometimes also to a form of commitment to them. If used pejoratively of someone, it may carry the implication that the "idealist" is so involved with his ideals that he overlooks "real" facts in human experience. In the narrower sense, however, idealism denotes a school of philosophy with a technically developed position within which the main arguments deal with ideas rather than ideals. It must be added immediately, however, that this does not mean that idealists have no interest in ideals: they do indeed, often in ways not shared by other philosophers. However, this is their interest as philosophers, not as "common sense" idealists.

With idealism, our study returns to a position within which the metaphysical impulse is strong. Idealism is in fact primarily a metaphysical vision which seeks—like all such visions—to present a coherent, inclusive view of the universe and of man's place within it. Unfortunately, however, it is difficult to provide an accurate and helpful introductory definition of idealism. The word itself is derived from the Greek *idein*, which means to see and also to know. The word goes back further to the Sanskrit root *vid,* to know or to learn. Such an etymology is filled with meanings that center on mind, for only minds or conscious persons can see, know, and learn. This suggests a definition of idealism as the philosophy for which mind, or what is most characteristic of mind, is the fundamental principle of explanation and understanding. As a metaphysics, idealism asserts that the real is mind or the mindlike; as an epistemology, it posits that knowledge is the result of mind's creative activity; and in axiology and related disciplines, it holds the dependency of values on mind. Idealist philosophies thus maintain that the universe, as well as man's experience of it is, in all three respects, the work or embodiment of mind.

While idealists generally accept this description of their position, they do differ in their respective emphases. These differences provide a convenient basis for distinguishing four major varieties of idealism.

First are the mentalists or subjective idealists who, following Bishop George Berkeley (1685–1753), deny the reality of matter and material substances, asserting that physical objects—"all the choir of heaven and furniture of the earth"—are of the same kind of being as is mind itself. A second group of idealists are the absolutists, who urge that certain logical concepts like system or universal best define reality, and that reality so characterized is one inclusive mindlike structure. In other words, knowledge, value, and the universe are most adequately understood when viewed in terms of such notions as systematic interrelation or the manifestation of universals. A third school of idealists seeks to discover the presuppositions or "transcendental conditions" (Kant) of experience, which they profess to find in mind and its activities. To know some particular fact, for example, is to know it as a kind of fact with relations to other facts, which presupposes the mental activities of classification and systematization. Among the presuppositions of factual knowledge, therefore, are these acts of mind. Finally, there are idealist philosophers who argue that values are in some sense objective and part of the nature of reality. Yet, because value implies mind—apart from mind there is no experience of, nor meaning to, value—they draw the idealist conclusion that reality is in its essence spiritual.

At the risk of some repetition, it may be helpful for understanding these idealistic assertions to survey briefly some of the major arguments for them. One such argument—in fact, group of arguments—attempts to show that knowledge of anything implies that it is relative to mind. Consider what is meant by a fact of experience, either taken simply or as part of the systems of science, art, or morality. Facts are always found within a set of relationships held together by consciousness. Thus, relationship presupposes a self-distinguishing consciousness—a consciousness of system or relation—that functions as a principle of synthesis uniting phenomena in a single, inclusive universe. Knowledge is a function of the human mind, to be sure; but the knowability of the universe—even of any single fact—implies that an objective spiritual principle, a Cosmic or Absolute Mind, is fundamental to and constitutes the reality of the universe.

Closely related to this epistemological argument is one based on value experience. For some idealists, in fact, the preceding argument is only a part of the larger problem of values. They urge that reason, if abstracted from ideals and values like system, coherence, truth, and intelligibility, is incapable of discharging its function of grasping reality. Only an ideal world, a world that embodies and fulfills man's ideals, is knowable and intelligible. This means that ideals are objective, for they form the structure (or part of the structure) of reality itself. In support of this conclusion, idealists assert that while the experience of value is "subjective" because it is always an experience of persons, there is also in that experience an "objective reference" to the claim that values *ought* to be appreciated whether or not one actually does appreciate them. The ground for holding the objectivity of value on the basis of this reference is that men's value judgments can be organized into an intelligible system when such judgments are interpreted as claims that reality makes upon men. However, a reality laying claims on men must itself be ideal, a spiritual principle that is both ultimate reality and the locus of ideals.

Through arguments of these kinds, idealists are led to posit an eternal consciousness or spiritual being as the ultimate reality.* This conclusion, however, is also built on the negative argument that any belief in matter or material substance existing independent of mind is unjustified. Thinking, willing, knowing: activities such as these make up human experience, and what we experience is always something within the framework of experience. No reality, idealists argue, can be admitted that does not fall within this framework. To be realities, things must be constituted within the system of relationships that, as was seen above, is supported by a spiritual principle. A completely independent reality, a reality totally unrelated to mind, is not only unknowable, but indeed unthinkable. Of course, the idealist does not argue that reality is limited to *human* experience: he is saying that to be real is to be an element in experience as such, the experience of the Absolute.

Idealist arguments are frequently difficult to follow at a first reading. They often appear to contradict what seems to be common sense in addition to being abstract and technical. Perhaps it will be helpful to say in summary that idealist arguments lead to the following basic assertions: the world of ordinary perceptual experience is not the real world—reality is a *spiritual* principle beyond everyday experience; ideals are objective and part of the real itself; and reality, since it embodies ideals, is knowable and intelligible.

The social philosophy of the great idealists is developed within this guiding metaphysical position. The task of philosophy, they argue, is to seek to know the various standards and values, ends and purposes, of human life; and this same task confronts the philosopher as he examines society. Working with their conceptions of reason, personality, and ideals, idealists find in man a fundamental social impulse that is also a moral impulse to achieve the ideal. When rightly organized, society tries to give this impulse realization in a form adequate to the full and ideal meaning of morality. And when rightly understood, idealistic theories of rationality, of ethics, and of society are interrelated if not identical. The selections given attempt to develop the idealistic perspective in terms of its distinctive emphasis in social philosophy.

Man and Society

For idealists, the heading "man and society" raises questions about the nature of human personality, the meaning of community, and the relationship between the two—matters to be examined within the framework of idealistic metaphysical assumptions. From that metaphysics come such ideas as purpose, ideal selfhood, self-

---

* There are two refinements here that students of the metaphysics of idealism may wish to pursue. One is the distinction between monism or absolutism, which views the universe ultimately as one mind, and pluralisms which hold that the real consists of many minds. The other refinement concerns personal and impersonal idealisms, which reflects the differing emphases of idealists on the mental or conscious nature of the Absolute.

realization, reason, and consciousness, all of which are peculiarly relevant to the idealist's understanding of the human condition. Their meaning for a theory of man will be explained first.

As was seen in the introduction above, knowledge is explained in idealistic theory on the supposition that facts are related in a system held together by consciousness; man is capable of knowledge because he is a being conscious of facts. In a similar way, man is viewed as capable of conduct or morality because he is conscious of objects and deeds. For something to be an object means that it is related to some desire. Moral action* occurs when a person identifies himself with an object of desire, thus seeking to fulfill a purpose, to make real the idea of some better state of being, and to satisfy himself.

In this explanation of conduct, consciousness is the critical point. Even the most objectless human life, idealists insist, forms a system in which particular desires meet and are qualified by the conception of something desirable on the whole. In so forming even an elementary system, desires are also permeated by reason. And, since objects and desires are related to consciousness and reason, the system they constitute points toward completion in an "ideal self" that serves as both goal and judge of individual conduct. The ethical task for each person is to realize the ideal self in his own life, thus to achieve full "self-realization," as the theory is commonly named.†

Idealists find that society also is best represented as a system that depends on the recognition of something desirable on the whole, of the "common good," that involves other persons and is at the same time one of the sources of true self-satisfaction for the individual. The moral impulse is a social impulse: man is conscious of himself as an end to himself, yet because he is so aware of himself, he also has consciousness of others similarly conceived. The social impulse is also moral, for society tries to support this impulse in a form adequate to the full meaning of self-realization. Thus, to paraphrase the English idealist, T. H. Green: social life is to human personality what language is to thought; for language presupposes thought as a capacity, but this capacity is actualized only in language. Similarly, society presupposes persons in capacity, but it is only in the intercourse of men, when they recognize each other as ends not merely as means and thus have reciprocal claims, that the capacity is actualized and men truly live as persons. To function in support of self-realization, every society rests on the reality of some shared and acknowledged conception of a good common to all its members. The spiritual principle of consciousness is the source of this common good, and human society is ultimately an achievement of rationality.

The conditions of community, as Josiah Royce (1855–1916) develops them in the following selection, reflect these idealistic teachings. A community, he writes, is neither a mere collection of individuals nor simply cooperative activities. Per-

---

* This expression as used here is largely descriptive. It means action capable of being judged in reference to some moral criterion. The idealist's criterion for normative judgment is given in the following paragraphs.

† Self-realization is also the name frequently associated with Aristotle's ethics, to which many idealists are heavily indebted. The latter, however, lay greater stress than Aristotle did on the relation of the ideal to consciousness and—as will be seen more fully in the discussion of law and rights—on mutual recognition for the analysis of rights.

sons constitute a community by reference to an ideal past and future that makes them members of a "spiritual body" whose activities are "the life of my own self writ large." The existence of communities depends on the power of the self to extend its life to past and future through deeds done and ends sought, on social communication, and on the identity of some events experienced by all members of the community. While thus rooted in human nature and needs, society is also one of the conditions of that realization of selfhood that is the moral ideal.

JOSIAH ROYCE   The Search for Community

As an essentially social being, man lives in communities, and depends upon his communities for all that makes his civilization articulate. His communities, as both Plato and Aristotle already observed, have a sort of organic life of their own, so that we can compare a highly developed community, such as a state, either to the soul of a man or to a living animal. A community is not a mere collection of individuals. It is a sort of live unit, that has organs, as the body of an individual has organs. A community grows or decays, is healthy or diseased, is young or aged, much as any individual member of the community possesses such characters. Each of the two, the community or the individual member, is as much a live creature as is the other. Not only does the community live, it has a mind of its own,—a mind whose psychology is not the same as the psychology of an individual human being. The social mind displays its psychological traits in its characteristic products,—in languages, in customs, in religions,—products which an individual human mind, or even a collection of such minds, when they are not somehow organized into a genuine community, cannot produce. Yet language, custom, religion are all of them genuinely mental products.

Communities, in their turn, tend, under certain conditions, to be organized into composite communities of still higher and higher grades. States are united in empires; languages coöperate in the production of universal literature; the corporate entities of many communities tend to organize that still very incomplete community which, if ever it comes into existence, will be the world-state, the community possessing the whole world's civilization.

So far, I have spoken only of the natural history of the social organization, and not of its value. But the history of thought shows how manifold are the ways in which, if once you grant that a community is or can be a living organic being, with a mind of its own, this doctrine about the natural facts can be used for ideal, for ethical, purposes. Few ideas have been, in fact, more fruitful than this one in their indirect consequences for ethical doctrines as well as for religion. . . .

We have repeatedly spoken of two levels of human life, the level of the individual and the level of the community. We have now in our hands the means for giving a more precise sense to this expression, and for furnishing a further verification of what we asserted about these two levels of life. We

From Josiah Royce, *The Problem of Christianity,* 2 vols., New York: The Macmillan Co., 1913.

have also repeatedly emphasized the ethical and religious significance of loyalty; but our definition will help us to throw clear light upon the sources of this worth. And by thus sharpening the outlines of our picture of what a real community is, we shall be made ready to consider whether the concept of the community possesses a more than human significance. Let us recall our new definition to mind, and then apply it to our main problems.

Our definition presupposes that there exist many individual selves. Suppose these selves to vary in their present experiences and purposes as widely as you will. Imagine them to be sundered from one another by such chasms of mutual mystery and independence as, in our natural social life, often seem hopelessly to divide and secrete the inner world of each of us from the direct knowledge and estimate of his fellows. But let these selves be able to look beyond their present chaos of fleeting ideas and of warring desires, far away into the past whence they came, and into the future whither their hopes lead them. As they thus look, let each one of them ideally enlarge his own individual life, extending himself into the past and future, so as to say of some far-off event, belonging, perhaps, to other generations of men, "I view that event as a part of my own life." "That former happening or achievement so predetermined the sense and the destiny which are now mine, that I am moved to regard it as belonging to my own past." Or again: "For that coming event I wait and hope as an event of my own future."

And further, let the various ideal extensions, forwards and backwards, include at least one common event, so that each of these selves regards that event as a part of his own life.

Then, *with reference to the ideal common past and future in question, I say that these selves constitute a community*. This is henceforth to be our definition of a community. The present variety of the selves who are the members of the spiritual body so defined, is not hereby either annulled or slighted. The motives which determine each of them thus ideally to extend his own life, may vary from self to self in the most manifold fashion.

Our definition will enable us, despite all these varieties of the members, to understand in what sense any such community as we have defined exists, and is one.

Into this form, which, when thus summarily described, seems so abstract and empty, life can and does pour the rich contents and ideals which make the communities of our human world so full of dramatic variety and significance.

The *first* condition upon which the existence of a community, in our sense of the word, depends, is the power of an individual self to extend his life, in ideal fashion, so as to regard it as including past and future events which lie far away in time, and which he does not now personally remember. That this power exists, and that man has a self which is thus ideally extensible in time without any definable limit, we all know.

This power itself rests upon the principle that, however a man may come by his idea of himself, the self is no mere datum, but is in its essence a life which is interpreted, and which interprets itself, and which, apart from some sort of ideal interpretation, is a mere flight of ideas, or a meaningless flow of feelings, or a vision that sees nothing, or else a barren abstract conception. How deep the process of interpretation goes in determining the real nature of the self, we shall only later be able to estimate.

There is no doubt that what we usually call our personal memory does indeed give us assurances regarding our own past, so far as memory extends and is trustworthy. But our trust in our memories is itself an interpretation of their data. All of us regard as belonging, even to our recent past life, much that we cannot just now remember. And the future self shrinks and expands with our hopes and our energies. No one can merely, from without, set for us the limits of the life of the self, and say to us: "Thus far and no farther."

In my ideal extensions of the life of the self, I am indeed subject to some sort of control,—to what control we need not here attempt to formulate. I must be able to give myself some sort of reason, personal, or social, or moral, or religious, or metaphysical, for taking on or throwing off the burden, the joy, the grief, the guilt, the hope, the glory of past and of future deeds and experiences; but I must also myself personally share in this task of determining how much of the past and the future shall ideally enter into my life, and shall contribute to the value of that life.

And if I choose to say, "There is a sense in which *all* the tragedy and the attainment of an endless past and future of deeds and of fortunes enter into my own life," I say only what saints and sages of the most various creeds and experiences have found their several reasons for saying. The fact and the importance of such ideal extensions of the self must therefore be recognized. Here is the first basis for every clear idea of what constitutes a community.

The ideal extensions of the self may also include, as is well known, not only past and future events and deeds, but also physical things, whether now existent or not, and many other sorts of objects which are neither events nor deeds. The knight or the samurai regarded his sword as a part of himself. One's treasures and one's home, one's tools, and the things that one's hands have made, frequently come to be interpreted as part of the self. And any object in heaven or earth may be thus ideally appropriated by a given self. The ideal self of the Stoic or of the Mystic may, in various fashions, identify its will, or its very essence, with the whole universe. The Hindoo seer seeks to realize the words: "I am Brahm"; "That art thou."

In case such ideal extensions of the self are consciously bound up with deeds, or with other events, such as belong to the past or future life which the self regards as its own, our definition of the community warrants us in saying that many selves form one community when all are ideally extended so as to include the same object. But unless the ideal extensions of the self thus consciously involve past and future deeds and events that have to do with the objects in question, we shall not use these extensions to help us to define communities.

For our purposes, the community is a being that attempts to accomplish something in time and through the deeds of its members. These deeds belong to the life which each member regards as, in ideal, his own. It is in this way that both the real and the ideal Church are intended by the members to be communities in our sense. An analogous truth holds for such other communities as we shall need to consider. The concept of the community is thus, for our purposes, a practical conception. It involves the idea of deeds done, and ends sought or attained.

Hence I shall define it in terms of members who themselves not only live in time, but conceive their own ideally extended personalities in terms of a time-process. In so far as these personalities possess a life that is for each of them his own, while it is, in some of its events, common to them all, they form a community.

Nothing important is lost, for our conception of the community, by this formal restriction, whereby common objects belong to a community only when these objects are bound up with the deeds of the community. For, when the warrior regards his sword as a part of himself, he does so because his sword is the instrument of his will, and because what he does with his sword belongs to his literal or ideal life. Even the mystic accomplishes his identification of the self and the world only through acts of renunciation or of inward triumph. And these acts are the goal of his life. Until he attains to them, they form part of his ideal future self. Whenever he fully accomplishes these crowning acts of identification, the separate self no longer exists. When knights or mystics form a community, in our sense, they therefore do so because they conceive of deeds done, in common, with their swords, or of mystical attainments that all of them win together.

Thus then, while no authoritative limit can be placed upon the ideal extensions of the self in time, those extensions of the self which need be considered for the purposes of our theory of the community are indeed extensions in time, past or future; or at all events involve such extensions in time.

Memory and hope constantly incite us to the extensions of the self which play so large a part in our daily life. Social motives of endlessly diverse sort move us to consider "far and forgot" as

if to us it were near, when we view ourselves in the vaster perspectives of time. It is, in fact, the ideally extended self, and not, in general, the momentary self, whose life is worth living, whose sense outlasts our fleeting days, and whose destiny may be worthy of the interest of beings who are above the level of human individuals. The present self, the fleeting individual of to-day, is a mere gesticulation of a self. The genuine person lives in the far-off past and future as well as in the present. It is, then, the ideally extended self that is worthy to belong to a significant community.

The *second* condition upon which the existence of a community depends is the fact that there are in the social world a number of distinct selves capable of social communication, and, in general, engaged in communication.

The distinctness of the selves we have illustrated at length in our previous discussion. We need not here dwell upon the matter further, except to say, expressly, that a community does *not* become one, in the sense of my definition, by virtue of any reduction or melting of these various selves into a single merely present self, or into a mass of passing experience. That mystical phenomena may indeed form part of the life of a community, just as they may also form part of the life of an individual human being, I fully recognize.

About such mystical or quasi-mystical phenomena, occurring in their own community, the Corinthians consulted Paul. And Paul, whose implied theory of the community is one which my own definition closely follows, assured them in his reply that mystical phenomena are not essential to the existence of the community; and that it is on the whole better for the life of such a community as he was addressing, if the individual member, instead of losing himself "in a mystery," kept his own individuality, in order to contribute his own edifying gift to the common life. Wherein this common life consists we have yet further to see in what follows.

The *third* of the conditions for the existence of the community which my definition emphasizes consists in the fact that the ideally extended past and future selves of the members include at least some events which are, for all these selves, identical. This third condition is the one which furnishes both the most exact, the most widely variable, and the most important of the motives which warrant us in calling a community a real unit. The Pauline metaphor of the body and the members finds, in this third condition, its most significant basis,—a basis capable of exact description. . . .

Men do not form a community, in our present restricted sense of that word, merely in so far as the men cooperate. They form a community, in our present limited sense, when they not only cooperate, but accompany this cooperation with that ideal extension of the lives of individuals whereby each cooperating member says: "This activity which we perform together, this work of ours, its past, its future, its sequence, its order, its sense,—all these enter into my life, and are the life of my own self writ large". . . .

A community thus constituted is essentially a community of those who are artists in some form of cooperation, and whose art constitutes, for each artist, his own ideally extended life. But the life of an artist depends upon his love for his art.

The community is made possible by the fact that each member includes in his own ideally extended life the deeds of cooperation which the members accomplish. When these deeds are hopelessly complex, how shall the individual member be able to regard them as genuinely belonging to his own ideally extended life? He can no longer understand them in any detail. He takes part in them, willingly or unwillingly. He does so because he is social, and because he must. He works in his factory, or has his share, whether greedily or honestly, in the world's commercial activities. And his cooperations may be skilful; and this fact also he may know. But his skill is largely due to external training, not to inner expansion of the ideals of the self. And the more complex the social order grows, the more all this cooperation must tend to appear to the individual as a mere process of nature, and not as his own work,—as a mechanism and not as an ideal extension of himself,—unless indeed love supplies what individual wit can no longer accomplish.

Social and Political Values

The idealist's teleological view of man and society reflects a set of values involved in the ideal of self-realization. This ideal is one of personal worth: "all other values are relative to value for, of, or in a person" (T. H. Green). So act, Kant (1724–1804) said, that you treat humanity, whether in your own person or in that of another, always as an end in itself, never merely as a means. This is a dictate of reason, which is the basis of society because it is the source of practical rules serving the common interest and of self-imposed subjection to these rules. Human communities are thus founded on the unity of consciousness with its capacity to grasp the idea of a common, permanent good and the duties it implies.

Immanuel Kant's writings provide a guide for following the idealistic theory of social values. Unlike most subsequent idealists, Kant accepts a version of the social compact theory to account for the nature of society, though he qualifies the theory to the extent that it is hardly recognizable. In no way does the compact refer to historic fact: it is an "idea of reason" signifying the union of wills that is the original condition for the existence of any society. This union of men must be viewed as an end in itself so that every person ought to carry it out as a primary and unconditional duty. This primary and unconditional duty is the realization of the capacities and rights of men under compulsory laws.

According to Kant, reason wills that a commonwealth be a relation of free men who live under law, a relation that is based on three rational principles of value that serve as the presuppositions making the commonwealth possible. The first principle is the *liberty* of every member of society as a man—a principle first in importance as well as in order. Idealists generally take freedom to be a "positive" conception. It is not just freedom from the interference of others, but a positive power of doing or enjoying something worth doing or enjoying. To do things worth doing means to act as one ought, to act rationally, and to be disciplined in discharging moral obligations. The "external right" of liberty arises out of this notion of human freedom, for "right" involves the limitation of the action of an individual to agree with the freedom of others.

The second principle is the *equality* of every member of society as a subject. Kant is writing here of legal and civil equality, not of social equality. In fact, he believes that legal equality is compatible with inequality of talents and possessions. As subjects, all persons must be compelled or coerced only by public law, and they may resist unlawful coercion by the same means.

The third rational principle of society is the *self-dependency* of every member as a citizen. Here Kant means that every qualified person must be considered equal in giving or enacting laws. A public law, he argues, is an act of a public will, and hence only the will of a whole people is competent to legislate for the whole. No particular will can be legislative rightfully for a commonwealth; liberty, equality, and the public will all require the independent (or self-dependent) participation of citizens in the formulation of rules for the public domain.

It is not a great oversimplification to view the idealistic theory of social values as a set of implications from the ethical theory of self-realization. No other person, no law, no society can be the agent of one's own conduct: moral action is always self-originating and a product of one's own will. But there are certain external conditions that must be fulfilled in order that individual self-realization may occur. These conditions—which may be called moral because they are necessary to self-realization—are the values defining the *telos* of society as well as, *mutatis mutandis,* of individual life.

IMMANUEL KANT Liberty, Equality,
and Self-Dependency

The establishment of a Civil Constitution in society is one of the most important facts in human history. In the principle on which it is founded this institution differs from all the other forms of social union among mankind. Viewed as a compact,[1] and compared with other modes of compact[2] by which numbers of men are united into one Society, the formation of a Civil Constitution has much in common with all other forms of Social Union in respect of the mode in which it is carried out in practice. But while all such compacts are established for the purpose of promoting in common some chosen End, the Civil Union is essentially distinguished from all others, by the principle on which it is based. In all social contracts we find a union of a number of persons for the purpose of carrying out some one End which they all have in common. But a Union of a multitude of men, viewed as an end in itself that every person ought to carry out, and which consequently is a primary and unconditional duty amid all the external relations of men who cannot help exercising a mutual influence on one another,—is at once peculiar and unique of its kind. Such a Union is only to be found in a Society which, by being formed into a Civil State, constitutes a Commonwealth. Now the End which in such external relations is itself a duty and even the highest formal condition— the *conditio sine qua non*—of all other external duties, is the realization of *the*

---

[1] *Pactum unionis civilis.*
[2] *Pactum Sociale.*

Rights of Men under public compulsory Laws, by which every individual can have what is his own assigned to him, and secured against the encroachments or assaults of others.

The idea of an external Right, however, arises wholly out of the idea of human Freedom or *Liberty,* in the external relations of men to one another. As such, it has nothing specially to do with the realization of Happiness as a purpose which all men naturally have, or with prescription of the means of attaining it; and it is absolutely necessary that this End shall not be mixed up with the Laws of Right as their motive. *Right* in general, may be defined as the limitation of the Freedom of any individual to the extent of its agreement with the freedom of all other individuals, in so far as this is possible by a universal Law. *Public Right,* again, is the sum of the external Laws which make such a complete agreement of freedom in Society possible. Now as all limitation of freedom by external acts of the will of another, is a mode of *coercion* or *compulsion,* it follows that the Civil Constitution is a relation of *free* men who live under coercive Laws, without prejudicing their liberty otherwise in the whole of their connection with others. For, Reason itself wills this. By "Reason" is here meant the pure innate law-giving Reason which gives no regard to any End that is derived from experience, such as are all comprehended under the general name of Happiness. In respect of any such End or in what any individual may place it, men may think

From Kant's essay, "Concerning the Common Saying: This May Be True in Theory, but Does Not Apply in Practice," in *Kant's Principles of Politics,* trans. W. Hastie, Edinburgh: T. & T. Clark, 1891.

quite differently, so that their wills could not be brought under any common principle, nor, consequently, under any External Laws that would be compatible with the liberty of all.

The Civil State, then, regarded merely as a social state that is regulated by laws of right, is founded upon the following rational principles:—

1. The *Liberty* of every Member of the Society *as a Man;*

2. The *Equality* of every Member of the Society with every other, *as a Subject;*

3. The *Self-dependency* of every Member of the Commonwealth, *as a Citizen.*

These Principles are not so much Laws given by the State when it is established, as rather fundamental conditions according to which alone the institution of a State is possible, in conformity with the pure rational Principles of external Human Right generally.

1. The *Liberty* of every Member of the State *as a Man,* is the first principle in the constitution of a rational Commonwealth. I would express this Principle in the following form:—"No one has a right to compel me to be happy in the peculiar way in which he may think of the well-being of other men; but everyone is entitled to seek his own happiness in the way that seems to him best, if it does not infringe the liberty of others in striving after a similar end for themselves when their Liberty is capable of consisting with the Right of Liberty in all others according to possible universal laws."—A Government founded upon the principle of Benevolence towards the people—after the analogy of a *father* to his children, and therefore called a *paternal Government*—would be one in which the Subjects would be regarded as children or minors unable to distinguish what is beneficial or in-

jurious to them. These subjects would be thus compelled to act in a merely passive way; and they would be trained to expect solely from the Judgment of the Sovereign and just as he might will it, merely out of his goodness, all that *ought* to make them happy. Such a Government would be the greatest conceivable *Despotism;* for it would present a Constitution that would abolish all Liberty in the Subjects and leave them no Rights. It is not a *paternal* Government, but only a *patriotic* Government that is adapted for men who are capable of Rights, and at the same time fitted to give scope to the goodwill of the ruler. By "patriotic" is meant that condition of mind in which everyone in the State —the Head of it not excepted—regards the Commonwealth as the maternal bosom, and the country as the paternal soil out of and on which he himself has sprung into being, and which he also must leave to others as a dear inheritance. Thus, and thus only, can he hold himself entitled to protect the Rights of his fatherland by laws of the common will, but not to subject it to an unconditional purpose of his own at pleasure.—This Right of Liberty thus belongs to him as a man, while he is a Member of the Commonwealth; or, in point of fact, so far as he is a being capable of rights generally.

2. The *Equality* of every member of the State *as a subject,* is the second Principle in the Constitution of a rational Commonwealth. The formula of this Principle may be put thus:—"Every Member of the Commonwealth has rights against every other that may be enforced by compulsory Laws, from which only the Sovereign or Supreme Ruler of the State is excepted, because he is regarded not as a mere Member of the Commonwealth, but as its Creator or Maintainer; and he alone has the

Right to compel without being himself subject to compulsory Law." All, however, who live *under* Laws in a State, are its subjects; and, consequently, they are subjected to the Compulsory law, like all other members of the Commonwealth, one only, whether an individual Sovereign or a collective body, constituting the Supreme Head of the State, and as such being accepted as the medium through which alone all rightful corecion or compulsion can be exercised. For, should the Head of the State also be subject to compulsion, there would no longer be a Supreme Head, and the series of members subordinate and superordinate would go on upwards *ad infinitum*. Again, were there in the State two such powers as persons exempt from legal compulsion, neither of them would be subject to compulsory Laws, and as such the one could do no wrong to the other; which is impossible.

This thoroughgoing Equality of the individual men in a State as its subjects, is, however, quite compatible with the greatest *Inequality* in the extent and degrees of their possessions, whether consisting in corporeal or spiritual superiority over others, or in the external gifts of fortune, or in rights generally— of which there may be many—in relation to others. Thus the prosperity of the one may greatly depend on the will of another as in the case of the poor in relation to the rich. One may even have of necessity to obey and another to command, as in the relation of children to parents, and of wife to husband. Again, one may have to work and another to pay, as in the case of a day laborer; and so on. But in relation to the involved law of Right, which as the expression of the universal Will of the State can be only one, and which regards the *form* of the Right, and not the matter or object to which the Right refers: in all cases, the persons as Subjects, are to be regarded as all equal to one another. For no one has a right to compel or coerce anyone whomsoever in the State, otherwise than by the public Law and through the Sovereign or Ruler executing it; and anyone may resist another thus far, and through the same medium. On the other hand, no one can lose this right, as a title to proceed by legal compulsion against others, except by his own fault or a criminal act. Nor can anyone divest himself of it voluntarily, or by a compact, so as to bring it about by a supposed act of Right, that he should have no rights but only duties towards others; for in so doing he would be depriving himself of the right of making a compact, and consequently the act would annul itself.

Out of this idea of the Equality of men as Subjects in the Commonwealth, there arises the following formula:— "Every Member of the State should have it made possible for him to attain to any position or rank that may belong to any subject, to which his talent, his industry or his fortune may be capable of raising him; and his fellow-subjects are not entitled to stand in the way by any *hereditary* prerogative, forming the exclusive privilege of a certain class, in order to keep him and his posterity forever below them."

For, all Right just consists in restriction of the Liberty of another to the condition that is consistent with my Liberty according to a universal Law; and Public Right in a Commonwealth is only the product of actual legislation conformable to this principle and conjoined with power, in virtue of which all who belong to a nation as its subjects find themselves in a rightful state—*status juridicus*—constituted and regulated by law. And, as such, this state is in fact a condition of Equality, inasmuch as it is determined by the action and reaction of free wills limiting one another, according to the universal law of Freedom; and it thus constitutes the Civil State of human Society. Hence the *inborn* Right of all individuals in this sphere (that is considered as being prior to their having actually entered upon juridical action) to bring compulsion to bear upon any others, is entirely *identical and equal throughout,* on the assumption that they are always to remain within the bounds of unanimity and concord in the mutual use of their Liberty. Now birth is not an *act* on the part of him who is born, and consequently it does not entail upon him any inequality in the state of Right, nor any subjection under laws of compulsion other than what is common to him, with all others, as a subject of the one supreme legislative Power; and, therefore, there can be no inborn privilege by way of Right in any member of the Commonwealth as a subject, before another fellow-subject. Nor, consequently has anyone a right to transmit the privilege or prerogative of the *Rank* which he holds in the Commonwealth to his posterity so that they should be, as it were, qualified by birth for the rank of nobility; nor should they be prevented from attaining to the higher stages in the gradations of social rank, by their own merit. Everything else that partakes of the nature of a thing and does not relate to personality, may be bequeathed; and, since such things may be acquired as property, they may also be alienated or disponed. Hence after a number of generations a considerable inequality in external circumstances may arise among the members of a Commonwealth, producing such relations as those of Master and Servant, Landlord and Tenant, etc. These circumstances and relations, however, ought not to hinder any of the subjects of the State from rising to such positions as their talent, their industry, and their fortune may make it possible for them to fill. For, otherwise such a one would be qualified to coerce without being liable to be coerced by the counter action of others in return; and he would rise above the stage of being a fellow-subject. Further, no man who lives under the legalised conditions of a Commonwealth, can fall out of this equality otherwise than by his own crime, and never either by compact or through any military occupancy.[3] For he cannot by any legal act, whether of himself or of another, cease to be the owner of himself, or enter into the class of domestic cattle, which are used for all sorts of services at will and are maintained in this condition without their consent as long as there is a will to do it, although under the limitation—which is sometimes sanctioned even by religion, as among the Hindoos—that they are not to be mutilated or slain. Under any conditions, he is to be regarded as happy who is conscious that it depends only on himself—that is on his faculty or earnest will—or on circumstances which he cannot impute to any other, and not on the irresistible will of others, that he does not rise to a stage of Equality with others who as his fellow-subjects have no advantage over him as far as Right is concerned.

3. The *Self-dependency*[4] of a member of the Commonwealth *as a citizen,* or fellow-legislator, is the third principle

---

[3] *Occupatio bellica.*

[4] The term *Selbständigkeit,* here rendered by "Self-dependency," is represented by Kant in his text by the Latin equivalent *Sibisufficientia.* The word "self-sufficiency," however, would be apt to mislead English readers. The term is commonly translated by "Independence," but "Self-dependency" has been preferred as more closely indicative of the form and connotation of the German word. *Tr.*

or condition of Right in the State. In the matter of the legislation itself, all are to be regarded as free and equal *under* the already existing public Laws; but they are not to be all regarded as equal in relation to the right to give or *enact* these laws. Those who are not capable of this right, are, notwithstanding, subjected to the observance of the laws as members of the Commonwealth, and thereby they participate in the protection which is in accordance therewith; they are, however, not to be regarded as *Citizens* but as protected fellow-subjects.—All right, in fact, depends on the laws. A public law, however, which determines for all what is to be legally allowed or not allowed in their regard, is the act of a public Will, from which all right proceeds and which therefore itself can do no wrong to anyone. For this, however, there is no other Will competent than that of the *whole* people, as it is only when all determine about all that each one in consequence determines about himself. For it is only to himself that one can do no wrong. But if it be another will that is in question, then the mere will of anyone different from it, could determine nothing for it which might not be wrong; and consequently the law of such a will would require another law to limit its legislation. And thus no particular will can be legislative for a Commonwealth.—Properly speaking, in order to make out this, the ideas of the external Liberty, Equality, and *Unity* of the will of all, are to be taken into account; and for the last of these *Self-dependency* is the condition, since the exercising of a vote is required when the former two ideas are taken along with it. The fundamental law thus indicated, which can only arise out of the universal united will of the people, is what is called the *"Original Contract."*

Now anyone who has the right of voting in this system of Legislation, is a *Citizen* as distinguished from a Burgess; he is a *citoyen* as distinguished from a *bourgeois*. The quality requisite for this status, in addition to the natural one of not being a child or a woman,— is solely this, that the individual is his *own master* by right (*sui juris*); and, consequently, that he has some property that supports him,—under which may be reckoned any art or handicraft, or any fine art or science. Otherwise put, the condition in those cases in which the citizen must acquire from others in order to live, is that he only acquires it by alienation of what is his own, and not by a consent given to others to make use of his powers; and consequently that he *serves* no one but the Commonwealth, in the proper sense of the term. In this relation those who are skilled in the arts, and large or small proprietors, are all equal to one another; as in fact each one is entitled only to one vote. As regards Proprietors, the question might be considered as to how it may have happened by right that anyone has got as his own more land than he can himself use with his own hands (for acquisition by military occupation is not primary acquisition); and how it has happened that many men, who otherwise might have altogether been able to acquire an independent possession, have been brought to the position of merely serving such a one in order to be able to live. But without entering here upon the consideration of this question, it is manifest that it would at once be contrary to the previous principle of Equality, if a law were to invest such persons with the privilege of a class, so that their descendants should either always continue to be great proprietors of land— in the manner of fiefs—without such being able to be sold or divided by in-heritance, and thus coming to be applied for the use of more of the people; or if, even in carrying out such divisions, that no one but he who belonged to a certain class, arbitrarily regulated in this connection, could acquire any part of such land. The great possessor of an estate, does in fact annihilate as many smaller owners and their voices as might occupy the place he takes up; he does not vote in their name, and he has consequently only one vote. It thus must be left to depend merely on the means, the industry, and the fortune of each member of the Commonwealth, that each one may acquire a part of it, and all of its members the whole. But these distinctions cannot be brought into consideration in connection with a uni-versal Legislation; and hence the num-ber of those qualified to have a voice in the legislation, must be reckoned by the heads of those who are in posses-sion and not according to the extent of their possessions.

Furthermore, *all* who have this right of voting must agree in order to realize the Laws of public justice, for other-wise there would arise a conflict of right between those who were not in agree-ment with it, and the others who were; and this would give rise to the need of a higher principle of right that the con-flict might be decided. A universal agree-ment cannot be expected from a whole people; and consequently it is only a plurality of voices, and not even of those who immediately vote in a large nation, but only of their delegates as repre-sentative of the people that can alone be foreseen as practically attainable. And hence, even the principle of making the majority of votes suffice as repre-senting the general consent, will have to be taken as by compact; and it must thus be regarded as the ultimate basis

of the establishment of any Civil Con-stitution. . . .

Hobbes is of the opposite opinion. In his view the sovereign as Head of the State is bound in nothing to the people by compact and can do no wrong to the citizens, however he act towards them. This proposition would be quite cor-rect, if by "wrong" we understand that kind of lesion which allows to the in-jured party a right of coercion against the one who does the wrong. So it is in the special relation, but taken generally the proposition is repulsive and appall-ing. Any Subject who is not utterly in-tractable, must be able to suppose that his Sovereign does not really *wish* to do him wrong. Moreover, every man must be held to have his own inalienable rights which he cannot give up though he wish to do it, and about which he is himself entitled to judge. But the wrong in question which in his opinion is done to him occurs according to that view only from error or ignorance of certain consequences that will ensue from the laws laid down by the sovereign power. Consequently the right must be con-ceded to the citizen, and with the direct consent of the sovereign, that he shall be able to make his opinion publicly known regarding what appears to him to be a wrong committed against the Com-monwealth by the enactments and ad-ministration of the Sovereign. For to assume that the Sovereign Power can never err, or never be ignorant of any-thing, would amount to regarding that Power as favored with heavenly inspira-tion and as exalted above the reach of mankind, which is absurd. Hence the *Liberty of the Press,* is the sole pal-ladium of the rights of the people. But it must be exercised within the limits of reverence and love for the constitution as it exists, while it must be sustained by the liberal spirit of the subjects, which the constitution itself tends to inspire; and it must be so limited by the wise percautions of those who exercise it that their freedom be not lost. To refuse this Liberty to the people amounts to taking from them all claim to right in relation to the supreme Power; and this is the view of Hobbes. But more than this is involved. As the will of the Sovereign only commands the subjects as citizens on the ground that he represents the general will of the people, to deprive the people of this liberty would be to withdraw from the Sovereign power all knowledge of what he would himself alter if he only knew it; and it would thus put him into contradiction with himself. Moreover to instill an anxiety into the sovereign that independent thinking and public utterance of it, would of themselves excite trouble in the State, would amount to exciting distrust against his own power or even awakening hatred against the people. There is then a general principle according to which the people may assert their rights *negatively,* so far as merely to judge that a certain thing is to be regarded as not *ordained* by the supreme legislation in accordance with their best will. This principle may be expressed in the following proposition: *What a People could not ordain over itself, ought not to be ordained by the Legislator over the People.*

For example, the question may be raised as to whether a Law, enacting that a certain regulated ecclesiastical constitution shall exist permanently and for all time, can be regarded as issuing from the proper will of the lawgiver according to his real intention. In dealing with it, the position which first arises, is whether a people *may* make a law to itself to the effect that certain dogmas and external forms of religion, when once adopted, shall continue to be adopted for all time; and, therefore, whether it may prevent itself in its own descendants from advancing further in religious insight, or from altering any old errors when they have become recognised as such? It will thus become clear, that an "original contract" of the people which made such a position a law, would be in itself null and void because it is inconsistent with the essential destination and purposes of mankind. Consequently, a law enacted to such an effect, is not to be regarded as the proper will of the monarch; and counter representations may therefore be made to him against it. In all cases, however, even when such things have been ordained by the supreme legislation, resistance is not to be offered to them in word or in deed, but they are only to be opposed by the influence of general and public judgments.

In every Commonwealth there must be *obedience* to coercive laws relating to the whole people and regulated by the mechanism of the political constitution. But at the same time there must be a *Spirit of Liberty* among the people; for every one needs to be convinced by reason in things relating to universal human duty, that such coercion is in accordance with Right. Without this he would be in contradiction with his own nature. Obedience without the Spirit of Liberty, is the cause and occasion of all *Secret* Societies. For there is a natural tendency implanted in mankind to communicate to one another what is in them, especially in what bears upon man generally. Such societies would therefore fall away if such liberty were more favored. And how can governments obtain the knowledge which is necessary for furthering their own essential object otherwise than by giving scope in its origin and in its effects, to this estimable spirit of human Liberty?

State, Power, and Authority

Idealists argue that human beings achieve maturity and self-realization only in communal life. Man is indeed a social animal. In communities, however, there is a special institution called the state that has a distinctive role to fill in relation to self-realization. The following selections from G. W. F. Hegel (1770–1831) and Bernard Bosanquet (1848–1923) present idealistic accounts of the state.

To understand Hegel's theory, it is necessary to introduce one of his most central conceptions, namely the dialectic. This term refers to his understanding of change and development, which he analyzed in a threefold series of states called thesis, antithesis, and synthesis. The thesis in any change is its starting point, or that from which the change ensues. The thesis is "abstract" in Hegel's view, for it is undifferentiated and separated from its relations. The antithesis is "other" than the thesis, related to the thesis and yet different from it. The third stage of change is the synthesis, which develops out of the difference and tension between thesis and antithesis. The synthesis cancels out both thesis and antithesis, yet it also preserves them in a higher unity. A synthesis is also more "concrete" because it is differentiated and includes more relations. Hegel teaches that all reality is dialectical in this sense: dialectic is the law both of thought and of being.

The dialectic is illustrated in Hegel's *Philosophy of Right,* from which the selection is taken. In this book Hegel attempts to show that society advances by continually making adjustments to the tensions created by internal factors. An overall triad is developed, consisting of abstract right, morality, and ethical life. The thesis, abstract right, is the level of life on which sheer individualism—individual wills—is asserted. The mere conflict of individuals tends to be destructive, so there is movement to the antithesis, morality, in which men are viewed as the bearers of rights and obligations. Even this level, however, is abstract and partial, for it omits all reference to society and men's dependence on it. Hence arises the synthesis, communal life, in which individual and society are interrelated and mutually dependent.

Within communal life a second triad—family, civil society, and the state—is developed by Hegel. Men find themselves socially organized first in family units. These break down, however, because of their inadequacy to the whole range of human interests—they are "abstract." An antithesis therefore develops, namely civil society, which is the realm of "blind inclination" and motivation by interests. But civil society is also inadequate for it depends on some higher institution to give it supervision and moral significance. This institution is the state, which is the synthesis of the triad. "Higher" than civil society, the state thus comes into being with genuine public authority. It seeks to establish an ethical order by action in obedience to conscious ends.

Hegel makes a number of different assertions about the state. It is the actuality of the ethical idea, meaning that the state maintains the conditions for the realization of the communal ethical life. Among the highest human needs is the need to participate in causes and purposes larger than private wants and satisfactions; only life in the state can provide such a social cause.* Perhaps Hegel's meaning can be made clearer by contrasting his view with liberalism. As Hegel understood it, liberalism fails to recognize that the citizen's personality is a social nature that must participate in the life of civil society and in the state as a condition of its moral significance. In this failure, liberalism falsifies the notion of social institutions; it regards them as accidental to the moral and spiritual development of personality. In the same vein, Hegel speaks of the state as objective mind. Conceptions of the state for other thinkers—Bentham or Hume, for example—would be inadequate for Hegel because they recognize only the pursuit of private ends, or argue that all ends are private. But Hegel teaches that private ends, which belong to the sphere of civil society, ultimately have no meaning apart from a social context of public ends needed for their realization. The state must coordinate private and public, particular and universal (substantial) interests, a coordination that leads Hegel to see the state as rational.

Finally, Hegel speaks of the state as the actuality of concrete freedom. Freedom for Hegel and many idealists is the ability to do what one deliberately chooses to do, and this positive ability is conceivable only for creatures who live in a moral order. Here again we met the idealist insistence on the connection between individual realization and the external conditions that support it. Only after a man is a moral being, after he has acquired some values, can he rationally prefer some of his impulses to others. Otherwise he is but a slave to his impulses, unable to control or select from among them. Freedom is the supreme value for spirit, and the state, Hegel concludes, is the highest type of community in which spirit is made actual.

The second selection is from the writings of the English idealist, Bernard Bosanquet. Bosanquet is arguing against critics who charge the idealist theory with political absolutism. Hegel, to whom he frequently refers, did find the unity of the state to be expressed ultimately in its sovereignty, and also occasionally used the term absolute, though he never meant by it "arbitrary." Writing without the apparatus of the dialectic, Bosanquet attempts to clarify the doctrine of the state by describing it as the "guardian of the whole moral world": it seeks to maintain the external conditions of the good life; and behind any use of force lies the general (rational) will. Neither absolutism nor less government is the basic issue, the basic issue is to have the best government.

---

* Hegel did not make social life the highest value: art, religion, and philosophy are yet more fulfilling activities.

G. W. F. HEGEL   The State as Ethical Idea

257. The state is the actuality of the ethical idea,—ethical mind as the substantial will manifest and revealed to itself, which thinks and knows itself, and fulfills what it knows in so far as it knows it. In custom it exists immedi-

---

Translated from the *Philosophie des Rechts* of Hegel, herausgeben von Eduard Gans, Berlin: Verlag von Duncker und Humblot, 1854.

ately, and mediately in individual self-consciousness, knowledge, and activity; so that through its sentiment toward the state, as its essence, end, and product of its activity, self-consciousness has its substantial freedom.

258. The state is in and for itself rational as the actuality of the substantial will, which it possesses in particular self-consciousness when that consciousness has been raised to consciousness of its universality. This substantial unity is an absolute unmoved end in itself, in which freedom comes into its supreme right; this final end has as well supreme right against the individual, whose supreme duty is to be a member of the state.

If the state is confused with civil society and its vocation is laid down as the security and protection of property and personal freedom, then the interest of individuals becomes the ultimate end for which they are united; and it follows that to be a member of the state is something optional. —But the state has an entirely different relation to the individual from this; since the state is mind objectified, the individual himself has objectivity, truth, and ethical life only as one of its members. Unification as such is the true content and aim of the individual, and the destiny of the individual is to lead a universal life; his further particular satisfaction, activity, and mode of conduct have this substantial and universally valid life as their starting point and result.—Rationality, taken abstractly, consists generally in the thorough-going unity of the universal and the single. Concrete in the state, rationality consists in its content in the unity of objective freedom, i.e. freedom of the universal substantial will, and of subjective freedom as the freedom of the individual will in its volition of particular ends—and consequently, so far as its form is concerned, in self-determining action on laws and principles that are thoughts and so universal.—But if it be asked what is or has been the historical origin of the state in general, or still more of the origin of any particular state, of its rights and institutions, or again if the state

originally arose out of patriarchal conditions, out of fear or trust, out of corporations, and so forth; or finally on what the state's rights have been based and established, whether in the consciousness of divine positive right, contract, or custom, and so forth: with all this the idea of the state has no concern. In regard to philosophic knowledge, of which here alone one speaks, these are mere appearance and a historical concern; in regard to the authority of an actual state, in so far as it admits reasons, these are taken from forms of valid laws within it. . . .

260. The state is the actuality of concrete freedom; but concrete freedom consists in this, that personal individuality and its particular interests achieve not only their complete development and recognition for their rights (as in the sphere of the family and civil society), but for one thing they pass over of themselves into the interest of the universal, for another thing, they know and will the universal. They even recognize it as their own substantial mind and are active for it as their ultimate purpose. Neither does the universal become valid and fulfilled without particular interests, knowledge, and will, nor do individuals live as private persons merely for themselves, not to will in and for the universal and have a consciousness of this end. The principle of modern states has this prodigious strength and depth because it allows the principle of subjectivity to progress to its culmination in the self-subsistent extreme of personal particularity, and at the same time brings it back to the substantial unity and so maintains this unity in the principle of subjectivity itself.

261. In contrast to the spheres of private rights and private welfare, the family and civil society, the state is on the one hand an external necessity and their higher authority whose nature is

such that their laws and interests are subordinate to it and are dependent on it. On the other hand, it is the end immanent within them, and has its strength in the unity of its own universal end and of the particular interests of individuals, wherein individuals have in so far duties to the state as they have rights against it.

. . . Duty is primarily a relation which for me is substantial and absolutely universal. A right, on the other hand, is generally the existence of this substance and is therewith the side of particularity and my particular freedom. Hence both right and duty on the formal level are allotted to different sides or persons. In the state, as ethical, as the inter-penetration of the substantial and the particular, my obligation to the substantial embodies at the same time my particular freedom. That is, in the state duty and right are united in one and the same relation. But further, since in the state the distinct moments acquire the shape and reality peculiar to each, and since the distinction between right and duty enters here again, it follows that while they are identical implicitly, i.e. in form, they at the same time differ in their content. In the spheres of personal rights and morality, the actual necessity of their relation is wanting, and there is therewith only an abstract similarity of content between them: what in those abstract spheres is one man's right ought also to be another's right and what is one man's duty ought also to be another's duty. That absolute identity of duty and right finds a place only as proportionate identity of content, in the determination that this content itself as wholly universal, namely the one principle of duty and right, is the personal freedom of men. . . .

264. Human beings *en masse* themselves comprise a mental nature and therewith a twofold moment, namely at one extreme, explicit knowing and willing individuality, and at the other extreme, knowing and willing universality of what is substantial. Hence they attain their right in both respects only in so far as they are actual as well as substantial persons;—to achieve their right in each sphere (family and civil society) partly in the first respect directly and partly in the second indirectly, so that they find their essential self-consciousness in institutions which are the universal implicit in their particular interests; and partly in the corporation that supplies them with occupation and activity directed on a universal end.

265. These institutions make up the constitution, that is developed and actualized rationality, in the sphere of particularity, and they are, therefore, the firm foundation of the state and of the individual's trust and sentiment in it. They are the pillars of public freedom, since in them particular freedom is realized and rational, and therefore in them implicitly present is the union of freedom and necessity.

266. But mind is objective and actual to itself not merely as this necessity and as a realm of appearance, but also as the ideality and heart of the same; so is this substantial universality of itself its own object and end, and that necessity appears to itself in the shape of freedom.

267. The necessity in ideality is the inner self-development of the idea itself; as subjective substance, it is political sentiment [patriotism], as objective in distinction from the organism of the state, it is the strictly political state and its constitution.

268. The political sentiment, patriotism generally, is assured conviction based in truth (mere subjective assurance is not the outcome of truth and is only opinion) and volition assured by habit; they are only a result of the institutions subsisting in the state, in which rationality is actually present, so that they are shown forth in suitable

deeds.—This sentiment is, in general, trust (which may pass over into greater or lesser educated insight),—the consciousness that my substantial and particular interest is contained and preserved in another's interest and end (here the state's), as in the other's relation to me as an individual. Wherewith this very other is immediately not an other for me, and in this consciousness I am free.

270. As the end of the state is the general interest as such and the maintenance of particular interests in its substance, one finds therein (1) its abstract actuality or substantiality. But this is (2) its necessity, since it is divided into distinct notions of its activity corresponding to the moments of its concept, which through that substantiality are fixed determinations, are its powers. (3) But this very substantiality is willing and knowing mind itself, after passing through the forming process of education. The state therefore knows what it wills, and knows it in its universality, as something thought; it thus works and acts according to conscious ends, known principles, and laws that are not only implicit but are present to consciousness. And further, in so far as its actions cover existing conditions and situations, it acts with precise knowledge of them.

BERNARD BOSANQUET   The Concept of the State

I wish to present a brief positive account of the theory of the state as I understand it, more particularly with reference to the state in its external relations, and the conditions essential to federations or a world-state.

It seems to me that much misconception is prevalent as to the views which in fact great philosophers have held upon this problem. But I do not wish to raise mere questions in the history of philosophy, but to meet the issue as it seems to me to stand to-day. The ideas which I express are therefore my own, in the sense that no one else is responsible for the form I give them. But, to the best of my judgment, they represent the Greek tradition as renewed by Hegel and by English thought.

In considering any problem affecting the state I take the primary question to be how self-government is possible. For anything which interferes with the possibility of self-government destroys altogether the conditions of true government. The answer is drawn, I take it, from the conception of the general will, which involves the existence of an actual community, of such a nature as to share an identical mind and feeling. There is no other way of explaining how a free man can put up with compulsion and even welcome it.

Here then we have the universal condition of legitimate outward authority. City-state, Nation-state, Commonwealth, Federation, World-state, it makes no difference. Behind all force there must be a general will, and the general will must represent a communal mind. All other contrivances for government are external and tyrannical.

1. This is the reason of the unique relation between the state and the individual which is caricatured by critics as state absolutism. Of course the state

From Bernard Bosanquet, *Social and International Ideals*, London: Macmillan & Co., Ltd., 1917. Used by permission of the publisher.

is not the ultimate end of life. The ultimate end, if we avoid religious phraseology, which would probably furnish the truest expression of it, is surely the best life. I understand by the state the power which, as the organ of a community, has the function of maintaining the external conditions necessary to the best life. These conditions are called rights. They are the claims recognised by the will of a community as the *sine qua non* of the highest obtainable fulfilment of the capacities for the best life possessed by its members.

Now the relation between the state and the individual is the external equivalent of that between the community and the individual. And it is a unique relation, because there is no other body that bears the same relation to the individual's will as that community which is represented by a state in the external world.

This can be said with as much precision as human affairs admit, because there is reason to expect that the community which organises itself as a state will be for every group the largest body which possesses the unity of experience necessary for constituting a general will. There is, as we shall see, no other body at all comparable with it in intensity of unity. "A national purpose is the most unconquerable and victorious of all things on earth." And the individual's private will, we must bear in mind, is certainly and literally a part of the communal will. There is no other material of which his will can be made. If he rejects the communal will in part, he rejects it on the basis of what it is in him, not from any will of his own which has a different source. This is the ground of the duty of rebellion.

This unique relation between the individual and the community which the state represents—it may be a nation or any other community—is what seems to me to dominate the whole problem. It is further determined when we add the consideration that the state is an organ of action in the external world. In this sphere, which is its special sphere as an organ exercising force, it may really be called absolute, that is, if power extending to life and death and complete disposal of property can be called absolute. This does not mean that it is the whole end of life,[1] nor that it is the only object of loyalty. It means, as I understand it, that, being the special organ of arrangement in the external world, corresponding to that particular community whose will *is* our own will when most highly organised, it has the distinctive function of dictating the final adjustment in matters of external action. This is the only sense in which I have called it absolute, and the ground is obvious and simple. It lies in the tendency of the world of action to bring into collision factors which, apart from action, might never conflict. However purely non-political two associations may be, and however cosmopolitan, if they claim the same funds or the same building they must come before a power which can adjust the difference without appeal. And if such a power were not single in respect of them, obviously there could be no certainty of adjustment without a conflict between the two or more powers which might claim jurisdiction. Cases like that supposed are frequent, of course, with churches.

---

[1] Hegel in one place calls the state an end-in-itself, when he is contrasting his view of it with the reduction of its purpose to the protection of property or the right of the stronger. He regards it as having in it some of the end of life, viz. the embodiment of liberty; of course, not the whole end. It is for him the basis of the further more specialised achievements (art, philosophy, and the like).—*Rechtsphilosophie*, Sect. 258.

Thus there are two connected points, which, I think, the critics confuse under the name of absolutism. One is the power of the state as sustainer of all adjustments in the world of external action, on the ground which has just been explained. The other is the unique relation to the individual of such a community as is at present exemplified by his nation-state, because it represents, as nothing else in the world does, that special system of rights and sentiments, the complement of his own being, which the general will of his group has formed a state to maintain.

It is the result, I take it, of these two grounds of unity co-operating, that in times of stress the state, as the organ of community, will suspend or subject to conditions any form of intercourse between its members and persons or associations within or without its territory, and will require any service that it thinks fit from any of its members. It does, in Mr. Bradley's words, "with the moral approval of all what the explicit theory of scarcely one will morally justify."[2] That it does not exercise such powers to anything like the same degree in ordinary times, and that it recognises the rights of conscience even in times of stress, flows from the fact that its primary end is the maintenance of rights, and it will override no right by force where an adjustment is possible compatibly with the good life of the whole. And of this possibility it is the sole judge. What it permits, it permits by reason of its end, and no theory can stand which will not justify in principle its habitual action in time of stress.

2. "The state," as I understand the words, is a phrase framed in the normal way, to express that one is dealing with the members of a class strictly according to the connotation of the class-name. If a plural noun is used, there can be no certainty whether we are speaking of characteristics which belong to the class-members as such, or of circumstances which may occur in each of them for independent reasons. "The state," in a word, is a brief expression for "states *qua* states." I confess that I am a good deal surprised that nearly all recent critics have stumbled, as it seems to me, in this simple matter of interpretation. Would they find the same difficulty in the title of a book on "the heart" or "the steam-engine"? It would be urged, perhaps, that a heart does not imply other hearts, but that a state does imply other states; but if the thing implies other things its name implies the reference to them.

And, indeed, the whole *raison d'être* of our theory is to show why, and in what sense, there must be states wherever there are groups of human beings, and to explain for what reasons men are distinguished into separate adjacent political bodies instead of forming a single system over the whole earth's surface.

Our theory has told us, for example, that states represent differentiations of the single human spirit (Hegel), whose extent and intensity determine and are determined by territorial limits. They are members, we are told by Plato and Hegel, of an ethical family of nations, so far, at least, as the European world is concerned; they are characterised— it is Mazzini's well-known doctrine—by individual missions or functions which furnish for every state its distinctive contribution to human life. They have a similar task to achieve, each within its territory allotted by history, so Green argues, and the more perfectly each of them attains its proper object of giving

---

[2] *Ethical Studies,* p. 166. [F. H. Bradley (1846–1924), contemporary of Bosanquet and important British idealist. *Ed.*]

free scope to the capacities of all persons living on a certain range of territory, the easier it is for others to do so. Obviously they are co-operating units. This is throughout the essence of the theory.

Now it is not, I think, unfair to point out that my critics, dealing unguardedly with "states" and not with "the state" or with "states *qua* states," have on the whole founded their account of states not upon what they are, so far as states, but just upon what, *qua* states, they are not; upon defects which appear unequally in the several communities, consisting in those evils which the organisation of the state exists in order to remove, and does progressively remove in so far as true self-government is attained. Such evils are war, exploitation within or without, class privilege, arbitrary authority, discontent directing ambitions to foreign conquest and to jealousy of other states, the doctrine that one state's gain is *ipso facto* another's loss. . . .

5. Thus every state as such—that is, "the state"—is "the guardian of a whole moral world," maintaining the peculiar contribution of its community to the total of human life and of human mind. We shall see why this double expression is necessary. And it is very important to observe that this moral world includes a whole distinctive attitude to life and humanity. It is an attitude *of* the community, but *to* the world. Thus you cannot get away from it. All individuals share it, more or less, and every relation of the group, external or internal, is brought to a meeting point within their consciousness, and elicits a response from it. . . .

Now I think that the critics of our theory speak uncertainly here. Is our fault in saying that the community which asserts itself through the state *is* a moral being, and *has* a conscience, or is not a moral being and has not a conscience? They seem to me in effect to say both at once. But only one can be true.

It is clear, I think, that we are accused of denying the moral responsibility of the community which has the state for its organ. But it can hardly be doubted that we are also accused of putting this moral responsibility much too high. Thus the critics find themselves driven to treat the community which is a state as a mere association of individuals, which cannot possess an organic moral conscience nor general will. Though in one passage disclaiming individualism, the argument breathes its spirit. If you call the state an association, you speak the language of individualism, and still more so, if you speak of individual rights which can be asserted against it, and of the individual judgment as ultimate. To call it an "association" is contrary, I think, both to usage and to truth. The word is, I presume, employed intentionally as paradoxical and aggressive.

It is really, then, the moral being and moral responsibility of the state which we affirm, and which the main attack desires to undermine. The opposite suggestion, that we do not recognise the moral responsibility of the members of a group for its action, is, as we shall see, a mere misconception, derived from the fact that we observe the moral action of a community not to be capable of being criticised by the method of comparison with that of an individual.

The unique position of the state springs, as I said at starting, from the fact that it is moulded, as no mere association is, by and for the special task of maintaining in a certain territory the external conditions of good life as a whole. Its territorial area adjusts itself to that unity of communal experience which is most favourable to the maintenance of an organised will, so that it tends to cover the largest area within which, for a certain group, the conditions of such an experience exist.

It is an error, I think, resting on a confusion regarding the sphere of the state, to suggest that obedience to it can conflict with the existence of loyalty to associations—I refuse to say *other* associations—at home or abroad. The state's peculiar function is in the world of external action, and it does not inquire into the sentiments of men and women further than to establish the *bona fide* intention which the law includes in the meaning of an act. But whatever loyalties may exist in the mind, the state will undoubtedly, when need arises, of which it through constitutional methods is the sole judge, prohibit and prevent the expression, in external acts, of any loyalty but that to the community which it represents. Absoluteness in this sense is inherent in the state, for the reason which we have noted. . . .

8. However this may be, whatever may prove to be the extent of the effective unity which at any time may be realised among mankind, the condition of its realisation, if our theory is sound,

admits of no dispute. The body which is to be in sole or supreme command of force for the common good must possess a true general will, and for that reason must be a genuine community sharing a common sentiment and animated by a common tradition. With less than this the supreme authority must become an administration of general rules, external to the needs and consciences of the communities which it is meant to unite, and incapable therefore of appreciating the more serious problems which will confront them, or those needs of their lives which demand a certain social structure. This is why I view with apprehension the tendency to minimise the function of the state which is current to-day, owing, as I believe, to a too special explanation of causes which led to the present conflict. The first thing needed is the better adjustment and maintenance of rights within the communities which form states at the present moment. That is to say, the more complete discharge of their functions by existing states, and, if need be, the formation of new ones, adapted to similar tasks. More of the state, that is, and not less, is required within communities.

Law and Rights

Idealists attempt to present their philosophy of law through a series of inferences from the self-consciousness of a reasonable being. Self-conscious and possessing the capacities of will and reason, man is also a moral being. His moral ideals remain abstract, however, until he lives in a society whose institutions embody the conditions for their realization. It is civil life that "gives reality" to man's personal capacities and makes their concrete exercise possible. Thus, idealists are led to argue that only the teleological view of man and society can provide an adequate theory of law and rights.

While law has its ground in man's moral capacities, ethics and law must be sharply distinguished. Legality relates to external human acts that can conform to some standard set by law; ethics concerns internal acts of will and motives. In fact, not even all external acts are within the province of legal obligations, but only those that must be regulated in order that the moral end of self-realization may be made possible to citizens. Thus, law is the rules issued and sanctioned by civil authority to order those actions of men related to the maintenance of the possibility of moral development.

As has been seen, however, idealists argue that the true political community does not consist in power alone: it is the process by which men are clothed with rights and duties and come to be conscious of their obligations. Once again, it is consciousness that makes possible the recognition of rights, which are of the same metal as law—in fact, the other side of the same coin. A right, as T. H. Green (1836–1882) develops his idealistic theory in the selection below, has two elements: a claim to freedom of action in order to realize one's inner powers and capacities; and the general social recognition that the claim is warranted, that the individual's freedom contributes to the general good. Thus idealists argue that there must be rights because moral personality ought to be developed, and the possession of rights, ascribed and guaranteed to individuals by law and the state, is the condition of that development. The second element in Green's view means that one has rights only in a society where some common good is recognized by the members of society as their own ideal good.* To summarize, then: the existence of rights ascribed to members of a community depends on moral personality, on the recognition by each of the moral personality of others, and on the consciousness by all of common interests and objects.

Such a view of rights involves a rejection of traditional theories of natural rights. As Green puts it, a law is good because it contributes to the realization of certain ends, not because it conforms to antecedent natural rights. Not natural law, but the "naturalness of law" is Green's view: if rights are still termed natural, it is "not in the sense that they actually exist when a man is born and that they have existed as long as the human race, but that they arise out of, and are necessary for the fulfillment of, a moral capacity without which a man would not be a man." The so-called law of nature, understood as an ethical law, must be based on consciousness. Only when men are conscious of it are they bound by it. But then, Green argues, it ceases to be a law of nature. In a similar way, Green rejects the notion of consent developed by liberals: the moral end, not consent, is the ground of law, rights, and the state itself.

---

* Strictly speaking, this interdependence of claim and recognition is an ethical rather than a juristic conception.

T. H. GREEN   Law and Self-realization

6. The condition of a moral life is the possession of will and reason. Will is the capacity in a man of being determined to action by the idea of a possible satisfaction of himself. An act of will is an action so determined. A state

---

From T. H. Green, *Lectures on the Principles of Political Obligation*, in *Works of Thomas Hill Green*, 3 vols., New York: Longmans, Green, and Co., 1886.

of will is the capacity as determined by the particular objects in which the man seeks self-satisfaction; and it becomes a character in so far as the self-satisfaction is habitually sought in objects of a particular kind. Practical reason is the capacity in a man of conceiving the perfection of his nature as an object to be attained by action. All moral ideas have their origin in reason, i.e. in the idea of a possible self-perfection to be attained by the moral agent. This does not mean that the moral agent in every stage of his progress could state this idea to himself in an abstract form, any more than in every stage in the acquisition of knowledge about nature a man can state to himself in an abstract form the conception of the unity of nature, which yet throughout conditions the acquisition of his knowledge. Ideas do not first come into existence, or begin to operate, upon the formation of an abstract expression for them. This expression is only arrived at upon analysis of a concrete experience, which they have rendered possible. Thus we only learn to express the idea of self-perfection in that abstract form upon an analysis of an experience of self-improvement which we have ourselves gone through, and which must have been gone through by those with whom we are connected by the possession of language and an organisation of life, however elementary: but the same analysis shows that the same idea must have been at work to make such experience possible. In this idea all particular moral ideas— all ideas of particular forms of conduct as estimable—originate, though an abstract expression for the latter is arrived at much sooner than such an expression for the idea in which they originate. They arise, as the individual's conception of the society on the well-being of which his own depends, and of the con-

stituents of that well-being, becomes wider and fuller; and they are embodied in the laws, institutions, and social expectation, which make conventional morality. This embodiment, again, constitutes the moral progress of mankind. This progress, however, is only a *moral* progress in so far as it tends to bring about the harmony of will and reason, in the only form in which it can really exist, viz. in the characters of persons. And this result is actually achieved, in so far as upon habits disciplined by conformity to conventional morality there supervenes an intelligent interest in some of the objects contributory to human perfection, which that conventional morality subserves, and in so far as that interest becomes the dominant interest of the character.

7. The value then of the institutions of civil life lies in their operation as giving reality to these capacities of will and reason, and enabling them to be really exercised. In their general effect, apart from particular aberrations, they render it possible for a man to be freely determined by the idea of a possible satisfaction of himself, instead of being driven this way and that by external forces, and thus they give reality to the capacity called will: and they enable him to realise his reason, i.e. his idea of self-perfection, by acting as a member of a social organisation in which each contributes to the better-being of all the rest. So far as they do in fact thus operate they are morally justified, and may be said to correspond to the "law of nature," the *jus naturæ,* according to the only sense in which that phrase can be intelligibly used.

14. . . . legal obligations—obligations which can possibly form the subject of positive law—can only be obligations to do or abstain from certain acts, not duties of acting from certain motives, or

with a certain disposition. It is not a question whether the law should or should not oblige to anything but performance of outward acts. It simply cannot oblige to anything else, because the only means at its command for obtaining the fulfilment of obligations are (1) threats of pain and offers of reward, by means of which it is possible indeed to secure the general performance of certain acts, but not their performance from the motive even of fear of the pain threatened or hope of the reward offered, much less from any higher motive; (2) the employment of physical force, (*a*) in restraining men disposed to violate obligations, (*b*) in forcibly applying the labour or the property of those who violate obligations to make good the breach, so far as is possible: (as, e.g., when the magistrate forestalls part of a man's wages to provide for a wife whom he has deserted, or when the property of a debtor is seized for the benefit of his creditors.)

15. Only outward acts, then, *can* be matter of legal obligation; but what sort of outward acts *should* be matter of legal obligation? The answer to this question arises out of the above consideration of the means which law employs to obtain the fulfilment of obligations, combined with the view of law as relative to a moral end, i.e. the formation of a society of persons, acting from a certain disposition, from interest in the society as such. Those acts only should be matter of legal injunction or prohibition of which the performance or omission, irrespectively of the motive from which it proceeds, is so necessary to the existence of a society in which the moral end stated can be realised, that it is better for them to be done or omitted from that unworthy motive which consists in fear or hope of legal consequences than not to be done at all.

20. A true theory of "jus naturæ," a rationale of law or ideal of what it should be, is not to be had by inquiring how far actual law corresponds to, and is derived from, the exercise of certain original or natural rights, if that is taken to mean that we know, or can ascertain, what rights are natural on grounds distinct from those on which we determine what laws are justifiable, and that then we can proceed to ascertain what laws are justifiable by deduction from such rights. "Natural rights," so far as there are such things, are themselves relative to the moral end to which perfect law is relative. A law is not good because it enforces "natural rights," but because it contributes to the realisation of a certain end. We only discover what rights are natural by considering what powers must be secured to a man in order to the attainment of this end. These powers a perfect law will secure to their full extent. Thus the consideration of what rights are "natural" (in the only legitimate sense) and the consideration what laws are justifiable form one and the same process, each presupposing a conception of the moral vocation of man.

21. The doctrine here asserted, that all rights are relative to moral ends or duties, must not be confused with the ordinary statement that every right implies a duty, or that rights and duties are correlative. This of course is true in the sense that possession of a right by any person both implies an obligation on the part of someone else, and is conditional upon the recognition of certain obligations on the part of the person possessing it. But what is meant is something different, viz. that the claim or right of the individual to have certain powers secured to him by society, and the counter-claim of society to exercise certain powers over the individual, alike rest on the fact that these powers are

necessary to the fulfilment of man's vocation as a moral being, to an effectual self-devotion to the work of developing the perfect character in himself and others.

24. Thus, though it may be possible and useful to show how the more seemingly artificial rights are derived from rights more simple and elementary, how the rights established by law in a political society are derived from rights that may be called natural, not in the sense of being prior to society, but in the sense of being prior to the existence of a society governed by written law or a recognised sovereign, still such derivation is no justification of them. It is no answer to the question why they should be respected; because this question remains to be asked in regard to the most primitive rights themselves. Political or civil rights, then, are not to be explained by derivation from natural rights, but in regard to both political and natural rights, in any sense in which there can be truly said to be natural rights, the question has to be asked, how it is that certain powers are recognised by men in their intercourse with each other as powers that should be exercised, or of which the possible exercise should be secured.

25. I have tried to show in lectures on morals that the conception expressed by the "should be" is not identical with the conception of a right possessed by some man or men, but one from which the latter conception is derived. It is, or implies on the part of whoever is capable of it, the conception of an ideal, unattained condition of himself, as an absolute end. Without this conception the recognition of a power as a right would be impossible. A power on the part of anyone is so recognised by others, as one which should be exercised, when these others regard it as in

some way a means to that ideal good of themselves which they alike conceive: and the possessor of the power comes to regard it as a right through consciousness of its being thus recognised as contributory to a good in which he too is interested. No one therefore can have a right except (1) as a member of a society, and (2) of a society in which some common good is recognised by the members of the society as their own ideal good, as that which should be for each of them. The capacity for being determined by a good so recognised is what constitutes personality in the ethical sense; and for this reason there is truth in saying that only among persons, in the ethical sense, can there come to be rights; (which is quite compatible with the fact that the logical disentanglement of the conception of rights precedes that of the conception of the legal person; and that the conception of the moral person, in its abstract and logical form, is not arrived at till after that of the legal person).

Conversely, everyone capable of being determined by the conception of a common good as his own ideal good, as that which unconditionally should be (of being in that sense an end to himself), in other words, every moral person, is capable of rights; i.e. of bearing his part in a society in which the free exercise of his powers is secured to each member through the recognition by each of the others as entitled to the same freedom with himself. To say that he is capable of rights, is to say that he ought to have them, in that sense of "ought" in which it expresses the relation of man to an end conceived as absolutely good, to an end which, whether desired or no, is conceived as intrinsically desirable. The moral capacity implies a consciousness on the part of the subject of the capacity that its realisation is an end desirable in itself, and rights are the condition of realising it. Only through the possession of rights can the power of the individual freely to make a common good his own have reality given to it. Rights are what may be called the negative realisation to this power. That is, they realise it in the sense of providing for its free exercise, of securing the treatment of one man by another as equally free with himself, but they do not realise it positively, because their possession does not imply that in any active way the individual makes a common good his own. The possession of them, however, is the condition of this positive realisation of the moral capacity, and they ought to be possessed because this end (in the sense explained) ought to be attained.

26. Hence on the part of every person ("person" in the moral sense explained) the claim, more or less articulate and reflected on, to rights on his own part is co-ordinate with his recognition of rights on the part of others. The capacity to conceive a common good as one's own, and to regulate the exercise of one's powers by reference to a good which others recognise, carries with it the consciousness that powers should be so exercised; which means that there should be rights, that powers should be regulated by mutual recognition. There ought to be rights, because the moral personality,—the capacity on the part of an individual for making a common good his own,—ought to be developed; and it is developed through rights; i.e. through the recognition by members of a society of powers in each other contributory to a common good, and the regulation of those powers by that recognition.

27. In saying that only among "persons" can there come to be rights, and that every "person" should have rights,

I have been careful to explain that I use "person" in the moral, not merely in the legal, sense. In dealing, then, with such phrases as "jura personarum" and "personal rights," we must keep in view the difference between the legal and ethical sense of the proposition that all rights are personal, or subsist as between persons. In the legal sense, so far as it is true,—and it is so only if "person" is used in the sense of Roman law,—it is an identical proposition. A person means a subject of rights and nothing more. Legal personality is derived from the possession of right, not *vice versa*. Like other identical propositions, its use is to bring out and emphasise in the predicate what is included in the understood connotation of the subject; to remind us that when we speak of rights we imply the existence of parties, in English phraseology, capable of suing and being sued. In the ethical sense, it means that rights are derived from the possession of personality as = a rational will (i.e. the capacity which man possesses of being determined to action by the conception of such a perfection of his being as involves the perfection of a society in which he lives), in the sense (*a*) that only among beings possessed of rational will can there come to be rights, (*b*) that they fulfil their idea, or are justifiable, or such rights as should be rights, only as contributing to the realisation of a rational will. It is important to bear this distinction in mind in order that the proposition in its ethical sense, which can stand on its own merits, may not derive apparent confirmation from a juristic truism.

28. The moral idea of personality is constantly tending to affect the legal conception of the relation between rights and persons. Thus the "jura personarum," which properly = either

rights arising out of "status," or rights which not only (like all rights) reside in someone having a legal status and are available against others having a legal status, but are exercised over, or in respect of, someone possessed of such status (e.g. a wife or a servant), come to be understood as rights derived from the human personality or belonging to man as man. It is with some such meaning that English writers on law speak of rights to life and liberty as personal rights. The expression might seem pleonastic, since no right can exist except as belonging to a person in the legal sense. They do not use the phrase either pleonastically or in the sense of the Roman lawyers' "jura personarum" above, but in the sense that these rights are immediately derived from, or necessarily attach to, the human personality in whatever that personality is supposed to consist. There is no doubt, however, that historically the conception of the moral person, in any abstract form, is not arrived at till after that of the legal person has been thus disentangled and formulated; and further that the abstract conception of the legal person, as the sustainer of rights, is not arrived at till long after rights have been actually recognised and established. But the disentanglement or abstract formulation of the conception of moral personality is quite a different thing from the action of the consciousness in which personality consists.

29. The capacity, then, on the part of the individual of conceiving a good as the same for himself and others, and of being determined to action by that conception, is the foundation of rights; and rights are the condition of that capacity being realised. No right is justifiable or should be a right except on the ground that directly or indirectly it serves this purpose. Conversely every power should be a right, i.e. society should secure to the individual every power, that is necessary for realising this capacity. Claims to such powers as are directly necessary to a man's acting as a moral person at all—acting under the conception of a good as the same for self and others— may be called in a special sense personal rights (though they will include more than Stephen includes under that designation); they may also be called, if we avoid misconceptions connected with these terms, "innate" or "natural" rights. They are thus distinguished from others which are (1) only indirectly necessary to the end stated, or (2) are so only under special conditions of society; as well as from claims which rest merely on legal enactment and might cease to be enforced without any violation of the "jus naturæ."

30. The objection to calling them "innate" or "natural," when once it is admitted on the one side that rights are not arbitrary creations of law or custom but that there are certain powers which ought to be secured as rights, on the other hand that there are no rights antecedent to society, none that men brought with them into a society which they contracted to form, is mainly one of words. They are "innate" or "natural" in the same sense in which according to Aristotle the state is natural; not in the sense that they actually exist when a man is born and that they have actually existed as long as the human race, but that they arise out of, and are necessary for the fulfilment of, a moral capacity without which a man would not be a man. There cannot be innate rights in any other sense than that in which there are innate duties, of which, however, much less has been heard. Because a group of beings are capable each of conceiving an absolute good of himself and of conceiving it to be good for himself as identical with, and because

identical with, the good of the rest of the group, there arises for each a consciousness that the common good should be the object of action, i.e. a duty, and a claim in each to a power of action that shall be at once secured and regulated by the consciousness of a common good on the part of the rest, i.e. a right. There is no ground for saying that the right arises out of a primary human capacity, and is thus "innate," which does not apply equally to the duty.

31. The dissociation of innate rights from innate duties has gone along with the delusion that such rights existed apart from society. Men were supposed to have existed in a state of nature, which was not a state of society, but in which certain rights attached to them as individuals, and then to have formed societies by contract or covenant. Society having been formed, certain other rights arose through positive enactment; but none of these, it was held, could interfere with the natural rights which belonged to men antecedently to the social contract or survived it.

Such a theory can only be stated by an application to an imaginary state of things, prior to the formation of societies as regulated by custom or law, of terms that have no meaning except in relation to such societies. "Natural right," as = right in a state of nature which is not a state of society, is a contradiction. There can be no right without a consciousness of common interest on the part of members of a society. Without this there might be certain powers on the part of individuals, but no recognition of these powers by others as powers of which they allow the exercise, nor any claim to such recognition; and without this recognition or claim to recognition there can be no right.

138. It is equally impossible, then, to hold that the right of the sovereign power in a state over its members is dependent on their consent, and, on the other hand, that these members have no rights except such as are constituted and conferred upon them by the sovereign. The sovereign, and the state itself as distinguished by the existence of a sovereign power, presupposes rights and is an institution for their maintenance. But these rights do not belong to individuals as they might be in a state of nature, or as they might be if each acted irrespectively of the others. They belong to them as members of a society in which each recognises the other as an originator of action in the same sense in which he is conscious of being so himself (as an "ego," as himself the object which determines the action), and thus regards the free exercise of his own powers as dependent upon his allowing an equally free exercise of his powers to every other member of the society. There is no harm in saying that they belong to individuals as such, if we understand what we mean by "individual," and if we mean by it a self-determining subject, conscious of itself as one among other such subjects, and of its relation to them as making it what it is; for then there is no opposition between the attachment of rights to the individuals as such and their derivation from society. They attach to the individual, but only as a member of a society of free agents, as recognising himself and recognised by others to be such a member, as doing and done by accordingly. A right, then, to act unsocially,—to act otherwise than as belonging to a society of which each member keeps the exercise of his powers within the limits necessary to the like exercise by all the other members, —is a contradiction. No one can say that, unless he has consented to such a limitation of his powers, he has a right to resist it. The fact of his not

consenting would be an extinction of all right on his part.

139. The state then presupposes rights, and rights of individuals. It is a form which society takes in order to maintain them. But rights have no being except in a society of men recognising each other as ἴσοι καὶ ὅμοιοι. They are constituted by that mutual recognition. In analysing the nature of any right, we may conveniently look at it on two sides, and consider it as on the one hand a claim of the individual, arising out of his rational nature, to the free exercise of some faculty; on the other, as a concession of that claim by society, a power given by it to the individual of putting the claim in force. But we must be on our guard against supposing that these distinguishable sides have any really separate existence. It is only a man's consciousness of having an object in common with others, a well-being which is consciously his in being theirs and theirs in being his,—only the fact that they are recognised by him and he by them as having this object,—that gives him the claim described. There can be no reciprocal claim on the part of a man and an animal each to exercise his powers unimpeded by the other, because there is no consciousness common to them. But a claim founded on such a common consciousness is already a claim conceded; already a claim to which reality is given by social recognition, and thus implicitly a right.

140. It is in this sense that a slave has "natural rights." They are "natural" in the sense of being independent of, and in conflict with, the laws of the state in which he lives, but they are not independent of social relations. They arise out of the fact that there is a consciousness of objects common to the slave with those among whom he lives,—whether other slaves or the family of his owner,

—and that this consciousness constitutes at once a claim on the part of each of those who share it to exercise a free activity conditionally upon his allowing a like activity in the others, and a recognition of this claim by the others through which it is realised. The slave thus derives from his social relations a real right which the law of the state refuses to admit. The law cannot prevent him from acting and being treated, within certain limits, as a member of a society of persons freely seeking a common good. Now that capability of living in a certain limited community with a certain limited number of human beings, which the slave cannot be prevented from exhibiting, is in principle a capability of living in community with any other human beings, supposing the necessary training to be allowed; and as every such capability constitutes a right, we are entitled to say that the slave has a right to citizenship, to a recognised equality of freedom with any and every one with whom he has to do, and that in refusing him not only citizenship but the means of training his capability of citizenship, the state is violating a right founded on that common human consciousness which is evinced both by the language which the slave speaks, and by actual social relations subsisting between him and others. And on the same principle upon which a state is violating natural rights in maintaining slavery, it does the same in using force, except under the necessity of self-defence, against members of another community. Membership of any community is so far, in principle, membership of all communities as to constitute a right to be treated as a freeman by all other men, to be exempt from subjection to force except for prevention of force.

141. A man may thus have rights as

a member of a family or of human society in any other form, without being a member of a state at all,—rights which remain rights though any particular state or all states refuse to recognise them; and a member of a state, on the ground of that capability of living as a freeman among freemen which is implied in his being a member of a state, has rights as against all other states and their members. These latter rights are in fact during peace recognised by all civilised states. It is the object of "private international law" to reduce them to a system. But though it follows from this that the state does not create rights, it may be still true to say that the members of a state derive their rights from the state and have no rights against it. We have already seen that a right against society, as such, is an impossibility; that every right is derived from some social relation; that a right against any group of associated men depends on association, as ἴσος καὶ ὅμοιος, with them and with some other men. Now for the member of a state to say that his rights are derived from his social relations, and to say that they are derived from his position as member of a state, are the same thing. The state is for him the complex of those social relations out of which rights arise, so far as those rights have come to be regulated and harmonised according to a general law, which is recognised by a certain multitude of persons, and which there is sufficient power to secure against violation from without and from within. The other forms of community which precede and are independent of the formation of the state, do not continue to exist outside it, nor yet are they superseded by it. They are carried on into it. They become its organic members, supporting its life and in turn maintained by it in a new harmony with each other. Thus the citizen's rights, e.g. as a husband or head of a family or a holder of property, though such rights, arising out of other social relations than that of citizen to citizen, existed when as yet there was no state, are yet to the citizen derived from the state, from that more highly developed form of society in which the association of the family and that of possessors who respect each other's possessions are included as in a fuller whole; which secures to the citizen his family rights and his rights as a holder of property, but under conditions and limitations which the membership of the fuller whole—the reconciliation of rights arising out of one sort of social capability with those arising out of another—renders necessary. Nor can the citizen have any right against the state, in the sense of a right to act otherwise than as a member of some society, the state being for its members the society of societies, the society in which all their claims upon each other are mutually adjusted.

142. But what exactly is meant by the citizen's acting "as a member of his state"? What does the assertion that he can have no right to act otherwise than as a member of his state amount to? Does it mean that he has no right to disobey the law of the state to which he belongs, whatever that law may be? that he is not entitled to exercise his powers in any way that the law forbids and to refuse to exercise them in any way that it commands? This question was virtually dealt with before in considering the justifiability of resistance to an ostensible sovereign. The only unqualified answer that can be given to it is one that may seem too general to be of much practical use, viz. that so far as the laws anywhere or at any time in force fulfil the idea of a state, there can be no right to disobey them; or, that

there can be no right to disobey the law of the state except in the interest of the state; i.e. for the purpose of making the state in respect of its actual laws more completely correspond to what it is in tendency or idea, viz. the reconciler and sustainer of the rights that arise out of the social relations of men. On this principle there can be no right to disobey or evade any particular law on the ground that it interferes with any freedom of action, any right of managing his children or "doing what he will with his own," which but for that law the individual would possess. Any power which has been allowed to the individual up to a certain time, he is apt to regard as permanently his right. It has, indeed, been so far his right, if the exercise of that power has been allowed with any reference to social good, but it does not, as he is apt to think, remain his right when a law has been enacted that interferes with it. A man e.g. has been allowed to drive at any pace he likes through the streets, to build houses without any reference to sanitary conditions, to keep his children at home or send them to work "analphabetic," to buy or sell alcoholic drinks at his pleasure. If laws are passed interfering with any or all of these powers, he says that his rights are being violated. But he only possessed these powers as rights through membership of a society which secured them to him, and of which the only permanent bond consists in the reference to the well-being of its members as a whole. It has been the social recognition grounded on that reference that has rendered certain of his powers rights. If upon new conditions arising, or upon elements of social good being taken account of which had been overlooked before, or upon persons being taken into the reckoning as capable of participation in the social well-being

who had previously been treated merely as means to its attainment,—if in any of these ways or otherwise the reference to social well-being suggest the necessity of some further regulation of the individual's liberty to do as he pleases, he can plead no right against this regulation, for every right that he has possessed has been dependent on that social judgment of its compatibility with general well-being which in respect to the liberties in question is now reversed.

143. "Is then," it may be asked, "the general judgment as to the requirements of social well-being so absolutely authoritative that no individual right can exist against it? What if according to this judgment the institution of slavery is so necessary that citizens are prohibited by law from teaching slaves to read and from harbouring runaways? or if according to it the maintenance of a certain form of worship is so necessary that no other worship can be allowed and no opinion expressed antagonistic to it? Has the individual no rights against enactments founded on such accepted views of social well-being?" We may answer: A right against society as such, a right to act without reference to the needs or good of society, is an impossibility, since every right depends on some social relation, and a right against any group of associated men depends upon association on some footing of equality with them or with some other men. We saw how the right of the slave really rested on this basis, on a social capacity shown in the footing on which he actually lives with other men. On this principle it would follow, if we regard the state as the sustainer and harmoniser of social relations, that the individual can have no right against the state; that its law must be to him of absolute authority. But in fact, as actual

states at best fulfil but partially their ideal function, we cannot apply this rule to practice. The general principle that the citizen must never act otherwise than as a citizen, does not carry with it an obligation under all conditions to conform to the law of his state, since those laws may be inconsistent with the true end of the state as the sustainer and harmoniser of social relations. The assertion, however, by the citizen of any right which the state does not recognise must be founded on a reference to an acknowledged social good. The fact that the individual would like to exercise the power claimed as a right does not render the exercise of it a right, nor does the fact that he has been hitherto allowed to exercise it render it a right, if social requirements have arisen under changed conditions, or have newly come to be recognised, with which its exercise is incompatible. The reason that the assertion of an illegal right must be founded on reference to acknowledged social good is that, as we have seen, no exercise of a power, however abstractedly desirable for the promotion of human good it might be, can be claimed as a right unless there is some common consciousness of utility shared by the person making the claim and those on whom it is made. It is not a question whether or no it ought to be claimed as a right; it simply cannot be claimed except on this condition. It would have been impossible, e.g., in an ancient state, where the symbol of social union was some local worship, for a monotheistic reformer to claim a right to attempt the subversion of that worship. If a duty to do so had suggested itself, consciousness of the duty could never have expressed itself in the form of a claim of right, in the absence of any possible sense of a public interest in the religious revolution to which the claim could be addressed. Thus, just as it is not the exercise of every power, properly claimable as a right, that is a right in the full or explicit sense of being legally established, so it is not every power, of which the exercise would be desirable in an ideal state of things, that is properly claimable as a right. The condition of its being so claimable is that its exercise should be contributory to some social good which the public conscience is capable of appreciating, not necessarily one which in the existing prevalence of private interests can obtain due acknowledgment, but still one of which men in their actions and language show themselves to be aware.

Political Obligation

According to some authorities, for example Professor A. P. D'Entrèves, the idealist T. H. Green was the first philosopher to use the phrase, "political obligation." While this does not at all mean that the problem of political obligation was absent from previous theories, it does suggest that idealists have isolated this problem and given it special attention. Green's own theory of obligation—followed by many idealists—always referred to man's purpose or goal present in his consciousness as the form of his ideal self. Man's capacity to grasp a common idea of a permanent good, a common or rational good, is presupposed in all groupings of men; it is in relation to this good that the problem of political obligation is to be solved.

Briefly put, the idealist theory is this: men have a common moral end that is the object of their permanent interest and rational will. The state is a device to help men realize this object; its authority—and men's obligation to it—therefore rests on the state's being necessary to that end. What this means is that men's rights, which have been seen to be the conditions of self-realization guaranteed by the state, do not depend on conventions or contracts, nor simply on a sovereign power, nor again on men's individual interests or immediate desires; they derive from that good which is common to all men and which defines their fulfillment and realization. As the instrument and protector of the common good, the state has rights against or over its citizens: it can compel them in their external actions to maintain the order dictated by the common good. Yet citizens are obliged to obey the state because it is the agent of their rational will or common good. It is this doctrine that Professor Brand Blanshard (1892–   ) develops in the next selection. He discusses it through four propositions: (1) there is a distinction between the immediate and the rational will, (2) the rational will is the same for all men, (3) men's common end is the basis of their rights, and (4) the justification of the state lies in furthering this end.

But does the state have obligations to its citizens? Or, what amounts to the same thing, can a citizen ever disobey his government? In general, idealists answer these questions affirmatively. Insofar as a state fulfills the idea of a state, there is no right to disobey it. But the state is an instrument, a means; it is obliged to maintain the common good. Should a state become so corrupt that it cuts men off from their proper ends, it not only may, sometimes it must be disobeyed. And yet the idealist would point out that the appeal to disobedience involves the same end as obedience, namely the common good. The general principle that one should always act as a citizen does not mean that one must always conform to the laws of his state. It does mean, however, that all assertions against the state must be founded on an acknowledged common and social good.

BRAND BLANSHARD   The Rational Will

13. . . . The rights to life and liberty do not depend on conventions because they exist before conventions and independently of them. They do not depend on the rational nature of their subjects (though duties do), for that nature may exist without them, and they without it. What is it, then, that *is* always present when rights are present, absent when they are absent, and variable as they vary? The answer is implicit in our criticism of all the previous positions. There is one circumstance that can over-ride any contrary claim, namely the general good. A man forfeits his right to life itself if he becomes sufficiently dangerous to the community; he forfeits his right to freedom if the exercise of that freedom would

From Brand Blanshard, *Reason and Goodness*, London: George Allen & Unwin Ltd., 1961. Used by permission of the publisher.

jeopardize the community. Now the suggestion is irresistible that if that which alone can modify or suspend a right is its relation to the general good, this must be what validates it also. If a man claims the right to do something that is clearly harmful to the community, we point to this consequence as full justification for refusing it to him. On the other hand, if he can show that what he is doing is of net value to those affected by it, we consider that he has made out his case and that to prevent his doing it would be an unjust restriction. Thus the variable element on which the justification of a right depends is prospective contributoriness to general good. The force of this conclusion is greatly strengthened when we note the connection of rights with duties. A right is the obverse side of a duty, a duty looked at from the other end. To say that I have a right to walk the streets unmolested is to say that it is your duty not to molest me. Now we have seen, at the cost of some effort, that the reason why an act is a duty is precisely that it promises the greatest good. If this is true of duties, and rights *are* duties, it must be true of rights as well.

14. In the end, then, every political right must be defended on moral grounds. But we cannot leave the matter there. For moral and political rights are not simply identical; there are many moral rights that no one would call political, for example, the right to be spoken to courteously and the right of parents to the consideration of their children. Political rights are rights that are, or appropriately may be, guaranteed by government, that is, by enforced law. Now it is clear that there are "rights" thus enforced by law for which many who must heed them can find no moral justification at all. But now for

the real difficulty. The state claims the right, for example, and enforces it by heavy penalties, to reach down into the pockets of its citizens and take a large part of their income for its own purposes. Many of these citizens are convinced not only that the particular purposes for which the state will use this money are bad, but also that an income tax as such is a policy opposed to the general good. To tell these people that what they regard as a wicked tax imposed for wicked purposes is a moral right, on all fours with the right to truthful speech and civil treatment, is not unlikely to provoke jeers. Clearly there is a missing link in the argument. These people are told that it is a moral obligation to do what produces the greatest good. They believe that a law passed by their government is inimical to the public good, and are told that they should obey it nevertheless. That may be a political obligation, but to call it a moral obligation looks very much like self-contradiction. How is one to make out that it is their moral duty to obey a law that they disapprove? This is probably the most searching question in political theory.

15. I believe that the true answer to this question has been given by philosophers over and over again, and that it is not the exclusive property of any school. But it has had a history so unfortunate as to rob it of much of its persuasiveness. It was suggested by Rousseau, but, as presented by him, was so embedded in mythology and bad argument that one can extract it only with difficulty from his incoherent text. It was stated again by Hegel, but was made an integral part of a system of logic and metaphysics which most philosophers have found it impossible to accept; besides, it came to be associated, partly by his own fault and partly not, with Prussian

nationalism, which after precipitating two wars, earned general detestation. The doctrine was taken over from Hegel by the British idealists and given a more judicious statement by T. H. Green, whose *Principles of Political Obligation* remains, I think, the weightiest work in English on political theory. It was presented again by Bosanquet in *The Philosophical Theory of the State,* but with needless obscurity and with certain expressions that sounded suspiciously like endorsements of absolutism and nationalism. These were seized upon by L. T. Hobhouse in his *Metaphysical Theory of the State* and made the focal points of the most thorough-going attack that has been made on the theory.

Rousseau called his version a theory of the "general will"; Hegel and Bosanquet talked, instead, of the "real will"; if the version about to be presented is to have a name, I should prefer the "rational will." It may be of interest to say that my own conviction of the truth of the theory came through reading Hobhouse's attack on it. It had been so long out of favour and was mentioned with such general deprecation that, having made no careful study of it, I had come to think of it as pretty certainly indefensible. Its association with the name of Hegel, and the many attempts to link Hegelianism with Fascism did not help, though I follow Principal Knox in holding that the occasional outbursts of Prussianism in Hegel are excrescences on his system, and not organic to it. When I approached the doctrine of the real will, I began by reading the critics of the theory, expecting at least to find some amusement in watching the work of demolition, and thinking I should be more likely to find intelligibility among the critics than among the exponents. The first two or three broadsides I reviewed left me in mild surprise, for the target was still visibly standing when the roar had subsided and the smoke cleared away. But these were guns of low calibre. So I turned to Hobhouse, who had, I understood, destroyed the theory utterly; and as I warmly admire his work, I sat down to him expectantly. But as the arguments in the heralded parade limped slowly past, a conviction gradually formed itself in my mind. If this was really the best that could be said against the theory of the real will, I had been deceived about it. Wave after wave of argument broke against it only to leave it, so far as I could see, standing aggressively intact. By the time I was half way through the book, I had begun to think the case *for* it impregnable; at the end, my conversion was complete. I thought then, and have never wavered in thinking since, that this doctrine, if one penetrates through the sorry form in which it has so often been expressed, and gets rid of associations that cling to it like barnacles, offers the firmest available core for political theory.

16. The doctrine is quite simple. It is that men have a common moral end which is the object of their rational will, that the state is a contrivance that they have worked out to help them realize that end, and that its authority over them rests on its being necessary for that end. If it is politically obligatory at times to obey a law that one regards as bad, that is because the state could not be run at all if the citizens could pick and choose which laws they would obey. Ultimately, therefore, political obligation, even that of obeying a morally bad law, *is* a moral obligation; and when, as occasionally happens, it becomes a duty to disobey, the ground is still the same. I believe that this simple doctrine is what all the philosophers who have defended a "real" or

"general" will, from Rousseau to Bosanquet and even Hobhouse himself, have in fact been arguing for. I shall not try to prove this by historical inquiry, for my prime concern is not whether the doctrine I seem to find in them is actually theirs, but whether it is true. The doctrine that does seem to me true may be expanded and made more explicit in four propositions. First, we can distinguish within our own minds between the end of our actual or immediate will, and the end of our rational will, which is what on reflection would commend itself as the greatest good. Secondly, this rational end is the same for all men. Thirdly, this end, because a common end, is the basis of our rights against each other. Fourthly, the justification of the state, and its true office, lie in furthering the realization of this end. Let us try to get these points clear.

17. (1) It is puzzling at first to hear of a real or rational will which can be set over against our actual will. Is not our actual will our only will, and whatever goes beyond this, myth? On the contrary, it is easy to see that what we have here is a distinction of the first importance.

A man goes to a dealer and buys a motor-car. There is no dispute about his actual will; it is simply to possess the car; that is what he immediately and unmistakably wants. Is there any sense in saying that he has a further and rational will that goes beyond this and might even veto it? Yes, undoubtedly; in fact, unless we concede such a will we shall never understand what really moves him. If possessing the car were an ultimate end, the question "Why buy it?" would be meaningless. But the buyer would be the first to insist that it was anything but meaningless, and if he were like other eager buyers he would readily explain that the car was a means

to all sorts of advantages, personal, professional, and social, and these, perhaps, means to still further advantages to a widening circle of beneficiaries. In short, he wills to buy the car, but he wills it subject to tacit conditions as to how it will contribute to an end beyond itself. The evidence that these conditions exist lies in what would dissuade him from the purchase. Convince him that through buying the car he will not advance his business, that his son and daughter being what they are, it will probably involve them in accidents, and that if he carries the purchase through, he cannot move into the larger house that is the family's most pressing need, and he will not improbably cut the whole business short. If his actual will were self-contained, if it were the end of the line rather than a link in a chain whose point of attachment lies far beyond it, all this would be irrelevant. It is only because his explicit will is *not* exhaustive, because its object is a means to a further end, or a piece in a larger picture which is more fervently wanted than itself, that his immediate will can admit such correction. He may hardly have known that he wanted these ulterior things; at the moment of buying he was probably not thinking of them; but if, the instant he sees how his will of the moment bears on them, he sets that will aside, is it not natural to say that in contrast to the objects of his actual will, they are the objects of his real or rational will?

This line of reasoning, we may be told, leads to an unplausible consequence. For if his present will is thus open to correction by ulterior considerations of advantage to himself and his family, these considerations themselves will in turn be open to correction by still further considerations, for example, his duty to his profession, his community, and his country. "What you are saying, then, is that the object of a man's real or rational will is that which an ideally competent reflection would show to be the greatest good attainable in the circumstances. No doubt with ideal powers this is what he ought to will. But you are saying that he does in fact will what he ideally ought to will, and that is absurd."

I do not think it is. To be sure, one may easily enough prove it absurd if one takes the two wills on the same level of explicitness. If to will something must mean to will it immediately and with full awareness, then the suggestion that we always will what it would be best to will *is* absurd. Very well then; out with the word "will"; we are not insisting on words; we are insisting on what we take to be a fact, and one of the prime facts of the moral life. Writers describe it variously. The theologian would say that at our best we remain miserable sinners; the moralist that we never do our whole duty; the poet that "what I sought to be, and was not, comforts me." However capricious or selfish or brutal a man may be in actual behaviour, if we are right in calling him a moral being at all, what he is trying to be and do is never exhausted in what he is. Whenever he makes a judgment of better or worse, whenever he does anything because he thinks he ought to do it, even when he thinks this without doing it, he is recognizing a claim as prior to the wants of the moment and conceding it the right to overrule them. A man may flout this claim to any extent in practice, and protest that he neither recognizes it nor tries to fulfil it. Is his protest to be accepted? Surely not. We could point, if we knew him well enough, to a thousand actions that belie his own report. He continually defers present good to a later and greater good,

corrects impulsive choices by reflection, recognizes the force of another's claim when at the moment he would prefer not to. In doing so, he concedes the claim of a rational good upon him, a claim which, if he is consistent, he must admit to have overwhelming force in confirmation or in veto of the will of the moment. We agree that he does know in detail the object of this larger will. We agree that it is not a will at all in the simple straightforward sense in which the will of the moment is such. But it remains a will in the extremely important sense of an ideal to which the man by implication commits himself every day of his life and whose claims he cannot repudiate without turning his back upon himself.

If this is true, the distinction must be accepted between a man's actual will and his ulterior will, his real or rational will. That was our first point. The others may be dealt with more briefly.

18. (2) The second was that the end or object of the rational will is the same in everyone. This looks questionable. But the fact is that we could not so much as argue with each with any point unless it were true. Consider the matter first on the side of theory. When we argue, we both assume that there is a truth to be found, that its discovery is our common end, and that there is a standard way of gaining it. If we differ as to whether President Madison preceded or followed President Monroe, we have no doubt that one did precede the other, or that if the evidence is rightly assessed, it will point one way. If this were really in doubt, there would be no sense in arguing at all. What would be the use of your trying to convince me if what was proof to you was in the end mere fallacy to me? The very essence of your attempt to show me my mistake lies in appealing to our common

end, namely to grasp what fact and logic require, and if you can show that in this respect or that I have fallen short of these requirements, you expect me to see and acknowledge my error. Unless our thinking is governed by the same ideal, unless what would ultimately satisfy you as cogent evidence or conclusive proof is assumed to be the same as what would satisfy me, argument is a waste of time. So long as we do make that assumption, there is hope. Argument is the joint appeal to a fundamental agreement in the hope of extending it to remove a relatively superficial disagreement.

The same holds on the practical side. Men expostulate with each other over wrongdoing just as they argue over fact. Now when another expostulates with me over an action that seems to him wrong, what sort of argument must he use if he is to convince me? He must show me that the action I am considering will not, as I suppose, subserve the sort of ends that we approve in common. Suppose he finds me set on buying the motorcar, and thinks it a madcap scheme; his argument will take essentially the following form: "You think it of the first importance, don't you, that one's family should be comfortably and healthfully housed?" "Yes." "Well, if you buy the car, you must sacrifice that end for occasional pleasures that you admit yourself to be less important." That is, he appeals to an end about which he feels confident that I agree with him, and tries to show me that the action I am proposing would defeat it rather than promote it. If I were to betray to him that I had no interest whatever in the welfare of my family, he would be at a loss how to proceed, for his argument assumes that I attach the same value to this that other sane men do. Put in the ab-stract, what he is saying is: "You agree with me that E is the important thing at stake; if you do M you will jeopardize it; if you do N you will get it; therefore you should do N." Unless there is some broad agreement on the ends that are worth pursuing, neither of us would have any purchase on the thought of the other.

There is, to be sure, an element of paradox in this view. If the Russians get involved with the Americans in an argument over practical politics, does it really make sense to say that they are both driving at the same ultimate end? Yes, I think it does, and thinking so increases my hope in the work of an international forum where they may meet and canvas their differences. Indeed, considering the bitterness of their differences, their professed ends are surprisingly near to identity. The Russians insist that they believe as strongly as the "democracies" in the dissemination of knowledge, in freedom for the masses of the people, in the cultivation of literature and the arts, and in the increase through applied knowledge of the comfort, health, and happiness of mankind. Their difference with the west is not in our accepting and their rejecting these goods, for both parties avow devotion to them; the difference is that whereas the communists think that capitalism is an atrociously bad means to these ends and communism an exceedingly good one, the west thinks that communism is a bungling and tyrannous means to them and a "free economy" a more effective one. The United Nations has been treated to many strange scenes and strange arguments, but it has not yet, I think, been invited to listen to a plea for ignorance, misery, and slavery as the true ends of man. Since all alike accept certain ends, they can argue with some point about the means. If the Russians were seeking ends that really had nothing in common with ours, if they were aiming, for example, at unhappiness in widest commonalty spread, discussion with them would take a remarkable form; when we offered an argument to show that a Russian move was calculated to increase human misery, we should be greeted at the end with applause and the exclamation, "Bravo; you put our case admirably." It is happily to be doubted whether among sane and candid men this ultimate difference about ends ever occurs.

19. (3) The third proposition is that our rights against each other are based on our common ends. Smith borrows money from Jones, and when the debt falls due, Jones claims the right to repayment. On what ground? Not, surely, on the ground alone that it furthers his own interest, since that might not be Smith's, nor on the ground alone that it is Smith's interest; to say that would too often be hypocritical and false. To get the key, we must ask another question, Is Jones's right to be repaid the same as Smith's duty to pay? We have seen that in substance it is, since a duty is the obverse side of a right. When Jones presses his claim against Smith, he is therefore insisting on Smith's duty to repay. Why is it Smith's duty to repay? Duty, as we have seen, is always based on the production of good. What is the good in this case? It is not merely Jones's satisfaction in getting his money back, though that will form part of the end for any considerate debtor. It is also the maintenance in society of a state of things in which promises are kept and debts repaid. When Jones presses his claim against Smith, he is saying in effect, "You believe, do you not, as I do, that this state of things is better than one in which promises are broken and debts repudiated? Very well,

if you do, your only consistent course is to pay." That this common end is the basis on which Jones is urging his right may be clearly seen by his helplessness if Smith rejects it. Suppose Smith rejoins, "I see no value whatever in a state of things in which promises may be relied on or debts repaid; this may be an end or good for you; it is not for me." What could Jones do? He could threaten him with the police, but that is not argument, and no argument he could offer would carry the least validity for Smith. To urge that Smith seek a good which for him was no good at all would be absurd. Jones's case in its entirety rests on the assumption that he and Smith are seeking a common end, and that when the repayment of the debt is seen to be required by that end, Smith will recognize it as his duty and do it. But that he should so recognize and do it is precisely what Jones is claiming as his right. To put it generally, your right against me and my duty to you rest on an identical ground, namely their necessity to our joint end.

20. (4) Now for the fourth proposition: it is because the state is the greatest of instruments to this common end that it has such rights as it possesses over its citizens. The state is more than a system of rights. If half a dozen hunters met by accident in the woods, such rights would hold among them, but this could not make them into a state. A state is a set of institutions—a legislature, courts, police, a chief executive —designed to give effect to these rights, to guarantee them in practice. The state is thus a means, not an end. It is a system of brakes and prods applied in the interest of reaching a goal beyond itself.

The simplest evidence for this lies in the answer we naturally give to two related questions, Why should I obey the law? and Why may I sometimes resist it? The answers to both are the same, and they amount to an admission that the state is an attempt at the embodiment of a common rational will, and is justified only as the instrument of that will. Why should I obey the law by doing anything so disagreeable as paying my income tax? Not because I have to, since with enough cleverness I might evade it, nor because I can point to any definite advantages to me or anyone else that would result from this particular act. I should obey it if at all because it belongs to a system of commands and restraints whose maintenance serves better than any available alternative as an instrument for the common good.

It is needless to work this out in detail. Everyone knows that a government is often a nuisance, whose rules about parking cars, stopping at street lights, paying taxes, keeping walks clear, and all the rest, are a source of endless major and minor frustrations. We all believe, nevertheless, that though government is a nuisance, it is a wholly indispensable nuisance. Why? Because without it the main goods of life, and for that matter life itself, would be insecure. If we can count on our house and its contents not being taken away from us, if the shops that supply our clothes and fuel and food are able to do their business, if there are roads on which we can get about, schools to send our children to, courts and police to deal with those who would take advantage of us, it is because behind these arrangements, protecting and guaranteeing them, is the power of the state. Without it we should be at the mercy of the worst elements in our society. We may concede to communists and anarchists that if the ends men are seeking in common could be realized without the complex and expensive machinery of government, it should be dispensed with. We cannot agree with them in supposing that, human nature being what it is, there is any prospect whatever of attaining these goods except with the aid of the state.

21. Does it follow that since the state is a necessary means to our major ends, we should in all circumstances obey it, that we never have the right to rebel? Not at all. Our view would not only justify disobedience in some cases; it would require it. If the state is regarded, not as sacrosanct or an end in itself, but as an instrument to certain great ends, then when it becomes so corrupt as to cut us off from those ends rather than further them, when it serves its purpose so badly that it is better to risk chaos for the sake of a better order than continue to suffer under the old, then resistance becomes a right and a duty. This will be an extreme and desperate case, since it will obviously be better as a rule to obey what we regard as a bad law and try by persuasion to get it amended than to seek the overthrow of the power which supports all laws alike. But there is no doubt that when government has ceased to serve its major ends, the people who have fashioned it to serve those ends have a right to replace it with something that serves these better. In doing so, they will appeal to the same ends that earlier led them to support it, and they will do so with full consistency and justification. Thus the theory of a rational will provides a natural and intelligible ground both for obedience in normal cases and for disobedience in abnormal cases. It is hard to conceive what better evidence could be offered for it.

22. Here then is a theory of political obligation. It holds that each of us is seeking an end that goes beyond the good of the moment, that besides his

will of the moment for food, drink, and comfort, he has a rational will directed far beyond these to what would satisfy in the light of a fully critical reflection. The nature of that end we have explored in earlier chapters. At best it is conceived vaguely and pursued waveringly, but its presence nevertheless is both the magnet that draws us on and the monitor that reproves when we stray out of the way. This end, we have held, is the end of all men. Because it is, each can justly claim of another that he should be loyal to it; that is what we mean by a right. The state itself is an arrangement accepted as a necessary means to this ultimate end, and on this necessity rests its right to obedience.

The Ideal of Justice

The various positions taken by idealists on the fundamental questions of social philosophy reflect concerns for personality, conscience and morality, and the "ideal" element in man's experience. All of these come together in the discussion of justice, the consummate political value and goal. For the presentation of this view, a selection from the writings of Sir Ernest Barker has been chosen. Influenced especially by T. H. Green, Ernest Barker (1874–1960) was a distinguished English historian and analyst of political ideas. Though he was not an idealistic metaphysician, his own constructive efforts in social philosophy give expression to the idealist perspective.

Justice, Barker writes, is "the reconciler and the synthesis of political values: it is their union in an adjusted whole." Justice is thus a term of synthesis, allotting to persons their rights. It seeks to balance and to reconcile the conflicting claims of persons and principles, and thus to produce that right order of right relations that guarantees to all persons the external conditions of their development.

Statements such as these, and perhaps many others throughout this section on idealism, raise questions about the relationship of ethics and law, a relationship whose clarification may aid the understanding of the conception of justice. The source of the principle of justice, Barker asserts, is ethics in the sense that justice is a kind of moral standard of the community, reinforced by the general moral conscience. Law, which is the impersonal expression of justice, has validity through declaration, recognition, and enforcement; it has value through its expression of the demands of moral conscience in the form of a rule of right for human relations. Given that ethics is thus the source of justice, in what sense is the state a moral agent? Fundamentally, it must be recognized that law *is not* ethics: ethics deals with inner motives, law can deal only with external acts, or acts that external sanctions can secure. This distinction means that it is impossible that the state be the actual agent of its citizens' morality.

Yet sharp as the distinction is, it does not abolish all relations between ethics and law. Both are concerned with what should be (an ideal element), both are expressed in imperatives, and both deal with roughly the same areas of life. How, then, can this relation be expressed? One view is that law and justice are the expression of the "moral minimum" of a community, with the state being a school-master to bring men to this minimum. Barker rejects this, for justice aims at something higher than a minimum, and the schoolmaster idea ultimately obliterates the distinction of law and ethics. Rather, he says, justice seeks to secure the external conditions needed by moral conscience for its effective growth and action.

Justice, with the state, thus supports the development of persons through "partnership" with them. And this it does because, as Green put it, all good is for, of, and in persons; and because, therefore, the intrinsic value of personality is the basis of political thought as it is of ethical thought. So based, justice is the "joining" of persons and principles as the expression of the final and ultimate social value.

ERNEST BARKER   Justice and Personality

It has already been noted that the root idea of the word *jus,* and therefore also the words *justus* and *justitia,* is the idea of joining or fitting, the idea of a bond or tie. Primarily, the joining or fitting implied in this root idea is that between *man and man* in an organized system of human relations. But we may also conceive of the "just" and "justice" as connected with, and expressed in, a joining or fitting between *value and value* in a general sum and synthesis of values. We recognize a number of different values as necessary to an organized system of human relations. There is the value of liberty: there is the value of equality: there is the value of fraternity, or (as it may also be called, and is perhaps better called) co-operation. All these values are present in any system of law; but they are present in different degrees at different periods of time, and there is a constant process of adjustment and readjustment between their claims. The claims of liberty have to be adjusted to those of equality; and the claims of both have also to be adjusted to those of co-operation. From this point

of view the function of justice may be said to be that of adjusting, joining, or fitting the different political values. Justice is the reconciler and the synthesis of political values: it is their union in an adjusted and integrated whole: it is, in Aristotle's words, "What answers to the whole of goodness . . . being the exercise of goodness as a whole . . . towards one's neighbour."[1] We must presently inquire into each of the values. But before we can do so, it is necessary to inquire into the origin and nature of the general notion of justice—the notion of the "first" or "total" value in which the others are all combined; by which they are all controlled; and in virtue of which their different claims (if and so far as a conflict arises) are reconciled and adjusted.

How do we discover, and from what source do we draw, the total notion of justice—the general and controlling idea of the right and the just—which we feel that the law of the State should express? We acknowledge that justice will justify

[1] *Ethics,* Book V, c. ii, ¶ 10 (1130b 18–19).

From Ernest Barker, *Principles of Social and Political Theory,* Oxford: The Clarendon Press, 1951. Used by permission of the publisher.

law to us; we admit that, in virtue of this justification, it finally ties and obliges us to law. But what is the source of its justifying grace and obliging power? . . .

Can we find this principle in ethics? If we answer in the affirmative, the moral standard of the community, precipitated in and enforced by the general moral conscience, will be the source of a notion of justice, containing a system or synthesis of values, which will be in its turn the impersonal source of positive law. We shall accordingly hold that if law is to have value as well as validity —value all round, and not some single "broken arc" of value called by the name of "solidarity" or by some other such name—it must satisfy, in the last resort, the demands of the general moral conscience, issuing and expressed in a general all-round notion of what is just and right in the conduct of human relations. In order that law may be valid, it is enough that it should satisfy the canon of declaration, recognition, and enforcement by a constituted authority acting on behalf of the community. In order that it may have value, over and above validity, law must also satisfy—*as much as it can, and so far as its strength avails* —the canon of conformity to the demands of moral conscience as expressed in the general notion of justice. In other words, and in simpler terms, law will have value only if it expresses and realizes—*so far as it can and in such ways as it can*—a rule of right for human relations ultimately derived from ethics.

Here we touch a difficulty, which the provisos already stated are meant to meet in advance. Law is not ethics; and legality, or obedience to law, is not the same as morality. Law is concerned with external acts, and its demands are satisfied by such acts because they are all that its sanctions, themselves external

acts of physical compulsion, can possibly secure. Ethics is concerned not only with external acts, but also with internal motive: its essence, as Aristotle said, is "a state of character, concerned with choice," which is freely determined in its choice by its own internal motive; and the demands of ethics are not satisfied unless an internal motive is present as well as an external act. An act is legal, whatever its motive, so long as it is the act demanded by the law. An act is not moral, whatever its outward show may be, if it is not inspired by an internal motive and does not proceed from a "state of a character concerned with choice."

But though we must draw a distinction between the nature of ethics and the nature of law, it does not follow that such a distinction abolishes any relation. Law and ethics are both concerned with what should be, and they both speak in the imperative mood: they both deal, in the main, with identical areas of life —marriage and its sanctities, the keeping of faith and the honouring of pledges, the duty of consideration for others, and man's general duty to his neighbour. How shall we express their relation? We may attempt two alternative methods of expression, and seek to discover which of the two expresses the relation best.

The first method of expression is based on the fact that law is a uniform rule of action binding on all men alike. Men in general run through the whole gamut of the moral scale: some act on this, and some on that standard: one standard is lower, and another higher. What law does, it may be argued, is to establish a moral minimum which every man must attain. It establishes, as it were, a lowest common measure of conduct which all can compass and which can therefore be made a uniform rule of action for all. If law bids me attach and keep burning a rear light on my bicycle when I am riding it in the dark, that is a lowest common measure of consideration for others, and it may, as such, be legally imposed. If law proceeds to fine me for riding without a rear light, it stimulates me into a disposition to obey the moral minimum—a disposition which itself is not moral (even though it results in obedience to the moral rule of consideration for others) because it is based on the negative and non-moral factor of force, and not on the positive and moral factor of an inward motive of spontaneous consideration. Law, when it is so considered, may be regarded as a schoolmaster to bring us to morality, through the enforcement of habits of action by the use of coercive discipline.

But there is an obvious objection to this view of law. A moral minimum, enforced by non-moral means, may have *some* relation to ethics; but it is not a relation which can stand the test of scrutiny, or prove itself to be anything more than a superficial relation. If law is connected with ethics in the sense that it is meant to enforce the rules of ethics on some sort of common standard, ought not the standard initially to be something higher than a mere minimum, and ought we not to be constantly engaged in screwing the strings tighter and tighter, in order to produce a fuller and truer note? And, even more, ought not the standard, whatever its pitch, to be enforced by means, such as reformatory punishment and moral education, which will themselves have a moral quality because they tend to promote a moral disposition? These questions suggest that if once we adopt the idea that law is a moral minimum, we shall soon be led to seek to obliterate any distinction between law and ethics, and to substitute law for ethics, with the result of eliminating ethics.

We may therefore turn to another method of expressing the relation between law and ethics. This second method, like the first, is based on the fact that law deals only with men in the mass, and is in its nature no more than a uniform rule of action binding equally on all alike. But the corollary which we now draw from that fact is that the only thing which law can get from man in the mass is external conduct, because the only thing which it can apply to men in the mass is external force. From this point of view, and bearing in mind the word "external," we arrive at another method of expressing the relation between law and ethics. We conclude that law is related to ethics in the sense that it seeks to secure the set of external conditions necessary for moral action, or the general framework of external order in which the moral conscience can act and determine itself most easily and most freely. Law, from this point of view, is not the lowest common measure of ethics, or the lowest story in the house of ethics: it is rather the best and highest set of conditions, set round the house and forming, as it were, a fence for its protection, which has to be assembled, and firmly established, before moral action can find a free space for its play and in order that moral development may unfold its energies freely. All moral development is inevitably confronted by external obstacles or hindrances: it is the function of law "to remove the obstacles" or "hinder the hindrances". . . .

The course of the argument has led to the conclusion that the idea of justice, which is the impersonal source of law, is an idea which itself has its source in ethics and ethical principles. But the foundation of ethics, and the source of all ethical principles, is the value and the worth of individual personality. The moral world is a world of individual persons, each intrinsically valuable, but all existing in time, and all accordingly subject to the conditions of a time-process. The intrinsic value of each personality is the basis of political thought, just as (and just because) it is the basis of moral thought; and worth of persons —individual persons; *all* individual persons—is the supreme worth in the State. Existing under, and subject to, the conditions of a time-process, these persons —not fixed substances, but so many *growing* nuclei—are engaged in a motion of development, which is the turning of capacity into energy or (as we may also say) of "potency" into "act." The end of any national society is to foster and encourage, in and through partnership, the highest possible development of all the capacities of personality in all of its members; and this end is the justice, or "right ordering," of such a society, and may accordingly be called by the name of social justice.[2] Similarly the end of any legal association or State, which is based and superimposed on a national society, is to assemble and establish the external conditions required by every citizen for the development of his capacities; and this end is the justice, or right ordering, of such a legal association, and may accordingly be called legal justice. . . .

Justice, as we are now in a position to see, is a term of synthesis. It is the final principle which controls the general distribution of rights and the various principles of their distribution. It is, in a word, the general right ordering of human relations in, and by, the association of the State. As such, it gives to each person rights, as his share in the whole system, and it thus "adjusts" person to person. As such, again, it gives to each principle of distribution (liberty, equality, and co-operation) its share and weight in determining the distribution actually made, and it thus "adjusts" principle to principle. This idea of justice as the general "right ordering of human relations," or the final adjustment of persons and principles, may appear to be an abstract conception if we compare it with actual concrete law, which is its visible expression and actual embodiment. But it is not abstract; nor does it reside merely in the speculative mind of the thinker, seeking, by an effort of his own reason, to separate and distil some sort of quintessence from the matter and practice of ordinary life. The idea of justice resides in *all* minds, and it has been created and developed through the ages by a process of historical social thought, which has made it a common inheritance. In that sense, and from that point of view, it is not an abstract conception but a social reality: an actual content of actual minds: a content progressively greater and clearer as those minds think out more fully and consciously the problems of a general right ordering of human relations. This justice is not morality, and its code is not that of ethics; it is not a rule of the inward life, but a rule of the outward life—the life of the relations between the members of an organized Society acting as such. On the other hand, this rule of the outward life of relations is vitally and intimately con-

---

[2] The term "social justice," in common usage, tends to be applied only to economics, and to be used only to denote a just distribution of economic duties and rewards. Justice of this economic order is indeed a necessary part of "social justice" in the larger sense of that term; for a just distribution of economic duties and rewards is a necessary means to the fostering and encouraging of general personal development. But social justice, in its broader sense, is a matter of something more than merely economic duties and rewards.

nected with the inward moral life: it is a condition, or set of conditions, needed and designed for the free movement of that life: it is a removal of the obstacles, or a hindrance of the hindrances, which may impede that movement. If justice is not morality it is based upon it. If its code is not that of ethics, it is a code which, as we have seen, is ultimately derived from ethics.

To elucidate the meaning of a term such as justice, built and vested with associations by an historical process of social thought, we shall do well to go back to its origin and the root from which it has grown. That root, which appears in many branches and has been prolific of many growths, would seem to be the notion of "joining" (as in the Latin *jungere* or the Greek *zeugnunai*): of "binding," or "fitting," or "tying together."[3] Justice is thus, in its original notion, the quality of aptitude of joining: it ties together whatever it touches. Primarily, it ties *men* together, by the common bond of a right and "fitting" order of relations, under which each has his position in the order and receives his due place (*suum cuique*); each has rights as his share of the general Right pervading and constituting the order; and each owns *jura* as the exemplification and concrete expression in his own case of the general *jus*. Accordingly the *Institutes* of Justinian define justice, considered as a subjective feeling and a consequent will for the general right and fitting order, as *constans et perpetua voluntas suum cuique tribuendi*. Similarly the *Institutes* define the three precepts of *jus,* considered as the objective

expression of the right order in a recognized and enforced body of rules, as consisting in *honeste vivere* ("living," as we say, "up to one's position"), *alterum non laedere* (not injuring the position of another), and *suum cuique tribuere* (actually and positively respecting another's position and rights). Aristotle, almost a thousand years earlier, had distinguished three different species of justice, as the *Institutes* afterwards distinguished and defined three precepts of *jus*. The first is "distributive" justice, which gives each person his proper position and due share in the political community: this is analogous to Justinian's *suum cuique tribuere,* but it also differs, as it is concerned only with the distribution by the city-state among its members of *public* or official position, and not with the giving of *general* position in the shape of a share in general rights. The second is "corrective" justice, which corrects a loss of position and rights involuntarily sustained in the course of transactions between individual members of the community:[4] this is analogous to Justinian's *alterum non laedere.* The third is "commutative" justice, or justice in exchange, which determines the proportion of one sort of goods or services to be rendered in return for another sort in voluntary transactions of

---

[3] The original Indo-European root was *yug,* which may be traced in the English "yoke." The Romans, as has already been noted, still used the word *jus* in the general sense of a bond or tie, as when they spoke of *jus amicitiae* (the bond of friendship), or *jura necessitudinis* (the ties of kinship).

[4] Aristotle cites, as examples of loss thus involuntarily sustained, clandestine injuries such as theft or perjury (leading to the loss of a man's goods or good name), and open and violent injuries such as assault or murder. In Aristotle's own terminology the one term "rectificatory" (or "diorthotic") is used to cover the two sorts of justice distinguished in the text as "corrective" and "commutative." Using that one term, he then proceeds to distinguish (1) the form of rectificatory justice which deals with losses involuntarily sustained, and (2) the form of rectificatory justice which is concerned with the voluntary transactions of exchange. But the meaning is made clearer if separate names are given to these two separate forms.

buying and selling or letting and hiring: this has no analogy with any of Justinian's three precepts—unless it be taken as another form of Justinian's *suum cuique tribuere*.

Such is the primary way in which justice performs its function of "joining" and "fitting together." But there is also a second and further way. Justice is a joining or fitting together not only of persons, but also of principles. It joins and knits together the claims of the principle of liberty with those of the principle of equality, and both with those of the principle of fraternity or co-operation: it adjusts them to one another in a right order of *their* relations. Equality may quarrel with liberty; for if its application be pushed to the length of what is called a "classless" society, with absolute equality of possessions, it is at once brought into conflict with the liberty of each to try himself out in the effort of acquiring for himself some individual "equipment." Similarly the principle of liberty may quarrel with that of co-operation: on the one hand, men may stand on the claims of their liberty (whether the civil liberty of the ordinary individual, or the economic liberty of the worker) to the detriment of the claims of the community for the co-operation of all its members; on the other hand, a party may press the claims of co-operation to the length of demanding the common provision and common possession of the whole equipment of life, and it may press them thereby to the detriment of the claims of the individual for civil liberty and personal freedom of effort. But not only may there be conflicts between one principle and another; there may also be internal conflicts inside the area of a single principle. In the area of liberty, for example, as the argument has previously suggested, civil liberty may be pleaded in support of claims which run contrary to those of economic liberty; and similarly political liberty may be on occasion the enemy, even if it is generally the friend, of either civil or economic liberty. There must therefore be some final principle transcending that of liberty, as it also transcends the principles of equality and co-operation: a principle which can balance each of these principles against the others, as it can also balance against one another the different and possibly divergent modes of interpretation that may be present within the area even of a single principle: a final principle which, in a word, *suum cuique tribuit*. That final principle is justice, which balances, and thus reconciles (and thus, in the issue, "joins"), the different claims. This balancing and reconciling, in its turn, implies some final and ultimate value in the light of which, and by reference to which, it is possible to strike a balance and achieve a reconciliation; for you can only balance different and possibly conflicting claims if you have something behind them all in terms of which you can measure the weight to be assigned to each. That final and ultimate value, on the basis of the argument previously advanced, is the highest possible development of the capacities of personality in the greatest possible number of persons. Justice is therefore an order of persons, and an order of the principles regulating the distribution of rights to persons, which is measured and determined by this final and ultimate value.

Communism

Together with his collaborator, Friedrich Engels, and his successor, V. I. Lenin, Karl Marx (1818–1883) is the founder of one of the most influential philosophies in the modern world. Born in Trier in west Germany, he showed a deep interest in culture early in life. His education was at first directed toward a career in law, but by 1839 he wished to become a professor of philosophy. His studies in philosophy included the works of Spinoza, Leibniz, Hume, Kant, Feuerbach, and above all, Hegel. In 1841 at Jena, Marx submitted his dissertation, a study of the differences in the materialism of Democritus and Epicurus. Almost immediately, however, he developed deep and abiding interests in social problems. In 1842 he met Engels, a man whose mind was exactly the same as his (Marx and Engels never differed on theoretical matters), and from then until his death in 1883, he worked as a writer and organizer for the communist movement.

The social interests Marx developed were rooted in his sympathy for the proletarian (worker's) revolution of his century. One of the keenest social observers, Marx saw that capitalism as an economic institution was producing a class of men who live solely from their wages. That is, workers were becoming little more than commodities, selling themselves on the labor market and relating themselves to society merely through a "cash nexus." Political relations such as power and law that control the social life of the proletariat are but reflections of the capitalist economic structure, and they served to maintain the servile and inhuman condition of the working class. Yet, Marx insisted, capitalism need not be accepted as the necessary economic system for Europe: it is not the result of timeless economic laws, as some of its theorists insisted. Marx saw capitalism as a phase in historical evolution that can be surpassed if conditions are right. Such an insight, Marx himself realized, contains the seeds of a revolutionary movement, and he set about to create a social philosophy for the rising proletariat and for the revolutionary role that he believed the proletariat would take.

That philosophy is dialectical materialism. The term dialectical reminds one of Hegel, and communism is indeed unthinkable apart from Hegel. That history is a process, that historical process is patterned in terms of thesis-antithesis-synthesis, that the driving force of the dialectical is tension and opposition, and that the dialectic moves toward an "end" that reconciles the conflicts of preceding stages: these notions were all accepted by Marx. Yet Marx was at the same time critical of Hegel for the dialectic must move in the realm of real forces, not logical abstractions. It is necessary, he said, to turn Hegel "right way up," and this he did in terms of his materialism. By materialism Marx meant economic determinism, which is the view that the process of economic production is the basic force in history and society. The character of production determines the character of social life because it makes social life possible and creates the need for social institutions.

This union of dialectic with materialism transformed Hegelianism into a revolutionary radicalism. Marx found what he took to be a revolutionary element in Hegel himself, particularly in the latter's dialectical treatment of religion which implied that the so-called absolute truths of particular religions are in fact relative to religious evolution. Generalizing from this application, Marx made economics a historical science as well, and thus he interpreted various economies such as feudalism and mercantilism as relative stages in economic evolution.

As Marx saw it, the history of the modern world can be understood in terms of a general triad whose thesis is feudalism, whose antithesis is capitalism, and whose synthesis is—or will be—communism. Though feudalism did not "depersonalize" labor as capitalism does, it had to be transcended because of its low productive capacities. Capitalism therefore emerged, and with it came high levels of production. (Marx did not deny the value of economic growth in capitalistic economies.) However, it also brought a number of evils, including the exploitation of man by man and the alienation of man from himself. Therefore, a higher synthesis is needed, which will retain the productivity of capitalism, yet eliminate its disvalues; and this Marx sketched in his ideal of the classless communist society.

The formulation of the theory of dialectical materialism belongs to the earlier part of Marx's career; his concern with economics—including his detailed critique of capitalism—belongs to the latter part. Perhaps the most important link between his major interests in these two periods is his high moralism and his concern for the values he thought appropriate to the human condition. Neither Marx nor Engels was a systematic philosopher in the sense of an Aristotle or a Hume, that is, in the sense of a systematic critic of the ideas men use to explain their world or their actions. They did not make any significant contributions to basic areas of philosophy such as metaphysics or epistemology, and they insisted that "philosophers have only interpreted the world differently—the main thing is to change it." They did offer, however, a philosophic interpretation of society and of the values and disvalues men may experience in society. The selections below seek to develop the details of that interpretation.

Man and Society

The fundamental assertion of dialectical materialism is that the system of production in any society determines the society's structure and the cultural institutions erected on it. Even men's consciousness is so determined. Does it require deep intuition, Marx asks, "to comprehend that man's ideas, views and conceptions, in one word, man's consciousness, changes with every change in the conditions of his material existence, in his social relations, and in his social life?" The question, of course, is only rhetorical, but to understand it fully requires linking this deterministic theory with another Marxist thesis, namely, that "the history of all hitherto existing society is the history of class struggles."

The notion of class is a crucial element in Marx's view of man's social condition. "Class" for Marx is a limited and economically determined concept: the class to which a man belongs depends on whether he owns property, and if so, what kind. Under capitalism, for example, the bourgeoisie constitutes one class, namely that which owns the means of production and distribution; and the proletariat is a second, distinct class because it is propertyless. So understood, class is Marx's replacement for Hegel's state as the unit of history, and the dialectic moves through the relations between classes. In turn, Marx made two further assumptions about classes: the relation between them is one of antagonism, and a single class always dominates and is the exploiter of all other classes. Antagonism and domination mark the existence of classes, Marx insists, because the interests of conflicting classes are irreconcilable. Class interests arise out of, and are relative to, the economic situations of classes, and from these diverse interests come diverse notions of justice, of morality, of religion—in short, of different *ideologies*.

This last conception is one of Marx's most interesting ideas. By an ideology he means the "superstructure" or system of ideas, especially normative ones, which reflects underlying economic realities and which is developed, not to explain the world (this task belongs to science), but to support class interests and social conditions. Because this is their function, Marx speaks of ideologies as "false consciousness" and as "illusion," though this does not mean that he denies their authority.* The opposite is true; established social relations are defended by the economically privileged class whose ideology is reflected in them. But Marx is insisting that, for economic determinism,

morality, religion, metaphysics, all the rest of ideology and their corresponding forms of consciousness, thus no longer retain the semblance of independence. They have no history, no development; but men, developing their material production and their material intercourse, alter, along with their real existence, their thinking and products of their thinking. Life is not determined by consciousness but consciousness by life.

But "life" or economic reality does not always determine consciousness in ways

---

* Engels, it may be noted, divided ideology into (1) science and technology and (2) law, morals, art, philosophy, and religion. Only the second is termed by him false consciousness.

consistent with man's fundamental capacities. This is especially true of the present conflict of bourgeoisie and proletariat within capitalism. Neither capitalism nor the ideology of the bourgeoisie is adequate to the meaning of human personality. In fact, man finds himself *alienated* from both self and society, because society sets up standards of behavior through its dominant ideology, yet it at the same time produces motives that move men to reject those standards. Incompatible passions arise that conflict with one another and with the rules and values men are taught to accept. They feel themselves to be rootless and impelled to take courses of action that are unsatisfying. Crime, disobedience, and sometimes destructive violence accompany this alienated condition.

Yet alienation need not be. To be sure, Marx says, great social changes must occur before a society adequate to human nature will emerge. Man is a creature whose view of himself and of his world is a product of what he does to satisfy his needs. He is also a creature who can come to understand himself and his world. Through understanding and by working on his environment, man can be "made whole" again. Alienation will end when man brings his passions into harmony with his values and his ambitions into relation to the means at his disposal.†

The major themes of the communist view of man and society are given in the selections that follow. The first is from the preface of Marx's work on political economy; it is the only brief summary he ever made of his conclusions on society and cultural development. The second selection is from the Communist Manifesto. This work was published in 1848 as the platform of the Communist League, a German workingmen's association. Though designed as much as a call to action as a theoretical statement, it remains a forceful summary of Marx and Engels' thought as it had developed up to this time.

---

† This point is relevant to Marx's treatment of religion. As indicated above, religion is ideology or false consciousness. It functions for alienated man as a comforter or opiate. So interpreted, however, religion will disappear in the ideal society where alienation is overcome.

KARL MARX   The Material Basis of Life

The first work undertaken for the solution of the question that troubled me, was a critical revision of Hegel's "Philosophy of Law"; the introduction to that work appeared in the "Deutsch-Französische Jahrbücher," published in Paris in 1844. I was led by my studies to the conclusion that legal relations as well as forms of state could neither be understood by themselves, nor explained by the so-called general progress of the human mind, but that they are rooted in the material conditions of life, which are summed up by Hegel after the fashion of the English and French of the eighteenth century under the name "civic society"; the anatomy of that civic society is to be sought in political economy. The study of the latter which I had taken up in Paris, I continued at Brussels whither I emigrated on account of an order of expulsion issued by Mr.

From Karl Marx, *A Contribution to the Critique of Political Economy,* trans. N. I. Stone, Chicago: Charles H. Kerr and Co., 1904.

Guizot. The general conclusion at which I arrived and which, once reached, continued to serve as the leading thread in my studies, may be briefly summed up as follows: In the social production which men carry on they enter into definite relations that are indispensable and independent of their will; these relations of production correspond to a definite stage of development of their material powers of production. The sum total of these relations of production constitutes the economic structure of society—the real foundation, on which rise legal and political superstructures and to which correspond definite forms of social consciousness. The mode of production in material life determines the general character of the social, political and spiritual processes of life. It is not the consciousness of men that determines their existence, but, on the contrary, their social existence determines their consciousness. At a certain stage of their development, the material forces of production in society come in conflict with the existing relations of production, or—what is but a legal expression for the same thing—with the property relations within which they had been at work before. From forms of development of the forces of production these relations turn into their fetters. Then comes the period of social revolution. With the change of the economic foundation the entire immense superstructure is more or less rapidly transformed. In considering such transformations the distinction should always be made between the material transformation of the economic conditions of production which can be determined with the precision of natural science, and the legal, political, religious, aesthetic or philosophic—in short ideologi-cal forms in which men become conscious of this conflict and fight it out. Just as our opinion of an individual is not based on what he thinks of himself, so can we not judge of such a period of transformation by its own consciousness; on the contrary, this consciousness must rather be explained from the contradictions of material life, from the existing conflict between the social forces of production and the relations of production. No social order ever disappears before all the productive forces, for which there is room in it, have been developed; and new higher relations of production never appear before the material conditions of their existence have matured in the womb of the old society. Therefore, mankind always takes up only such problems as it can solve; since, looking at the matter more closely, we will always find that the problem itself arises only when the material conditions necessary for its solution already exist or are at least in the process of formation. In broad outlines we can designate the Asiatic, the ancient, the feudal, and the modern bourgeois methods of production as so many epochs in the progress of the economic formation of society. The bourgeois relations of production· are the last antagonistic form of the social process of production—antagonistic not in the sense of individual antagonism, but of one arising from conditions surrounding the life of individuals in society; at the same time the productive forces developing in the womb of bourgeois society create the material conditions for the solution of that antagonism. This social formation constitutes, therefore, the closing chapter of the prehistoric stage of human society.

COMMUNIST MANIFESTO
Marx and Engels

History as Class Struggle

The history of all hitherto existing society is the history of class struggles.

Freeman and slave, patrician and plebeian, lord and serf, guild-master and journeyman, in a word, oppressor and oppressed, stood in constant opposition to one another, carried on an uninterrupted, now hidden, now open fight, a fight that each time ended, either in a revolutionary re-constitution of society at large, or in the common ruin of the contending classes.

In the earlier epochs of history, we find almost everywhere a complicated arrangement of society into various orders, a manifold gradation of social rank. In ancient Rome we have patricians, knights, plebians, slaves; in the Middle Ages, feudal lords, vassals, guild-masters, journeymen, apprentices, serfs; in almost all of these classes, again, subordinate gradations.

The modern bourgeois society that has sprouted from the ruins of feudal society has not done away with class antagonisms. It has but established new classes, new conditions of oppression, new forms of struggle in place of the old ones.

Our epoch, the epoch of the bourgeoisie, possesses, however, this distinctive feature: it has simplified the class antagonisms. Society as a whole is more and more splitting up into two great hostile camps, into two great classes directly facing each other: Bourgeoisie and Proletariat. . . .

Each step in the development of the bourgeoisie was accompanied by a corresponding political advance of that class. An oppressed class under the sway of the feudal nobility, an armed and self-governing association in the mediaeval commune, here independent urban republic (as in Italy and Germany), there taxable "third estate" of the monarchy (as in France), afterwards, in the period of manufacture proper, serving either the semi-feudal or the absolute monarchy as a counterpoise against the nobility, and, in fact, cornerstone of the great monarchies in general, the bourgeoisie has at last, since the establishment of Modern Industry and of the world-market, conquered for itself, in the modern representative State, exclusive political sway. The executive of the modern State is but a committee for managing the common affairs of the whole bourgeoisie.

The bourgeoisie, historically, has played a most revolutionary part.

The bourgeoisie, wherever it has got the upper hand, has put an end to all feudal, patriarchal, idyllic relations. It has pitilessly torn asunder the motley feudal ties that bound man to his "natural superiors," and has left remaining no other nexus between man and man than naked self-interest, than callous "cash payment." It has drowned the most heavenly ecstasies of religious fervour, of chivalrous enthusiasm, of philistine sentimentalism, in the icy water of egotistical calculation. It has resolved personal worth into exchange value, and

From the *Manifesto of the Communist Party* by Karl Marx and Friedrich Engels, authorized English translation, ed. Engels, Chicago: Charles H. Kerr and Co., 1888.

in place of the numberless indefeasible chartered freedoms, has set up that single, unconscionable freedom—Free Trade. In one word, for exploitation, veiled by religious and political illusions, it has substituted naked, shameless, direct, brutal exploitation.

The bourgeoisie has stripped of its halo every occupation hitherto honoured and looked up to with reverent awe. It has converted the physician, the lawyer, the priest, the poet, the man of science, into its paid wage-labourers.

The bourgeoisie has torn away from the family its sentimental veil, and has reduced the family relation to a mere money relation.

The bourgeoisie has disclosed how it came to pass that the brutal display of vigour in the Middle Ages, which Reactionists so much admire, found its fitting complement in the most slothful indolence. It has been the first to show what man's activity can bring about. It has accomplished wonders far surpassing Egyptian pyramids, Roman aqueducts, and Gothic cathedrals; it has conducted expeditions that put in the shade all former Exoduses of nations and crusades.

The bourgeoisie cannot exist without constantly revolutionising the instruments of production, and thereby the relations of production, and with them the whole relations of society. Conservation of the old modes of production in unaltered form, was on the contrary, the first condition of existence for all earlier industrial classes. Constant revolutionising of production, uninterrupted disturbance of all social conditions, everlasting uncertainty and agitation distinguish the bourgeois epoch from all earlier ones. All fixed, fast-frozen relations, with their train of ancient and venerable prejudices and opinions, are swept away, all new-formed ones become antiquated before they can ossify. All that is solid melts into air, all that is holy is profaned, and man is at last compelled to face with sober senses, his real conditions of life, and his relations with his kind.

The need of a constantly expanding market for its products chases the bourgeoisie over the whole surface of the globe. It must nestle everywhere, settle everywhere, establish connexions everywhere. . . .

The bourgeoisie, during its rule of scarce one hundred years, has created more massive and more colossal productive forces than have all preceding generations together. Subjection of Nature's forces to man, machinery, application of chemistry to industry and agriculture, steam-navigation, railways, electric telegraphs, clearing of whole continents for cultivation, canalisation of rivers, whole populations conjured out of the ground—what earlier century had even a presentiment that such productive forces slumbered in the lap of social labour?

We see then: the means of production and of exchange, on whose foundation the bourgeoisie built itself up, were generated in feudal society. At a certain stage in the development of these means of production and of exchange, the conditions under which feudal society produced and exchanged, the feudal organisation of agriculture and manufacturing industry, in one word, the feudal relations of property became no longer compatible with the already developed productive forces; they became so many fetters. They had to be burst asunder; they were burst asunder.

Into their place stepped free competition, accompanied by a social and political constitution adapted to it, and by the economical and political sway of the bourgeois class.

A similar movement is going on before our own eyes. Modern bourgeois society with its relations of production, of exchange and of property, a society that has conjured up such gigantic means of production and of exchange, is like the sorcerer, who is no longer able to control the powers of the nether world whom he has called up by his spells. For many a decade past the history of industry and commerce is but the history of the revolt of modern productive forces against modern conditions of production, against the property relations that are the conditions for the existence of the bourgeoisie and of its rule. It is enough to mention the commercial crises that by their periodical return put on its trial, each time more threateningly, the existence of the entire bourgeois society. In these crises a great part not only of the existing products, but also of the previously created productive forces, are periodically destroyed. In these crises there breaks out an epidemic that, in all earlier epochs, would have seemed an absurdity—the epidemic of over-production. Society suddenly finds itself put back into a state of momentary barbarism; it appears as if a famine, a universal war of devastation had cut off the supply of every means of subsistence; industry and commerce seem to be destroyed; and why? Because there is too much civilisation, too much means of subsistence, too much industry, too much commerce. The productive forces at the disposal of society no longer tend to further the development of the conditions of bourgeois property; on the contrary, they have become too powerful for these conditions, by which they are fettered, and so soon as they overcome these fetters, they bring disorder into the whole of bourgeois society, endanger the existence of bourgeois property. The condi-

tions of bourgeois society are too narrow to comprise the wealth created by them. And how does the bourgeoisie get over these crises? On the one hand by enforced destruction of a mass of productive forces; on the other, by the conquest of new markets, and by the more thorough exploitation of the old ones. That is to say, by paving the way for more extensive and more destructive crises, and by diminishing the means whereby crises are prevented.

The weapons with which the bourgeoisie felled feudalism to the ground are now turned against the bourgeoisie itself.

But not only has the bourgeoisie forged the weapons that bring death to itself; it has also called into existence the men who are to wield those weapons —the modern working class—the proletarians.

In proportion as the bourgeoisie, *i.e.,* capital, is developed, in the same proportion is the proletariat, the modern working class, developed—a class of labourers, who live only so long as they find work, and who find work only so long as their labour increases capital. These labourers, who must sell themselves piecemeal, are a commodity, like every other article of commerce, and are consequently exposed to all the vicissitudes of competition, to all the fluctuations of the market.

Owing to the extensive use of machinery and to division of labour, the work of the proletarians has lost all individual character, and, consequently, all charm for the workman. He becomes an appendage of the machine, and it is only the most simple, most monotonous, and most easily acquired knack, that is required of him. Hence, the cost of production of a workman is restricted, almost entirely, to the means of subsistence that he requires for his maintenance, and for the propagation of his race. But the price of a commodity, and therefore also of labour, is equal to its cost of production. In proportion, therefore, as the repulsiveness of the work increases, the wage decreases. Nay more, in proportion as the use of machinery and division of labour increases, in the same proportion the burden of toil also increases, whether by prolongation of the working hours, by increase of the work exacted in a given time or by increased speed of the machinery, etc.

Modern industry has converted the little workshop of the patriarchal master into the great factory of the industrial capitalist. Masses of labourers, crowded into the factory, are organised like soldiers. As privates of the industrial army they are placed under the command of a perfect hierarchy of officers and sergeants. Not only are they slaves of the bourgeois class, and of the bourgeois State; they are daily and hourly enslaved by the machine, by the overlooker, and, above all, by the individual bourgeois manufacturer himself. The more openly this despotism proclaims gain to be its end and aim, the more petty, the more hateful and the more embittering it is. . . .

The proletariat goes through various stages of development. With its birth begins its struggle with the bourgeoisie. At first the contest is carried on by individual labourers, then by the workpeople of a factory, then by the operatives of one trade, in one locality, against the individual bourgeois who directly exploits them. They direct their attacks not against the bourgeois conditions of production, but against the instruments of production themselves; they destroy imported wares that compete with their labour, they smash to pieces machinery, they set factories ablaze, they seek to restore by force the vanished

status of the workman of the Middle Ages.

At this stage the labourers still form an incoherent mass scattered over the whole country, and broken up by their mutual competition. If anywhere they unite to form more compact bodies, this is not yet the consequence of their own active union, but of the union of the bourgeoisie, which class, in order to attain its own political ends, is compelled to set the whole proletariat in motion, and is moreover yet, for a time, able to do so. At this stage, therefore, the proletarians do not fight their enemies, but the enemies of their enemies, the remnants of absolute monarchy, the landowners, the non-industrial bourgeois, the petty bourgeoisie. Thus the whole historical movement is concentrated in the hands of the bourgeoisie; every victory so obtained is a victory for the bourgeoisie.

But with the development of industry the proletariat not only increases in number; it becomes concentrated in greater masses, its strength grows, and it feels that strength more. The various interests and conditions of life within the ranks of the proletariat are more and more equalised, in proportion as machinery obliterates all distinctions of labour, and nearly everywhere reduces wages to the same low level. The growing competition among the bourgeois, and the resulting commercial crises, make the wages of the workers ever more fluctuating. The unceasing improvement of machinery, ever more rapidly developing, makes their livelihood more and more precarious; the collisions between individual workmen and individual bourgeois take more and more the character of collisions between two classes. Thereupon the workers begin to form combinations (Trades' Unions) against the bourgeois; they club together in order to keep up the rate of wages; they found permanent associations in order to make provision beforehand for these occasional revolts. Here and there the contest breaks out into riots.

Now and then the workers are victorious, but only for a time. The real fruit of their battles lies, not in the immediate result, but in the ever-expanding union of the workers. This union is helped on by the improved means of communication that are created by modern industry and that place the workers of different localities in contact with one another. It was just this contact that was needed to centralise the numerous local struggles, all of the same character, into one national struggle between classes. But every class struggle is a political struggle. And that union, to attain which the burghers of the Middle Ages, with their miserable highways, required centuries, the modern proletarians, thanks to railways, achieve in a few years.

This organisation of the proletarians into a class, and consequently into a political party, is continually being upset again by the competition between the workers themselves. But it ever rises up again, stronger, firmer, mightier. It compels legislative recognition of particular interests of the workers, by taking advantage of the divisions among the bourgeoisie itself. Thus the ten-hours' bill in England was carried.

Altogether collisions between the classes of the old society further, in many ways, the course of development of the proletariat. The bourgeoisie finds itself involved in a constant battle. At first with the aristocracy; later on, with those portions of the bourgeoisie itself, whose interests have become antagonistic to the progress of industry; at all times, with the bourgeoisie of foreign countries. In all these battles it sees itself compelled to appeal to the proletariat, to ask for its help, and thus, to drag it into the political arena. The bourgeoisie itself, therefore, supplies the proletariat with its own elements of political and general education, in other words, it furnishes the proletariat with weapons for fighting the bourgeoisie.

Further, as we have already seen, entire sections of the ruling classes are, by the advance of industry, precipitated into the proletariat, or are at least threatened in their conditions of existence. These also supply the proletariat with fresh elements of enlightenment and progress.

Finally, in times when the class struggle nears the decisive hour, the process of dissolution going on within the ruling class, in fact within the whole range of old society, assumes such a violent, glaring character, that a small section of the ruling class cuts itself adrift, and joins the revolutionary class, the class that holds the future in its hands. Just as, therefore, at an earlier period, a section of the nobility went over to the bourgeoisie, so now a portion of the bourgeoisie goes over to the proletariat, and in particular, a portion of the bourgeois ideologists, who have raised themselves to the level of comprehending theoretically the historical movement as a whole.

Of all the classes that stand face to face with the bourgeoisie today, the proletariat alone is a really revolutionary class. The other classes decay and finally disappear in the face of Modern Industry; the proletariat is its special and essential product.

The lower middle class, the small manufacturer, the shopkeeper, the artisan, the peasant, all these fight against the bourgeoisie, to save from extinction their existence as fractions of the middle class. They are therefore not revolutionary, but conservative. Nay more, they are reactionary, for they try to roll back the wheel of history. If by chance they are revolutionary, they are so only in view of their impending transfer into the proletariat, they thus defend not their present, but their future interests, they desert their own standpoint to place themselves at that of the proletariat.

The "dangerous class," the social scum, that passively rotting mass thrown off by the lowest layers of old society, may, here and there, be swept into the movement by a proletarian revolution, its conditions of life, however, prepare it far more for the part of a bribed tool of reactionary intrigue.

In the conditions of the proletariat, those of old society at large are already virtually swamped. The proletarian is without property; his relation to his wife and children has no longer anything in common with the bourgeois family-relations; modern industrial labour, modern subjection to capital, the same in England as in France, in America as in Germany, has stripped him of every trace of national character. Law, morality, religion, are to him so many bourgeois prejudices, behind which lurk in ambush just as many bourgeois interests.

All the preceding classes that got the upper hand, sought to fortify their already acquired status by subjecting society at large to their conditions of appropriation. The proletarians cannot become masters of the productive forces of society, except by abolishing their own previous mode of appropriation, and thereby also every other previous mode of appropriation. They have nothing of their own to secure and to fortify; their mission is to destroy all previous securities for, and insurances of, individual property.

All previous historical movements were movements of minorities, or in the interest of minorities. The proletarian movement is the self-conscious, independent movement of the immense majority, in the interests of the immense majority. The proletariat, the lowest stratum of our present society, cannot stir, cannot raise itself up, without the whole superincumbent strata of official society being sprung into the air.

Though not in substance, yet in form, the struggle of the proletariat with the bourgeoisie is at first a national struggle. The proletariat of each country must, of course, first of all settle matters with its own bourgeoisie.

In depicting the most general phases of the development of the proletariat, we traced the more or less veiled civil war, raging within existing society, up to the point where that war breaks out into open revolution, and where the violent overthrow of the bourgeoisie lays the foundation for the sway of the proletariat.

Hitherto, every form of society has been based, as we have already seen, on the antagonism of oppressing and oppressed classes. But in order to oppress a class, certain conditions must be assured to it under which it can, at least, continue its slavish existence. The serf, in the period of serfdom, raised himself to membership in the commune, just as the petty bourgeois, under the yoke of feudal absolutism, managed to develop into a bourgeois. The modern labourer, on the contrary, instead of rising with the progress of industry, sinks deeper and deeper below the conditions of existence of his own class. He becomes a pauper, and pauperism develops more rapidly than population and wealth. And here it becomes evident, that the bourgeoisie is unfit any longer to be the ruling class in society, and to impose its conditions of existence upon society as an over-riding law. It is unfit to rule because it is incompetent to assure an existence to its slave within his slavery, because it cannot help letting him sink into such a state, that it has to feed him, instead of being fed by him. Society can no longer live under this bourgeoisie, in other words, its existence is no longer compatible with society.

The essential condition for the existence, and for the sway of the bourgeois class, is the formation and augmentation of capital; the condition for capital is wage-labour. Wage-labour rests exclusively on competition between the labourers. The advance of industry, whose involuntary promoter is the bourgeoisie, replaces the isolation of the labourers, due to competition, by their revolutionary combination, due to association. The development of Modern Industry, therefore, cuts from under its feet the very foundation on which the bourgeoisie produces and appropriates products. What the bourgeoisie, therefore, produces, above all, is its own grave-diggers. Its fall and the victory of the proletariat are equally inevitable.

Social and Political Values

Implicit in the first selections, and continuing through much communist literature, is the moral stance that places it within the moralistic tradition of political philosophy. Both in its critiques and its positive suggestions, this tradition works in relation to moral values and ideals, attempting to judge and to propose for society ways in which to promote those values. To be sure, individual thinkers have their various and differing value systems as has been seen in some of the preceding selections, but Marx agrees with Plato, St. Thomas, Locke, and a host of others that moral criticism of society is an essential part of the philosopher's work.

This value system may be approached through its analysis of capitalism, and Marx criticizes capitalism as much on moral as on economic grounds. The key term in this criticism is *exploitation,* which is the appropriation by the bourgeoisie of the surplus value produced by workers. In turn, the notion of surplus value is related to the labor theory of value, which Marx accepts from such classical economists as Adam Smith (1723–1790) and David Ricardo (1772–1823). According to this theory, the value of any commodity is determined by the amount of labor put into it. This means, in effect, that workers create the values of things. Of course workers do not receive in wages what they have created in value: their wages are geared to a minimal level of subsistence. Over and above wages is surplus value, which the owners of the means of production (the bourgeoisie) appropriate as profit.

The result is that workers are exploited, for profit making takes away from workers something they create. Even worse, however, is the tendency, resulting from efforts to minimize costs and wages and to increase profits, to treat workers simply as means to profits. Workers must sell themselves, and the only relations between them and society—remembering that economic power is political power— are callous economic ones. Workers are slaves in the machinery of production. In effect, they are stripped of their humanity and, since the product of their labor is denied them and society is organized for the class interests of the bourgeoisie, workers experience greater alienation from themselves and society. There are no derived benefits of capitalism for the proletariat, for however organized the productive process, there is only anarchy in exchange. Goods and services are distributed according to money (which the proletariat does not have) rather than according to need.

Behind these judgments on capitalism are two chief values. The first is freedom, which, as Friedrich Engels (1820–1895) writes in the following selection, can be achieved when men come to understand social forces and then subject them to their own wills. The second is the principle of respect for personality, of the treatment of persons as ends rather than as means only. This principle can be realized only when three conditions have been met. Private property—that is, property in the form of means to profits—must be abolished. The means of production must become communal property, so that the anarchy of capitalism will be replaced with social regulation. With the abolition of private property will come, secondly, the abolition of class distinctions. Exploitation of class by class will be impossible, and men may finally become masters of their own social organization. Finally, the principle, "From each according to his ability, to each according to his needs," which is the summary statement of communist values, will be fulfilled and realized.

Marx and his followers thus propose a new society, classless and cooperative, which will be the embodiment of a new morality. Perhaps the moral principles as such are not new: indeed, Marx recognized them to be as old as the Judeo-Christian tradition. But their acceptance for social organization—their social realization—would be new; and this would mean nothing less than "the ascent of man from the kingdom of necessity to the kingdom of freedom."

FRIEDRICH ENGELS   Exploitation and Freedom

The idea that all men have something in common as men and that they are equal with respect to that common quality is naturally older than history. But the modern doctrine of equality is something quite different than that. This derives from the property of humanity, common to man, the equality of man, as man, or at least of all citizens of a given state or of all members of a given society. Until the conclusion of equality of rights in the state and society was deduced from the original notion of relative equality, and until this conclusion was to be stated as something natural and self evident, many thousands of years had to pass and indeed have passed. In the oldest and most elementary communities it may be said that equality of rights among the members existed in the highest degree, women, slaves, and foreigners, however, being

From Friedrich Engels, *Landmarks of Scientific Socialism: Anti-Dühring,* trans. Austin Lewis, Chicago: Charles H. Kerr and Co., 1907, and *Socialism: Utopian and Scientific,* trans. Edward Aveling, Chicago: Charles H. Kerr and Co., 1908.

excluded. Among the Greeks and Romans inequality existed to a greater degree. Greeks and barbarians, freemen and slaves, citizens and subjects, Roman citizens and Roman subjects (to employ a comprehensive expression) that these should have any claim to equality of political rights would have been regarded by the ancients necessarily as madness. Under the Roman Empire there was a complete elimination of all these distinctions with the exception of those of freemen and slaves. There arose therefore as far as the freemen were concerned that equality of private individuals upon which Roman law was founded and developed as the most perfect system of jurisprudence based on private property with which we are acquainted. But while the contradiction of freemen and slaves existed there could be no statement based upon the universal equality of man as such, as was recently shown in the slave states of the Northern American Union.

Christianity recognised one equality on the part of all men, that of an equal taint of original sin, which entirely corresponded with its character as a religion of slaves and the oppressed. In the next place it recognised completely the equality of the elect but it only declared this at the beginning of its teaching. The traces of common property in possessions which may be found occasionally in the earliest days of the religion was based rather upon the mutual assistance which persecuted people hold out to each other, than upon any real concepts of human equality. Very soon the establishment of the antithesis between the priesthood and the laity put an end to even this expression of Christian equality. The inundation of Western Europe by the Germans abolished for centuries all concepts of equality by the creation of a universal, social and political gradation of rank of a much more complicated nature than had existed up to that time. Contemporaneously with this Western and Middle Europe entered upon a historical development, shaped for the first time a compact civilisation, and a system which was on the one hand dynamic and on the other conservative, the leading national states. Thereupon a soil was prepared for the declaration of the equality of human rights so recently made.

The feudal middle ages moreover developed the class in its womb destined to be the apostle of the modern agitation for equality, the bourgeois class. In the beginning even under the feudal system the bourgeois class had developed the prevalent hand-industry and the exchange of products even within feudal society to a high degree considering the circumstances, until with the close of the fifteenth century the great discoveries of lands beyond the seas opened before it a new and individual course. The trade beyond Europe which up to that time had been carried on between the Italians and the Levant was now extended to America and the Indies and soon exceeded in amount the reciprocal trade of the European countries as well as the internal commerce of any particular land. American gold and silver flooded Europe and like a decomposing element penetrated all the fissures, crevices and pores of feudal society. The system of hand-labor was no longer sufficient for the growing demand, it was replaced by manufacture in the leading industries of the most highly developed peoples.

A corresponding change in the political structure followed this powerful revolution in the economic conditions of society but by no means immediately. The organisation of the State remained feudal in form while society became more and more bourgeois. Trade, particularly international, and to a greater degree world-commerce demanded for its development the free and unrestricted possessors of commodities, who have equality of right to exchange commodities at least in one and the same place. The transition from hand labor to manufacture presupposes the existence of a number of free laborers, free on the one hand from the fetters of the gild and on the other free to employ their labor force in their own behalf, who could make contracts for the hire of their labor force to the manufacturers and therefore face him as if endowed with equal rights as contracting parties. At last then there arose equality of rights and actual equality of all human labor, for labor force finds its unconscious but strongest expression in the law of value of modern bourgeois economy according to which the value of a commodity finds its measure in the socially necessary labor incorporated in it. But where the economic circumstances render freedom and equality of rights necessary, the political code, gild restrictions and peculiar privileges oppose them at every step. Local provisions of a legal character, differential taxation, exceptional laws of every description, interfere not only with foreigners or colonials but frequently enough also with whole categories of citizens in the nation itself. Gild privileges in particular constituted a continual impediment to the development of manufacture. The course was nowhere open and the chances of the bourgeois victory were by no means equal, but to make the course open was the first and ever more pressing necessity.

As soon as the demand for the abolition of feudalism and for the equality of rights was set on the order of the day it had necessarily to take an ever widening scope. As soon as the claim was made in behalf of commerce and industry it had also to be made in behalf of the peasants who, being in every stage of slavery from serfdom labored for the most part without any return for the feudal lords and were obliged in addition to perform innumerable services for them and for the State. Also it became desirable to abolish feudal privileges, the immunity of the nobility from taxation, and the superiority which attached to a certain status. And as men no longer lived in a world empire like the Roman, but in an independent system with states which approximated to a similar degree of bourgeois development and which had intercourse with one another on an equal footing, the demand took on necessarily a universal character reaching beyond the individual state, and freedom and equality were thus proclaimed as human rights. But as regards the special bourgeois character of these human rights, it is significant that the American Constitution which was the first to recognise these rights of man in the same breath established slavery among the colored people: class privileges were cursed, race privileges were blessed.

As is well known, the bourgeois class as soon as it escaped from the domination of the ruling class in the cities, by which process the medieval stage passes into the modern, has been steadily and inevitably dogged by a shadow, the proletariat. So also the bourgeois demands for equality are accompanied by the proletarian demands for equality. Directly the demand for the abolition of class privileges was made by the bourgeois there succeeded the proletarian demand for the abolition of classes themselves. This was first made in a religious form and was based upon early Christianity, but later derived its support from the bourgeois theories of equality. The proletarians take the bourgeois at their word, they demand the realisation of equality not merely apparently, not merely in the sphere of government but actually in the sphere of society and economics. Since the French bourgeoisie of the great Revolution placed equality in the foreground of their movement, the French proletariat has answered it blow for blow with the demand for social and economic equality, and equality has become the special battle cry of the French proletariat.

The demand for equality as made by the proletariat has a double significance. Either it is, as was particularly the case at first, in the Peasants' War, for example, a natural reaction against social inequalities which were obvious, against the contrast between rich and poor, masters and slaves, luxurious and hungry, and as such it is simply an expression of revolutionary instinct finding its justification in that fact and in that fact alone. On the other hand it may arise from reaction against the bourgeois claims of equality for which it deduces more or less just and far reaching claims, serves as a means of agitation to stir the workers, by means of a cry adopted by the capitalists themselves, against the capitalists, and in this case stands or falls with bourgeois equality itself. In both cases the real content of the proletarian claims of equality is the abolition of classes. Every demand for equality transcending this is of necessity absurd. We have already given examples and can furnish many more when we come to consider Herr Duehring's prophecies of the future.

So the notion of equality, in its proletarian as well as in its bourgeois form, is itself a historic product. Certain circumstances were required to produce it and these in their turn proceeded from a long anterior history. It is therefore anything but an eternal truth. And if the public regards it as self-evident in one sense or another if it, as Marx remarks "already occupies the position of a popular prejudice" it is not due to its being an axiomatic truth but to the universal broadening of conception in accordance with the spirit of the eighteenth century. . . .

Hegel was the first man to make a proper explanation of the relations of freedom and necessity. In his eyes freedom is the recognition of necessity. "Necessity is blind only in so far as it is not understood." Freedom does not consist in an imaginary independence of natural laws but in a knowledge of these laws and in the possibility thence derived of applying them intelligently to given ends. This is true both as regards the laws of nature and of those which control the spiritual and physical existence of man himself,—two classes of laws which we can distinguish as an abstraction but not in reality. Freedom of the will consists in nothing but the ability to come to a decision when one is in possession of a knowledge of the facts. The freer the judgment of a man then in relation to a given subject of discussion so much the more necessity is there for his arrival at a positive decision. On the other hand lack of certainty arising from ignorance which apparently chooses voluntarily between many different and contradictory possibilities of decision shows thereby its want of freedom, its control by things which it should in reality control. Freedom, therefore, consists in mastery over ourselves and external nature founded upon knowledge of the necessities of nature, it is, therefore, necessarily a product of historical development. The first human beings to become differentiated from the lower animals were in all essentials as devoid of freedom as these animals themselves but each step in human development was a step towards freedom. At the threshold of human history stands the discovery of the transformation of mechanical motion in heat, the generation of fire by friction; at the close of development up to the present stands the discovery of the transformation of heat into mechanical motion, the steam engine. In spite of the tremendous revolution in the direction of freedom which the steam engine has produced in society it is not yet half complete. There is no question that the production of fire by friction still surpasses it as an agent in the liberation of humanity. Because the production of fire by friction for the first time gave man power over the forces of nature and separated him for ever from the lower animals. The steam engine can never bridge so wide a chasm. It appears however as the representative of all those productive forces by the help of which alone a state of society is rendered possible in which no class subjection or pain will be produced by reason of the lack of means for the sustenance of the individual, in which moreover it will be possible to speak of real human freedom as arising from living in accordance with the recognised laws of nature. But considering the youth of humanity it would be absurd to wish to impute any universal absolute validity to our present philosophical views, and it follows from the mere facts that the whole of history up to the present time is to be regarded as the history of the period extending from the time of the practical discovery of the transformation of mechanical movement into heat to that of the transformation of heat into mechanical movement. . . .

The modern State, no matter what its form, is essentially a capitalist machine, the state of the capitalists, the ideal personification of the total national capital. The more it proceeds to the taking over of productive forces, the more does it actually become the national capitalist, the more citizens does it exploit. The workers remain wage-workers—proletarians. The capitalist relation is not done away with. It is rather brought to a head. But, brought to a head, it topples over. State-ownership of the productive forces is not the solution of the conflict, but concealed within it are the technical conditions that form the elements of that solution.

This solution can only consist in the practical recognition of the social nature of the modern forces of production, and therefore in the harmonizing the modes of production, appropriation, and exchange with the socialized character of the means of production. And this can only come about by society openly and directly taking possession of the productive forces which have outgrown all control except that of society as a whole. The social character of the means of production and of the products to-day reacts against the producers, periodically disrupts all production and exchange, acts only like a law of Nature working blindly, forcibly, destructively. But with the taking over by society of the productive forces, the social character of the means of production and of the products will be utilized by the producers with a perfect understanding of its nature, and instead of being a source of disturbance and periodical collapse, will become the most powerful lever of production itself.

Active social forces work exactly like natural forces; blindly, forcibly, destructively, so long as we do not understand, and reckon with, them. But when once we understand them, when once we grasp their action, their direction, their effects, it depends only upon ourselves to subject them more and more to our own will, and by means of them to reach our own ends. And this holds quite especially of the mighty productive forces of to-day. As long as we obstinately refuse to understand the nature and the character of these social means of action—and this understanding goes against the grain of the capitalist mode of production and its defenders—so long these forces are at work in spite of us, in opposition to us, so long they master us, as we have shown above in detail.

But when once their nature is understood, they can, in the hands of the producers working together, be transformed from master demons into willing servants. The difference is as that between the destructive force of electricity in the lightning of the storm, and electricity under command in the telegraph and the voltaic arc; the difference between a conflagration, and fire working in the service of man. With this recognition at last of the real nature of the productive forces of to-day, the social anarchy of production gives place to a social regulation of production upon a definite plan, according to the needs of the community and of each individual. Then the capitalist mode of appropriation, in which the product enslaves first the producer and then the appropriator, is replaced by the mode of appropriation of the products that is based upon the nature of the modern means of production; upon the one hand, direct social appropriation, as means to the maintenance and extension of production— on the other, direct individual appropriation, as means of subsistence and of enjoyment.

Whilst the capitalist mode of production more and more completely transforms the great majority of the population into proletarians, it creates the power which, under penalty of its own destruction, is forced to accomplish this revolution. Whilst it forces on more and more the transformation of the vast means of production, already socialized, into State property, it shows itself the way to accomplishing this revolution. *The proletariat seizes political power and turns the means of production into State property.*

But in doing this, it abolishes itself as proletariat, abolishes all class distinctions and class antagonisms, abolishes also the State as State. Society thus far, based upon class antagonisms, had need of the State. That is, of an organization of the particular class which was *pro tempore* the exploiting class, an organization for the purpose of preventing any interference from without with the existing conditions of production, and therefore, especially, for the purpose of forcibly keeping the exploited classes in the condition of oppression corresponding with the given mode of production (slavery, serfdom, wage-labor). The State was the official representative of society as a whole; the gathering of it together into a visible embodiment. But it was this only in so far as it was the State of that class which itself represented, for the time being, society as a whole; in ancient times, the State of slave-owning citizens; in the middle ages, the feudal lords; in our own time, the bourgeoisie. When at last it becomes the real representative of the whole of society, it renders itself unnecessary. As soon as there is no longer any social class to be held in subjection; as soon as class rule, and the individual struggle for existence based upon our present anarchy in production, with the collisions and excesses arising from these, are removed, nothing more remains to be repressed, and a special repressive force, a State, is no longer necessary. The first act by virtue of which the State really constitutes itself the representative of the whole of society—the taking possession of the means of production in the name of society—this is, at the same time, its last independent act as a State. State interference in social relations becomes, in one domain after another, superfluous, and then dies out of itself; the government of persons is replaced by the administration of things, and by the conduct of processes of production. The State is not "abolished." *It dies out*. This gives the measure of the value of the phrase "a free State," both as to its justifiable use at times by agitators, and as to its ultimate scientific insufficiency; and also of the demands of the so-called anarchists for the abolition of the State out of hand.

Since the historical appearance of the capitalist mode of production, the appropriation by society of all the means of production has often been dreamed of, more or less vaguely, by individuals, as well as by sects, as the ideal of the future. But it could become possible, could become a historical necessity, only when the actual conditions for its realization were there. Like every other social advance, it becomes practicable, not by men understanding that the existence of classes is in contradiction to justice, equality, etc., not by the mere willingness to abolish these classes, but by virtue of certain new economic conditions. The separation of society into an exploiting and an exploited class, a ruling and an oppressed class, was the necessary consequence of the deficient and restricted development of production in former times. So long as the total social labor only yields a produce which but slightly exceeds that barely necessary for the existence of all; so long, therefore, as labor engages all or almost all the time of the great majority of the members of society—so long, of necessity, this society is divided into classes. Side by side with the great majority, exclusively bond slaves to labor, arises a class freed from directly productive labor, which looks after the general affairs of society; the direction of labor, State business, law, science, art, etc. It is, therefore, the law of division of labor that lies at the basis of the division into classes. But this does not prevent this division into classes from being carried out by means of violence and robbery, trickery and fraud. It does not prevent the ruling class, once having the upper hand, from consolidating its power at the expense of the working-class, from turning their social leadership into an intensified exploitation of the masses.

But if, upon this showing, division into classes has a certain historical justification, it has this only for a given period, only under given social conditions. It was based upon the insufficiency of production. It will be swept away by the complete development of modern productive forces. And, in fact, the abolition of classes in society presupposes a degree of historical evolution, at which the existence, not simply of this or that particular ruling class, but of any ruling class at all, and, therefore, the existence of class distinction itself has become an obsolete anachronism. It presupposes, therefore, the development of production carried out to a degree at which appropriation of the means of production and of the products, and, with this, of political domination, of the monopoly of culture, and of intellectual leadership by a particular class of society, has become not only superfluous, but economically, politically, intellectually a hindrance to development.

This point is now reached. Their political and intellectual bankruptcy is scarcely any longer a secret to the bourgeoisie themselves. Their economic bankruptcy recurs regularly every ten years. In every crisis, society is suffocated beneath the weight of its own productive forces and products, which it cannot use, and stands helpless, face to face with the absurd contradiction that the producers have nothing to consume, because consumers are wanting. The expansive force of the means of production bursts the bonds that the capitalist mode of production had imposed upon them. Their deliverance from these bonds is the one precondition for an unbroken, constantly-accelerated development of the productive forces, and therewith for a practically unlimited increase of production itself. Nor is this all. The socialized appropriation of the means of production does away, not only with the present artificial restrictions upon production, but also with the positive waste and devastation of productive forces and products that are at the present time the inevitable concomitants of production, and that reach their height in the crises. Further, it sets free for the community at large a mass of means of production and of products, by doing away with the senseless extravagance of the ruling classes of to-day, and their political representatives. The possibility of securing for every member of society, by means of socialized production, an existence not only fully sufficient materially, and becoming day by day more full, but an existence guaranteeing to all the free development and exercise of their physical and mental faculties—this possibility is now for the first time here, but *it is here*.

With the seizing of the means of production by society, production of commodities is done away with, and, simultaneously, the mastery of the product over the producer. Anarchy in social production is replaced by systematic, definite organization. The struggle for individual existence disappears. Then for the first time, man, in a certain sense, is finally marked off from the rest of the animal kingdom, and emerges from mere animal conditions of existence into really human ones. The whole sphere of the conditions of life which environ man, and which have hitherto ruled man, now comes under the dominion and control of man, who for the first time becomes the real, conscious lord of Nature, because he has now become master of his own social organization. The laws of his own social action, hitherto standing face to face with man as laws of Nature foreign to, and dominating, him, will then be used with full understanding, and so mastered by him. Man's own social organization, hitherto confronting him as a necessity imposed by Nature and history, now becomes the result of his own free action. The extraneous objective forces that have hitherto governed history, pass under the control of man himself. Only from that time will man himself, more and more consciously, make his own history—only from that time will the social causes set in movement by him have, in the main and in a constantly growing measure, the results intended by him. It is the ascent of man from the kingdom of necessity to the kingdom of freedom.

State, Power, and Authority

The communist theory of the state, power, and authority may be developed under three headings: the analysis of the state as a historical product, the use of the state in the communist revolution, and the disappearance of the state in the classless society. The first of these is given in the selection by Engels. The state, Engels insists, is not an institution forced on society from the outside, nor is it in Hegelian fashion the ultimate realization of the ethical ideal. It is a product of historical evolution, where it arises at a certain stage in the dialectical development of society, and where it will—when conditions are right—eventually disappear.

What is the stage of the state? Primarily it is when society divides itself into classes (understood in the technical sense), so that men become divided in their activities and interests. As has been seen, communists believe that the existence of classes leads inevitably to class conflicts, with one class becoming dominant and the exploiter of other classes. There is tension and resistance between classes, and consequently there is also need for some coercive power to control and keep down class conflicts. Just how any particular state is organized depends on the way its society is organized, but all states have the same function, namely to keep social peace. Yet the peace is kept in a special way: economic power is political power, which means that the class having control of economic matters also controls the state. This means in turn that the state becomes the agent of the dominant class, securing its interests at the expense and sacrifice of the interests of other classes. In brief, the state is a coercive power serving the purposes of exploitation.

The state does not exist for all eternity: it will in time be taken over and used to bring about its own destruction. This is the second communist teaching, presented here in the selection from Lenin (1870–1924) on the dictatorship of the proletariat.* Given that the state is the organization of force in society maintaining the interests of exploiters, it follows that any revolutionary class bent on changing the social order must turn the power of the state to its own purposes. Force must be used to suppress the exploiters, and such use will be conducted by the proletariat. Interestingly, communism teaches that the revolutionary class is the oppressed: it is they rather than the oppressor who makes progress, for they are enlightened and disciplined by work. Establishing its own dictatorship for this purpose, the proletariat will crush the bourgeoisie and lead the masses to socialism.†

In nearly all communist literature is the third teaching on the state, namely its disappearance in the classless society. Summarizing his work in a letter written in 1852, Marx emphasized the transitional nature of the dictatorship of the proletariat:

---

* Lenin's role in the development of communist thought is given below in the section on "Political Obligation." Further reference, in a different context, is also given there to the doctrine of the dictatorship of the proletariat.

† Communism, it may be noted, is one type of socialism. It agrees with other socialist theories in such aims as the abolition of private property, but differs from them on the means of social change. Most other forms of socialism reject communist ideas of violent revolution and the dictatorship of the proletariat.

What I did that was new was to prove: (1) that the *existence of classes* is only bound up with *particular, historic phases in the development of production;* (2) that the class struggle necessarily leads to the *dictatorship of the proletariat;* (3) that this dictatorship itself only constitutes the transition to the *abolition of all classes* and to a *classless society.*

Having defined the state as organized force serving exploitation, Marx is led further to hold that in the classless society the state will disappear. There will be no class interests that political power must maintain, for private property—the property used for profit—will be eliminated. There will not be a need for force because there will no longer be alienation, which is the basic cause of crime and antisocial behavior. To be sure, Marx believed (with other socialists such as the Saint-Simonians) that there will still be the need for "administration," understood as business management and the arbitration of disputes. Since, however, men and society no longer are divided and antithetical (since society conforms to men's capacities), force is unnecessary for the acceptance of management and arbitration. The social good supports, indeed is, the individual good, which is another way of observing that the classless society is the realm of freedom.

FRIEDRICH ENGELS   The State as Coercive Power

In preceding chapters we have shown by three concrete examples the three main forms in which the state was built up on the ruins of gentilism. Athens represented the simplest, the classic type: the state grew directly and mainly out of class divisions that developed within gentile society. In Rome the gentile organization became an exclusive aristocracy amid a numerous plebs of outsiders who had only duties, but no rights. The victory of the plebs burst the old gentile order asunder and erected on its remains the state which soon engulfed both gentile aristocracy and plebs. Finally, among the German conquerors of the Roman empire, the state grew as a direct result of the conquest of large foreign territories which the gentile constitution was powerless to control. But this conquest did not necessitate either a serious fight with the former population or a more advanced division of labor. Conquerors and conquered were almost in the same stage of economic development, so that the economic basis of society remained undisturbed. Hence gentilism could preserve for many centuries an unchanged territorial character in the form of mark communes, and even rejuvenate itself in the nobility and patrician families of later years, or in the peasantry, as e.g. in Dithmarsia.

The state, then, is by no means a power forced on society from outside; neither is it the "realization of the ethical idea," "the image and the realization of reason," as Hegel maintains. It is simply a product of society at a certain stage of evolution. It is the confession that this society has become hopelessly divided against itself, has entangled itself in irreconcilable contradictions which it is powerless to banish. In order that these contradictions, these classes

From Friedrich Engels, *The Origin of the Family, Private Property and the State,* trans. Ernest Untermann, Chicago: Charles H. Kerr and Co., 1902.

with conflicting economic interests, may not annihilate themselves and society in a useless struggle, a power becomes necessarily that stands apparently above society and has the function of keeping down the conflicts and maintaining "order." And this power, the outgrowth of society, but assuming supremacy over it and becoming more and more divorced from it, is the state.

The state differs from gentilism in that it first divides its members by territories. As we have seen, the old bonds of blood kinship uniting the gentile bodies had become inefficient, because they were dependent on the condition, now no longer a fact, that all gentiles should live on a certain territory. The territory was the same; but the human beings had changed. Hence the division by territories was chosen as the point of departure, and citizens had to exercise their rights and duties wherever they chose their abode without regard to gens and tribe. This organization of inhabitants by localities is a common feature of all states. It seems natural to us now. But we have seen what long and hard fighting was required before it could take, in Athens and Rome, the place of the old organization by blood kinship.

In the second place, the state created a public power of coërcion that did no longer coincide with the old self-organized and armed population. This special power of coërcion is necessary, because a self-organized army of the people has become impossible since the division of society into classes took place. For the slaves belonged also to society. The 90,000 citizens of Athens formed only a privileged class compared to the 365,000 slaves. The popular army of the Athenian democracy was an aristocratic public power designed to keep the slaves down. But we have

seen that a police force became also necessary to maintain order among the citizens. This public power of coërcion exists in every state. It is not composed of armed men alone, but has also such objects as prisons and correction houses attached to it, that were unknown to gentilism. It may be very small, almost infinitesimal, in societies with feebly developed class antagonisms and in out of the way places, as was once the case in certain regions of the United States. But it increases in the same ratio in which the class antagonisms become more pronounced, and in which neighboring states become larger and more populous. A conspicuous example is modern Europe, where the class struggles and wars of conquest have nursed the public power to such a size that it threatens to swallow the whole society and the state itself.

In order to maintain this public power, contributions of the citizens become necessary—the taxes. These were absolutely unknown in gentile society. But today we get our full measure of them. As civilization makes further progress, these taxes are no longer sufficient to cover public expenses. The state makes drafts on the future, contracts loans, public debts. Old Europe can tell a story of them.

In possession of the public power and of the right of taxation, the officials in their capacity as state organs are now exalted above society. The free and voluntary respect that was accorded to the organs of gentilism does not satisfy them any more, even if they might have it. Representatives of a power that is divorced from society, they must enforce respect by exceptional laws that render them specially sacred and inviolable. The lowest police employee of the civilized state has more "authority" than all the organs of gentilism combined.

But the mightiest prince and the greatest statesman or general of civilization may look with envy on the spontaneous and undisputed esteem that was the privilege of the least gentile sachem. The one stands in the middle of society, the other is forced to assume a position outside and above it.

The state is the result of the desire to keep down class conflicts. But having arisen amid these conflicts, it is as a rule the state of the most powerful economic class that by force of its economic supremacy becomes also the ruling political class and thus acquires new means of subduing and exploiting the oppressed masses. The antique state was, therefore, the state of the slave owners for the purpose of holding the slaves in check. The feudal state was the organ of the nobility for the oppression of the serfs and dependent farmers. The modern representative state is the tool of the capitalist exploiters of wage labor. At certain periods it occurs exceptionally that the struggling classes balance each other so nearly that the public power gains a certain degree of independence by posing as the mediator between them. The absolute monarchy of the seventeenth and eighteenth century was in such a position, balancing the nobles and the burghers against one another. So was the Bonapartism of the first, and still more of the second, empire, playing the proletariat against the bourgeoisie and vice versa. The latest performance of this kind, in which ruler and ruled appear equally ridiculous, is the new German empire of Bismarkian make, in which capitalists and laborers are balanced against one another and equally cheated for the benefit of the degenerate Prussian cabbage junkers.

In most of the historical states, the rights of the citizens are differentiated according to their wealth. This is a direct confirmation of the fact that the state is organized for the protection of the possessing against the non-possessing classes. The Athenian and Roman classification by incomes shows this. It is also seen in the medieval state of feudalism in which the political power depended on the quantity of real estate. It is again seen in the electoral qualifications of the modern representative state. The political recognition of the differences in wealth is by no means essential. On the contrary, it marks a low stage of state development. The highest form of the state, the democratic republic, knows officially nothing of property distinctions. It is that form of the state which under modern conditions of society becomes more and more an unavoidable necessity. The last decisive struggle between proletariat and bourgeoisie can only be fought out under this state form. In such a state, wealth exerts its power indirectly, but all the more safely. This is done partly in the form of direct corruption of officials, after the classical type of the United States, or in the form of an alliance between government and bankers which is established all the more easily when the public debt increases and when corporations concentrate in their hands not only the means of transportation, but also production itself, using the stock exchange as a center. The United States and the latest French republic are striking examples, and good old Switzerland has contributed its share to illustrate this point. That a democratic republic is not necessary for this fraternal bond between stock exchange and government is proved by England and last, not least, Germany, where it is doubtful whether Bismarck or Bleichroeder was more favored by the introduction of universal suffrage. The possessing class rules directly through universal suffrage. For as long as the oppressed class, in this case the proletariat, is not ripe for its economic emancipation, just so long will its majority regard the existing order of society as the only one possible, and form the tail, the extreme left wing, of the capitalist class. But the more the proletariat matures toward its self-emancipation, the more does it constitute itself as a separate class and elect its own representatives in place of the capitalists. Universal suffrage is the gauge of the maturity of the working class. It can and will never be anything else but that in the modern state. But that is sufficient. On the day when the thermometer of universal suffrage reaches its boiling point among the laborers, they as well as the capitalists will know what to do.

The state, then, did not exist from all eternity. There have been societies without it, that had no idea of any state or public power. At a certain stage of economic development, which was of necessity accompanied by a division of society into classes, the state became the inevitable result of this division. We are now rapidly approaching a stage of evolution in production, in which the existence of classes has not only ceased to be a necessity, but becomes a positive fetter on production. Hence these classes must fall as inevitably as they once arose. The state must irrevocably fall with them. The society that is to reorganize production on the basis of a free and equal association of the producers, will transfer the machinery of state where it will then belong: into the Museum of Antiquities by the side of the spinning wheel and the bronze ax.

VLADIMIR I. LENIN   Dictatorship of the Proletariat

In the first place, according to Marx, the proletariat needs only a state which is withering away, *i.e.,* a state so constituted that it begins to wither away immediately, and cannot but wither away. Secondly, the toilers need a "state," *i.e.,* "the proletariat organised as the ruling class."

The state is a special organisation of force; it is the organisation of violence for the suppression of some class. What class must the proletariat suppress? Naturally, only the exploiting class, *i.e.,* the bourgeoisie. The toilers need a state only to overcome the resistance of the exploiters, and only the proletariat can direct this suppression, carry it out; for the proletariat is the only class that is consistently revolutionary, the only class that can unite all the toilers and the exploited in the struggle against the bourgeoisie, in completely displacing it.

The exploiting classes need political rule in order to maintain exploitation, *i.e.,* in the selfish interests of an insignificant minority and against the interests of the vast majority of the people. The exploited classes need political rule in order completely to abolish all exploitation, *i.e.,* in the interests of the vast majority of the people, and against the interests of the insignificant minority consisting of the modern slave-owners— the landlords and the capitalists.

The petty-bourgeois democrats, those alleged Socialists who substituted

From V. I. Lenin, *The State and Revolution: The Marxist Doctrine of the State and the Tasks of the Proletariat in the Revolution,* New York: International Publishers, n.d. Used by permission of International Publishers Co., Inc.

dreams of class harmony for the class struggle, even pictured the socialist reformation in a dreamy fashion—not in the form of the overthrow of the rule of the exploiting class, but in the form of the peaceful submission of the minority to the majority which has become conscious of its aims. This petty-bourgeois utopia, which is inseparably bound up with the idea of the state being above classes, led in practice to the betrayal of the interests of the toiling classes, as was shown, for example, by the history of the French revolutions of 1848 and 1871, and by the "Socialists" joining bourgeois cabinets in England, France, Italy and other countries at the end of the nineteenth and the beginning of the twentieth centuries.

Marx fought all his life against this petty-bourgeois socialism—now resurrected in Russia by the Socialist-Revolutionary and Menshevik Parties. He logically pursued his doctrine of the class struggle to the doctrine of political power, the doctrine of the state.

The overthrow of bourgeois rule can be accomplished only by the proletariat, as the particular class whose economic conditions of existence train it for this task and provide it with the opportunity and the power to perform it. While the bourgeoisie breaks up and disintegrates the peasantry and all the petty-bourgeois strata, it welds together, unites and organises the proletariat. Only the proletariat—by virtue of the economic role it plays in large-scale production—is capable of acting as the leader of *all* the toiling and exploited masses, whom the bourgeoisie exploits, oppresses and crushes not less, and often more, than it does the proletarians, but who are incapable of waging an *independent* struggle for their emancipation.

The doctrine of the class struggle, as applied by Marx to the question of the state and of the socialist revolution, leads inevitably to the recognition of the *political rule* of the proletariat, of its dictatorship, *i.e.,* of power shared with none and relying directly upon the armed force of the masses. The overthrow of the bourgeoisie can be achieved only by the proletariat becoming transformed into the *ruling class,* capable of crushing the inevitable and desperate resistance of the bourgeoisie, and of organising *all* the toiling and exploited masses for the new economic order.

The proletariat needs state power, the centralised organisation of force, the organisation of violence, for the purpose of crushing the resistance of the exploiters and for the purpose of *leading* the great mass of the population—the peasantry, the petty bourgeoisie, the semi-proletarians—in the work of organising socialist economy.

By educating the workers' party, Marxism educates the vanguard of the proletariat which is capable of assuming power and of *leading the whole people* to socialism, of directing and organising the new order, of being the teacher, guide and leader of all the toiling and exploited in the task of building up their social life without the bourgeoisie and against the bourgeoisie. As against this, the now prevailing opportunism breeds in the ranks of the workers' party representatives of the better paid workers, who lose touch with the rank and file, "get along" fairly well under capitalism, and sell their birthright for a mess of pottage, *i.e.,* renounce their role of revolutionary leaders of the people against the bourgeoisie.

Marx's theory: "The state, *i.e.,* the proletariat organised as the ruling class," is inseparably bound up with all he taught on the revolutionary role of the proletariat in history. The culmination of this role is the proletarian dictatorship, the political rule of the proletariat. . . . The essence of Marx's doctrine of the state is assimilated only by those who understand that the dictatorship of a *single* class is necessary not only for class society in general, not only for the *proletariat* which has overthrown the bourgeoisie, but for the entire *historical period* between capitalism and "classless society," communism. The forms of the bourgeois state are extremely varied, but in essence they are all the same: in one way or another, in the last analysis, all these states are inevitably the *dictatorship of the bourgeoisie.* The transition from capitalism to communism will certainly create a great variety and abundance of political forms, but in essence there will inevitably be only one: *the dictatorship of the proletariat.*

Law and Rights

Two ideas—both of which have been met in preceding selections—are basic for understanding the communist approach to law. The first is economic determinism, which teaches that the level of economic development is decisive for the form of any society and its culture. "The sum total of these relations of production," says Marx, "constitutes the economic structure of society—the real foundation, on which rise legal and political superstructures and to which correspond definite forms of social consciousness." Thus belonging to the "superstructure," law, with morality, manners, and religion, is never higher than the economic substructure of society; it is always effect, Marx says in the first selection below, and never cause.

The second idea is that the whole conception of law is linked with the state. This is true both of private law which aims at individual security and of public law which controls utility. In all forms, law is analyzed exclusively as a means of control serving class interests. More precisely, property relations (to which law is ultimately reduced) are the legal expression of relations of production, and the function of law is to maintain that class structure of society which enables some classes to exploit others.* But this idea must be pursued with reference to the theory of economic and historical development, for as the state is destined to wither away, so too is law. During the dictatorship of the proletariat, there is need for a "revolutionary legality," which is the coercive power to suppress opponents. Then will follow a development when, as Marx says, the narrow horizon of bourgeois law will be fully crossed and when the principle, "From each according to his ability, to each according to his needs," will be a social reality. At this point, the ideal is really one of the identity of law and moral consciousness such that there will be no need for the sanctions of law.

---

* As Engels puts it, if the state reflects economic conditions, so does the law. This dependence is often forgotten, however, so that the superstructure is pursued for its own sake. The result is professionalism and formalism in legal practice.

In general, it must be said that these statements about law are largely passive, for little basis is provided by them for the construction of an affirmative philosophy of law. Later communists have however recognized this, with the result that there has been a development in law beyond the views found in classic sources. Engels himself came to admit that he and Marx had overstated the extent to which economic causes could be found for political and legal institutions. This seems to be an admission that, to some extent at least, law is an independent domain with principles of its own. Also, with the recognition of the need for administrative procedures in a socialist society, further modification of Marx's views becomes necessary. Later communist philosophers have therefore addressed themselves to this need to create a legal norm fully adequate to all the trends of social development.

KARL MARX Right and Inequality

One man is superior to another physically or mentally and so supplies more labour in the same time, or can labour for a longer time; and labour, to serve as a measure, must be defined by its duration or intensity, otherwise it ceases to be a standard of measurement. This *equal* right is an unequal right for unequal labour. It recognizes no class differences, because everyone is only a worker like everyone else; but it tacitly recognizes unequal individual endowment and thus productive capacity as natural privileges. *It is, therefore, a right of inequality, in its content, like every right.* Right by its very nature can consist only in the application of an equal standard; but unequal individuals (and they would not be different individuals if they were not unequal) are measureable only by an equal standard in so far as they are brought under an equal point of view, are taken from one *definite* side only, for instance, in the present case, are regarded *only as workers* and nothing more is seen in them, everything else being ignored.

Further, one worker is married, another not; one has more children than another, and so on and so forth. Thus, with an equal performance of labour, and hence an equal share in the social consumption fund, one will in fact receive more than another, one will be richer than another, and so on. To avoid all these defects, right instead of being equal would have to be unequal.

But these defects are inevitable in the first phase of communist society as it is when it has just emerged after prolonged birth pangs from capitalist society. Right can never be higher than the economic structure of society and its cultural development conditioned thereby.

In a higher phase of communist society, after the enslaving subordination of the individual to the division of labour, and therewith also the antithesis between mental and physical labour, has vanished; after labour has become not only a means of life but life's prime want; after the productive forces have

From Karl Marx, "Critique of the Gotha Programme," in *Selected Works,* Moscow: Foreign Languages Publishing House, 1958. Used by permission of Progress Publishers, Moscow.

also increased with the all-round development of the individual, and all the springs of co-operative wealth flow more abundantly—only then can the narrow horizon of bourgeois right be crossed in its entirety and society inscribe on its banners: From each according to his ability, to each according to his needs!

FRIEDRICH ENGELS Law and Economic Conditions

In modern history, at least, it is therefore proved that all political contests are class contests and that all fights of classes for emancipation, in spite of their necessarily political form (for every class struggle is a political struggle), finally, are directed towards economic emancipation. Here, at least, therefore, the State, the political arrangement is the subordinate, bourgeois society, the rule of economic relations, the deciding element. The old fashioned philosophy which even Hegel respected saw in the State the determining element and in bourgeois society the element determined by it. Appearances corresponded with this idea. As all the impulses of each single agent pass through his individual brain and must transform themselves into motives of his will in order to set him to work, so must also the desires of bourgeois society, no matter which class happens to be dominant, penetrate the will of the state in order to secure universal validity in the form of laws. That is the formal side of the matter which is self evident, the question only is what content has this merely formal will—of the individual as well as of the State—and whence comes this content—why is just this desired and nothing else? And if we enquire into this we discover that in modern history the will of the State, as

a whole, is declared through the changing needs of bourgeois society, through the domination of this or that class, in the last instance through the development of the forces of production and the conditions of exchange.

But if in our modern times, with their gigantic methods of production and commerce, the State is not an independent affair with an independent development, but its existence as well as its evolution is to be explained in the last resort from the economic conditions of the life of society, so much the more must the same thing be true of all earlier times when the production of the necessities of existence was not furthered by these extensive aids, where, therefore, the necessities of this production must exercise a greater control over men. If the State is today, at the time of the great industries and steam railways, merely, as a whole, the summarized, reflected form of the economic desires of the class which controls production, it must, therefore, have been still more so at a period when a generation of men must spend the greater portion of their united life-time in the satisfaction of their material needs, and man was, therefore, much more dependent on them than we are today. The examination of the earlier epochs of history, as far as it is earnestly con-

From Friedrich Engels, *Feuerbach: The Roots of the Socialist Philosophy,* trans. Austin Lewis, Chicago: Charles H. Kerr and Co., 1903, and "Letter to C. Schmidt, October 27, 1890," in *Selected Works,* Moscow: Foreign Languages Publishing House, 1958. The latter is used by permission of Progress Publishers, Moscow.

ducted in this direction, establishes this abundantly, but manifestly this cannot here be taken in hand.

If the State and public law are the creatures of economic conditions, so, obviously, is private law, which only sanctions relations between individuals under given normal economic circumstances. The form in which this appears may, however, vary considerably. One can, as happened in England in accordance with the whole national development, retain, for the most part, the forms of the old feudal law, and give them a middle-class content, even read a middle-class meaning into the feudal names, but one may also, as in the western part of the European continent, use as a foundation the first general law of a society producing commodities, the Roman, with its unsurpassably keen elaboration, of all the legal relations of possessions of commodities (sellers and buyers, creditors and debtors, obligations, etc.), by which we can bring it down as common-law to the use and benefit of a still small bourgeois and half feudal society; or, with the help of pseudo-enlightened and moralizing jurists, a code (which is bad from a legal point of view) can be worked out suitable to the conditions of the particular society (as the Prussian land law). And, still again, after a great bourgeois revolution, a classical code for bourgeois society, such as the French "Code Civil," may be worked out. If, therefore, the bourgeois laws only declare the economic circumstances of society, these may be good or bad according to conditions.

In the State appears the first ideological force over men. Society shapes for itself an organ for the protection of its general interests against attack from the outside or inside. This organ is the force of the State. Hardly did it come into being before this organ dominated society, and as a matter of fact, in proportion as it becomes the organ of a particular class, it brings into existence the supremacy of that class. The fight of the subject against the dominant class becomes of necessity political, a fight in the next place against the political control of this latter class. This consciousness of the connection of the political fight with its underlying economic causes becomes more and more obscure and may be altogether lost. Where this is not altogether the case with the combatants it becomes nearly altogether so with the historians. Of the ancient sources of history with regard to the contest within the Roman Republic, Appian alone gives us plain and clear information respecting its final cause, which was property in land. But the State, once become an independent power over society, forthwith displayed a further ideology. Among the practical politicians and the theorists in jurisprudence, and among the jurists in particular, this fact is first completely lost sight of. Since in each single instance the economic facts must take the form of juristic motives so as to be sanctioned in the form of law, and since, therefore, a backward view must be taken over the whole existing system of law, it follows therefrom that the juristic form appears to be the whole and the economic content nothing at all. Public and private law are considered as independent realms which have their own independent historic evolution, which are considered capable of a systematic representation, and stand in need of it through persistent elimination of all inner contradictions. . . .

The reaction of the state power upon economic development can be one of three kinds: it can run in the same direction, and then development is more rapid; it can oppose the line of development, in which case nowadays state power in every great people will go to pieces in the long run; or it can cut off the economic development from certain paths, and prescribe certain others. This case ultimately reduces itself to one of the two previous ones. But it is obvious that in cases two and three the political power can do great damage to the economic development and result in the squandering of great masses of energy and material.

Then there is also the case of the conquest and brutal destruction of economic resources, by which, in certain circumstances, a whole local or national economic development could formerly be ruined. Nowadays such a case usually has the opposite effect, at least among great peoples: in the long run the vanquished often gains more economically, politically and morally than the victor.

Similarly with law. As soon as the new division of labor which creates professional lawyers becomes necessary, another new and independent sphere is opened up which, for all its general dependence on production and trade, still has also a special capacity for reacting upon these spheres. In a modern state, law must not only correspond to the general economic condition and be its expression, but must also be an *internally coherent* expression which does not, owing to inner contradictions, reduce itself to nought. And in order to achieve this, the faithful reflection of economic conditions suffers increasingly. All the more so the more rarely it happens that a code of law is the blunt, unmitigated, unadulterated expression of the domination of a class—

this in itself would offend the "conception of right." Even in the *Code Napoléon* the pure, consistent conception of right held by the revolutionary bourgeoisie of 1792–96 is already adulterated in many ways, and, in so far as it is embodied there, has daily to undergo all sorts of attenuations owing to the rising power of the proletariat. Which does not prevent the *Code Napoléon* from being the statute book which serves as a basis for every new code of law in every part of the world. Thus to a great extent the course of the "development of right" only consists, first, in the attempt to do away with the contradictions arising from the direct translation of economic relations into legal principles, and to establish a harmonious system of law, and then in the repeated breaches made in this system by the influence and pressure of further economic development, which involves it in further contradictions. (I am speaking here only of civil law for the moment.)

The reflection of economic relations as legal principles is necessarily also a topsy-turvy one: it goes on without the person who is acting being conscious of it; the jurist imagines he is operating with *a priori* propositions, whereas they are really only economic reflexes; so everything is upside down. And it seems to me obvious that this inversion, which, so long as it remains unrecognized, forms what we call *ideological conception,* reacts in its turn upon the economic basis and may, within certain limits, modify it. The basis of the law of inheritance—assuming that the stages reached in the development of the family are equal—is an economic one. Nevertheless, it would be difficult to prove, for instance, that the absolute liberty of the testator in England and the severe restrictions imposed upon him in France are only due in every detail to economic causes. Both react back, however, on the economic sphere to a very considerable extent, because they influence the distribution of property.

Political Obligation

Why is a citizen obliged to obey the state or society of which he is a member? For the communist, this question is in the end meaningless—or at least unnecessary. The reason is that a society conformable to man's nature, a society that has overcome alienation and exploitation, will be willingly obeyed. No chasm would exist between individual and society, and social life would be seen by individuals as the fulfillment, or condition of the fulfillment, of their own inner being. But this, of course, is the communist ideal. In capitalist societies, the situation is very different: citizens, especially proletarians, obey out of force and fear, not out of a sense of moral duty. The important element in the problem of political obligation is not, therefore, some theoretical answer, but rather the development of a practical program by which the ideal may be attained. The writings of Lenin provide some of the details of that program.

Supple leader of the October Revolution, Lenin adopted Marx's teaching to the Russian situation, yet at the same time he always appeared "orthodox." The clue to his revision of Marx is his theory of the party and of party organization. Such is needed, Lenin taught, if a social class is to act as a group, and especially if a class is to be revolutionary. The development of class consciousness, which occurs when a class learns what its interests are, is primarily the result of party activity. Lenin also sought to bring the "dictatorship of the proletariat" in its Russian form into communist theory. In making communism even more explicitly a theory of social revolution, he accepted the idea that the "new state" produced by the revolution is itself an instrument of power. In effect, therefore, he came to understand the dictatorship of the proletariat as the dictatorship of the party, emphasizing therewith the notion of a conspiratorial underground movement and giving Russian communism its political character.

These ideas received expression in Lenin's first theoretical work, *What Is to Be Done?*, from which the selection is taken. In it, Lenin insists that the masses must be trained for their revolutionary activity by complete political exposure. The political consciousness they achieve by this exposure comes from without rather than from within, and its source is a disciplined party organization that is the "vanguard of the revolutionary forces in our time." For Lenin communism is a dogma eliciting loyalty and serving as a scientific guide to action. When the work of the party is completed and the classless society achieved, the problem of political obligation will be resolved.

VLADIMIR I. LENIN   Political Consciousness

One of the fundamental conditions for the necessary expansion of political agitation is the organisation of *all-sided* political exposure. In *no other way* can the masses be trained in political consciousness and revolutionary activity except by means of such exposures. Hence, to conduct such activity is one of the most important functions of international Social-Democracy as a whole, for even the existence of political liberty does not remove the necessity for such exposures; it merely changes the sphere against which they are directed. For example, the German Party is strengthening its position and spreading its influence, thanks particularly to the untiring energy with which it is conducting a campaign of political exposure. Working class consciousness cannot be genuinely political consciousness unless the workers are trained to respond to *all cases* of tyranny, oppression, violence and abuse, no matter *what class* is affected. Moreover, that response must be a Social-Democratic response, and not one from any other point of view. The consciousness of the masses of the workers cannot be genuine class consciousness, unless the workers learn to observe from concrete, and above all from topical, political facts and events, *every* other social class and *all* the manifestations of the intellectual, ethical and political life of these classes; unless they learn to apply practically the materialist analysis and the materialist estimate of *all* aspects of the life and activity of *all* classes, strata and groups of the population. Those who concentrate the at-

tention, observation and the consciousness of the working class exclusively, or even mainly, upon itself alone are not Social-Democrats; because, for its self-realisation the working class must not only have a theoretical . . . rather it would be more true to say . . . not so much a theoretical as a practical understanding, acquired through experience of political life, of the relationships between *all* the various classes of modern society. That is why the idea preached by our Economists, that the economic struggle is the most widely applicable means of drawing the masses into the political movement, is so extremely harmful and extremely reactionary in practice. In order to become a Social-Democrat, a workingman must have a clear picture in his mind of the economic nature and the social and political features of the landlord, of the priest, of the high state official and of the peasant, of the student and of the tramp; he must know their strong and weak sides; he must understand all the catchwords and sophisms by which each class and each stratum *camouflages* its selfish strivings and its real "nature"; he must understand what interests certain institutions and certain laws reflect and how they reflect them. This "clear picture" cannot be obtained from books. It can be obtained only from living examples and from exposures, following hot after their occurrence, of what goes on around us at a given moment, of what is being discussed, in whispers perhaps, by each one in his own way, of the meaning of such and such events, of such and such

From V. I. Lenin, "What Is to Be Done? Burning Questions of Our Movement," in *Selected Works,* New York: International Publishers, n.d. Used by permission of International Publishers Co., Inc.

statistics, of such and such court sentences, etc., etc., etc. These universal political exposures are an essential and *fundamental* condition for training the masses in revolutionary activity. . . .

Class political consciousness can be brought to the workers *only from without,* that is, only outside of the economic struggle, outside of the sphere of relations between workers and employers. The sphere from which alone it is possible to obtain this knowledge is the sphere of relationships between *all* the various classes and strata and the state and the government—the sphere of the interrelations between *all* the various classes. For that reason, the reply to the question: what must be done in order to bring political knowledge to the workers? cannot be merely the one which, in the majority of cases, the practical workers, especially those who are inclined towards Economism, usually content themselves with, *i.e.,* "go among the workers." To bring political knowledge to the *workers* the Social-Democrats must *go among all classes of the population,* must despatch units of their army *in all directions.*

We deliberately select this awkward formula, we deliberately express ourselves in a simple, forcible way, not because we desire to indulge in paradoxes, but in order to "stimulate" the Economists to take up their tasks which they unpardonably ignore, to make them understand the difference between trade union and Social-Democratic politics, which they refuse to understand. Therefore, we beg the reader not to get excited, but to listen patiently to the end.

Take the type of Social-Democratic circle that has been most widespread during the past few years, and examine its work. It has "contacts with the workers," it issues leaflets—in which abuses in the factories, the government's par-

tiality towards the capitalists and the tyranny of the police are strongly condemned—and it rests content with this. At meetings of workers the discussions never, or rarely, go beyond the limits of these subjects. Lectures and discussions on the history of the revolutionary movement, on questions of the home and foreign policy of our government, on questions of the economic evolution of Russia and of Europe, and the position of the various classes in modern society, etc., are extremely rare. Of systematically acquiring and extending contact with other classes or society, no one even dreams. The ideal leader, as the majority of the members of such circles picture him, is something more in the nature of a trade union secretary than a Socialist political leader. Any trade union secretary, an English one for instance, helps the workers to conduct the economic struggle, helps to expose factory abuses, explains the injustice of the laws and of measures which hamper the freedom to strike and the freedom to picket (*i.e.,* to warn all and sundry that a strike is proceeding at a certain factory), explains the partiality of arbitration court judges who belong to the bourgeois classes, etc., etc. In a word, every trade union secretary conducts and helps to conduct "the economic struggle against the employers and the government." It cannot be too strongly insisted that *this is not* enough to constitute Social-Democracy. The Social-Democrat's ideal should not be a trade union secretary, but *a tribune of the people,* able to react to every manifestation of tyranny and oppression, no matter where it takes place, no matter what stratum or class of the people it affects; he must be able to group all these manifestations into a single picture of police violence and capitalist exploitation; he must be able to take advantage of every petty event in order to explain his socialistic convictions and his Social-Democratic demands *to all,* in order to explain to *all* and everyone the world-historic significance of the struggle for the emancipation of the proletariat. . . .

Is there scope for activity among all classes of the population? Those who fail to see this also lag behind the spontaneous awakening of the masses as far as class consciousness is concerned. The labour movement has aroused and is continuing to arouse discontent in some, hopes for support for the opposition in others, and the consciousness of the intolerableness and inevitable downfall of autocracy in still others. We would be "politicians" and Social-Democrats only in name (as very often happens), if we failed to realise that our task is to utilise every manifestation of discontent, and to collect and utilise every grain of even rudimentary protest. This is quite apart from the fact that many millions of the peasantry, handicraftsmen, petty artisans, etc., always listen eagerly to the preachings of any Social-Democrat who is at all intelligent. Is there a single class of the population in which no individuals, groups or circles are to be found who are discontented with the state of tyranny and, therefore, accessible to the propaganda of Social-Democrats as the spokesmen of the most pressing general democratic needs? To those who desire to have a clear idea of what the political agitation of a Social-Democrat *among all* classes and strata of the population should be like, we would point to *political exposures* in the broad sense of the word as the principal (but of course not the sole) form of this agitation.

We must "arouse in every section of the population that is at all enlight-ened a passion for *political* exposure," I wrote in my article "Where to Begin?" (*Iskra,* No. 4, May 1901), with which I shall deal in greater detail later.

We must not allow ourselves to be discouraged by the fact that the voice of political exposure is still feeble, rare and timid. This is not because of a general submission to political despotism, but because those who are able and ready to expose have no tribune from which to speak, because there is no audience to listen eagerly to and approve of what the orators say, and because the latter do not see anywhere among the people forces to whom it would be worth while directing their complaint against the "omnipotent" Russian government. . . . We are now in a position, and it is our duty, to set up a tribune for the national exposure of the tsarist government. That tribune must be a Social-Democratic paper.

The ideal audience for these political exposures is the working class, which is first and foremost in need of universal and live political knowledge, which is most capable of converting this knowledge into active struggle, even if it does not promise "palpable results." The only platform from which *public* exposures can be made is an all-Russian newspaper. "Without a political organ, a political movement deserving that name is inconceivable in modern Europe." In this connection Russia must undoubtedly be included in modern Europe. The press has long ago become a power in our country, otherwise the government would not spend tens of thousands of rubles to bribe it, and to subsidise the Katkovs and Meshcherskys. And it is no novelty in autocratic Russia for the underground press to break through the wall of censorship and *compel* the legal and conservative press to speak openly of it. This was the case in the 'seventies and even in the 'fifties. How much broader and deeper are now the strata of the people willing to read the illegal underground press, and to learn from it "how to live and how to die," to use the expression of the worker who sent a letter to *Iskra*. (No. 7.) Political exposures are as much a declaration of war against the *government* as economic exposures are a declaration of war against the employers. And the wider and more powerful this campaign of exposure is, the more numerous and determined the social *class,* which has *declared war in order to commence the war,* will be, the greater will be the moral significance of this declaration of war. Hence, political exposures in themselves serve as a powerful instrument for *disintegrating* the system we oppose, the means for diverting from the enemy his casual or temporary allies, the means for spreading enmity and distrust among those who permanently share power with the autocracy.

Only a party that will *organise* real, *public* exposures can become the vanguard of the revolutionary forces in our time. The word "public" has a very profound meaning. The overwhelming majority of the non-working class exposers (and in order to become the vanguard, we must attract other classes) are sober politicians and cool businessmen. They know perfectly well how dangerous it is to "complain" even against a minor official, let alone against the "omnipotent" Russian government. And they will come *to us* with their complaints only when they see that these complaints really have effect, and when they see that we represent a *political* force. In order to become this political force in the eyes of outsiders, much persistent and stubborn work is required to *raise* our own consciousness, initiative and energy. For this, is it not sufficient to stick the label "vanguard" on rearguard theory and practice.

But if we have to undertake the organisation of the real, public exposure of the government, in what way will the class character of our movement be expressed?—the over-zealous advocates of "close organic contact with the proletarian struggle" will ask us. The reply is: in that we *Social-Democrats* will *organise* these public exposures; in that all the questions that are brought up by the agitation will be explained in the spirit of Social-Democracy, without any concessions to deliberate or unconscious distortions of Marxism: in the fact that *the Party* will carry on this universal political agitation, uniting into one inseparable whole the pressure upon the government in the name of the whole people, the revolutionary training of the proletariat—while preserving its political independence—the guidance of the economic struggle of the working class, the utilisation of all its spontaneous conflicts with its exploiters, which rouse and bring into our camp increasing numbers of the proletariat.

The Ideal of Justice

In general, ideals of justice are derived from political theories, and this is true of communism too. At the center of the theoretical apparatus of the position is a call to social justice: communism demands as well as rests on an ideal of justice that would eliminate the causes of social inequality by abolishing private ownership of the means of production. Whether discussing dialectical materialism, exploitation, classes, or alienation, Marx and his important followers were moved by the conviction that injustice can be overcome, and that, with the proper understanding of himself and society, man can establish a society that will make injustice impossible.

The moral principle supporting this ideal of justice has been met before: "From each according to his abilities, to each according to his needs." In turn, this principle reflects an even more fundamental ethical assumption, namely respect for personality. Marx was convinced, on the one hand, that capitalist society violates this principle. His attacks on the effects of capitalism—its resolving of personal worth into exchange value—are a documentation of this. On the other hand, he sought to formulate a social vision and the means to realize it that would maintain the conditions for the exercise of personal rights. His conception of justice may thus be said to be a social expression of the ethical principle of respect for personality.

Marx believed that history is inevitably moving toward this ideal. No other outcome of the class struggle is possible. And yet he also was an activist who believed that men must strive and work to achieve justice. Communism is thus a call to action, guided, communists believe, by accurate, scientific knowledge of the laws of historical evolution. The following selection from the Communist International Program (September 1, 1928) conveys both the theoretical and practical aspects of communism. The movement of history is toward world communism, which will eliminate exploitation through the abolition of private property. The means to this goal is the dictatorship of the proletariat, which will use power not as an end in itself but to overcome class divisions altogether. The outcome of this period of social reorganization will lead to the achievement of true (rather than bourgeois) justice, and will secure individual rights fully consistent with the dignity of the human person. In this realm of freedom with its release of human powers, culture will flourish, and an "all-conquering scientific knowledge" will guide men to their true destiny.

COMMUNIST   "To Each According
INTERNATIONAL PROGRAM   to His Needs"

THE ULTIMATE AIM OF THE COMMUNIST INTERNATIONAL— WORLD COMMUNISM

The ultimate aim of the Communist International is to replace world capitalist economy by a world system of Communism. Communist society, the basis for which has been prepared by the whole course of historical development, is mankind's only way out, for it alone can abolish the contradictions of the capitalist system which threaten to degrade and destroy the human race.

Communist society will abolish the

From the Communist International Program (6th World Congress of the Comintern), in *The Strategy and Tactics of World Communism,* House Document No. 619, 80th Congress, 2d Session, Washington: United States Government Printing Office, 1948.

class division of society, i.e., simultaneously with the abolition of anarchy in production, it will abolish all forces of exploitation and oppression of man by man. Society will no longer consist of antagonistic classes in conflict with each other, but will represent a united commonwealth of labor. For the first time in its history mankind will take its fate into its own hands. Instead of destroying innumerable human lives and incalculable wealth in struggles between classes and nations, mankind will devote all its energy to the struggle against the forces of nature, to the development and strengthening of its own collective might.

After abolishing private ownership in the means of production and converting them into social property, the world system of Communism will replace the elemental forces of the world market, of competition and the blind process of social production, by consciously organized and planned production for the purpose of satisfying rapidly growing social needs. With the abolition of competition and anarchy in production, devastating crises and still more devastating wars will disappear. Instead of colossal waste of productive forces and spasmodic development of society— there will be planned utilization of all material resources and painless economic development on the basis of unrestricted, smooth and rapid development of productive forces.

The abolition of private property and the disappearance of classes will do away with the exploitation of man by man. Work will cease to be toiling for the benefit of a class enemy: instead of being merely a means of livelihood it will become a necessity of life: want and economic inequality, the misery of enslaved classes, and a wretched standard of life generally will disappear; the

hierarchy created in the division of labor system will be abolished together with the antagonism between mental and manual labor; and the last vestige of the social inequality of sexes will be removed. At the same time, the organs of class domination, and the State in the first place, will disappear also. The State, being the embodiment of class domination, will die out insofar as classes die out, and with it all measures of coercion will expire.

With the disappearance of classes the monopoly of education in every form will be abolished. Culture will become the acquirement of all and the class ideologies of the past will give place to scientific materialist philosophy. Under such circumstances, the domination of man over man, in any form, becomes impossible, and a great field will be opened for the social selection and the harmonious development of all the talents inherent in humanity.

In Communist society no social restrictions will be imposed upon the growth of the forces of production. Private ownership in the means of production, the selfish lust for profits, the artificial retention of the masses in a state of ignorance, poverty—which retards technical progress in capitalist society, and unproductive expenditures will have no place in a Communist society. The most expedient utilization of the forces of nature and of the natural conditions of production in the various parts of the world; the removal of the antagonism between town and country, that under capitalism results from the low technical level of agriculture and its systematic lagging behind industry; the closest possible cooperation between science and technics, the utmost encouragement of research work and the practical application of its results on the widest possible social scale; planned organization of scientific work; the application of the most perfect methods of statistical accounting and planned regulation of economy; the rapidly growing social need, which is the most powerful internal driving force of the whole system—all these will secure the maximum productivity of social labor, which in turn will release human energy for the powerful development of science and art.

The development of the productive forces of world Communist society will make it possible to raise the well-being of the whole of humanity and to reduce to a minimum the time devoted to material production and, consequently, will enable culture to flourish as never before in history. This new culture of a humanity that is united for the first time in history, and has abolished all State boundaries, will, unlike capitalist culture, be based upon clear and transparent human relationships. Hence, it will bury forever all mysticism, religion, prejudice and superstition and will give a powerful impetus to the development of all-conquering scientific knowledge.

This higher stage of Communism, the stage in which Communist society has already developed on its own foundation, in which an enormous growth of social productive forces has accompanied the manifold development of man, in which humanity has already inscribed on its banner: "From each according to his abilities to each according to his needs!"—presupposes, as an historical condition precedent, a lower stage of development, the stage of Socialism. At this lower stage, Communist society only just emerges from capitalist society and bears all the economic, ethical and intellectual birthmarks it has inherited from the society from whose womb it is just emerging. The productive forces of Socialism are not yet sufficiently developed to assure a distribution of the products of labor according to needs: these are distributed according to the amount of labor expended. Division of labor, i.e. the system whereby certain groups perform certain labor function, and especially the distinction between mental and manual labor, still exists. Although classes are abolished, traces of the old class division of society and, consequently, remnants of the Proletarian State power, coercion, laws, still exist. Consequently, certain traces of inequality, which have not yet managed to die out altogether, still remain. The antagonism between town and country has not yet been entirely removed. But none of these survivals of former society is protected or defended by any social force. Being the product of a definite level of development of productive forces, they will disappear as rapidly as mankind, freed from the fetters of the capitalist system, subjugates the forces of nature, re-educates itself in the spirit of Communism, and passes from Socialism to complete Communism.

2. THE FUNDAMENTAL TASKS OF COMMUNIST STRATEGY AND TACTICS

The successful struggle of the Communist International for the dictatorship of the proletariat presupposes the existence in every country of a compact Communist Party, hardened in the struggle, disciplined, centralized, and closely linked up with the masses.

The Party is the vanguard of the working class and consists of the best, most class-conscious, most active, and most courageous members of that class. It incorporates the whole body of experience of the proletariat struggle. Basing itself upon the revolutionary theory of Marxism and representing the general and lasting interests of the whole of the working class, the Party personifies the unity of proletarian principles, of proletarian will and of proletarian revolutionary action. It is a revolutionary organization, bound by iron discipline and strict revolutionary rules of democratic centralism, which can be carried out thanks to the class-consciousness of the proletarian vanguard, to its loyalty to the revolution, its ability to maintain inseparable ties with the proletarian masses and to its correct political leadership, which is constantly verified and clarified by the experiences of the masses themselves.

In order that it may fulfill its historic mission of achieving the dictatorship of the proletariat, the Communist Party must first of all set itself and accomplish the following fundamental strategic aims:

Extend its influence over the majority of the members of its own class, including working women and the working youth. To achieve this the Communist Party must secure predominant influence in the broad mass proletarian organizations (Soviets, trade unions, factory councils, cooperative societies, sport organizations, cultural organizations, etc.). It is particularly important for the purpose of winning over the majority of the proletariat, to capture the trade unions, which are genuine mass working-class organizations closely bound up with the everyday struggles of the working class. To work in reactionary trade unions and skillfully to capture them, to win the confidence of the broad masses of the industrially organized workers, to change and "remove from their posts" the reformist leaders, represent important tasks in the preparatory period.

The achievement of the dictatorship of the proletariat presupposes also that the proletariat acquires hegemony over wide sections of the toiling masses. To accomplish this the Communist Party must extend its influence over the masses of the urban and rural poor, over the lower strata of the intelligentsia and over the so-called "small man," i.e. the petty-bourgeois strata generally. It is particularly important that work be carried on for the purpose of extending the Party's influence over the peasantry. The Communist Party must secure for itself the whole-hearted support of that stratum of the rural population that stands closest to the proletariat, i. e. the agricultural laborers and the rural poor. To this end, the agricultural laborers must be organized in separate organizations; all possible support must be given them in their struggles against the rural bourgeoisie, and strenuous work must be carried on among the small allotment farmers and small peasants. In regard to the middle strata of the peasantry in developed capitalist countries, the Communist Parties must conduct a policy to secure their neutrality. The fulfillment of all these tasks by the proletariat— the champion of the interests of the whole people and the leader of the broad masses in their struggle against the oppression of finance capital—is an essential condition precedent for the victorious Communist revolution.

The tasks of the Communist International connected with the revolutionary struggle in colonies, semi-colonies and dependencies are extremely important strategical tasks in the world proletarian struggle. The colonial struggle presupposes that the broad masses of the working class and of the peasantry in the colonies be rallied round the banner of the revolution; but this cannot be achieved unless the closest cooperation is maintained between the proletariat in the oppressing countries and the toiling masses in the oppressed countries.

While organizing, under the banner of the proletarian dictatorship, the revolution against imperialism in the so-called civilized States, the Communist International supports every movement against imperialist violence in the colonies, semi-colonies and dependencies themselves (for example Latin-America); it carries on propaganda against all forms of chauvinism and against the imperialist maltreatment of enslaved peoples and races, big and small (treatment of Negroes, "yellow labor," anti-semitism, etc.) and supports their struggles against the bourgeoisie of the oppressing nations. The Communist International especially combats the chauvinism that is preached in the Empire-owning countries by the imperialist bourgeoisie as well as by its Social-Democratic agency, the Second International, and constantly holds up in contrast to the practices of the imperialist bourgeoisie the practice of the Soviet Union, which has established relations of fraternity and equality among the nationalities inhabiting it.

The Communist Parties in the imperialist countries must render systematic aid to the colonial revolutionary liberation movement and to the movement of oppressed nationalities generally. The duty of rendering active support to these movements rests primarily upon the workers in the countries upon which the oppressed nations are economically, financially or politically dependent. The Communist Parties must openly recognize the right of the colonies to separation and their right to carry on propaganda for this separation, i.e. propaganda in favor of the independence of the colonies from the imperialist State; they must recognize their right of armed defense against imperialism (i.e. the right of rebellion and revolutionary war) and advocate and give active support to this defense by all the means in their power. The Communist Parties must adopt this line of policy in regard to all oppressed nations.

The Communist Parties in the colonial and semi-colonial countries must carry on a bold and consistent struggle against foreign imperialism and unfailingly conduct propaganda in favor of friendship and unity with the proletariat in the imperialist countries. They must openly advance, conduct propaganda for and carry out the slogan of agrarian revolution, rouse the broad masses of the peasantry for the overthrow of the landlords and combat the reactionary and mediaeval influence of the clergy, of the missionaries and other similar elements.

In these countries, the principal task is to organize the workers and the peasantry independently (to establish class Communist Parties of the proletariat, trade unions, peasant leagues and committees and, in a revolutionary situation, Soviets, etc.) and to free them from the influence of the national bourgeoisie, with whom temporary agreements may be made only on the condition that they, the bourgeoisie, do not hamper the revolutionary organization of the workers and peasants, and that they carry on a genuine struggle against imperialism. . . .

The Communist International must devote itself especially to systematic preparation for the struggle against the danger of imperialist wars. Ruthless exposure of social chauvinism, of social imperialism and of pacifist phrase-mongering intended to camouflage the imperialist plans of the bourgeoisie; propaganda in favor of the principal slogans of the Communist International; every day organizational work in connection with this, in the course of which work legal methods must unfailingly be combined with illegal methods; organized work in the army and navy—such must be the activity of the Communist Parties in this connection. The fundamental slogans of the Communist International in this connection must be the following: Convert imperialist war into civil war; defeat the "home" imperialist government; defend the U.S.S.R. and the colonies by every possible means in the event of imperialist war against them. It is the bounden duty of all Sections of the Communist International, and of every one of its members, to carry on propaganda for these slogans, to expose the "Socialistic" sophisms and the "Socialistic" camouflage of the League of Nations and constantly to keep to the front the experiences of the war of 1914–1918.

In order that revolutionary work and revolutionary action may be coordinated and in order that these activities may be guided most successfully, the international proletariat must be bound by international class discipline, for which, first of all, it is most important to have the strictest international discipline in the Communist ranks.

This international Communist discipline must find expression in the subordination of the partial and local interests of the movement to its general and lasting interests and in the strict fulfillment, by all members, of the decisions passed by the leading bodies of the Communist International.

Unlike the Social-Democratic, Second International, each section of which submits to the discipline of "its own" national bourgeoisie and of its own "fatherland," the sections of the Communist International submit to only one discipline, viz., international proletarian discipline, which guarantees victory in the struggle of the world's workers for world proletarian dictatorship. Unlike the Second International, which splits the trade unions, fights against colonial peoples, and practices unity with the bourgeoisie, the Communist International is an organization that guards proletarian unity in all countries and the unity of the toilers of all races and all peoples in their struggle against the yoke of imperialism.

Despite the bloody terror of the bourgeoisie, the Communists fight with courage and devotion on all sectors of the international class front, in the firm conviction that the victory of the proletariat is inevitable and cannot be averted.

"The Communists disdain to conceal their views and aims. They openly declare that their aims can be attained only by the forcible overthrow of all the existing social conditions. Let the ruling class tremble at a Communist revolution. The proletarians have nothing to lose but their chains. They have a world to win.

"Workers of all countries, unite!"

Pragmatism

Pragmatism is America's most distinctive contribution to the world community of philosophy. Developed partly in interaction with the American experience, partly in relation to the continually maturing science of the nineteenth century, and especially influenced by the theory of evolution, it became a many-sided movement that affected much of American culture, including law, education, and political thought. Its chief philosophic spokesmen were Charles Sanders Peirce (1839–1914), William James, and John Dewey, though lesser known philosophers like Chauncey Wright (1830–1875) and lawyers like Nicholas St. John Green (1835–1876) and Oliver Wendell Holmes, Jr., contributed to the movement and helped to bring the pragmatic spirit into many areas of intellectual concern.

What is pragmatism? Writing for the *Century Dictionary* in 1909, Dewey gave the following as the basic meaning of the term amid all its uses: "The theory that the processes and the materials of knowledge are determined by practical or purposive considerations—that there is no such thing as knowledge determined by exclusively theoretical, speculative, or abstract intellectual considerations." Two years earlier, James published an essay on "What Pragmatism Means"* in which he asserted in a similar vein that any purely objective truth, that is, any truth supposedly established apart from the function of giving human satisfaction, is nowhere to be found. To illustrate this point (and others), James begins his article with an anecdote about a "metaphysical" problem. Imagine a squirrel clinging to one side of a tree and a human witness standing on the opposite side. The witness tries to sight the squirrel by moving around the tree, but the squirrel moves fast enough in the opposite direction that it is never seen. Now the man goes around the tree and the squirrel is on the tree. The vexing question is, does

---

* Lecture II in *Pragmatism. A New Name for Some Old Ways of Thinking,* New York: Longmans, Green & Co., 1907.

the man go around the squirrel? To take sides on this question, however, is to begin an interminable dispute unless one condition is met, namely to decide what is *practically meant* by "going around" the squirrel. If one's meaning is to occupy positions of east, north, west, and south of the squirrel, the man does go around it; if one means to stand in front, then to the side, and then to the rear of the squirrel, he does not go around the squirrel. With this distinction made, there is no longer really any dispute: "You are both right and both wrong according as you conceive the verb 'to go round' on one practical fashion or the other."

This illustration suggests that pragmatism is both a theory of meaning and knowledge and a revolt against certain speculative, abstract philosophies. The key notions for these sides of pragmatism are "purpose in thought" and "practical consequences." Before analyzing their meaning more carefully, however, it may be helpful to look first at two of the influences on pragmatism mentioned above, namely the theory of evolution and experimental science. Writing of evolutionary theory, Dewey said that "the influence of Darwin upon philosophy resides in his having conquered the phenomena of life for the principle of transition, and thereby freed the new logic for application to mind, life, and morals."† Three ideas are contained in this quotation. Having conquered the phenomena of life, Darwin showed, first, that nature includes man and intelligence. No supernatural or extra-natural principle is needed to account for man or his capacities: they are products of the evolutionary process itself. Secondly, Darwin suggested the priority of transition over permanence, of becoming over being. No fixed species, no eternal forms, are necessary or warranted. Thirdly, therefore, intelligence itself is natural-ized. The function of thought can no longer be to conceive eternal principles or natural laws. It cannot "look back" to grasp fixed structures. Mind attempts to control events by looking forward to consequences in order to secure those condi-tions that will best serve human purposes. A new logic will stress methods for such control rather than so-called timeless laws of thought.

These same interpretations, pragmatists believe, are given support by the practices of experimental science. In the "laboratory method," as Peirce called it, ideas are basically hypotheses or proposed solutions to felt problems. Hypotheses predict consequences, and methods of verification are pursued by scientists to determine which consequences can be found in experience and which hypotheses, therefore, are confirmed. Experimental thinking is related to doing in terms of purpose, for it involves the manipulation of present means according to con-ceived consequences for the purpose of subsequent control.

As a philosophic revolt, then, pragmatism is a movement that rejects philoso-phies which speculate on abstractions or empty first principles. It looks to con-crete cases, to particular consequences, and to ideas and meanings that will "make a difference." It is also against monistic and absolutistic positions: there are no "wholesale views" of reality (Dewey) or single solutions for the problems of men. Pragmatists also reject purely logical procedures such as coherence as a method of thought for either facts or values. Thought is experimental, and its full meaning includes active manipulation and control beyond logical inference.

---

† "The Influence of Darwin on Philosophy," *The Influence of Darwin on Philosophy and Other Essays in Contemporary Thought*, New York: Henry Holt and Co., 1910. This whole essay is important for details on Darwin's influence on pragmatism.

Positively, pragmatists developed a new theory of knowledge and truth. An idea is a plan of action, a hypothesis to be tested, an instrument‡ whose function is to guide inquiries to the satisfactory resolution of problematic situations. Mind is best understood as response to the doubtful, and knowledge "is the fruit of the undertakings that transform a problematic situation into a resolved one" (Dewey). Truth is a matter of successful resolution of problems, and the test of truth lies in practical consequences that are satisfying.

Thus the true is "that which works," that which is successful in solving problems. Properly understood, this brief statement provides a convenient summary of pragmatic epistemology. But it also raises one more introductory matter that must be treated, for pragmatists have differed somewhat in their views about what practical consequences are to be considered satisfactory. These differences also provide a convenient basis for distinguishing the main varieties of pragmatism. To the question, then, of what satisfactory consequence is the test of truth, there is the answer of *humanistic* pragmatism: that what fulfills human purposes and desires is true. In some of his writings, particularly on ethics and religion, James took this position, as did the English pragmatist, F. C. S. Schiller (1864–1937). A second answer is *experimental:* truth is what works in the sense of the experimentally verified. A subform of experimentalism is *nominalistic* pragmatism. The results of ideas are expected in the form of particular perceptual facts in future experiences. The meaning of, and true statements about, human nature, for example, are not about some essence "Man," but are rather about the particular doings of particular men. Peirce and James (in his "tough-minded" writings) took an experimental, and occasionally nominalistic, position. Finally is the *biological* version of pragmatism associated with Dewey. Thought is purposive in seeking to help the organism adapt to its environment, and successful adaptation in terms of survival and growth provides the criterion for the truth of ideas.

In its emphasis on science and experimental method, pragmatism has something in common with positivism, and its stress on consequences links it with utilitarianism. Despite this indebtedness, however, it differs from them both: from positivism because of its concern with an experimentalist approach to values,§ and from utilitarianism because of its evolutionary and instrumentalist view of mind and its interest in all shared values rather than pleasures alone. Thus, while its relations with earlier theories may easily be traced, pragmatism constitutes a distinctive philosophic perspective.

Man and Society

The pragmatist's attention to consequences and their control through intelligence is the basis of his understanding of man and society: he appeals neither to special forces outside the course of observable phenomena nor to fictional devices or

---

‡ Dewey often used the term instrumentalism because of this understanding of the function of ideas.

§ This matter is treated below in the section on "Social and Political Values."

special causes to account for man's social behavior. Man is a social animal for association rather than isolation is a law of everything that exists; he becomes a social animal because the content of his developing experience is itself social. The question, therefore, of how individuals come to be associated in their various groups is hardly a proper question at all.

Yet the question of how social connections develop in the ways they do is a proper question, and it arises because individuals are led in terms of their interests to think of the consequences of their behavior on themselves and others. These consequences become matters of observation and possible control, and therewith they take on a new value in relation to intelligence. Interest in the consequences of associative life turns to such matters as survival, habits of action, and thought as well as choice in terms of consequences. These ends are served by numerous social groups, each of which is formed when shared interests are felt and consequences are appreciated.

Thus, society is to be viewed, not as an entity in itself, but as a collection of interacting "primary groups." Many of these groups, however, have consequences on persons other than those who participate in them. Hence there arises a distinct, though secondary, interest in public forms of associative life including the state. To these forms belongs the supervision of the consequences of primary groups, which do not themselves go beyond their own shared interests.

This pragmatic understanding of society in terms of pluralism of groups, interests, and consequences is developed in the selection below by John Dewey (1859–1952). After his presentation of these themes, Dewey provides a summary of his approach in the following assertions. Associated action is a universal trait of existence. Such action has results, and some results of human action are perceived or noted. Then come purposes and plans to secure those consequences that are desired. Since some interests concern only the group while others have broader consequences, a common interest is also generated. Hence arises the "public," whose interest is directed toward the control of these broader consequences.

JOHN DEWEY   Association and Society

While the doctrine [of individualism] is false, it sets out from a fact. Wants, choices and purposes have their locus in single beings; behavior which manifests desire, intent and resolution proceeds from them in their singularity. But only intellectual laziness leads us to conclude that since the form of thought and decision is individual, their content, their subject-matter, is also something purely personal. Even if "consciousness" were the wholly private matter that the individualistic tradition in philosophy and psychology supposes it to be, it would still be true that consciousness is *of* objects, not of itself. Association in the sense of connection and combination is a "law" of everything known to exist. Singular things act, but they act together. Nothing has been discovered which acts in entire isolation. The action of everything is along with the action of other things. The "along with" is of such a kind that the behavior of each is modified by its connection with others. There are trees which can grow only in a forest. Seeds of many plants can successfully germinate and develop only under conditions furnished by the presence of other plants. Reproduction of kind is dependent upon the activities of insects which bring about fertilization. The life-history of an animal cell is conditioned upon connection with what other cells are doing. Electrons, atoms and molecules exemplify the omnipresence of conjoint behavior.

There is no mystery about the fact of association, of an interconnected action which affects the activity of singular elements. There is no sense in asking how individuals come to be associated. They exist and operate in association. If there is any mystery about the matter, it is the mystery that the universe is the kind of universe it is. Such a mystery could not be explained without going outside the universe. And if one should go to an outside source to account for it, some logician, without an excessive draft upon his ingenuity, would rise to remark that the outsider would have to be connected with the universe in order to account for anything in it. We should still be just where we started, with the fact of connection as a fact to be accepted.

There is, however, an intelligible question about human association:— Not the question how individuals or singular beings come to be connected, but how they come to be connected in just those ways which give human communities traits so different from those which mark assemblies of electrons, unions of trees in forests, swarms of in-

sects, herds of sheep, and constellations of stars. When we consider the difference we at once come upon the fact that the consequences of conjoint action take on a new value when they are observed. For notice of the effects of connected action forces men to reflect upon the connection itself; it makes it an object of attention and interest. Each acts, in so far as the connection is known, in view of the connection. Individuals still do the thinking, desiring and purposing, but *what* they think of is the consequences of their behavior upon that of others and that of others upon themselves.

Each human being is born an infant. He is immature, helpless, dependent upon the activities of others. That many of these dependent beings survive is proof that others in some measure look out for them, take care of them. Mature and better equipped beings are aware of the consequences of their acts upon those of the young. They not only act conjointly with them, but they act in that especial kind of association which manifests interest in the consequences of their conduct upon the life and growth of the young.

Continued physiological existence of the young is only one phase of interest in the consequences of association. Adults are equally concerned to act so that the immature learn to think, feel, desire and habitually conduct themselves in certain ways. Not the least of the consequences which are striven for is that the young shall themselves learn to judge, purpose and choose from the standpoint of associated behavior and its consequences. In fact, only too often this interest takes the form of endeavoring to make the young believe and plan just as adults do. This instance alone is enough to show that while singular beings in their singularity think, want and decide, *what* they think and strive for, the content of their beliefs and intentions is a subject-matter provided by association. Thus man is not merely *de facto* associated, but he *becomes* a social animal in the make-up of his ideas, sentiments and deliberate behavior. *What* he believes, hopes for and aims at is the outcome of association and intercourse. The only thing which imports obscurity and mystery into the influence of association upon what individual persons want and act for is the effort to discover alleged, special, original, society-making causal forces, whether instincts, fiats of will, personal, or an immanent, universal, practical reason, or an indwelling, metaphysical, social essence and nature. These things do not explain, for they are more mysterious than are the facts they are evoked to account for. The planets in a constellation would form a community if they were aware of the connections of the activities of each with those of the others and could use this knowledge to direct behavior.

We have made a digression from consideration of the state to the wider topic of society. However, the excursion enables us to distinguish the state from other forms of social life. There is an old tradition which regards the state and completely organized society as the same thing. The state is said to be the complete and inclusive realization of all social institutions. Whatever values result from any and every social arrangement are gathered together and asserted to be the work of the state. The counterpart of this method is that philosophical anarchism which assembles all the evils that result from all forms of human grouping and attributes them *en masse* to the state, whose elimination would then bring in a millennium of voluntary fraternal organization. That the state

should be to some a deity and to others a devil is another evidence of the defects of the premises from which discussion sets out. One theory is as indiscriminate as the other.

There is, however, a definite criterion by which to demarcate the organized public from other modes of community life. Friendships, for example, are non-political forms of association. They are characterized by an intimate and subtle sense of the fruits of intercourse. They contribute to experience some of its most precious values. Only the exigencies of a preconceived theory would confuse with the state that texture of friendships and attachments which is the chief bond in any community, or would insist that the former depends upon the latter for existence. Men group themselves also for scientific inquiry, for religious worship, for artistic production and enjoyment, for sport, for giving and receiving instruction, for industrial and commercial undertakings. In each case some combined or conjoint action, which has grown up out of "natural," that is, biological, conditions and from local contiguity, results in producing distinctive consequences—that is, consequences which differ in kind from those of isolated behavior.

When these consequences are intellectually and emotionally appreciated, a shared interest is generated and the nature of the interconnected behavior is thereby transformed. Each form of association has its own peculiar quality and value, and no person in his senses confuses one with another. The characteristic of the public as a state springs from the fact that all modes of associated behavior may have extensive and enduring consequences which involve others beyond those directly engaged in them. When these consequences are in turn realized in thought and sentiment, recognition of them reacts to remake the conditions out of which they arose. Consequences have to be taken care of, looked out for. This supervision and regulation cannot be effected by the primary groupings themselves. For the essence of the consequences which call a public into being is the fact that they expand beyond those directly engaged in producing them. Consequently special agencies and measures must be formed if they are to be attended to; or else some existing group must take on new functions. The obvious external mark of the organization of a public or of a state is thus the existence of officials. Government is not the state, for that includes the public as well as the rulers charged with special duties and powers. The public, however, is organized in and through those officers who act in behalf of its interests.

Thus the state represents an important although distinctive and restricted social interest. From this point of view there is nothing extraordinary in the preëminence of the claims of the organized public over other interests when once they are called into play, nor in its total indifference and irrelevancy to friendships, associations for science, art and religion under most circumstances. If the consequences of a friendship threaten the public, then it is treated as a conspiracy; usually it is not the state's business or concern. Men join each other in partnership as a matter of course to do a piece of work more profitably or for mutual defense. Let its operations exceed a certain limit, and others not participating in it find their security or prosperity menaced by it, and suddenly the gears of the state are in mesh. Thus it happens that the state, instead of being all absorbing and inclusive, is under some circumstances the most idle and empty of social arrangements. Nevertheless, the temptation to generalize from these instances and conclude that the state generically is of no significance is at once challenged by the fact that when a family connection, a church, a trade union, a business corporation, or an educational institution conducts itself so as to affect large numbers outside of itself, those who are affected form a public which endeavors to act through suitable structures, and thus to organize itself for oversight and regulation. . . .

Thus the problem of discovering the state is not a problem for theoretical inquirers engaged solely in surveying institutions which already exist. It is a practical problem of human beings living in association with one another, of mankind generically. It is a complex problem. It demands power to perceive and recognize the consequences of the behavior of individuals joined in groups and to trace them to their source and origin. It involves selection of persons to serve as representatives of the interests created by these perceived consequences and to define the functions which they shall possess and employ. It requires institution of a government such that those having the renown and power which goes with the exercise of these functions shall employ them for the public and not turn them to their own private benefit. It is no cause for wonder, then, that states have been many, not only in number but in type and kind. For there have been countless forms of joint activity with correspondingly diverse consequences. Power to detect consequences has varied especially with the instrumentalities of knowledge at hand. Rulers have been selected on all kinds of different grounds. Their functions have varied and so have their will and zeal to represent common interests. Only the exigencies of a rigid philosophy can lead us to suppose that there is some one form or idea of The State which these protean historic states have realized in various degrees of perfection. The only statement which can be made is a purely formal one: the state is the organization of the public effected through officials for the protection of the interests shared by its members. But what the public may be, what the officials are, how adequately they perform their function, are things we have to go to history to discover. . . .

As the argument has moved to and fro, it will conduce to clearness to summarize its steps. Conjoint, combined, associated action is a universal trait of the behavior of things. Such action has results. Some of the results of human collective action are perceived, that is, they are noted in such ways that they are taken account of. Then there arise purposes, plans, measures and means, to secure consequences which are liked and eliminate those which are found obnoxious. Thus perception generates a common interest; that is, those affected by the consequences are perforce concerned in conduct of all those who along with themselves share in bringing about the results. Sometimes the consequences are confined to those who directly share in the transaction which produces them. In other cases they extend far beyond those immediately engaged in producing them. Thus two kinds of interests and of measures of regulation of acts in view of consequences are generated. In the first, interest and control are limited to those directly engaged; in the second, they extend to those who do not directly share in the performance of acts. If, then, the interest constituted by their being affected by the actions in question is to have any practical influence, control over the actions which produce them must occur by some indirect means.

So far the statements, it is submitted, set forth matters of actual and ascertainable fact. Now follows the hypothesis. Those indirectly and seriously affected for good or for evil form a group distinctive enough to require recognition and a name. The name selected is The Public. This public is organized and made effective by means of representatives who as guardians of custom, as legislators, as executives, judges, etc., care for its especial interests by methods intended to regulate the conjoint actions of individuals and groups. Then and in so far, association adds to itself political organization, and something which may be government comes into being: the public is a political state.

The direct confirmation of the hypothesis is found in the statement of the series of observable and verifiable matters of fact. These constitute conditions which are sufficient to account, so it is held, for the characteristic phenomena of political life, or state activity. If they do, it is superfluous to seek for other explanation. In conclusion, two qualifications should be added. The account just given is meant to be generic; it is consequently schematic, and omits many differential conditions, some of which receive attention in subsequent chapters. The other point is that in the negative part of the argument, the attack upon theories which would explain the state by means of special causal forces and agencies, there is no denial of causal relations or connections among phenomena themselves. That is obviously assumed at every point. There can be no consequences and measures to regulate the mode and quality of their occurrence without the causal nexus. What is denied is an appeal to *special* forces outside the series of observable connected phenomena. Such causal powers are no different in kind to the occult forces from which physical science had to emancipate itself. At best, they are but phases of the related phenomena themselves which are then employed to account for the facts. What is needed to direct and make fruitful social inquiry is a method which proceeds on the basis of the interrelations of observable acts and their results. . . .

The discussion also returns with some added illumination to the problem of the relation of state and society. The problem of the relation of individuals to associations—sometimes posed as the relation of *the* individual to society—is a meaningless one. We might as well make a problem out of the relation of the letters of an alphabet to the alphabet. An alphabet *is* letters, and "society" is individuals in their connections with one another. The mode of combination of letters with one another is obviously a matter of importance; letters form words and sentences when combined, and have no point nor sense except in some combination. I would not say that the latter statement applies literally to individuals, but it cannot be gainsaid that singular human beings exist and behave in constant and varied association with one another. These modes of conjoint action and their consequences profoundly affect not only the outer habits of singular persons, but their dispositions in emotion, desire, planning and valuing.

"Society," however, is either an abstract or a collective noun. In the concrete, there are societies, associations, groups of an immense number of kinds, having different ties and instituting different interests. They may be gangs, criminal bands; clubs for sport, sociability and eating; scientific and professional organizations; political parties and

unions within them; families; religious denominations, business partnerships and corporations; and so on in an endless list. The associations may be local, nation-wide and trans-national. Since there is no one *thing* which may be called society, except their indefinite overlapping, there is no unqualified eulogistic connotation adhering to the term "society." Some societies are in the main to be approved; some to be condemned, on account of their consequences upon the character and conduct of those engaged in them and because of their remoter consequences upon others. All of them, like all things human, are mixed in quality; "society" is something to be approached and judged critically and discriminatingly. "Socialization" of some sort—that is, the reflex modification of wants, beliefs and work because of share in a united action—is inevitable. But it is as marked in the formation of frivolous, dissipated, fanatical, narrow-minded and criminal persons as in that of competent inquirers, learned scholars, creative artists and good neighbors.

Confining our notice to the results which are desirable, it appears that there is no reason for assigning all the values which are generated and maintained by means of human associations to the work of states. Yet the same unbridled generalizing and fixating tendency of the mind which leads to a monistic fixation of society has extended beyond the hypostatizing of "society" and produced a magnified idealization of The State. All values which result from any kind of association are habitually imputed by one school of social philosophers to the state. Naturally the result is to place the state beyond criticism. Revolt against the state is then thought to be the one unforgivable social sin. Sometimes the deification proceeds from a special need of the time, as in the cases of Spinoza and Hegel. Sometimes it springs from a prior belief in universal will and reason and a consequent need of finding some empirical phenomena which may be identified with the externalization of this absolute spirit. Then this is employed, by circular logic, as evidence for the existence of such a spirit. The net import of our discussion is that a state is a distinctive and secondary form of association, having a specifiable work to do and specified organs of operation.

It is quite true that most states, after they have been brought into being, react upon the primary groupings. When a state is a good state, when the officers of the public genuinely serve the public interests, this reflex effect is of great importance. It renders the desirable associations solider and more coherent; indirectly it clarifies their aims and purges their activities. It places a discount upon injurious groupings and renders their tenure of life precarious. In performing these services, it gives the individual members of valued associations greater liberty and security: it relieves them of hampering conditions which if they had to cope with personally would absorb their energies in mere negative struggle against evils. It enables individual members to count with reasonable certainty upon what others will do, and thus facilitates mutually helpful cooperations. It creates respect for others and for one's self. A measure of the goodness of a state is the degree in which it relieves individuals from the waste of negative struggle and needless conflict and confers upon him positive assurance and reënforcement in what he undertakes. This is a great service, and there is no call to be niggardly in acknowledging the transformations of group and personal action which states have historically effected.

But this recognition cannot be legitimately converted into the monopolistic absorption of all associations into The State, nor of all social values into political value. The all-inclusive nature of the state signifies only that officers of the public (including, of course, lawmakers) may act so as to fix conditions under which *any* form of association operates; its comprehensive character refers only to the impact of its behavior. A war like an earthquake may "include" in its consequences all elements in a given territory, but the inclusion is by way of effects, not by inherent nature or right. A beneficent law, like a condition of general economic prosperity, may favorably affect all interests in a particular region, but it cannot be called a whole of which the elements influenced are parts. Nor can the liberating and confirming results of public action be construed to yield a wholesale idealization of states in contrast with other associations. For state activity is often injurious to the latter. One of the chief occupations of states has been the waging of war and the suppression of dissentient minorities. Moreover, their action, even when benign, presupposes values due to nonpolitical forms of living together which are but extended and reënforced by the public through its agents.

The hypothesis which we have supported has obvious points of contact with what is known as the pluralistic conception of the state. It presents also a marked point of difference. Our doctrine of plural forms is a statement of a fact: that there exist a plurality of social groupings, good, bad and indifferent. It is not a doctrine which prescribes inherent limits to state action. It does not intimate that the function of the state is limited to settling conflicts among other groups, as if each one of them had a fixed scope of action of its own. Were that true, the state would be only an umpire to avert and remedy trespasses of one group upon another. Our hypothesis is neutral as to any general, sweeping implications as to how far state activity may extend. It does not indicate any particular polity of public action. At times, the consequences of the conjoint behavior of some persons may be such that a large public interest is generated which can be fulfilled only by laying down conditions which involve a large measure of reconstruction within that group. There is no more an inherent sanctity in a

church, trade-union, business corporation, or family institution than there is in the state. Their value is also to be measured by their consequences. The consequences vary with concrete conditions; hence at one time and place a large measure of state activity may be indicated and at another time a policy of quiescence and *laissez-faire*. Just as publics and states vary with conditions of time and place, so do the concrete functions which should be carried on by states. There is no antecedent universal proposition which can be laid down because of which the functions of a state should be limited or should be expanded. Their scope is something to be critically and experimentally determined.

Social and Political Values

Rejecting eternal truths and fixed patterns in the study of fact, pragmatists similarly deny that value can be understood by reference to ready-made and over-all patterns or objective structures. Value and disvalue are qualities that arise within the context of human experience, attaching themselves to the consequences of courses of action. Further, the problem of value relates to that control of experience which will establish values, not to merely theoretical manipulation of general concepts.

Dewey's efforts to develop a logic of valuation have had a wide influence. Like all inquiries, valuation begins with the recognition of a problematic situation—in this case, a conflict in desires. Using knowledge gained in previous inquiries, one sets up a hypothesis or proposed solution to the conflict that serves as an end-in-view. The end-in-view guides subsequent actions that create the objective conditions and control the consequences through which a value is instituted and the original conflict resolved. The movement is thus from the desired to the desirable; the method followed is the tentative, experimental method of intelligence; and—as is true of pragmatism generally—the direction of control is toward consequences.

Two selections follow to present the pragmatic approach to value. In the first, William James (1842–1910) begins with the assertion that value is not some principle rooted in antecedent being, but is consequent upon human feelings and desires. Sentient life is the "habitat of value," and apart from persons, terms like good and bad have no meaning or application. That is, the universe itself—or anything else—cannot be considered good or bad except in relation to desires. But, says James, one other condition is needed for the existence of an ethical world, and this is the requirement of many persons. Given a pluralism of desiring beings, there arises the conflict of interests and ideals, as well as the claims of individuals to fulfill their desires and to oblige others to respect their fulfillment.

Thus there are opposing claims and values and it must be decided how to choose among them. Not, James insists, "by any abstract moral 'nature of things' existing antecedently to the concrete thinkers themselves with their ideals." Any desire is imperative, and every claim produces an obligation. The rightness that is sought must be concrete, a right after—and by virtue of—the fact that claims are actually made. No single abstract principle is useful, accurate, or indeed even possible. The best act is the one that makes for the "best whole" of goods, in the sense of provoking the least amount of dissatisfaction.

The second selection is from one of Dewey's works on social value. With James, Dewey rejects discussions of individual and society that are based on a logic of general concepts. The need is for concrete guidance and inquiry. Social arrangements, Dewey says, must not be viewed as means to progress or as the guarantee of happiness: they are means for creating individuals. So understood, these arrangements become the object of detailed inquiry about how to release and strengthen human capacities. The release of capacities, however, is possible only through communication, sharing, and joint participation in society's goods. Thus, the general problem of social and political values is the institution of those social conditions whose consequences insure the joint participation of persons in shared experiences. The growth of persons through such participation, Dewey concludes, gives freedom its meaning, and conjoint and communicated experience is the defining phrase for democracy.

While both of these presentations fall clearly within pragmatism, they also reflect two sides or emphases of the tradition. On the whole, James's views are more individualistic, more subjectivist, even more romantic. Pragmatists who follow James are likely to retain this same emphasis. The instrumentalism of Dewey, on the other hand, is more social, objectivist, and scientific in nature. The import of James's position is thus primarily, though not exclusively, in the area of individual choice and conduct; the stress of Dewey's is on society and culture. Dewey in fact understood philosophy to be the critic of culture, and to have a normative function. On the whole, therefore, his writings have a wider relevance to social philosophy than do James's, though the indirect influence of the latter on social discussion should not be underemphasized.

WILLIAM JAMES   Value and Desire

[We turn next to] the metaphysical question, of what we mean by the words "obligation," "good," and "ill."

First of all, it appears that such words can have no application or relevancy in a world in which no sentient life exists.

From William James, "The Moral Philosopher and the Moral Life," in *The Will to Believe and Other Essays in Popular Philosophy*, New York: Longmans, Green, and Co., 1909.

Imagine an absolutely material world, containing only physical and chemical facts, and existing from eternity without a God, without even an interested spectator: would there be any sense in saying of that world that one of its states is better than another? Or if there were two such worlds possible, would there be any rhyme or reason in calling one good and the other bad,—good or bad positively, I mean, and apart from the fact that one might relate itself better than the other to the philosopher's private interests? But we must leave these private interests out of the account, for the philosopher is a mental fact, and we are asking whether goods and evils and obligations exist in physical facts *per se.* Surely there is no *status* for good and evil to exist in, in a purely insentient world. How can one physical fact, considered simply as a physical fact, be "better" than another? Betterness is not a physical relation. In its mere material capacity, a thing can no more be good or bad than it can be pleasant or painful. Good for what? Good for the production of another physical fact, do you say? But what in a purely physical universe demands the production of that other fact? Physical facts simply *are* or are *not;* and neither when present or absent, can they be supposed to make demands. If they do, they can only do so by having desires; and then they have ceased to be purely physical facts, and have become facts of conscious sensibility. Goodness, badness, and obligation must be *realized* somewhere in order really to exist; and the first step in ethical philosophy is to see that no merely inorganic "nature of things" can realize them. Neither moral relations nor the moral law can swing *in vacuo.* Their only habitat can be a mind which feels them; and no world composed of merely physical facts can possibly be a world to which ethical propositions apply.

The moment one sentient being, however, is made a part of the universe, there is a chance for goods and evils really to exist. Moral relations now have their *status,* in that being's consciousness. So far as he feels anything to be good, he *makes* it good. It *is* good, for him; and being good for him, is absolutely good, for he is the sole creator of values in that universe, and outside of his opinion things have no moral character at all.

In such a universe as that it would of course be absurd to raise the question of whether the solitary thinker's judgments of good and ill are true or not. Truth supposes a standard outside of the thinker to which he must conform; but here the thinker is a sort of divinity, subject to no higher judge. Let us call the supposed universe which he inhabits a *moral solitude.* In such a moral solitude it is clear that there can be no outward obligation, and that the only trouble the god-like thinker is liable to have will be over the consistency of his own several ideals with one another. Some of these will no doubt be more pungent and appealing than the rest, their goodness will have a profounder, more penetrating taste; they will return to haunt him with more obstinate regrets if violated. So the thinker will have to order his life with them as its chief determinants, or else remain inwardly discordant and unhappy. Into whatever equilibrium he may settle, though, and however he may straighten out his system, it will be a right system; for beyond the facts of his own subjectivity there is nothing moral in the world.

If now we introduce a second thinker with his likes and dislikes into the universe, the ethical situation becomes much more complex, and several possibilities are immediately seen to obtain.

One of these is that the thinkers may ignore each other's attitude about good and evil altogether, and each continue to indulge his own preferences, indifferent to what the other may feel or do. In such a case we have a world with twice as much of the ethical quality in it as our moral solitude, only it is without ethical unity. The same object is good or bad there, according as you measure it by the view which this one or that one of the thinkers takes. Nor can you find any possible ground in such a world for saying that one thinker's opinion is more correct than the other's, or that either has the truer moral sense. Such a world, in short, is not a moral universe but a moral dualism. Not only is there no single point of view within it from which the values of things can be unequivocally judged, but there is not even a demand for such a point of view, since the two thinkers are supposed to be indifferent to each other's thoughts and acts. Multiply the thinkers into a pluralism, and we find realized for us in the ethical sphere something like that world which the antique sceptics conceived of,—in which individual minds are the measures of all things, and in which no one "objective" truth, but only a multitude of "subjective" opinions, can be found.

But this is the kind of world with which the philosopher, so long as he holds to the hope of a philosophy, will not put up. Among the various ideals represented, there must be, he thinks, some which have the more truth or authority; and to these the others *ought* to yield, so that system and subordination may reign. Here in the word "ought" the notion of *obligation* comes emphatically into view, and the next

thing in order must be to make its meaning clear.

Since the outcome of the discussion so far has been to show us that nothing can be good or right except so far as some consciousness feels it to be good or thinks it to be right, we perceive on the very threshold that the real superiority and authority which are postulated by the philosopher to reside in some of the opinions, and the really inferior character which he supposes must belong to others, cannot be explained by any abstract moral "nature of things" existing antecedently to the concrete thinkers themselves with their ideals. Like the positive attributes good and bad, the comparative ones better and worse must be *realized* in order to be real. If one ideal judgment be objectively better than another, that betterness must be made flesh by being lodged concretely in some one's actual perception. It cannot float in the atmosphere, for it is not a sort of meteorological phenomenon, like the aurora borealis or the zodiacal light. Its *esse* is *percipi,* like the *esse* of the ideals themselves between which it obtains. The philosopher, therefore, who seeks to know which ideal ought to have supreme weight and which one ought to be subordinated, must trace the *ought* itself to the *de facto* constitution of some existing consciousness, behind which, as one of the data of the universe, he as a purely ethical philosopher is unable to go. This consciousness must make the one ideal right by feeling it to be right, the other wrong by feeling it to be wrong. But now what particular consciousness in the universe *can* enjoy this prerogative of obliging others to conform to a rule which it lays down?

If one of the thinkers were obviously divine, while all the rest were human, there would probably be no practical dispute about the matter. The divine thought would be the model, to which the others should conform. But still the theoretic question would remain, What is the ground of the obligation, even here?

In our first essays at answering this question, there is an inevitable tendency to slip into an assumption which ordinary men follow when they are disputing with one another about questions of good and bad. They imagine an abstract moral order in which the objective truth resides; and each tries to prove that this pre-existing order is more accurately reflected in his own ideas than in those of his adversary. It is because one disputant is backed by this overarching abstract order that we think the other should submit. Even so, when it is a question no longer of two finite thinkers, but of God and ourselves,—we follow our usual habit, and imagine a sort of *de jure* relation, which antedates and overarches the mere facts, and would make it right that we should conform our thoughts to God's thoughts, even though he made no claim to that effect, and though we preferred *de facto* to go on thinking for ourselves.

But the moment we take a steady look at the question, *we see not only that without a claim actually made by some concrete person there can be no obligation, but that there is some obligation wherever there is a claim.* Claim and obligation are, in fact, coextensive terms; they cover each other exactly. Our ordinary attitude of regarding ourselves as subject to an overarching system of moral relations, true "in themselves," is therefore either an out-and-out superstition, or else it must be treated as a merely provisional abstraction from that real Thinker in whose actual demand upon us to think as he does our obligation must be ultimately based. In a theistic-ethical philosophy

that thinker in question is, of course, the Deity to whom the existence of the universe is due.

I know well how hard it is for those who are accustomed to what I have called the superstitious view, to realize that every *de facto* claim creates in so far forth an obligation. We inveterately think that something which we call the "validity" of the claim is what gives to it its obligatory character, and that this validity is something outside of the claim's mere existence as a matter of fact. It rains down upon the claim, we think, from some sublime dimension of being, which the moral law inhabits, much as upon the steel of the compass-needle the influence of the Pole rains down from out of the starry heavens. But again, how can such an inorganic abstract character of imperativeness, additional to the imperativeness which is in the concrete claim itself, *exist?* Take any demand, however slight, which any creature, however weak, may make. Ought it not, for its own sole sake, to be satisfied? If not, prove why not. The only possible kind of proof you could adduce would be the exhibition of another creature who should make a demand that ran the other way. The only possible reason there can be why any phenomenon ought to exist is that such a phenomenon actually is desired. Any desire is imperative to the extent of its amount; it *makes* itself by the fact that it exists at all. Some desires, truly enough, are small desires; they are put forward by insignificant persons, and we customarily make light of the obligations which they bring. But the fact that such personal demands as these impose small obligations does not keep the largest obligations from being personal demands.

If we must talk impersonally, to be sure we can say that "the universe" requires, exacts, or makes obligatory such or such an action, whenever it expresses itself through the desires of such or such a creature. But it is better not to talk about the universe in this personified way, unless we believe in a universal or divine consciousness which actually exists. If there be such a consciousness, then its demands carry the most of obligation simply because they are the greatest in amount. But it is even then not *abstractly* right that we should respect them. It is only *concretely* right,— or right after the fact, and by virtue of the fact, that they are actually made. Suppose we do not respect them, as seems largely to be the case in this queer world. That ought not to be, we say; that is wrong. But in what way is this fact of wrongness made more acceptable or intelligible when we imagine it to consist rather in the laceration of an *à priori* ideal order than in the disappointment of a living personal God? Do we, perhaps, think that we cover God and protect him and make his impotence over us less ultimate, when we back him up with this *à priori* blanket from which he may draw some warmth of further appeal? But the only force of appeal to *us,* which either a living God or an abstract ideal order can wield, is found in the "everlasting ruby vaults" of our own human hearts, as they happen to beat responsive and not irresponsive to the claim. So far as they do feel it when made by a living consciousness, it is life answering to life. A claim thus livingly acknowledged is acknowledged with a solidity and fulness which no thought of an "ideal" backing can render more complete; while if, on the other hand, the heart's response is withheld, the stubborn phenomenon is there of an impotence in the claims which the universe embodies, which no talk about an eternal nature of things can gloze over or dispel. An ineffective *à priori* order is as important a thing as an ineffective God; and in the eye of philosophy, it is as hard a thing to explain.

We may now consider that what we distinguished as the metaphysical question in ethical philosophy is sufficiently answered, and that we have learned what the words "good," "bad," and "obligation" severally mean. They mean no absolute natures, independent of personal support. They are objects of feeling and desire, which have no foothold or anchorage in Being, apart from the existence of actually living minds.

JOHN DEWEY Shared Experience

How can philosophic change seriously affect social philosophy? As far as fundamentals are concerned, every view and combination appears to have been formulated already. Society is composed of individuals: this obvious and basic fact no philosophy, whatever its pretensions to novelty, can question or alter. Hence these three alternatives: Society must exist for the sake of individuals; or individuals must have their ends and ways of living set for them by society; or else society and individuals are correlative, organic, to one another, society requiring the service and subordination of individuals and at the same time existing to serve them. Beyond these three views, none seems to be logically conceivable. Moreover, while each of the three types includes many subspecies and variations within itself, yet the changes seem to have been so thoroughly rung that at most only minor variations are now possible.

Especially would it seem true that the "organic" conception meets all the objections to the extreme individualistic and extreme socialistic theories, avoiding the errors alike of Plato and Bentham. Just because society is composed of individuals, it would seem that individuals and the associative relations that hold them together must be of coequal importance. Without strong and competent individuals, the bonds and ties that form society have nothing to lay hold on. Apart from associations with one another, individuals are isolated from one another and fade and wither; or are opposed to one another and their conflicts injure individual development. Law, state, church, family, friendship, industrial association, these and other institutions and arrangements are necessary in order that individuals may grow and find their specific capacities and functions. Without their aid and support human life is, as Hobbes said, brutish, solitary, nasty.

We plunge into the heart of the matter, by asserting that these various theories suffer from a common defect. They are all committed to the logic of general notions under which specific situations are to be brought. What we want light upon is this or that group of individuals, this or that concrete human being, this or that special institution or social arrangement. For such a logic of inquiry, the traditionally accepted logic substitutes discussion of the meaning of concepts and their dialectical relationship to one another. The discussion goes on in terms of *the* state, *the* individual; the nature of institutions as such, society in general.

We need guidance in dealing with particular perplexities in domestic life, and are met by dissertations on the Family or by assertions of the sacredness of individual Personality. We want to know about the worth of the institution of private property as it operates under given conditions of definite time and place. We meet with the reply of Proudhon that property generally is theft, or with that of Hegel that the realization of will is the end of all institutions, and that private ownership as the expression of mastery of personality over physical nature is a necessary element in such realization. Both answers may have a certain suggestiveness in connection with specific situations. But the conceptions are not proffered for what they may be worth in connection with special historic phenomena. They are general answers supposed to have a universal meaning that covers and dominates all particulars. Hence they do not assist inquiry. They close it. They are not instrumentalities to be employed and tested in clarifying concrete social difficulties. They are ready-made principles to be imposed upon particulars in order to determine their nature. They tell us about *the* state when we want to know about *some* state. But the implication is that what is said about *the* state applies to any state that we happen to wish to know about. . . .

Consider [also] the conception of the individual self. The individualistic school of England and France in the eighteenth and nineteenth centuries was empirical in intent. It based its individualism, philosophically speaking, upon the belief that individuals are alone real, that classes and organizations are secondary and derived. They are artificial, while individuals are natural. In what way then can individualism be said to come under the animadversions that have been passed? To say the defect was that this school overlooked those connections with other persons which are a part of the constitution of every individual is true as far as it goes; but unfortunately it rarely goes beyond the point of just that wholesale justification of institutions which has been criticized.

The real difficulty is that the individual is regarded as something *given,* something already there. Consequently, he can only be something to be catered to, something whose pleasures are to be magnified and possessions multiplied. When the individual is taken as something given already, anything that can be done to him or for him it can only be by way of external impressions and belongings: sensations of pleasure and pain, comforts, securities. Now it is true that social arrangements, laws, institutions are made for man, rather than that man is made for them; that they are means and agencies of human welfare and progress. But they are not means for obtaining something for individuals, not even happiness. They are means of *creating* individuals. Only in the physical sense of physical bodies that to the senses are separate is individuality an original datum. Individuality in a social and moral sense is something to be wrought out. It means initiative, inventiveness, varied resourcefulness, assumption of responsibility in choice of belief and conduct. These are not gifts, but achievements. As achievements, they are not absolute but relative to the use that is to be made of them. And this use varies with the environment. . . .

Consequently we cannot be satisfied with the general statement that society and the state is organic to the individual.

The question is one of specific causations. Just what response does *this* social arrangement, political or economic, evoke, and what effect does it have upon the disposition of those who engage in it? Does it release capacity? If so, how widely? Among a few, with a corresponding depression in others, or in an extensive and equitable way? Is the capacity which is set free also directed in some coherent way, so that it becomes a power, or its manifestation spasmodic and capricious? Since responses are of an indefinite diversity of kind, these inquiries have to be detailed and specific. Are man's senses rendered more delicately sensitive and appreciative, or are they blunted and dulled by this and that form of social organization? Are their minds trained so that the hands are more deft and cunning? Is curiosity awakened or blunted? What is its quality: is it merely esthetic, dwelling on the forms and surfaces of things or is it also an intellectual searching into their meaning? Such questions as these (as well as the more obvious ones about the qualities conventionally labelled moral), become the starting-points of inquiries about every institution of the community when it is recognized that individuality is not originally given but is created under the influences of associated life. Like utilitarianism, the theory subjects every form of organization to continual scrutiny and criticism. But instead of leading us to ask what it does in the way of causing pains and pleasures to individuals already in existence, it inquires what is done to release specific capacities and co-ordinate them into working powers. What sort of individuals are created? . . .

Society, as was said, is many associations not a single organization. Society means association; coming together in joint intercourse and action for the better realization of any form of experience which is augmented and confirmed by being shared. Hence there are as many associations as there are goods which are enhanced by being mutually communicated and participated in. And these are literally indefinite in number. Indeed, capacity to endure publicity and communication is the test by which it is decided whether a pretended good is genuine or spurious. Moralists have always insisted upon the fact that good is universal, objective, not just private, particular. But too often, like Plato, they have been content with a metaphysical universality or, like Kant, with a logical universality. Communication, sharing, joint participation are the only actual ways of universalizing the moral law and end. We insisted at the last hour upon the unique character of every intrinsic good. But the counterpart of this proposition is that the situation in which a good is consciously realized is not one of transient sensations or private appetites but one of sharing and communication—public, social. Even the hermit communes with gods or spirits; even misery loves company; and the most extreme selfishness includes a band of followers or some partner to share in the attained good. Universalization means socialization, the extension of the area and range of those who share in a good.

The increasing acknowledgment that goods exist and endure only through being communicated and that association is the means of conjoint sharing lies back of the modern sense of humanity and democracy. It is the saving salt in altruism and philanthropy, which without this factor degenerate into moral condescension and moral interference, taking the form of trying to regulate the affairs of others under the guise of doing them good or of conferring upon them some right as if it were a gift of charity. It follows that organization is never an end in itself. It is a means of promoting *association,* of multiplying effective points of contact between persons, directing their intercourse into the modes of greatest fruitfulness.

The tendency to treat organization as an end in itself is responsible for all the exaggerated theories in which individuals are subordinated to some institution to which is given the noble name of society. Society is the *process* of associating in such ways that experiences, ideas, emotions, values are transmitted and made common. To this active process, both the individual and the institutionally organized may truly be said to be subordinate. The individual is subordinate because except in and through communication of experience from and to others, he remains dumb, merely sentient, a brute animal. Only in association with fellows does he become a conscious centre of experience. Organization, which is what traditional theory has generally meant by the term Society or State, is also subordinate because it becomes static, rigid, institutionalized whenever it is not employed to facilitate and enrich the contacts of human beings with one another.

The long-time controversy between rights and duties, law and freedom is another version of the strife between the Individual and Society as fixed concepts. Freedom for an individual means growth, ready change when modification is required. . . .

We began by pointing out that European philosophy arose when intellectual methods and scientific results moved away from social traditions which had consolidated and embodied the fruits of spontaneous desire and fancy. It was pointed out that philosophy had ever since had the problem of adjusting the dry, thin and meagre scientific standpoint with the obstinately persisting body of warm and abounding imaginative beliefs. Conceptions of possibility, progress, free movement and infinitely diversified opportunity have been suggested by modern science. But until they have displaced from *imagination* the heritage of the immutable and the once-for-all ordered and systematized, the ideas of mechanism and matter will lie like a dead weight upon the emotions, paralyzing religion and distorting art. When the liberation of capacity no longer seems a menace to organization and established institutions, something that cannot be avoided practically and yet something that is a threat to conservation of the most precious values of the past, when the liberating of human capacity operates as a socially creative force, art will not be a luxury, a stranger to the daily occupations of making a living. Making a living economically speaking, will be at one with making a life that is worth living. And when the emotional force, the mystic force one might say, of communication, of the miracle of shared life and shared experience is spontaneously felt, the hardness and crudeness of contemporary life will be bathed in the light that never was on land or sea.

State, Power, and Authority

Dewey's theory of man and society assigns a fundamental role to interests in associative phenomena. Rejecting attempts to understand society through abstractions like State, Law, and Sovereignty, he begins with the existence of many groups resting on shared interests and pursuing desired consequences. Within this pluralistically conceived society, however, there arises a general or common interest relating to the consequences of group activity on those not participating in that activity. The state develops from this interest.

Further analysis of this account of the state is given in the following selection by R. M. MacIver (1882–   ). Having its basis in human interests, the state is but one association among many others. Yet it is a distinctive kind of association, with a unique function of its own. That function is to give unity to the whole system of social relationships, sustaining and controlling them as well as making them possible. More simply, the state supports the "business of life," for within its unity all the different primary groups of society may find their proper place. This it does because it is given the power to dispense and guarantee rights to groups and individuals.

Such power is universal in principle: it extends over all members of a society and even to the entire human race. What is the source of this authority and power? Since the pragmatist insists that all relations and values derive from the subjective valuations of human beings, he answers this question by holding that the state is sustained by the general community as the expression of common interest. It is thus the community that gives the state its functions and powers—though the community itself is not an organization, but the source of organization.

It may be asked, how can the power that determines rights be itself limited?

In two ways, MacIver answers: the state is limited by its function, and by the community that assigns to it that function. To be sure, particular states may overstep these bounds and become oppressive agents; yet they thereby lose their effectiveness as the sustainers of communities. The state is and remains a true unifying agent, MacIver concludes, only as it has evolved toward a democracy. Its character is that of a corporation, and its true nature is revealed in the fundamental meaning of law.

R. M. MACIVER   The State as Organ of Community

In our last chapter we approached the great dilemma with which the political thought of the present is faced. We showed not only that the state must be regarded as an association among others, but also that it has, partly in fact and wholly in the logic of its function, the character of a corporation. It commands only because it serves; it owns only because it owes. It creates rights not as the lordly dispenser of gifts, but as the agent of society for the creation of rights. The servant is not greater than his master. As other rights are relative to function and are recognized as limited by it, so too the rights of the state *should* be. It has the function of guaranteeing rights. To exercise this function it needs and receives certain powers. These powers should be limited just as the function is limited. The function is limited both by its own nature and by the capacity of the agent, and that capacity becomes known to us by experience of its conduct, in the light of the means at its command. The state is not exempt from the imperative, "thus far and no further," to which all agencies are subject.

But here the dilemma threatens us again. How can the power which determines rights be itself subject to obligation? How can the authority which alone has compulsive power be itself controlled? If the state be not the final authority, how can there be any other? And if there be none, how can order be secured? Who assigns to each association its place, who establishes its bounds, unless it is the state? How can law itself be supreme, unless the state also is supreme? And yet again, how can the state be supreme in the face of the indubitable fact that other associations are not its creatures, and that they possess powers and spheres of their own, which are not those of the state?

If we turn again, and for the last time to the criterion of law, we find the answer. Let us for a moment contrast law with custom. There are many customs which are observed at least as faithfully as political laws. Now customs are sustained by the community as such, not as a rule by the aid of any organization. Law, on the other hand, is sustained by the state. But ultimately they rest alike on the same basis, for the state itself is sustained by the community. Ultimately they are both expressions of the social sense, the sense of solidarity, the sense of common interest. In this subjective fact we find the root of the

From R. M. MacIver, *The Modern State,* Oxford: The Clarendon Press, 1926. Used by permission of The Clarendon Press.

unity of society, not in the state, which is only a form through which that unity is expressed. We are here in the sphere of values, which must be felt before they are established. Just as, for example, all the objective values of the economic sphere, together with all the institutions and associations by which they are maintained and pursued, derive from the subjective valuations of economically minded beings, so in the whole area of society all forms of relationship, including those protected by the state, derive from the subjective valuations of social beings. It is they who create, according to the range of felt or recognized solidarity, states and churches and trade-unions and employers' associations. It is they who say what the state shall or shall not do or be, and set limits, directly or indirectly, to the activity of groups to which they belong or do not belong. The community is the matrix of all its inclusive and exclusive forms. It is not an organization but the source of organization. No structure, no form of government, can assure social unity. The final unity lies in the solidarity of men, not in the power of the state. There is social unity just in so far as the sense of common interest or common nature is stronger than that of dividing interests. Man is a social animal and the more fully he comes to realize it the stronger and the greater does the order of society become. In that realization lies the source of what unity exists or can exist.

The state is, as it were, the paved highway of social life, bordered by fields and cities. It is the common way which serves them all. All the business of life is rendered possible by its aid, and all who live along it must contribute to its upkeep. It is the basis of all social communications. Therefore, whatever else a man may be, he *must* be a member, or at least a subject, of the state. If he does not share the responsibility for the highway he must at least observe its rules. But he does not live on the highway, nor does man live for the state. His home is in the fields or the cities, and there he gathers the fruits of his labour. In the simpler days when there were only a few scattered houses along the highway, men learned to speak of it as if it included all that belonged to them. So the rule of the highway became a tyranny, because its guardians claimed to control the whole lives of men. Very slowly have they learned its true significance. They are only now learning that although they all have duties towards the upkeep of the highway, this universal obligation does not sum up their social life. The fields and cities now stretch far away from the thoroughfare. So the many memberships of social life have grown explicit, and refuse any longer to be summed in the one membership of the state.

The one membership remains still as a condition of all the rest. It too has grown fuller and richer, the greater means of more manifold purposes. The highway is broader and more necessary than ever before. Now it is the means whereby great groups and centres of social life are kept in due relation to each other and to the whole. But we must not on that account restore its ancient claim, the former claim of its guardians, that they should control the centres of life to which it ministers. The highway is for the sake of the life that is lived along it and beyond it. Nor, dismissing that false claim, should we take the opposing extreme, which would make the centres independent of the highway. The greater community is still a community, and the highway is still the chief external means that makes it one.

All civilized men must be members or subjects of a state, because they are all members of some community and must share its external social conditions.[1] In this sense the state is universal in extension, though on that very account it is peculiarly limited in its *mode* of action. Ideally the order of the state includes everybody everywhere, and its end is not fully achieved until all states are parts of a universal political order as extensive as humanity itself. This order may be achieved through the consent of particular states, each maintaining, to return to our metaphor, its own part of the one great highway. But the logic of political order requires a unity of system over the whole earth, and our traditions of independent and exclusive sovereignties have become mere obstacles to the recognition of this indefeasible truth. Within this unity all the intrinsic differences of groups can find their proper place; apart from it they are distorted or exaggerated because they ignore the intrinsic likenesses, the common social nature, of

---

[1] This distinction between the membership of the state and that of other associations is generally put in a misleading way, and consequently false deductions are made from it. Thus a recent writer, Mr. Norman Wilde, in a generally well-balanced work (*The Ethical Basis of the State*), remarks that "all men are members of the state, but not of any other association" (p. 135). All men are subject to some one state, but not all are members of it. Moreover, all men are members of families, and all men are bound together in some economic system, though there is here no association co-extensive with the system. The same writer adds that the state "is not merely one institution among many, but the condition of all." This is true, at any rate if we substitute "association" for "institution." But it is a statement which can be made with equal truth of the family, and also, in the modern world, of its economic associations. If the state is unique in its own way, so are other associations in their ways. And if the state is absolutely necessary to our social life, so are they also.

humanity. If all men *must,* no matter what their differences, be included in some political system, all men should, by the logic of the same necessity, be included in one still greater order, the unbounded rule of law.

The same logic opposes the conception of a pluralistic society wherein great associations seek their several aims and when these clash must somehow decide their differences by the mere impact on one another of their respective forces. We too have insisted that the state is but one among the great associations, but its own peculiar function is no other than this, of giving a form of unity to the whole system of social relationships. It can achieve this end, as successfully as other associations achieve their ends, without arrogating to itself again that omnicompetence which it has vainly sought to establish. There are times when it fails, as every human organization fails, but its success is far more notable and enduring. Ultimately it succeeds, because it does not act merely in its own right, because it is an organ of society maintained by it for that very purpose. It is the community, including therefore the members of all other associations, which assigns to it its function and lends it power.

We see this too if we reflect on the actual clashes which do occur between associations. We speak, for instance, of the conflicts between church and state, or between the state and the trade-union. But such conflicts have a very different interpretation from those that occur, say between church and church or between trade-union and employers' union. In the latter cases there is a sheer difference of attitude or of interest. The particular groups, wholly as groups, deny and oppose the aims of one another. The aims are themselves particular, and the conflict can be waged on a ground which leaves intact the general order of society. But it is otherwise when the issue involves the state and another association. It is never simply a conflict of two distinct groups, two distinct sects of interest, of which one is at stake. Take for example the Scottish Disruption or the Kulturkampf. These were conflicts *within* a state, because all directly concerned were its citizens. In the first instance it was also a conflict *within* a church. In the second it was a conflict, touching the proper spheres of state and church, between those citizens who accepted certain claims of the Catholic Church and those who denied them. In the strict sense there cannot be a conflict between the state as a whole and any other association. The claims of the state, as insisted upon by a government or by a majority of its citizens, may be opposed to the claims of other associations. But it is always an internal struggle, and therefore, unless the state be dissolved altogether in the process, one modified by the common fact of citizenship. As the state has grown in experience, it has learned the unwisdom of making such claims as endanger the vital principle or the autonomy of any of the great associations to which its members may also belong.

The state can act thus as a unifying agent, but only in so far as it has itself undergone evolution towards democracy. For this reason we regard democracy as the form of the state proper, for only under democratic conditions can it achieve this proper function, this function, in other words, which it and it alone is capable of performing. Historically the interest of the state has been identified with that of ruler or ruling caste, military or landed oligarchy or later plutocracy. In these forms it was the organization of a class, and instead of standing for the interests we have shown to be its true concern it stood for the whole complex of interests belonging to a class. The land laws, enclosure acts, anti-labour acts, and so forth, which states have enforced were contradictory of the universality of law—they were not directed towards the common interests of those who were subject to the laws. The true nature of the state, here as always, is revealed in the fundamental character of law.

Law and Rights

Two schools of jurisprudence have developed under the influence of pragmatism. One is known as sociological jurisprudence and is associated especially with Roscoe Pound,* who wrote of it that

the sociological movement in jurisprudence is a movement for pragmatism as a philosophy of law; for the adjustment of principles and doctrines to the human conditions they are to govern rather than to assumed first principles; for putting the human factor in the central place and relegating logic to its true position as an instrument.

This brief quotation contains or alludes to the chief elements of the pragmatic view of law. There is the rejection of appeals to so-called first principles, to self-evident assumptions, and to rationalistic theories of natural law. Decisions must be made

---

* The selection below in "The Ideal of Justice" gives Pound's views more fully.

with reference to their specific consequences; antecedent material such as tradition and precedent serves as a guide for analysis, but not as a norm for evaluation.

Rules of law are projections into the future. They attempt to prophesy the effect
on the social order of the conduct they regulate. More broadly put, law and the
courts constitute a scheme of instruments for readaptation, for assisting society
in experiments of readjustment. There is also the centrality of the human factor,
of needs and interests. Law is not logical deduction, it is a kind of "social engineering" that aims at maximizing satisfactions and minimizing wants. As Pound put
it in another place, "For the purpose of understanding the law of today, I am
content with a picture of satisfying as much of the whole body of human wants
as we may with the least sacrifice."

The second school, influenced by Oliver Wendell Holmes (1841–1935), is
legal realism. Many scholars find it difficult to distinguish sharply between realism
and sociological jurisprudence: the former seems to be a subdivision of the latter.
Legal realism's emphasis is more scientific, even positivistic—though it will be
remembered that pragmatism has affinities with positivism—and it lays greater
stress on the implicit relativism of pragmatic value theory. While accepting with
sociological jurisprudence the understanding of law as prophecy as to what the
courts lay down, realists tend to limit themselves to "scientific" descriptions of the
legal process, and thus also to exclude consideration of legal ideals.

The selection below is from one of Justice Holmes's many influential papers,
"The Path of the Law." In it Holmes calls his reader's attention to how the rules
of law actually work, not to what they may be on paper. Thus he is led to his
famous definition of law as a prophecy of what the courts will do in fact. This
notion applies to rights and duties also, for there is no right or duty independent
of the consequences of its breach. A right, therefore, may similarly be defined as
a prediction that if a man does (or does not do) a certain thing, he will suffer
in certain ways by judgment of the court.

In addition to this question of definition, two other matters concern Holmes.
The first is the distinction between law and morals. Failure to make this distinction,
he says, is not only conceptually confusing, but it may lead to the failure to see
the nature of law as prophecy. The second point is that logic is not the only
force at work in law: experience is there in an even more important way. Almost
any conclusion can be given logical form. The truer stuff of the law is human
needs and purposes, and the goal of the law is to develop a civilized, rational
system where "every rule it contains is referred articulately and definitely to an
end it subserves, and when the grounds for desiring that end are stated or are
ready to be stated in words."

OLIVER WENDELL HOLMES   The Path of the Law

When we study law we are not studying a mystery but a well-known profession. We are studying what we shall
want in order to appear before judges,

From Oliver Wendell Holmes, "The Path of the Law," *Harvard Law Review,* 10 (1897).
An address delivered at the dedication of the new hall of the Boston University School of
Law on January 8, 1897.

or to advise people in such a way as to keep them out of court. The reason why it is a profession, why people will pay lawyers to argue for them or to advise them, is that in societies like ours the command of the public force is intrusted to the judges in certain cases, and the whole power of the state will be put forth, if necessary, to carry out their judgments and decrees. People want to know under what circumstances and how far they will run the risk of coming against what is so much stronger than themselves, and hence it becomes a business to find out when this danger is to be feared. The object of our study, then, is prediction, the prediction of the incidence of the public force through the instrumentality of the courts.

The means of the study are a body of reports, or treatises, and of statutes, in this country and in England, extending back for six hundred years, and now increasing annually by hundreds. In these sibylline leaves are gathered the scattered prophecies of the past upon the cases in which the axe will fall. These are what properly have been called the oracles of the law. Far the most important and pretty nearly the whole meaning of every new effort of legal thought is to make these prophecies more precise, and to generalize them into a thoroughly connected system. The process is one, from a lawyer's statement of a case, eliminating as it does all the dramatic elements with which his client's story has clothed it, and retaining only the facts of legal import, up to the final analyses and abstract universals of theoretic jurisprudence. The reason why a lawyer does not mention that his client wore a white hat when he made a contract, while Mrs. Quickly would be sure to dwell upon it along with the parcel gilt goblet and the sea-coal fire, is that he foresees that the public force will act in the same way whatever his client had upon his head. It is to make the prophecies easier to be remembered and to be understood that the teachings of the decisions of the past are put into general propositions and gathered into text-books, or that statutes are passed in a general form. The primary rights and duties with which jurisprudence busies itself again are nothing but prophecies. One of the many evil effects of the confusion between legal and moral ideas, about which I shall have something to say in a moment, is that theory is apt to get the cart before the horse, and to consider the right or the duty as something existing apart from and independent of the consequences of its breach, to which certain sanctions are added afterward. But, as I shall try to show, a legal duty so called is nothing but a prediction that if a man does or omits certain things he will be made to suffer in this or that way by judgment of the court;—and so of a legal right.

The number of our predictions when generalized and reduced to a system is not unmanageably large. They present themselves as a finite body of dogma which may be mastered within a reasonable time. It is a great mistake to be frightened by the ever-increasing number of reports. The reports of a given jurisdiction in the course of a generation take up pretty much the whole body of the law, and restate it from the present point of view. We could reconstruct the corpus from them if all that went before were burned. The use of the earlier reports is mainly historical, a use about which I shall have something to say before I have finished.

I wish, if I can, to lay down some first principles for the study of this body of dogma or systematized prediction which we call the law, for men who want to use it as the instrument of their business to enable them to prophesy in their turn, and, as bearing upon the study, I wish to point out an ideal which as yet our law has not attained.

The first thing for a business-like understanding of the matter is to understand its limits, and therefore I think it desirable at once to point out and dispel a confusion between morality and law, which sometimes rises to the height of conscious theory, and more often and indeed constantly is making trouble in detail without reaching the point of consciousness. You can see very plainly that a bad man has as much reason as a good one for wishing to avoid an encounter with the public force, and therefore you can see the practical importance of the distinction between morality and law. A man who cares nothing for an ethical rule which is believed and practised by his neighbors is likely nevertheless to care a good deal to avoid being made to pay money, and will want to keep out of jail if he can.

I take it for granted that no hearer of mine will misinterpret what I have to say as the language of cynicism. The law is the witness and external deposit of our moral life. Its history is the history of the moral development of the race. The practice of it, in spite of popular jests, tends to make good citizens and good men. When I emphasize the difference between law and morals I do so with reference to a single end, that of learning and understanding the law. For that purpose you must definitely master its specific marks, and it is for that I ask you for the moment to imagine yourselves indifferent to other and greater things.

I do not say that there is not a wider point of view from which the distinction between law and morals becomes of secondary or no importance, as all mathematical distinctions vanish in presence of the infinite. But I do say that that distinction is of the first importance for the object which we are here to consider—a right study and mastery of the law as a business with well understood limits, a body of dogma enclosed within definite lines. I have just shown the practical reason for saying so. If you want to know the law and nothing else, you must look at it as a bad man, who cares only for the material consequences which such knowledge enables him to predict, not as a good one, who finds his reasons for conduct, whether inside the law or outside of it, in the vaguer sanctions of conscience. The theoretical importance of the distinction is no less, if you would reason on your subject aright. The law is full of phraseology drawn from morals, and by the mere force of language continually invites us to pass from one domain to the other without perceiving it, as we are sure to do unless we have the boundary constantly before our minds. The law talks about rights, and duties, and malice, and intent, and negligence, and so forth, and nothing is easier, or, I may say, more common in legal reasoning, than to take these words in their moral sense, at some stage of the argument, and so to drop into fallacy. For instance, when we speak of the rights of man in a moral sense, we mean to mark the limits of interference with individual freedom which we think are prescribed by conscience, or by our ideal, however reached. Yet it is certain that many laws have been enforced in the past, and it is likely that some are enforced now, which are condemned by the most enlightened opinion of the time, or which at all events pass the limit of interference as many consciences would draw it. Manifestly, therefore, nothing but confusion of thought can result from assuming that the rights of man in a moral sense are equally rights in the sense of the Constitution and the law. No doubt simple and extreme cases can be put of imaginable laws which the statute-making power would not dare to enact, even in the absence of written constitutional prohibitions, because the community would rise in rebellion and fight; and this gives some plausibility to the proposition that the law, if not a part of morality, is limited by it. But this limit of power is not coextensive with any system of morals. For the most part it falls far within the lines of any such system, and in some cases may extend beyond them, for reasons drawn from the habits of a particular people at a particular time. I once heard the late Professor Agassiz say that a German population would rise if you added two cents to the price of a glass of beer. A statute in such a case would be empty words, not because it was wrong, but because it could not be enforced. No one will deny that wrong statutes can be and are enforced, and we should not all agree as to which were the wrong ones.

The confusion with which I am dealing besets confessedly legal conceptions. Take the fundamental question, What constitutes the law? You will find some text writers telling you that it is something different from what is decided by the courts of Massachusetts or England, that it is a system of reason, that it is a deduction from principles of ethics or admitted axioms or what not, which may or may not coincide with the decisions. But if we take the view of our friend the bad man we shall find that he does not care two straws for the axioms or deductions, but that he does want to know what the Massachusetts or English courts are likely to do in fact. I am much of his mind. The prophecies of what the courts will do in fact, and nothing more pretentious, are what I mean by the law.

Take again a notion which as popularly understood is the widest conception which the law contains—the notion of legal duty, to which already I have referred. We fill the word with all the content which we draw from morals. But what does it mean to a bad man? Mainly, and in the first place, a prophecy that if he does certain things he will be subjected to disagreeable consequences by way of imprisonment or compulsory payment of money. But from his point of view, what is the difference between being fined and being taxed a certain sum of doing a certain thing? That his point of view is the test of legal principles is shown by the many discussions which have arisen in the courts on the very question whether a given statutory liability is a penalty or a tax. On the answer to this question depends the decision whether conduct is legally wrong or right, and also whether a man is under compulsion or free. Leaving the criminal law on one side, what is the difference between the liability under the mill acts or statutes authorizing a taking by eminent domain and the liability for what we call a wrongful conversion of property where restoration is out of the question. In both cases the party taking another man's property has to pay its fair value as assessed by a jury, and no more. What significance is there in calling one taking right and another wrong from the point of view of the law? It does not matter, so far as the given consequence, the compulsory payment, is concerned, whether the act to which it is attached is described in terms of praise or in terms of blame, or whether the law purports to prohibit it or to allow it. If it matters at all, still speaking from the bad man's point of view, it must be because in one case and not in the other some further disadvantages, or at least some further consequences, are attached to the act by the law. The only other disadvantages thus attached to it which I ever have been able to think of are to be found in two somewhat insignificant legal doctrines, both of which might be abolished without much disturbance. One is, that a contract to do a prohibited act is unlawful, and the other, that, if one of two or more joint wrongdoers has to pay all the damages, he cannot recover contribution from his fellows. And that I believe is all. You see how the vague circumference of the notion of duty shrinks and at the same time grows more precise when we wash it with cynical acid and expel everything except the object of our study, the operations of the law. . . .

So much for the limits of the law. The next thing which I wish to consider is what are the forces which determine its content and its growth. You may assume, with Hobbes and Bentham and Austin, that all law emanates from the sovereign, even when the first human beings to enunciate it are the judges, or you may think that law is the voice of the Zeitgeist, or what you like. It is all one to my present purpose. Even if every decision required the sanction of an emperor with despotic power and a whimsical turn of mind, we should be interested none the less, still with a view to prediction, in discovering some order, some rational explanation, and some principle of growth for the rules which he laid down. In every system there are such explanations and principles to be found. It is with regard to them that a second fallacy comes in, which I think it important to expose.

The fallacy to which I refer is the notion that the only force at work in the development of the law is logic. In the broadest sense, indeed, that notion would be true. The postulate on which we think about the universe is that there is a fixed quantitative relation between every phenomenon and its antecedents and consequents. If there is such a thing as a phenomenon without these fixed quantitative relations, it is a miracle. It is outside the law of cause and effect, and as such transcends our power of thought, or at least is something to or from which we cannot reason. The condition of our thinking about the universe is that it is capable of being thought about rationally, or, in other words, that every part of it is effect and cause in the same sense in which those parts are with which we are most familiar. So in the broadest sense it is true that the law is a logical development, like everything else. The danger of which I speak is not the admission that the principles governing other phenomena also govern the law, but the notion that a given system, ours, for instance, can be worked out like mathematics from some general axioms of conduct. This is the natural error of the schools, but it is not confined to them. I once heard a very eminent judge say that he never let a decision go until he was absolutely sure that it was right. So judicial dissent often is blamed, as if it meant simply that one side or the other were not doing their sums right, and, if they would take more trouble, agreement inevitably would come.

This mode of thinking is entirely natural. The training of lawyers is a training in logic. The processes of analogy, discrimination, and deduction are those in which they are most at home. The language of judicial decision is mainly the language of logic. And the logical method and form flatter that longing for certainty and for repose which is in every human mind. But certainty generally is illusion, and repose is not the destiny of man. Behind the logical form lies a judgment as to the relative worth and importance of competing legislative grounds, often an inarticulate and unconscious judgment, it is true, and yet the very root and nerve of the whole proceeding. You can give any conclusion a logical form. You always can imply a condition in a contract. But why do you imply it? It is because of some belief as to the practice of the community or of a class, or because of some opinion as to policy, or, in short, because of some attitude of yours upon a matter not capable of exact quantitative measurement, and therefore not capable of founding exact logical conclusions. Such matters really are battle grounds where the means do not exist for determinations that shall be good for all time, and where the decision can do no more than embody the preference of a given body in a given time and place. We do not realize how large a part of our law is open to reconsideration upon a slight change in the habit of the public mind. No concrete proposition is self evident, no matter how ready we may be to accept it, not even Mr. Herbert Spencer's Every man has a right to do what he wills, provided he interferes not with a like right on the part of his neighbors.

Why is a false and injurious statement privileged, if it is made honestly in giving information about a servant. It is because it has been thought more important that information should be given freely, than that a man should be protected from what under other circumstances would be an actionable wrong. Why is a man at liberty to set up a business which he knows will ruin his neighbor? It is because the public good is supposed to be best subserved by free competition. Obviously such judgments of relative importance may vary in different times and places. Why does a judge instruct a jury that an employer is not liable to an employee for an injury received in the course of his employment unless he is negligent, and why do the jury generally find for the plaintiff if the case is allowed to go to them? It is because the traditional policy of our law is to confine liability to cases where a prudent man might have foreseen the injury, or at least the danger, while the inclination of a very large part of the community is to make certain classes of persons insure the safety of those with whom they deal. Since the last words were written, I have seen the requirement of such insurance put forth as part of the programme of one of the best known labor organizations. There is a concealed, half conscious battle on the question of legislative policy, and if any one thinks that it can be settled deductively, or once for all, I only can say that I think he is theoretically wrong, and that I am certain that his conclusion will not be accepted in practice *semper ubique et ab omnibus*. . . .

So much for the fallacy of logical form. Now let us consider the present condition of the law as a subject for study, and the ideal toward which it tends. We still are far from the point of view which I desire to see reached. No one has reached it or can reach it as yet. We are only at the beginning of a philosophical reaction, and of a reconsideration of the worth of doctrines which for the most part still are taken for granted without any deliberate, conscious, and systematic questioning of their grounds. The development of our law has gone on for nearly a thousand years, like the development of a plant, each generation taking the inevitable next step, mind, like matter, simply obeying a law of spontaneous growth. It is perfectly natural and right that it should have been so. Imitation is a necessity of human nature, as has been illustrated by a remarkable French writer, M. Tarde, in an admirable book, *Les Lois de l'Imitation*. Most of the things we do, we do for no better reason than that our fathers have done them or that our neighbors do them, and the same is true of a larger part than we suspect of what we think. The reason is a good one, because our short life gives us no time for a better, but it is not the best. It does not follow, because we all are compelled to take on faith at second hand most of the rules on which we base our action and our thought, that each of us may not try to set some corner of his world in the order of reason, or that all of us collectively should not aspire to carry reason as far as it will go throughout the whole domain. In regard to the law, it is true, no doubt, that an evolutionist will hesitate to affirm universal validity for his social ideals, or for the principles which he thinks should be embodied in legislation. He is content if he can prove them best for here and now. He may be ready to admit that he knows nothing about an absolute best in the cosmos, and even that he knows next to nothing about a permanent best for men. Still it is true that a body of law is more rational and more civilized when every rule it contains is referred articulately and definitely to an end which it subserves, and when the grounds for desiring that end are stated or are ready to be stated in words.

At present, in very many cases, if we want to know why a rule of law has taken its particular shape, and more or less if we want to know why it exists

at all, we go to tradition. We follow it into the Year Books, and perhaps beyond them to the customs of the Salian Franks, and somewhere in the past, in the German forests, in the needs of Norman kings, in the assumptions of a dominant class, in the absence of generalized ideas, we find out the practical motive for what now best is justified by the mere fact of its acceptance and that men are accustomed to it. The rational study of law is still to a large extent the study of history. History must be a part of the study, because without it we cannot know the precise scope of rules which it is our business to know. It is a part of the rational study, because it is the first step toward an enlightened scepticism, that is, toward a deliberate reconsideration of the worth of those rules. When you get the dragon out of his cave on to the plain and in the daylight, you can count his teeth and claws, and see just what is his strength. But to get him out is only the first step. The next is either to kill him, or to tame him and make him a useful animal. For the rational study of the law the black-letter man may be the man of the present, but the man of the future is the man of statistics and the master of economics. It is revolting to have no better reason for a rule of law than that so it was laid down in the time of Henry IV. It is still more revolting if the grounds upon which it was laid down have vanished long since, and the rule simply persists from blind imitation of the past. . . .

Since I wrote this discourse I have come on a very good example of the way in which tradition not only overrides rational policy, but overrides it after first having been misunderstood and having been given a new and broader scope than it had when it had a meaning. It is the settled law of England that a material alteration of a written contract by a party avoids it as against him. The doctrine is contrary to the general tendency of the law. We do not tell a jury that if a man ever has lied in one particular he is to be presumed to lie in all. Even if a man has tried to defraud, it seems no sufficient reason for preventing him from proving the truth. Objections of like nature in general go to the weight, not to the admissibility, of evidence. Moreover, this rule is irrespective of fraud, and is not confined to evidence. It is not merely that you cannot use the writing, but that the contract is at an end. What does this mean? The existence of a written contract depends on the fact that the offerer and offeree have interchanged their written expressions, not on the continued existence of those expressions. But in the case of a bond, the primitive notion was different. The contract was inseparable from the parchment. If a stranger destroyed it, or tore off the seal, or altered it, the obligee could not recover, however free from fault, because the defendant's contract, that is, the actual tangible bond which he had sealed, could not be produced in the form in which it bound him. About a hundred years ago Lord Kenyon undertook to use his reason on this tradition, as he sometimes did to the detriment of the law, and, not understanding

it, said he could see no reason why what was true of a bond should not be true of other contracts. His decision happened to be right, as it concerned a promissory note, where again the common law regarded the contract as inseparable from the paper on which it was written, but the reasoning was general, and soon was extended to other written contracts, and various absurd and unreal grounds of policy were invented to account for the enlarged rule.

I trust that no one will understand me to be speaking with disrespect of the law, because I criticise it so freely. I venerate the law, and especially our system of law, as one of the vastest products of the human mind. No one knows better than I do the countless number of great intellects that have spent themselves in making some addition or improvement, the greatest of which is trifling when compared with the mighty whole. It has the final title to respect that it exists, that it is not a Hegelian dream, but a part of the lives of men. But one may criticise even what one reveres. Law is the business to which my life is devoted, and I should show less than devotion if I did not do what in me lies to improve it, and, when I perceive what seems to me the ideal of its future, if I hesitated to point it out and to press toward it with all my heart.

Political Obligation

The grounds for the pragmatist's treatment of political obligation have now been given. They include the basic associative nature of human experience, the diversity of interests, the appeal to intelligence as a means of control, and the determination of value in terms of desirable consequences. The presentation of this treatment is by Harold J. Laski (1893–1950), an English political theorist who acknowledges James as the philosophical source and inspiration of his own views. This influence is central to Laski's theory of value: "What I mean by 'right,'" he said, "is something the pragmatist will understand. It is something the individual ought to concede because experience has proved it to be good."

Laski's theory of political obligation rests on the assumptions that the good of individuals cannot, over the long run, be separated from the goods of other men, and that intelligence is valuable as it helps to make possible the future harmony of interests. Man, Laski says, is a community-building animal, for his many and diverse interests are fundamentally social in nature. But in any community, private or group decisions are insufficient for the good of the whole, and spontaneity of action is impractical if not occasionally dangerous. Hence arises the necessity of government as "the final depository of the social will." The ideal for government is that the general purpose it supports will embody individual purposes, and that it will provide the means for developing human capacities. Should the mechanisms of state and society fail, human faculties remain to that degree unrealized.

Society and government are thus rooted in the complex facts of human nature. The obligation to obey arises from these same facts. Human beings develop their capacities in the shared experience of social groups, and at the same time, they are largely determined by social institutions. Men's allegiance to social institutions, however, cannot be explained in purely rational terms, for these institutions—including the state—reflect a variety of yearnings and interests. Allegiance comes as authority, and the maintenance of rules is experienced as an instrumentality for the control of desirable consequences. Realized desires, even freedom itself, rest on obedience to the common interest reflected in rules of order; the obligation to obey that order rests on the fact that it is in the individual's interest that there be a common interest.

Laski concludes with the observation that his theory is a revised Benthamism. Once again the influence of utilitarianism on pragmatism must be noted. The pragmatic theory of political obligation rests on the general utility of society to mankind, and yet important differences between the positions remain. Pragmatists reject the hedonism of utilitarians, and insist on an instrumentalist role for intelligence in the control of consequences.

HAROLD J. LASKI   Allegiance and Human Nature

Man finds himself, in the modern world, living under the authority of governments; and the obligation to obey their orders arises from the facts of his nature. For he is a community-building animal, driven by inherited instinct to live with his fellows. Crusoe on his desert island, or St. Simon Stylites upon his pillar, may defy the normal impulses which make them men; but, for the vast majority, to live with others is the condition of a rational existence.

Therein, at the outset, is implied the necessity of government. If the habits of peaceful fellowship are to be maintained, there are certain uniformities of

From Harold J. Laski, *A Grammar of Politics,* London: George Allen & Unwin, Ltd., 1939. Used by permission of the publisher.

conduct which must be observed. The activities of a civilised community are too complex and too manifold to be left to the blind regulation of impulse; and even if each man could be relied upon to act consistently in terms of intelligence there would be need for a customary standard by which the society in its organised form agreed to differentiate right from wrong. The theory of philosophic anarchy is impossible, in fact, so long as men move differently to the attainment of opposed desires. The effort involved in the peaceful maintenance of a common life does not permit the making of private decisions upon what the society deems essential to its existence. At some point, that is, spontaneity ceases to be practical, and the enforced acceptance of a common way of action becomes the necessary condition of a corporate civilisation.

Nor is the absence of such spontaneity a limitation upon freedom; it is rather its primary safeguard. For once it is admitted that no man is sufficient unto himself, there must be rules to govern the habits of his intercourse. His freedom is largely born from the maintenance of those rules. They define the conditions of his personal security. They maintain his health and the standards, spiritual, not less than material, of his life. Without them he is the prey of uncertainties far more terrible than the uniformities by which the sea of his experience is charted. No society is known in which the individual can, in any final way, mould the tradition to his desires. Everywhere the historic environment shapes its substance and limits its possibilities. It is only on the moon that men can cry for the moon.

Man is not, in fact, born free, and it is the price he pays for his past that he should be everywhere in chains. The illusion of an assured release from captivity will deceive few who have the patience to examine his situation. He comes into a society the institutions of which are in large part beyond his individual control. He learns that they will inevitably shape at least the general outlines of what fortune he may encounter. The organised effort of a determined group of men may, with patience, change the character of those institutions; but the individual who stands apart from his fellows is unlikely to be their master. The capacity, indeed, of most men will be exhausted by the mere effort to live; and the search to understand life will lead them into complexities they have rarely the energy, and seldom the leisure, to penetrate. For it is a grave error to assume that men in general are, at least actively and continuously, political creatures. The context of their lives which is, for the majority, the most important is a private context. They are conscious of their neighbours; they rarely grasp the essential fact that their neighbours are, in truth, the whole world. They set their wills by the wills of institutions they rarely explore. They do not examine those wills to give their own a rational relationship to them. They obey the orders of government from inertia; and even their resistance is too often a blind resentment rather than a reasoned desire to secure an alternative. No faculty, indeed, is more rare than that sense of the State which enables a few thinkers —Hobbes, Locke, Rousseau, Marx— to move their fellows to the measure of their thought. With most, even the interest to grasp the expression is uncommon. The characteristic of social life is the unthinking obedience of the many to the will of the few: It is the sudden invasion of our lives by unwonted experience that drives most of us to realise the vast discipline in which we are involved. . . .

It is a big world, about which, at our peril, we have to find our way. For the theory upon which the government to which we give our obedience acts is that its will somehow embodies the wills of us all. It professes, if not in detail, then at least in large outline, to embody within its general purpose the individual purpose we believe ourselves to embody at moments of clearest consciousness. The faith of civilisation is built upon the assumption that by reason of its mechanisms an increasing number of human beings realise at their best their highest faculties. To the extent that those mechanisms fail, so do our faculties, at their best, remain unrealised. In such a background, it is clear that the prospects of civilisation depend, in large degree, upon our ability to work its institutions. Our awareness of their nature will be, also, the degree in which we perceive their fragility. For we can have none of the comfortable assurance of a century ago that, whatever our errors, we may rest confident in the knowledge of progress. Our civilisation is held together by fear rather than by good will. The rivalry of States, the war of classes, the clash of colour—these haunt its margins as prospects instinct with disaster. It is not uncommon for men to sacrifice the welfare of their fellows to a private end. It is not infrequently that from the analysis of their relationships, honourable and selfless men have judged that modern civilisation is vicious at its foundations. Science may have given us the weapons of a creative life; but those weapons are, as we have become aware, the instruments of destruction. It does not seem likely that society will, in any coherent form, survive their devotion to ends of conflict.

In such an analysis, the study of modern politics can hardly avoid becoming an inquiry into the dynamics of peace. We seek to know what will bind men's allegiance, not inertly, but with passion, to its preservation and enlargement. We seek to find the ways in which their impulses as men may be satisfied at a level which secures the enrichment of the common life. We begin with the State because the context of men's lives is set most firmly in the background of its institutions. For there is no area of activity that is not, at least in theory, within the ambit of its control. The modern State is a territorial society divided into government and subjects claiming, within its allotted physical area, a supremacy over all other institutions. It is, in fact, the final legal depository of the social will. It sets the perspective of all other organisations. It brings within its power all forms of human activity the control of which it deems desirable. It is, moreover, the implied logic of this supremacy that whatever remains free of its control does so by its permission. The State does not permit that men should marry their sisters; it is by its graciousness that they are allowed to marry their cousins. The State is the keystone of the social arch. It moulds the form and substance of the myriad human lives with whose destinies it is charged.

This does not mean that the State is an unchanging organisation. It has been subject at every point to the laws of an unceasing evolution. New forms of property, an alteration in the character of religious belief, physical conditions at the moment of their coming beyond the control of men—these and things like these have shaped its substance. Nor are its forms unmoving. It has been monarchic, aristocratic, democratic; it has been in the control of the rich and of the poor. Men have ruled it by reason of their birth or by their position in a religious fellowship.

What, as a matter of history, can alone be predicted of the State is that it has always presented the striking phenomenon of a vast multitude owing allegiance to a comparatively small number of men. Thinkers since the time of Socrates have sought to explain that curiosity. To some it has seemed that men obey their masters because, at least ultimately, the will of the few is sufficiently the will of the many to secure obedience. Consent, it is said, is the basis of the State. But if by consent be meant anything more than an inert acceptance of orders obeyed without scrutiny, it is clear that there has not yet been an epoch in the history of the State in which this is true. Nor can we accept as obvious the view of Hobbes that men obey the State through fear. Something of this, indeed, may colour the attitude of men to particular laws. I may refrain from murder upon a nice balance of consequences. But I send my children to school from motives far more complex than that of self-interest built upon fear. It is far nearer the truth to urge, as Sir Henry Maine would have us admit, that the State is built upon habit; but this still leaves unexplored the dispositions which enter into habit, and the point at which their infraction, as in the France of the Revolution, becomes possible. And if, as with Bentham and the Utilitarians, we ground the whole upon utility, the difficulty arises of explaining to whom the particular State is useful, and why (as in pre-Revolutionary Russia) the character of its utility should not provoke dissent instead of obedience.

The answer to the problem of obedience is, of course, that all theories which strive to explain it in purely rational terms are beside the mark; for no man is a purely rational animal. The State as it was and is finds the roots of allegiance in all the complex facts of human nature; and a theory of obedience would have to weight them differently for each epoch in the history of the State if it were to approximate to the truth. In a social situation which made thought itself a danger, it was natural for Hobbes to seek in fear the ultimate source of men's acts; just as the eighteenth-century moralist tended to make of benevolence the basic spring of action. In fact, nothing is gained by the postulation of separate forces of this kind as socially predominant. Distinct impulses, of whatever sort, operating to lead men to obey the State are as unreal as an explanation of the facts they resume as a fire-principle is worthless as an explanation of the character of fire. We meet man as a bundle of impulses which act together as a total personality. He will want to live with his fellows. He will build churches that he may worship with them, and clubs that he may enjoy the peace of silence. He will fall in love and marry and have children; and he will fiercely protect what he deems their interests against the demands the world will make upon them. He will be curious in the face of nature, and that curiosity will lead in most to a constructiveness which, as William James said, is "a genuine and irresistible instinct in man, as in the bee and the beaver." He will seek to acquire things, and that collector's zest will, for the majority, translate itself into whatever forms the society holds of greatest worth. A hatred of insecurity, a desire to build a home, a yearning to move into unknown regions from the place where he was born, a hunter's impulse which may take him to the African desert, or, less romantically, satisfy him by saturation in detective stories—all these are yearnings written into the fabric of our institutions. Man is a pugnacious animal; and the task of finding an outlet for that fruitful source of destruction is omnipresent. He desires to master his environment, to be the leader in his platoon; yet, under fitting conditions, he finds pleasure also in submission which, as in military organisation, can be turned to effective ends. He is a vain creature, seeking, as Veblen has shown, to waste his substance conspicuously, anxious, often enough, to be judged by the transient display rather than the solid achievement; so the workman will buy the piano he cannot play as an index to respectability, and the social leader will offer to the Moloch of fashion the income which might educate her children to social usefulness.

Hunger, drink, sex, and the need of shelter and clothing seem the irreducible minimum of human wants. All else is capable of transmutation into forms as various as the history of society. All that we know with certainty is that the wants are there. Some, as hunger, we cannot deny in general measure if the society is to live; others we can meet with response so complex as almost to conceal the true desire beneath. But what, above all, is urgent is that we should realise that our institutions are the response to the totality of these impulses. They are inexplicable save in terms of their formidable complexity.

It is, of course, vital to the structure of political philosophy that man should be not merely a creature of impulse, but also the possessor of reason. He can reflect upon his conduct. He can observe disharmonies, correlate means and ends. He can, that is to say, so observe the results of his activity as to rectify the ills from which he suffers by directing into them a principle of conduct that increases his chance of self-fulfilment.

Where the tiger and the cuckoo hit upon that principle by accident, men can achieve its discovery by deliberate thought. It is here that there enters the concept of a social good. For good, it must be emphasised, is either social, or it is not good at all. If man is to live in community with his fellows it is a necessary condition of his life that what he attains should, at least in the long run, involve benefit also to others. Social good, therefore, seems to consist in the unity our nature attains when the working of our impulses results in a satisfied activity. It is a full response to the forces of human nature as these work in the lives of the myriad men about us. The substance of that good may vary; a changing tradition implies a difference from age to age. As the body of our knowledge grows we become, at least as a matter of doctrine, the better able intelligently to organise the method and degree of response. The unification that is achieved demands, of course, close scrutiny lest falsehood be mistaken for truth. In the long run, for example, the desire to acquire property is hardly satisfied by the consistent flotation of fraudulent companies. What is rather wanted is a certain balance of forces within our nature that, when achieved, relieves the pressure of gnawing want and, more positively, makes possible the continuous satisfaction of initiative. It is not a question of attaining a static environment in which immobile habits may be satisfied. All situations that we confront are ultimately unique; and experiment is the condition of survival. Since the same good never occurs twice, immobility in a changing world must spell disaster; and the unification we must seek is one that intelligently anticipates the future as it reasonably interprets the past.

All this, it may be noted, is a special

adaptation of the Benthamite theory to the special needs of our time. It follows Bentham in its insistence that social good is the product of co-ordinated intelligence; that, though the difficulties be admittedly great, we must plan our way to the end in view. It follows Bentham, also, though from a different basis, in urging that social good means the avoidance of misery and the attainment of happiness. It applies reason, that is, to the task of discovering ways in which wants can be satisfied; and it evaluates the quality of wants according to the degree in which, when satisfied, they minister to the permanent happiness of the whole community. Where it differs from the Utilitarian outlook is in its rejection of the egoistic nature of impulse

and the elaborate calculus of pains and pleasures which, though couched in the terminology of the Industrial Revolution, was in fact derived from evangelistic assumptions. Our view is rather, first, that individual good cannot, over a long period, be usefully abstracted from the good of other men and, second, that the value of reason is to be found in the degree to which it makes possible the future, not less than the immediate, harmony of impulses. For, otherwise, these war within us to frustrate the realisation of what is best both for ourselves and others. Social good is thus such an ordering of our personality that we are driven to search for things it is worth while to obtain that, thereby, we may enrich the great fellowship we serve.

The Ideal of Justice

As law is the prophecy of what the courts will do, so pragmatists assert that just law means the prophecy of what will produce the most satisfactory consequences. Justice becomes an attribute of a legal rule through its relation to subsequent experience, or put another way, every rule of law is just or unjust according to its subsequent justification. Indeed, the justice of a rule is the process of its justification, which means that the "just" is the expedient in adapting the legal order to an order of wants and interests.*

These general statements are developed in the selection by Roscoe Pound (1870–1964). Long-time dean of the Harvard Law School, Pound exerted a great influence on American jurisprudence, not only within sociological jurisprudence with which he was closely identified, but on legal realism and analytic jurisprudence as well. Resting his analysis on a theory of interests—"Individual interests are the only real interests"—Pound accepts the pragmatic formula that "the essence of good is to satisfy demand." He classifies interests as public, social, and private, and believes that the task of law is to balance interests at the least cost by "social engineering" (another term associated with his name).

Unlike some pragmatists, Pound rejected complete relativism and skepticism,

---

* See also James in "Pragmatism's Conception of Truth": "Truth *happens* to an idea. It *becomes* true, is *made* true by events." And again, " 'The true,' to put it very briefly, is only the expedient in the way of our thinking, just as 'the right' is only the expedient in the way of our behaving."

and toward the end of his long career, he favored a definition of law that includes reference to an ideal of justice. Thus, while recognizing an ideal element,† Pound retains the link with individual interests and offers no definition of justice himself.

Pound begins the selection by reviewing theories of the authority of law, including those based on force, on consent, and on political ethics. Finding that the legal order keeps its authority because it harmonizes conflicting human demands and thereby maintains civilization, he rejects these theories. He accepts the theory of obedience to the law as motivated primarily by *habits* of obedience. To draw this conclusion is also to reject theories of the legal order based on divine or natural order, on pure reason, and on historical experience: none of these provides a measure or a standard—"justice"—that is applicable in legal experience.

How, then, does the law go about measuring value in practice? Three methods are possible: by experience, through which men learn the rules and procedures that will adjust interests and demands; by reason, by which men can formulate "jural postulates" as the presuppositions of civilized society; and by an ideal of legal order, against which men can judge authoritatively the value of particular rules. Pound concludes that philosophers do not agree on this ideal, and yet the law must go on. It must rely, therefore, on the first two methods, developing by reason and experience those ways of adjusting relations that, with the least waste, will give the greatest effect to the whole scheme of interests.

---

† This is not necessarily inconsistent with other pragmatists, but is more a matter of emphasis. Dewey, for example, acknowledged the role of ideals in inquiry where they indicate possibilities for realization.

ROSCOE POUND   The Harmony of Interests

What is the source of authority of the legal order? When we ask this much-debated question we may mean the immediate practical source or the ultimate practical source or the ultimate moral source. Hence we cannot give one answer to a question which, seemingly simple, contains at least three questions, each with a different answer. The immediate practical source is to be found in the lawmaking and law-administering organs of a politically organized society, and behind them, as has been said, is the force of that society. So say the jurists. The ultimate practical source is a question for the science of politics. In our classical political theory we have been taught that it is consent; the consent of a free people to be ruled by a constitution and under it by laws made by legislators and administered by officials whom the people have freely chosen. Austin and Maine taught that it is a habit of obedience on the part of people generally, a phase, perhaps, of that control over internal nature which is half of civilization, making it unnecessary to apply force except in a relatively small number of the controversies which arise in daily life and to the conduct of a relatively small proportion of the population. Then there are those in recent times who tell us it is the self-interest of the dominant social and eco-

---

From Roscoe Pound, *Social Control through Law*, New Haven: Yale University Press, 1942. Used by permission of the publisher.

nomic class. That class, we are told, imposes its will upon those who are not in a position or are too weak or too economically dependent to resist, and thus there arises the habit of obedience. When we come to the third question, we are in the domain of political ethics and political and legal philosophy. But there are those who tell us that the question is superfluous. It is not a question of ought to be at all. In the ideal society of the future there will be no law since there will be no classes seeking one to impose its will upon others. With the disappearance of property, classes will disappear and law with them. Thus all question of ought is eliminated. Law has binding force because or when it is backed by a force imposing itself on all other forces. The classical juristic theory is that law may be deduced directly from justice, from the ideal relation between men, and owes its binding force to the binding force of justice which it declares. The dominant legal philosophy of today tells us that we cannot answer this question. As between the force theory and the consent theory and the justice theory, an assured choice is impossible. They express elements in the law which are in an irreducible antinomy, an ineradicable contradiction.

But the legal order goes on, whatever may be the basis of whatever rightful authority it has, and I submit it has kept and holds an actual authority because it performs, and performs well, its task of reconciling and harmonizing conflicting and overlapping human demands and so maintains a social order in which we may maintain and further civilization. So long as it does this well there will be the habit of obedience that makes practicable the employment of force upon those who require it. . . .

Jurists have conceived of a legal order patterned upon a divine order and so have turned to authority to provide a canon. They have thought of conformity to a moral order as revealed by the analogy of the order of physical nature, or as partly ascertained from revelation and partly discoverable by reason. At other times, they have conceived of the legal order as a rational order and so of a canon of values derived from pure reason. Reason, in this mode of thought, was taken to reveal a natural or ideal law of universal and unchallengeable validity, even if, as we see it now, an ideal version of the positive law and legal institutions of the time and place. At still other times they have thought of the legal order as resting upon experience, and so of a canon of values representing experience of life in civilized society. In that mode of thought, experience of life was conceived of as developed by experience in adjusting relations and ordering conduct through political and legal institutions, put into formulas by lawmakers and judges and doctrinal writers, and criticized and systematized by jurists. Thus they have conceived of the legal order as a historical order. At still other times, they have thought of the legal order as an order of freedom, as a regime of securing to everyone the maximum of free exertion of his will consonant with a like measure of free exertion of his will by everyone else. In this view there is a canon of values demonstrated by metaphysics. More recently there have been attempts to found a canon of values upon economics or to derive one from a theory of class war, attributing value to a class rather than to individuals and to claims urged in title of a class rather than in title of individual life or of social life, looking at society as a whole.

Where are we in juristic theory today? Some urge a maximum satisfaction of material wants. More argue that it is impossible to arrive at any measure of values or for judges and officials to hew to one if it is established. The former put this on epistemological grounds. The latter base the conclusion on Freudian psychology. Be the criterion of values in the books what it may, the actual behavior of judges and officials will be motivated by wish, and reason and authority will be conjured up afterward to satisfy another wish, namely, to appear reasonable. The former hold that a law is a threat of exercise of state force and so conceive of an order of force. The latter interpret judicial and administrative action in terms of individual psychology and so conceive of an order of impulse. . . .

How has the law gone about this matter of a measure of values in practice?

If we look at the actual working out, development, and application of legal precepts rather than at juristic theory, we may say that three methods have obtained. One is a finding out by experience of what will achieve an adjustment of conflicting and overlapping interests with the least impairment of the scheme of interests as a whole and giving that experience a reasoned development. Thus the measure becomes a practical one of what will adjust relations and order conduct with the least friction and waste. . . .

But the practical process of the legal order does not stop at finding by experience—by trial and error and judicial inclusion and exclusion—what will serve to adjust conflicting or overlapping interests. Reason has its part as well as experience. Jurists work out the jural postulates, the presuppositions as to relations and conduct, of civilized society in the time and place, and arrive in this way at authoritative starting points for legal reasoning. Experience is

developed by reason on this basis, and reason is tested by experience. Thus we get a second method, namely, valuing with reference to the jural postulates of civilization in the time and place. Newly arising claims are measured by these postulates when they push for recognition. When recognized they are adjusted to other recognized interests by this measure. When they are delimited with reference to other interests the means of securing them are determined by this same measure. . . .

A third measure of values, used in the classical era both in Roman law and in the law of the modern world, and well established in the maturity of law, is found in a received, traditionally authoritative idea of the social order and hence of the legal order, and of what legal institutions and doctrines should be and what the results of applying them to controversies should be.

It need scarcely be said that such pictures of an ideal social order, which come to enter into the law as part of the authoritative guides to determination of controversies, are not photographs or even idealized photographs of the social order of the time and place. They are instead much more idealized pictures of the social order of the past, undergoing a gradual process of retouching with reference to details of the social order of the present. Thus the received ideals of American law, as they took shape in our formative era in the fore part of the nineteenth century, are much closer to the pioneer agricultural society of our past than to the typically urban, industrial society of twentieth-century America. In general, men have sought to explain the institutions of the present in terms of a picture of the social order of the past. . . .

It will have been seen that of the

three methods of valuing interests open to lawmakers and courts and jurists, the third, which has been the main reliance of the jurist, and the second, much urged in the present century, are now less useful, indeed are embarrassed in their operation, because of transition from a social order for which the received ideal had been shaped and the jural postulates of which were clearly understood, to one which has not sufficiently found itself to admit of formulating an ideal which all will accept (as all the schools accepted that of the last century) or formulating jural postulates of the validity of which we may be assured. Yet the practical work of the courts in adjusting relations and ordering conduct must go on. The legal order cannot stand still until philosophers can agree, as they did in the last century, on an ideal, and the legal profession and the courts can be induced or educated to receive it as authoritative. It cannot stand still until the social order has settled down for a time in a condition of stability in which its jural postulates can be recognized and formulated and the principles derived from them can be received into the authoritative guides to determination of controversies. In the meantime the courts must, as in the past, go on finding out by experience and developing by reason the modes of adjusting relations and ordering conduct which will give the most effect to the whole scheme of interests with the least friction and the least waste.

Existentialism

Widely read and discussed, existentialism is viewed by many as an expression of the moods and experiences of twentieth-century man. To a large extent, it is a protest. It speaks out against various forms of dehumanization that it believes result from industrial technology, nationalism, militarism, and scientific "objectivism." Modern mass society, existentialists find, leads to alienation, to self-deception, and to the denial of nobility. Modern man's penchant for systematization—in science, in philosophy, in social theory—issues in the loss of subjectivity. Events and tendencies such as these mean that human values are in a state of crisis, and that human freedom is threatened with extinction.

What is existentialism? When used broadly, the term refers to a type of thinking that emphasizes human existence and the qualities peculiar to it rather than to nature or the physical world. Man centered and individualistic, existentialism seeks to probe the often darker corners of the human situation. Yet "emphasis on human existence," though the beginning of a definition, is actually too vague for use in reference to this contemporary philosophy. Many, if not most, philosophers of the past have also been concerned about the human condition, and religion addresses itself to human life as well.

The existentialist's attention to man grows out of specifically modern conditions and concludes in unique insights. As suggested above, these conditions include the loss of the individual in mass culture and technology, the consequent alienation of the human person from himself as well as from his productions, and the evaporation of meaning in life through divisions within the human spirit. The response of persons to them is frequently called the "existentialist experience." Recorded by many artists and writers as well as by philosophers, it is a sense of the decomposition of man's experienced world—first, of all rational concepts and systems, next of stable objects, then of time and history, until finally all coherence, meaning, and value are gone—to the point where one faces only the Nothing and experiences only despair. Together with the description of this decomposition, existentialists analyze men's anxieties in such boundary or "limit" situations as guilt and death. This experience, sometimes also called an experience of crisis, has arisen in times of social and personal catastrophe in the twentieth century.

Existentialism is not simply a philosophy of despair and crisis, whatever conditions produce it. A second expression, "the existentialist attitude," indicates that reflection on the existentialist experience can result in an important philosophical position. This attitude is also directed toward human existence. Other philosophers study man, but they view him in terms of some systematic concept or essence derived from reason. Existentialists oppose such traditional conceptualism and its abstract, general concepts of existence and individuality. Neither systems of thought nor rational definitions can capture individual human existence. Man must be understood, existentialists insist, in terms of possibilities, anxieties, and decisions; in terms of the tragic and absurd situations in which he finds himself. Man is not an image or reflection of an antecedently existing essence that determines his actions and his values; he is a free being. *What* man is can only be inferred from *how* he is, that is, man's essence is to be found only in his concrete existence. The desire to know the meaning of the individual man in a more radical way than have other philosophers leads existentialists to hold that the starting point of philosophy is the concrete situation of man in the world.

Much of existentialist writing aims to describe the whole of human life—not just reason but emotional and conative states as well. Reason and rational structure are not equivalent to human life: feeling, passion, and decision are equally if not more important clues to man's being. Yet existentialism is more than phenomenology, great as is its reliance on descriptive techniques. It also seeks to know the reality of human existence and, for some existentialists, to produce a theory of being. The phenomenological interest is directed toward an ontological goal, though the latter can be achieved only through the former.

This ontological interest links existentialism with certain aspects of traditional philosophy, though it would agree to some extent with positivism and other anti-metaphysical positions in their distrust of philosophic rationalism. Existentialism, in turn, has questions about these latter philosophies and, in particular, takes issue with efforts to make philosophy another technology. It doubts that science or reason can interpret the whole universe, and it is suspicious of the "disinterestedness" of modern objective thought. Its closer tie is with realism and idealism although, as has been suggested in these paragraphs, its approach to human existence is unique.

It is difficult to go beyond these introductory generalizations in describing existentialism. Writing of individuality as a constant theme, existentialists are themselves fervidly individual: they refuse to belong to schools and systems and, for the most part, they do not offer doctrines in the traditional sense. Indeed, they more often speak of philosophizing than philosophy, for their message is as much a call to self-examination and decision as the giving of new information. Some existentialists such as Jean-Paul Sartre (1905–   ) have produced atheistic versions of existentialism; others like Karl Jaspers (1883–   ) and Gabriel Marcel (1887–   ) have produced theistic versions (the former nondenominational, the latter Roman Catholic); and yet others have followed Martin Heidegger

(1889–   ), who has left the religious question open. Even the use of the term existentialist is disputed, some of these men accepting it, others rejecting it.

Because of these observations, it might be more accurate to say that this section attempts to develop certain existentialist ideas rather than existentialism as a single position. There is much debate in the literature as to who are and who are not existentialists, and as just indicated, some of the men usually called existentialist have themselves rejected the label. Little mention, therefore, is made in the following materials of the problem of proper classification (though it is recognized that, while Jaspers would ordinarily be placed in the position, Niebuhr ordinarily would not); instead, attention is given to the social implications of existentialist themes.

The individuality and uniqueness of existentialists are carried over into their social philosophy. No "system" of government and society is given: existentialists are more interested in man than in government, in how man feels about law and society than in what these are in themselves. As a protest movement, existentialism provides more criticism than construction. Yet, here too, certain themes are identifiable. In general, stable social forms and processes are desirable, but often men tend to divide the ends sought from the means taken to realize them. There is, so to speak, an alienation of means and ends, with a consequent loss of ends and a brutalization of means. There is little agreement among existentialists on the meaning of social ends: Pascal accepted the absolute monarchy under which he was born, for he saw nothing better; Sartre has embraced a version of Marxism; Kierkegaard was suspicious of democracy; and Nietzsche seems at times to have been almost an anarchist. But existentialists have agreed that only disaster can result if trust is placed in social organizations and ideologies for the wrong reasons. Such trust may lead to a failure to take "risks" against abuses, it may involve a retreat from freedom, and it may issue in destructive idolization of power and organization.

Existentialism thus entails no specific political program—perhaps even no social philosophy—in the sense that other philosophies produce them. With Pascal, most existentialists view society and government as objects of neither esteem nor contempt. They claim these contribute little or nothing to man's perfection, though they can be sources of degradation and therefore must be carefully watched. Not systematic social philosophy, existentialist writings nevertheless provide important source materials for the student of society.

Man and Society

Although the number of thinkers before the nineteenth and twentieth centuries who reflect the existentialist position is small, one—the French mathematician and philosopher Blaise Pascal (1623–1662)—surely belongs within the stream of existentialism. Caught in the religious strife of his day and yet also a contributor to the rising science of the seventeenth century, he was a sensitive observer of the human condition with its frailty, uncertainty, and despair.

Pascal is well aware of man's need to feel at home in the world. As man looks at himself in relation to the world, he is caught between Nothing and the Infinite, a something yet not everything. Still, he has looked, and perhaps also has aspired to everything, though the only result is a sense of his own insignificance. This awareness of insignificance points to man as a being with reason, man looks for what only a thinking being can seek—and he sees only misery. Pascal teaches that man's sense of insignificance comes paradoxically from what is most excellent in him, namely reason.

Reason, moreover, is an even more basic source of human wretchedness: not only can man think, but he can think about himself. He is thus led to make himself the center of everything, becoming irksome to others because of his wish to enslave them. Each self is the enemy of all other selves and aspires to tyranny over them; in his self-centeredness man spends his life concerned about some "image" of himself in the minds of others. In fact, he is concerned about this image to himself. Unable to face himself as he is, he masks his true motives and lives in the untruth of self-deception. Once again, man's highest excellence, reason, becomes the source of his deepest misery, for the triviality of man comes from his fear of truth. To escape this wretched condition, man must learn to see himself as he really is. The pursuit of this truth—of what is high and what is base in man —leads ultimately to God. Before man finds God, however, he is afflicted by vanity and by the need to escape from himself, and this is the condition for which social order and government are the remedies.

Like Hobbes, Pascal teaches that men are enemies of each other and that government is a curb on passion and pride (though his assumptions differ radically from those of Hobbes). Indeed, men are also enemies of themselves, and only divine grace can save them from the consequences of this. The basis of society is thus might and necessity. Pascal posits no ideal of justice for society and he remained as skeptical about reason as Hume: if there is a real or essential justice, it eludes man. He is also indifferent to questions of political obligation and the legitimacy of government. The legal order adds nothing to man's perfection; perfection must be found in man's spiritual dimension.

Pascal's writings touch on many of the recurring themes of existentialist thought: the problem of knowing oneself, the distrust of science and reason for existential concerns, the uncertainties of existence, the nothingness of man's being, the elusiveness of finality, the reality of temporality and change, and man's corruption— his untruth—as revealed in disguise, falsehood, and hypocrisy. Many of them will be met again in subsequent selections.

BLAISE PASCAL   The Social Condition of Man

72

Man's disproportion. [This is where our innate knowledge leads us. If it be not true, there is no truth in man; and if it be true, he finds therein great cause for humiliation, being compelled to abase himself in one way or another.

From Blaise Pascal, *Thoughts,* trans. W. F. Trotter, New York: P. F. Collier and Son, 1910.

And since he cannot exist without this knowledge, I wish that, before entering on deeper researches into nature, he would consider her both seriously and at leisure, that he would reflect upon himself also, and knowing what proportion there is . . . .] Let man then contemplate the whole of nature in her full and grand majesty, and turn his vision from the low objects which surround him. Let him gaze on that brilliant light, set like an eternal lamp to illumine the universe; let the earth appear to him a point in comparison with the vast circle described by the sun; and let him wonder at the fact that this vast circle is itself but a very fine point in comparison with that described by the stars in their revolution round the firmament. But if our view be arrested there, let our imagination pass beyond; it will sooner exhaust the power of conception than nature that of supplying material for conception. The whole visible world is only an imperceptible atom in the ample bosom of nature. No idea approaches it. We may enlarge our conceptions beyond all imaginable space; we only produce atoms in comparison with the reality of things. It is an infinite sphere, the centre of which is everywhere, the circumference nowhere. In short it is the greatest sensible mark of the almighty power of God, that imagination loses itself in that thought.

Returning to himself, let man consider what he is in comparison with all existence; let him regard himself as lost in this remote corner of nature; and from the little cell in which he finds himself lodged, I mean the universe, let him estimate at their true value the earth, kingdoms, cities, and himself. What is a man in the Infinite?

But to show him another prodigy equally astonishing, let him examine the most delicate things he knows. Let a mite be given him, with its minute body and parts incomparably more minute, limbs with their joints, veins in the limbs, blood in the veins, humours in the blood, drops in the humours, vapours in the drops. Dividing these last things again, let him exhaust his powers of conception, and let the last object at which he can arrive be now that of our discourse. Perhaps he will think that here is the smallest point in nature. I will let him see therein a new abyss. I will paint for him not only the visible universe, but all that he can conceive of nature's immensity in the womb of this abridged atom. Let him see therein an infinity of universes, each of which has its firmament, its planets, its earth, in the same proportion as in the visible world; in each earth animals, and in the last mites, in which he will find again all that the first had, finding still in these others the same thing without end and without cessation. Let him lose himself in wonders as amazing in their littleness as the others in their vastness. For who will not be astounded at the fact that our body, which a little ago was imperceptible in the universe, itself imperceptible in the bosom of the whole, is now a colossus, a world, or rather a whole, in respect of the nothingness which we cannot reach? He who regards himself in this light will be afraid of himself, and observing himself sustained in the body given him by nature between those two abysses of the Infinite and Nothing, will tremble at the sight of these marvels; and I think that, as his curiosity changes into admiration, he will be more disposed to contemplate them in silence than to examine them with presumption.

For in fact what is man in nature? A Nothing in comparison with the Infinite, an All in comparison with the Nothing, a mean between nothing and everything.

Since he is infinitely removed from comprehending the extremes, the end of things and their beginning are hopelessly hidden from him in an impenetrable secret; he is equally incapable of seeing the Nothing from which he was made, and the Infinite in which he is swallowed up.

What will he do then, but perceive the appearance of the middle of things, in an eternal despair of knowing either their beginning or their end. All things proceed from the Nothing, and are borne towards the Infinite. Who will follow these marvellous processes? The Author of these wonders understands them. None other can do so.

Through failure to contemplate these Infinites, men have rashly rushed into the examination of nature, as though they bore some proportion to her. It is strange that they have wished to understand the beginnings of things, and thence to arrive at the knowledge of the whole, with a presumption as infinite as their object. For surely this design cannot be formed without presumption or without a capacity infinite like nature.

If we are well-informed, we understand that, as nature has graven her image and that of her Author on all things, they almost all partake of her double infinity. Thus we see that all the sciences are infinite in the extent of their researches. For who doubts that geometry, for instance, has an infinite infinity of problems to solve? They are also infinite in the multitude and fineness of their premises; for it is clear that those which are put forward as ultimate are not self-supporting, but are based on others which, again having others for their support, do not permit of finality. But we represent some as ultimate for reason, in the same way as in regard to material objects we call that an indivisible point beyond which our senses can no longer perceive anything, although by its nature it is infinitely divisible.

Of these two Infinites of science, that of greatness is the most palpable, and hence a few persons have pretended to know all things. "I will speak of the whole," said Democritus.

But the infinitely little is the least obvious. Philosophers have much oftener claimed to have reached it, and it is here they have all stumbled. This has given rise to such common titles as *First Principles, Principles of Philosophy,* and the like, as ostentatious in fact, though not in appearance, as that one which blinds us, *De omni scibili.*[1]

We naturally believe ourselves far more capable of reaching the centre of things than of embracing their circumference. The visible extent of the world visibly exceeds us, but as we exceed little things, we think ourselves more capable of knowing them. And yet we need no less capacity for attaining the Nothing than the All. Infinite capacity is required for both, and it seems to me that whoever shall have understood the ultimate principles of being might also attain to the knowledge of the Infinite. The one depends on the other, and one leads to the other. These extremes meet and reunite by force of distance, and find each other in God, and in God alone.

Let us then take our compass; we are something, and we are not everything. The nature of our existence hides from us the knowledge of first beginnings which are born of the Nothing; and the

---

[1] "Concerning everything knowable"—the title under which Pico della Mirandola announced the 900 propositions which he undertook to defend in 1486. *Tr.*

littleness of our being conceals from us the sight of the Infinite.

Our intellect holds the same position in the world of thought as our body occupies in the expanse of nature.

Limited as we are in every way, this state which holds the mean between two extremes is present in all our impotence. (Our senses perceive no extreme.) Too much sound deafens us; too much light dazzles us; too great distance or proximity hinders our view. Too great length and too great brevity of discourse tend to obscurity; too much truth is paralysing; (I know some who cannot understand that to take four from nothing leaves nothing). First principles are too self-evident for us; too much pleasure disagrees with us. Too many concords are annoying in music; too many benefits irritate us; we wish to have the wherewithal to over-pay our debts. *Beneficia eo usque læta sunt dum videntur exsolvi posse; ubi multum antevenere, pro gratia odium redditur.*[2] We feel neither extreme heat nor extreme cold. Excessive qualities are prejudicial to us and not perceptible by the senses; we do not feel but suffer them. Extreme youth and extreme age hinder the mind, as also too much and too little education. In short, extremes are for us as though they were not, and we are not within their notice. They escape us, or we them.

This is our true state; this is what makes us incapable of certain knowledge and of absolute ignorance. We sail within a vast sphere, ever drifting in uncertainty, driven from end to end. When we think to attach ourselves to any point and to fasten to it, it wavers and leaves us; and if we follow it, it eludes our grasp, slips past us, and

vanishes for ever. Nothing stays for us. This is our natural condition, and yet most contrary to our inclination; we burn with desire to find solid ground and an ultimate sure foundation whereon to build a tower reaching to the Infinite. But our whole groundwork cracks, and the earth opens to abysses.

Let us therefore not look for certainty and stability. Our reason is always deceived by fickle shadows; nothing can fix the finite between the two Infinites, which both enclose and fly from it.

If this be well understood, I think that we shall remain at rest, each in the state wherein nature has placed him. As this sphere which has fallen to us as our lot is always distant from either extreme, what matters it that man should have a little more knowledge of the universe? If he has it, he but gets a little higher. Is he not always infinitely removed from the end, and is not the duration of our life equally removed from eternity, even if it lasts ten years longer?

In comparison with these Infinites all finites are equal, and I see no reason for fixing our imagination on one more than on another. The only comparison which we make of ourselves to the finite is painful to us.

If man made himself the first object of study, he would see how incapable he is of going further. How can a part know the whole? But he may perhaps aspire to know at least the parts to which he bears some proportion. But the parts of the world are all so related and linked to one another, that I believe it impossible to know one without the other and without the whole.

Man, for instance, is related to all he knows. He needs a place wherein to abide, time through which to live, motion in order to live, elements to com-

---

[2] "Benefits are pleasant while it seems possible to requite them; when they become much greater, they produce hatred rather than gratitude."—Tacitus. *Tr.*

pose him, warmth and food to nourish him, air to breathe. He sees light; he feels bodies; in short, he is in a dependent alliance with everything. To know man, then, it is necessary to know how it happens that he needs air to live, and, to know the air, we must know how it is thus related to the life of man, etc. Flame cannot exist without air; therefore to understand the one, we must understand the other.

Since everything then is cause and effect, dependant and supporting, mediate and immediate, and all is held together by a natural though imperceptible chain, which binds together things most distant and most different, I hold it equally impossible to know the parts without knowing the whole, and to know the whole without knowing the parts in detail.

[The eternity of things in itself or in God must also astonish our brief duration. The fixed and constant immobility of nature, in comparison with the continual change which goes on within us, must have the same effect.]

And what completes our incapability of knowing things, is the fact that they are simple, and that we are composed of two opposite natures, different in kind, soul and body. For it is impossible that our rational part should be other than spiritual; and if any one maintain that we are simply corporeal, this would far more exclude us from the knowledge of things, there being nothing so inconceivable as to say that matter knows itself. It is impossible to imagine how it should know itself.

So if we are simply material, we can know nothing at all; and if we are composed of mind and matter, we cannot know perfectly things which are simple, whether spiritual or corporeal. Hence it comes that almost all philosophers have confused ideas of things, and speak of

material things in spiritual terms, and of spiritual things in material terms. For they say boldly that bodies have a tendency to fall, that they seek after their centre, that they fly from destruction, that they fear the void, that they have inclinations, sympathies, antipathies, all of which attributes pertain only to mind. And in speaking of minds, they consider them as in a place, and attribute to them movement from one place to another; and these are qualities which belong only to bodies.

Instead of receiving the ideas of these things in their purity, we colour them with our own qualities, and stamp with our composite being all the simple things which we contemplate.

Who would not think, seeing us compose all things of mind and body, but that this mixture would be quite intelligible to us? Yet it is the very thing we least understand. Man is to himself the most wonderful object in nature; for he cannot conceive what the body is, still less what the mind is, and least of all how a body should be united to a mind. This is the consummation of his difficulties, and yet it is his very being. *Modus quo corporibus adhærent spiritus comprehendi ab hominibus non potest, et hoc tamen homo est.*[3] . . .

294

. . . On what shall man found the order of the world which he would govern? Shall it be on the caprice of each individual? What confusion! Shall it be on justice? Man is ignorant of it.

Certainly had he known it, he would not have established this maxim, the most general of all that obtain among

---

[3] "The manner in which spirits are united to bodies cannot be understood by men, yet such is man."—St. Augustine. *Tr.*

men, that each should follow the customs of his own country. The glory of true equity would have brought all nations under subjection, and legislators would not have taken as their model the fancies and caprice of Persians and Germans instead of this unchanging justice. We should have seen it set up in all the States on earth and in all times; whereas we see neither justice nor injustice which does not change its nature with change in climate. Three degrees of latitude reverse all jurisprudence; a meridian decides the truth. Fundamental laws change after a few years of possession; right has its epochs; the entry of Saturn into the lion marks to us the origin of such and such a crime. A strange justice that is bounded by a river! Truth on this side of the Pyrenees, error on the other side.

Men admit that justice does not consist in these customs, but that it resides in natural laws, common to every country. They would certainly maintain it obstinately, if reckless chance which has distributed human laws has encountered even one which was universal; but the farce is that the caprice of men has so many vagaries that there is no such law.

Theft, incest, infanticide, patricide, have all had a place among virtuous actions. Can anything be more ridiculous than that a man should have the right to kill me because he lives on the other side of the water, and because his ruler has a quarrel with mine, though I have none with him?

Doubtless there are natural laws; but good reason once corrupted has corrupted all. *Nihil amplius nostrum est; quod nostrum dicimus, artis est.*[4] *Ex senatus consultis et plebiscitis crimina exercentur.*[5] *Ut olim vitiis, sic nunc legibus laboramus.*[6]

The result of this confusion is that one affirms the essence of justice to be the authority of the legislator; another, the interest of the sovereign; another, present custom, and this is the most sure. Nothing, according to reason alone, is just in itself; all changes with time. Custom creates the whole of equity, for the simple reason that it is accepted. It is the mystical foundation of its authority; whoever carries it back to first principles destroys it. Nothing is so faulty as those laws which correct faults. He who obeys them because they are just, obeys a justice which is imaginary, and not the essence of law; it is quite self-contained, it is law and nothing more. He who will examine its motive will find it so feeble and so trifling that if he be not accustomed to contemplate the wonders of human imagination, he will marvel that one century has gained for it so much pomp and reverence. The art of opposition and of revolution is to unsettle established customs, sounding them even to their source, to point out their want of authority and justice. We must, it is said, get back to the natural and fundamental laws of the State, which an unjust custom has abolished. It is a game certain to result in the loss of all; nothing will be just on the balance. Yet people readily lend their ear to such arguments. They shake off the yoke as soon as they recognize it; and the great profit by their ruin, and by that of these curious investigators of accepted customs. But from a contrary mistake men sometimes think they can justly do everything which

---

4 "We can claim nothing more; what we call ours is art's." *Tr.*

5 "Decrees of the senate and of the people are responsible for crimes." *Tr.*

6 "As once we suffered from vices, so now from laws." *Tr.*

is not without an example. That is why the wisest of legislators said that it was often necessary to deceive men for their own good; and another, a good politician, *Cum veritatem qua liberetur ignoret, expedit quod fallatur.*[7] We must not see the fact of usurpation; law was once introduced without reason, and has become reasonable. We must make it regarded as authoritative, eternal, and conceal its origin, if we do not wish that it should soon come to an end.

301

Why do we follow the majority? Is it because they have more reason? No, because they have more power.

Why do we follow ancient laws and opinions? Is it because they are more sound? No, but because they are unique; and remove from us the root of difference.

302

. . . It is the effect of might, not of custom. For those who are capable of originality are few; the greater number will only follow, and refuse glory to those inventors who seek it by their inventions. And if these are obstinate in their wish to obtain glory, and despise those who do not invent, the latter will call them ridiculous names, and would beat them with a stick. Let no one then boast of his subtility, or let him keep his complacency to himself.

303

Might is the sovereign of the world, and not opinion.—But opinion makes

---

[7] "When a man does not understand the truth by which he might be freed, it is expedient that he should be deceived."—St. Augustine. *Tr.*

use of might.—It is might that makes opinion. Gentleness is beautiful in our opinion. Why? Because he who will dance on a rope will be alone, and I will gather a stronger mob of people who will say that it is unbecoming.

304

The cords which bind the respect of men to each other are in general cords of necessity; for there must be different degrees, all men wishing to rule, and not all being able to do so, but some being able.

Let us then imagine we see society in the process of formation. Men will doubtless fight till the stronger party overcomes the weaker, and a dominant party is established. But when this is once determined, the masters, who do not desire the continuation of strife, then decree that the power which is in their hands shall be transmitted as they please. Some place it in election by the people, others in hereditary succession, &c.

And this is the point where imagination begins to play its part. Till now power makes fact; now power is sustained by imagination in a certain party, in France in the nobility, in Switzerland in the burgesses, &c.

These cords which bind the respect of men to such and such an individual are therefore the cords of imagination.

320

The most unreasonable things in the world become most reasonable, because of the unruliness of men. What is less reasonable than to choose the eldest son of a queen to rule a State? We do not choose as captain of a ship the passenger who is of the best family.

This law would be absurd and unjust; but because men are so themselves, and always will be so, it becomes reasonable and just. For whom will men choose, as the most virtuous and able? We at once come to blows, as each claims to be the most virtuous and able. Let us then attach this quality to something indisputable. This is the king's eldest son. That is clear, and there is no dispute. Reason can do no better, for civil war is the greatest of evils.

325

Montaigne is wrong. Custom should be followed only because it is custom, and not because it is reasonable or just. But people follow it for this sole reason, that they think it just. Otherwise they would follow it no longer, although it were the custom; for will only submit to reason or justice. Custom without this would pass for tyranny; but the sovereignty of reason and justice is no more tyrannical than that of desire. They are principles natural to man.

It would therefore be right to obey laws and customs, because they are laws; but we should know that there is neither truth nor justice to introduce into them, that we know nothing of these, and so must follow what is accepted. By this means we would never depart from them. But the people cannot accept this doctrine; and, as they believe that truth can be found, and that it exists in law and custom, they believe them, and take their antiquity as a proof of their truth, and not simply of their authority apart from truth. Thus they obey laws, but they are liable to revolt when these are proved to be valueless; and this can be shown of all, looked at from a certain aspect.

330

The power of kings is founded on the reason and on the folly of the people, and specially on their folly. The greatest and most important thing in the world has weakness for its foundation, and this foundation is wonderfully sure; for there is nothing more sure than this, that the people will be weak. What is based on sound reason is very ill founded, as the estimate of wisdom.

332

Tyranny consists in the desire of universal power beyond its scope.

There are different assemblies of the strong, the fair, the sensible, the pious, in which each man rules at home, not elsewhere. And sometimes they meet, and the strong and the fair foolishly fight as to who shall be master, for their mastery is of different kinds. They do not understand one another, and their fault is the desire to rule everywhere. Nothing can effect this, not even might, which is of no use in the kingdom of the wise, and is only mistress of external actions.

Tyranny. . . . So these expressions are false and tyrannical: "I am fair, therefore I must be feared. I am strong, therefore I must be loved. I am . . . ."

Tyranny is the wish to have in one way what can only be had in another. We render different duties to different merits; the duty of love to the pleasant; the duty of fear to the strong; the duty of belief to the learned.

We must render these duties; it is unjust to refuse them, and unjust to ask others. And so it is false and tyrannical to say, "He is not strong, therefore I will not esteem him; he is not able, therefore I will not fear him."

Social and Political Values

While Pascal's writings are an important anticipation of existentialism, the real origin of the movement is with another thinker, Soren Kierkegaard (1813–1855), although mention must be made again of the difficulty of classification, for it has been debated whether Kierkegaard was in fact an existentialist. Kierkegaard's central theme is how one may become a Christian—he was essentially a religious author—and much of his writing defends Christianity against false values. His own age, he believed, had forgotten what it means to be a Christian, or even what it means *to be*. Hence he was led, many say for the first time, to introduce into Western thought the categories of "existence" and "individual."

By existence, Kierkegaard means the striving of a person to fulfill himself at the highest level of development. Concrete and individual, existence is also unique, irreducible, and not conceptualizable: more technically, it is possibility. Since men must strive and decide in relation to the possible, their lives point to a tension within their very being. In describing and analyzing various experiences such as dread and despair, Kierkegaard finds this tension to be a result of the fact that man is a synthesis of the temporal and eternal, of the finite and infinite—in short, that man is a spiritual being.

Ultimately, for Kierkegaard, existence means to stand "before God." To exist simply as a synthesis is not yet to be a spiritual being, for meaning and purpose have not been achieved. True selfhood can be reached only when the self is related to the Power that constitutes the synthesis (even though men may try to find substitutes for God in pleasure, duty, or some totalitarian political program). Only decision or faith can bring meaning into the individual human life, and the achievement of meaning is "subjective truth."

Kierkegaard's writings on political and social values are mainly critical, for his concern in this area was with the convergence of movements in his century against the individual. In brief, Kierkegaard believed that his age was witnessing an abdication of selfhood: democracy was trusting the crowd, the power of reason, and the spread of progress. But the multitude is an absurd monster: "the crowd, regarded as a judge over ethical and religious matters, is untruth." Reason seeks man-made absolutes—which means no absolutes—so that the whole of existence sinks into "average behavior" without passion or individual existence. The "progress" of the age is science and technology, which are but tools that will only hasten the loss of the individual in urban and industrial masses. Reason and progress lead to secularism, the "levelling process," "faceless multitudes," and therewith the deification of state or society. Kierkegaard, in fact, described secular social movements such as socialism and communism as religions of salvation, though idolatrous ones because they assume that society is everything. As one critic has put it, "Kierkegaard understood better than anyone and before anyone the creative diabolical *principle* of the mass: fleeing from one's own person, no longer being responsible, and therefore no longer guilty, and becoming at one stroke a participant in the divinized power of the Anonymous."*

Kierkegaard describes the dehumanization of the individual in many places in his writings, of which the following selection is only a sample. On the more positive side, he suggests for society a transformation based on preserving the individual. "Religion [that is, for Kierkegaard Christianity] is the true humanity"; and religious existence—persons personally related to a personal God—rather than to the anonymous "public" is needed if society is to be remade, if the resources for its renewal are to be provided, and if people are to be prevented from being stampeded into impersonal totalitarian movements.

* Denis de Rougemont, *The Devil's Share,* New York: Pantheon (Bollingen Series), 1944, p. 141.

SOREN KIERKEGAARD   The Present Age

Our age is essentially one of understanding and reflection, without passion, momentarily bursting into enthusiasm, and shrewdly relapsing into repose.

If we had statistical tables of the consumption of intelligence from generation to generation as we have for spirits, we should be astounded at the enormous amount of scruple and deliberation consumed by even small, well-to-do families living quietly, and at the amount which the young, and even children, use. For just as the children's crusade may be said to typify the Middle Ages, precocious children are typical of the present age. In fact one is tempted to ask whether there is a single man left who, for once, commits an outrageous folly.

Nowadays not even a suicide kills himself in desperation. Before taking the step he deliberates so long and so carefully that he literally chokes with thought. It is even questionable whether he ought to be called a suicide, since it is really thought which takes his life. He does not die *with* deliberation but *from* deliberation.

It would therefore be very difficult to prosecute the present generation because of its legal quibbles: in fact, all its ability, virtuosity and good sense consists in trying to get a judgment and a decision without ever going as far as action. If one may say of the revolutionary period that it runs wild, one would have to say of the present that it runs badly. Between them, the individual and his generation always bring each other to a standstill, with the result that the prosecuting attorney would find it next to impossible to get any fact admitted—because nothing ever happens. To judge from innumerable indications, one would conclude that something quite exceptional had either just happened or was just about to happen. Yet any such conclusion would be quite wrong. Indications are, indeed, the only achievements of the age; and its skill and inventiveness in constructing fascinating illusions, its burst of enthusiasm, using as a deceitful escape some projected change of form, must be rated as high in the scale of cleverness and of the negative use of strength as the passionate, creative energy of the revolution in the corresponding scale of energy. But the present generation, wearied by its chimerical efforts, relapses into complete indolence. Its condition is that of a man who has only fallen asleep towards morning: first of all come great dreams, then a feeling of laziness, and finally a witty or clever excuse for remaining in bed.

However well-meaning and strong the individual man may be (if he could only use his strength), he still has not the passion to be able to tear himself from the coils and seductive uncertainty of reflection. Nor do his surroundings supply the events or produce the general enthusiasm necessary in order to free him. Instead of coming to his help, his *milieu* forms around him a negative intellectual opposition, which juggles for a moment with a deceptive prospect, only to deceive him in the end by pointing to a brilliant way out of the difficulty —by showing him that the shrewdest thing of all is to do nothing. For at the bottom of the tergiversation of the present age is *vis inertiae,* and every one without passion congratulates himself upon being the first to discover it, and so becomes cleverer still. During the revolution arms were distributed freely, just as during the Crusades the insignia of the exploit were bestowed upon men, and nowadays people are supplied with the rules of careful conduct and ready-reckoners to facilitate judgement. If a generation were given the diplomatic task of postponing all action in such a way as to make it seem as if something were just about to happen, then we should have to admit that our age had performed as remarkable a feat as the revolutionary age. Let any one try forgetting all he knows of the age and its actual relativity which is so enhanced by

familiarity, and then arrive, as it were, from another world: if he were then to read a book or an article in the papers, or merely to speak to some passer-by, his impression would be: "Good heavens, something is going to happen to-night—or perhaps something happened the night before last."

A revolutionary age is an age of action; ours is the age of advertisement and publicity. Nothing ever happens but there is immediate publicity everywhere. In the present age a rebellion is, of all things, the most unthinkable. Such an expression of strength would seem ridiculous to the calculating intelligence of our times. On the other hand a political virtuoso might bring off a feat almost as remarkable. He might write a manifesto suggesting a general assembly at which people should decide upon a rebellion, and it would be so carefully worded that even the censor would let it pass. At the meeting itself he would be able to create the impression that his audience has rebelled, after which they would all go quietly home—having spent a very pleasant evening. Among the young men of today a profound and prodigious learning is almost unthinkable; they would find it ridiculous. On the other hand a scientific virtuoso might draw up a subscription form outlining an all-embracing system which he purposed to write and, what is more, in such a way that the reader would feel he had already read the system; for the age of encyclopaedists, when men wrote gigantic folios with unremitting pains, is gone. Now it is the turn of those lightweight encyclopaedists who, *en passant,* settle with all the sciences and the whole of existence. Equally unthinkable among the young men of today is a truly religious renunciation of the world, adhered to with daily self-denial. On the other hand almost any theological student is capable of something far more wonderful. He could found a society with the sole object of saving all those who are lost. The age of great and good actions is past, the present is the age of anticipation when even recognition is received in advance. No one is satisfied with doing something definite, every one wants to feel flattered by reflection with the illusion of having discovered at the very least a new continent. Like a young man who decides to work for his examination in all earnest from September 1st, and in order to strengthen his resolution decides to take a holiday during August, so the present generation seems—though this is decidedly more difficult to understand—to have made a solemn resolution that the next generation should set to work seriously, and in order to avoid disturbing or delaying the next generation, the present attends to—the banquets. Only there is a difference: the young man understands himself in the light-heartedness of youth, whereas our generation is serious—even at banquets. . . .

Throughout many changes the tendency in modern times has remained a levelling one. These changes themselves have not, however, all of them, been levelling, for they are none of them abstract enough, each having a certain concrete reality. To some extent it is true that the levelling process goes on when one great man attacks another, so that both are weakened, or when one is neutralized by the other, or when an association of people, in themselves weak, grow stronger than the eminent. Levelling can also be accomplished by one particular caste, e.g. the clergy, the bourgeois, the peasants, by the people themselves. But all that is only the first movement of an abstract power within the concreteness of individuality.

In order that everything should be reduced to the same level, it is first of all necessary to procure a phantom, its spirit, a monstrous abstraction, an all-embracing something which is nothing, a mirage—and that phantom is *the public*. It is only in an age which is without passion, yet reflective, that such a phantom can develop itself with the help of the Press which itself becomes an abstraction. In times of passion and tumult and enthusiasm, even when a people desire to realize a fruitless idea and lay waste and destroy everything: even then there is no such thing as a public. There are parties and they are concrete. The Press, in times such as those, takes on a concrete character according to the division of parties. But just as sedentary professional people are the first to take up any fantastic illusion which comes their way, so a passionless, sedentary, reflective age, in which only the Press exhibits a vague sort of life, fosters this phantom. The public is, in fact, the real Levelling-Master rather than the actual leveller, for whenever levelling is only approximately accomplished it is done by something, but the public is a monstrous nothing. The public is a concept which could not have occurred in antiquity because the people *en masse, in corpore* took part in any situation which arose and were responsible for the actions of the individual, and, moreover, the individual was personally present and had to submit at once to applause or disapproval for his decision. Only when the sense of association in society is no longer strong enough to give life to concrete realities is the Press able to create that abstraction "the public," consisting of unreal individuals who never are and never can be united in an actual situation or organization—and yet are held together as a whole.

The public is a host, more numerous

than all the peoples together, but it is a body which can never be reviewed, it cannot even be represented, because it is an abstraction. Nevertheless, when the age is reflective and passionless and destroys everything concrete, the public becomes everything and is supposed to include everything. And that again shows how the individual is thrown back upon himself.

The real moment in time and the real situation being simultaneous with real people, each of whom is something: that is what helps to sustain the individual. But the existence of a public produces neither a situation nor simultaneity. The individual reader of the Press is not the public, and even though little by little a number of individuals or even all of them should read it, the simultaneity is lacking. Years might be spent gathering the public together, and still it would not be there. This abstraction, which the individuals so illogically form, quite rightly repulses the individual instead of coming to his help. The man who has no opinion of an event at the actual moment accepts the opinion of the majority, or, if he is quarrelsome, of the minority. But it must be remembered that both majority and minority are real people, and that is why the individual is assisted by adhering to them. A public, on the contrary, is an abstraction. To adopt the opinion of this or that man means that one knows that they will be subjected to the same dangers as oneself, that they will go astray with one if the opinion goes astray. But to adopt the same opinion as the public is a deceptive consolation because the public is only there *in abstracto*. Whilst, therefore, no majority has ever been so certain of being right and victorious as the public, that is not much consolation to the individual, for a public is a phantom which forbids all personal con-

tact. And if a man adopts public opinion today and is hissed tomorrow he is hissed by the public.

A generation, a people, an assembly of the people, a meeting or a man, are responsible for what they are and can be made ashamed if they are inconstant and unfaithful; but a public remains a public. A people, an assembly or a man can change to such an extent that one may say: they are no longer the same; a public on the other hand can become the very opposite and still be the same —a public. But it is precisely by means of this abstraction and this abstract discipline that the individual will be formed (in so far as the individual is not already formed by his inner life), if he does not succumb in the process, taught to be content, in the highest religious sense, with himself and his relation to God, to be at one with himself instead of being in agreement with a public which destroys everything that is relative, concrete and particular in life; educated to find peace within himself and with God, instead of counting hands. And the ultimate difference between the modern world and antiquity is: that "the whole" is not concrete and is therefore unable to support the individual, or to educate him as the concrete should (though without developing him absolutely), but is an abstraction which by its abstract equality repels him and thus helps him to be educated absolutely—unless he succumbs in the process. The *taedium vitae* so constant in antiquity was due to the fact that the outstanding individual was what others *could not be;* the inspiration of modern times will be that any man who finds himself, religiously speaking, has only achieved what *every one can achieve.*

A public is neither a nation, nor a generation, nor a community, nor a society, nor these particular men, for all these are only what they are through the concrete; no single person who belongs to the public makes a real commitment; for some hours of the day, perhaps, he belongs to the public—at moments when he is nothing else, since when he really is what he is he does not form part of the public. Made up of such individuals, of individuals at the moments when they are nothing, a public is a kind of gigantic something, an abstract and deserted void which is everything and nothing. But on this basis any one can arrogate to himself a public, and just as the Roman Church chimerically extended its frontier by appointing bishops *in partibus infidelium,* so a public is something which every one can claim, and even a drunken sailor exhibiting a "peep-show" has dialectically absolutely the same right to a public as the greatest man; he has just as logical a right to put all those many noughts *in front* of his single number.

A public is everything and nothing, the most dangerous of all powers and the most insignificant: one can speak to a whole nation in the name of the public, and still the public will be less than a single real man, however unimportant. The qualification "public" is produced by the deceptive juggling of an age of reflection, which makes it appear flattering to the individual who in this way can arrogate to himself this monster, in comparison with which concrete realities seem poor. The public is the fairy story of an age of understanding, which in imagination makes the individual into something even greater than a king above his people;[1] but the public is also a gruesome abstraction through which the individual will receive his religious formation—or sink.

---

[1] As an author I have fortunately never sought for or had a public, but have contented myself with "the individual," and on account of that limitation have almost become a proverb.

[All Kierkegaard's religious discourses, which form a large part of his works, were dedicated to " 'that individual,' whom with joy and thankfulness I call my reader because he reads, not thinking of the author, but of God." *Tr.*]

State, Power, and Authority

Already suggested in the preceding readings is the existentialist's distrust of political power and the state. Too often these become the object of idolatrous adoration and commitment that block individual self-realization. Some of the most forceful statements of this theme are found in the writings of the late nineteenth-century German philosopher, Friedrich Nietzsche (1844–1900).

Nietzsche's thought begins with the observation that "God is dead," and he adds that "we have killed him." This widely quoted statement meant for Nietzsche that in the modern scientific and industrial age—the result of men's efforts—the existence of God is no longer believable. To be sure, millions of individuals may claim to believe, but the God hypothesis is neither supported by nor relevant to modern culture. Still, the death of God, Nietzsche says, is not an event for rejoicing, for also dead with him are the old theological picture of man and the commitment to values it entailed. In fact, the implication of the death of God for European civilization is a nihilistic loss of all meaning and value.

Nietzsche's problem is to develop a new picture of man without theological assumptions and to restate the conditions for meaningful valuation. His doctrine of man is expressed in the image of the "superman" (*Übermensch*), a morally new type of individual who through dedicated commitments—the "will to power"—will be a creator of values in the very presence of nihilism. The values of the superman will be naturalistic rather than theological, and though Nietzsche speaks of a transvaluation of values, his real concern is to war against accepted valuations that prevent the realization of selfhood and the attainment of culture. Mankind needs courage to live by the highest values, which are the personal or existential qualities of integrity, honesty, and generosity.

Nietzsche is unsure which is the more universal characteristic—fear or laziness. Both keep men from culture and self-realization for men fear social retaliation, and so they do not strive to be uniquely themselves. The State thus appears almost as a Devil in Nietzsche's ethical vision. It intimidates men into conformity and denies them their proper destiny. The State embodies mediocrity rather than fulfillment, and the power it has moves men to conformity. Even more, Nietzsche opposes all overvaluations of political life: it is sheer idolatry to seek salvation in political programs and state power, whether they be democratic, socialist, or communist.

As a philosopher, Nietzsche lacked both systematic commitments and developed premises. His observations on the state and society are largely negative, and one might infer that his position ultimately is political anarchy. Yet Nietzsche's purpose as a writer was—with most existentialists—less to present doctrines than to "disturb" his readers and to issue a call for moral courage and personal integrity. Man's social dimension has an importance appropriate to it, but it is neither the highest dimension nor a self-fulfilling one. In an age tending to absolutize and worship the State, Nietzsche saw depersonalization and destruction. Only courage and personal valuations can prevent the total loss of the individual.

FRIEDRICH NIETZSCHE   The New Idol

Somewhere there are still peoples and herds, but not with us, my brethren: here there are states.

A state? What is that? Well! open now your ears unto me, for now will I say unto you my word concerning the death of peoples.

A state, is called the coldest of all cold monsters. Coldly lieth it also; and this lie creepeth from its mouth: "I, the state, am the people."

It is a lie! Creators were they who created peoples, and hung a faith and a love over them: thus they served life.

Destroyers, are they who lay snares for many, and call it the state: they hang

From Friedrich Nietzsche, *Thus Spake Zarathustra*, trans. Thomas Common, and *Beyond Good and Evil*, trans. Helen Zimmern, in *The Philosophy of Nietzsche*, London: George Allen & Unwin, Ltd., n.d. Used by permission of the publisher.

a sword and a hundred cravings over them.

Where there is still a people, there the state is not understood, but hated as the evil eye, and as sin against laws and customs.

This sign I give unto you: every people speaketh its language of good and evil: this its neighbour understandeth not. Its language hath it devised for itself in laws and customs.

But the state lieth in all languages of good and evil; and whatever it saith it lieth; and whatever it hath it hath stolen.

False is everything in it; with stolen teeth it biteth, the biting one. False are even its bowels.

Confusion of language of good and evil; this sign I give unto you as the sign of the state. Verily, the will to death, indicateth this sign! Verily, it beckoneth unto the preachers of death!

Many too many are born: for the superfluous ones was the state devised!

See just how it enticeth them to it, the many-too-many! How it swalloweth and cheweth and recheweth them!

"On earth there is nothing greater than I: it is I who am the regulating finger of God"—thus roareth the monster. And not only the long-eared and short-sighted fall upon their knees!

Ah! even in your ears, ye great souls, it whispereth its gloomy lies! Ah! it findeth out the rich hearts which willingly lavish themselves!

Yea, it findeth you out too, ye conquerors of the old God! Weary ye become of the conflict, and now your weariness serveth the new idol!

Heroes and honourable ones, it would fain set up around it, the new idol! Gladly it basketh in the sunshine of good consciences,—the cold monster!

Everything will it give *you,* if ye worship it, the new idol: thus it pur-

chaseth the lustre of your virtue, and the glance of your proud eyes.

It seeketh to allure by means of you, the many-too-many! Yea, a hellish artifice hath here been devised, a death-horse jingling with the trappings of divine honours!

Yea, a dying for many hath here been devised, which glorifieth itself as life: verily, a hearty service unto all preachers of death!

The state, I call it, where all are poison-drinkers, the good and the bad: the state, where all lose themselves, the good and the bad: the state, where the slow suicide of all—is called "life."

Just see these superfluous ones! They steal the works of the inventors and the treasures of the wise. Culture, they call their theft—and everything becometh sickness and trouble unto them!

Just see these superfluous ones! Sick are they always; they vomit their bile and call it a newspaper. They devour one another, and cannot even digest themselves.

Just see these superfluous ones! Wealth they acquire and become poorer thereby. Power they seek for, and above all, the lever of power, much money— these impotent ones!

See them clamber, these nimble apes! They clamber over one another, and thus scuffle into the mud and the abyss.

Towards the throne they all strive: it is their madness—as if happiness sat on the throne! Ofttimes sitteth filth on the throne.—and ofttimes also the throne on filth.

Madmen they all seem to me, and clambering apes, and too eager. Badly smelleth their idol to me, the cold monster: badly they all smell to me, these idolaters.

My brethren, will ye suffocate in the fumes of their maws and appetites!

Better break the windows and jump into the open air!

Do go out of the way of the bad odour! Withdraw from the idolatry of the superfluous!

Do go out of the way of the bad odour! Withdrawn from the steam of these human sacrifices!

Open still remaineth the earth for great souls. Empty are still many sites for lone ones and twain ones, around which floateth the odour of tranquil seas.

Open still remaineth a free life for great souls. Verily, he who possesseth little is so much the less possessed: blessed be moderate poverty!

There, where the state ceaseth—there only commenceth the man who is not superfluous: there commenceth the song of the necessary ones, the single and irreplaceable melody.

There, where the state *ceaseth*—pray look thither, my brethren! Do ye not see it, the rainbow and the bridges of the Superman?—Thus spake Zarathustra.

Whether we call it "civilisation," or "humanising," or "progress," which now distinguishes the European; whether we call it simply, without praise or blame, by the political formula: the *democratic* movement in Europe—behind all the moral and political foregrounds pointed to by such formulas, an immense *physiological process* goes on, which is ever extending: the process of the assimilation of Europeans; their increasing detachment from the conditions under which, climatically and hereditarily, united races originate; their increasing independence of every definite *milieu,* that for centuries would fain inscribe itself with equal demands on soul and body;—that is to say, the slow emergence of an essentially *super-national* and nomadic species of man, who possesses, physiological speaking, a maximum of the art and power of adaptation as his typical distinction. This process of the *evolving European,* which can be retarded in its *tempo* by great relapses, but will perhaps just gain and grow thereby in vehemence and depth—the still raging storm and stress of "national sentiment" pertains to it, and also the anarchism which is appearing at present —this process will probably arrive at results on which its naïve propagators and panegyrists, the apostles of "modern ideas," would least care to reckon. The same new conditions under which on an average a levelling and mediocrising of man will take place—a useful, industrious, variously serviceable and clever gregarious man—are in the highest degree suitable to give rise to exceptional men of the most dangerous and attractive qualities. For, while the capacity for adaptation, which is every day trying changing conditions, and begins a new work with every generation, almost with every decade, makes the *powerfulness* of the type impossible; while the collective impression of such future Europeans will probably be that of numerous, talkative, weakwilled, and very handy workmen who *require* a master, a commander, as they require their daily bread; while, therefore, the democratising of Europe will tend to the production of a type prepared for *slavery* in the most subtle sense of the term: the *strong* man will necessarily in individual and exceptional cases, become stronger and richer than he has perhaps ever been before—owing to the unprejudicedness of his schooling, owing to the immense variety of practice, art, and disguise. I meant to say that the democratising of Europe is

at the same time an involuntary arrangement for the rearing of *tyrants*—taking
the word in all its meanings, even in its
most spiritual sense.

Law and Rights

The following selection is quite different from others that have been met under this title. It deals with law and rights very indirectly, facing rather the general problem of a "life-order," whether economic, social or legal. The position of its author, Karl Jaspers (1883–   ) is that the construction and maintenance of any absolutely valid and inclusive life-order is impossible.

Influenced especially by Kierkegaard, Jaspers' voluminous writings seem pledged to the over-all goal of breaking down modern man's trust in science, in theology, indeed in rational endeavor anywhere. Offering no philosophic doctrines himself, Jaspers seeks to show the limits of science and thereby to loosen man from the fetters of determinate thinking. Yet, it is inaccurate to classify Jaspers as an irrationalist: he suggests that rational thought is really subphilosophical, and that "philosophizing" lies above reason and must replace it.

This polemic against rationalism rests on Jaspers' belief that the foundation of all knowledge is "out of possible Existence"—a truth that rationalism easily forgets. Possible Existence is met in the concrete situation of the striving, existing individual, but such situations in many ways are incompatible with the claims of reason. The world, therefore, is not reducible to a single philosophical principle, and to acknowledge this incompatibility prepares the way for a movement away from the objective world toward Existence.

Existence can never be grasped by rationalistic thought: it is the beginning or ground of thought, not an end or object. This means that an existing person cannot be transformed into some kind of impersonal thing. I am "the being who is not, but who can and ought to be and, therefore, decides in time whether he is eternal." That is, one experiences a need to be oneself in an absolute way; one can accept this or sink into nothingness. To exist, therefore, is to be free.

At the highest moments of existence, personality cannot remain satisfied merely with social and legal levels, even though it also cannot forget its roots in the community. This dissatisfaction results in part from the recognition that no steadfast life-order is possible. Life in its expressiveness is always seeking new forms, and even a machinelike organization of society cannot repress it. Furthermore, any given life-order contains internal oppositions, not only of state to state and of class to class, but within life itself, as for example, in the creativity yet destruction of self-interest. Human life, therefore, is impossible in mechanical production and social or legal rational systems. It is possible only as historical destiny, by which Jaspers means the human effort to bring a world of purposive order into existence. That this is man's task shows that his being is not exhausted in techniques, apparatus, political programs, legal systems, or mass-life.

KARL JASPERS   Limits of the Life-Order

IMPOSSIBILITY OF A STEAD-FAST LIFE-ORDER

If life could be satisfactorily arranged, one would have to presuppose the possibility of a steadfast life-order. It is obvious, however, that no such stable condition is possible. Life, being essentially imperfect, and, as we know it, intolerable, is continually seeking to re-fashion the life-order under new forms.

Not even the technical apparatus can attain finality. We might conceive of the using-up of our planet as the locale and substance of a gigantic factory, run by the masses of mankind. In the planet as thus conceived, there would no longer persist anything purely and directly natural. The material out of which the apparatus was made would, of course, be a gift of nature, but, having been applied to human purposes, would have been used up and would no longer have an independent being. The only substance remaining in the world would be that which had already been moulded by man. The world itself would be like an artificial landscape, consisting exclusively of this man-made apparatus in space and time, a unique product each of whose parts would be kept in touch with one another by incessantly-working means of communication, human beings being fettered to the apparatus in order, by their joint labour, to continue to make for themselves the necessaries of life. Thus a stable condition would have been achieved. We may suppose that all the matter and all the energy in the world would be continually utilised without reserve. Population would be regulated by birth control. The sciences of eugenics and hygiene would see to it that the best possible human beings were being bred. Diseases would have been abolished. There would be a purposive economy wherein, by compulsory social service, the needs of all would be supplied. No further decisions would have to be made. In the cycle of the recurring generations, everything would go on unchanged. Without struggle and without the spice of hazard, the joys of life would be provided for all in unalterable allotments, with the expenditure of little labour and with ample scope for pastime.

In truth, however, such a condition of affairs is impossible. It is prevented by the working of incalculable natural forces, whose devastating effects can become intensified to technical catastrophes. There may also be the specific misfortune of a failure of technique. Perhaps the persistence of the scientific campaign against diseases, temporarily to all appearance overwhelming in its success, will rob human beings of their immunity, will deprive them of it so completely that an unanticipated pestilence will sweep away the whole race. The notion that people will generally and for an indefinite period remain content to practise birth control has been too readily adopted; the struggles that have to be faced by an indefinitely-increasing population will be renewed through the working of the will to reproduction, which is stronger in some members of our species than in others. Eugenics will prove unable to hinder the

From Karl Jaspers, *Man in the Modern Age*, trans. Eden and Cedar Paul, London: Routledge & Kegan Paul Ltd., 1951. Used by permission of the publisher.

survival of the weakly, and will fail to prevent that racial deterioration which would seem unavoidable amid the conditions of modern civilisation—for we have no objective standard of values to guide us in eugenic selection, and the idea of such a standard becomes almost unthinkable in view of the multiplicity of the primitive stocks out of which the human species has sprung.

Nor can we conceive of any permanent condition which would bring content. Technical advances do not create a perfected world, but at every stage introduce fresh difficulties and therewith new tasks into an imperfect world. Not merely does improved technique bring about an increasing discontent with its lack of perfection, but it has to remain imperfect under pain of collapse. Whatever frontiers technique may have momentarily reached, it cannot continue to subsist without the spirit of discovery, invention, planning, and new creation; and these will force it to overstep the aforesaid frontiers.

We learn from a study of the whole that mankind can never definitively attain a thoroughly purposive life-order, inasmuch as this order itself is rent in sunder by internal oppositions. The result of this internecine struggle is that the life-order moves restlessly onward through the ages in inevitable imperfection. Not merely do we find that, concretely, State wars against State, party against party, the sense of the State against economic interests, class against class, and one economic interest against another—but that the very forces which bring our life into being are themselves full of antinomies. Self-interest as the working motor of individual activity fashions, at one time, vital conditions which promote the general interest, and, at another time, destroys these same conditions. The orderly machinery, with

its sharply delimitated functions, duties, and rights of atomised human beings all regarded as perfectly interchangeable, arms itself against initiative, against individual venturesomeness, which threatens orderliness—and yet this machinery itself could not, in the absence of such initiative, continue to adapt itself to the perpetually changing situations of its environment.

Unless organisation be held in check by contraposing forces, it will ruin what it would fain safeguard, man as man. A bee community is possible as a static structure, perpetually reproducible; but human life, whether for the individual or for the community at large, is only possible as historical destiny, only as the incalculable course of technical achievements, economic enterprise, political ordinances.

Man can live only when, using his reason and working in co-operation with his fellows, he busies himself about the ordering of the technical supply of mass-needs. He must, therefore, devote himself with ardour to the cares of this world unless he is himself to perish amid its decay. He brings a world of purposive order into existence by striving to transcend its limitations wherever they show themselves. The limits of the life-order are in this matter his adversaries; and yet, in such limitations, he himself, since he is not absorbed into the order, is likewise personally present. Were he to become unreservedly master of the adversaries of the life-order, he would be hopelessly merged in the world of his own creation. Man's situation does not become a truly mental one until he grows aware of himself in these limitary positions. There he is truly living as himself when life, instead of rounding itself off, forces upon him continually-renewed antinomies.

Attempts to Justify the Establishing of a Life-Order That Shall Have Been Rendered Absolute (Modern Sophistry)

The realisation of the existence of economic forces, of masses, of apparatus, of mechanisation, has, through research, led to the growth of a science which claims universal validity. In actual fact the reality embodied in it is a mighty one. It has become a new, and at length a spiritual force. Nevertheless, insofar as it claims to be anything more than the rational control of purposive activity, insofar as it puts forward a claim to absolute status as a picture of life in its entirety, it has become, so to say, a creed or a faith which the spirit must either accept or resist. Whilst scientific research in particular (as far as this field is concerned) is occupied in the study of the qualities and quantities of economic forces, what is decisive in our consciousness of the mental situation is the answer we give to the question whether these economic forces and their results are the only and the universally dominant realities for mankind.

The claim that an all-embracing life-order shall have an absolute validity is based in some such fashion as the following. Life is to be regarded as the purposive satisfaction of the elementary vital needs of all. The human mind enters into this world, claiming it for its own. Joy in work must not be in any way diminished, but must, rather, promote the satisfaction of needs, and must contribute to the improvement of working methods, technique, and sociological apparatus. The individual's life must be entirely devoted to the service of the whole, thanks to which he simultaneously achieves the partial gratification of his own self-seeking (within the limits of the possible). Thus there arises the closed circuit of self-preserving human life, an orbit wherein life must revolve for ever—for it is utopian to imagine that joy in the general life will become identical with joy in the work which makes life possible for all. Judged by the standard of the greatest happiness of the greatest number, the meaning of human life is the economic provision of the largest possible mass of people with the amplest opportunities for gratifying their manifold needs.

All the same, the trend of this realisation cannot be pursued to its logical end, and, furthermore, the dominance of such images in the modern consciousness is by no means an absolute one. Technique, apparatus, and mass-life are far from exhausting the being of man. It is true that the titanic tools and forms of this life-world, the instruments of his own making, react upon him; but they do not wholly or unreservedly control his being. They influence him, but he remains different from them. Man cannot be deduced from a restricted number of principles. The construction of such principles, while throwing light upon certain relationships, makes it all the plainer that there is much which lies altogether outside of them.

Consequently, with the science of this life-order (insofar as it is regarded as having an absolute validity), there is unwittingly associated, either an erroneous belief in the possibility of attaining a definitively stable and sound world-organisation, or else an utter hopelessness in respect of all human life. Those who look forward to a routinist satisfaction with the welfare of the whole, to such a degree of welfare as might conceivably be attainable, tacitly ignore undesirable but undeniable facts. But instead of swinging like a pendulum between affirmation and denial of life as thus contemplated, we should continually strive to keep ourselves aware of the limits of the life-order. When we do this, the notion that the life-order can be rendered absolute becomes impossible for us to entertain; and our consciousness, relieved of its burden, recognising a reality that is knowable in its relativity, is free to turn to another possibility.

But if the notion that the life-order for the supply of mass-needs can have an absolute validity be allowed to persist, this inevitably leads to a mental attitude (that of the modern sophists) which manifests the unfathomability of the mind in respect of a reality thus rendered absolute. . . .

Irresolution. The life-order has a pre-eminent need of tranquillity as its safeguard, and its champions sophistically represent their dread of coming to a decision as the best way of promoting the general interest.

The insatiability of desire is restrained in individuals, in groups, in organisations, and in parties, by all agreeing to resist one another's encroachments. That is why compromise so often masquerades as justice. But compromise is either an artificial binding together of heterogeneous interests to form the specious unity of a life-institution, or else it is nothing more than a reciprocal yielding of points in order to avoid having to come to a decision. It is true that in community life any one who encounters an opposing activity is constrained to desire understanding and not struggle, if he desires this community life to continue. He therefore, within limits, renounces self-seeking, that he may render the continuance of life pos-

sible in the long run. He distinguishes his selfhood, which is unconditioned, from life, which is relative, and thus, as selfhood, has the power for compromise. But the question necessarily arises, what is the boundary between the compromise whose presupposition is the energy of deciding selfhood, and the compromise which leads to the dissolution of selfhood by becoming no more than the extremity of leveling co-operation on the part of all.

For when, in any matter, a man is wholly himself, he recognizes that there are alternatives, and then his action will not be a compromise. He will want to force a decision between the alternatives he has recognised. He knows that he may come to wreck, is well acquainted with primitive resignation as regards the duration of life, and is aware that a sincere failure may but emphasise the reality of his being. But for one who is exclusively animated by self-seeking impulses, so that in the life-order he makes partial renunciation merely in order to safeguard himself in the whole, the struggle brings risks which he cannot face. He only uses force when the big battalions are on his side, and shuns decision which involves danger. As long as his present life remains possible under tolerable conditions, he will accept whatever comes, and will always favour those of moderate views as against the extremists. He abjures anything that seems to him highflown, demanding adaptableness and a peaceful disposition. A frictionless functioning of the enterprise remains the ideal of such persons. They are willing to merge themselves in the co-operative body, pretending that therein each member is supplemented and enlarged by all the others. Not the individual takes precedence, but the general interest which (when it happens to be definite) is in truth simultaneously particular, and as a "general" interest remains void. The suppression of competition by the formation of cartels is trimmed with frills called the "general interest." Jealousy is neutralised by reciprocally tolerant changes of occupation, and an endeavour is made to mitigate the severity of the struggle for truth by a synthesis of every possibility. Justice becomes unsubstantial, imprecise, as if every one could be ranged upon the same plane as all others. To strive for a decision no longer means to come to grips with fate but to act forcibly in a strongly authoritative position.

But when, thereupon, a revolt occurs, it likewise, owing to the sophistical perversion of opinion and behaviour, leads to no decision, resulting only in a ruinous turning of things topsy-turvy, which, if not controlled by the life-order, must inevitably lead to chaos.

The Mind as a Means. Insofar as everything has been made dependent upon the rendering of the life-order absolute; insofar as the economic forces and situations, the possible powers, strive towards this end—so likewise is mental activity similarly directed, as if this were the one thing that mattered. The mind has ceased to believe in itself, as self-arising, and becomes a means to an end. Having thus grown fully mobile as a mere instrument of sophistry, it can serve any master. It discovers justification for any state of affairs, either extant or regarded as desirable by the powers that be. Yet the mind knows, all the time, that its working cannot be seriously regarded so long as it works on these lines, and it marks its secret knowledge of itself by the emotionalism of an assumed conviction. Since the awareness of the real powers of life does not only demand this insincerity, but also refuses to allow a veil to be drawn over the essential dependence of all life, there does, indeed, arise a new straightforwardness in the knowledge of the inevitable. All the same, forthwith the demand for a sober sense of reality becomes the sophistical instrument of everything which is not perfectly obvious, and man's true will is thereby ruined. This insincerity in its incredible manifoldedness cannot fail to result from the perversion of human possibilities if life continues to be regarded as the order or system for supplying the masses with the general necessaries of life.

Political Obligation

The problem of political obligation is directed toward the nature and basis of the bond that links individuals and society. That there is such a bond is indisputable, though its moral legitimacy and justification remain as philosophical problems even when the fact is recognized. Men are—and perhaps ought to be—bound and determined by the social order, yet few if any theories omit reference to some limitation on the completeness of such determination. The possibility of rejection, of revolt, is linked with and often is part of the very meaning of man's obligation to society.

This possibility of rebellion is used by the French writer and Nobel prize winner,

Albert Camus (1913–1960), as the basis for an analysis of man's social and historical existence. Rebellion is a dimension of man's being: it removes the individual from his solitude, founding its first value on the whole human race. If a man decides to rebel, it is because he has decided that human society has some value. Rebellion, therefore, Camus observes, is never nihilistic. It is "born of the spectacle of irrationality, confronted with an unjust and incomprehensible condition." The rebel asks not simply for life, but for reasons for living; he thus fights to preserve the integrity of one part of his own being. Rebellion is "the secular will not to surrender"; "it keeps us always erect in the savage, formless movement of history."

And yet, Camus says, there is a necessary limit to rebellion. Indeed, every thought or action that goes beyond limits negates itself. The freedom and justice for which the rebel fights are never simply given. They derive from the conditions of living, which must be accepted along with the suffering entailed by the limits of the possible. The logic of the rebel is to try to serve justice, not to add to injustice, but he must face the tensions resulting from the opposition of violence and nonviolence and of absolute justice and freedom. Violence destroys life and absolute justice destroys freedom. Rebellion without limits means slavery.

The revolutionary mind must therefore return to the only system of thought that is faithful to its origins, namely thought that recognizes limits. Such thought must apply the law of moderation to the contradictions and oppositions of rebellious thought. Moderation teaches that some element of realism is necessary to every ethic, even an ethic of rebellion, and that the irrational poses limits on the rational. Yet moderation must not be viewed as the opposite of rebellion: these are born and can only live in relation to each other, the one finding its limit in the other.

The limit of rebellion, however, is finally met in the "We are" that also must have its place in history. Every form of society presupposes a discipline and an order, but if the "We are" be denied, society and discipline lose all their direction. When rebellion is taken as the sole value, there are duties but no rights. The absence of rights implies the absence of social obligations, and the absence of obligations denies the possibility of the very values the rebel seeks to realize. Rebellion thus also reveals a limit in human nature itself, namely the limit of man's social dimension and his consequent dependence upon and obligation to the social order. Rebellion, moderation, and society, tragically opposed as they often are, are all conditions for and limitations of each other.

ALBERT CAMUS   Rebellion and Limit

The errors of contemporary revolution are first of all explained by the ignorance or systematic misconception of that limit which seems inseparable from human nature and which rebellion reveals. Nihilist thought, because it neglects this frontier, ends by precipitating itself into a uniformly accelerated

From Albert Camus, *The Rebel,* trans. Anthony Bower, New York: Alfred A. Knopf, Inc.; London: Hamish Hamilton, Ltd., 1956. Used by permission of the publishers.

movement. Nothing any longer checks it in its course and it reaches the point of justifying total destruction or unlimited conquest. We now know, at the end of this long inquiry into rebellion and nihilism, that rebellion with no other limits but historical expediency signifies unlimited slavery. To escape this fate, the revolutionary mind, if it wants to remain alive, must therefore return again to the sources of rebellion and draw its inspiration from the only system of thought which is faithful to its origins: thought that recognizes limits. If the limit discovered by rebellion transfigures everything, if every thought, every action that goes beyond a certain point negates itself, there is, in fact, a measure by which to judge events and men. In history, as in psychology, rebellion is an irregular pendulum, which swings in an erratic arc because it is looking for its most perfect and profound rhythm. But its irregularity is not total: it functions around a pivot. Rebellion, at the same time that it suggests a nature common to all men, brings to light the measure and the limit which are the very principle of this nature.

Every reflection today, whether nihilist or positivist, gives birth, sometimes without knowing it, to standards that science itself confirms. The quantum theory, relativity, the uncertainty of interrelationships, define a world that has no definable reality except on the scale of average greatness, which is our own. The ideologies which guide our world were born in the time of absolute scientific discoveries. Our real knowledge, on the other hand, only justifies a system of thought based on relative discoveries. "Intelligence," says Lazare Bickel, "is our faculty for not developing what we think to the very end, so that we can still believe in reality." Approximative thought is the only creator of reality.[1]

The very forces of matter, in their blind advance, impose their own limits. That is why it is useless to want to reverse the advance of technology. The age of the spinning-wheel is over and the dream of a civilization of artisans is vain. The machine is bad only in the way that it is now employed. Its benefits must be accepted even if its ravages are rejected. The truck, driven day and night, does not humiliate its driver, who knows it inside out and treats it with affection and efficiency. The real and inhuman excess lies in the division of labor. But by dint of this excess, a day comes when a machine capable of a hundred operations, operated by one man, creates one sole object. This man, on a different scale, will have partially rediscovered the power of creation which he possessed in the days of the artisan. The anonymous producer then more nearly approaches the creator. It is not certain, naturally, that industrial excess will immediately embark on this path. But it already demonstrates, by the way it functions, the necessity for moderation and gives rise to reflections on the proper way to organize this moderation. Either this value of limitation will be realized, or contemporary excesses will only find their principle and peace in universal destruction.

This law of moderation equally well extends to all the contradictions of rebellious thought. The real is not entirely

---

[1] Science today betrays its origins and denies its own acquisitions in allowing itself to be put to the service of State terrorism and the desire for power. Its punishment and its degradation lie in only being able to produce, in an abstract world, the means of destruction and enslavement. But when the limit is reached, science will perhaps serve the individual rebellion. This terrible necessity will mark the decisive turning-point.

rational, nor is the rational entirely real. As we have seen in regard to surrealism, the desire for unity not only demands that everything should be rational. It also wishes that the irrational should not be sacrificed. One cannot say that nothing has any meaning, because in doing so one affirms a value sanctified by an opinion; nor that everything has a meaning, because the word everything has no meaning for us. The irrational imposes limits on the rational, which, in its turn, gives it its moderation. Something has a meaning, finally, which we must obtain from meaninglessness. In the same way, it cannot be said that existence takes place only on the level of essence. Where could one perceive essense except on the level of existence and evolution? But nor can it be said that being is only existence. Something that is always in the process of development could not exist—there must be a beginning. Being can only prove itself in development, and development is nothing without being. The world is not in a condition of pure stability; nor is it only movement. It is both movement and stability. The historical dialectic, for example, is not in continuous pursuit of an unknown value. It revolves around the limit, which is its prime value. Heraclitus, the discoverer of the constant change of things, nevertheless set a limit to this perpetual process. This limit was symbolized by Nemesis, the goddess of moderation and the implacable enemy of the immoderate. A process of thought which wanted to take into account the contemporary contradictions of rebellion should seek its inspiration from this goddess.

As for the moral contradictions, they too begin to become soluble in the light of this conciliatory value. Virtue cannot separate itself from reality without becoming a principle of evil. Nor can it identify itself completely with reality without denying itself. The moral value brought to light by rebellion, finally, is no farther above life and history than history and life are above it. In actual truth, it assumes no reality in history until man gives his life for it or dedicates himself entirely to it. Jacobin and bourgeois civilization presumes that values are above history, and its formal virtues then lay the foundation of a repugnant form of mystification. The revolution of the twentieth century decrees that values are intermingled with the movement of history and that their historical foundations justify a new form of mystification. Moderation, confronted with this irregularity, teaches us that at least one part of realism is necessary to every ethic: pure and unadulterated virtue is homicidal. And one part of ethics is necessary to all realism: cynicism is homicidal. That is why humanitarian cant has no more basis than cynical provocation. Finally, man is not entirely to blame; it was not he who started history; nor is he entirely innocent, since he continues it. Those who go beyond this limit and affirm his total innocence end in the insanity of definitive culpability. Rebellion, on the contrary, sets us on the path of calculated culpability. Its sole but invincible hope is incarnated, in the final analysis, in innocent murderers.

At this limit, the "We are" paradoxically defines a new form of individualism. "We are" in terms of history, and history must reckon with this "We are," which must in its turn keep its place in history. I have need of others who have need of me and of each other. Every collective action, every form of society, supposes a discipline, and the individual, without this discipline, is only a stranger, bowed down under the weight of an inimical collectivity. But society and discipline lose their direction if they deny the "We are." I alone, in one sense, support the common dignity that I cannot allow either myself or others to debase. This individualism is in no sense pleasure; it is perpetual struggle, and, sometimes, unparalleled joy when it reaches the heights of proud compassion. . . .

In the common condition of misery, the eternal demand is heard again; nature once more takes up the fight against history. Naturally, it is not a question of despising anything, or of exalting one civilization at the expense of another, but of simply saying that it is a thought which the world today cannot do without for very much longer. There is, undoubtedly, in the Russian people something to inspire Europe with the potency of sacrifice, and in America a necessary power of construction. But the youth of the world always find themselves standing on the same shore. Thrown into the unworthy melting-pot of Europe, deprived of beauty and friendship, we Mediterraneans, the proudest of races, live always by the same light. In the depths of the European night, solar thought, the civilization facing two ways awaits its dawn. But it already illuminates the paths of real mastery.

Real mastery consists in refuting the prejudices of the time, initially the deepest and most malignant of them, which would reduce man, after his deliverance from excess, to a barren wisdom. It is very true that excess can be a form of sanctity when it is paid for by the madness of Nietzsche. But is this intoxication of the soul which is exhibited on the scene of our culture always the madness of excess, the folly of attempting the impossible, of which the brand can never be removed from him who has, once at least, abandoned himself to it? Has Prometheus ever had

this fanatical or accusing aspect? No, our civilization survives in the complacency of cowardly or malignant minds—a sacrifice to the vanity of aging adolescents. Lucifer also has died with God, and from his ashes has arisen a spiteful demon who does not even understand the object of his venture. In 1950, excess is always a comfort, and sometimes a career. Moderation, on the one hand, is nothing but pure tension. It smiles, no doubt, and our Convulsionists, dedicated to elaborate apocalypses, despise it. But its smile shines brightly at the climax of an interminable effort: it is in itself a supplementary source of strength. Why do these petty-minded Europeans who show us an avaricious face, if they no longer have the strength to smile, claim that their desperate convulsions are examples of superiority?

The real madness of excess dies or creates its own moderation. It does not cause the death of others in order to create an alibi for itself. In its most extreme manifestations, it finds its limit, on which, like Kaliayev, it sacrifices itself if necessary. Moderation is not the opposite of rebellion. Rebellion in itself is moderation, and it demands, defends, and re-creates it throughout history and its eternal disturbances. The very origin of this value guarantees us that it can only be partially destroyed. Moderation, born of rebellion, can only live by rebellion. It is a perpetual conflict, continually created and mastered by the intelligence. It does not triumph either in the impossible or in the abyss. It finds its equilibrium through them. Whatever we may do, excess will always keep its place in the heart of man, in the place where solitude is found. We all carry within us our places of exile, our crimes and our ravages. But our task is not to unleash them on the world; it is to fight them in ourselves and in others. Rebellion, the secular will not to surrender of which Barrès speaks, is still today at the basis of the struggle. Origin of form, source of real life, it keeps us always erect in the savage, formless movement of history.

The Ideal of Justice

Various existentialist themes have particular relevance to the problem of justice. Usually viewed as the consummate political and social value, justice is understood as an order among persons that secures certain conditions for their lives. As an order, it has also frequently been taken as a rational ideal in the sense that rational insight is necessary to and can give the principles of the ideal; as the consummate political value, it has been taken as the "saving" principle for society.

While recognizing the importance of justice to any society, existentialists have certain doubts about it. Their distrust of reason for existential concerns leads them to judge that belief in achieved rationality is illusory. The uncertainties of existence constantly present a challenge to the adequacy of any proposed structure of justice, and the elusiveness of finality means that such structures can never be taken as fully reliable. Man's corruption suggests that rules of justice in any living society can never be wholly free from the self-interests of dominant individuals and groups. In sum, both the nature of existence and the complexity of justice preclude the possibility that full justice is ever achievable, or that confidence in justice will ever be adequate to man's ultimate concerns.

Among the more forceful writers enunciating these themes is the Protestant theologian and social critic, Reinhold Niebuhr (1892–   ). Hardly classifiable as an existentialist—he would reject the appellation in many of its connotations—he nevertheless reflects and develops existentialist themes in his analyses of social issues. Particularly relevant to all discussions of justice for Niebuhr is the complexity of the concept and of its relations to ideals of brotherhood and love.

Justice may be considered in two ways: as a set of abstract rules and as structures of justice within historical conditions. Rules of justice are instruments of community serving to establish obligations that go beyond merely egotistic ones and to develop syntheses of interests. There is no need, Niebuhr believes, to be completely pessimistic about the ability of communities to achieve solutions on these matters. Rules of justice are not merely the product of selfish interests or the unstable compromises of power. The actual structures of justice in society, however, do not fulfill the law of brotherhood—human sin is the social reality preventing such fulfillment. The harmony achieved by justice can remain only an approximation of brotherhood for three reasons: all rational estimates of rights are infected by the contingent and finite character of human reason; complete impartiality is illusory; and rules of justice—caught in the relativities of history as they are—can never be unconditional.

Yet Niebuhr concludes with a position that is neither relativistic nor optimistic. There are relativities in the ideals of justice held by various societies, and there are also certain approximately universal rules and duties. There is evidence of progress, but there is also no ground for believing that the transcendent ideal of justice will ever be fully realized—or even known. With the existentialists, Niebuhr affirms that man is more than a social animal, and that his existence has more than the one social dimension. However important the ideal of justice is, it is not the final source of man's perfection; and the belief that it is, is idolatry.

REINHOLD NIEBUHR   The Relativity of Justice

The relation of justice to love contains complexities analogous to the dialectical relation of mutual to sacrificial love. These complexities may be clarified by considering them in two dimensions. The first is the dimension of rules and laws of justice. The second is the dimension of structures of justice, of social and political organizations in their relation to brotherhood. The difference between the first and second dimension obviously lies in the fact that laws and principles of justice are abstractly conceived, while structures and organizations embody the vitalities of history. The contradiction between actual social institutions and arrangements and the ideal of brotherhood is obviously greater than between love and the rules and laws of justice.

All systems, rules and laws governing social relations are on the one hand instruments of mutuality and community; and they contain on the other hand mere approximations of, and positive contradictions to, the ideal of brotherhood. These aspects of the character of rules of justice must be examined in turn.

Systems and principles of justice are the servants and instruments of the spirit of brotherhood in so far as they extend the sense of obligation towards the other, (*a*) from an immediately felt obligation, prompted by obvious need, to a continued obligation expressed in fixed principles of mutual support; (*b*) from a simple relation between a self and one "other" to the complex relations of the self and the "others"; and (*c*) finally from the obligations, discerned by the individual self, to the wider obligations which the community defines from its more impartial perspective. These communal definitions evolve slowly in custom and in law. They all contain some higher elements of disinterestedness, which would not be possible to the individual self.

In these three ways rules and laws of justice stand in a positive relation to the law of love. It is significant that the rational element is constitutive in each of them. An immediately felt obligation towards obvious need may be prompted by the emotion of pity. But a continued sense of obligation rests upon and expresses itself in rational calculations of the needs of others as compared with our own interests. A relation between the self and one other may be partly ecstatic; and in any case the calculation of relative interests may be reduced to a minimum. But as soon as a third person is introduced into the relation even

Reprinted with the permission of Charles Scribner's Sons from Volume II of *The Nature and Destiny of Man,* pages 247–256, by Reinhold Niebuhr. Copyright 1943 Charles Scribner's Sons. And by permission of the British publisher, James Nisbet and Company, Limited.

the most perfect love requires a rational estimate of conflicting needs and interests. Even the love within a family avails itself of customs and usages which stereotype given adjustments between various members of the family in such a way that each action need not be oriented by a fresh calculation of competing interests.

The definitions of justice arrived at in a given community are the product of a social mind. Various perspectives upon common problems have been merged and have achieved a result, different from that at which any individual, class or group in the community would have arrived. The fact that various conceptions of a just solution of a common problem can be finally synthesized into a common solution disproves the idea that the approach of each individual or group is consistently egoistic. If it were, society would be an anarchy of rival interests until power from above subdued the anarchy.

Interests may indeed clash to such a degree that no arbitration of the conflict is possible, in which case the conflict is ended either by the victory of one side or the other, or by the submission of both to a superior coercive force. Martin Luther's and Thomas Hobbes' political views are informed by the belief that all conflicts of interest are of such a nature.

The achievements of democratic societies refute this pessimism; and with it the purely negative conception of the relation of government and systems of justice to the ideal of brotherhood. History reveals adjustments of interest to interest without the interposition of superior coercive force to be possible within wide limits. The capacity of communities to synthesize divergent approaches to a common problem and to arrive at a tolerably just solution proves man's capacity to consider interests other than his own. Nevertheless, the fact that a synthesis of conflicting interests and viewpoints is not easy, and may become impossible under certain conditions, is a refutation of a too simple trust in the impartial character of reason. It would be as false to regard rules and principles of justice, slowly elaborated in collective experience, as merely the instruments of the sense of social obligation, as to regard them merely as tools of egoistic interest.

An analysis of the development of social conscience on any current social issue, as for instance the community's sense of obligation to the unemployed, may clarify the complex factors involved in this development. The unemployment benefits which the community pays to those who are out of work is partly an expression of the sense of obligation of the more privileged members of the community towards those who are less fortunate. They find an advantage in meeting this obligation according to fixed principles instead of relying upon their own occasional feeling of pity for this or that needy person. They know furthermore that their own knowledge of comparative needs is very inadequate and that they require the more impartial and comprehensive perspective of the total community, functioning through its proper agencies. This function of principles of unemployment relief presents the most positive relation between specific rules and the sense of brotherhood.

On the other hand the benefits which are paid to the unemployed are almost always higher than the privileged would like to pay, even though they may be lower than the poor would like to receive. Some members of the privileged classes in modern communities have in fact obscured the issue of justice in regard to this problem by the most obvious and transparent of all ideologies. They have sought to maintain that the unemployed are the victims of sloth rather than of the caprices of an intricate industrial process; and that the fear of hunger might cure their sloth. The actual schedule of payments upon which the community finally decides represents the conclusions of the social, rather than any individual, mind, and is the consequence of a perennial debate upon the subject. It is probably a compromise between conflicting viewpoints and interests. It certainly is not an unconditionedly "just" solution of the social problem involved. The privileged may in fact accept it for no better reason than that they fear the revolt of the poor. This aspect of the situation proves the impossibility of completely separating the concept of "principles of justice" from the hopes and fears, the pressures and counter-pressures, of living communities, expressed below the level of a rational calculation of rights and interests.

The solution may nevertheless become a generally accepted social standard; and some privileged members of the community may welcome it, because it expresses their considered sense of social obligation upon which they would prefer to rely rather than upon the momentary power of pity. The poor as a whole may receive less from these benefits than an individual needy person might secure by appealing to a given sensitive and opulent individual. But they will certainly receive more than if all of them were dependent upon nothing but vagrant, momentary and capricious impulses of pity, dormant unless awakened by obvious need.

This positive relation between rules of justice and the law of love must be emphasized in opposition to sentimental versions of the love commandment, according to which only the most personal individual and direct expressions of social obligation are manifestations of Christian *agape*. Both sectarian and Lutheran analyses of the relation of love to justice easily fall into the error of excluding rules of justice from the domain of love.[1]

Laws and systems of justice do, however, have a negative as well as a positive relation to mutual love and brotherhood. They contain both approximations of and contradictions to the spirit of brotherhood. This aspect of their character is derived from the sinful element in all social reality. They are merely approximations in so far as justice presupposes a tendency of various members of a community to take advantage of each other, or to be more concerned with their own weal than with that of others. Because of this tendency all systems of justice make careful distinctions between the rights and interests of various members of a

---

[1] Emil Brunner succumbs to this error when he writes: "The believer's most important duty . . . always remains that of pouring the vitality of love into the necessarily rigid forms of the order [structure of justice]. . . . The end is the personal relation itself. . . . To improve it [the order] is not a hopeless task, nor is it unnecessary but it is still only a matter of *secondary importance*. The one thing that matters is to do what can be done only from the standpoint of faith, namely, to love our neighbour 'In Christ,' and to serve him in any way we can. . . . It is supremely important to emphasize the truth that what is decisive always takes place in the realm of personal relations and not in the political sphere, save where we are concerned with preserving the whole order from a general breakdown." *The Divine Imperative,* p. 233.

Brunner's consistently negative interpretations of the political task and his idea of its secondary importance is a Lutheran heritage in his thought. He is, of course, correct in asserting that no systems and schemes of justice fulfill the law of love so that the possibility of giving them a higher content by personal attitudes and actions is obviated.

community. The fence and the boundary line are the symbols of the spirit of justice. They set the limits upon each man's interest to prevent one from taking advantage of the other. A harmony achieved through justice is therefore only an approximation of brotherhood. It is the best possible harmony within the conditions created by human egoism. This negative aspect of justice is not its only characteristic, as has been previously observed. Even if perfect love were presupposed, complex relations, involving more than two persons, require the calculation of rights. The negative aspect is nevertheless important.

The more positive contradiction to brotherhood in all schemes of justice is introduced by the contingent and finite character of rational estimates of rights and interests and by the taint of passion and self-interest upon calculations of the rights of others. There is no universal reason in history, and no impartial perspective upon the whole field of vital interests, which compete with and mutually support each other. Even the comparatively impartial view of the whole of a society, as expressed particularly in the carefully guarded objectivity of its juridical institutions, participates in the contingent character of all human viewpoints.

Such rules of justice as we have known in history have been arrived at by a social process in which various partial perspectives have been synthesized into a more inclusive one. But even the inclusive perspective is contingent to time and place. The Marxist cynicism in regard to the pretended moral purity of all laws and rules of justice is justified. Marxism is right, furthermore, in regarding them as primarily rationalizations of the interests of the dominant elements of a society. The requirements of "natural law" in

the medieval period were obviously conceived in a feudal society; just as the supposed absolute and "self-evident" demands of eighteenth-century natural law were bourgeois in origin.

The relative and contingent character of these ideals and rules of justice refutes the claim of their unconditioned character, made alike by Catholic, liberal and even Marxist social theorists.[2] Both Catholic and liberal social theories (and for that matter the Stoic theories in which both had their origin) make a distinction between "natural law" and the "positive" or "civil" law. The latter represents the actual and imperfect embodiment of the rules of justice in specific historical communities. The contingent and relative character of the latter type of law is recognized; but finality is ascribed to the former. This fundamental distinction must be challenged. It rests upon an untenable faith in the purity of reason; and it is merely another of the many efforts which men make to find a vantage point of the unconditioned in history. The effect of this pretended finality of "natural law" is obvious. It raises "ideology" to a higher degree of pretension, and is another of the many illustrations in history of the force of sin in the claim of sinlessness.[3]

---

[2] Marxist theory as usual detects the taint of interest in theories other than its own. But it also has the equivalent of a "natural law." In that law the dominance of the ideal of equality is, for instance, clearly "ideological." It is informed by a justified resentment of the poor against inequality but fails to recognize the inevitability of functional inequalities in society.

[3] Catholic theories of "natural law" are no less pretentious than secular theories, even though they subordinate the virtue of justice, enjoined in the natural law, to the virtue of love, achieved by grace. According to Catholic theory "natural law" is the part of the "divine" or the "eternal" law which is manifested in human reason. The endless relativi-

There is of course a tenable distinction between ideals of justice and their embodiment in historical or "civil" law. The latter is the consequence of pressures and counter-pressures in a living community. It is therefore subject to a greater degree of historical relativity than "natural law." In so far as thought is purer than action "natural law" is purer than "civil law." Furthermore it is important to recognize the validity of principles of justice, rationally conceived, as sources of criticism for the historical achievements of justice in living communities. If the medieval and modern secular theories of natural law claim too much for these rational principles of justice, both secular and Reformation relativists frequently dismiss them as irrelevant or dangerous. Karl Barth's belief that the moral life of man would possess no valid principles of guidance, if the Ten Commandments had not introduced such principles by revelation, is as absurd as it is unscriptural.[4]

The practical universality of the prohibition of murder for instance in the moral codes of mankind is just as significant as the endless relativities which manifest themselves in the practical application of the general prohibition. There are essentially universal "principles" of justice moreover, by which

the formulation of specific rules and systems of justice is oriented. Both "equality" and "liberty" are recognized in Stoic, medieval and modern theories of natural law as transcendent principles of justice; though the modern theories (both bourgeois and Marxist) falsely regard them as realizable rather than as transcendent principles. An analysis of one of them, the principle of equality, will serve to reveal the validity of both as transcendent principles of justice.

The perpetual recurrence of the principle of equality in social theory is a refutation of purely pessimistic conceptions of human nature, whether secular or religious. Its influence proves that men do not simply use social theory to rationalize their own interest. Equality as a pinnacle of the ideal of justice implicitly points towards love as the final norm of justice; for equal justice is the approximation of brotherhood under the conditions of sin. A higher justice always means a more equal justice. Special privilege may be frowned upon more severely by those who want it than those who have it; but those who have it are uneasy in their conscience about it. The ideological taint enters into the discussion of equality when those who suffer from inequality raise the principle of equality to the definitive principle of justice without recognizing that differences of need or of social function make the attainment of complete equality in society impossible.[5] The beneficiaries of special privilege emphasize, on the other hand, that inequalities of social function justify corresponding inequalities of privilege. They may also assert, with some, but less, justification, that inequality of reward is a necessary induce-

---

ties of historical rational perspectives are obscured. This unconditioned claim for an essentially universal reason is the basis of the remarkable degree of certainty with which Catholic moral theology is able to define "justice" and "injustice" in every possible situation. *Cf.* Vol. I, Ch. X.

[4] It is in conflict with the Pauline assertion: "For when the Gentiles which have not the law, do by nature the things contained in the law, these, having not the law, are a law unto themselves." Romans 2:14. Barth's exegetical effort to eliminate the force of this Pauline doctrine is tortuous. *Cf.* his *Epistle to the Romans,* pp. 65–68.

[5] This is the aspect of the problem recognized in Stoic and medieval theories, according to which equality belongs to the golden age or to the perfection before the fall.

ment for the proper performance of social function. But they will seek to hide the historic fact that privileged members of the community invariably use their higher degree of social power to appropriate an excess of privileges not required by their function; and certainly not in accord with differences of need.

The validity of the principle of equality on the one hand and the impossibility of realizing it fully on the other, illustrates the relation of absolute norms of justice to the relativities of history. The fact that one class will tend to emphasize the absolute validity of the norm unduly, while another class will be inclined to emphasize the impossibility of achieving it fully, illustrates the inevitable "ideological taint" in the application of a generally valid principle, even if the principle itself achieves a high measure of transcendence over partial interest.[6]

---

[6] The Stoic and Catholic distinction between relative and absolute natural law is a helpful recognition of the necessity of accommodating absolute principles to relative and "sinful" historic situations. But the idea that the requirements of "relative" natural law can be stated absolutely proceeds from the failure to include the human mind in the relativities of history. Here Emil Brunner's criticisms of this distinction are admirable. Cf. The Divine Imperative, pp. 626–632.

Brunner, however, erroneously follows the Reformation disparagement of the function of reason in the realm of social ethics and arrives at a consequent dismissal of the ideal of equality as merely a "rational" and therefore unchristian norm. He writes: "The egalitarian law of nature does not belong to the world of the Bible but to the context of Stoic rationalism. The egalitarian ideal does not arise out of reverence for the Creator but out

The complex character of all historic conceptions of justice thus refutes both the relativists who see no possibility of finding valid principles of justice, and the rationalists and optimists who imagine it possible to arrive at completely valid principles, free of every taint of special interest and historical passion.

The positive relation of principles of justice to the ideal of brotherhood makes an indeterminate approximation of love in the realm of justice possible. The negative relation means that all historic conceptions of justice will embody some elements which contradict the law of love. The interests of a class, the viewpoint of a nation, the prejudices of an age and the illusions of a culture are consciously and unconsciously insinuated into the norms by which men regulate their common life. They are intended to give one group an advantage over another. Or if that is not their intention, it is at least the unvarying consequence.

---

of the desire to dictate to the Creator how things ought to be, or the presupposition that the Creator ought to treat every one alike." Ibid., p. 407.

Any parent who has sought to administer justice and to compose childish disputes will know how spontaneously children appeal to the principle of equality as the correct principle of arbitrament, and with what difficulty they must, on occasion, be persuaded that differences of age, function and need, render the principle inoperative, or make it only indirectly relevant. The children may lack proper reverence for the Creator of inequalities; but on the other hand they have certainly never heard of, or been spoiled by, "Stoic rationalism."

Analytic Philosophy

In many ways an even more radical "revolution" in philosophy than the existentialist protest is the movement variously known as linguistic, ordinary language, and analytic philosophy. The term revolution is used advisedly. Analytic philosophers claim to present not another doctrine, but a new conception of philosophical activity, which they insist goes to the very nature of philosophy itself.

The most general characterization that can be made of this perspective—and one must be careful of generalizations here for analytic philosophers like existentialists do not form a "school" in the traditional sense—is that philosophy has become language oriented. Analytic philosophers share the conviction that the perennial problems of philosophy can be clarified, if not resolved, by careful attention to the ways in which languages are actually used. Metaphysical questions, which analysts believe are never genuine questions at all, are the objects of critical attention. These questions are considered mere confusions resulting when language is used in peculiar and illegitimate ways. Offering no new or "higher" knowledge, philosophy becomes the activity of clarifying and removing the conceptual puzzles into which language can occasionally lead one. No longer is philosophy to be pursued in the "grand manner" of building systems of ultimate propositions: it is rather a piecemeal effort to achieve clarity through the resolution of particular issues arising from linguistic confusion.

To say that philosophy is concerned with language is itself no revolutionary statement. Philosophers have always found it important to give careful attention to language and linguistic forms. Analytic philosophers go further than this: philosophy is the activity of finding meaning, and in no way is it the pursuit of truth. Why should philosophy be so restricted? The first—and earlier—answer was given by a form of linguistic philosophy usually called "logical positivism." Agreeing with the antimetaphysical and scientific stress of earlier positivism,* this twentieth-century philosophy began its work with this observation: true and false are terms having application to propositions or statements, but before it is possible to decide whether any given statement is true or false, it is first necessary to know what it means. How can one determine the meaning or sense of a statement? Logical positivists answered: one knows the meaning when one is able to indicate the circumstances under which the statement would be true (or the circumstances that would make it false): The only way the meaning of any sentence can be made clear is to describe these circumstances. Meaning is reference to verification.

Of the many statements that purport to be cognitive, there is a group found in logic and mathematics whose truth can be determined simply by the principle of noncontradiction. Given the meanings of 2, 4, 5, plus, and equals, it is true that $2 + 2 = 4$ and false that $2 + 2 = 5$ because the former is consistent, the latter inconsistent. Unfortunately, however, while these *analytic* propositions are necessarily true or false, they give no knowledge of reality. Their sole function is to relate symbols to each other. The propositions that give knowledge of the world are *synthetic*. Their meaning lies in their relation to possible verification in sense experience. If it is possible to specify the circumstances under which the proposition could be so verified (or falsified), it is meaningful; if it is not possible, the proposition is meaningless and "non-sense." All meaningful synthetic propositions, positivists assert, belong to the sciences. There are also propositions enunciating value judgments, such as Lying is wrong. These, however, are neither analytic (since they cannot be proven by their consistency) nor synthetic (since no sense experience could possibly verify them), but *emotive* for they involve the expression of emotion rather than any cognitive function.

With their threefold distinction of types of propositions—analytic, synthetic, and emotive—logical positivists are able to resolve traditional philosophical problems in two ways. Some of them will dissolve away upon analysis: they may look like problems and questions because they are framed in a certain grammatical order, but the words as they are put together do not make logical sense. Secondly, some philosophical problems will prove to be real; but if so, then they are capable of being solved by the methods of science. That is, if such problems are answerable in principle, the answer can be given only by scientific investigation. Thus, the fate of all philosophical problems is that some will disappear by being shown to be mistakes and misunderstandings in the use of language; others will be found to be ordinary scientific questions in disguise.

A second and more recent answer to the question of restricting philosophy to language analysis is given by a group of scholars who find traditional philosophy less nonsense than puzzlement. While agreeing with the logical positivists in the rejection of metaphysics and the prevention of linguistic confusion, these analysts differ from them in three important ways. First, they generally reject the verification principle. For them, it is either a kind of metaphysical principle itself or it is highly reductive in its restriction of cognitive meaning to relation to sense experi-

---

* The chief influences on logical positivism, however, came mainly from advances in science and logic, not from the positivistic sources used in Section Two above. Hume's critique of reason is important for logical positivists also.

ence. To use a slogan of the analysts, "the meaning is the use," not verification.†
Next, analytic philosophers reject any rigid interpretation of the analytic-synthetic
distinction. In certain types of discourse, to be sure, this distinction can be maintained, but in actual and living languages, it does not hold. Finally, analysts reject
any simple classification of uses of language such as cognitive, directive, and emotive, insisting that sentences perform an indefinitely large number of tasks. To use a
second slogan, "every statement has its own logic"; that is, the uses and functions
of words are richer and more varied than a rigid classification would imply.

The analyst's view of philosophy may now be stated as "conceptual elucidation,"
which must be pursued to prevent misconceptions in language itself. Misconceptions
arise because, as Professor Gilbert Ryle has written,‡ some expressions are
"systematically misleading." For example, the statement, "Mr. Baldwin is a
politician," is not misleading, for it states a fact in a straightforward way. The
statement, "Mr. Baldwin is objective," however, though similar in structure, does
not exhibit the form of the fact for which it is being used (if any), and is misleading without analysis. The analyst holds that traditional philosophy has been
particularly susceptible to error because of such expressions, and he seeks to
detect "the sources in linguistic idioms of recurrent misconstructions and absurd
theories," which he believes is "the sole and whole function of philosophy" (Ryle).

Philosophy thus shifts from questions like What is the nature of x? to questions
like What does x do in a language, and how does it do it? Elucidation involves
the description of the roles of certain concepts and the conditions under which
they function. Doubting that philosophers can give any systematic account of
reality, analysts may, with G. E. Moore (1873–1958) defend common sense,
with Ludwig Wittgenstein (1889–1951) remove philosophical perplexities, with
John Wisdom (1904–   ) point out the unique anxieties underlying philosophical puzzles, or with John Austin (1911–1960) search out the ways in which
language can be legitimately employed. The general aim is the same, namely to
clear up puzzlement, to prevent misconceptions in language, and to expose absurd
theories.

Man and Society

The quest for clarity in social philosophy follows the directions outlined above.
Offering no special philosophical wisdom for society, either as a kind of unique
knowledge or as higher moral guidance, analysts find that many of the central

---

† A more technical way of putting this slogan is this. Logical positivists often assumed that
meaning must be understood as denotation or naming. Analysts recognize, however, that language is exceedingly more complex than this. Attention is therefore given to such problems as
how children actually learn to understand an expression. Central to this achievement is the
mastery of rules, and hence, sense or meaning is the rule for the employment of an expression.

‡ See his article, "Systematically Misleading Expressions," *Proceedings of the Aristotelian
Society,* 1931–1932.

concepts of traditional social philosophy like group, society, state, and law are vague, formless, and misleading. Therefore, their use is accompanied often by perplexity and confusion, which may issue in social theories that are extreme, if not absurd. The logic* of these concepts must be properly mapped out if this consequence is to be avoided.

In the following selection, Professor Jan Srzednicki (1923–   ) observes these difficulties in social and political concepts, and he seeks to offer certain "opening moves" for discussions of them. The path he follows lies between giving up in the midst of confusion and providing a "pure" analysis of basic concepts; it is one that seeks to relate political concepts to actual usage. He begins with "group-structure," which is essentially a relation structure, and then moves to other concepts such as group, voluntary behavior, regulation, status, institution, and social system. He also finds it necessary to explore several interrelations of these concepts, such as that of society to behavior controlled by regulations, and of the latter to an individual's acting for reasons. The result of his work is not to offer new facts about man and society as a social scientist might do, but to provide an elucidation of key concepts that can serve as a prolegomenon to further exploration.

---

* This frequently used word suggests an important point that should not be missed. The task of conceptual elucidation must not be confused with the work of the linguist or grammarian. The "logic" of an expression is a matter of the rules governing its coemployment with other expressions in communication situations.

JAN SRZEDNICKI   Basic Political Concepts

Political Philosophy is a very unsatisfactory discipline. In it, it is possible to find: bits of analysis, pseudo-science, empirical investigation, reformatory attempts, political programming, utopia building, and some other odds and ends. One is tempted either to give it up altogether, or to provide a solid basis for it by thorough analysis of concepts. There one is faced by a difficulty —political and social terms are vague and formless; everybody bends them to their own use. The case is even worse than the case of aesthetics. For here it is not only the philosopher and the critic that indulge in this pastime, but also the various practitioners of political arts and the general public. Since the

practice is universal it cannot be called improper, unless it be in a moral sense. It is also very difficult to find a solid basis for analytical treatment of the concepts involved. It has been maintained sometimes that this is a wholly unprofitable occupation, or even that no special or specific concepts are involved in political practice and discourse. On the one hand I cannot agree with this opinion; on the other, I find it very difficult to provide a pure analysis of the basic concepts. I have therefore adopted a middle course. I shall discuss and analyse concepts and their relations in a way that has solid basis in actual usage. However, I shall select the concepts that I feel are basic, and those features of

From Jan Srzednicki, "Basic Political Concepts," *The Philosophical Quarterly,* 13 (1963). Used by permission of the editor and the author.

them that appear more important or more central; the analysis will therefore be slightly "biased." The only purpose of this treatment is to provide a reasonably clear framework for discussion of further issues of political philosophy. I might add that the concepts as presented here seem to me to be significant in that with their help the other concepts and other mutations of similar concepts can be understood more readily than with the aid of other similar selections. In this sense then I claim that the concepts as analysed and presented here are genuinely *basic political concepts*.

The first of the important concepts is somewhat similar to the concept of social-structure as used by anthropologists. I shall use the term *group-structure* in order to avoid confusion and purely terminological argument. I would say, for instance, that a state,[1] a nomadic community, a tribe, etc., could be group-structures, but the English legal system and the communist legal system are not. A different group-structure would exist in two societies if one of them had, and the other did not have, a legal system. These two would be societies of different type *qua* societies. Distinction between two group-structures would rest usually on the existence of differences of the following kind: on the one hand there exists an apparatus for interpreting and enforcing law, on the other hand there is none; a division of labour and trade unions exists in the one case but not in the other, and so on. When I speak about differences in group-structure, I am not referring to differences of the following type: between two primitive taboo systems; between two similar systems of codified law, between two

religious marriage systems where, for example, the exact ceremony, the period of engagement, and the number of days per year the mother-in-law is allowed in the home of a married couple, are different. This does not mean that the distinctions in group-structure are gross or crude; there may be subtle differences which are of this kind. However, the group-structure names mentioned above: "state," "tribe," "community," are general and consequently lack precision in a way common to all very general terms. The existence of group-structure presupposes the existence of a group. To say about any group that it exhibits a certain group-structure is to describe or classify it by reference to the kind of arrangements that exist within it; to refer to the types of relations that exist between its members rather than referring to the particular relations that exist between them. Group-structure is the relation-structure of a group where all the relations are between, and concerning, members of this group as such. The concept of group-structure nearly ceases to apply in the case of a group such that a number of individuals come into contact with each other more or less frequently, but there do not exist any standing relationships between them nor yet any rules concerning their behaviour towards each other. On the other hand, should there be 20 people on an island, completely isolated from each other, one could not even ask, "What sort of group-structure exists among these people?"; here there is not even a group to talk about. A group can exist only where individuals are in contact with each other. A mere group is then the limiting case of a group-structure. An ant-hill and a pack of wolves are already less primitive; not even a flock of sheep is a mere group. The sheep keep together, and follow the first among themselves that

---

[1] I mean to use "state" in the sense in which we say that Great Britain is a *state,* not in the sense in which we talk about the *British State.*

moves away in any direction. In this they are, or at least I imagine that they are, different from a colony of bacteria in a test-tube. Thus one is able to describe and mark at least some distinctions of group-structure without making any reference to the distinction between voluntary and involuntary behaviour.

Voluntary behaviour could, however, be regarded as a *conditio sine qua non* for the existence of social or political phenomena. We do not talk about a society unless we can point to the existence of some institutions or, at the very least, some regulations. All group-structures below this level are pre- or non-social. We do not think of an ant-hill as a society because we would not say that ants have chosen to behave in an orderly manner for this or that reason, or indeed that they are following any rules at all. Ant behaviour can be causally explained, hence it is neither social nor political. We are not prepared to talk about the existence of institutions or regulations unless the behaviour of individuals forming the group is controlled by something else than their instincts and other natural urges. It is this sort of behaviour to which I have referred as voluntary, and which I can perhaps describe more precisely as *behaviour controlled by regulations*. A little reflection will suffice to show that the above view is correct. If one man, or even if every man on the planet Pincus No. 7 had the habit of straightening his tie every 7¾ minutes, we would not be prepared to say that those people act according to the rule, "Straighten your tie every 7¾ minutes." The difference between this sort of behaviour and behaviour controlled by regulations can be put in a nutshell by saying that though a Pincushion straightening his tie acts in a way in which we expect him to act, yet he cannot be described as doing what is

expected of him. He is simply doing what we have come to expect him to do. When we say that someone has done what was expected of him, we mean to imply that he did it *because* it was expected of him. It is easily seen that this is the case whenever people do something in accordance with any rules. In these cases they do "what is done" or "what is prescribed" or "what should be done" or "what they are supposed to do" and so on. When a man ceases to perform a habitual action we are usually surprised; but when a man ceases to do what he is supposed to do, we are not surprised, we are either angry or pleased with him, as the case may be. In many cases we come to expect people to do what they are not supposed to do, i.e. we expect them to do what is not expected of them. In such cases we are likely to punish a person rather than try to cure him. We would ask for his reasons rather than investigate the cause of his unorthodox behaviour. We would describe people's behaviour as controlled by regulations if, and only if, *people behave in a specified way because[2] other people behave in this way, or because other people expect people to behave in this way.*[3]

I have said that the existence of society presupposes *behaviour controlled by regulations,* rather than saying that it presupposes that individuals *act for reasons*. The reason for doing this is easy to see—we are not prepared to talk about society and institutions unless we are prepared to talk about group behaviour as well. In Hobbes's "state of

---

[2] "Because" here refers to reasons for acting in this way.

[3] "To behave in a specified way" is meant here to indicate a mode of behaviour which becomes standardised in a given sort of situation. The very least that is thus indicated is that broadly the same behaviour occurs repeatedly in broadly the same situation.

warre" people act for reasons, but there is no group behaviour in the required sense. Group behaviour arises where there emerges behaviour controlled by regulations. It is however quite true, (and important to notice,) that behaviour controlled by regulations presupposes that individuals act for reasons. The above description of behaviour controlled by regulations leaves open the questions: "How are the regulations established?" and "Why do people let their behaviour be controlled by regulations?"; these, however, are not questions which are my concern in this paper.

The concept of group-structure is relevant to any group. But the concepts of "society," "community," "institution," "law," "legal system," etc., are only applicable where the behaviour of individuals is, at least to some extent, controlled by regulations. Some structure words like "state," "tribe" and "community" cannot be used below this level. Let us now ask: "What sort of reasons can be given for having regulations?" I do not wish to ask the question in a way which presupposes that a regulation is always established deliberately and for a deliberate purpose. It is quite sufficient to observe that each regulation, if effective, can be said to do a job, and that a question like: "What sort of function can this regulation have?" or "What sort of function can this regulation be supposed to have?" always make sense. Regulations then seem to have a purpose or a function. Let us also ask: "How are regulations stated?" Once again I am not trying to imply that all regulations are expressly stated, but only that it is logically possible to state any regulation by using a more or less complex imperative formula. A typical simple formula would be: "Don't hit a woman with a flower" or "Don't spit through the window" or "Take your hat

off in church" and so on. The order: "Tomorrow at 11.00 hours release the pigeons" is not a regulation, even though the order: "Soldiers are to remove their caps in church" is one. This is so because a regulation is a standing directive. However, we would not say that a complex directive contained in 145 pages and dealing with all aspects of behaviour of soldiers of different ranks towards each other is a regulation—we would say that it is a *code* or an organised cluster of regulations. It is the purpose of a regulation to control the behaviour of individuals. But since the *scope* of a regulation *is limited,* its purpose is to control people's behaviour in a specific situation, or with respect to a particular type of contingency. In saying that a regulation is a *standing directive,* I mean to indicate that it is the purpose of a regulation to control people's behaviour at any time, when the contingency to which the given regulation is relevant, should arise. It is not the purpose of a regulation to select the time at which it is to apply. If a regulation is established and is supposed to come into force on 1st January, and to lapse on 10th November, then these limits of its operation are established by an order or agreement concerning the regulation in question, but not by the regulation itself.[4] When we use the word "always" in a regulation (e.g. "Always respect the Pope"), we mean to say that there are no exceptions to the rule, and not that the principle applied 2,000 years ago and will apply 5,000 years hence. A statement to the effect that *a regulation*

---

[4] An order directing a soldier to report to the Officer of the Day, three times a day, in full dress, for five consecutive days, is not a regulation because, *inter alia,* the time at which the soldier is bound by the uncomfortable behaviour directive is specified in the order itself.

cannot or will not ever lapse, cannot be contained within the regulation itself. It is part of the meaning of "standing directive" or "regulation" that it applies over an *indefinite* period of time.

A regulation is not an institution. An institution is not even a number of regulations, because a number of regulations scattered, and each dealing with a totally different matter, could not even form a basis for an institution. In order to have an institution we have to have at least a *code,* i.e. a cluster of regulations controlling the behaviour of individuals in a systematic manner. One would like to say that such systematic coverage exists where one regulation supplements another, e.g. when one takes over where the other leaves off, where the effects of one limit the effect of another, or, very generally, in any case where they can be said to have a joint effect. For illustration one could list the code of table manners, the code of morals, the traffic code and others. These examples will also serve to stress the interesting fact that we distinguish between different codes *by the way* of distinguishing between the fields in which they operate. None of these areas of human behaviour could possibly be covered by a single regulation, because to refer to a field in this sense is to refer to a type of activity which permits of an indefinite number of particular types of contingencies, each of which could be covered by a behavioural directive or regulation. To say that a code is supposed to give a consistent coverage of a given field involves more than may be apparent at the first glance. A code consists of directives, hence having a consistent code implies enforcing a policy aimed at a certain goal or goals. To illustrate—one of the goals of the football code is to prevent a football game from deteriorating into a series of

wrestling matches; another is to let the players show a certain type of skill with the ball; another to put a premium on teamwork; yet another to enable the referee to reach a fair decision and so on. On the other hand one could say that the goal of the code is to provide a spectator drawcard, to fill the stadium and the cashbox of the League. The question "What is the aim of this code?" can be answered in different ways, some more pertinent than others, but always by mentioning a general effect as the aim of the code. It always makes sense to ask this question of any possible code, exactly in the same way as it makes sense to ask "What is its purpose?" of any possible regulation. I said that in order to have an institution one must have a code and not merely a number of regulations. The next question which comes naturally to one's mind is whether it is sufficient to have a code[5] in order to have an institution. As an example for discussion let us consider a court of law. A court could not exist without a cluster of regulations designed to enable it to consider systematically any matter brought before it in a proper way, and to reach a legally satisfying decision having regard for the law and the facts as presented to the court. These regulations determine all the proceedings of the court in fair detail. But this is not enough. Let us observe:

Firstly that not all the regulations relevant to court proceedings apply equally to all persons involved. The judge, and nobody else, can adjourn the court and instruct the jury. The counsel for defence, not a jury member, can cross-examine a witness. It is the de-

---

[5] I am using the word "code" in a very wide sense, where e.g. a procedure can be called a code, and any cluster of regulations, even when sub-divided into smaller units, can be called a code.

fendant, not anybody else, who is presumed innocent till proved guilty, etc., etc. It is apparent *both that* the regulations differentiate between different persons involved in a court case; *and* that this discrimination is not directed against anybody personally—*the discrimination applies to people having different status with regard to the court* in virtue of their status. When I say someone is the presiding judge, the defendant, a witness, a jury member, in a court case, I am referring to this person by his status with respect to the given court.[6] It is clearly essential to determine the status of actors in order to establish the institution of a court; in the absence of status distinctions we could not even state the necessary regulations. By saying this, however, I do not wish to imply that a status within an institution must be always established in a deliberate, explicit and formal way, nor do I wish to say that it must precede the regulations in time. I am saying that an institution cannot be established without the status of the people involved being determined. In this case, it is also true that one cannot have a status independently of institutions. Generally "status" is not an independent concept. Even though the "status of the most privileged person in Melbourne"[7] can be established independently of any given institution, it cannot be maintained independently of all political and social institutions. A physical feature, e.g. an ability or disability, e.g. being a mathematical prodigy, or a typhoid carrier, is not in itself a status, but can, and often does, give rise to a status.

---

[6] Smith could be the judge in one case, and a witness in another court case.

[7] If this is a status, although I am willing to accept it as a status for the sake of argument; I have used inverted commas to mark my doubt.

Secondly we should notice that rights, duties, liberties, powers, etc., are vested in members of the institution as such, and so:

We talk of a *right* when the regulations within the institution forbid others to interfere with some wishes or claims of certain persons. For instance, courts' regulations forbid anybody to interfere with a witness's wish to refuse to give answers which might incriminate him.

We talk about *liberties* when those regulations permit somebody to do something, for instance the counsel is permitted by court rules to ask any questions relevant to the case if he wishes to do so.

We talk about *duties* when regulations within an institution make it necessary for someone to do something. For instance, according to court rules, a witness is required to give truthful answers to questions put to him.

We talk about *powers* or *authority* when these regulations make it necessary for others to comply with directives issued by someone having a certain status within the institution. All people concerned are, for example, required to comply if the presiding judge directs the court to adjourn. Where there is a cluster of institutions, certain complications will arise, since a person's status, duties, liberties, etc., in some of the institutions may have an effect on his status, etc., in other institutions. But with regard to a single institution, let us observe that these rights, duties and even the status itself, are established within the institution provided only that the directives and regulations necessary for maintaining them are established; and independently of whether they are really effective. It is also important to see that regulations discriminate between people only in virtue of their status, and therefore rights, duties, powers and liberties are attached to positions:[8] I shall then call them *"concepts appertaining to status."* All these elements, i.e. regulations, status concepts, and concepts appertaining to status, are equally essential for the existence of the institution. A code is not an institution, since when one refers to a code one does not imply the existence of any status concepts or any concepts appertaining to status. It could be maintained that whenever there is a code, some status must be established, be it only the status of a member to whom the code is meant to apply. Such would be the case, for example, with table manners, and the status of a diner. This suggestion is unacceptable. Regulations operating within an institution can only discriminate between its members; distinctions established by these directives must be contained within it. The membership of the institution is a distinction established outside of it.[9] The rules of an institution can apply only to its members and cannot therefore establish that they are members. The problem, to whom a given code is to apply, must be decided outside and independently of this code. For example, an order of the Governor in Council can, at the same time, establish a code and determine to whom this code is to apply.

The concepts of "group," "group-structure," "regulation," "institution," "status" and the concepts appertaining to status are as yet insufficient to explain the whole complexity of political group-structures such as state. We have therefore to introduce the concept of a social system. The legal system, the economic system, etc., are the models. Very roughly one could say that a social system is a fairly comprehensive structure within and often an integral part of a group-structure. It will typically consist of a cluster of institutions. These institutions will have definite relations to each other, etc. There again the law presents the best example—our legal system comprises a number of standing courts, which are institutions; these form a clearly defined cluster, such that one might be tempted to say that the system is in fact an institution, the members of which are other institutions. The impression is strengthened if one reflects on the laws and procedural rules appertaining to all the courts. The position is complicated by the fact that members of the legal profession have a status within it, and that this status determines to a large extent their possible rôles in particular courts, so it looks almost as if the legal system were a second order institution. Pursuing this line of thought might seem profitable, and it might well be, provided that we remember what we are doing. It is fatally easy to make the concepts too sharp and in this way to produce a conceptual framework that lacks the necessary degree of flexibility. For that reason I think that it is better to point out a few ways in which a social system can be conceived and to make it quite plain that the particular character of a social system must be determined in each particular case. Thus if we look at the system of commerce, the relations of particular institutions involved and the relations of individuals have different characters from those in

---

[8] I mean by this that they are vested in persons in virtue of these persons having certain status, which does not exclude the possibility that, e.g., some rights could be vested in anybody having any status within the institution.

[9] It is possible to have a status within a community, this depending *inter alia* on a man's membership of certain institutions and his status within them.

the case of the legal system. Let us also remember that there are other systems —like the system of education and that of civil administration. However, there are clear similarities between all the systems. In each case more is involved than is involved in a particular institution. We might perhaps say that a system must involve: institutions, in the widest sense of the word, individuals as members of these institutions and also having a second order status with respect to the system; and regulations over and above the regulations that go into the making of institutions and such that they give the cluster its particular character. In the case of social systems as well as in the case of institutions and particular regulations, one has to remember that within the limits of practicability these social forms can come into being without explicit agreements, proclamations, etc. An example of a whole system that could grow in this fashion is the family structure of a group. However, with growing complexity, explicit formulation and its correlates quickly become necessary.

It is obvious that social systems can be, and in fact are, related to each other. For example, the legal system of a country has a definite bearing on its administrative, commercial and other systems. Again, it is impossible to specify in advance the exact nature of the relations between these systems, and resultant relations between the institutions and individuals involved. We can see that the sophisticated group-structure is a cluster of systems; in fact it can be described as the ultimate system since it does not operate within a greater system. The nature of the structure will be determined by the character of the above mentioned relations. We could,

for instance, distinguish political and pre-political; feudal, totalitarian and democratic; agricultural and nomadic; urbanised and non-urbanised; centralised and decentralised groups. It will be clear that many classifications are possible, and that the choice depends on our interest and purpose. The above considerations are sometimes implemented by others, e.g. it is generally held that the concept of a state involves certain territorial claims, in addition to claims of independent jurisdiction over its members. But it might be argued plausibly that in present conditions any completely separate group must have a claim to a separate territory, otherwise its group-structure could never be completely independent, and in this way the territorial claim would be involved in the concept of this particular group-structure. Questions of this type, however, can be settled only when they arise.

Regarding complex political group-structures, e.g. the state, let us notice that when we say that such group-structures must be independent of each other, we do not imply that relations could not exist between such groups. Nor are we denying that relations can exist between individual members belonging to different groups. One example is the U.N.—there exists an association of independent states, but their independence is maintained since the relations exist only on this level. The Common Market association comes nearer to developing a single group-structure since at least some of the institutions existing within, and individual members of, the component states have acquired a special status with respect to the whole organisation. The process is of course complete in the United States and the Commonwealth of Australia. It is, however, a matter of degree. Particular international organisations present no difficulty since their members join them in their special capacities of e.g. physicists, stamp collectors or pacifists and not *qua* members of their respective states, social systems and institutions.

Clearly the reasons for the existence of any such social group, even when the groups are on the same level and of the same type, might be different in different cases, but this much must be true: any group-structure is based on some community of interest between the members of this group. This community of interest is presupposed by the simplest group-structure and the most primitive form of behaviour controlled by regulations. As the relations between people grow more complex, more complex dependencies of common and opposing interests are created and more complex group-structures make their appearance. It would be out of place, and completely profitless, to speculate here on how community and diversity of interests result,

in practice, in the growth of social and political forms. We must, however, insist that it is in terms of those features and the related regulations, institutions and social-systems, that we shall understand each particular group-structure, its character, its strength and its development. If the term "community of interests" is taken widely enough, and the nature of the interest is not specified, it will be obvious that such a view is correct. This is simply because one cannot think of other reasons for behaviour controlled by regulations. Instinctive concerted action arises sometimes at pre-social level, but then it takes place for no reason at all and a causal explanation is indicated.

Thus the basis for understanding and discussing social and political problems has been provided. To do this is not to do overmuch, but these are opening moves in prolegomena to political philosophy. They are intended as such, and their main purpose is to stimulate discussion.

Social and Political Values

For analytic philosophers, discussion about values is discussion of the language of values. Offering neither prescriptions for individuals or society nor possessing any higher wisdom concerning ethical and political values, analysts attempt to clarify the logic of statements expressing valuations. That these statements require special clarification seems obvious enough. To say that one ought not to steal or that laws should be just, is to make neither a logical nor an empirical assertion: not logical, for its truth cannot be determined by logical analysis alone; not empirical, for no fact seems to be asserted and no factual verification can be given.

The first attempts by linguistic philosophers to analyze value sentences followed the logical positivist's classification of cognitive, emotive, and imperative uses of language. Since they are obviously not cognitive nor do they take the form of commands, value sentences fall under the heading of emotive, and the resultant theory is called emotivism. According to this theory, a judgment like stealing is wrong really makes no assertion at all: it is an expression of the speaker's emotion. Roughly translated, it would mean, "I dislike stealing," and its role in language would be similar to an interjection.

Later analysts, however, find this emotivism an oversimplification for it gives no explanation of the fact that people disagree and dispute over ethical judgments, and it overlooks the influence that such judgments have on the conduct of people. More subtle analyses are therefore needed, and many linguistic philosophers have fulfilled this need. One influential theory has been developed by J. O. Urmson in his article, "On Grading."* To call things good or bad, Urmson writes, is to grade them, as for example apples might be graded in terms of their qualities. Such grading is not simply an interjection, it is an act—the making of a choice—with a commitment to similar choices in like situations. A second theory is that of R. M. Hare,† who distinguishes descriptive and prescriptive uses of language. Ethical statements are clearly not descriptive but prescriptive, and hence they function as imperatives or commendations.

These various theories have been developed in subtle ways that an introductory statement of them cannot fully reflect. Reference must be made to them, however, because, in facing the problem of social and political values, Professor W. B. Gallie (1912–   ) notes a further issue beyond linguistic analysis. Values, he writes, have varied greatly in different societies; how can one interpret these differences? Or, more simply, he asks whether morality is one or many. Analyzing the question, he finds that four answers have been given to it. The "monarchic" view says that only one set of moral canons exists, that only one right judgment about values is possible. Yet there are many possibilities for error, which explain the differences in men's moral and political beliefs. The "polyarchic" view suggests that there is not one but an indefinite number of value standards, and that therefore there are many fundamentally different moralities. Ethical relativism is like the polyarchic view in admitting a number of moral standards, but differs in holding that they are always relative to other and more basic differences (for example, economic differences) among groups of people. Finally, idealism teaches that there is one absolute, eternal morality that inevitably differentiates itself into distinct forms or phases.

Professor Gallie believes that the issue of one or more moralities is the most important question facing moral philosophy today. He suggests, however, that logical analysis alone does not settle it, for it is really a question of fact. His own hypothesis is that certain facts do attest to the polyarchic view, which implies that it is possible to say that both sides in a value dispute are right in at least some of their claims. The procedures‡ he suggests for resolving this factual question include a concentration on issues in political morality and fundamental discussion that would unmask truly basic differences rather than seek to reach superficial agreements.

---

* *Mind,* 59(1950), 145–169.

† *The Language of Morals,* Oxford: The Clarendon Press, 1952.

‡ In the original article, Professor Gallie also touches on factual matters, with particular reference to liberal morality and socialist morality, as his title indicates. These have not been included in the selection, although interested students may pursue the discussion further by consulting the whole of his paper.

W. B. GALLIE   Types of Morality

One Morality or many?   Liberal morality and Socialist morality; bourgeois morality and Georges Sorel's "morality of producers"; Protestant morality and Catholic; Greek morality and Christian; "aristocratic" morality and "slave" morality, "open" morality and "closed" morality—what, if any, is the relevance of such distinctions as these to moral philosophy?

Looked at from one angle they suggest something obvious enough; the fact that in different times and places different systems or aggregates of moral belief have prevailed, and the fact that sometimes in one and the same community different groups of people have adhered to different, in some cases to violently conflicting, moral beliefs. While no intelligent and informed person has ever denied these facts, moral philosophers have disagreed greatly as to their interpretation: I think, however, that their disagreements can be fairly summed up under the four following lines of interpretation.

First, what I shall call the "monarchic" view explains the existence of moral cleavages and conflicts in a very simple way. It points out that, although in every moral situation there is only one right judgment to be made or action to be chosen, yet the possibilities of moral error or failure are in every case enormous; and this simple fact explains all the real or basic differences in men's moral beliefs which history discloses. It may, of course, be granted on the monarchic view, that in any actual situation the right moral judgment or decision must take notice of many "non-moral"

(factual) features of that situation, and that, since adequate knowledge of these is not always equally available to different (and let us assume equally conscientious) agents, apparent (but only apparent) moral disagreements may be inevitable between them. And it may further be granted that differences in the non-moral features of situations typical of two different communities, e.g. differences in respect of the experimental knowledge and administrative skill possessed by them, may be so great, and may affect all moral questions arising within either community so profoundly, that it is perfectly natural (though it can be dangerously misleading) to talk about two different moralities, and to label them with the names of the communities or types of community in which they are found. But these admissions, for the monarchic view, in no way alter the fact that the cardinal moral attributes, right and wrong, good and bad, etc., apply and apply univocally in every situation to which moral considerations are in any way relevant. Thus, on the monarchic view, it should be possible theoretically (for all that it is in fact causally impossible) for a Chinese gentleman of the fifth century B.C., an Athenian citizen of the same period, a medieval monk and a contemporary citizen of Ealing or Nijni-Norgorod, to settle down and reach agreed and valid conclusions as to the duties of *any* man in certain well-defined moral situations, e.g. to decide in what circumstances, if any, a man should actively resist the commands of his government. On the monarchic view, there-

From W. B. Gallie, "Liberal Morality and Socialist Morality," *Philosophy*, 24(1949). Used by permission of the editor and the author.

fore, phrases such as Liberal morality and Socialist morality are ethically unimportant; since on this view moral philosophy is concerned only with those supreme moral principles and notions which are always applicable in no matter how widely divergent situations.

The monarchic view has, I think, been held by almost every great moral philosopher up to the present century. Certainly it possesses the attraction of logical simplicity and certain tonic properties highly relevant to moral practice; for, as a rule (though there is no logical necessity about this) adherents of the monarchic view assume that the particular moral beliefs to which they subscribe at least exemplify the one and only valid set of moral canons that exists; and surely no higher-order belief could be more important than this for inspiring and sustaining moral steadfastness. On the other hand, I must confess that the almost Augustinian exclusiveness of the monarchic view distresses me. Not so much because I dread being classed with the vast variety of moral goats who roam the wide pastures of error; nor yet because I think that adherents of the view are necessarily committed to a kind of higher-order self-righteousness; but rather because I suspect the parochial narrowness of their moral perspective. How often, I wonder, do adherents of the monarchic view reflect seriously on the range and variety of men's moral experience—from the men of Cro-Magnon to the present day? Moreover, I find highly suspicious the studied lack of interest, shown by most adherents of this view, to our rapidly accumulating knowledge of the different ways in which, in different communities, morality is learnt.

The second line of interpretation I call the polyarchic view. This, as its name suggests, stands in radical opposition to the monarchic view, maintaining that, far from there being one single set of valid moral standards, there are an indefinite number of these, embodied in different moralities whose cardinal principles are not mutually corrigible. Hence our previous happy picture of the Chinese Mandarin and his friends was a wholly misleading one; for the participants in the imaginary discussion would have been simply unable to comprehend each other's moral viewpoints. That there are and have been fundamentally different moralities is, for the polyarchic view, no more surprising than that there are and have been fundamentally different forms of human community, and of human language, art, religion and education: forms so different, that is to say, that even the theoretical possibility of mutual correction and supplementation between them doesn't arise. Within any given morality, different commands, appeals, valuations, etc., may be criticized, may be compared and classified as absolute, conditional, etc.; but between different moralities—well, the commands simply don't carry, the appeals don't work, the valuations and judgments lose their singleness of meaning; consequently comparisons and classifications can be of interest only to ignorant busybodies.

Now this, the polyarchic view, suffers from lack of a distinguished ancestry, although I suspect that something of Aristotle's and much of Hume's view of morality might be retained within a polyarchic framework. Lack of long ancestry should not, however, be counted against the polyarchic view; since the considerations that lend it weight—mainly historical, anthropological and psychological—could hardly have suggested themselves before the nineteenth century. Among recent writers of repute, Bergson, Sorel and Santayana seem to me, in their different ways, to be poly-archic moralists. None of these writers, however, has paid anything like suffi-cient attention to the logical difficulties that their view involves: in particular the difficulty of deciding at what point divergences in moral practice and belief should be taken as signs of the existence of two or more distinct moralities. In general, it seems to me, the difficulty with the polyarchic view is not to defend it—it is easy enough to appreciate the strength of the evidence that *might* be brought forward in support of it: the difficulty is, rather, first to state it in consistent and logically manageable form, and, secondly, really to believe it, or to "live with it" if that expression may be allowed; since, if true, the poly-archic view means that we should aban-don all hope of settling major moral disagreements by discussion. And this is a conclusion which I, for one, feel very uncomfortable about accepting.

The two remaining lines of interpreta-tion can be dealt with more briefly. The first, ethical relativism, resembles the polyarchic view superficially, since it agrees that there are and have been dif-ferent moralities which are not mutually corrigible; but, further, it maintains that different moralities are always relative to other and more basic differences be-tween groups, communities, civilizations: they are relative to—and this I suppose means theoretically deducible from if not reducible to—differences in, for in-stance, experimental and historical knowledge, forms and traditions of tribal and national life, methods of organizing production and distribution of goods, and so on. In effect, then, ethical relativ-ism can be considered as the polyarchic view qualified (or perhaps we should say neutralized) by a very simple-minded and dogmatic theory of scientific and other forms of explanation. From

the point of view of theoretical ethics, therefore, ethical relativism is not of great importance: it involves all the difficulties of the polyarchic view, and others which call for criticism from logic and metaphysics rather than from ethics. From the practical standpoint, how-ever, ethical relativism is of the first importance; since one extreme and widely accepted form of it is Marxism.

Lastly, we have the Idealist inter-pretation which represents morality as essentially one and absolute and eternal, and yet such that it inevitably differ-entiates itself into radically conflicting forms or phases. Happy reconciliation, it might seem, of the monarchic and polyarchic views, each of which has such obvious attractions and at the same time such apparently inescapable defects. But, alas, few competent thinkers to-day would be willing to accept the argu-ments (if this word can be used) by which Hegel and his followers advanced their at once uplifting and comfortable conclusions. I mention the Idealist view, however, because it may, however ob-liquely, throw light on what has become, in my belief, the most important prob-lem facing moral philosophy to-day. Namely: How, or on the basis of what sorts of consideration, should we seek to decide between the monarchic and the polyarchic view of moral differences? Or, more simply, Is Morality one or many?

Recent writers on ethics, it seems to me, have either shirked this question or tried to approach it along altogether unpromising lines. For the last four decades the ablest moral philosophers, in this country at any rate, have been preoccupied almost exclusively with cer-tain problems in the "logic of ethics": questions as to the definability or in-definability of key ethical expressions, and as to the possibility, or "correctness," in any language, of combining certain ethical expressions or of analysing certain of these in terms of certain others. Some of these questions are of great logical interest; but if anyone has thought that answers to any of them would suffice to answer our question, "One morality or many?" then he was certainly mistaken; and if anyone makes the milder claim that answers to the above questions are a necessary prerequisite of answering our question, I would say that he is very probably mistaken. My reason for saying this is simply that the "logic of ethics" is, like all logic, concerned solely with consistency and inconsistency of meanings and usages—and is concerned, in particular, with meanings and usages used within a given language *to express a given morality:* it is powerless to decide whether or not different languages, or for that matter any one language, can be used to express a number of different moralities. The question, One morality or many?—in this like the questions, One time-series or many? One God or many? One set of aesthetic values or many?—being a question of fact, is one that no amount of logical analysis can ever possibly decide. . . .

Concluding Remarks. What I have tried to do in this paper is to urge the importance for moral philosophy of certain facts which, no matter how difficult they are to describe, classify and interpret, do give the polyarchic view of moral differences what plausibility it possesses. And I would urge all adherents to the monarchic view to give these facts their most careful attention; and more, to give the polyarchic interpretation of them—considered as an hypothesis—a fair run for its money. For instance, with regard to the Liberal-Socialist conflict as I have presented it,

it seems to me simply useless to say that evidently both sides cannot be right in all they claim, though both may be wrong, but that much the most likely explanation of the conflict is that both sides are right in some of their claims and wrong in others. For this simple-minded solution neglects entirely the systematic character of the conflict. It is not a conflict at one point only (as are most of the conflicts of *prima facie* duties discussed in contemporary ethics), but at a number of intimately related points: conflict along a whole front, so to say. More generally—and more audaciously—I would urge that the monarchic view of moral differences deserves to be taken seriously from now onwards only in so far as it is prepared to meet and counter the polyarchic view on the latter's own ground. Moreover I would say that this means a pretty well continuous task for adherents to the monarchic view: they must be prepared to examine carefully and fairly any facts, arising from whatever quarter, that can reasonably suggest the existence of two or more conflicting moralities, with their own autonomous, i.e. not mutually corrigible, aims and standards.

Whether the monarchic view could sustain this task I do not know. I will only say here that, in my opinion, it would be quite possible for adherents to the monarchic view to hold that single, absolute morality admits—and perhaps requires—unbridgeable conflicts and cleavages between equally conscientious people on *certain* moral issues. But to say that this is possible is a very different thing from showing, in terms of actual moral conflicts which we can all recognize as important, that this situation obtains; and to show this would, I think, call for an infinitely deeper, more searching examination and illumination of moral life than has been attempted by any moral philosopher in the last hundred years.

This brings me to the last remark I wish to make. I have said that the question "One morality or many?" is the most important question facing moral philosophy to-day; and the methods of investigation I have been suggesting are of course aimed at settling this crucial question, however slowly and painfully. But now it seems perfectly clear to me that the value of a moral philosophy lies less in the conclusions it reaches (and the logic by which it reaches them) than in something which it achieves as it goes along: something which I can only describe as illumination of moral life. This again, I must admit, is a wretchedly vague phrase; but perhaps I can show what I mean by it by saying that it is the function which, to this day, Plato's moral philosophy discharges far more adequately than any other. Plato's dialogues do not explicitly describe, but they do nevertheless illuminate in a re-markable way the moral world of his contemporaries. That moral world is a vastly different one from our own; and yet it is curiously familiar—we can find our way about it, so to speak, with a surprising confidence. Now I believe that some of the methods I have suggested— in particular concentration on current issues relating closely to political mo-rality, and the possibilities of a new kind of discussion aimed at unmasking funda-mental differences rather than at reach-ing superficial agreement—*might* do something towards illuminating our con-temporary moral world: *might* help to dispel that thin but bewildering fog which seems to surround so much cur-rent ethical discussion and to make its terms and distinctions so unearthly and unreal. This at least is my hope, and my suggestion to those who have that rare combination of gifts which the practice of moral philosophy requires.

Each may think for himself what those qualities are and whether he pos-sesses them.

State, Power, and Authority

From the time of Bodin, at least, much of social philosophy has centered on issues concerning the state, power, and authority or—as Bodin put it—on sov-ereignty. Yet many contemporary political theorists have abandoned the concept, seeking to develop their views without it. Professor W. J. Rees (1914–   ) be-lieves there has been a twofold reason for this: sovereignty is subject to conceptual confusions and logical difficulties; and, partly related thereto, it is a difficult concept to apply to the complex political organizations of the modern world. The task of the philosopher, therefore, is to clarify the concept and the questions pertaining to it.

Consider the question, Is it necessary that there should be a sovereign in every state? An analytic professor like Professor Rees invites his readers to consider the kind of question this is. Is it a genuine question, that is, one that does not rule out a possible answer because of logical contradictions (What is there outside the universe?), or one that does not indicate what kind of information is relevant to an answer (Is everything twice as big today as it was yesterday?)? Questions about sovereignty do not seem to involve these difficulties, but they are affected by another complication: they are really complex questions, actually involving many rather than one question. Therefore, Professor Rees argues, it is necessary to clarify the key terms in questions about sovereignty, and then to replace the complex questions with unambiguous ones to which answers can be given.

Six different uses of the term sovereign are specified in the selection. Sovereign may refer to (1) the supreme legal authority, (2) the supreme legal authority in so far as it is also a moral authority, (3) a coercive power exercised by a determinate body, (4) a coercive power exercised by all the members of a community, (5) the strongest political influence in a community, and (6) the permanent interest therein. Since the concept state is closely related to sovereignty and is often used with it, Rees also distinguishes three of its meanings as (1) a politically organized society, (2) a politically organized society in so far as it is ideally organized, and (3) government considered as an institution. In terms of these distinctions, it is possible to give real answers to the traditional questions about sovereignty and therewith also to retain the concept for possible use in current political theory.

This selection is valuable not only for its elucidation of a central political concept, but also because of its clear use of analytic philosophic techniques. Scrutinizing carefully the questions asked about sovereignty, Professor Rees first determines their genuineness, and then isolates the conceptual problems connected with them. As is so often necessary, the next step is to unravel the variety of meanings associated with key terms that are the usual cause of difficulty. Third, is the reformulation of the original questions so that their complexity and ambiguity are removed. Then answers are often provided or, where not, at least it is clearer how inquiry must proceed if answers are to be forthcoming. As analysts view it, philosophy has this function rather than speculative, normative, or phenomenological goals.

W. J. REES Sovereignty Restated

There is a tendency among present-day political theorists to work without the aid of the concept of sovereignty. This is due partly to the logical difficulties inherent in the concept, and partly to the fact that certain modern political developments, such as the growth of democracy, federalism and public law, have made the concept a difficult one to apply in present conditions. The purpose of this article will be to re-examine the traditional use of the concept, and to enquire whether it still cannot be used in such a way as to avoid the objections now usually raised against it.

The strength of the logical objection to the traditional theory can be seen if we merely examine the following traditional questions: (1) Is it necessary that there should be a sovereign, or an ultimate source of authority or power,

From W. J. Rees, "The Theory of Sovereignty Restated," *Mind,* 59 (1950). Used by permission of the editor and the author.

in every state? (2) It is necessary that the authority or power of the sovereign should be indivisible? (3) It is necessary that the authority or power of the sovereign should be unlimited? and (4) Where is the sovereign located? It is notorious that no unambiguous answer is possible to these questions. What then is the point of asking them, and what is the point of a concept which merely enables us to ask pointless questions? Nor is the criticism obviously exaggerated. The evidence of some three and a half centuries of political theory is largely on the side of the critics.

There are, however, two different reasons why it may not be possible to give a straight answer to a seemingly straight question. In the first place, the question may not be a genuine question. This may be either because it involves a logical contradiction, *e.g.,* What is there outside the universe? or because we do not know what information would be relevant to determining the answer to the question, *e.g.,* Is everything twice as big to-day as it was yesterday? But in the second place, the question may be more than one question. This would be the case when the terms in which the question is stated are capable of having more than one meaning, *e.g.,* Is justice the interest of the stronger? where "justice" may mean "legal justice" or "ideal justice," and where the answer may be different according to the sense in which the word is used.

The traditional questions about sovereignty, it seems to me, are questions of the latter and not of the former kind. They cannot be satisfactorily answered, not because they are not genuine questions, but because each question consists of several questions which have never been clearly distinguished.

Once the proper distinctions are drawn, therefore, they may be replaced by other questions to which unambiguous answers can always be given. To show that this is so, all that is necessary is to analyse the possible meanings of the terms we are using.

In the traditional questions about sovereignty, the words which have been most often used ambiguously are the words "sovereign" and "state." My first task, therefore, must be to analyse the different meanings which different philosophers, and sometimes the same philosophers, have given to these two words. I shall take, first of all, the word "sovereign."

1. The word has been used by some as equivalent to a *supreme legal authority*. Those who have used the word in this way have not usually thought it necessary to define what they mean by authority, or to say how authority is to be distinguished from power or influence. It is clear, however, from the way in which they have written, that they have meant to draw some important distinction between these concepts. "Let us notice in the first place," writes Lord Lindsay, "that the doctrine of sovereignty is properly concerned with the question of authority. It is not properly concerned with questions of force or power as such."[1] This is predominantly the sense in which the word was used by John Austin, and by the lawyers of the Austinian school. I shall call this, sovereignty in the legal sense.

A word of further explanation, however, is needed. Theorists who have adopted the doctrine of the separation of powers have used the word "sovereign" to mean either (*a*) a supreme legislative authority, as for instance in

[1] *The Modern Democratic State,* vol. i, pp. 217–218.

the case of Dicey, or (*b*) a supreme legislative or executive authority, as in the case of Lord Bryce. Those who have denied the separation of powers, on the other hand, have used the word to mean (*c*) a supreme legal authority, irrespective of whether it is the authority of a Parliament, a Ministry, or a Court; that is, they have used it to mean what would, on a separationist view, be regarded as a supreme legislative, executive or judicial authority.[2] In order to avoid over-burdening the present analysis, and in order also not to prejudge the case for or against the doctrine of the separation of powers, I shall use the words "supreme legal authority" in this latter sense. I shall use them, that is to say, in what a separationist may regard as a generic sense, and what an anti-separationist may regard as the only appropriate sense. This will preclude any direct discussion of sovereignty in senses (*a*) and (*b*) above, but that will not affect my general argument. If the separationist view is the correct one, and if clear answers can be given to the traditional questions, using the present generic sense, then the same answers can always be given to the same questions, using senses (*a*) or (*b*). If, however, the separationist view is not the correct view, then the need to discuss senses (*a*) and (*b*) does not arise in any case.

2. The word "sovereign" has been used by others to mean a *supreme legal authority in so far as it also a completely moral authority*. This is sovereignty as understood by Rousseau and the Hegelians. "The Sovereign," says Rousseau, "merely by virtue of what it is, is always what it should be." "Sovereignty," says Bosanquet, "is the exercise of the Gen-

eral Will," which "is expressed in law, in so far as law is what it ought to be."[3] It is, therefore, a species of sovereignty in the previous sense. For that reason, it is not always clear that a person who uses the word in this way is using it necessarily in a way which is different from the previous one. But we can, in fact, be sure that a different sense is involved wherever there is clear evidence that the writer would, in addition, deny the title of sovereign to a supreme legal authority which is not, in his opinion, a completely moral authority. When the word is used in this way, I shall say that it is used in the moral sense.

3. For another group of philosophers the word has meant a *supreme coercive power exercised by a determinate body of persons possessing a monopoly of certain instruments of coercion*. They have not usually defined what they mean by coercive power, nor clearly stated how it is to be distinguished from legal authority or political influence. But it has been generally understood that power in this sense is to be distinguished from legal authority at least in one respect, namely, that its exercise may sometimes be extra-legal. In this sense, the sovereign is a determinate body of persons capable of *enforcing* decisions against any likely opposition, no matter who *makes,* or *otherwise carries out,* those decisions. Usually such a body consists of a professional police or a standing army; usually, too, the decisions which it enforces are those of Parliaments, Ministries and Courts, but they may be the analogous decisions of persons who have no legal authority to make such decisions, although such persons may acquire such legal authority in virtue of their decisions being en-

---

[2] *Cf.* Finer, *The Theory and Practice of Modern Government,* vol. i, chap. 1.

[3] *The Philosophical Theory of the State,* pp. 232 and 107.

forced, *e.g.,* the dissolution of the Long Parliament by Cromwell, or the overthrow of the Directory by Napoleon. This use of the word "sovereign" is implied in Lord Bryce's concept of the Practical Sovereign, which he defined as "the strongest force in the State, whether that force has or has not any recognised legal supremacy."[4] T. H. Green also wrote as if he thought the word should ordinarily be used in this or some similar sense: "the term 'sovereign' is best kept to the ordinary usage in which it signifies a determinate person or persons charged with the supreme coercive function of the state."[5] I shall call this, sovereignty in the institutionally coercive sense.

4. The word has again been used by some as equivalent to a *supreme coercive power exercised habitually and co-operatively by all, or nearly all, the members of a community.* Locke speaks variously of this kind of supreme coercive power as "the force of the community," "the force of the majority," and "all the force of all the people," in such a way as to imply a distinction between this and the coercive power of a professional police or a standing army.[6] T. H. Green, although he did not favour the usage, held that the word *could* be used in this, or a very similar, way. "A majority of citizens *can* be conceived as exercising a supreme coercive power. . . . But as the multitude is not everywhere supreme, the assertion of its sovereignty has to be put in the form that it is sovereign 'de jure'." (p. 109.) This is also a meaning of the word which has sometimes, though not necessarily, al-

ways, been implied both by those who have spoken of the "sovereignty of the people," and by those who have spoken of the "tyranny of the majority." When the word is used in this way, it will be convenient to say that it is used in the socially coercive sense.

5. It may now be noted that these four different senses of the word "sovereign" refer to supreme authorities or powers, each of a different kind. But the fact that they are sovereigns of a different kind does not mean that they cannot, in some cases, be subordinated one to another according to some principle of subordination other than those already indicated. Some philosophers have, indeed, held that they can be so subordinated, and have tried to show accordingly which of these sovereigns is "really sovereign." By so doing, they have used the word "sovereign" in yet another sense. They have used it in a sense which is equivalent to what one might call the *strongest political influence,* where political influence is to be distinguished, in some way yet to be determined, both from legal authority and from coercive power. Many things may be regarded as sovereign in this sense, but usually this kind of sovereignty has been attributed to the popular majority, irrespective of whether the popular majority be also regarded as the coercive sovereign or not. The following examples from Locke and Dicey will indicate how the concept has been generally used. "Though in a constituted commonwealth," writes Locke, "there can be but one supreme power, which is the legislative, to which all the rest are and must be subordinate, yet the legislative power being only a fiduciary power to act for certain ends, there remains still in the people a supreme power to remove or alter the legislative, when they find the legislative act contrary to the

---

[4] *Studies in History and Jurisprudence,* p. 511.

[5] *Lectures on the Principles of Political Obligation,* p. 103.

[6] For examples see *Treatise,* Book II, paras. 3, 88, 89, 96, 130, 131.

trust reposed in them." (para. 149.) "The plain truth," says Dicey, "is that as a matter of law Parliament is the sovereign power in the state. . . . It is, however, equally true that in a political sense the electors are the most important part of, we may even say are actually, the sovereign power, since their will is under the present constitution sure to obtain ultimate obedience."[7] This I shall call sovereignty in the influential sense.

6. There is, finally, a usage of the word "sovereign" which would make it equivalent to a *permanently supreme authority, power or influence*—the significant word in this case being the word "permanent." It seems to be a matter of custom among political theorists to make statements such as the following: "Force is not sovereign in the state, for no state can be perpetually ruled by force alone." Those who make such statements as this would not usually deny that a state may for some time be ruled by force alone; force may well be sovereign for some time, assuming some meaning of the word "sovereign" already given. But if now the title of sovereign is to be denied to a "sovereign" of this kind, clearly the word has once again shifted its meaning. It has shifted its meaning to the extent that a sovereign, in any of our previous senses, is no longer to be called sovereign unless it continues to exist for an indefinitely long time. Duguit says of Bodin, for instance, that "he defines sovereignty as 'the absolute and perpetual power in the state' ";[8] and Professor Laski, with this definition apparently in mind, argues against Bodin as follows: "The government which acts as its (Professor Laski

means the state's) sovereign organ never, as a matter of history, has the prospect of permanence if it consistently seeks to be absolute. Civil War and Revolution in the England of the seventeenth century, 1789 in France, 1917 in Russia, are all of them footnotes to the problem of sovereignty."[9] I shall call this, sovereignty in the permanent sense.

So much for the word "sovereign." It is necessary now to consider the word "state."

The word "state" has been used by philosophers in at least three different ways. (1) To some, it has meant a *politically organised society*. "The state," says Sorley, "is not something separate from the citizen, and it is not something separate from the community or society to which it belongs. It is this society organised as a whole and able to act as a unity."[10] This is the sense of the word "state" which we usually have in mind when we are dealing with matters of international politics, *e.g.*, when we speak of small and large states, backward states, industrial states, European states, etc. (2) To others, it has meant a *politically organised society in so far as it is ideally organised*. This, in the main, is the Hegelian use of the term. "By the State, then," says Bosanquet, "we mean Society as a unit, recognised as rightly exercising control over its members through absolute physical power." (p. 184.) Since this is a species of the state in the previous sense, it is not always clear that a person who uses the term in this way is using it in a sense which is different from the previous one. But, as with the moral sense of the word "sovereign," we can be sure that a different sense is involved whenever the writer is prepared to deny the

---

[7] *The Law of the Constitution*, eighth ed., p. 73.

[8] *Law in the Modern State*, trans. F. and H. Laski, p. 9.

[9] *Grammar of Politics*, p. 49.

[10] Creighton and others, *The Theory of the State*, p. 32.

title of state to a politically organised society which is not, in his opinion, ideally organised. (3) More often in ordinary speech, however, and sometimes in political theory, the word "state" has meant *government as an institution*. "The state," says Professor R. M. MacIver, "exists within society, but it is not even the *form* of society"; it is "a structure not coeval and co-extensive with society, but built within it as a determinate order for the attainment of specific ends."[11] This is the sense of the word which we usually have in mind when we are discussing matters of domestic politics, *e.g.,* when we speak of state enterprise, state employees, the revenues of the state, the machinery of the state, etc.

It may be that the word "sovereign" and "state" have been used in some senses other than these which I have indicated, but these at least are definite, it seems to me, as far as the history of political theory is concerned. Admittedly some of these senses are arbitrary, in that they are not the senses which are implied in the common use of the words by persons who are not political theorists; but to determine which is arbitrary and which is not is a question which need not concern us here, since it would not in any case affect any of the conclusions which may be derived from the foregoing analysis.

We are now in a position to answer the first of the traditional questions about sovereignty, namely, Is it necessary that there should be a sovereign in every state?

1. If we are using the word "sovereign" in the legal sense, it is not *logically* necessary that there should exist a sovereign in every state, on any of the three definitions of the word "state," since it is clearly not self-contradictory

to say that there does not exist in a state a supreme legal authority. But it is, however, *causally* necessary that there should exist a sovereign in every state, on any of our three definitions. I am now using the word "cause" in the sense in which it is normally used in the practical sciences, and which has been defined by Collingwood to mean "an event or state of things which it is in our power to produce or prevent, and by producing or preventing which we can produce or prevent that whose cause it is said to be." In this sense it is causally necessary that a sovereign should exist in every state, since, in practice, government can only be carried on by means of laws, and laws can only be effectively administered if there exists some final legal authority beyond which there is no further legal appeal. In the absence of such a final legal authority no legal issue could ever be certainly decided, and government would become impossible.

2. If, however, we take the word "sovereign" in the moral sense, and if, in addition, we use the word "state" in its second, or Hegelian, sense, then it is *logically* necessary that there should exist a sovereign in every state. For if the supreme legal authority which exists in a "state" is not a completely moral authority, that "state" is not an ideally organised society, that is, it is not a state on the present definition. This is an analytical proposition derived solely from the definitions of the terms used. But on any other use of the word "state," of course, it is neither logically nor causally necessary that there should exist in any state a sovereign in this sense.

3. It is not *logically* necessary that there should exist in a state, on any of the three definitions, a sovereign in the coercive sense, since again, it is not self-

---

[11] *The Modern State,* pp. 5 and 40.

contradictory to say that there does not exist in a state a supreme coercive power. But it is, nevertheless, *causally* necessary, in the present state of society, that there should exist in the state— senses (1) and (2)—a sovereign either in the socially coercive or in the institutionally coercive sense. Since it is a fact that many men in their present state are prone to disobey the law, it is necessary, if laws are to be effective, that they should be capable of being enforced. But laws can only be enforced in one of two ways, either by the habitual and co-operative exercise of coercive power in support of the law by indeterminate but exceedingly numerous persons in society, or else by the exercise of coercive power by a determinate body of persons, who are fewer in number, but who possess a monopoly of the instruments of coercion. Assuming, for the time being, that these two ways represent genuine practical alternatives, it is not causally necessary that there should exist in the state, as now defined, a sovereign in both the above senses, but only that there should exist a sovereign in the one sense or the other. But if, however, we are using the word "state" in the third sense, the same facts would need to be stated rather differently. In this case we should have to say that it is causally necessary that an institutionally coercive sovereign should exist in the state, if there does not exist in society a sovereign of the socially coercive kind. That is, the state must possess a monopoly of the instruments of coercion, as long as there does not exist in society a sufficiently large number of persons capable of co-operating to enforce the state's decisions.

4. If now we use the word "sovereign" in the influential sense, it is neither logically nor causally necessary that there should exist a sovereign in every state. This is true on any use of the word "state," since the strongest political influence may be exercised by bodies which exist, or events which occur, outside the boundaries of the state, *e.g.,* the influence of another powerful state, or of international economic events, etc. If we use the word "state" in sense (3), moreover, there is the additional reason that the strongest political influence may be that of public opinion, which itself lies outside the state as the state is now being defined.

5. It is, finally, neither logically nor causally necessary that there should exist in the state, on any of the given definitions, a sovereign in the permanent sense. In order, for instance, that the King in Parliament may be the legal sovereign to-day, it does not seem to be either logically or causally necessary that he should continue to be the legal sovereign for an indefinitely long time.

Summing up now the above argument, it is possible to say (*a*) that it is necessary, *in the sense of logically necessary,* that there should exist a sovereign in every state, if we use the word "sovereign" in the moral sense and the word "state" in the sense of a political society ideally organised. It is also possible to say (*b*) that it is necessary, *in the sense of causally necessary,* that there should exist a sovereign in every state, if we use the word "sovereign" in the legal sense or generically in the coercive sense, and if we use the word "state" in any of the three senses indicated. On no other usages of the words "sovereign" and "state" can it be said to be necessary that a sovereign should exist in every state.

The three remaining traditional questions may be dealt with more briefly, since we shall no longer be concerned with the variations in the meaning of the word "state." The answers may be given in three groups corresponding to the three traditional questions.

1. To the question, Is it necessary that the sovereign, if it exists, should be indivisible? the following answers may be given: (*a*) If by the word "sovereign" we mean the legal sovereign, it is in one sense logically necessary that the sovereign should be indivisible, since it would be self-contradictory to hold that there could be more than one final decision on any one legal question; but it is neither logically nor causally necessary that the sovereign should be indivisible in the sense that every legal question should be finally decided by one and the same legal authority. This is equally true, if by the word "sovereign" we mean a moral sovereign, since sovereignty of this kind is only a special case of sovereignty in the legal sense. (*b*) The same would also be true, *mutatis mutandis,* if by the word "sovereign" we meant the institutionally coercive sovereign, the socially coercive sovereign or the influential sovereign. It is, in one sense, logically necessary that these sovereigns should be indivisible, since it would be self-contradictory to say of any two coercive powers which were of the same kind, or of any two political influences, that they were both at one and the same time the strongest. But it is neither logically nor causally necessary that these sovereigns should be indivisible in the sense that the power or influence in question may not be divided between two or more bodies. (*c*) If, however, we use the word "sovereign" in the permanent sense, no questions about indivisibility arise, other than those already answered in connection with its other meanings. The additional qualification of permanence now introduced does not affect the present issue.

2. The answers to the third of the traditional questions, namely the question, Is it necessary that the authority or power or influence of the sovereign should be unlimited? will depend on what political theorists have meant when they have used the word "unlimited." The word has been used in at least two different ways. (*a*) Some have used it as equivalent to "omnipotent."[12] When it is used in this way, it is clearly neither logically nor causally necessary that sovereignty, in any sense, should be unlimited. In the United States, for instance, there exists no legal authority which can legally deprive any State within the Union of its equal representation in the Senate. Standing armies everywhere are dependent on other persons for their supplies of arms and equipment, and the larger the army the greater its dependence, in this respect, on the rest of the population. Equally, there are few political groups which can successfully influence legislation without compromising to some extent with rival groups. On no usage of the word "sovereign," therefore, is it necessary that sovereignty should be unlimited in this sense. (*b*) The word "unlimited" has often been used, however, in a weaker sense, to mean "exceedingly great" or "superior to any other."[13] When the word is used in this way, it is logically necessary that sovereignty, in any sense of the word, should be unlimited. But to say that it is, is now to utter rather a pointless tautology. It is simply to say that a supreme legal authority must be supreme, and so on, *mutatis mutandis,* for any other use of the word "sovereign."

3. The fourth of the traditional questions, namely, Where is the sovereign

---

12 *E.g.* Laski, *op. cit.,* pp. 51–53; Popper, *The Open Society and its Enemies,* vol. i, p. 107.
13 *E.g.* Bryce, *op. cit.,* pp. 522–523; Laird, *The Device of Government,* pp. 83 f.

located? may now be easily dealt with, since it resolves itself into a series of entirely empirical questions requiring straightforward historical, legal or sociological answers. It is not necessary here, therefore, to establish what the correct answers are in this case, but merely to indicate what kinds of answers would be appropriate. It would be appropriate, for instance, though not necessarily true, to say that the sovereign was located in the King in Parliament, or the Cabinet, or the House of Lords (legal or moral sense), or in the bulk of the people or in the army (coercive sense), or in the electoral majority or in the economically dominant class (influential sense), or nowhere, because no such sovereign at present exists (moral or permanent or any other sense). Needless to say, this question, or rather these series of questions, may still be difficult to answer, but if so, that is now due to insufficient empirical evidence, rather than to any ambiguity or other logical impropriety in the question. Not all questions which are difficult to answer are logically improper questions.

Answers have now been given to the traditional questions about sovereignty. If these are satisfactory, and I trust they are, then the traditional questions are not pointless questions, however much they may require analysis, and the theory of sovereignty may still be used in such a way as to present at least a consistent theory of politics.

Law and Rights

One of the most frequently asked questions takes the form, What is x? In many circumstances, this form causes no special difficulty, yet it can occasion a whole series of perplexities and confusions. This happens when one believes that his answer to it is a real or "true" definition giving the "essential nature" of the term being defined. An example would be, What is law?, with the answer, It is the command of a sovereign—an answer purporting to be the true definition of law.

Yet, this effort to find a true definition is misplaced for, linguistic philosophers believe, it is connected with failures to understand meaning and symbolism. It is, in fact, an effort resulting from a number of errors about language. First among them is the belief that there is some kind of *real connection* between a word and an object, so that words are taken to have "proper" meanings. A second error results from thinking that the use of a word *guarantees* that the fact or object to which it refers exists. A third arises from a conviction or assumption that words have a *magical use* to affect the course of natural events. And a fourth error of symbolism occurs when one uses a word with *no referent* in mind at all. All these errors follow from the root mistake of the "proper meaning fallacy," or overlooking the fact that the meaning of words is *conventional,* not real, causal, or natural.

Another group of mistakes follows upon these errors of symbolism. They concern confusions among types of questions, especially verbal, factual, and value ones. An important need for conceptual clarity is to distinguish these types of questions, for language often conceals them. Thus, for example, one asks about the nature of *x*—but is this factual? Usually it is not. It is a request for a definition of a word. One may also search for definitions on the supposition that there is a natural basis of classification, hoping thereby that one's definition reflects the objective structures of things. Or, putting the same point somewhat more technically, one may in his definitions seek the "natural essences" of things. But this is false procedure: neither natural essences nor natural classifications exist—they are the result of language functions.

In discussions of law and rights, theorists are especially prone to error because they seem to gravitate toward questions like, What is law? and What is a right? Writing with reference to the problems of meaning and definition Glanville Williams (1911–   ) finds only endless controversy and misunderstanding resulting from attempts to answer them. Proper attention to linguistic errors will have important consequences for controversies concerning the definition of law—though they are only consequences of word usage. Freeing discussions of law from all verbal matters, Mr. Williams seeks to overcome controversy about law by giving it up, which is the only way to deal with a verbal question. What remains as the proper talk about law is the particular rule-systems of actual societies and the questions associated with those systems.

Analytic philosophers have given great attention to problems of law, and though much of their work aligns them with the school of analytic jurisprudence, they have had a general influence on philosophy of law. Some observers, in fact, have suggested that linguistic philosophy is most at home in this area of social philosophy. In any case, its contributions here are significant.

GLANVILLE L. WILLIAMS Concerning the Word "Law"

. . . The error as to the "proper" meaning of words and as to "true" definitions is still widespread. For this there seem to be several reasons. For convenience of discussion they will here be considered in separate numbered sections, though to prevent possible misunderstanding it must be premised that some of the sections are simply different aspects of each other.

1. The first misconception is the idea that a controversy as to concepts is not a verbal but a scientific controversy. Thus Professor Lauterpacht quotes Somló as denying that international law

partakes of the character of law, while maintaining that this is not merely a matter of terminology, "for [Somló] says, if we describe the rules of so-called international law as rules of law we thereby obscure the conception of law as generally used."[1] Before considering this, let us get clear what we mean by a concept or conception. A concept is simply a universal notion (such as *space, time, causality, bird, law*) symbolized by a word. "Investigating (or analysing)

[1] Lauterpacht, *The Function of Law in the International Community,* 403, quoting Somló, *Juristische Grundlehre,* 2nd ed. (1927), 153–73.

From Glanville L. Williams, "International Law and the Controversy Concerning the Word 'Law,'" *The British Year Book of International Law* (Oxford: Oxford University Press, 1945). Published under the auspices of the Royal Institute of International Affairs. Used by permission of the publisher.

concepts" means exactly the same thing as defining the corresponding words. Now when Somló refers to "the conception of law as generally used" he evidently means by the word "law" municipal law. But this is only one use of the word; there is also its use to symbolize international law, which has many affinities to municipal law. It is easy to construct a concept that will cover both municipal and international law. Why should we not symbolize this concept by the word "law"? Somló objects; he wishes to confine the term "law" to municipal law. But this is a mere matter of terminology, a fact that Somló expressly refuses to admit.

2. The second reason for the misunderstanding considered in this paper is our tendency to conceal by our language the difference between a verbal and a scientific (factual) question. Four words that tend to conceal this difference are the copula "to be," "exist," "nature," and "theory."

As to the first, a sentence beginning "Law is . . ." may seem to state a fact; but it can practically always be translated by the words "The word 'law' means . . . ," when it clearly introduces a definition. The only case where this translation is not permissible is where the word "law" is independently defined.

Then, as to the word "exist," consider its use in the proposition: "international law does not exist." This may mean two different things: (*i*) that states do not observe any rules in their mutual dealings, or (*ii*) that, although states observe rules in their mutual dealings, these rules are not to be given the name "law." The first assertion is a factual one; it can be verified or disproved by looking at the conduct of States. The second is purely verbal. Yet both assertions alike can be expressed by reference to the "existence" of in-

ternational law. This word "existence" seems to refer to a matter of fact, and may well in some contexts mislead the reader into thinking that a mere definition of terms is a scientific proposition.[2]

Again, an inquiry into the "nature" of a concept like "law" is simply a search for a definition of a word. But the word "nature" seems to refer to a matter of empirical fact, and is therefore misleading.

The fourth offender is the word "theory." A scientific theory is an attempt to express facts in words or other symbols. But a "theory of law" or "legal theory" is not a statement of fact; it is a definition of words, or a value-judgment as to what the law ought to be or do, or both.

3. The third reason is our tendency to conceal the difference between a verbal question and a question of value-judgment. No one would be awarded a doctorate for asserting that in his opinion a State ought to rest on the consent of its subjects. Yet if he writes a book asserting that a State *is* an association resting on the consent of its subjects, academic honours may well follow. What is in truth a value-judgment is disguised as a definition of terms, and the definition of terms is itself erroneously regarded by the academic world as a scientific investigation.[3]

---

[2] Again to prevent misunderstanding it may be pointed out that there is a sense in which a definition is a statement of fact. A definition may be understood as stating the way in which the speaker chooses to use words, and the way in which one chooses to use words is a fact. Nevertheless a definition is not a proposition about a datum: it is a proposition which is itself a datum.

[3] The result of this technique may be surprising, as T. H. Green discovered when he found himself obliged by his own terminology to affirm that Czarist Russia could be counted as a State only "by a sort of courtesy" (*Lectures on the Principles of Political Obligation*, 1927 reprint, 137). A similar difficulty is ex-

4. The fourth reason is our tendency to hypostatize (objectify) abstractions. We take a word like "bird" or "law" and assume that somewhere in the universe there must be some entity corresponding to the word, an investigation into which is just as scientific and factual as the dissection of an individual sparrow in a laboratory. We assume, further, that our definition of the word must be an "accurate" word-picture of this "thing" in the universe to which the word belongs. It is this idea that causes us to speak so frequently of "true" definitions. As soon as we realize that *bird* and *law* are simply mental abstractions from the raw material of the universe, and that they do not exist by themselves separately anywhere, we realize that the idea of a true definition is a superstition. A description of an individual bird now before us, or of an agreed legal system, may be true or untrue, because we can verify it by reference to the facts; but a definition of "bird" or "law" cannot be true or untrue, because we can verify it by referfacts by which it can be checked. A definition can indeed be true in the sense that it is a representation of the ordinary meaning of the word: but the use of the adjective "true" in this context is so likely to cause misconception that it is better to avoid it.

Philosophers of the so-called "realist" school have a great deal to answer for in this matter, for it is they who have stuck so stubbornly to the idea of the "reality" of universals, and consequently to the idea of "true" definitions and

perienced with definitions of law, advanced by theorists like Duguit and Krabbe, which link it with natural law, "social solidarity," the "sense of right," or such-like. The consequence is that any particular rule that happens to be unjust, or anti-social, has to be denied the name "law," even though it be enforced by the tribunals of a State.

"true" meaning. Writing in the volume entitled *Modern Theories of Law,*[4] Professor C. A. W. Manning says: " 'What is philosophy?' is doubtless a philosophical question: for amongst other things philosophy concerns itself with the true meaning of terms." Perhaps the learned writer will agree that if this means anything it must mean that philosophy concerns itself with the ordinary meaning of terms, or with suggested new meanings, or both. There is no other possibility. This is not to disparage philosophy, for much useful work can be done in investigating the ordinary meanings of words (e.g., the functions of the copula), and making suggestions for improvement. What is true for philosophy is true for more specialized investigations of a kindred nature, such as analytical jurisprudence. The point to insist on is that such studies must start from words as they are actually used; it is unhelpful to frame definitions *a priori* and immediately to proceed to pronounce them "true" or "proper."

5. Arising out of the proper-meaning fallacy is the idea that words have not only a proper meaning but a single proper meaning. This involves a denial of the fact that words change their meanings from one context to another. To illustrate the difficulties into which this idea lands one: we commonly speak of "early customary law," yet a municipal lawyer refuses to say that all social customs at the present day are law. Conventions of the constitution, for instance, are not usually called "law" by the modern lawyer. Now it is a fact that it is practically impossible to frame a definition of "law" in general terms that will *both* include early customary law *and* exclude modern conventions of the constitution. If it includes the one it

[4] (1933), p. 184.

will include the other, and if it excludes the one it will exclude the other. This leads the single-proper-meaning theorists to argue among themselves whether conventions are to be put in or early custom to be left out. Again the misconception comes from supposing that there is an entity suspended somewhere in the universe called "law," which cannot truthfully be described as both including custom and excluding custom. When we get rid of the entity idea and realize that we are defining words, we see also that there is no need to use words consistently. The word "law" has one meaning in relation to early customary law and a different meaning in relation to municipal law.[5]

6. Closely connected with the last misconception is the idea that there are natural differences of "kind" quite independent of human classification. Thus Leslie Stephen, in a discussion of Austin, asks whether the fact that Austin's "laws improperly so called" do not conform to his definition of law "corresponds to a vital difference in their real nature. Is he simply saying, 'I do not call them laws,' or really pointing out an essential and relevant difference of 'kind?' " And again: "The question then arises whether the distinction between laws and customs is essential or superficial—a real distinction of kinds or only important in classification."[6] This language is misleading because it overlooks the fact that the concept of kind results from the process of classification, and that all classification is a man-made affair. An inquiry into whether a given difference is one of kind or of degree is a verbal, not a scientific inquiry.

7. This error as to the existence of natural kinds is again closely connected with, if not simply an aspect of, the error as to the existence of natural essences. The latter error consists in the idea that the search for "essences" or "fundamental features" is in some way a factual investigation, and not merely an inquiry into the meaning of words. Enough has been said in general opposition to this idea, but it may be useful to examine in detail certain contentions of an influential text-book on logic by Cohen and Nagel.[7] The deserved esteem of this book makes the views expressed in it worthy of serious consideration.

After pointing out that disputes over definitions are frequently the result of a conflict of emotional attitudes, the authors go on to say:

However, issues other than emotional ones may also be involved. Religion, for example, has sometimes been defined in terms of some dogma, sometimes in terms of a social organisation and ritual, and sometimes in terms of emotional experiences. The resulting conflicts over the meaning or essence of religion have been regarded, perhaps not without some justice, as conflicts over words. But this is only a half-truth. For the disputants frequently have their eye on a concrete phenomenon which presents all these aspects. The quarrels over the right definition of religion

---

[5] A recent illustration of this error is Dr. Timasheff's *Introduction to the Sociology of Law* (1939). Dr. Timasheff first advances what he calls a "working hypothesis" of what law is, and then proceeds to try to "prove" this "hypothesis" by reference to the "facts." He does not perceive that his "hypothesis" is a definition and that a definition can neither be proved nor refuted. Thus he is led to challenge Malinowski's definition of law (advanced in a discussion of primitive law), arguing that it does not "work" as applied to later societies because it would turn rules regulating duels into legal rules (p. 277; reprinted in Hall, *Readings in Jurisprudence* (1938), 871). The error is well pointed out by Kantorowicz in (1940) 56 *L.Q.R.*, 115.

[6] *The English Utilitarians* (1900), iii. 322, 324.

[7] *Introduction to Logic and Scientific Method,* 2nd ed. (1943), 233.

are attempts to locate the fundamental features of a social phenomenon. For if those features are taken as the definition of religion, it is possible to deduce many important consequences from it. Thus if belief in some doctrine is the essence of religion, other things follow than if some type of emotional experience is taken as defining religion: in the one case there is an emphaiss upon intellectual discipline and conformity, in the other, an emphasis upon aesthetic elements and a neglect of theology.

It is submitted that "attempts to locate the fundamental features of a social phenomenon" are attempts at definition, not scientific observation. Therefore the proposition in which these words appear does not advance the authors' argument that the conflict over the meaning of religion is over something other than words and emotion. Also, it is difficult to understand what "consequences" can be deduced from definitions, other than consequences as to the use of words. The authors say that if belief in some doctrine is regarded as the essence of religion, the "consequence" will be an emphasis upon intellectual discipline and conformity. But this is in effect a tautology, for it simply means that those who desire to see religion maintained, and who think that religion involves fixed tenets, necessarily desire to see these tenets maintained. The "consequence" follows not simply from the idea that religion involves fixed tenets, but from that idea plus the desire to see religion maintained; and the consequence is only a consequence in the logical sense, being in fact contained already in the premises. To put this in another way, the fact that a particular sect in real life insists upon intellectual discipline is not the effect of a definition of the word "religion." On the contrary, the word "religion" is merely a symbol for the practices of such a sect.

Cohen and Nagel proceed:

The age-long dispute about the nature of law involves similar issues. Is "law" to be construed as a command, as a principle certified by reason, or as an agreement? The controversy is not simply about words. It is concerned with making one rather than another aspect of law central, so that the appropriate consequences may be drawn from it. A schoolroom illustration is the question, "Is a bat a bird?" The two parties to the dispute concerning the answer may agree that a bird is a warm-blooded vertebrate having its fore limbs modified as wings, and yet not agree as to whether a bat is a bird. Why? Because one party to the dispute may believe there is a closer affinity of the bat to rodents than to birds, and may wish to regard those common features of rodents as central to the bat.

This, again, is difficult to follow. The "schoolroom illustration" seems to be plainly a dispute over verbal classification (as Locke held[8]) and thus to prove the opposite of what the authors contend. We are given the fact that there is no dispute over any of the features of the bat; so what is the dispute about if it be not over the application of words? It is difficult to see what is meant by "making one rather than another aspect of law central" unless the phrase have reference to the application of words. Those who construe law as command refuse to apply the *word* law to any system of rules that cannot be regarded as a command. Those who construe law as a principle certified by reason refuse to apply the *word* law to any system of rules that cannot be regarded as certified by reason. And so on. In each case the controversy is simply as to the application of a word, not as to the characteristics of any particular system of rules under dispute.

The answer to the argument that

---

[8] *Essay Concerning the Human Understanding* (1690), 13. 9. 15–16, 3. 11. 6–7.

"consequences" can be drawn from the definition of "law" is the same as before: such consequences are only consequences as to the use of words. For instance, if "law" be construed as a command, the consequence will be that international law will not be called "law"; but this will not in itself wipe out the body of rules that are now accepted for determining the conduct of States. It is true that if the phrase "international law" be replaced in current usage by some such phrase as "international custom," these international rules may lose some of the respect in which they are now held. But this consequence will not follow merely from the definition of law as a command. It will follow from the fact that the word "law" is nowadays more highly charged with a certain kind of emotion (namely, the emotion of unquestioning obedience) than the word "custom."

Must these quarrels over definitions last for ever? They will unless we bring ourselves to realize that definitions have no importance of themselves, no importance apart from the ascertainment of meaning. The only intelligent way to deal with a verbal question like that concerning the definition of the word "law" is to give up thinking and arguing about it. By no other means can the controversy be brought to an end.

However, when jurisprudence comes to shake itself free from verbal controversies, there will still be some questions, hitherto discussed in connection with verbal ones, that may usefully be saved for discussion on their own account. Thus a comparison of international law with municipal law would be a factual, not a verbal, discussion. Again, one may usefully hold debate over the reasons why men observe rules; how far rules are observed; the reasons for non-observance; how far a particular rule-system is adequate to the needs of society; and how its sanctions can be improved. Any of these matters may be discussed in its own right; but to discuss it as an incident to the question whether a system of rules is properly called law is to consign the issue to sterility.

Political Obligation

That analysts find much of traditional political theory to consist of verbal definitions and strange uses of ordinary words is now apparent. Still, if this be the understanding of philosophic statements about society, one can ask what kind of propositions they really are, and why—if they do not express fact—people use them. There is, in other words, a need to understand the effects of political language even when it gives no information. Margaret Macdonald (1905?–1956) presents the view in the selection following that philosophical statements function as linguistic recommendations. Predicting nothing about behavior and empty of fact, philosophical statements are invitations to "picture" facts in various (and sometimes strange) ways.

Miss Macdonald believes that different pictures of political relations, such as those offered by contract and organic theories, carry with them their own psychological effects and suggest, therefore, alternative insights into situations. In this regard, philosophical remarks are more like poetry than, say scientific analogy; people are led to use them because of their psychological effects even though nothing can be learned about political affairs from them. This likeness to poetry (but philosophy *is not* poetry) helps to explain the peculiarity and puzzlement of political theory.

The authors of traditional political theories see themselves doing more than writing poetry; they are seeking explanations to the problems of social life. Perhaps the most basic of social problems concerns political obligation, and to it have been given a number of proposed solutions. Consent theorists point to an original binding contract; idealists posit a higher self from which issue obligations of self-realization in society; and utilitarians suggest the advantage of society as the ground of obligation. Upon examination, Miss Macdonald finds each of these theories is wanting. Contract theory leads to no empirical original; the higher self is misleading in talking of a person one can never meet; and utilitarianism reduces to the tautology that only the governments we ought to support are those we ought to support because they promote the social good.

What is the secret of this ineptitude? Two observations help to answer this question. The first is that the use to which traditional theorists put language is confusing and illegitimate. The second is that theorists are searching for *general* answers to the questions they put. Such general answers are really metaphysical for they are offered as unique and almost magical formulas to resolve inquiry. Such formulas are impossible and unnecessary: there are only specific solutions to specific questions.

These observations apply to the problem of political obligation. To the question, Why ought I obey?, no general answer can be given. Obedience is related to particular matters such as a given law or a special authority, and only varied and shifting criteria are available for these situations. At this point, in fact, many traditional theories supply valuable insights since there are situations where consent, ideals, or consequences do offer the criteria for answering questions about obedience. But to ask about obedience in general is to ask a senseless question, and of course the answer to a senseless question is itself without sense. Responsible citizens, Miss Macdonald concludes, can never know once and for all what their political duties are, "and so we can never go to sleep."

MARGARET MACDONALD   Puzzles in "Obligation"

I have rashly chosen a subject about which I am more than usually likely to talk nonsense. For I know little about either history or politics. But having recently been forced to read a fair amount of what is called political theory or political philosophy, I have become both puzzled and interested by the curious notation in which much of it seems to be written. One meets here a "contract" which one is carefully warned was never contracted; an "organism"

From Margaret Macdonald, "The Language of Political Theory," *Proceedings of the Aristotelian Society,* 41(1940–1941). Used by permission of the editor of The Aristotelian Society.

unknown to biology; a superior "person" or higher "self" with whom one can never converse; an "association" or "corporation," whose objects are obscure and which is not listed in any of the recognized Directories. All these descriptions, analogies or pictures have been applied to the State. One or other of them can be found in the works of the most notable political philosophers from Plato and Hobbes to Laski and MacIver. Here, too, will be found elaborate discussions and disputes about whether men are or are not "naturally" social; whether they "really" will what they don't will; whether there is a Law of Nature or a "natural law" not established by any known empirical methods; whether freedom or "objective" freedom is not properly judicious coercion in the interests of order, etc.

There is a genuinely philosophic air about these strange uses of ordinary words. They seem to resemble the replies sometimes given to the haunting doubts which attack us when we reflect on other subjects. On our sensible experience, for example. Is it perhaps only a perpetual illusion? Or on moral actions. Can an action ever be completely disinterested? Or on other people. Do they have feelings as we do, or are they merely perfectly acting automata? How can we ever be sure? It seems, then, likely that the tales about the social contract and the unmeetable person will be related to similar puzzles. I do not, however, intend to expound in detail any of the answers in which the words I have given are key words. I shall avoid exegesis of Hobbes or of Hegel. I want rather to discuss how the uses of these words with the pictures or analogies they embody are related to the puzzles by which they were suggested and to the ordinary uses of language about social relationships and political affairs. What

sort of propositions are they and how do they function? For, at first glance, they seem very peculiar. To be told you are party to a contract, of which you were unaware, and which is nothing like what anyone would ever call a contract, seems to have little to do with giving your vote at a general election, sending your child to a State school, or paying a fine for exceeding the speed limit. Nor is your depression at the Labour Exchange likely to be much relieved by being told that you "really" willed your unemployment (you would never have thought so, unaided) or that the State is a very superior moral person, only even more anonymous and inaccessible than the Permanent Secretary to the Ministry of Labour.

One trouble in politics is to determine how far the questions are empirical and to what extent they are linguistic. Another is to discover what are the ordinary uses of the words involved. For many important words used in political discussion have a degree of vagueness which makes it even easier in political than in other branches of philosophy to disguise a linguistic elucidation or recommendation as an important factual discovery. A further problem is the causation of these puzzles. Is it merely philosophical discomfort about language that induces people to ask certain questions about their social life and accept these answers? If not, is this philosophically important?

I said that I had little knowledge of history. It is sometimes said that no one can understand or criticise political theories without a thorough knowledge of history. Hobbes and Locke cannot be properly understood without knowing the history of the English Civil War, the Revolution of 1688 and their relation to these events. Rousseau cannot be detached from the conditions in France immediately before the French Revolution of 1789. Hegel is inexplicable apart from the luscious yet strenuous atmosphere of the Romantic Movement and the beginnings of German nationalism. All these theories arose in peculiar circumstances of crisis in the particular societies of which their writers formed part and cannot be discussed as though they were of general application like the propositions of mathematics. This, however, is not quite true. It is certainly true that the propositions of politics are not like those of mathematics and it does indicate that practical as well as purely philosophical dissatisfactions have frequently co-operated to move philosophers to write political philosophy. Indeed, they have usually done so with the avowed intention of influencing political affairs. Nevertheless, they never supposed themselves merely to be writing tracts for their times. Locke doubtless wished to justify the Revolution Settlement, but not merely by considering how a reasonable social life was possible in seventeenth century England, but upon what relationship the life of the members of any community, divided into rulers and ruled, must be based if it is not to appear contemptible to rational human beings. What justifies us in forming political societies, in obeying laws, in being subjected to other persons? This is not a puzzle peculiar to any age. Moreover, so far from having died with the controversies of the seventeenth and eighteenth centuries, the "contract theory" is now being revived.[1] But even this may be philosophically as well as historically important. For present political conditions may be somewhat similar to those in which contract

theories formerly flourished. Historical circumstances then may be important in answering the question, "Why have philosophers been induced to ask these questions and accept these answers?" It may be objected that this is to confuse causes and reasons. A philosopher may be moved to doubt the existence of matter because he has swallowed too much opium, but this would be completely irrelevant to any reason with which he supported his view. Why, then, should it be philosophically important that he asks certain philosophical questions because he feels oppressed by the government, or, alternatively, because, like Hobbes, he is worried by the lack of order in the country? It is because the circumstances in which they are asked and answered may work differently for different kinds of philosophical propositions in influencing their effects. And this may be connected with their philosophical "point." With some, e.g., those of "pure epistemology," their importance may be negligible; with others, those of ethics, perhaps, and, even more, those of politics, they may be more important.

What must also be considered, then, are the practical and psychological effects of these problems and their answers. No one will deny that in political affairs philosophical nonsense may have serious effects. Is this philosophically relevant, or not? To deny that it is seems to reduce philosophising to mere scholastic verbalism. Not for any moral reason. Not because philosophers ruin themselves and their subject by sitting in ivory towers and talking about the uses of words instead of considering how the people perish (or flourish) on nonsensical theories and slogans. But simply because, not to try to understand how this language has effects, even though it may give no information, is to miss half

[1] Cf. Gough, *The Social Contract*, 1936. Introduction and last chapter. H. D. Lewis, "Is there a Social Contract." *Philosophy*, January and April, 1940.

its philosophical point and so is bad philosophy. The philosophical "point" of a remark (or the "point" of a remark which is of philosophical interest) is, at least partly, connected with the cause or reason which induces people to go on making it, though it can neither be supported nor refuted by any empirical evidence. It may be false, it may, if taken literally, be meaningless, but they feel that it has some use. This does seem to be relevant to the understanding of some philosophical remarks, if not of all.

It is true that no solipsist refuses to converse with others, unless he is also suffering from incipient schizophrenia. Nor does the sceptic about the existence of material objects sit down very gingerly on every chair for fear it isn't really there. For these problems have not, usually, been suggested by any practical difficulties about communication or knowledge in ordinary life. Nor will any answer which the philosopher gives to them be likely to alter his subsequent behavior. The problems of epistemology are mainly academic. Their practical causation and effects, therefore, are unimportant. That is perhaps why it is easier to see from such examples the predominantly linguistic character of philosophical problems, so emphasised recently by Wittgenstein, Wisdom and others. They can be traced, roughly, to a certain discomfort which the philosopher obscurely feels about what seem to be unjustifiable inconsistencies in our uses of certain words, e.g., those of "know" and "feel." And once he can be made to realise this and that no linguistic change which he may wish to suggest will give him that super-empirical information about the world which he supposed possible, he will cease asking unanswerable questions. The whole drama might be played by two solitary sages on a desert island. But I am not convinced that Butler, e.g., was merely puzzled about the use or misuse of the word "interest" or that he supposed that such misuse was the only mistake of his opponents. He was worried because their philosophical remark that "All action is really selfish" was seducing many people to a disregard of their duties. And though Burke, quite rightly, thought most of what Rousseau wrote was, strictly, nonsense, he did not underestimate his influence on the French Revolution. For whereas a person would be thought slightly crazy who took seriously his doubts about the uniformity of nature and refused to eat his dinner for fear the laws of nature might have changed since yesterday and it would now poison him, many people would not think it at all *absurd* that anyone who said, "An action is right only if by doing it the agent will promote his own advantage" should so interpret this as to neglect most of the actions that would ordinarily be called his duties. They might think he would come to a bad end, but not necessarily in Bethlem. Yet, in a sense, to ask whether all action isn't really selfish is a senseless question. And to assert that all action is "really" selfish is to make not an empirical but a grammatical statement. It expresses either .a misuse of or an intention to extend the use of "selfish" to cover actions to which it does not ordinarily apply. But the distinctions formerly marked by the ordinary uses of "selfish/unselfish" must reappear in the new notation if it is to fulfil all the tasks of the old. Nor does this change give us any fresh information about our duties to others. In this it resembles the epistemological puzzle about "know." When clearly stated, it takes the form of a linguistic recommendation. Yet it has, or may have, or perhaps only seems to have, certain effects which have been considered important. Not that it predicts any such effects. A linguistic recommendation predicts nothing about behaviour. It is empty of factual content. How then does it work so as to seem to need taking seriously in practical life? How does anyone "act" on a purely grammatical statement, except in speech and writing? Yet it does seem sometimes as if they do. The connection of utilitarianism with social reform is another instance. So that completely to understand ethical problems and theories, more than linguistic considerations are required. Or rather, perhaps, different sorts of elements may be involved in linguistic considerations.

If this is true of ethics, it is even more true of politics. Consider the statement, "The authority of the State derives from the contract or agreement by which men consented to give up certain liberties, to form a society and submit to government in order to obtain greater benefits. The interests of a State, therefore, are subordinate to the interests of its members." The attitude thus expressed may have importantly different results from the one expressed by "The authority of the State is absolute for it embodies the 'real' will and permanent interests of its members. It does, moreover, further certain historical and/or divine purposes incapable of fulfilment by any or all of its members. The State, therefore, is a moral person of a higher type than its members who must be subordinated to it." There may be a sense in which neither of the theories epitomized in these statements is directly verifiable by the facts. For the "contract" and the "real will" may correspond to nothing directly discoverable. There may be another sense in which all the facts to which both theories ap-

peal are the same for each. There is then no empirical means of deciding between them. But do not two statements or theories mean the same if all their empirical consequences are identical? Yet the "contractual" and the "organic" views of political relations would never be ordinarily said to mean the same and they have had very different effects. If the difference is not an empirical one of finding facts which will support the one and refute the other; if it is not a difference in their truth or falsity, what sort of difference is it? How can they differ in meaning without differing in verifiable consequences? But how *do* they differ? They differ, obviously, in picturing political relationships with the help of two very different images. One represents them under the guise of a contract freely entered into between responsible agents who understand the provisions and are prepared to keep them unless infringed by the other party. Joining society in general and keeping its laws is rather like joining a Trade Union and agreeing not to blackleg or work for less than the minimum rates, so long as the Union, on its side, agrees to maintain and improve the conditions of labour. Or it is like undertaking to provide goods or services in return for certain payment. Most people have had some experience of such agreements. They know what they imply and how they feel about them. If they have accepted the terms, they do not resent being bound by them, so long as they are observed by the other contractees. And, if not, either the law will enforce the terms or they will be released from their share of the obligation. They do not regard themselves, after entering such agreements, as being any "higher" or "lower" than they were before. Such contracts are convenient devices to secure desired social ends. They are useful, and their obligations should be respected, but no sensible person would rhapsodize about them. If then, people picture the relation between themselves, the State and the Government in these terms, certain consequences will tend to follow. They will tend to be affected, emotionally as well as intellectually, in some ways rather than others. They will probably tend to stress the fact or the need for the *consent* of the governed to its governors. For no one can enter a contract without consenting to it. They will emphasise the importance of the *responsibility* of governors to the governed. No contract can be solely one-sided. Because of the reciprocal nature of contract, their attitude to rulers will be critical rather than reverential. Certainly nothing done by rulers to fulfil their part of the bargain will be accepted because proceeding from a higher moral authority than that of mere individuals. The attitude induced by the "contract" picture might be expected to stress personal freedom and the existence on sufferance of all governments; to be, in general, liberal, democratic and unmystical. And it has, historically, tended to produce this result. It encourages the view that social arrangements of all kinds are made by men for their own ends and can be altered and even ended at their will and pleasure. This does not preclude acknowledging that some arrangements, *e.g.,* those comprised by the State, are very important, even that they function as fundamental conditions for most others. Only that they are not sacrosanct. Nor does it follow that changes must or will be undertaken without due regard for the customs and traditions of the past and the welfare of the future as well as of the present. But only that if, in spite of all this, they are *consented* to by a majority of the present members of a society, no higher

authority can be found with a *right* to prevent them. The "contract" view can take account of every fact stressed by other views, but its own difference of emphasis alters their point or effects. In political theory, as, indeed, in philosophy generally, it is very often not what is said, but the spirit in which it is said, which makes the difference.

The other picture tells a very different story. My relation to an organism of which I form part or to my "higher" self is not determined by free choice. "The State," said Burke,[2] "ought not to be considered as nothing better than a partnership agreement in a trade of pepper and coffee, calico or tobacco, or some other such low concern, to be taken up for a little temporary interest, and to be dissolved by the fancy of the parties. It is to be looked on with other reverence. . . . It is a partnership in all science, a partnership in all art, a partnership in every virtue and in all perfection . . . it is a partnership not only between those who are living, but between those who are living, those who are dead, and those who are to be born . . . linking the lower with the higher natures, connecting the visible and invisible world, according to a fixed compact sanctioned by the inviolable oath which holds all physical and all moral natures each in their appointed place." Compared with this splendid spectacle we, who compose any society here and now, are very small fry indeed. Should we not accept with becoming gratitude the fortunate chance that permits us to abase ourselves before this embodiment of "all virtue and all perfection"? "Consent," "choice," can mean only acceptance of what seems good to it, and not to our unimportant selves. This is the attitude of submission to and reverence

----

[2] Burke. *Reflections on the Revolution in France.*

for what is done by Authority, especially if the Authority is or represents what is old and respectable—or, now-a-days, if it commands forces of great physical power—which is induced by this language. Consent, freedom, criticism, which the contract picture emphasised, are not necessarily denied, but they are minimised or re-interpreted. I am no foe to liberty, said Burke, but it must be a liberty connected with *order*. If a man is misguided enough to resist the General Will, say Rousseau and Bosanquet, he must be forced to be free. The individual is trivial; the social organism or organisation is almost sacred.

These two ways of picturing political relationships may, then, have very different practical and psychological effects which may induce people to want to go on using them, although they learn nothing much from them about political affairs. Some people like to feel part of a vast and important organisation in which their chief function is to admire and obey. The picture of themselves deliberating about contracts, making decisions, criticising representatives, is much too fatiguing. For others, any picture in which they were wholly subordinate would be intolerable. A similar situation sometimes occurs in science. It is true, I believe, that all the planetary motions could, with suitable complications, be described as well by the Ptolemaic as by the Copernican system. In one sense, therefore, they mean the same. But that in another they do not is shown by the fierce resistance met by Copernicus and his followers. It had very little connection with the scientific value of their theory. The Ptolemaic theory included the picture of man and his world at the centre of the universe with the heavens revolving round them in cosy circles. The alternative Copernican picture terrified people. They felt lost, insecure,

unimportant. Something had gone for ever. Yet nothing had gone, for the facts were precisely the same for each. But the *point* of the two notations, with their accompanying pictures, used to describe the facts was very different. In their psychological effects they were very different theories.

It may be objected that this use of the words "picture" and "image" is itself a misuse, or, at least, an extension of the ordinary use of these words.[3] This is true. I cannot draw the social organism as I can a rat, nor paint a portrait of the "higher" self. And though I can imagine the scene when King John signed Magna Carta, I cannot similarly imagine that when Hobbes' pre-social beings contracted to form society. I can have an image of signing a building contract but not of signing the social contract. But, it may be urged, when it is said that the State resembles an organism or is based on contract, no particular organism or contract is meant. What is thus asserted is a general resemblance between political relationships and those between the parts of *any* organism or *any* contractees. But this seems very peculiar. I cannot have an image or paint a picture of a general resemblance. The words "image" and "picture" appear to be used for something which cannot be imaged or pictured at all, in the ordinary senses of these words. But this peculiar usage can be recommended. It emphasises the fact that philosophical remarks resemble poetic imagery rather than scientific analogy.[4] There is a pictorial or analogical element in most theories, scientific as well as philosophical. In poetry there are metaphors and images, but no theories. And philosophical theories have always seemed

[3] I owe this point to Mr. G. Ryle.
[4] Cf. Wisdom. "Other Minds." *Mind*, Vols. 49 and 50.

slightly odd, if not bogus. The use of "analogy" suggests "argument by analogy," *i.e.,* the deduction of new verifiable facts from a suggested resemblance which increases our knowledge about the world. Philosophical theories have no such application. Nevertheless, in common with the scientific analogies they have other, psychological and semi-logical effects. Compare, *e.g.,* the different effects of the planetary theories already mentioned or of the "mechanistic" and "purposive" hypotheses in biology. Philosophical remarks about social contracts and higher selves work chiefly in these ways. Perhaps to look for a contract or a new biological entity after reading Locke and Hegel on the State is only slightly less absurd than to look for flaming tigers after reading Blake or to ask how Wordsworth knew "at a glance" that he saw ten thousand daffodils. The theories of the scientist give new information about empirical facts; they also induce certain emotional and intellectual attitudes. The language of the poet is predominantly emotive; that of the philosopher less so, but both also have some relation to certain facts, though not that involved in the application of a scientific analogy. They do, however, partly by the use of certain images and metaphors express or call attention in a very vivid way to facts and experiences of whose existence we all know but which, for some reason, it seems important to emphasise.[5] I do not wish to say that philosophy *is* (inferior) poetry and not (pseudo) science, for it is neither, but philosophy. But it is sometimes useful when considering philosophical theories, and particularly political theories, to realise how unlike

scientific theories they are, in some respects, and how much, in others, they resemble the works of the poets. Rousseau is far more like Shelley than he is like Lavoisier. The use of the words "picture" and "image" stresses this resemblance and avoids the scientific associations of the word "analogy." This gives some justification for the extended use of these words.

But, according to their authors, political theories profess to explain certain puzzles about social life which must now be examined.

The surprising fact about political life, according to Hume, is the ease with which the many are governed by the few. Why should people thus submit to the jurisdiction of others of their own kind? Obviously, it is not solely because of the constant exercise or threat of physical force to compel conformity. The ruled, as Hume said, are always more numerous and therefore more powerful than the rulers. Not even Hitler can literally turn the whole of Germany into a concentration camp. For if he did, one result would be, presumably, that production would cease, and power would soon be useless. Nor is force any explanation. For it is conceivable that someone should prefer, and many people have preferred, to die rather than obey rulers of whom they disapproved. Nevertheless, most people most of the time do obey laws and accept the control of governments. It must then be either because they want to, or because they believe they ought to do so. But they do not always want to, and sometimes when they do want to they think they ought not to. The fundamental puzzle of political philosophy, then, is to find a valid reason for political obligation. Why should men be obliged to obey laws and be penalised if they do not? This leads to consideration of the

---

[5] I think this is true of some poetry, at least, but I do not wish to dogmatise about the function of poetry.

nature of that which appears to command and enforce laws, viz., the State. And there is perhaps an even more "fundamental" puzzle. Why should man live with others of his own kind at all? The laws which political obligation acknowledges are the rules of societies. But is it necessary to form political societies? Is man "naturally" social or only by convention? If the second, why was this convention adopted, and how? We all know how individuals join a trade union, a church, a club. These are particular societies. But how and why did we all join society in general? What sort of process was this?

These questions have the familiar tone. Philosophers do not ask whether Zulus or Dodos exist, but whether *any* material objects exist: not whether I can climb Mount Everest, if I choose, but whether I can do *any* action, however carefully I choose. So the political question is not "Why should I pay income tax?" or "Why should I support the present British Government?" but "Why should I obey *any* law, support *any* Government, acknowledge the authority of *any* State?" Why, indeed, should I be a member of *any* civil society?

I cannot consider all the answers which have been suggested to all these questions. Two have already been mentioned. If I have contracted with others to form a society and obey certain rules then my justification for keeping the laws will be that I formerly promised to do so, at least as long as they were generally observed by the other parties to the contract. But this theory leads to no original in the facts. When did I sign this agreement and with whom? One answer is, you did not sign it, but your ancestors did, only so long ago that all trace of it has been lost. The original Magna Carta of society has

vanished. Can it really be on account of this undiscoverable transaction that we keep the laws of England in 1941? For suppose, after incredible labour, archæologists found the lost document, should we feel happier about observing the Education Acts? Ah, that settles it. Now we know why we should send Johnny to school at five instead of into the fields to mind the sheep. Absurd, of course. And what are the provisions of the contract? Am I bound by it to observe laws yet to be made, of which I know nothing, just because they are laws of the contracted society and government? That would be a very peculiar contract to sign. No, the existence of a contract which could be discovered would answer our question. This is always admitted by political philosophers. "The social contract theory is really an attempt at analysing the logical presuppositions rather than the historical antecedents of the State,"[6] says Mr. Gough. The answer it gives to the question of political obligation is that our only justification for obeying laws and governments is that we have consented to do so and that political obligation is not an asymmetrical relationship between rulers and ruled. Hence the use of the contract picture in supporting the claims of individuals and groups against despotic governments.

The word "contract" then is admittedly not used in its ordinary legal sense of the State and the basis of political obligation. It is only "as if" we had signed a contract. The contract theory points not to a contract but to the fact that what we mean by saying that we ought to obey a law is that we have consented to it. But, as Hume said, unless habit, indolence and indifference are to be taken as consent,

---

[6] The Social Contract, p. 4.

very few laws would be obeyed at all on this criterion. To how many do we individually consent, and how do we do so? However important, this cannot be the whole story.

What then of the view that the laws of the State ought to be obeyed because they are the edicts of some higher being with which each of us is for the time being identified, or because they represent what we ourselves "really" will in our best moments? According to Rousseau, by the act of social union a moral and collective person, endowed with the general will, is thereby brought into existence and thereafter known as the State or Sovereign. Nor, he is careful to add, must this person be regarded as fictitious because not a man.[7] For Bosanquet, the State and its system of law and order represents my "higher" self, and its actions, even those which I explicitly reject, ought to be accepted because they are willed by the General Will which is my "real" will as opposed to my selfish and trivial actual will. The earlier quotation from Burke expresses a similar view. The essential point of this view is that the State or Society (no distinction is usually made between them) is something of far greater value than any or all of the individuals at any one time who compose it. What it ordains, therefore, and expresses as law must be good and must, therefore, be what I should also will if I were as wise as it is. In fact, it is what my higher self wills though I do not. Therefore, I "really" will it and I ought to do what I "really" want to do although I actually don't want to do it. I do not intend to examine all the linguistic shifts and ambiguities of this theory. The use of "self" and "will," *e.g.,* and the tendentious use of "higher" and "lower" where

difference of value should be proved and not merely asserted. In fact, the extremely perverse use of language by these philosophers often blinds one to the undoubted facts which they emphasise and which are neglected by alternative theories. The State is not identified with any one or with the whole collection of its members but is something over and above them. That is to say, propositions can be made about the State which would be nonsense if made about any or all of its members. *E.g.,* "The English State has been established for at least four hundred years." The State is a moral person. That is to say, it is sensible to say of actions which we ascribe to the State that they are right—or wrong. The sense in which these words are used is different from that for individuals but it is not nonsense to say "I think the State acts rightly in providing Old Age pensions," though the analysis of this statement would be very complicated. The State is greater and more permanent than the individual. That is true. The generations pass, but English state power remains. It is, therefore, likely that laws made according to the Constitution will be such as may reasonably be accepted. There is a presumption in their favour. Nor will responsible citizens wish rashly to destroy an established power and order which has served the past and serves the present moderately well and may be valued by future generations. The State serves more important purposes than the individual. Without accepting a mystical march of history, this also may be admitted. The actions of few individuals, *e.g.,* are likely to affect so many people for so long a time as do most State actions. The State has international functions, relations to colonies, to other States which may have lastingly bad or good effects. No in-

---

[7] *The Social Contract,* Chapters 6 and 7.

dividuals, in their private capacity, could perform such functions. None of these facts about the difference between the State and the individual need be denied. Indeed, they are important criteria for the use of "political obligation." But they are *differences* merely. It does not follow from them that the State is either morally better or worse than any individual. Nor are any or all of them a sufficient basis for political obligation. I do not mean by saying that "I ought to obey this law," that I was born, without my choice, a member of English society from which I received education, culture, the means of livelihood and the general system of law and order without which these would be impossible. Even though it may be true that all that one is and can do, is due to the facilities provided by the State and the social order, it does not follow that all State action is right and that all laws should be obeyed. For it is not self-contradictory to say "This is an English law but it is a bad law and ought not to be kept." Moreover, this view leads to the absurd conclusion that the laws of any community are equally good. The Nuremberg laws, therefore, are good for the Germans, though they are bad for everyone else. But if they are bad, they are bad also for the Germans, though they may not recognise this.

Then is it perhaps because of their social effects that laws ought to be obeyed? Do we mean by the State, the dispenser of social benefits on the largest possible scale? This is the Utilitarian or realist view of the State. The State, like any other institution, is justified by its works. It does not depend on mythical contracts or mystical organisms but on a pragmatic sanction. "The State is an organisation for enabling the mass of men to realise social good on the larg-

est possible scale" and social good "consists in the unity our nature attains when the working of our impulses results in a satisfied activity."[8] I am justified in obeying the laws only if I am tolerably satisfied with my life in the community. And anyone's life will or ought to be tolerably satisfactory if his "impulses" are being satisfied. But what is the criterion that they are? I can know whether I am satisfied with my life, but even if I am, what follows? Does it follow that I am justified in obeying the laws because the State does or will provide the conditions of such satisfaction? Or that I am entitled to rebel if my impulses are not satisfied? Could I not be satisfied as the result of a bad law and dissatisfied as the result of a good? But Laski would say, it will be urged, that the good must be social. State action should be approved only if it promotes this desirable unity for all or most people. But what exactly *is* this desirable state and how do we know whether it has been achieved for everyone? Without an adequate criterion of this, how do we know what laws to obey and what governments to approve? The conditions of personal satisfaction are numerous and many could not be provided by the most benevolent State. I do not wish to suggest that Laski, or any other philosopher, supposes that all the conditions of a happy life can be provided by the State. But it is not easy to see from his remarks on the social good why any should be excluded. The utilitarian criterion, which seems so practical, is not one of the easiest to apply, or even to state clearly. Bentham's criterion is at least clear, if impossible to accept. Once this is discarded what *is* the "social good" or the "general welfare" whose

[8] Laski. *Grammar of Politics,* pp. 24, 25. London, 1925.

promotion is the purpose of the State and the criterion of the goodness or badness of its actions and laws? Only the vaguest statements ever seem to be offered. This may be condemned as pedantic. To say that the State is justified by its works is to say, and this is known by all but the perverse, that it should be judged by the way in which it makes possible for all citizens the material and cultural conditions of good living. The laws of a State should be chiefly directed to securing for all its members, employment, a reasonable income, health, education, good houses, etc. Certainly not all the conditions can be provided communally but a great many can and should, and the more a State provides the more it should be approved. In fact, only if it tends to maximize certain obvious benefits should any law be obeyed. No laws ought to be partial. That is, I think, the point of the theory, which is generally favoured by social reformers. Far be it from me to minimise its importance. But again, I think, it is not and cannot be the whole story. For is it not conceivable that all these desirable objects might be promoted by what everyone would call a bad, e.g., a completely tyrannous State? The government of such a State might be exceedingly efficient in promoting social welfare to obtain popular support and the majority of its citizens might be thoroughly satisfied that all their impulses were satisfactorily fulfilled. Ought one then to support such a government and respect its laws? The usual reply is, "Ah, but there must always be some important impulses left unsatisfied by such a Government; no bad governments could possibly promote the general good." But now, is this an empirical statement? Suppose people no longer feel these important impulses, why should they bother about their satisfaction? Does this remove the difficulty? If people no longer resent actions which would normally be called tyrannical, do they cease to be tyrannical? Is contented slavery not repulsive? Utilitarian philosophers would probably not agree. They would say, as most people would, that such actions *ought* to be resented, and that they are not does not make them good. But then the utilitarian view can surely be expressed in the tautology, "Only the governments which we ought to support are those which we ought to support because they promote general social good." This is not very enlightening.

The utilitarian view, then, which pictures the State as an institution or association for promoting the interests of its members is not adequate. The picture likens the State to any other association with a specific purpose, e.g., a trade union, a college, a commercial company or a church. But the difference is that the objects of these associations can all be fairly clearly stated and, indeed, must be before they are given legal status. The object of the State itself cannot be thus stated. High wages and good working conditions might conceivably be achieved by other means than combining in trade unions: a copper mine might be discovered and worked without floating a commercial company, but there is no describable purpose or object of social life as such any more than of human life as such, which could be obtained by some alternative means. This picture then remains as inapplicable as the others. But it, too, points to important criteria for our use of "political obligation." That some laws promote desirable social improvements in the general conditions of living for the majority of people, is a good reason for accepting them. But it is not the sole justification for accepting any and every law.

What then is the answer to the original puzzle, "Why should I obey *any* law or acknowledge the authority of *any* State or Government?" to solve which these pictures were invented. The discussion of the three most prominent types of answer seems to show that even discounting nonsense or picturesque terminology, none of them alone is sufficient. May it not also suggest that no such general answer is either possible or necessary? This would not be surprising. A general proof of the existence of material objects seems impossible, and to ask for it, absurd. No general criterion of all right actions can be supplied. Similarly, the answer to "Why should I obey *any* law, acknowledge the authority of *any* State or support *any* Government?" is that this is a senseless question. Therefore, any attempted reply to it is bound to be senseless, though it may perform certain other useful or harmful functions. It makes sense to ask "Why should I obey the Conscription Act?" or "Why should I oppose the present German Government?" because by considering the particular circumstances and the characteristics of all concerned, it is possible to decide for or against obedience and support. We all know the kind of criteria according to which we should decide these two issues. But although it looks harmless and even very philosophical to generalise from these instances to "Why should I obey *any* law or support *any* government?" the significance of the question then evaporates. For the general question suggests an equally general answer and this is what every political philosopher has tried to give. But no general criterion applies to every instance. To ask why I should obey *any* laws is to ask whether there might be a political society without political obligations, which is absurd. For we mean by political society, groups of

people organised according to rules enforced by some of their number. A state of anarchy is just not a state of political society and to ask whether, since laws are not obeyed in the first state they ought to be obeyed in the second is to ask a nonsensical question. But neither does it follow, as some idealists seem to suppose, that all laws should be equally accepted because commanded by a political authority. For this is, in fact, only another attempt to find a general criterion for political obligation. But it is not that which we always apply when considering political action. The political theorists want an answer which is always and infallibly right, just as the epistemologists want a guarantee that there are material objects or that generalisation to the unexamined must be valid. But these are all equally senseless requests, for they result from stretching language beyond the bounds of significance. I know how to determine on any particular occasion whether or not I am suffering from an optical illusion. Therefore, it is sensible to ask "Is this line really crooked or does it only seem to be?" But to ask whether, after applying all the relevant tests unsuccessfully, I am still and always deluded, is senseless. For the word "deluded" has now lost all significance since however hard and carefully I look I can never find a veridical perception with which to compare my delusions. The word "delusion" no longer significantly opposed to "veridical" becomes meaningless. Similarly, I can determine whether or not I ought to observe the Education Acts or the Income Tax law. Obviously, I think I ought partly because they were passed by a freely elected Parliament, according to all the usual procedure, so that in some complicated and indirect sense I have consented to them. Then, too, they promote useful social ends and there may be other criteria for rightly obeying them. One or two of these criteria might be absent and I should not think it right to resist, if too many of them were I might get restive but not yet rebellious. A trade unionist, *e.g.,* might rightly think that the Trade Union Disputes Act passed after the general strike was harsh and unfair but not sufficient in itself to risk civil war about, especially since a new government which trade unionists could help to elect might repeal the Act. But if too many acts are passed in suspicious circumstances and with dubious objects, the duty to resist tyranny will over-rule the duty to obey law. When or how cannot be stated in advance. Nor can the criteria for accepting a law be precisely stated. Consent, tradition, objects promoted, all the criteria emphasised by the political theorists are important, but not all are equally important on every occasion, though if one or more were persistently absent over a long period we should, rightly, object. The manner in which they (and probably others) are blended is indefinitely various and no precise definition could describe our usage. Nevertheless, it does not in the least follow that we do not very often know that a law should be obeyed and a government supported and sometimes that both should be resisted. Just as we know very well that the pillar box is red and that Jane Austen was not vulgar, although both "red" and "vulgar" are used vaguely.

This may seem a disappointing conclusion and not likely to have the stirring effects of the homeric stories of the social contract and the "higher" self or even of Burke's rhapsodies on the British Constitution. But I think it has some practical value. The general, meta-physical theories are really very simple. They seek to reduce all political obligation to the application of an almost magical formula. All laws which should be obeyed result from the social contract, or the general will, or promote the greatest happiness of the greatest number, so in order to know your political duties look for the trade mark and leave the rest to government. They do imply that we can know once and for all almost by learning a single sentence, how and when political obedience is justified. But if there is no general criterion, but an indefinite set of vaguely shifting criteria, differing for different times and circumstances, then it may often, if not nearly always, be necessary to scrutinize our political relations to see whether we are on this particular occasion justified in giving or withholding our support to a measure or a government. The value of the political theorists, however, is not in the general information they give about the basis of political obligation but in their skill in emphasizing at a critical moment a criterion which is tending to be overlooked or denied. The common sense of Locke and the eloquence of Rousseau reinforced and guided the revolt against dogmatic authority by vividly isolating and underlining with the contract metaphor the fact that no one is obliged to obey laws concerning none of which he has had a chance to express consent or dissent. It does not follow that this is the sole criterion of political obedience, still less that having derived all political obligations from a social contract or a general will we can accept them all happily and go to sleep. As rational and responsible citizens we can never hope to know once and for all what our political duties are. And so we can never go to sleep.

The Ideal of Justice

Proper attention to the concept of justice, argues the author of the following selection, Professor H. L. A. Hart (1907–   ), shows that while it is a concept of appraisal, it belongs to a distinct section of moral words. Justice seems to have a special character and to be more specific than such more general words as good and bad. Its closest relative seems to be "fair" and—for injustice—"unfair." This is easily shown by the fact that while many words of commendation cannot be substituted for just, fair usually can.

Yet analysis has not gone far enough merely in noting this relation to fairness. It is necessary, Hart argues, to find the specific character of justice. This is done by observing that the principle justice denotes is that individuals are entitled to a certain relative position of equality or inequality in respect to each other (hence the traditional interpretation of justice as balance or proportion). In simpler words, the central idea in the concept of justice is to "treat like cases alike and different cases differently." Even this statement needs to be supplemented, for appraisals of law as just or unjust require knowledge of what similarities and differences among human beings are relevant.

Hence it is necessary to distinguish two parts of the idea of justice. The first part is the invariant formal principle expressed by treating like cases alike. Sound as this principle is, it is by itself useless for criticizing law apart from the second element in justice, namely a criterion by which to determine when cases are alike or different. The first part of justice is close in meaning to the idea of proceeding by a rule without bias and is relatively stable. The criterion of relevant differences, however, is a varying criterion and depends on nonlegal factors as well. The reason for this is that the law itself cannot say what similarities and differences the law must recognize. Differences in political and moral outlooks are reflected in the formulation and application of this criterion.

Justice, Professor Hart concludes, is thus a specific form of excellence attributed to laws. His analysis shows that it is a value distinct from other values and may, in fact, conflict with some of them such as the general welfare. Nevertheless, the analytic techniques he applies to the ideal of justice seek to bring greater clarity to the understanding of the ideal itself, as well as to certain puzzles that may arise as men apply the ideal in the concrete appraisals of laws and decisions.

H. L. A. HART   The Principles of Justice

The terms most frequently used by lawyers in the praise or condemnation of law or its administration are the words "just" and "unjust" and very

From H. L. A. Hart, *The Concept of Law,* Oxford: The Clarendon Press, 1961. Used by permission of the publisher.

often they write as if the ideas of justice and morality were coextensive. There are indeed very good reasons why justice should have a most prominent place in the criticism of legal arrangements; yet it is important to see that it is a distinct segment of morality, and that laws and the administration of laws may have or lack excellences of different kinds. Very little reflection on some common types of moral judgment is enough to show this special character of justice. A man guilty of gross cruelty to his child would often be judged to have done something morally *wrong, bad,* or even *wicked* or to have disregarded his moral *obligation* or duty to his child. But it would be strange to criticize his conduct as *unjust.* This is not because the word "unjust" is too weak in condemnatory force, but because the point of moral criticism in terms of justice or injustice is usually different from, and more specific than, the other types of general moral criticism which are appropriate in this particular case and are expressed by words like "wrong," "bad," or "wicked." "Unjust" would become appropriate if the man had arbitrarily selected one of his children for severer punishment than those given to others guilty of the same fault, or if he had punished the child for some offence without taking steps to see that he really was the wrongdoer. Similarly, when we turn from the criticism of individual conduct to the criticism of law, we might express our approval of a law requiring parents to send their children to school, by saying that it was a good law and our disapproval of a law forbidding the criticism of the Government, as by calling it a bad law. Such criticisms would not normally be couched in terms of "justice" and "injustice." "Just," on the other hand, would be the appropriate expression of approval of a law distributing the burden of taxation according to wealth; so "unjust" would be appropriate for the expression of disapproval of a law which forbade coloured people to use the public means of transport or the parks. That just and unjust are more specific forms of moral criticism than good and bad or right and wrong, is plain from the fact that we might intelligibly claim that a law was good because it was just, or that it was bad because it was unjust, but not that it was just because good, or unjust because bad.

The distinctive features of justice and their special connexion with law begin to emerge if it is observed that most of the criticisms made in terms of just and unjust could almost equally well be conveyed by the words "fair" and "unfair." Fairness is plainly not coextensive with morality in general; references to it are mainly relevant in two situations in social life. One is when we are concerned not with a single individual's conduct but with the way in which *classes* of individuals are treated, when some burden or benefit falls to be distributed among them. Hence what is typically fair or unfair is a "share." The second situation is when some injury has been done and compensation or redress is claimed. These are not the only contexts where appraisals in terms of justice or fairness are made. We speak not only of distributions or compensations as just or fair but also of a judge as just or unjust; a trial as fair or unfair; and a person as justly or unjustly convicted. These are derivative applications of the notion of justice which are explicable once the primary application of justice to matters of distribution and compensation is understood.

The general principle latent in these diverse applications of the idea of justice is that individuals are entitled in respect of each other to a certain relative position of equality or inequality. This is something to be respected in the vicissitudes of social life when burdens or benefits fall to be distributed; it is also something to be restored when it is disturbed. Hence justice is traditionally thought of as maintaining or restoring a *balance* or *proportion,* and its leading precept is often formulated as "Treat like cases alike"; though we need to add to the latter "and treat different cases differently." So when, in the name of justice, we protest against a law forbidding coloured people the use of the public parks, the point of such criticism is that such a law is bad, because in distributing the benefits of public amenities among the population it discriminates between persons who are, in all relevant respects, alike. Conversely, if a law is praised as just because it withdraws from some special section some privilege or immunity, e.g. in taxation, the guiding thought is that there is no such relevant difference between the privileged class and the rest of the community as to entitle them to the special treatment. These simple examples are, however, enough to show that, though "Treat like cases alike and different cases differently" is a central element in the idea of justice, it is by itself incomplete and, until supplemented, cannot afford any determinate guide to conduct. This is so because any set of human beings will resemble each other in some respects and differ from each other in others and, until it is established what resemblance and differences are relevant, "Treat like cases alike" must remain an empty form. To fill it we must know when, for the purposes in hand, cases are to be regarded as alike and what differences are relevant. Without this further supplement we cannot proceed to criticize laws or other social arrangements as unjust. It is not unjust for the law

when it forbids homicide to treat the red-haired murderers in the same way as others; indeed it would be as unjust if it treated them differently, as it would be if it refused to treat differently the sane and the insane.

There is therefore a certain complexity in the structure of the idea of justice. We may say that it consists of two parts: a uniform or constant feature, summarized in the precept "Treat like cases alike" and a shifting or varying criterion used in determining when, for any given purpose, cases are alike or different. In this respect justice is like the notion of what is genuine, or tall, or warm, which contain an implicit reference to a standard which varies with the classification of the thing to which they are applied. A tall child may be the same height as a short man, a warm winter the same temperature as a cold summer, and a fake diamond may be a genuine antique. But justice is far more complicated than these notions because the shifting standard of relevant resemblance between different cases incorporated in it not only varies with the type of subject to which it is applied, but may often be open to challenge even in relation to a single type of subject.

In certain cases, indeed, the resemblances and differences between human beings which are relevant for the criticism of legal arrangements as just or unjust are quite obvious. This is preeminently the case when we are concerned not with the justice or injustice of the *law* but of its *application* in particular cases. For here the relevant resemblances and differences between individuals, to which the person who administers the law must attend, are determined by the law itself. To say that the law against murder is justly applied is to say that it is impartially applied to all those and only those who are alike in having done what the law forbids; no prejudice or interest has deflected the administrator from treating them "equally." Consistently with this the procedural standards such as "*audi alteram partem*" "let no one be a judge in his own cause" are thought of as requirements of justice, and in England and America are often referred to as principles of Natural Justice. This is so because they are guarantees of impartiality or objectivity, designed to secure that the law is applied to all those and only to those who are alike in the relevant respect marked out by the law itself.

The connexion between this aspect of justice and the very notion of proceeding by rule is obviously very close. Indeed, it might be said that to apply a law justly to different cases is simply to take seriously the assertion that what is to be applied in different cases is the same general rule, without prejudice, interest, or caprice. This close connexion between justice in the administration of the law and the very notion of a rule has tempted some famous thinkers to identify justice with conformity to law. Yet plainly this is an error unless "law" is given some specially wide meaning; for such an account of justice leaves unexplained the fact that criticism in the name of justice is not confined to the administration of the law in particular cases, but the laws themselves are often criticized as just or unjust. Indeed there is no absurdity in conceding that an unjust law forbidding the access of coloured persons to the parks has been justly administered, in that only persons genuinely guilty of breaking the law were punished under it and then only after a fair trial.

When we turn from the justice or injustice of the administration of the law to the criticism of the law itself in these terms, it is plain that the law itself cannot now determine what resemblances and differences among individuals the law must recognize if its rules are to treat like cases alike and so be just. Here accordingly there is much room for doubt and dispute. Fundamental differences, in general moral and political outlook, may lead to irreconcilable differences and disagreement as to what characteristics of human beings are to be taken as relevant for the criticism of law as unjust. Thus, when in the previous example we stigmatized as unjust a law forbidding coloured people access to the parks, this was on the footing that, at least in the distribution of such amenities, differences of colour are irrelevant. Certainly in the modern world, the fact that human beings, of whatever colour, are capable of thought, feeling, and self-control, would be generally though not universally accepted as constituting crucial resemblances between them to which the law should attend. Hence, in most civilized countries there is a great measure of agreement that both the criminal law (conceived not only as restricting liberty but as providing protection from various sorts of harm) and the civil law (conceived as offering redress for harm), would be unjust if in the distribution of these burdens and benefits they discriminated between persons, by reference to such characteristics as colour or religious belief. And if, instead of these well-known *foci* of human prejudice, the law discriminated by reference to such obvious irrelevancies as height, weight, or beauty it would be both unjust and ludicrous. If murderers belonging to the established church were exempt from capital punishment, if only members of the peerage could sue for libel, if assaults on coloured persons were punished less severely than those on whites, the laws would in most modern communities be condemned as unjust on the footing that *prima facie* human beings should be treated alike and these privileges and immunities rested on no relevant ground.

Indeed so deeply embedded in modern man is the principle that *prima facie* human beings are entitled to be treated alike that almost universally where the laws do discriminate by deference to such matters as colour and race, lip service at least is still widely paid to this principle. If such discriminations are attacked they are often defended by the assertion that the class discriminated against lack, or have not yet developed, certain essential human attributes; or it may be said that, regrettable though it is, the demands of justice requiring their equal treatment must be overridden in order to preserve something held to be of greater value, which would be jeopardized if such discriminations were not made. Yet though lip service is now general, it is certainly possible to conceive of a morality which did not resort to these often disingenuous devices to justify discrimination and inequalities, but openly rejected the principle that *prima facie* human beings were to be treated alike. Instead, human beings might be thought of as falling naturally and unalterably into certain classes, so that some were naturally fitted to be free and others to be their slaves or, as Aristotle expressed it, the living instruments of others. Here the sense of *prima facie* equality among men would be absent. Something of this view is to be found in Aristotle and Plato, though even there, there is more than a hint that any full defence of slavery would involve showing that those enslaved lacked the capacity for independent existence or differed from the free in their capacity to realize some ideal of the good life.

It is therefore clear that the criteria of relevant resemblances and differences may often vary with the fundamental moral outlook of a given person or society. Where this is so, assessments of the justice or injustice of the law may be met with counter-assertions inspired by a different morality. But sometimes a consideration of the object which the law in question is admittedly designed to realize may make clear the resemblances and differences which a just law should recognize and they may then be scarcely open to dispute. If a law provides for the relief of poverty then the requirement of the principle that "Like cases be treated alike" would surely involve attention to the *need* of different claimants for relief. A similar criterion of need is implicitly recognized when the burden of taxation is adjusted by a graded income tax to the wealth of the individuals taxed. Sometimes what is relevant are the *capacities* of persons for a specific function with which the exercise of the law in question may be concerned. Laws which exclude from the franchise, or withhold the power to make wills or contracts from children, or the insane, are regarded as just because such persons lack the capacity, which sane adults are presumed to have, to make a rational use of these facilities. Such discriminations are made on grounds which are obviously relevant, whereas discriminations in these matters between the sexes or between persons of different colour are not; though of course it has been argued in defence of the subjection of women, or coloured people, that women or coloured people lack the white male's capacity for rational thought and decision. To argue thus is of course to admit that equal capacity for a particular function is the criterion of justice in the case of such law, though in the absence of any evidence that such capacity is lacking in women or coloured persons, again only lip service is paid to this principle.

So far we have considered the justice or injustice of laws which may be viewed as *distributing* among individuals burdens and benefits. Some of the benefits are tangible, like poor relief, or food rations; others are intangible, like the protection from bodily harm given by the criminal law, or the facilities afforded by laws relating to testamentary or contractual capacity, or the right to vote. From distribution in this wide sense, we must distinguish *compensation* for injury done by one person to another. Here the connexion between what is just and the central precept of justice "Treat like cases alike and different cases differently" is certainly less direct. Yet it is not too indirect to be traced and may be seen in the following way. The laws which provide for the compensation by one person of another for torts or civil injuries might be considered unjust for two different reasons. They might, on the one hand, establish unfair privileges or immunities. This would be so if only peers could sue for libel, or if no white person were liable to a colored person for trespass or assault. Such laws would violate, in a straightforward way, principles of fair distribution of the rights and duties of compensation. But such laws might also be unjust in a quite different way: for while making no unfair discriminations they might fail altogether to provide a remedy for certain types of injury inflicted by one person on another, even though morally compensation would be thought due. In this matter the law might be unjust while treating all alike.

The vice of such laws would then not be the maldistribution, but the refusal to all alike, of compensation for injuries which it was morally wrong to inflict on others. The crudest case of such unjust refusal of redress would be a system in which no one could obtain damages for physical harm wantonly inflicted. It is worth observing that *this* injustice would still remain even if the criminal law prohibited such assaults under penalty. Few instances of anything so crude can be found, but the failure of English law to provide compensation for invasions of privacy, often found profitable by advertisers, has often been criticized in this way. Failure to provide compensation where morally it is held due is, however, also the gravamen of the charge of injustice against technicalities of the law of tort or contract which permit "unjust enrichment" of the expense of another by some action considered morally wrong.

The connexion between the justice and injustice of the compensation for injury, and the principle "Treat like cases alike and different cases differently," lies in the fact that outside the law there is a moral conviction that those with whom the law is concerned have a right to mutual forbearance from certain kinds of harmful conduct. Such a structure of reciprocal rights and obligations proscribing at least the grosser sorts of harm, constitutes the basis, though not the whole, of the morality of every social group. Its effect is to create among individuals a moral and, in a sense, an artificial equality to offset the inequalities of nature. For when the moral code forbids one man to rob or use violence on another even when superior strength or cunning would enable him to do so with impunity, the strong and cunning are put on a level with the weak and simple. Their cases are made morally alike. Hence the strong man who disregards morality and takes advantage of his strength to injure another is conceived as upsetting this equilibrium, or order of equality, established by morals; justice then requires that this moral *status quo* should as far as possible be restored by the wrongdoer. In simple cases of theft this would simply involve giving back the thing taken; and compensation for other injuries is an extension of this primitive notion. One who has physically injured another either intentionally or through negligence is thought of as having taken something from his victim; and though he has not literally done this, the figure is not too far fetched: for he has profited at his victim's expense, even if it is only by indulging his wish to injure him or not sacrificing his ease to the duty of taking adequate precautions. Thus when laws provide compensation where justice demands it, they recognize indirectly the principle "Treat like cases alike" by providing for the restoration, after disturbance, of the moral *status quo* in which victim and wrongdoer are on a footing of equality and so alike. Again, it is conceivable that there might be a moral outlook which did not put individuals on a footing of reciprocal equality in these matters. The moral code might forbid Barbarians to assault Greeks but allow Greeks to assault Barbarians. In such cases a Barbarian may be thought morally bound to compensate a Greek for injuries done though entitled to no such compensation himself. The moral order here would be one of inequality in which victim and wrongdoer were treated differently. For such an outlook, repellant though it may be to us, the law would be just only if it reflected this difference and treated different cases differently.

In this brief outline of justice we have considered only some of its simpler applications in order to show the specific form of excellence attributed to laws which are appraised as just. Not only is this distinct from other values which laws may have or lack, but sometimes the demands of justice may conflict with other values. This may occur, when a court, in sentencing a particular offender for a crime which has become prevalent, passes a severer sentence than that passed in other similar cases, and avowedly does this "as a warning." There is here a sacrifice of the principle "Treat like cases alike" to the general security or welfare of society. In civil cases, a similar conflict between justice and the general good is resolved in favour of the latter, when the law provides no remedy for some moral wrong because to enforce compensation in such cases might involve great difficulties of proof, or overburden the courts, or unduly hamper enterprise. There is a limit to the amount of law enforcement which any society can afford, even when moral wrong has been done. Conversely the law, in the name of the general welfare of society, may enforce compensation from one who has injured another, even where morally, as a matter of justice, it might not be thought due. This is often said to be the case when liability in tort is strict, i.e. independent of the intention to injure or failure to take care. This form of liability is sometimes defended on the ground that it is in the interest of "society" that those accidentally injured should be compensated; and it is claimed that the easiest way of doing this is to place the burden on those whose activities, however carefully controlled, result in such accidents. They commonly have deep pockets and opportunities to insure. When this defence is made, there is in it an implicit appeal to the general welfare of society which, though it may be morally acceptable and sometimes even called "*social* justice," differs from the primary forms of justice which are concerned simply to redress, as far as possible, the *status quo* as between two individuals.

An important juncture point between ideas of justice and social good or welfare should be noticed. Very few social changes or laws are agreeable to or advance the welfare of all individuals alike. Only laws which provide for the most elementary needs, such as police protection or roads, come near to this. In most cases the law provides benefits for one class of the population only at the cost of depriving others of what they prefer. Provision for the poor can be made only out of the goods of others; compulsory school education for all may mean not only loss of liberty for those who wish to educate their children privately, but may be financed only at the cost of reducing or sacrificing capital investment in industry or old-age pensions or free medical services. When a choice has been made between such competing alternatives it may be defended as proper on the ground that it was for the "public good" or the "common good." It is not clear what these phrases mean, since there seems to be no scale by which contributions of the various alternatives to the common good can be measured and the greater identified. It is, however, clear that a choice, made without prior consideration of the interests of all sections of the community would be open to criticism as merely partisan and unjust. It would, however, be rescued from *this* imputation if the claims of all had been impartially considered before legislation, even though in the result the claims of one section were subordinated to those of others.

Some might indeed argue that all that in fact could be meant by the claim that a choice between the competing claims of different classes or interests was made "for the common good," was that the claims of all had been thus impartially surveyed before decision. Whether this is true or not, it seems clear that justice in this sense is at least a necessary condition to be satisfied by any legislative choice which purports to be for the common good. We have here a further aspect of distributive justice, differing from those simple forms which we have discussed. For here what is justly "distributed" is not some specific benefit among a class of claimants to it, but impartial attention to and consideration of competing claims to different benefits.

Bibliographical Essay

Though it is touched upon in most textbooks, social philosophy has not been treated in book-length introductory works as frequently as other areas of philosophy. Among the available texts, however, are A. R. M. Murray, *An Introduction to Political Philosophy*, New York, 1953; H. R. G. Greaves, *The Foundations of Political Theory*, London, 1958; Whitaker T. Deininger, *Problems in Social and Political Thought*, New York, 1965; and Charles Vereker, *The Development of Political Theory*, New York, 1965. Somewhat more advanced is Leo Strauss, *What Is Political Philosophy? And Other Studies*, Gencoe, Ill., 1959. Valuable introductions are also found in many anthologies; see, for example, F. A. Olafson (ed.), *Society, Law, and Morality*, New York, 1961; Alan Gewirth (ed.), *Political Philosophy*, New York, 1965; and R. F. Wolff (ed.), *Political Man and Social Man*, New York, 1966.

Many materials for the study of social philosophy are presented in historically oriented works. The student should familiarize himself with his library's collections in history and political science as well as in philosophy. A great variety of books on individual thinkers and on movements and schools will be found. Among these are the Home University Library series; the series edited by F. J. C. Hearnshaw from 1923 on, which includes volumes from medieval thought through the Victorian age; John Bowle's two volumes, *Western Political Thought*, London, 1947, and *Politics and Opinion in the Nineteenth Century*, Oxford, 1954; W. A. Dunning, *A History of Political Theories*, 3 vols., New York, 1910–1920; vol. 4 C. E. Merriam and H. E. Barnes (ed.), 1924; John Plamenatz, *Man and Society*, 2 vols., New York, 1963; and G. H. Sabine, *A History of Political Theory*, New York, 1937, and later editions. William Ebenstein, *Great Political Thinkers*, 3d ed., New York, 1960, contains a valuable annotated bibliography.

Students may also find it helpful in many instances to consult the complete works from which selections have been taken.

1. Classical Realism

Systematic introductions to classical realism are given in such volumes as Jacques Maritain, *An Introduction to Philosophy*, London, 1930; and John Wild, *Introduction to Realistic Philosophy*, New York, 1948. For further intensive study, the student must turn to the basic texts of the great figures in classical realism—Plato, Aristotle, and St. Thomas Aquinas. Their works are available in many editions and compilations. Of value in studying them are commentaries by Jacques Maritain,

Saint Thomas Aquinas, London, 1933; W. D. Ross, *Aristotle,* 5th ed., London, 1949; F. C. Copleston, *Aquinas,* Harmondsworth, England, 1955; Étienne Gilson, *The Christian Philosophy of St. Thomas Aquinas,* New York, 1956; A. E. Taylor, *Plato, the Man and His Work,* 4th ed., New York, 1956; G. M. A. Grube, *Plato's Thought,* Boston, 1958; and Robert S. Brumbaugh, *Plato for the Modern Age,* New York, 1962. Sir Ernest Barker's works on Plato and Aristotle, as well as relevant books mentioned above, are also helpful on the social philosophy of the important figures in realism. Many books exist on the history of realism; see, for example, Maurice de Wulf, *History of Medieval Philosophy,* New York, 1909; the interpretative and excellent study by Gilson, *The Spirit of Medieval Philosophy,* New York, 1940; and Émile Bréhier, *The Middle Ages and the Renaissance,* trans. Wade Baskin, Chicago, 1965. Contemporary work by thinkers of a realistic persuasion is found in such volumes as John Wild (ed.), *The Return to Reason,* Chicago, 1953, the *Proceedings of the American Catholic Philosophic Association,* and the many publications of Gilson and Maritain, who have written on all the major fields of philosophical concern.

Selections in the text have been taken from ancient and medieval realistic sources. While relying on these sources, contemporary realists have attempted to restate older insights in ways relevant to the modern world. Widely read have been such writings of Jacques Maritain as *True Humanism,* New York, 1938, *Scholasticism and Politics,* New York, 1940, and *The Person and the Common Good,* New York, 1947. Other works include A. P. d'Entrèves, *Natural Law: An Introduction to Legal Philosophy,* London, 1951; Yves Simon, *The Tradition of Natural Law: A Philosopher's Reflections,* New York, 1965; and John Wild, *Plato's Modern Enemies and the Theory of Natural Law,* Chicago, 1953.

2. Positivism

Much of the literature covering positivistic theories centers on Machiavelli, Hobbes, and Comte. Standard histories of philosophy are helpful, as are the following studies that provide a basic literature on the movement: J. S. Mill, *Auguste Comte and Positivism,* 5th ed., London, 1907; J. W. Allen, *Political Thought in the Sixteenth Century,* London, 1928; Herbert Butterfield, *The Statecraft of Machiavelli,* London, 1940; James Burnham, *The Machiavellians,* New York, 1943; Friedrich Meinecke, *Machiavellism: The Doctrine of Raison d'État and Its Place in Modern History,* New Haven, 1957; and two books by Leo Strauss, *The Political Philosophy of Hobbes,* Oxford, 1936 and Chicago, 1952, and *Thoughts on Machiavelli,* Glencoe, Ill., 1958. An important work in social philosophy by a contemporary positivist is Karl Popper's *The Open Society and Its Enemies,* Princeton, 1950, 4th ed., 1963. Students may also find interesting the book by R. L. Hawkins on *Positivism in the United States,* Cambridge, Mass., 1938.

Bibliographical materials on contemporary positivism are given below under analytic philosophy.

3. Liberalism

Liberal thought in the sense defined in this book has been given extensive treatment by historians and philosophers. Nearly all the volumes mentioned in the introduction of the bibliography contain chapters on that movement, as well as further bibliographical materials. Among the basic studies of liberalism is the following sample: G. P. Gooch, *The History of English Democratic Ideas in the Seventeenth Century,* New York, 1912; T. H. Green, *Four Lectures on the English Revolution,* which is reprinted from his *Works;* and Kingsley Martin, *French Liberal Thought in the Eighteenth Century,* 2d ed., London, 1954. Liberalism in America is treated in such works as C. E. Merriam, *A History of American Political Theories,* New York, 1928; Louis Hartz, *The Liberal Tradition in America,* New York, 1955; and Robert N. Beck, *The Meaning of Americanism,* New York, 1956.

4. UTILITARIANISM

Most students will find the primary source materials on utilitarianism easily available and readable, both in respect to its ethical foundations and social philosophy. A number of important descriptive studies are nevertheless available which provide historical perspective and explanation. Standard works include Ernest Albee. *A History of English Utilitarianism,* New York, 1901, reprinted 1962; David Baumgardt, *Bentham and the Ethics of Today,* Princeton, 1952, a valuable book in relating utilitarianism to contemporay thought; William L. Davidson, *Political Thought in England: The Utilitarians from Bentham to J. S. Mill,* London, 1935; Elie Halévy, *The Growth of Philosophical Radicalism,* trans. Mary Morris, London, 1928; G. W. Keeton and G. Schwarzenberger (eds.), *Jeremy Bentham and the Law,* London, 1948; John Plamenatz, *The English Utilitarians,* Oxford, 1949; and Leslie Stephen, *The English Utilitarians,* 3 vols., London, 1900, reprinted 1950.

5. IDEALISM

For purposes of introduction to basic idealistic arguments, two surveys of idealism by Josiah Royce are important, *Lectures on Modern Idealism,* New Haven, 1919, reprinted 1964 and, in the relevant chapters, *The Spirit of Modern Philosophy,* New York, 1892. An anthology edited by A. C. Ewing, *The Idealistic Tradition,* Glencoe, Ill., 1957, presents an interesting collection of papers and includes a bibliography that students may consult for intensive reading in idealism. An introductory text covering idealism is E. S. Brightman and Robert N. Beck, *An Introduction to Philosophy,* 3d ed., New York, 1963. Somewhat more advanced are discussions of idealism in such books as Clifford Barrett (ed.), *Contemporary Idealism in America,* New York, 1932; G. W. Cunningham, *The Idealistic Argument in Recent British and American Philosophy,* New York, 1933; and A. C. Ewing, *Idealism: A Critical Survey,* London, 1934.

The social philosophy of idealism and major idealists is treated in such works as: M. B. Foster, *The Political Philosophy of Plato and Hegel,* Oxford, 1935; Norman Wilde, *The Ethical Basis of the State,* Princeton, 1924; Francis B. Harman, *The Social Philosophy of the St. Louis Hegelians,* New York, 1943; John E. Smith, *Royce's Social Infinite,* New York, 1950; A. J. M. Milne, *The Social Philosophy of English Idealism,* London, 1962; T. M. Knox, trans., *Hegel's Politi-*

cal Writings, Oxford, 1964; Melvin Richter, *The Politics of Conscience: T. H. Green and His Age,* Cambridge, Mass., 1964; and Peter Fuss, *The Moral Philosophy of Josiah Royce,* Cambridge, Mass., 1965.

6. Communism

A great number of studies and anthologies—usually with introductory essays—have been published on communist thought. Among them are: Max Beer, *The Life and Teaching of Karl Marx,* London, 1925; Sidney Hook, *Towards the Understanding of Karl Marx,* New York, 1933, as well as other works; Emile Burns (ed.), *A Handbook of Marxism,* New York, 1935; Isaiah Berlin, *Karl Marx,* 2d ed., London, 1948; Jacques Barzun, *Darwin, Marx, Wagner,* Boston, 1941; R. N. C. Hunt, *The Theory and Practice of Communism,* New York, 1950; G. D. H. Cole, *A History of Socialist Thought,* 4 vols., New York, 1953–1958; Herbert Marcuse, *Soviet Marxism: A Critical Analysis,* New York, 1958; Raymond Polin, *Marxian Foundations of Communism,* Chicago, 1966; and many works by Maurice Cornforth.

The materials used in the text are from writings of Marx, Engels, and Lenin, but there is continuing development of communist thought, from Stalin on as well as in many countries. A bibliography of soviet philosophy, now in five volumes, is edited by J. M. Bocheński and published by D. Reidel Publishing Co. Many of the books listed above touch on later developments, and a number of journals reprint important Russian and communist philosophical papers in English, including *Science and Society, Praexis,* and *Soviet Studies in Philosophy.*

7. Pragmatism

The various meanings of pragmatism were first analyzed in a classic paper by Arthur O. Lovejoy, "The Thirteen Pragmatisms," *Journal of Philosophy,* 5(1908); it has been reprinted in many anthologies, such as Muelder, Sears, and Schlabach, *The Development of American Philosophy,* 2d ed., Boston, 1960. Good statements on pragmatism are found in this work (see Section Six) and in other books such as Herbert W. Schneider, *A History of American Philosophy,* New York, 1946; W. H. Werkmeister, *A History of Philosophical Ideas in America,* New York, 1949; Stow Persons, *American Minds: A History of Ideas,* New York, 1958; and John E. Smith, *The Spirit of American Philosophy,* New York, 1963. Especially interesting are the studies by John Dewey, "The Development of American Pragmatism," in *Studies in the History of Ideas,* New York, 1925; G. H. Mead, "The Philosophies of Royce, James, and Dewey in Their American Setting," *Ethics,* 40(1929); and Philip P. Wiener, *Evolution and the Founders of Pragmatism,* Cambridge, Mass., 1949.

A general though critical treatment of pragmatic social philosophy is found in W. Y. Elliott, *The Pragmatic Revolt in Politics,* New York, 1928. Many shorter studies may be found in philosophical journals. Two other books touching on pragmatism in this area may be mentioned: Morton White, *Social Thought in America: The Revolt Against Formalism,* New York, 1949; and Richard Hofstadter, *Social Darwinism in American Thought, 1860–1915,* rev. ed., Boston, 1955.

8. Existentialism

A number of fine surveys of existentialist thought have been written; among them are Marjorie Grene, *Dreadful Freedom,* Chicago, 1948, reissued as *Introduction to Existentialism;* Emmanuel Mounier, *Existentialist Philosophies,* New York, 1949; Ronald Grimsley, *Existentialist Thought,* Cardiff, Wales, 1955; Walter A. Kaufmann (ed.), *Existentialism from Dostoevsky to Sartre,* New York, 1956; F. H. Heinemann, *Existentialism and the Modern Predicament,* New York, 1958; H. J. Blackham, *Six Existentialist Thinkers,* New York, 1959; F. Molina, *Existentialism as Philosophy,* Englewood Cliffs, N.J., 1962; and R. G. Olson, *An Introduction to Existentialism,* New York, 1962. These works touch on major figures in the movement as well as on many topics of interest to the social philosopher. Though they are not ordinarily classified as existentialists, the following works may also be mentioned as reflecting certain existentialistic themes: Reinhold Niebuhr, *The Children of Light and the Children of Darkness,* New York, 1946; John Wild, *Human Freedom and Social Order,* Durham, N.C., 1959; and many books by Paul Tillich.

9. Analytic Philosophy

Introductory textbooks reflecting logical positivism include Arthur Pap, *Elements of Analytic Philosophy,* New York, 1949; Hans Reichenbach, *The Rise of Scientific Philosophy,* Berkeley, 1951; and Richard von Mises, *Positivism: A Study in Human Understanding,* Cambridge, Mass., 1951. The classic work of the movement is A. J. Ayer's *Language, Truth and Logic,* 2d ed., London, 1949. Many important papers are collected in such anthologies and compilations as H. Feigl and W. Sellars (eds.), *Readings in Philosophical Analysis,* New York, 1949; H. Feigl and M. Brodbeck (eds.), *Readings in the Philosophy of Science,* New York, 1953; *International Encyclopedia of Unified Science;* and the *Minnesota Studies in the Philosophy of Science.* A. J. Ayer's *Logical Positivism,* Glencoe, Ill., 1959, is a broad anthology with excellent bibliographical material.

Analytic philosophy of the more recent linguistic variety is treated in such works as A. J. Ayer and Others, *The Revolution in Philosophy,* London, 1956; J. O. Urmson, *Philosophical Analysis,* Oxford, 1956; J. Passmore, *A Hundred Years of Philosophy,* London, 1957; D. F. Pears (ed.), *The Nature of Metaphysics,* London, 1957; and G. J. Warnock, *English Philosophy Since 1900,* London, 1958. Somewhat more advanced is F. Waismann, *The Principles of Linguistic Philosophy,* London, 1965. Anthologies of important discussions from an analytic point of view are: A. G. N. Flew (ed.), *Logic and Language,* First Series, Oxford, 1951, Second Series, Oxford, 1953; M. Macdonald (ed.), *Philosophy and Analysis,* Oxford, 1954; C. A. Mace (ed.), *British Philosophy in the Mid-Century,* London, 1957; and Morris Weitz (ed.), *20th-Century Philosophy: The Analytic Tradition,* New York, 1966.

Except in philosophy of law, analytic philosophers have paid relatively less attention to social philosophy than to other philosophic problems. Unlike their positivistic predecessors in the eighteenth and nineteenth centuries, logical positivists produced little on social thought. The important studies of analytic philosophers have been collected in two anthologies, P. Laslett (ed.), *Philosophy, Politics and Society,* Oxford, 1956, and P. Laslett and W. G. Runciman (eds.), *Philosophy, Politics and Society,* Second Series, Oxford, 1962. No work, however, seems to have supplanted T. D. Weldon's *The Vocabulary of Politics,* Harmondsworth, England, 1953, as the standard approach to social philosophy by linguistic philosophers. A forthcoming work is Jan Srzednicki, *Prolegomena to Social Philosophy.*

Finally, mention may be made of various treatments of special topics in social philosophy. Numerous studies have been made of all the major problems in this field, and only a sample of them may be given here. They indicate something of the range of books, however, and they may also be a guide to other studies: D. C. Ritchie, *Natural Rights,* London, 1903; John Plamenatz, *Consent, Freedom and Political Obligation,* Oxford, 1938; H. E. Brunner, *Justice and the Social Order,* trans. M. Hottinger, New York, 1945; J. W. Gough, *The Social Contract,* 2d ed., Oxford, 1957; Bertrand de Jouvenal, *Sovereignty,* Cambridge, Mass., 1957; Hans Kelson, *What is Justice?,* Berkeley, 1957; I. Berlin, *Two Concepts of Liberty,* Oxford, 1958; C. J. Friedrich, *The Philosophy of Law in Historical Perspective,* Chicago, 1958; F. A. Hayek, *The Constitution of Liberty,* Chicago, 1960; Sidney Hook (ed.), *Law and Philosophy,* New York, 1964; Sanford A. Lakoff, *Equality in Political Philosophy,* Cambridge, Mass., 1964; Morris Ginsberg, *On Justice in Society,* Harmondsworth, England, 1965; and M. P. Golding (ed.), *The Nature of Law: Readings in Legal Philosophy,* New York, 1966. Eight valuable collections of papers in the *Nomos* series, yearbooks of The American Society for Political and Legal Philosophy, have been edited by C. J. Friedrich, including volumes on *Authority, Community, Responsibility, Liberty, The Public Interest, Justice, Rational Decision,* and *Revolution.*

Index*

---

* Numbers in italics refer to topics in selections in the text and to their authors.

Date Due

MAY 7 '88			